A Memorial to the Jewish Community of Zhetl (Dzyatlava, Belarus)

Translation of
Pinkus Zhetl

Original Book Edited by: Baruch Kaplinski

Originally published in Tel Aviv 1957
By the Zhetl Association in Israel

JewishGen
מרכז עולמי לגנאלוגיה יהודית
The Global Home for Jewish Genealogy

A Publication of JewishGen, INC
Edmond J. Safra Plaza, 36 Battery Place, New York, NY 10280
646.494.5972 | info@JewishGen.org | www.jewishgen.org

MUSEUM OF
JEWISH HERITAGE
A LIVING MEMORIAL
TO THE HOLOCAUST

A Memorial to the Jewish Community of Zhetl (Dzyatlava, Belarus)
Translation of *Pinkus Zhetl*

Editor of Original Yizkor Book: Baruch Kaplinski
Project Coordinator: Sam Bayer
Layout and Name Indexing: Jonathan Wind
Reproduction of Photographs: Sondra Ettlinger
Cover Design: Rachel Kolokoff Hopper

Printed in the United States of America by Lightning Source, Inc.

Library of Congress Control Number (LCCN): 2021952234

ISBN: 978-1-954176-29-4 (hard cover: 688 pages, alk. paper)

About JewishGen.org

JewishGen, an affiliate of the Museum of Jewish Heritage - A Living Memorial to the Holocaust, serves as the global home for Jewish genealogy.

Featuring unparalleled access to 30+ million records, it offers unique search tools, along with opportunities for researchers to connect with others who share similar interests. Award winning resources such as the Family Finder, Discussion Groups, and ViewMate, are relied upon by thousands each day.

In addition, JewishGen's extensive informational, educational and historical offerings, such as the Jewish Communities Database, Yizkor Book translations, InfoFiles, Family Tree of the Jewish People, and KehilaLinks, provide critical insights, first-hand accounts, and context about Jewish communal and familial life throughout the world.

Offered as a free resource, JewishGen.org has facilitated thousands of family connections and success stories, and is currently engaged in an intensive expansion effort that will bring many more records, tools, and resources to its collections.

Please visit https://www.jewishgen.org/ to learn more.

Executive Director: Avraham Groll

About the JewishGen Yizkor Book Project

Yizkor Books (Memorial Books) were traditionally written to memorialize the names of departed family and martyrs during holiday services in the synagogue (a practice that still exists in many synagogues today).

Over the centuries, as a result of countless persecutions and horrific atrocities committed against the Jews, Yizkor Books (Sefer Zikaron in Hebrew) were expanded to include more historical information, such as biographical sketches of famous personalities and descriptions of daily town life.

Following the Holocaust, the idea of remembrance and learning took on an urgent and crucial importance. Survivors of the Holocaust sought out other surviving residents of their former towns to memorialize and document the names and way of life of those who were ruthlessly murdered by the Nazis. These remembrances were documented in Yizkor Books, hundreds of which were published in the first decades after the Holocaust.

Most of these books were published privately, or through landsmanshaftn (social organizations comprised of members originating from the same European town or region) that still existed, and were often distributed free of charge. Sadly, the languages used to document these crucial histories and links to our past, Yiddish and Hebrew, are no longer commonly understood by a significant percentage of Jews today. As a result, JewishGen has undertaken the sacred responsibility of translating these books into English so that the culture and way of life of these communities will be preserved and transmitted to future generations.

In 1986, a group of farsighted JewishGenners started a project to pool their efforts together in groups based upon their ancestors from each town and donate money to get the Yizkor books of their ancestral towns translated into English. As the translated material became available, it was made accessible for free at www.JewishGen.org/Yizkor. Hardcover copies can be purchased by visiting www.JewishGen.org/Yizkor/ybip.html (see below).

It is our hope that the translation of these books into English (and other languages) will assist the countless Jewish family researchers who are so desperately seeking to forge a connection with their heritage.

Director of JewishGen Yizkor Book Project: Lance Ackerfeld

About the JewishGen Press

JewishGen Press (formerly the Yizkor Books-in-Print Project) is the publishing division of JewishGen.org, and provides a venue for the publication of non-fiction books pertaining to Jewish genealogy, history, culture, and heritage.

In addition to the Yizkor Book category, publications in the Other Non-Fiction category include Shoah memoirs and research, genealogical research, collections of genealogical and historical materials, biographies, diaries and letters, studies of Jewish experience and cultural life in the past, academic theses, and other books of interest to the Jewish community.

Please visit https://www.jewishgen.org/Yizkor/ybip.html to learn more.

Director of JewishGen Press: Joel Alpert
Managing Editor - Jessica Feinstein
Publications Manager - Susan Rosin

Notes to the Reader

The images in the original book were reproduced from photographs from the time of the first edition. These reproductions were already of poor quality, being pre-war and at least 30 or more years old. As a result the images in the book are not very good and the best achievable.

A reader can view the original scans of the book on the websites listed below.

The original book can be seen online at the New York Public Library site:

https://digitalcollections.nypl.org/items/f36172c0-6ebb-0133-71d6-00505686a51c

or

at the Yiddish Book Center web site:

https://www.yiddishbookcenter.org/collections/yizkor-books/yzk-nybc314123/kaplinski-baruch-pinkes-zshetl-tsum-15-tn-yortog-nokh-dem-groyzamen-hurbn

To obtain a list of all Shoah victims from Zhetl (Dzyatlava), the reader should access the Yad Vashem web site listed below; one can also search for specific family names using family name option. These lists are continually updated by Yad Vashem, so it is worthwhile to periodically search these lists.

There is more valuable information (including the Pages of Testimony, etc.) available on this website: http://yvng.yadvashem.org

A list of all books available from JewishGen Press along with prices is available at:
https://www.jewishgen.org/Yizkor/ybip.html

Acknowledgements

If you're reading this it's because you want to learn about the now extinct Jewish village of Zhetl, known today as Dyatlovo, Belarus. Unfortunately, you can't read it in Yiddish. Sixty-Five years after this Zhetl Yizkor book was originally published, I am honored to make it available to the English-speaking world.

Why do you care about Zhetl?

If you're like me, it's probably because your parents, grandparents, great-grandparents, uncles, aunts or cousins were born and lived in Zhetl. A few of them survived, all of them tried to, but most of them were savagely murdered during humanity's lowest point in modern history: the Holocaust of World War II.
If you're like me, you've heard bits and pieces of your family's Zhetl's stories over the years. Some of them get repeated to the point where you no longer hear them. Then one day you wake up and want to know more. You want to ask the questions which your youthful self didn't have the time, nor interest, to ask.

But alas, our Zhetl is gone.

Therein lies the wisdom of our dear Zhetl relatives. They knew this day would come.

We all owe a debt of gratitude to all the authors who made the time to tell their stories, as painful as it was. To Baruch Kaplinski (z"l) for editing the original 1957 version and to Mordecai (Motl) Dunetz (z"l), for passionately gathering and editing materials from former Zhetl residents and survivors the world over for nearly a decade in order to drive the project through to its completion.

As for this English translation, I want to thank Ronnie Dunetz for making me aware of the Zhetl Yizkor Book's existence and for encouraging me to take on this project.

Of course this project is what it is only because of the hard work and professionalism of the members of the project team:

- Janie Respitz, now an honorary Zhetlite, translated all of the Yiddish pages, captions and lists of the book. She is the consummate professional and I am happy that this project reunited our families.
- Judy Montel bravely overcame her reluctance to confront some of the more painful stories in the book to translate them from Hebrew into English.
- Lance Ackerfeld, and the JewishGen staff, managed the logistics of the project and made it feel effortless.

In the end, I took on this project so that my direct connections to Zhetl, my great-grandfather Shlomo Zalman Dunetz, and his son, my namesake, Shmuel Dunetz, could meet my children, Tovah Karl and Adam Bayer, and my grandchildren, Colden and Reese Karl.

Hopefully, someday after I'm long gone, my grandchildren's grandchildren and their grandchildren will all say "we are survivors from Zhetl".

May we never forget.

Sam (Shmuel) Bayer
Durham, NC
December 12, 2021

Credits for Book Cover

Front Cover:

Front Cover Photograph Courtesy of Sam Bayer. Photo taken in Zhetl, Belarus circa April 1934.

Standing left to right: Mordecai (Motl) Dunetz, Fanya Dunetz, Bracha (Belagrudsky) Dunetz, Shmuel Dunetz, Shifra Dunetz. Sitting left to right: Yoel David Dunetz, Anzel Dunetz (on the lap), Sarah Rochel Dunetz, Basya Golda Dunetz and Roselein Bitensky.

Front and back cover background photograph: The Synagogue of Dzyatlava (Zhetel) at the onset of World War II. Pinkas Zhetl: A Memorial to the Jewish community Zetel / Ed. B. Kaplinski. Tel Aviv: Zetel Association in Israel, 1957. P. 2. Unknown author. From Wikipedia: https://tinyurl.com/2nvj4fut

Back Cover Poem: My Small Jewish Town by Pesieh Mayevsky. Page 405 *[Page 304]*.

GeoPolitical Information

Dzyatlava, Belarus is located at 53°28' N 25°24' E, 94 miles WSW of Minsk

	Town	District	Province	Country
Before WWI (c. 1900):	Dyatlovo	Slonim	Grodno	Russian Empire
Between the wars (c. 1930):	Zdzięcioł	Nowogródek	Nowogródek	Poland
After WWII (c. 1950):	Dyatlovo			Soviet Union
Today (c. 2000):	Dzyatlava			Belarus

Alternate Names for the Town:
Dzyatlava [Bel], Zdzięcioł [Pol], Dyatlovo [Rus], Zhetl [Yid], Zietela [Lith], Dsjatlawa [Ger], Zdjatlava, Zdzentsyul, Dzentsel, Zhetel, Zetel, Zetl, Zietil, Zitl, Zozhetsiol, Zsetl, Dzięcioł, Dzięciołki, Dzdietel

Nearby Jewish Communities:

Novoyel'nya 8 miles E
Dvarets 8 miles ESE
Kozlovshchyna 11 miles SSW
Belitsa 13 miles NNW
Dubrovo 15 miles WNW
Molchad 16 miles SE
Orlya 17 miles W
Zheludok 19 miles WNW
Navahrudak 20 miles ENE
Hałynka 23 miles SW
Vselyub 24 miles NE
Derechin 25 miles SW
Polonka 25 miles SSE
Slonim 27 miles S
Haradzishcha 27 miles ESE
Gav'ya 28 miles NNE
Rozhanka 28 miles W
Lida 29 miles N
Shchuchyn 29 miles WNW

Jewish Population: 3,033 (in 1897), 3,450 (in 1926)

Map of Belarus with Dzyatlava (Zhetl) indicated

TABLE OF CONTENTS

The First World War

Between the two world wars

Political Parties

Institutions

Memories

The Folklore of Zhetl

Under Soviet Rule

In the forests

A Memorial to the
Jewish Community of Zhetl
(Dzyatlava, Belarus)

53°28' / 25°24'

Translation of
Pinkus Zhetl

Edited by Baruch Kaplinski

Published by the Zhetl Association in Israel

Acknowledgments

Project Coordinator

Sam Bayer

Emerita Project Coordinator: Becky Diamond

Our sincere appreciation to Stefanie Holzman for extracting the pictures
from the original book, enabling their addition to the project.

This is a translation from *Pinkus Zhetl*,
(A memorial to the Jewish community of Zhetl),
Editors: Baruch Kaplinski, Published by the Zhetl Association in Israel,
Tel Aviv 1957 (H,Y 482 pages).

Note: The original book can be seen online at the NY Public Library site: Dziatlava

Please contribute to our translation fund to see the translation of this book completed.

JewishGen's Translation Fund Donation Form provides a secure way to make donations,
either on-line or by mail, to help continue this project. Donations to JewishGen are tax-deductible for U.S. citizens.

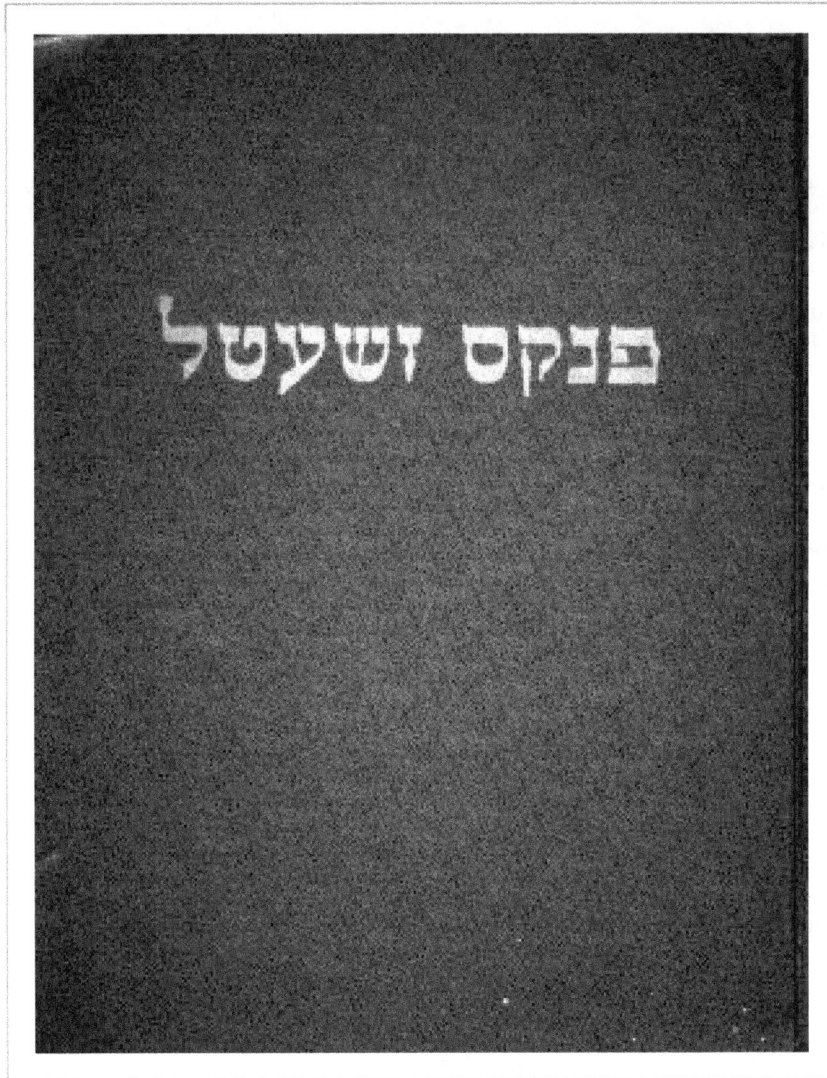

פנקס זשעטל

Pinkas Zhetl

A memorial to the Jewish community of Zhetl

**Published by the Zhetl Association in Israel
in Participation with the Zhetl Attociations*
in the United States of America, Argentina and Canada**
Tel-Aviv 1957

[Page 9]

Introduction

Translated by Janie Respitz

The chronicles of Zhetl are not simply a book.

It is a memorial tablet on the grave of three thousand bodies from a productive Jewish community, an endeavour from a total of 450 years of Jewish life in a Jewish town (Shtetl) in White Russia (Belarus).

Not Your Average Shtetl

Zhetl was not your average town, it was enterprising, lively and progressive. It was a town with higher religious, national and social force, and a small base for growing Zionism and militant socialism.

Its businessmen were active, devoted and prominent.

Its institutions possessed a lot of initiative and zest.

The Jews were proud fighters and pioneers of untraversed paths.

They were among the pioneers to fulfill the good deed to settle in the Land of Israel in the first half of the 19th century.

They were among the first immigrants to America, in search for bread and freedom in the second half of the 19th century.

They were among the daring partisans who sowed revenge and death on the Nazi fascists in the 40s of this century.

The orthodox wing put forth religious authority and clever teachings.

The national wing excelled with progressive enlightened Jews, passionate Zionists and pugnacious pioneers.

The socialist group generated flaming revolutionaries who preached Marxism and rebelled against the Czarist regime.

Zhetl Takes Pride in her Sons

Two of her sons were the greatest rabbinic authorities in the 18th, 19th and 20th centuries: The Preacher of Dubne, Rabbi Yakov Krantz of blessed memory, and the Chefetz Chaim (Desire of Life), Rabbi Yisroel Meir HaCohen, of blessed memory. (Translator's note: Many great Jewish scholars were known by the titles of their books).

Another son of Zhetl was the well known Hebrew writer A. Ben– Avigdor.

The great Zionist dreamer and fighter: Yehoshua Barzilay – Eyznshtat, of blessed memory.

For many years the chair of Chief Rabbi was held by Rabbi Zalman Sarartzky, a great rabbinic authority in Poland, now in Israel.

In the chronicle we take into account many businessmen on local and national levels, who illuminated the eastern wall of communal life in Zhetl.

This was Zhetl. A town which excelled in the collective and the individual.

Could we allow all of this to be forgotten?

No!

Therefore we are publishing this chronicle. Did we achieve our goal?

We believe we did, despite the many difficulties we stumbled upon.

Sources

Perhaps there are materials about the history of the Jews from Zhetl and vicinity in Soviet Russia and Poland. However, here in Israel there is very little, except for a few notices in the Hebrew press, a few court documents and scant notices in Polish and Russian encyclopaedias. We have not found substantive material. All of this is not enough to restore the past of the Jews of Zhetl.

[Page 10]

Memoirs

Zhetl excelled with a lively communal life, but only a small portion of these activities were recorded. We hoped to get most of our information from memoirs. It turns out the survivors from Zhetl can be divided in two groups: those who have already forgot a little and those who do not remember because they were too young. The consequence therefore is not enough attention has been payed to: certain Zhetl institutions and issues, customs and lifestyle, which should have been illuminated.

The Nature of This Chronicle

The Zhetl Chronicle is a collective creation by 100 authors who were unable to collaborate on the content of their work, even if they wanted to. Therefore this chronicle is not free of repetition, even thought the editor was strict, and removed a lot with his pen, of course with compassion.

It was not easy for us to decide to give almost all people from Zhetl the opportunity to tell about themselves and the town in their own language and style. The result therefore, is that a few works are a bit drawn out, but with great simplicity and even more authenticity.

Language

We really wanted this chronicle to appear in the language of the record books of the Zhetl societies: the Free Loan Society and the Burial Society, in the language of the State of Israel, in the language of our children, the Sabras (born in Israel). Finally, our chronicle is not intended for those who know and remember Zhetl, rather for our children who know very little about it.

After long deliberation we decided to publish this chronicle almost exclusively in Yiddish, in the daily language of Zhetl and the language which is understood by everyone from Zhetl in all countries all over the world.

Spelling

It was not easy to arrive at an agreement on spelling from among the many writers and various Yiddish spellings. In order to solve this we turned, early in this project to instructions from the following friends: Y. Paner and S. Pines to whom we are very grateful. Thanks to their instructions we published in a uniform spelling.

The Zhetl Chronicle – A Collective Work

The Zhetl Chronicle is a collective work of initiators, memoirists, collectors of material, editors and fund raisers. Thanks to their effort and tight collaboration we were able to publish this chronicle in this format and with this content.

Permit us here to thank all the pioneers of this chronicle, especially the tireless initiators, our friends Dr. Avraham Alpert (Ramat – Gan) and Mordkhai Dunitz (The United States), who took the first steps in the realization of this chronicle and with great devotion collected material in Israel and the United States.

Congratulations to our many friends in Israel, the United States, Argentina and Canada who wrote and collected memoirs.

Congratulations to our friends who searched for documents and newspaper notices, compiled a list of the martyrs, identified photographs and collected funds.

Congratulations to our fellow townspeople in America, especially our friend Efraim Pasaf (New York), whose efforts resulted in the book being printed on extraordinarily good paper.

Our deepest appreciation to all!

Thanks to them, the Zhetl Chronicle is lying in front of me!

Tel Aviv, July, 1957. The editor and book committee in Israel

[Page 12]

Pictures tell Stories

By Borukh Kaplinsky

Translated by Janie Respitz

Do you remember Zhetl?

In a fog? Like in a dream?

It's no surprise. You left Zhetl 10, 20, 30 or 40 years ago. But now, wherever you are, in Israel or America, in Europe or Africa, I'm sure you want, occasionally, even for a short time, to walk down its streets, see the houses and people, and glance at their faces.

Yes?

So come. Take this book. Turn the pages and look at the pictures. What stories do they tell?

Here stands Zhetl, here are the lanes and streets, the people and houses. They are running, hustling and bustling.

Where to?

They do not even know themselves. It is before 1939 and of course, before the sorrowful 1942. Look further. Remember the warm houses and complete families. What a pleasure!

Everything becomes so warm and homey, and for a moment it seems nothing has happened.

Zhetl is still alive!

Everyone is still alive! All the fathers, mothers, all the women and children, all the brothers and sisters.

Although far, far from here…

You have arrived from the outside world in Zhetl and are greeted by Novoredek Street. This was the gate to the city. A mixed street where both Christians and Jews lived. Leybe Kaplinsky's house stood at the entrance of town, nicely fenced and surrounded by white birch trees. The neighbouring houses were thatched roofed Christian houses. Their hats and waistcoats remind us of Zhetl 30 -35 years ago.

Page 13]

We are nearing the market place. The following live on the right side: Velvl Alpert, Yoyne Leyb Khlebnik, Artchik Efraim Hirshl's and on the other side of the street – Yisakhar Berman.
The First World War is raging in the outside world, but all is quiet and calm in Zhetl. Germans march through the streets and farmers from the region rush to church to pray.

The marketplace is the heart of the town. It is quadrilateral and wide. Nine streets lead from town to the marketplace. Here you will find the pharmacy and the church, the shops and hotels. Only Jews live here. Christians come here to pray to God and do business with Jews. Here is a bird's eye view of the Zhetl marketplace. You can see the church and the shops, the roofs and chimneys of the Jewish houses and in the middle of the marketplace, a few tables with merchandise and lots of movement.

The marketplace from north-west. When you come from Novolienie you are standing at this part of the marketplace. Wagons are standing behind the church and big and small are posing for the camera, in an attempt to perpetuate their faces.

Majestically standing out from the marketplace are Avrom Moishe's porch, Hendl's fence, Khaim Koyfman's two story house and nearby, military trucks, a few wagons and many Germans. Is this perhaps 1915 or 1917?

Here is the other end of the marketplace. Two streets lead out from here: the Priest's Street and Estate Street. Here you can find the pharmacy and Binyomin Krigel's brick house with its characteristic four steps to the porch and the attic with two windows. The revolutionary Dovid Nadlshteyn lived in the attic. In 1905 Zhetl's youth would gather there for secret meetings where they would read the works of Karl Marx and plan on how to get rid of Czar Nikolai. (Nicholas II).

[Page 14]

A stampede. What happened? The bus Novolienie – Zhetl has arrived. Everyone runs to see. Perhaps an acquaintance has arrived?

It is apparently Friday. A small market. Wagons wait, farmers have come to buy and they look upon the large signs: pharmacy, warehouse etc…

The eastern part of the marketplace where the finest houses in Zhetl are situated. The brick houses stand like a line of soldiers with sloping roofs and closed porches. The following live here: Shmuel Shvedsky's family, Berl Rabinovitch (previously Feyvl from Skvid), Solomiyansky and the three Dvoretzky families. From the idleness we can assume this was not a Sunday, Tuesday and also not Friday.

We are in the Synagogue courtyard. Here are the old and the middle Houses of Study. The inscription of the middle House of Study reads: Year - but the year is illegible. There are one or two notices on the door. Where are the rest? Maybe there is no news in Zhetl. The old cemetery. This is where our great grandfather's grandfathers are buried. The Jewish community in Zhetl began in this area.

[Page 15]

The bathhouse and the first power station.

Here is the Talmud Torah on the bank of the Pomeraika. It has already been renovated, however there are holes in the chimney. Apparently some guys climbed up onto the roof and took a few shingles to make guns. Now they are "dignified". They are posing for the camera with their teacher.

A little further, behind the Talmud Torah you can see the tower of the fire station and the church in a rare picture. A Polish nobleman is riding in a carriage drawn by two horses and surrounding him are farmers wearing shoes made of hemp, fur lined coats and characteristic hats.

[Page 16]

A few steps further stands the "Balnitza", this is what we called the hospital and public clinic. When was this building built? By whom? I think it was one of Yisroel Ozer's accomplishments. He bought it from the Russian authorities.

On the other side of Lisagura, on a hill, is the place where Zhetl buried its dead for over 200 years. Reb Yisroel Ber the undertaker lives in the small house with his family. However, behind the fence, in the shade of many branched trees, 8 generations of Zhetl Jews rest eternally. Oh, if only we could take a peek at the other side of the fence, if we could just copy the texts on tombstones, we would trace our origins back to the 18th century. This is also the place of the mass grave of 2,000 of Zhetl's holy martyrs.

We jump from the new cemetery. Now we are at the banks of the Zhetlka. From a distance we can see the wooden shingled roofs on Slonim Street. Closer, we see three young men from Zhetl posing on the bridge which the Germans destroyed. Back in the olden days, this was a moveable bridge which protected the palace from enemy attacks.

[Page 17]

Here is the Post Office, or as we called it in Zhetl the "Potcht". This house connected Zhetl with the rest of the world. This is where a package from America would arrive, or a love letter from a young man to his girlfriend. The Party secretaries would rush here to pick up circulars that arrived from the central office.

Four streets meet here. Everyone runs to Yatre's stoop. The kids just smelled the camera and gathered. Maybe you are looking at yourself in this crowd and you don't recognize yourself.

This is what Estate Street looked like. In the distance, the church. Up close, wooden and brick houses. Mordkhaithe shoemaker and Issar the baker lived here. The latter folds his arms and smiles.

This is a bird's eye view of Estate Street. It turns like a question mark with many sloping roofs and four cornered chimneys. Generations of Zhetl's Jews lived on these streets, in these houses, on the balconies and stoops. Today, no trace of them remains, just pictures…and a long list of Jews who were killed just because they were Jews!

[Page 18]

אל

מלא רחמים שוכן במרומים, המצא
מנוחה נכונה על כנפי השכינה,
במעלות קדושים וטהורים, כזהר
הרקיע מזהירים, לנשמותיהם של
שלושת אלפי בני הקהילה הקדושה

ז'טל

אנשים, נשים וטף
שנהרגו, נשחטו, נשרפו, נחנקו ונקברו
חיים בידי הלויני היטלר ומסיתיהם
הרשעים, ימח שמם, בשנים 1941–1944.
בגן עדן תהא מנוחתם.
לכן בעל הרחמים יסתיר בצל כנפיו
את נשמותיהם,
ה' הוא נחלתם,
וינוחו בשלום על משכבם
ונאמר: אמן!

Translated by Judy Montel

Merciful God

in heaven, grant perfect repose to the souls of the three thousand members of the holy community of

Zhetl

men, women and children,
who were murdered, slaughtered, burned, strangled and buried alive
by the hangmen of Hitler and their evil servants,
may their names be erased, during the years 1941-1944;
may they be under thy divine wings among the holy and pure who shine bright as the sky;
may their place of rest be in paradise.
Merciful One, O keep their souls forever alive in thy protective wings.
The Lord being their heritage,
may they rest in peace
and let us say, Amen.

[Page 19]

By the graves of the martyrs of Zhetl on the sixth anniversary of their death

Zhetl Martyrs

Who were shot to bestial perfection by the Hitlerist executioners
in Zhetl, Dvoretz and neighboring communities in 1941-1944

Translated by David Goldman

א Alef

ABRANAK	Mordechai, Miriam and son
ABELEVITCH	Yaakov and Yosef
ABELEVITCH	Yisrael, wife and child
ABERSTEIN	Yaakov, Pessya, Sheyna, Zechariah and wife
ABERSTEIN	Leib and Yisrael
ABRAMOVITCH	Chaim, Perl and Fruma
AGULNICK	Motleya and two children
AGUSHEVITCH	Yitzchak and Yenta
AVZEROVITCH	Zeidel, Leiba, Feigel and a little brother
OTKIN	Malka
OVSEYEVITCH	Yehoshua, Etel and Dina
OVSEYEVITCH	Yosef and Chaya
OVSEYEVITCH	Yitzchak
ORINOVITCH	Leah, husband and son
IVENITZKY	Avraham, Esther, Berl and Sarah
IZBARNITZKY	Chaim Berl, Yehudis and Sheyna Chana
EINBINDER	Pesach, Chaya, Sarah, Berl and Yehudis
EINSTEIN	Hinda, Shlomo and Devorah
INDERSTEIN	Avraham, Zlata, Sarah Leah, and Leib
INDERSTEIN	Fruma, Lyuba, Sarah Musha, Yosef, Mayrim and Yaakov
INDERSTEIN	Moshe, Zlata and two children
INDERSTEIN	David, Avraham and Malka
INDERSTEIN	Dvosha and mother
INDERSTEIN	Moshe, Yehudis and two children
INDERSTEIN	Necha and Masha

Remember what Amalek did to you!

[Page 20]

INDERSTEIN	Dvosha and Moshe's mother
INDERSTEIN	Alta and Zalman
ITZKOVITCH	Sarah and three children
OCHONOVSKY	Leah, Yedidiah, son and daughter
ALPERT	Chana Rachel, Chaya, Berl, Yosef and Baruch
ALPERT	Aharon
ALPERT	Mordechai and Michla
ALPERT	Sula, Chana, Lyuba, Shlomo and Gedaliah
ALPERT	Sarah and son
ALPERT	Falka, Chaya and Yitzchak
ALPERT	Moshe and Freidel
ALPERT	Hirsh, Sarah, Ozer and Devorah
ALPERT	Esther and Chana
ALPERT	Yisrael, Malka, Avraham, Berl and Moshe
ALPERT	Shimon, wife and children
ALPERT	Wolf, Chaya Sarah and Reizel
ALPERT	Keyla, Ozer and Yocha
ALPERT	Moshe, wife and two children
ALPERT	Devorah and three children
ALPERSTEIN	Chaim, Sarah, Moshe, Chaya, Yehudis and Liba
ALPERSTEIN	Chaya Esther, her husband David and children
ALPERSTEIN	Zerach, Basha, Pesha, Mottel, Henya and and Leib
ALPERSTEIN	Zalman, Frida, Sheina Beyla and Reuven
ALPERSTEIN	Shosha, husband and children
ALPERSTEIN	Reuven
ALPERSTEIN	(wife of Yudel Zerach) and child
ALPERSTEIN	Velvel
ARONOVITCH	Ezriel
ORLINSKY	Leib, Rikla, Chana, Reizel, Faya and Henech
ORLINSKY	Baruch, Liba, Devorah, Chaya and Yaakov
ORLINSKY	Rivka Rachel
ORLINSKY	Leah, Yitzchak, Meir and Izak
ORLINSKY	Moshe, wife and three children
ARKIN	Yitzchak and son

ב Beit

BAGDANOVITCH	Yosef, Malka and Yehudis
BAYER	Moshe, Feigel, Musha, Guta and Anshel
BOYER	Musha, Guta and Anshel
BACHRACH	Chana, Bella and son
BAM	Beyla
BAM	wife and child
BAM	Chaya (Berkovsky), her husband and child
BARISHANSKY	Yisrael Ozer, Chaya, Rivka, Sarah, Hillel, Tchira Mera and husband
BARISHANSKY	Avraham Moshe, Guta Minya, Yudel, Binyamin, Aharon and Rachel
BULANSKY	Eliezer, Sima, Miriam and Chaim Yitzchak
BUSSELL	Baruch, Bracha and Pesach
BUSSELL	Eliyahu, Shasha and Feigel
BUSSELL	Hirsh, Leah, Malka, Shlomo, Maryasha and child
BUSSELL	Meir, wife and three children
BUSSELL	Kalman, Blyuma, Moshe and another child
BUSSELL	Reizshe Mera, Zviya and Leah
BUSSELL	Avraham, wife and child
BUSSELL	Yitzchak, Chaya and three children
BUSSELL	Betzalel, wife, Chaya and Avraham
BUSSELL	Izak Hershel, Mera and Chana
BUSSELL	Yisrael
BUSSELL	Izak Hershel, Miriam and Esther
BUSHLIN	Betzalel, Frida and Chaya
BUSHLIN	Yosef, Miriam and Rivka
BUSHLIN	Chaya Hodel, Yosef, Rivka, Chaim and Sarah
BUTKOVSKY	Hirsh and Rivka
BITENSKY	Moshe
BYELITSKY	Chyenka, Betzalel, Sarah and child
BYELITSKY	Shimon, Chaya and two children
BYELITSKY	Sarah, Benya and three children
BYELITSKY	Guta
BYELITSKY	Rachel, Etel, Yudel, wife and child

BYELITSKY	Mordechai
BYELITSKY	Yitzchak, Etel, and two children
BYELITSKY	Moshe, Pessya and two children
BELAUS	Yisrael, Chana and Chaim
BENSKY	Malka and Dina
BENYAMINOVITCH	Devorah

May G-D avenge their blood!

[Page 21]

BENYAMINOVITCH	Avraham Chaim, Sarah, Yosef and Leibel
BENYAMINOVITCH	Hirsh, Nechama, Yosef, Moshe and Yerachmiel
BENYAMINOVITCH	Yitzchak, Rivka, Zlata and Velvel
BECKENSTEIN	Chaim, Chasha, Devorah and son
BERMAN	Zelik, Tamara and Minya
BERMAN	Meir, Gittel and three children
BERMAN	Beyla, Leah and child
BERMAN	Eidela
BERMAN	Leib, Sula, Rachel, Minya and another child
BERMAN	Teyba, Melech, Avraham, Yehudis, Rachel and her husband
BERMAN	Hirsh, Tsippa, Avraham, Shlomo, Chana and two children
BERMAN	Elka, Feigel, her husband and two children and Eliezer
BERMAN	Avraham Eliezer
BERMAN	Esther
BERMAN	Yissachar, Mila, Nachum, Avraham and Lyuba
BERMAN	Zalman and Elka Chaya
BERNICKER	Avraham, Chaya Sarah, Michel and Yaakov
BERNICKER	Alta, Yosef and Yaakov
BERNICKER	Vela Zelda, Yehudis and two children
BERKOVSKY	Shneur, Sarah and Etel
BERKOVSKY	Moshe, Yenta and child
BERKOVITCH	Rivka and child
BERKOVITCH	David, wife and five children
BERKOVSKY	Reuven, Sarah Leah, Fruma, Miriam anda child
BECKSTEIN	Leib, Bobel, Masha, Frida and Shlomo

BRONSTEIN	Leah, Shachna and Basha Devorah
BRESKIN	Sheina, Betzalel, Mordechai, Rivka, child, Moshe, Sarah Liba and husband
BRESKIN	Sarah Pesha
BRESKIN	Avraham Aharon, wife, Mila and Rivka
BRESKIN	Chaim, Meyta, Ita and Nechama
BRESTOVSKY	Avraham, Rivka, and child

ג Gimel

GOVRIN	Rachel Leah and Chaim Leib
GOL	Avraham Nachman and Miriam
GOLDBERG	Feivel, Shprintsa, Feigel and Nechama
GOLDMAN	Leah
GOLDSTEIN	Shlomo Chaim and Zlata
GOLDSTEIN	Moshe, Ladka, Breina, Molya, and and Fruma Chyenka
GOLDSTEIN	RIvka, Yosef, Michel, Reizel, Eliezer and Bracha
GOLDSTEIN	Aharon, Sima and children
GOLDSTEIN	mother of Sima
GANUZOVITCH	Chaya Leah
GANUZOVITCH	Chiam, Chasya, Frida, Sarah and Feivel her husband
GANTCHAROVSKY	Kreina and three children
GANKOVSKY	Netta, Sarah, Ita, Michel and son
GAFANOVITCH	Pesha, Malka, Chana, Shifra, Michlia
GAFANOVITCH	Michla
GARBER	Chaim Eliyahu, Zlata and Yechezkel
GORDON	Yitzchak, Rivka, Chaya and Hinda
GORDON	Yitzchak, Sima, Yaakov, Yisrael, Rashel and daughter
GUZOVSKY	Avraham
GUZOVSKY	Avraham, Sima, Leib and Binyamin
GERLING	Simela
GERTSOVSKY	Leib, Mina, Miriam and Gittel
GERTSOVSKY	Yosef
GERTSOVSKY	Asna, Berl and Henya
GERTSOVSKY	Isser, Rosa and Asher
GERTSOVSKY	Alter, Chaya Lyuba, Hirsh and Aharon

GERTSOVSKY	Zalman, Sarah, Ephraim, Avraham and Zevulun
GERTSOVSKY	Gutel's wife and two children
GERTSOVSKY	Wolf and Sarah Leah
GERTSOVSKY	Blyuma Tsippa
GERTSOVSKY	Avraham and Fruma
GERTSOVSKY	Sima and Meyriam
GERTSOVSKY	Shmuel and Leah Michla
GERSHOVSKY	Chanan, Tsirel, Elka, Henya, Chaya and Hinda
GREEN	Zalman, Chana and Henya
GREEN	Binyamin, Masha, Rivka, Shmuel and Genya
GREEN	Pinchas, Feigel and child
GREEN	Liza and husband

War for G-d Against Amalek From Generation to Generation! (Exodus 17)

[Page 22]

ד **Dalet**

DAREVSKY	Leib, Chaya, Teyba and two sons
DVORETSKY	Chaya and three children
DVORETSKY	Henya, Alter, Raya and Yoel
DVORETSKY	Berl, Sarah and Etel
DVORETSKY	Moshe, Esther and Meyriam
DVORETSKY	Yehoshua, Chana, Feigel, Leah and two sons
DVORETSKY	Yitzchak, Alta and son
DVORETSKY	Chaim Meir, Chava, Nishka and Rivka
DONYETZ	Yoel David, Basha, Shifra and Antsel
DONYETZ	Sarah Rachel
JENTCHELSKY	Leib, Beyla, Rivka, Mordechai, Naftali, Miriam and Chyena
JENTCHELSKY	Yonah, Devorah, and son
JENTCHELSKY	Chyenka, Yacha, Yechiel, wife and child
DYCHOVSKY	Leib, Leah and Shulamis
DELATISKY	mother, Aharon, Moshe and two children
DERETCHINSKY	Tuvia, Miriam and three children

DERETCHINSKY	husband and wife

ה Heh

HANDELSON	and his wife, Masha, Devorah and Chaya
HANDELSON	Chana
HORNSTEIN	Yitzchak and Regina
HORNSTEIN	Yisrael, Feigel, Wolf, Mendel and Yetta
HEIDUKOVSKY	Avraham, Zelda, Berl, Ita and son
HEIDUKOVSKY	Dvosha, Zelda and Hinda
HEIDUKOVSKY	Gershon, Eidela, Zelik and Rachel
HEIDUKOVSKY	Yehoshua, Cherna, Feigel and Chaim Eliezer
HEIDUKOVSKY	Golda, Zelik, Aharon and Berl
HEIDUKOVSKY	Sarah and three children

ו Vav

WOLFOVITCH	Hirsh Aharon, Dina, Baruch and Yonah
WOLFOVITCH	Yaakov and Devorah
WOLFOVITCH	Avraham, Devorah and Musha
WOLFOVITCH	Meir, Sarah, Zelik, Baruch and Mordechai
WOLFOVITCH	Asher, Liba and Eliezer
WOLFOVITCH	Yitzchak, Yenta and Yonah
WOLFOVITCH	Henya
WEINSTEIN	Shmuel, David, Teyba, Henech and Meyriam
WEINSTEIN	Shmuel David's mother
WEINSTEIN	Binyamin, Cherna, Chana, Mordechai and Sheyna
WEINSTEIN	Zelda
WEINSTEIN	Zelda (Eta's)
VINOKUR	Moshe, Pessya Berl and Leibel
VINICK	Yaakov and Frida
VINARSKY	Aharon, Rachel and two children
VINYETSKY	Sonia
VISMANSKY	Yitzchak, Fruma and Chaya Tolya
VELIKANSKY	Alta
VERNICK	Reizel and son

ז Zayin

ZABLATSKY	Yisrael and Golda
ZABELINSKY	Avraham and Malka
ZABELINSKY	Elyusha, Ida and Alec
ZAYANTCHEK	Mina
ZALTSSTEIN	Shlomo, Ita, Sarah and son
ZAMASHCHIK	Alter, Hinda, Zalman, Nisan and Chaya
ZAMASHCHIK	Michla
ZAMASHCHIK	Nachum, Rachel and Chaya
ZAMASHCHIK	Yaakov and Golda
ZAMASHCHIK	Isser, wife and two children
ZAMASHCHIK	Yosef, Esther Malka and two children
ZANARATSKY	Yisrael and Dina
ZATSEPITSKY	Nachum and Rivka
ZAKANOVITCH	Eliyahu, Sarah, Liba and Yitzchak Isaac
ZAKREISKY	Avraham and Basha
ZAKREISKY	Nechama, her husband and child
ZAKREISKY	Frida , Mordechai and Shmuel
ZAKREISKY	Chaya, husband and two children
ZLOTSKOVSKY	Shlomo, Miriam and two children

Write This As a Memorial in a Book (Exodus 17)

[Page 23]

ZELIKOVITCH	Yaakov, Sheina Chana and David
ZERNITSKY	Chaya, Alter and Miriam
ZSHUCHOVITSKY	Gershon, Zelda, Leah, Leib and Risha
ZSHUCHOVITSKY	Hinda and child

ח Chet

KHURGIN	Rabbi Zvi, his brother-in-law Yosef and sister-in-law Basya
KHAITOVITCH	Zlata, her husband, Reuven and Michla
KHASID	Moshe and wife

KHANANKIND   Hirsh and Sarah

ט Tet

TURETSKY	Berl and Liba
TURETSKY	Mordechai, Liba and children
TURETSKY	Moshe, Chana and son
TILEVITCH	Gershon, Etel and two children
TINKOVITSKY	Esther Leah, and Rivka
TROTSKY	Reuven, Hinda and Sonia
TREGER	Yosef and Pessya
TREGER	Zvia, Meir and two children
TCHATCHINA	Shmuel, Frida and two daughters
CHEMERINSKY	Leah and Dalia
CHMERINSKY	Chaim and Frida
CHESSLER	Chaim, Chana, Leib and Malka
CHEPLAVODSKY	Yoel, Rachel and three children
CHEPLAVODSKSY	Shlomo and Tsirel

י Yud

YATVITSKY	Mordechai, Sarah and two children
YATVITSKY	Binyamin, Beyla, Asna and three children
YANKELOVITCH	Shlomo, Chana, Tzvia, Hershel and Ezriel
YANKELOVITCH	Gershon and Zvia
YOSSELOVITCH	Aharon, Elka, Nasan, Efraim and Feigel
YOSSELOVITCH	Moshe Wolf
YOSSELOVITCH	Chaim Feivel, wife, Yaakov and Ita
YOSSELOVITCH	Pinchas, wife, Guta and Menucha
YARMOVSKY	Yisrael
YUDELEVITCH	Chava and Yosef
YUDELEVITCH	Elya, Chana and Neta
YEVELEVITCH	Yeshayahu and Hinda
YELLIN	Devorah
YERUCHIMOVITCH	Esther

כ Khaf

CHARABRAVITSKY	Mendel and two children
CHLEBNIK	Henya Leah, Yudel, Liba, Reuven and Yisrael
KATZ	Chaya Leah and Reuven

ל Lamed

LOZOVSKY	Yosef and Meita
LANGBART	Aharon Hirsh and wife
LANGBART	Avraham and Pessya
LANTZEVITSKY	Eliyahu and child
LANTZEVITSKY	Meir, Hinya, Liba Leah, Sarah and Motel
LANTZEVITSKY	Breina and two children
LASH	Alter, wife and child
LUBETKIN	Asher
LUBETKIN	Noach, Liba, Sheina, Beyla, Reuven and Frida
LUSKY	Chaya Leah and Beyla
LUSKY	Rivka and husband
LUSKY	Asher and Sarah Chana
LUSKY	Rafael, Liba Chana and Avigdor
LUSKY	Moshe Izshik and Sheyna
LUSKY	Pinchas, Hinda and Eidel
LUSKY	Chana Rivka
LUSKY	Rachel and Masha
LUSKY	Yaakov, Rachel and two children
LUSKY	Meir, Rivka, Chan and Eliezer
LUSKY	Yehuda and Liba
LUSKY	Yosef, Yachna and Chana
LUSKY	Mordechai, Perl, Mitya and Elyusha
LUSKY	Mordechai, Pesha, Yitzchak and Leah
LUSKY	Avraham, Babel, her mother Kreina Chaya and Yitzchak
LUSKY	Yehoshua, Sarah, Malka, Dova and David
LIASSY	Eshka and Liba
LIASS	Lyuba and Chaim
LIDSKY	Yisrael, Risha, Feigel, Chaim and Sarah

| LIDSKY | Shlom, Nechama and Basya |
| LIDSKY | Nachman, Liba, Aharon, Nisan and Moshe |

The Revenge of a Small Child – Satan has no yet created!

[Page 24]

LIDSKY	Yisrael, wife and three children
LIDSKY	Feigel and Chana
LEIBOVITCH	Mordechai, Zlata and Hadassah
LEIBOVITCH	Wolf and Rachel
LEIBOVITCH	Yaakov, Chana, Chanan and Yehuda
LEIBOVITCH	Leah and Basha
LEIBOVITCH	Eliyahu, Shulamis, Falka, Sarah and Etele
LEIBOVITCH	Yechezkel, Eliezer and Dvosha
LEIBOVITCH	Sheina and Yehuda
LEIZEROVITCH	Faya, Hinda, Feigel and Avraham
LICHTER	Rivka, Isser, Yerachmiel, David and Zalman
LISAGORSKY	Baruch, wife and three children
LYEVARONTSHIK	Noach, wife and Sarah
LYEVARONTSHIK	Noach and Miriam
LYEVARONTSHIK	Sarah and husband
LYEVARONTSHIK	Binyamin, Dvosha, Yehoshua, Fruma and Henech
LIPSKY	Yaakov, wife and Baruch
LIFSHITZ	Aharon and Etel
LEV	Avraham and wife
LEVITT	Miriam, Moshe, Avraham and son
LEVITT	Yaakov and Faya
LEVITT	Chaim Eliezer, Devorah, Avraham Simcha, Sarah, Nachum, Moshe, Shifra, and Frida Hinda
LEVITT	Sarah and two children
LEVITT	Hirsh, Chaya and Betzalel
LEVITT	Chaya Sarah, Isser, Hoda and Hinda
LEVITT	Moshe and Kalman
LEVITT	Alter, Yehudis, Sarah Rachel, and Yisrael
LEVITT	Wolf, Chaya and Rachel

LEVITT	Kalman, Etel, Motel, Guta and Frida
LEVITT	Dvosha and Pessya
LEVITT	Asher, Fruma Sarah, Lyuba and Rivka
LEVITT	Chaim, Chava, Chana and Yoel
LEVITT	Berl and Sheyna
LEVITT	Yehuda, Henya and Chaya
LEVITT	Yehoshua, Hinda and son
LEVITT	Meir, Sarah, Rivka and two children
LEVENBUK	Michla, Hirsh, Chaya, Miriam, Rachel and Hillel
LEVKOVITCH	Dr.

מ Mem

MOVSHOVITCH	Pincas, Pesha, Leah and second child
MOVSHOVITCH	Yitzchak, Feigel, Reizel and brother
MOVSHOVITCH	Yitzchak, wife and daughter
MAYEVSKY	Yisrael, Asher, Chaya, Chanan and Hinda
MAYEVSKY	Meir, Pesya, Sarah, Avraham and Feivel
MAYEVSKY	Moshe Gedaliah, Yenta Rivka, Freidela and David
MAYEVSKY	Yehuda, Chaya Sarah, and Yitzchak
MAYEVSKY	Dvosya, Pinchas and Chaim
MALACHOVSKY	Reuven, wife and two children
MANN	Chaim Hershel
MANKOVITCH	Chana, Esther, Ephraim, Yosef and Avraham
MANKOVITCH	Meir, Reizel, Berl, Mendel and Fruma
MANKOVITCH	Baruch and Zavel
MANKOVITCH	Rikla and Zavel [sic]
MANKOVITCH	Meir, wife and child
MORDKOVSKY	Hodel and Yocha
MORDKOVSKY	Etel and husband
MORDKOVSKY	Rachel, Ita and Aharon
MARCUS	Shmerl
MOSHKOVSKY	Betzalel, Necha, Masha, Mordechai and Sarah
MAGID	Bracha, Yechezkel and Chanan
MILKOVSKY	Noach, wife and child

MIRSKY	Chaya, Gershon, Rachel and Fruma
MIRSKY	Avraham, wife and two children
MIRSKY	Shmuel and Moshe
MIRSKY	Zalman, Elka and two children
MIRSKY	Pinchas, Beyla, Yosef, Eliezer, Yaakov and Basya
MIRSKY	Leibel
MIRSKY	Sonia and Fruma
MENUSKIN	Noach, Chana and two children
MENUSKIN	Ita, Cherna and husband
MENUSKIN	Yosef, Devorah and Freidel
MENUSKIN	Beyla and Rosha
MENUSKIN	Aharon
MENUSKIN	Berl and Shpetl
MEDVETSKY	David Wolf and Miriam
MEDVETSKY	David Hirsh
MEDVETSKY	Eliyahu and Mirel
MEDVETSKY	Michel Baruch, wife and two daughters

Pursue Our Killers In Anger And Exterminate Them From Under The Heavens!

[Page 25]

MEDVETSKY	Esther and four children
MEDVETSKY	David, Leah, Shimon, Yaakov and Yisrael
MEDVETSKY	Babel, Yenta and Yonah
MELNIKOVSKY	Meir, Sarah, Chaya, Rivka and Yaakov

נ Nun

NODELSTEIN	Michla, Babel and Henya
NODELSTEIN	Gelya
NOVOGRODSKY	Avraham Moshe, Rivka, Gavriel, Chaya, Yosef and Aharon Eliezer
NOVOGRODSKY	Henech
NOVOGRODSKY	Eliezer, Sheina and child
NOVOGRODSKY	Reuven, Yenta and two children
NOVOLENSKY	Eliyahu, Sarah, Yehoshua and two children

NATKOVITCH	Chaim, Toyba, Avraham, Guta, Moshe and [sic] another child
NACHIMOVSKY	Aharon, Leah and daughter
NACHIMOVSKY	Wolf and wife
NACHIMOVSKY	Eliyahu Zvi, Malka and Noach
NAMIAT	Nechama, Moshe, Yerucham and Shepsel
NAMIAT	Yaakov, Nechama and two children
NIGNYENVITSKY	Chaim Eliyahu, Rashe, Sonia, Yocha, Michla, and Yisrael
NYESVIZSHESKY	Chaya Friedel, her husband Yosha and Yekusiel
NIKOLAYEVSKY	Mera, Sarah, Chana and child
NIKOLAYEVSKY	Chana and three children
NISHVITSKY	Moshe, Fruma, Masha and Yitzchak
NEVACHOVITCH	Noach and Chana

ס **Samech**

SAVITSKY	Elka and Sheyna
SAVITSKY	Beinish, Beyla, Sheyna and Rachel
SAVITSKY	Kalman
SAVITSKY	Moshe, wife and two children
SAVITSKY	Yosha, Fruma Leah, Avigdor and two children
SAVITSKY	Mordechai and Chaya
SAVITSKY	Yitzchak, wife and child
SAVITSKY	Shaul, Leah and children
SAVITSKY	Michel, Miriam, Chana and Meir
SAVITSKY	Alter, Yachna and Hershel
SAVITSKY	Avraham, Basha, Efraim and Frida
SAVITSKY	Hershel Meir, Minya, Alter, Yocha, David and Yehudis
SAVITSKY	Binyamin, Shifra and two children
SAVITSKY	Yaakov Shimon, Hinda and Avraham
SAVITSKY	Grones, Frida, Rachel and Mordechai Aharon
SAVITSKY	Henya, Chaya, Yisrael and children
SAVITSKY	Meir, Isaac, Reuven, Liba, Reizel, Yitzchak Ber and another child
SAVITSKY	Mordechai and son
SAVITSKY	Leah, her husband and children
SAVITSKY	Leah, and two children

SAVITSKY	Meita, Avraham Yosef, and child
SAVITSKY	Yehuda and Shifra
SALMON	Yitzchak, Leah Sarah, Masha, and Mordechai Velvel
SOLOMON	[sic]Yeshayahu, Beyla, Moshe and Reizel
SOKOLVSKY	Chaim, Zelda, Shifra and Chanan
SOKOLOVSKY	Alter, Esther, Felta, and Risha
SOKOLOVSKY	Antzel, Necha and two children
SOKOLOVSKY	Avraham Izshik, Feigel, Sonia and Minya
SOKOLOVSKY	Yitzchak, wife and two children
SOKOLOVSKY	Feivel, Dova and children
SOKOLOVSKY	Feigel, Sonia and Mina
SOKOLOVSKY	Shifra and husband
SOKOLOVSKY	Gela and son
SLUTSKY	Kreina and Nachman
SLUTSKY	Moshe and Kuna
SLUTSKY	Gershon, Sarah and two children
SLUTSKY	Leizer Eliyahu, Chaya Rachel and Zelik
SLONIMSKY	Avraham, Henya Leah, Berl, Pinchas
SLONIMSKY	Shmuel, his wife and three children
SNAVSKY	Berl and Leah
SENDEROVSKY	Leizer, Rivka and GIttel
SENDEROVSKY	Rivka
SENDEROVSKY	Menachem, Shalom, Moshe and Reizel
SENDEROVSKY	Yisrael and wife
SENDEROVSKY	Hillel and Malka
SENDEROVSKY	David, Maryasha and Yisrael
SENDEROVSKY	Mordechai, Manya and Berl
SENDEROVSKY	Hinda and child
SENDEROVSKY	Avraham, Henya, Risha and Sheyna

Thus Shall Your Persecutors Be Destroyed, O Israel!

[Page 26]

SENDEROVSKY	Rivka, husband and son
SENDEROVSKY	Chyena, Rivka, Miriam, Meir and Eliezer

SENDEROVSKY	Michael and Zelda
SENDEROVSKY	Chanan, Rivka, Eliezer Miriam and Meir
SENDEROVSKY	Yehuda, Rivka, Zilpa and brother
SENDEROVSKY	Leizer Chaim, Mirel and child
SENDEROVSKY	Kalman, Shepsel, Avraham and sister
SENDEROVSKY	Ben-zion, Chava, Shepsel, brother and
SENDEROVSKY	Freidel, Leah and Sonia
SENDEROVSKY	Asher, Rachel and child
SENDEROVSKY	David, Devorah, Yosef and Sarah
SENDEROVSKY	Aharon and Sarah Leah
SENDEROVSKY	Yaakov and Chaya
SENDEROVSKY	Isser, Feigel, Michla and another two children
SKROBUN	Tsirel, Elka and Mera
SKROBUN	Eliyahu, Chaim, Rachel and two children

ע Ayin

EPSTEIN	Aharon Zelik, Yitzchak, Avraham, Eliyahu, Chaim and Asna
EPSTEIN	Masha and Yaakov
EPSTEIN	Miriam, Yaakov, Yosef and Avraham
EPSTEIN	Tanchum, Sarah, Rivka, Yitzchak, Chaya and Sheyna
EPSTEIN	Moshe Avraham, Feivel and Mulik
EPSTEIN	Feigel, Lyuba, and Mira
EPSTEIN	Yisrael Ber, Reizel, Henya and Mina
EPSTEIN	Chaim Meir, Basya and Velya
EPSTEIN	Rachel
EPSTEIN	Dr., his wife, Rafael, Daniel and Lusik
EPSTEIN	Hirsh, Chasya, and two children
EPSTEIN	Sarah and Feivel

פ Peh

PODLASKY	Yechezkel and Fruma
PODLASKY	Mordechai, Basya and mother
PODLASKY	(teacher), wife and two children
PODLISHEVSKY	Leib, Minya, Leah and two children

PAZDUNSKY	Rivka, Moshe, wife and daughter
POTASHNIK	and wife
POLIAK	Tuvia, Feigel Sarah, Chasha and Beyla
PATSOVSKY	Yaakov, Zlata and Hirsh
PORETSKY	Moshe, Gnesha, Reizel and Mulya
FARFEL	Wolf, Eidele, Betya and Solik
FUNT	Shaul, Sima and Tsila
FYALON	Shalom
FYVUZSHINSKY	Shmerl, Frida and four children
FYVUZSHINSKY	Pesach, Betsalel, Breina, Shmuel, Velvel, and a child
FILOTOVITCH	Devorah, Michla, Basha and Leib
PILNIK	Yitzchak, Esther and two children
PILNIK	Yeshayahu Moshe, Mera and Michla
PILNIK	Yaakov, Rivka and two children
FILIN	Mendel and Necha
FIN	Reuven, Chava Leah, Shlomo, Chaim and Zlata
FIN	Liba
PINTSHUK	Berl, Rivka, Sonia, and two other children
PINTSHUK	Yaakov, Miriam, Nechama, Noach and a child
PINTEL	Menashe, Sarah and Yudel Moshe
PINSKY	Baruch Lipa, Henya and Rachel
PISHKOVITCH	Berl, Shasha, Zelda and Ita
PESKOVSKY	Ben-Zion, Malka and Leibel
PERSKY	Yaakov
PERGOMENIK	YIsrael, Miriam, Henya and Rachel
FRIEDSON	Dr. and wife and child
FRIEDBERG	Basha

צ Tsadi

TSEITLIN	Sonia and daughter

ק Kof

KABAK	Yerucham, Miriam, Chinka and Shalom
KABAK	Zelda and two children

KAGAN	Yisrael
KAGAN	Mendel, Rivka and two children
KAGAN	Yaakov, Dr., [sic] Rachel and Aviva
KAGAN	Yitzchak, Etel, Elka, Rachel, Alter and Pinchas
KOVENSKY	Eliezer and Eshka
KOVENSKY	Aharon David, Teibel and two children
KAVENSKY	Yehuda, Pesha and child

I Conferred My Revenge Upon Edom (Ezekiel 25)

[Page 27]

KAVENSKY	Leib and Yisrael
KAVENSKY	Shmuel and wife
KAVENSKY	Feigel, Avraham and Matlia
KAVENSKY	Zelik, Devorah, Hirsh and two other children
KAVENSKY	Kalman, Alta and son
KAVENSKY	Michael, Frida and husband
KAVENSKY	Moshe and Rachel
KALBSTEIN	Meir, Leah, Itel, Esther, Avraham and Sarah
KALBSTEIN	Chaim Velvel, Elka, Yisrael, Chana, Ita, Rashel and Henya
KALBSTEIN	Michel, Tamara, and two children
KALTON	Shalom, wife and three children
KALAMANOVSKY	Michel
KOLEDITSKY	Yitzhak, Bracha, Mordechai and Henech
KAMINSKY	and daughter
KANTROVITCH	Berl, wife, Tsippa, Gnesha, Chasya and three other children
KANTROVITCH	Binyamin, Mera, Berl and son
KANTROVITCH	Reizel, Masha, and Yechezkel
KANTESBART	Musha, Meir, Chana and two children
KONTSEVIK	Aharon and Teyba
KAPLAN	Mordechai, Leah, Chaya and David
KAPLAN	Yaakov
KAPLAN	Yosef, Shasha, husband and child
KAPLINSKY	Shaul and Rafael
KAPLINSKY	Nyutka

KAPLINSKY	Etel, Yosef, and daughter
KAPLINSKY	Chaim, Liba, Necha and brother
KAPLINSKY	Yaakov Baruch and Sarah
KAPLINSKY	Hirsh, Chasya and child
KAPLINSKY	Yitzchak, Tila, Pinchas and Berl
KAPLINSKY	Cherna and Feigel
KAPLINSKY	Eliyahu, Babel, and three children
KAPLINSKY	Leib, Rosa, Asya, Lalya and Sonia
KAPLINSKY	Yenta
KOPA	(teacher)
KARABELNIK	David, Rashel and son
KORELISHKY	Chana and Moshe
KRAVETSKY	Yirmiyahu, Beyla, Mordechai, Chaya and Yocha
KRAVETZ	Avraham Moshe, and Minya
KRAVETZ	Yitzchak, wife and child
KRAVETZ	Mala
KRAVETZ	Pesha and Maya
KRAVETZ	Yochka and child
KRASHINSKY	Shalom, Rachel, Michla, Frida and Feigel
KRASHINSKY	Yosef, Henya, Basha, Teyba and Gedaliah
KRASHINSKY	(wife of Yitzchak), Tsirel and two other children
KRASHINSKY	Mordechai and Alta
KRUGMAN	Beyla, Chaya, Sarah And Reuven
KRUGMAN	Yehuda, Chaya and Hershele
KRUGMAN	Berl
KROLEVETSKY	Yehoshua, Etsha, Chashka, and Michel
KROLEVETSKY	Tirtsa, Moshe Aharon, wife and children
KRIEGEL	Binyamin, Yenta and Baruch
KORELITSKY	alter, wife, Chaim David, Chaya, Chana, Doba and Miriam
KORELITSKY	Chaya and child
KOSTIN	Shmuel and Chasya
COOPERMAN	Zelik, Alia, Mina and Feivel
COOPERMAN	Yehuda, Rozsha and Yisrae
KLIATSHKA	Dr.
KESTEIN	Hirsh and wife

| KESTEIN | Alta |
| KRAVETSKY | Feigel |

ר Resh

RABINOVITCH	Mordechai, Chaya and Leah
RABINOVITCH	Henya
RABINOVITCH	Ita, Beyla, and Mera
RABINOVITCH	Berl and Beyla
RABINOVITCH	Shlomo
RABINOVITCH	Mordechai
RABINOVITCH	Yoel, Nechama, Malka and son
RABINSTEIN	Gittel
RAVETZ	Simcha, Chaya, Hirsh, Shifra, Shmuel and Mordechai
RAVETZ	Dina and daughter

Pour Out Your Anger On The Murderers!

[Page 28]

RAVETZ	Musha, Rafael, Chaya Sarah, and Musha [sic]
ROSOVSKY	Tuvia, Idel, Ita, Beyla, Sarah, Yisrael Meir, Michel and Rikla
ROSOVSKY	Yehoshua, Freidel, Yosef and Chaya
ROSOVSKY	David, Basha and Yechiel
ROSOVSKY	Berl Moshe and Beyla
ROSOVSKY	Yosef
ROSOVSKY	Moshe and wife
ROSOVSKY	Mordechai, Feigel and Basya
ROSOVSKY	Elyakim, Yenta, Wolf, Michel and Perl
ROSOVSKY	David and two children
ROSOVSKY	Zeidel, Frida, Henya, Feigel and Yehoshua
ROSOVSKY	Hirsh, Elka and child
ROSOVSKY	Elka and child
ROSOVSKY	Yitzchak and Minya Bracha
ROSOVSKY	Pesach, Masha, Chaya and Devorah
ROSOVSKY	Avraham, Zelda, Ben-Zion, Aharon, Chana and Esther Rivka

ROSNOV	Chana Rashka
ROSENFELD	Eliezer, Sarah and Etel
ROZSHANSKY	Feigel
ROZSHANSKY	Tamar, Zelig, Alta, her husband and child
ROZSHANSKY	Hertz and wife
ROZSHANSKY	Yaakov, Felta and son
ROMANOVSKY	Yosef, Doba, Mina and sister
RAMIROVSKY	Yonah, Sarah, Shifra and brother
RAKOVITSKY	Shmuel, Zelda, Sarah and three children
RASHKIN	Yudel Chaim and Menucha
RASHKIN	Avraham, Chaya Rachel, Sarah and sister
RASHKIN	Gershon, Rivka and child
RUBINSTEIN	Henya and Leah
REITZER	Yitzchak the rabbi, and wife
REITZER	Beinish
REITZER	Yisrael, wife and child
REITZER	Sheyna, Tsippora and husband
RESNIK	Shlomo Chaim, Sheyna Hinda and three children
REZNITSKY	Hirsh and Rachel
REZNITSKY	Chana and Zechariah
REZNITSKY	Hirsh and Rachel

ש Shin

SHABAKOVSKY	David and child
SHAYA	(teacher), wife and child
SHOLKOVITCH	Gershon, Malka, Rachel, Sarah and Pinchas
SHOLKOVITCH	Hillel, Ita, Michla, Esther and Henya
SHOLKOVITCH	Shaul, Sheyna, Basha and Noach
SHOLKOVITCH	Chaya, Yitzchak and two children
SHAPIRO	Chana, husband and child
SHAPIRO	Moshe and wife
SHAPIRO	Tana, Sima, Yitzchak, Meir and Yehudis
SHAPIRO	Shmuel, Rachel and two children
SHATZKES	Asna

SHATZKES	Rivka, Leibel, Lyuba and Feigel
SHARLOT	Yitzchak, Chaya and Rivka
SHABSAY	Rivka and Malka
SHVEDSKY	Aharon Leib, Frida, Chaya, Liba, Mei and Zalman
SHVEDSKY	Meir, Golda and child
SHUSHAN	Yehoshua, Sonia, Asher and Yisrael
SHUSHAN	Yehuda, Rachel and two children
SHUSHAN	Menachem
SHTCHIRANSKY	Malka and husband
SHILOVITSKY	Chaim Yonah, Keyla, Sonia, Chasya, Shasha and Nechama
SHILOVITSKY	Chaim and Yaakov
SHILOVITSK	(wife of Chaim), Sonia, Fruma and Yosef
SHIMSHELEVITCH	Keyla, Shimon, Perl and Yitzchak
SHLYAPAK	his wife and child
SHLEP	Yaakov, Zelda, and his sister
SHMAYEVSKY	Aharon, Rachel Leah, Ita and three children
SHMULEVITCH	Ben-Zion, Chaya, Sarah, Malka and Nisan
SHMUSHKOVITCH	Zalman Yitzchak, Cherna and Simcha
SHELUBSKY	Yitzchak Zelik and Beyla
SHEPETNITSKY	David, Sarah, Eliezer and Lyuba
SHEPSHELEVITCH	Zalman
SHEPSHELEVITCH	Michel, Alta, Sheyna and Sarah Liba
SHEPSHELEVITCH	Avraham, Basya, Bracha and Rachel
SHREIBMAN	Noach and Bashka
SHREIBMAN	Shaul, Toyba and Noach

Earth – Do Not Cover Up Their Blood!

[Page 29]

Tragic Dates in the Destruction of Zhetl

June 30, 1941	-	Germans entered Zhetl
July 14, 1941	-	The decree about the yellow patch was published
July 15, 1941	-	The first six Jews of Zhetl were murdered
July 23, 1941	-	Murder of 120 Jews was carried out
October 1, 1941	-	German headquarters was set up in Zhetl
November 28, 1941	-	Zhetl Jews gave up their gold, silver and copper
December 15, 1941	-	400 Zhetl Jews were send to Dvoretz
February 22, 1942	-	Zhetl Jews were confined to the ghetto
April 30, 1942	-	The first massacre of 1000 Zhetl Jews took place
May 11, 1942	-	Alter Dvoretsky and his friends were murdered in the forest
August 6, 1942	-	The last massacre

On the anniversary for the martyrs of Zhetl

Town of Zhetl drawn from memory by Ruven (Rubin) Mirsky.

1. The Public School (Folk School)
2. The Catholic Church
3. The Public Bank (Folk Bank)
4. The New House of Study
5. The Old and Middle House of Study
6. The Bathhouse
7. The Talmud Torah
8. The Hospital
9. The New Cemetery

[Page 31]

"The Market" drawn by the artist Ben (Paris)

The Old Zhetl

"Novoredker Street" drawn by the artist Ben (Paris)

[Page 32]

Zetel on the map of Vaad Arbah Haaratzot

Zhetl and surroundings.

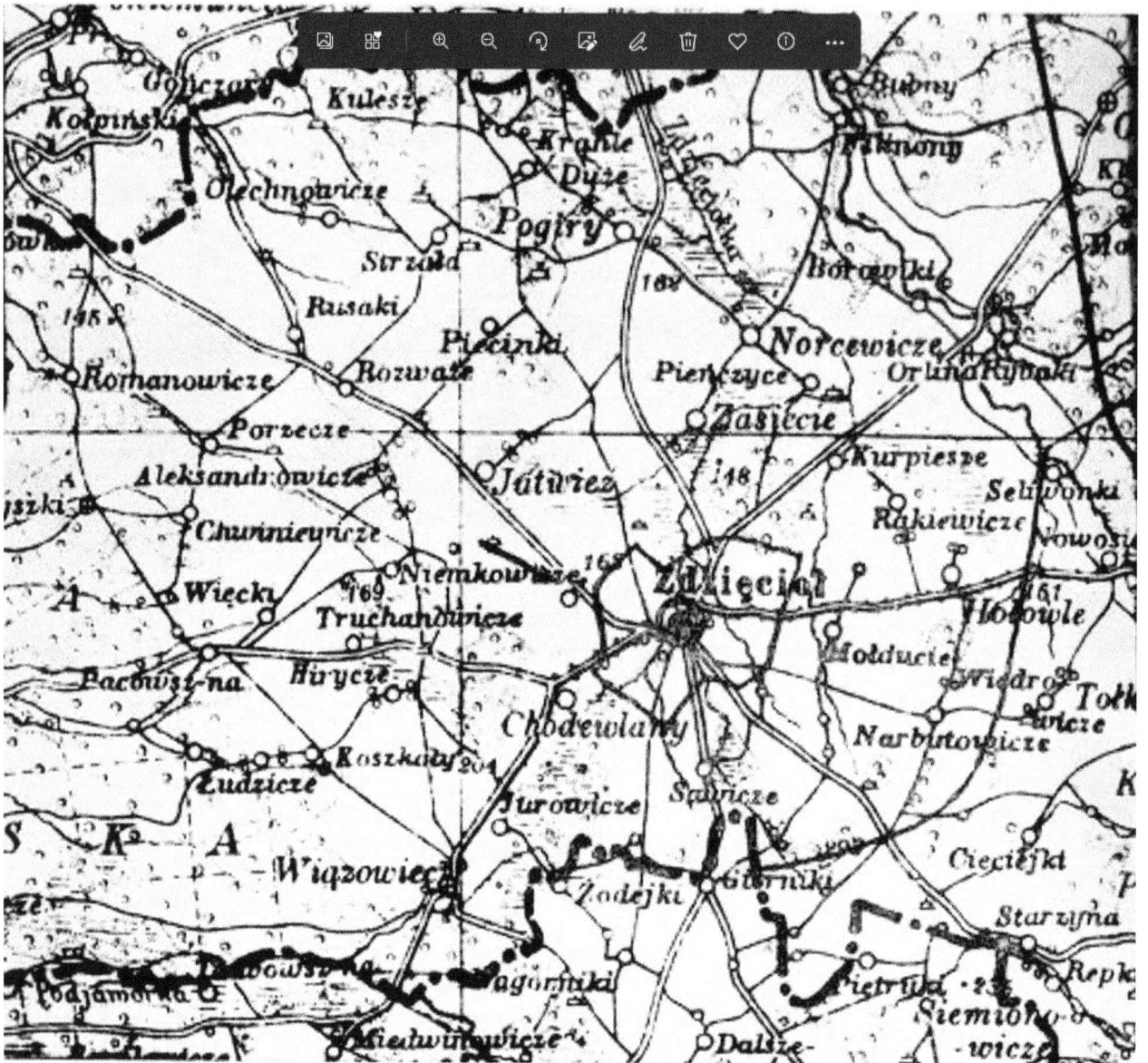

[Page 33]

The History of the Jews of Zhetl

by Borukh Kaplinsky (Tel Aviv)

Translated by Janie Respitz

On the unending plains of White Russia, between Slonim and Novogrudek, in the heart of the district marked by the Nieman and Tchare rivers, lay our town: Zhetl.

Zhetl was not an administrative centre, not a business centre, nor a communications centre and of course not an industrial centre. However, it was a small Jewish centre for three thousand Jewish people.

Borukh Kaplinsky

The three thousand Zhetl Jews earned their meagre living through handiwork and business with the agricultural Christian hinterland, for about 4 ½ centuries.

Despite the economic hardships and the geographic seclusion a lively enterprising spirit pulsated through the community. Zhetl did not miss out on the general and Jewish new political orientations that were emerging. Every new ideology found its supporters and activists. Among the population there were religious zealots, ingenious scholars, orthodox enlighteners, passionate revolutionaries, devoted Zionists, and when adversity demanded – heroic partisans. This existed for 18 generations.

Jews prospered spiritually, but vegetated materially, and founded a community of three thousand Jews with many philanthropic and self help institutions.

As in all Jewish towns and cities Zhetl also had communal activities accompanied by friction and division. There was a time when the town was divided in two camps: artisans and proprietors. Later these two side were called: Zionists and Yiddishists. Sometimes the fight was about a doctor, sometimes a school and sometimes idealistic. However in the unending struggle for material existence and social matters Zhetl Jews displayed a lot of heart and love and solidarity towards fellow Jews.

Lack of Sources

Unfortunately it is not easy for us to describe 18 generations of Zhetl Jewry. Forgetfulness, destruction and the Iron Curtain prevent us from reconstructing the societal life structure which Zhetl Jewry built over the generations.

Many events of the Zhetl Jewish community are recorded in the record books of the Burial Society and the Interest Free Loan Society, but fires and wars destroyed these records. Perhaps the character of the Jews is described in the parish records of the Zhetl Catholic Church and the Zhetl Orthodox Church but the Iron Curtain separates us from both.

Many events were never even recorded. Obviously the history of the Zhetl Jewish community would be enriched if we could see the tombstones at the cemetery.

Unfortunately the majority of sources on the history of Zhetl Jews has been lost or is locked up. We will just have to get a taste through leftovers, crumbs, and small pieces which we have collected in Israel and North America over the last two years.

From these pieces we will attempt to draw a picture of the Jewish community in Zhetl on the backdrop of its general history.

The Founding of Zhetl

This was 458 years ago, the 6th of June 1498. Duke Konstantin Ostrogsky received the right from the Lithuanian Grand Duke Alexander Yogelonchik to found a city on the Zdzietyl estates. Duke Konstantin Ostrogsky, of Belorussian descent and an Orthodox Christian just returned from many years in captivity after the defeat in the war against Moscow. He received this right in recognition of his suffering in captivity.

Later privileges were granted in: 1507, 1509, and 1514 which confirmed the rights of Duke Ostrogsky on the Zdietyl estates, freed him from taxes and allowed him to deal freely on the Nieman.

This is how the history of the Zdzietyl court began and later became a (Shtetl) small town.

Unfortunately we do not have documents about the beginning of Jewish settlement in Zhetl, but one thing is clear. When Zhetl was founded there were no Jews in Lithuania. Three years earlier, in 1495, this same Duke Alexander expelled the Jews from Lithuania.

[Page 34]

Only in 1505 did they return and until this time there were no Jews in Zhetl. From where did the Jews come to Zhetl?

Perhaps from the three large Lithuanian cities: Brisk, Grodno and Trak, perhaps from surrounding towns, or from east and west like all other Lithuanian Jews. At this opportunity here are a few words about Lithuanian Jews.

When Did Jews Arrive in Lithuania?

According to all probabilities Jews came to Lithuania in the 14th century. The tolerant Lithuanian ruler Gediminas (1316–1341) expanded the borders of Lithuania until the Nieman and Bug. He gladly took over foreign lands including their Jews. Gediminas' grandson Vitold (1386– 1430) displayed a tolerant attitude toward the Jews. Thanks to the liberal attitude of both these Lithuanian rulers three large Jewish communities were founded in: Brisk, Grodno and Trak.

The Settlement of Jews in Lithuania

Not only the rulers, but the local population had a milder attitude toward the Jews than in other countries. There were many reasons for this. Firstly, until the second half of the 14th century the Lithuanians were pagans and had no notion of antisemitism. Secondly, later Lithuanian Catholicism was far from fanatic. The main point is: the peasant population of Lithuania needed an intermediary element. The Jews fulfilled this task.

The liberal attitude to Jews in Lithuania is noted in a series of privileges which Duke Vitold gave to the Jews of Brisk, Grodno and Trak.

What Privileges Were Granted?

The privileges granted by Duke Vitold were similar to those granted by Duke Boleslav from Kalisz to the Jews of Poland. They allowed the Jews : 1) Free movement throughout the country; 2) the right to do business; 3) protection of religion; 4) Jewish jurisdiction in conflicts between Jews, and between others: A) a Christian who does not respond to a Jew's cry for help at night – will be accused of robbery, B) a Christian who forcibly enters a Jewish home will be accused of stealing from the state; C) if a Christian kills a Jew he will be accused according to the general code and his belongings will be confiscated; D) a blood libel must be witnessed by three Christians and three Jews; E) throwing stones at a Jewish House of Study or a cemetery results in confiscation of belongings; F) a Jew can be accused by the virtue of two witnesses: one Christian and one Jew; G) religious substance of an allegation is only a Jewish witness when carried out Jewishly; H) A Jewish money lender does not have to give his pledge on the Sabbath.

Lithuanian Jews Settle on Estates and in Villages

As we have seen, elementary privileges and rights were promised to Jews in the cities but many Jews gladly went to villages, estates, crossroads, and borders of the land due to the following reasons: 1) Jews did not enjoy the privileges of Duke Vitold in all cities; 2) Many cities enjoyed the right "No tolerance of Jews"; 3) in the cities there was competition with bourgeoisie. This is why the Jews of Vilna in the 16th century were forbidden to deal in salt, herring and flax or do a job that a Christian could have done.

However besides the material persecution, Jews in the cities, despite the relatively mild attitude in Lithuania, were physically persecuted. An attack on a Jewish quarter was not a rare occurrence.

The First Documented Information About a Jew Called Nisn

The first Jews came to Zhetl in search of bread and security. They probably came right after the expulsion from Lithuania. Here we find the first documented information of a Jew in Zhetl dated April 24th, 1580. In the acts of the Vilna archgeographic commission (Vol. 14 p. 203) we find an announcement under the following headline: "Inventory of the Zdzietyl Estate which belong s to Duke Konstantin Ostrogsky". The text of this announcement reads: in the market in the town of Zdietyl the Jew Mison (a mistaken spelling of Nisn) occupies 8 rods ."

From this announcement we can attain: A) This Jewish man Nisn lived in Zhetl before 1580, as assets were usually registered long after one had settled at that place; 2) from the word "occupy" we assume he is using these rods on a settled piece of land; 3) Zhetl was already a Jewish settlement which had a market, and this Jew Nisn was apparently an inn keeper who built an inn and a house on his 8 rods. He was probably the only Jew in the marketplace, but it is possible that others lived nearby.

[Page 35]

Be that as it may, Nisn the Jew is the historic father of Jewish settlement in Zhetl. We do not know where he came from. We also do not know who his descendants in town were. It is possible that someone reading this book is a great – great grandchild of Reb Nisn who occupied 8 rods in the Zhetl marketplace.

Interestingly, Jewish settlement in Zhetl is not much younger than Jewish settlement in Vilna. The first information about the first two Jews in Vilna dates back to 1551, meaning 29 years earlier than the first Zhetl Jew, Nisn.

There were probably Jews in Zhetl a lot earlier but unfortunately no historical footprints have survived.

Aharon Goshkevitch Litigates

The second piece of information concerning Jews in Zhetl dates from 1598. In a publication from Vilna published in 1901 we read that a Jew from Mizyevets (a village near Zhetl), Aharon Goshkevitch, accuses the Zhetl village elder Andrei Viltchuk with Zhetl nobleman Yarosh Zhibart.

We learn a lot of interesting facts from this act. Firstly, that Aharon Goshkevitch from Mizyevetz was a lessee of the nobleman Mikolai Rey from Naglovitz and moreover he demands the state taxes for beer, honey and whisky, according to the agreement with the village elder (starosta).

The Jew, Aharon Goshkevitch accuses the nobleman Yarosh Zhibart of a few claims. Firstly, he demanded state taxes for the year 1596. Two Zhetl Jews appear in this claim: Meir Levkovitch and Aharon Goshkevitch's son in law, Merl Yuditch. Both Jews were employed by Ahaorn Goshkevitch and demand the taxes from him. From their account we know that Zhibart paid taxes for three quarters of the year and is honouring his debt of a quarter year. Aharon Goshkevitch estimated his loss at 120 Polish groschen but the court ruled only 60.

In a second claim the court ruled Ahahron Goshkevitch did not have to pay Zhibart for measures of barley and grain which he ordered to grind at his mill.

From a third claim we learn that Aharon Goshkevitch rented an apartment from Zhibart. He only lived there for half a year and instead of rent, he freed him from the honey tax.

In another claim, the Jew Aharon Goshkevitch demands from Zhibart 120 groschen for whisky and beer tax. Zhibart presented two witnesses who testified that his wife had paid the tax to the Jew. Aharon denies this and takes pains to reject the witnesses and the document ascertains that due to the Jew's stubbornness there was no judgement delivered on this claim.

From this document we learn: 1) Jews lived in Zhetl: Meir Levkovitch and Merl Yudiych, and the Jew Aharon Goshkevitch lives near Zhetl. All of them work to collect taxes for the starosta of Zhetl. In their conflict with Zhetl nobility they litigate before the starosta who displays objectivity.

We observe Jewish – Christian relations. The Jew, Aharon lives at the Polish nobleman's, grinds at his mill and frees him from honey tax. There is commercial solidity lacking in this relationship and the impression is, Aharon's claims are not always grounded.

We must presume that besides these three Jews, by the end of the 16th century more Jews were living in Zhetl who served the nobleman and the surrounding area with their business and artisanal talents.

Jews in Zhetl at the end of the 16th Century

It is difficult to establish exactly how many Jews lived in Zhetl, but probably less than a few dozen families. In all of Lithuania in 1578 there were 27 thousand Jews. In Brisk, the largest Jewish community in Lithuania, there were 90 Jewish households in 1552, 60 in Grodno and understandably, the amount in Zhetl was much less.

Jews in Zhetl in the 17th Century

Slowly, in the span of a generation, we see lessees, inn keepers, artisans and shopkeepers arrive and begin to build a Jewish community. At first the community was small. In nearby Dvoretz it was much bigger. But in 1627 the Jewish community of Zhetl was recorded in the record books of Council of Lithuanian Jews with the following announcement: "Dvoretz and Zhetl owe 360 groschen from the year 5387.

For 43 years Zhetl and Dvoretz paid taxes to the Council of Lithuanian Jews (from 1627 until 1670).

[Page 36]

However in 1670 Zhetl became an independent community. Apparently during those forty odd years the Jewish community of Zhetl grew.

In comparison to the head tax paid by other communities Zhetl paid half of what Novaradek paid and 60% of Slonim.

We have more proof that the Zhetl Jewish community grew in the 17th century. This was largely thanks to the dukes of the Safyeha family who in 1646 took over the Zhetl estates. They expanded the Christian population, built a church and brought about a general vitality to Zhetl. As a result, the Jewish community also grew. Around 1670 the old synagogue was built.

Understandably, before this time there were Houses of Study (Bet Midrash) in Zhetl. However the building of a synagogue was a sign the Zhetl community was materially established.

Exactly at this time, the second half of the 17th century, the Jewish communities in Poland and Lithuania were shaken by Cossack revolts (1648) and the war with Sweden (1655– 59). Both events brought about epidemics and ruin among the Jewish population. Despite all these troubles the Jewish population in Lithuania grew, including Zhetl.

Reb Khaim Hirsh Segal

In the record books of the Council of Lithuanian Jews 1673– 1687, the name Reb Khaim Hirsh Segal of Zhetl is mentioned, a wealthy Jew who paid 1/5 of the taxes imposed on the Zhetl Jewish community. Besides Reb Khaim Hirsh Segal there were other wealthy Jews living in Zhetl. Rabbi Reb Yekhezkl Katzenelnboygn tell us in his book "The Congregation of Yekhezkl" about a wealthy Jew Reb Yisroel Bar Yeshayahu. Reb Yisroel Bar Yeshayahu dealt in leather goods and his business dealings spanned from Zhetl to Telz. He was killed there during a robbery and Reb Yekhezkl authorized his wife as an Agunnah (an abandoned woman who cannot prove the death of her husband or does not have an official divorce and therefore cannot remarry).

Spiritual Renaissance at the end of the 17th Century

As mentioned, the Zhetl Jewish community grew in numbers, importance and established itself materially. The material revival led to a spiritual one. Besides wealthy men we also find in Zhetl, at the end of the 17th century, great scholars. One of these great scholars was the rabbi Reb Arye Leyb Segal Hurvitz, the author of "Nature – Daisy" a commentary on Maimonides' Book of Good Deeds.

In 1696 Reb Arye Leyb left Zhetl to take the post of rabbi in Minsk. He did not serve as Chief Rabbi of Zhetl because in his book he is referred to as Arye Leyb Zhetl Segal (assistant Cohen) Hurvitz and not Chief Judge of the Jewish court. In the introduction to his book we read: "In my opinion he was the friend of great renowned deceased rabbi, Arye Leyb Zhetl Segal Hurvitz who was the Chief Judge of the Jewish court in Minsk". It is most probable that the rabbi Reb Arye Leyb Segal Hurvitz had a connection to the wealthy Zhetl Jew Reb Khaim Hirsh Segal who is mentioned in the records of the Council of Jews in Lithuania in the years 1673– 1683.

If Reb Nisn was historically the first Jew in Zhetl, Reb Arye Leyb was the first Talmudic scholar. There were probably scholars earlier but these are the first for which we have historic documentation.

Zhetl is Taken Over by the Radziwills

For almost 40 years Zhetl was in the possession of Duke Sofyeha. At the end of the 17th century in 1685 the Zhetl estates changed over to the family of Princes Radziwill. The princes in this family, especially Prince Dominic and Mikolai Faustin made a great effort to enrich and establish the town. They rebuilt the old castle and the church and concerned themselves with the Christian and Jewish populations.

The Accusations Against 5 Leaders of the Jewish Community

Proof of the concern Prince Mikolai Radzwill had for the Jewish population can be seen in the trial he carried out in 1712 before the Lithuanian Tribunal in Vilna against 5 leaders of the Jewish community from the Council of Jews in Lithuania (Vilna, Grodno, Brisk, Pinsk and Slutsk). In his accusation Prince Radziwill wrote the Zhetl Jewish community was supposed to pay 625 Zlotys head tax, but the unbelieving 5 community leaders decided to ruin the poor Jews of Zhetl who were already punished by God, and raised the tax to 3000 Zlotys. Prince Radziwill also used the argument that this could also bring harm to the principality.

The 5 accused heads of the Jewish community did not appear in court and the tribunal judged in favour of his claim. According to the verdict the 5 heads of the Jewish community had to pay the Jews of Zhetl 3000 Zlotys compensation for the unfounded raising of the head tax, 310 Zlotys court costs and an infamy was placed on them.

[Page 37]

As we do not have any documents to support this from the Jewish perspective, it is hard to judge this action of our ancestors in Zhetl. It is hard to believe they went to the nobleman directly against the 5 leaders of the Jewish community. Perhaps Prince Mikolai Radziwill learnt about this and on his own initiative accused the 5 leaders of the Jewish community. We have no confirmation of this trial from Jewish sources, nor of its outcome. Therefore it is difficult to draw a conclusion about this issue. However, one thing is clear:

the document reeks of Polish, characteristic antisemitism. The 5 Jewish community leaders were depicted in black colours. They wanted to ruin Zhetl and united against her. They are called heretics – unbelievers. This document respects the Jews of Zhetl who were lessees and merchants and had already punished them enough. The attitude was characteristic of a Polish magnate, who hated all Jews, except his own humble Jew with no status.

Rabbi Khaim HaCohen Rappaport

In the early years of the 18th century, Rabbi Khaim HaCohen Rappaport was the chief rabbi of Zhetl. This has been documented in a book about prominent men by Rabbi Aharon Vildn who wrote: "The revered Rabbi Khaim HaCohen Rappaport is a true Talmudic genius, a marvel of his generation, the light of the diaspora and the head judge of the Jewish court in Lvov". In a second posting we read: "The Talmudic genius Rabbi Khaim HaCohen was also the head of the Jewish court in Zhetl". We do not know exactly when Reb Khaim HaCohen was in Zhetl, but it was probably from 1720–1729.

The rabbi Reb Khaim HaCohen was one of the greatest rabbis of his time. He probably also has a secular education as he was one of three rabbis to debate the Frankists in Lemberg in 1759. To learn more about the rabbi Reb Khaim HaCohen – see in our list of "Zhetl Rabbis" the article by A. Shepetnitsky.

The Rabbi Reb Zev Krantz and His Son the Preacher from Dubne

The second most important rabbi in Zhetl in the 18th century was Reb Zev Wolf Krantz. He was the son in law of the Kobrin rabbi Reb Nokhem and the father of the well known preacher from Dubne.

The preacher from Dubno, Reb Yakov Krantz, to whom we have dedicated a separate article was born in Zhetl in 1740 and lived there until 1758. When the rabbi Reb Yakov Krantz left Zhetl for Mezrich he was already 18 years old and brought enthusiasm to the scholarly world.

It was an injustice for Zhetl that one of her finest sons who grew up in her Houses of Study was called the Dubne Preacher and not the Zhetl Preacher.

Rabbis in the Second Half of the 18th Century

During the second half of the 18th century the following occupied the chair of chief rabbi of Zhetl: the rabbi Reb Boruk Bendit, author of the book "The Eternal Light", the rabbi Reb Moishe, the rabbi Reb Eliezer Namyat, and the rabbi Reb Nisn. For more information about these rabbis see the list "Zhetl Rabbis" by A. Shepetniksky.

Zhetl in the 18th Century

The Jewish community in Zhetl was founded in the 16th century. In the 17th century it grew in numbers and importance. In the 18th century her spiritual strength was developed. Important rabbis occupied the chair of chief rabbi. We are familiar with seven names. Two of them are important authorities in the rabbinic world: the rabbi Reb Khaim HaCohen Rappaport and the Preacher of Dubne.

Unfortunately, no documents of material and spiritual life of this period have remained. We know that sometime around 1743 a great fire broke out in Zhetl which destroyed practically the entire town. The new cemetery opened in 1750s behind the city. Around 1781 Zhetl welcomed two messengers from the Land of Israel: Reb Avram HaCohen Mlask and Reb Hillel Mizrachi.

The Demands of the Russian Occupation

By the end of the 18th century the estates of Zhetl were taken over by the Saltan nobles.

Ten years later, in 1795, the united Polish – Lithuanian state experienced its greatest political shock: the final partition of the land.

The provinces of Slonim and Vilna were occupied by the Russians in 1795 and were transformed into a North West region of the Russian Empire. Their fate included Zhetl.

The demands of the Russian occupation were felt immediately. The autonomy of the Jewish community decreased and Jews are now forbidden to lease taverns in the villages.

[Page 38]

There was now a tendency to remove Jews from the villages and move them to cities. Jews had not yet adjusted to the new authority and edicts when they faced a second political shock: the Napoleonic War in 1812.

Political Changes in the 19th Century

19 years after the Napoleonic War, Poland, including Zhetl experienced the Polish Uprising of 1831. The owners of the Zhetl estates, the Saltans took part in the uprising and therefore their estates were confiscated by the state. This is when the Zhetl palace was rebuilt and transformed into barracks.

At the same time, in 1823, the Russian government renewed Jewish expulsions from the villages. In 1827 they began to kidnap Jewish children for military service. A little later in 1844 they began to liquidate Jewish communities. All these changes were brought upon by the reactionary Czar Nilolai I and had a great impact on our grandfathers in Zhetl.

Another change for the better that occurred was the abolition of serfdom after the Polish uprising in 1863. In the industrial centres the freeing of the peasants brought competition and loss of livelihood for the Jews. However in Zhetl the effect was the opposite. The new independent producers, the peasants, became good customers for the Zhetl merchants and artisans.

The wave of pogroms which befell Poland and Russia in the 1880s evaded Zhetl, yet their effect was deeply felt.

Societal Changes

In the 19th century three social movements were born: the Jewish Enlightenment, Zionism and immigration. All three found supporters in Zhetl. It was not easy for the first enlighteners and Zionists in Zhetl but they slowly gained a place of honour in society. In our section about Hovevei Zion (Lovers of Zion), we describe the first steps of Zionism in Zhetl. We have scant information about the enlighteners in Zhetl, but we must assume that all the enlighteners in Zhetl later became members of Hovevi Zion and Zionists.

In the 1880s an intensive wave of immigration began to America. Individuals went to the Land of Israel but masses went to America. Unfortunately we do not have material about the immigration but according to the numbers provided by A. Pasaf, there are 500 Jewish families from Zhetl today in the United States. In Canada, Argentina and other countries in the Americas there are over 100 Zhetl families. There are 300 Zhetl families in Israel. These one thousand families left Zhetl between 1880–1945.

Zhetl Rabbis in the 19th Century

We have gathered information from various sources about the rabbis from this period. We offer them here chronologically: the rabbi Reb Khaim Lifshitz, the rabbi Reb Avrom, the rabbi Reb Zev Wolf Halevi, the rabbi Reb Zvi Hirsh HaCohen Dvoretsky, and the rabbi Reb Borukh Avrom Mirsky. As in the previous century, a great authority in the rabbinic world was born in Zhetl in the 19th century: the rabbi Reb Yisroel Meir HaCohen, known as Khefetz Khaim (Love of Life).

The Khefetz Khaim was born in Zhetl in 1839. Later when his father Reb Arye Zev died he moved with his mother to Vilna. At 18 he married and moved to Radin and was known as the Genius of Radin, although his cradle stood in Zhetl. This is where he took his first steps as a small boy and began his learning in the Houses of Study there. He would become the greatest authority in the rabbinic world in the 19th and 20th centuries.

The Rabbi Reb Zev Wolf Halevy Writes About the Jews of Zhetl

When the Khefetz Khaim, was a young child there was a rabbi who was a great authority in the rabbinic world: the rabbi Reb Zev Wolf Halevy. Before him the chief rabbis of Zhetl were: the rabbi Reb Khaim Lifshitz, (1806–1813) and the rabbi Reb Moishe Avrom Eyznshtat until 1836. The rabbi Reb Zev Wolf occupied this position from 1840– 1850. He was the author of the book "Emek Halakha" containing questions and answers dealing with the Code of Jewish Law. The book was published in 1845 in Vilna. In the introduction he wrote the following about Zhetl: (In Hebrew)

[Page 39]

This is what the rabbi Reb Zev Wolf Halevy had to say about Zhetl Jews in 1845. He praises them as scholarly, generous hones good hearted Jews. He thanks them for contributing toward the publication of his book and he blesses their children's children.

In the book there is a list of Zhetl Jews who contributed: Reb Eliezer son of Khaim, Reb Avrom son of Moishe, Reb Aharon son of Yakov, Reb Eli Shatz, Reb Zalman Zekharia son of Binyomin, Reb Yehuda Leyb son of Tankhum, Reb Yisroel Dov, Reb Yehuda son of Yisroel Katz, Reb Yisroel son of Khaim Segal, Reb Yehuda son of Ezriel Epshteyn, Reb Yehoshua Zelik Menavin, Reb Nisn Baharav son of Yisroel, Reb Peysakh Mavotskevitch, Reb Moishe Mordkhai son of Pinkhas, Reb Moishe son of Yitzkhak Izik, Reb Moishe Yitzkhak son of Binyomin, Reb Meir Yitzkhak son of Yehuda Leyb.

This is a list of 19 well off men in Zhetl who lived 110 years ago and fortuitously their names have been written down. Perhaps Jews from Zhetl will find the names of their grandfathers or great grandfathers.

The two rabbis that held the chief rabbi position in Zhetl during the second half of the 19th century were Rabbi Zvi Hirsh HaCohen (1850–1892), a great scholar with a keen mind and Rabbi Borukh Avrom Mirsky (1892–1912) who was very active in the Hovevei Zion and about whom we speak about in detail in our chapter "Rabbis of Zhetl" as well as in specific articles by Rabbi Y.L Maimotn and Moishe Tsinovitch.

At the Threshold of the 20th Century

At the threshold of the 20th century Zhetl was still a very religious town, but slowly but surely winds of change were blowing through particularly influencing the youth who organized two revolutionary parties: the "Bund" and the S.R.(Social Revolutionaries).

We speak about the activities of both parties in the works of Yekhiel Kuznyetsky and H. Khabibi.

Both the Bundists and the Social Revolutionaries placed all the faith they inherited from their parents into their holy beliefs in the revolution. They dreamt and fought for a new, just world order.

The 20th Century

The largest portion of our book is dedicated to the Jewish community of Zhetl in the 20th century. During this century the Jewish community of Zhetl experienced two horrific world wars.

During the First World War Zhetl was covered in blood and impoverished. However this did not last long and after the war they managed to rebuild their material and spiritual lives.

The period between the two wars were the golden years of the Jewish community in Zhetl. During this period there were three camps struggling against each other: orthodox, Zionists, and Yiddishists. Each camp organized its own schools, youth groups, institutions and even theatres. Together they created a symphony of Jewish society.

During this period the Jewish community went through some changes. New elements were penetrating the religious lives of our parents: National, social and secular. In a short time these elements changed the face of the Zhetl Jewish community which was building national and secular institutions parallel to the old religious ones.

The interesting development of the Zhetl Jewish community after the First World War was torn to pieces by the cruel Second World War. In almost four years they annihilated all that was built over four hundred years. This happened in two short time periods.

The Destruction of Zhetl

In the first period from 1939–1941 Zhetl was sovietised. The second period, 1941–1942, the Jewish community of Zhetl was massacred. By the end of both these periods Zhetl was a destroyed town, without Jews. Only a few remaining fighters walked bloodied through the forest.

This period is described in our chronicle by dozens of witnesses of this cruel extermination of the Jews. We would like to however emphasize a few moments.

During the years 1939–1941 the Jewish community in Zhetl was declassified, writhed in pain and convulsed with a constant fear of what lay ahead.

From 1941–1944 the Zhetl Jewish community displayed solidarity in the ghetto and a will to fight in the forests.

This is the history of the Zhetl Jewish community. How it grew, lived and was annihilated.

Today, 14 years after this cruel extermination, let these lines serve as a monument on the grave of the Jewish community of Zhetl.

[Page 40]

Zhetl in the Budget of the Jewish Council of Lithuania

by Mordkhai V. Bernshteyn (Buenos Aires)

Translated by Janie Respitz

My work on the theme: "Zhetl in the Budget of the Jewish Council of Lithuania" was assembled from "The Records of the State" (Records of the Councils of the Leading Jewish Communities in Lithuania), which was published in Berlin in 1925 by Prof. Shimon Dubnov. The text was taken from the manuscript which was kept in Grodno and was complemented and compared with copies of the records which were found in Brisk of Lithuania and Vilna.

These "Records of the State" contain rules and statutes decided by the council at its sessions which took place in various cities between the years (1623 – 1761), approximately 150 years.

One of the most important issues dealt with at the above mentioned 33 sessions was the budget of the Lithuanian council. Every Jewish community from the biggest to the smallest was taxed an established amount for the general budget. The lists of taxes are an important source for the history of dozens of Jewish communities. Often the fact that a Jewish community appears on a list is the only proof that at that time an organized Jewish community existed there. The evolution of the Jewish community tax also tells us about the development of the contributing community: if it grows or shrunk.

We received our facts about Zhetl from protocols of individual sessions. From time to time we will offer Zhetl's position in relation to other cities.

When and Where Did These 33 Sessions Take Place?

Firstly I will tell you a bit about when and in which cities these sessions were held. This is important in order not to repeat when quoting the budget statements from various sessions.

As mentioned the Jewish Council of Lithuania held 33 sessions in the following places:

1. In Brisk – Lithuania 1623
2. In Brisk – Lithuania 1626
3. In Brisk – Lithuania 1627
4. In Pruzhene 1628
5. In Brisk – Lithuania 1631
6. In Seltz 1632
7. In Seltz 1634
8. In Seltz 1637
9. In seltz 1639
10. In Seltz 1644
11. In Seltz 1647
12. In Mistetzky 1649

13. In Zabludeve 1650
14. In Khomsk 1652
15. In Seltz 1656
16. In Seltz 1662
17. In Zabludeve 1664
18. In Khomsk 1667
19. In Seltz1670
20. In Seltz 1673
21. In Zabludeve 1676
22. In Khomsk 1679
23. In Seltz 1684
24. In Krinki 1687
25. In Khomsk 1691
26. In Olkenik 1695
27. In Seltz 1700
28. In Amdor 1720
29. In Khomsk 1721
30. In Grodno 1727
31. In Grodno 1731
32. In Mir 1752
33. In Slutzk 1761

Although we are not dealing here with the history of the Council of Jews in Lithuania the fact must be noted that in the early years of its existence the sessions took place more or less every year. The last sessions take place about once every 10 years.

As already said money matters held an important place in these sessions. Financial difficulties, debts to high officials and the central Polish authority, special expenditures during a Blood Libel, or the building of a synagogues, help for refugees after the pogroms of 1648–49 (the <u>Chmielnicki Massacres</u>) and for the families of the Ruzhne martyrs. These prosaic money matters mirror the size of each community, its rise or decline.

[Page 41]

Let us observe from session to session the contribution from Zhetl to the communal tax.

I am bringing the financial statements in the language and spelling of the original (often with mistakes) without any changes. All the initials and abbreviations are from the original. (Translator's note: I will provide correct spellings where possible).

The Boundaries of the Jewish Council of Lithuania

In paragraph 89 of the first session of the Council we find the boundaries of the Council. The three regions which belonged at the time were: Brisk, Grodno and Pinsk.

In order to familiarize ourselves with these regions it is worthwhile to bring forth the designation from paragraph 89. The names in parenthesis are how they appeared in the second version.

"89. These are the boundaries and surroundings of the region of Brisk:

Mezrich, Varin (Vayn), Yanovi, Rashs (Rashi), Lomz (Lomoz), Bila, Beshtz, Vlaudvi (Vladvi), Slavitz, Karni, Visaki, Amstibava (Amstibavi) Kobrin, Hordetz, Prushna, Mltcha, Seltz, Chernoytzitz (Chernovitz), Kamnitz, Shershavi, Razanik (Razanay), Slonim, Dvortz, Nvarodek (Navrodek), Neshvitz, Slutzk, Minsk, Mahlaboni (Mahlobni), Ursha, residents of Russia.

These are the boundaries of Hurodna:Amdor, Mistetzky, Kuznitsa, Navidbor, Ustrin, Radin, Lida.
These are the boundaries of the region of Pinsk:
Kletzk, Lekhvitch, Khomsk, Brehin, Dubrovitch, Visotzk, Turava and the residents of N"Z.

As we can see Zhetl does not appear on these lists of Jewish settlements. This is not evidence that there was no Jewish community there. We find, for example, in the handling of various matters at the same session, names of towns not included in the former list. We are speaking about the towns: Kapulie, Mush, Smorgon, Polonke, Ivye, Polotzk, Krashin, Kosve, Zelve, Trok and others. No mention of Zhetl is not proof that there was no Jewish community there.

Dvoretz and Vicinity

In clause 97 of the session we find the contributions each community had to pay in head taxes (which Jews in Lithuania had to pay the government). The Council of Four Lands in Poland and the Jewish Council of Lithuania were responsible for collecting this tax. It was usually between 1–3 Polish guldens. It was first implemented by the Polish Sejm in 1581.

We see there that "Dvoretz and Vicinity" had to pay 14 shok, shok standing for 60 (840).

Zhetl is not mentioned in these records, however in later sessions, Zhetl is connected to Dvoretz. We must assume, Zhetl was included in "Vicinity". The following communities paid these head taxes: Novaredok – 12 shok (720), Slonim – 20 shok (1,200), Minsk 10 shok (600). From this we can gather, the 14 shok "Dvoretz and Vicinity" had to pay a large amount.

In the same clause 97 we see the Jews had to pay another tax. (This was a return tax imposed on Jews after they were permitted to return to Lithuania after the expulsion). Dvoretz had to pay 10 red guldens, the same as Minsk, more than Novaredok, which had to pay 8 red guldens.

Zhetl is Mentioned for the First Time

Zhetl is mentioned for the first time in the session of 1627. In clause 225 debts that individual communities owed are calculated. Among the debts owed we see: Dvoretz with Zhetl owed debts from 1627 – 6 shok. Here we also have proof of the communal connection of these two communities.

At the fifth session of the Council in 1631 Zhetl figures in two places in clause 255 of the records. We read:

[Page 42]

From the years 1628 until 1632 Zhetl paid its contribution together with Dvoretz: 5 shok. In the same clause 225 we see the contribution of head the tax to the government and once again we see Dvoretz and Zhetl together. Novaredok paid 12 shok and Dvoretz and Zhetl paid 9 shok.

In the same clause we find a list of debts owed to the Council. Among others we see a debt from Dvoretz for 55 goldens. We must understand this debt was also shared.

The Session of 1639

In clause 388 of the session of 1639 there is a list of debts owed to the Council. Dvoretz and Zhetl appear together: we see here that over time the earlier communal debt of 55 goldens was reduced to 12 and a half.

In this session a list was presented for the debts owed for the right to return tax. Among others we see Dvoretz and Zhetl owed seven and a half red guldens. Let us compare this amount to amounts owed by other Jewish communities. How much did they owe for the same tax?

Novaredok – 11 red guldens; Slonim 12 red guldens; Niesviezh – 12 red guldens; Bielitze – 5 red guldens; Mush – 2 red guldens; Polonke – 1 red gulden.

In clause 400 from the same session we find a list from the session in Seltz from 1637. Here we learn the general budget of the Council of the Jews of Lithuania. Among others we see the debt owed by Dvoretz – Zhetl totalling 186 goldens. Both towns owed this money to the Council budget.

This was what they owed, but the amount they had to pay for a Jewish community tax is not clear.

The Session of 1644

At the session of the Council in 1644 the amount both communities had to pay is mentioned. It is worthwhile to present the entire budget of this Council. In clause 422 we read:

"This budget ends on the 5th day of Elul (September 1644)."
Brisk and vicinity – 270 shok
Huradna – 40 shok
Vicinity of Huradna – 26 shok
Pinsk and vicinity – 70 shok
Vilna and vicinity – 100 shok
The Land of Russia – 60 shok
Minsk – 25 shok
Minsk Region – 100 (200) shok
Slutsk – 62 shok
Neshviz – 14 shok
Slonim – 11 shok
Novardok – 17 shok
Dvoretz Zhetl – 7 shok, 12 Polish groschen
Mush with Reb Borukh Mistolovitch – 5 shok
Polnki – 36 Polish groschen
Reb Feyvl from Krashin – 48 Lithuanian groschen
Poltzki – 11 shok
Kapulie – 4 shok
Bielitze and vicinity – 3 shok Tomkovitz – 33 Lithuanian groschen
Traka, Zmoyt in Vilna, Smorgon…
Total – 733 shok

In short, we have a picture here of the entire budget. 733 Lithuanian shok. The position of Dvoretz and Zhetl on this list is not among the first but far from the last. We must also keep in mind that only a few communities appear on their own as independent contributors. Most of the Jewish communities are included in the "vicinities" of Brisk, Gordno, Pinsk, Minsk, Vilna and the Land of Russia. We have to then assume the position of the allocated communities was important, including Dvoretz and Zhetl.

The session of 1647

In clause 449 from the session of 1647 we find a new budget. Now we see 1,741 and a half. In this budget we see Dvoretz and Zhetl with 7 Lithuanian shok and 12 groschen.

In the same clause we see debts owed from various taxes.

We read:

These are the debts owed to the Council by Dvoretz and Zhetl 406 goldens. (Goldens mean groschen, there were Polish and Lithuanian groschen, the Lituanian was worth more. There were 30 groschen to one gulden. In Czarist Russia 15 Kopeks equalled one gulden, or 30 groschen.)

[Page 43]

Also in the list of outstanding debts to the Council, Dvoretz – Zhetl appear owing 240 goldens and 5 groschen in a profit fund of 15 Lithuanian shok. Separate capital and interest appear in this total. This means those who did not pay on time had to pay interest.

The Session of 1650

In the session of 1650 Dvoretz and Zhetl appear in clause 481 with the amount of 5 and a half Lithuanian shok. This budget was generally smaller. Brisk and vicinity previously paid 270 shok combined, now only 100 shok; Grodno and vicinity previously had to pay 26 shok, now – 13 shok.

In clause 482 from the same session a list of debts can be found which had been paid. The first one we see is:

"Dvoretz – Zhetl 100 goldens and 14 goldens – paid ".

In a later list in the same clause we see Dvoretz and Zhetl must together pay debts for a special Jewish communal tax of 50 in the winter of 1648. It appears by this account Dvoretz –Zhetl had to pay 900 goldens but only paid 338 and a half. According to this same clause, Dvoretz – Zhetl paid 45 goldens for the right to return tax.

After the Pogroms of 1648–49

At the session in 1652 the budget of the Council was presented again. This time Dvoretz and Zhetl with 4 Lithuanian shok. Other communities were also assessed for less than in previous years. (Brisk – 88 shok, Grodno and vicinity 11 shok and so on).

The following clause can serve as proof of the impoverishment of the Jewish communities. Brought forth is a list of long standing debts for taxes for both the Council and the government. This list shows debts amounting to tens of thousands of goldens. Dvoretz – Zhetl appears on this list owing 3, 016 and a half goldens.

This session also dealt with the difficult situation of communities who suffered pogroms.

The Session of 1656

In the session in 1656 Dvoretz – Zhetl appeared with 2 Lithuanian shok and 18 groschen. The amounts at this session were much smaller than in previous years with a total amount of 213 Lithuanian shok.

Therefore the list of long standing debts grew. Here we learn the communities of Dvoretz – Zhetl owed 3286 goldens!

The Session of 1662

During this session in 1662 a new Jewish community tax was introduced. Dvoretz and Zhetl appear together but the amount is not known. We know the tax was small from the amounts paid by Brisk, all told, 11 shok, and Grodno and vicinity, not more than 6 shok. We can assume the communities had local expenditures and consequently the Council decreased their taxes.

The Session of 1664

The Jewish communal tax which was decided on at the session in 1664 was even smaller – Dvoretz and Zhetl appear owing only 1 Lithuanian shok, Brisk and vicinity 10 shok, Vilna and vicinity – 5 shok. At the same session Dvoretz and Zhetl are mentioned together having a debt of 1250 goldens.

The Session of 1667

At the beginning of the session in 1667 we see Zhetl, to a certain extent, independent. In clause 4223 of this session they talk about quittances and banknotes. (These were receipts for paid taxes. Communities would receive receipts for their taxes and then collect them from other places. The banknotes had the value of a state document. One could, with administrative force, collect the amount from the banknotes).

The Council distributed these quittances to various communities at the expense of their community taxes. These were loans which the Council gave to the communities which they had to deduct from their taxes which they owed the Council. Zhetl appears here twice. The Council owes Zhetl a quittance "For Dvoretz and Zhetl for 25 goldens" and a separate one "For Zhetl 35 goldens" – which means, besides the 25 goldens which Zhetl paid together with Dvoretz, there was a separate quittance for Zhetl alone for 35 gulden.

[Page 44]

Zhetl Becomes Independent

In the session of 1670 we already have a clear picture about the place Zhetl held in its partnership with Dvoretz; we begin to see its emergence as an independent community. There is a clause from this session which reads:

…"Dvoretz – Zhetl 3 goldens, namely Dvoretz with Maytshet 47 goldens and Zhetl 31 Polish groschens…"

For the first time we have information that Maytshet also entered the community. We also see the place Zhetl occupied in the common sum.

In a later clause from the session in 1670 we find the distribution of the head tax in the Jewish Council of Lithuania. We can learn from this how many in general paid head taxes in Lithuania that year. It is worthwhile to present the entire list. The clause says this:

"The regions of Lithuania"

Brisk and vicinity – 900 goldens
Horadna and vicinity – 400 goldens
Pinsk – 280 goldens
Vilna – 180 goldens
Krayim – (an autonomous region in Lithuania) 207
Zamoyt – 400 goldens
Slutzk – 300 goldens
Slonim – 55 goldens
Navardok – 75 goldens
Dvoretz – 45 goldens Zhetl – 35 goldens
Mush and Polonki – 27 goldens
Minsk – 67 goldens
Minsk region – 120 goldens
The Land of Russia – 150 goldens
Smorgon and the region – 40 goldens
Neshviz and Mir – 45 goldens
Bilitza – 20 goldens
Residents of Kashin – 3 goldens

This list of head tax shows us the exact position and size of the Zhetl Jewish community. It is listed with the independent communities and not part of "vicinity" or "region". It also shows proportionally where Zhetl stands in relation to other communities.

In the same clause we see the distribution of the return tax. Here too we see Dvoretz and Zhetl listed separately.

Dvoretz – 20 goldens
Zhetl – 20 goldens
Consequently, the same amount.

In a later part of the same clause old debts are calculated. Here they appear together:

The communities of Dvoretz and Zhetl owe 1,403 goldens.

The Session of 1673

In the budget of the Lithuanian Jewish Council of 1673 we find the next stage of Zhetl independence. There are three things we learn from this budget:

Zhetl was an independent community in the Council of Jews in Lithuania;

In Zhetl there was a Jew, Khaim Hirsh who paid for himself, meaning he was very wealthy;

Dvoretz was already in a community with Maytshet.

In the same session they put forth a register of debts. Here Zhetl appears with Reb Hirsh – this is certainly the above mentioned Khaim Hirsh, who is also referred to as Reb Hirsh Segal.

The Session of 1676

In the subsequent sessions Zhetl appears as an independent community. In the session of 1676 the Zhetl community tax is:

"Zhetl with Reb Hirsh 52 Polish groschens.

In the list of debtors:

Zhetl's debt is 1500 goldens which could be paid

[Page 45]

in 5 installments, 300 goldens per installment. We learn when the installments have to be paid and to whom:

the first installment must be at the Stolovitch Fair in 1676, 150 gulden to the Amstibev Rabbi, Reb Mordkhai, and 150 gulden to the Brisk Rabbi, Reb Leyzer.

To whom and when the subsequent installments must be paid is not calculated in this clause. Also, the second installment is more than the decided 300 goldens.

The Session of 1679

Zhetl appears in the budget passed at this session and it seems to have surpassed many other communities. The following appear in the same budget:

Minsk – 2 gulden and 8 groschen;
Slonim and vicinity – 1 gulden 8 groschen;
Novaredok and vicinity – 1 gulden 5 groschen
Dvoretz and Maytshet – 26 groschen
Zhetl (together with Reb Hirsh) 1 gulden 12 groschen.

The Session of 1684

In the budget of the session in 1684 Zhetl appears (together with Reb Hirsh) with the sum of 27 groschen. Dvoretz with Maytshet – 18 groschen; Novaredok – 18 groschen;

Also at this session a list of debts was presented. We find here an important annotation about Zhetl:

We see that Zhetl's debt was not small. It reaches beyond 2300 goldens. Interestingly, the Zhetl Jewish community and Reb Hirsh Segal needed money to pay installments for a girl orphaned as a result of a martyrdom. She was the grandchild of a rabbi.

The Session of 1687

In the session of 1687 Zhetl appears in the taxes of the Council with 24 groschen and again together with Reb Hirsh Segal. We can see here that Zhetl's debt had decreased. In one entry Zhetl owed 710 goldens, 219 in another entry and Reb Hirsh Segal owed 120.

The Session of 1691

At this session it was decided to take an extraordinary action to liquidate the debts of the Council of Jews in Lithuania. It was decided to raise 1500 in community taxes and pay it in 6 installments.

We see there were yearly installments to be paid at the fairs in Nesviezh and Kapulie. Of these 1500 of community tax Zhetl was taxed with 1,000 goldens with each installment being 160 goldens and 20 groschen.

In the session of 1691 Zhetl now appears (without Reb Hirsh Segal) with 20 Polish groschen. We also see that Dvoretz is now separated from Maytshet. Dvoretz is now independent with 12 groschen and Maytshet 7 groschen.

The Session of 1695

In this session Zhetl appears in the budget of the Council with 15 groschen, Dvoretz 6 and Maytshet 7.

The Session of 1700

In the session of 1700 Zhetl appears in the budget with 20 groschen to be paid in the manner of debenture. Dvoretz had to pay 6 groschen.

The Session of 1720

At this session in 1720 Zhetl was taxed 18 Polish groschen.

The Session of 1731

At this session a list of debts was presented which had to be paid to a sequence of nobility and priests.

[Page 46]

These debts were distributed to various communities. Among others, Zhetl had to pay 300 golden to the nobleman Borkovsky.

The Session of 1752

In the session of 1752 there was a list of communities and how much each to pay for the "register of tariffs of the regions". They had to raise sixty thousand Polish goldens.

Appearing on this list was: the community of Zhetl with Vidovitz and Rahtna owing 800 Polish golden…

Rahatna was a small village and Vidovitz was apparently a place where Jews lived as well.

In comparison to the earlier towns which Zhetl was connected to, we will add here that on the same list Dvoretz owed 370 golden and Maytshet 370 as well.

The Session of 1761

In the session of 1761 Zhetl does not appear in a list of communities which owed regional fees. All the surrounding communities do appear so this must have been an omission when transcribing the records. Zhetl does appear in the same session in a list of communities owing community tax where they had to pay twenty groschen.

The Outcome:

During the 150 years of the existence of the Council of Jews of Lithuania Zhetl was an active member in this Jewish autonomous organization and participated carrying the common burden of the community at large.

We can observe the development of Zhetl, beginning as a "Supplement" of Dvoretz and then becoming an independent community, growing in importance and surpassing other neighbouring communities. These dry budget entries are important milestones in the history of our holy community of Zhetl between the years 1623 – 1761.

[Page 47]

Zhetl From the Past

by Avrom Ivenitsky of blessed memory

Translated by Janie Respitz

According to a local legend the town Zhetl received its name when the first resident saw his first bird which was a woodpecker, Dzicciol in Polish.

The Geographic Situation

Avrom Ivenitsky, of blessed memory

Zhetl is situated 12 kilometres from the train station in Novolyelne, on the highway which runs from Novoredok through Zhetl, Derechin, Zelve, Volkovisk, Bialystok, Warsaw, all the way to the German border; it is 45 kilometres north of Slonim and 55 kilometres north of Baranovich. To the east there are no larger cities close by; Novoredok is 35 kilometres north east; 50 kilometres north is Lida. There are no large centres close toward the west. Volkovisk is 12 miles west and Grodno is 16 miles North West. The closest largest river, the Nieman, flows 20 kilometres north of Zhetl. Two small rivers cut through Zhetl: the Zhetlke and the Pomerayke.

A Bit of History

From documents found in the Polish National Museum in Grodno, we know that in 1498 the Lithuanian Grand Duke Alexander Yagelonchik, by means of a privilege from June 6th, gave the Duke Konstantin Ostrogsky the right to found the city. Zhetl can calculate its existence from then on.

Later Zhetl was taken over by the Sofyehas and after, the Radziwills. From a Latin inscription on the church we learn the church was built in 1646 by the administrator in Slonim, Duke Kazimierz Leo Sofyehas. We calculate the rounded stores which stretched along the length of the church were built in this same period. They decorated the western wall of the brick surrounding enclosure.

The last owner of Zhetl was Adam Saltan. After the Polish uprising in 1831, Adam Saltan ran away and the town, as well as all the land owned by the Saltans which stretched around 10 kilometres was taken over by the state.

The only remnant of magnate ownership of Zhetl is a palace with the coat of arms of the Saltans on the cornices. Until the German occupation in 1915 there were remnants of a draw bridge which crossed the Zhetlke to the palace where Zhetl actually began.

From the town on the estate there was a tree lined path of very old, wide, beautiful poplar trees. The Germans cut them all down. All the land owned by Zhetl magnates was divided up. Before the war the palace was used as a Russian teacher's seminary. After the First World War it became a Polish trade school for orphaned girls.

Vestiges of Old Jewish Zhetl

The only vestige of old Jewish Zhetl is the old cemetery in the Synagogue court yard. There are no written recollections of that Zhetl. In the old cemetery all the inscriptions on the tombstones are wiped out. There is a record book from the new cemetery which began in 1748. There are no records from the Houses of Study.

Old people tell us that the spot where the present old House of Study stands used to be where the Rabbi's wooden house stood. The house was rebuilt one hundred years ago and is now a walled House of Study. The "middle" House of study was built beside the "old" one and a few steps away from these two a third was built by Zhetl's wealthy Jews 150 years later.

Behind these Houses of Study, on the other side of the Pomerayke, which flows very close to them, stood the walled Hasidic Prayer House. The old synagogue once stood in the Synagogue yard which burned down during the big fire 55 years ago. At that time almost the entire town burned down.

The Rabbi Reb Khaim HaKohen Rappaprt – The First Rabbi

Old Zhetl was known for its Talmudic scholars and great rabbis. Approximately 200 years ago there was a rabbi, the Gaon (Genius), Reb Khaim son of Simkha HaKohen Rappaport, who was brought to Slutsk and then to Lemberg.

[Page 48]

In 1759 the rabbi went to Lemberg with 40 other rabbis from Poland and had to take part in a debate with the Frankists. From the 40 rabbis, he was chosen together with Rabbi Dubner, the chief judge of the Jewish court in Biazlovitz and Reb Yisroel Besht to debate which resulted in a victory for the rabbis. The debate was chaired by the bishop of Lemberg, Mikolsky who was also the organizer according to the initiative of the Frankists. Reb Khaim HaKohen Rappaport was already the rabbi of Slutsk.

After the debate the Jewish community of Lemberg kept him as their rabbi. Among his most important works were "Questions and Answers" (Lemberg 1861) and "Life Memory" (1865).

Interestingly, in the Russian Jewish Encyclopedia it says he was the rabbi in Slutsk and Lemberg. It was news for Prof. M. Balaban to learn Reb Khayim was rabbi in Zhetl for many years.

Therefore in Duber's "Well Known People" there is a monograph about Khaim son of Simkha HaKohen Rappaport and says his first post as rabbi was in Zhetl. (1729).

The Rabbi Reb Zev Wolf Segal

One hundred years ago there was a rabbi in Zhetl, Reb Zev Wolf Segal, and author of "Emek Halakha". Reb Zev Wolf Segal was the Gaon (Genius) of the Jewish community of Zhetl, is mentioned by commentators of "Yoreh Daya" whose work is based on his "Questions and Answers". Reb Zev Wolf Segal was invited to come to Zhetl from Germany* (Reb Zev Wolf Segal came to Zhetl from Zabludove. The author is certainly mistaken).It happened like this: German Jews, merchants, passing through came to Reb Zev Wolf Segal with a religious question for judgement. The question was very complicated. The Rabbi interpreted it so well and judged so cleverly, they returned home to Germany and made him very popular and brought him to be their rabbi.

Reb Zev Wolf was the first to sign the protocol in the record book of the Interest Free Loan Society 100 years ago as one of its first founders.

The Old and New Talmud Society

The most significant role in the old Zhetl Jewish cultural – spiritual life was played by the old Talmud Society. Forty years ago the old Talmud Society had among its members such great scholars as the old Zhetl rabbi Reb Borukh Avrom Mirsky, one of the first founders of "Mizrachi". Besides his great scholarship he was also an expert in Hebrew language and old Hebrew literature. Another member of the Talmud Society was the deceased rabbi from Moscow, Reb Shmuel Rabinovitch, and the son in law of a Zhetl Jew. He was known for his rabbinic pedigree, his brilliant mind and his vast knowledge of Talmud.

It was very difficult to make one's way into the old Zhetl Talmud Society. Belonging to the society was a sign you were a great scholar. Due to these difficulties a new Talmud Society was founded in Zhetl 50 years ago which did not demand as much from its members but was held up to the high esteem of the old Talmud Society.

After the Talmud Society came the old Zhetl Yeshiva which was famous for its prodigies. Boys came there to study from all corners of Poland, Lithuania and Belarus. A specific Gemara melody rang through the town.

Revolutionaries in Zhetl

In general Zhetl stood at meaningful spiritual heights. In the first years of this century new winds began to blow through old Zhetl. The former Zhetl good boys, in the years of "Storm and Drive" , generated heroic socialist and revolutionary fighters for the Jewish and Russian worker's movement.

Zhetl was then the centre of the Jewish Workers's Movement in our region and played an important role. Many young Jews were sent to Siberia, forced labour camps and died on Russian gallows. As a remembrance of those revolutionaries in Zhetl: Khaim Kaplinsky and Yitzkhak Rabinovitch, a worker in leather factory, an anarchist who organized and carried out the famous expropriation of Ponarny Pereulak in St. Petersburg in 1905. When he ran away he shot a few policemen. He was hanged.

Many Zhetl revolutionaries have already died. Those who survived are spread throughout the world. Perhaps they remember the past at times, stare at the world with a thoughtful smile on their lips.

("Chronicles of Yekopo")

Zhetl's Rabbis
(This work was supplemented by material gathered by Moishe Tzinovitch)

by Avrom Shepetnitsky (Kfar Hasidim)

Translated by Janie Respitz

Avrom Shepetnitsky

Zhetl was recognized in the Jewish world by its great Rabbis. Great scholars served as chief rabbi of Zhetl in the 18th, 19th, and 20th centuries. It is very possible that Zhetl had a rabbi as early as the 16th century. Unfortunately no evidence about this has remained.

The Rabbi Reb Arye – Leyb Segal Hurvitz

The first evidence we have of a rabbi in Zhetl was the rabbi Reb Arye – Leyb Segal Hurvitz. We gathered this information from a recommendation printed on the front page of the book "Marganita Ha Tova" written by Reb Arye Leyb which reads: "Reb Arye Leyb from Zhetl who became chief judge of the Jewish court of Minsk."

According to this Reb Arye Leyb was a resident of Zhetl and was hired as rabbi in Minsk. This essay was a commentary on Maimonides' "Book of Good Deeds" which was published by his son after his death in 1755.

The Rabbi Reb Khaim HaKohen Rappaport

The rabbi Reb Khaim HaKohen Rappaport was the son of Simkha HaKohen Rappaport, one of the greatest rabbis of his time, who was a rabbi in Zhetl. We find proof of this in the book "The New Book of Important Men" by Rabbi Aharon Voldin who wrote: "the Gaon (Talmudic Genius) Reb Khaim HaKohen was the chief judge of the Jewish court in the holy community of Zhetl". A second piece of evidence is from the rabbi Reb Arye – Leyb Epshteyn from Grodno who wrote in his "Sefer HaPardes" (Book of the Grove), that his brother, our esteemed teacher Zev Wolf of blessed memory, studied in Zhetl with the famous Gaon Reb Khaim ben Simkha, who was later the rabbi in Lemberg. A third piece of evidence: in his book "Questions and Answers of our Rabbi Khaim HaKohen" we find the following passage: the well known Reb Khaim Arye – Leyb Segal Hurvitz, author of Marganita Tova, was in Zhetl.

By 1750 he was already rabbi in Slutsk.

הקדמת בן הרב המחבר, אשר לכבוד אביו הגאון ז"ל מדבר.

The preface of "Marganita Tova" by Rabbi Arye Leyb Segal Hurvitz of Zhetl

[Page 50] We learn this from the book "Seder Dorot" (Order of generations) by the rabbi Reb Yekhiel Halprin, chief judge of the Jewish court in Minsk. In 1741 he took over the position of chief rabbi of Lemberg, where he died in 1771. According to all probabilities he was rabbi in Zhetl from 1720 – 1729.

In 1759 he was one of the three rabbis who participated in the debate with the Frankists, which took place in Lemberg, in the presence of priests and Polish statesmen. Thanks to his defense the Talmud was not burned.

His books remained in manuscript form and 90 years after his death one of his grandsons Reb Ruven HaKohen Rappaport from Tarnopol had them published. His most important work was "Questions and Answers of Rabbi Khaim HaKohen" (Lemberg 1861). The second is a book of his sermons and eulogies called "Memory of Life" (Lemberg 1865).

His grandsons were great rabbis. Among them was Reb Khaim Hakohen Rappaport (the second), who was the rabbi in Ostrog, who refers to his important grandfather in his book "Questions and Answers". He brings forth his grandfather's will where he asks that there should be no words of praise engraved on his tombstone.

The Rabbi Reb Zev Wolf Krantz

The rabbi Reb Zev Wolf Krantz was the father of the Preacher of Dubno, Reb Yakov Krantz. In "The New Book of Important Men" we read the following about him: "The great rabbi Reb Zev Wolf from the city of Zhetl was the son in law of the holy Gaon Reb Nokhem, chief rabbi of the Jewish court of Kobrin, and father the righteous rabbi Reb Yakov from Dubno". From this list it is hard to affirm if he was a rabbi in Zhetl, but there is no doubt he was a great scholar.

The Rabbi Reb Borukh Son of Moishe Bendit

The rabbi Reb Borukh Bendit was the rabbi in Zhetl and Zabludove. He is the author of two books: 1) "Ner Elohim" (Light of God) and 2) "Ner Tamid" (Eternal Light). Both these books were published in 1789 in Navidvor.

In the recommendation in the front of his book "Ner Tamid" by Rabbi Reb Eliezer son of Zvi Hirsh from Grodno, he writes: "Borukh Bendit, chief judge of the Jewish court in Zhetl– I knew this man and his words".

The Rabbi Reb Moishe

The rabbi Reb Moishe was the son of the Vilna preacher Reb Shloime Zalman, and according to the book "Nachlat Avot" (Patrimony) was the rabbi in Zhetl in the second half of the 18th century. His brother, Reb Khaim Meseraya was a representative of Gaon of Vilna in his battle against Hasidism. He died in 1795. It is probable, in those years Reb Moishe was the rabbi in Zhetl. His son, Reb Nokhem was the rabbi in Turetz, Lubsht and Karelitch.

The Rabbi Reb Eliezer Namiat

The rabbi Reb Eliezer Namiat was the rabbi in Zhetl. The inscription on his tombstone reads: Eliezer, servant of God.

The Rabbi Reb Zekharia Mendl Namiat

The rabbi Reb Zekharia Mendl was the rabbi in Zhetl fro 40 years. We learn this from the book "The Words of Moshe" by Dov Moishe son of Yekhiel Mikhl Namiat, born in Zhetl. We read the following in this book: "Zekharia Mendl of blessed memory, son of the righteous rabbi, the famous rabbi Duber of sacred blessed memory was known by the name Reb Ber Yezharan, son of the righteous Gaon Zekharia Mendl who was the chief judge of the Jewish court in his birthplace Zhetl for 40 years".

We don't know when Reb Zekharia Mendl was rabbi in Zhetl.

The Rabbi Reb Nisn Radiner

The rabbi Reb Nisn Radiner was, according to the book "Nachlat Avot" (Patrimony) a rabbi in Zhetl. He was also rabbi in Radin and Bielitza. Reb Nisn wrote an almanac for the years 1789–1864. At the end of the book he published customs of the whole year written by his father Reb Aron, a rabbi in Lithuania and author of "Even Tkumah".

When the rabbi Reb Nisn published his book in the Jewish publishing house in Grodno, he was the rabbi in Zhetl. He writes in the introduction of this book that his family descends from Reb Shaul Wohl.

The Rabbi Reb Khaim Lifshitz

According to the book "Nachlat Avot" (Patrimony) Reb Khaim Lifshitz was rabbi in Zhetl from 1806– 1813. He left Zhetl for Srednik where he served as rabbi for 43 years. Reb Khaim was the son of Reb Eliezer, a student of the Gaon of Vilna. He received his ordination at the fair in Zelve which was signed by the greatest rabbis of the day: Reb Khaim Volazhner, Reb Avrom Ably, and Reb Shaulke Katznelboygn from Vilna.

Reb Khaim Lifshitz passed away in 1856. His position in Srednik was taken over by his son Rabbi Dov Ber who wrote many books: "Bar Khaim" (Son of Khaim), "Shir Khaim" (Song of Khaim or life), "Mayan Khaim" (Source of Khaim or Life) and "Ruakh Khaim" (Spirit of Khaim or Life). The introduction to his book "Ruakh Khaim" was written by his father Reb Khaim who wrote under the name Khaim son of Eliezer who was the chief judge of the Jewish court in Zhetl, as well as the branch in Lithuania which was close to Slonim.

Reb Dover Lifshitz, known as Berchik Sredniker is the father of the Lifshitz rabbinic family.

[Page 51]

His sons were: the rabbi Reb Hillel Arye Lifshitz – rabbi in Plongian, Subalk and Lublin, the rabbi Reb Yekhezkl Lifshitz – rabbi in Brisk, Plotzk and Kalicz, the rabbi Reb Eliezer – rabbi in Zdunska, Valya, and the rabbi Reb Yakov – rabbi in Kanin.

The Rabbi Reb Moishe Avrom Eisenshtat

The rabbi Reb Moishe Eisenshtat was born in Mir in 1814. His father Reb Yosef Dovid was the local rabbi. He was the son of a Zhetl resident Reb Zvi Hirsh Eisneshtat. Reb Yosef Eisenshtat was also born in Zhetl. According to the book "Garden of Flowers" he received ordination in Zhetl from Rabbi Reb Khaim (probably Lifshitz).

In 1836 Reb Moishe left the rabbinate in Zhetl and moved to Mir to help his father administer the Mir Yeshiva. After his father died he became rabbi of Mir.

Reb Moishe Avrom was the son in law of the renowned teacher from Slonim, Reb Shimon author of "Manche Blula".

In the book "Toldot Noah" by Reb Noakh Rabinovitch (born in Zhetl) we read a eulogy after the death of the rabbi Reb Moishe Avrom.

One of Reb Moishe Avrom's brothers, Reb Yisroel, is the father of the banking family Shereshevsky in Warsaw.

In the book "From One Generation to Another" by M. Lifson, it is told that one day butchers from Zhetl came to Reb Moishe Avrom and complained, they had borrowed money at interest and if God forbid he bans their ox they will not have money to pay their debt.

When the judge from town saw the rabbi was inclined to kosher the ox they observed he was ruling against the RAMA (Moses Isserles, eminent Rabbi in Poland). The Rabbi replied to them:

If I ban the ox, I will have to deal with these butchers in the world to come and they will never forgive me, but with the RAMA I can reach an agreement. I will ask for his forgiveness and he will forgive.

A second story was told about Reb Avrom. Once, some well off Jews from Zhetl came to him and told him a Jew in Zhetl died from hunger. The rabbi wondered. Anyone he would have asked to give him food would have given. The wealthy men replied:

The man had been rich and lost all he had. He was ashamed to ask for alms.

If so – said the rabbi – he did not die of hunger but from pride.

The Rabbi Reb Zev – Wolf son of Yehuda Halevy

The rabbi Reb Zev– Wolf Halevy was the rabbi in Zhetl from 1840 – 1850.

He is the author of the book "Emek Halacha" which was highly respected in the rabbinic world. Great rabbinic authorities subscribed to this book.

ס פ ר

עמק הלכה

הוא קבוצת חידושי דינים , כידך שאלות ותשובות כחלק אורח חיים ויורת דעה
אשר העלתי בעומק העיון לכן בעומקה של הלכה , וכם התלמוד ופוסקים
ראשונים ואחרונים , אשר על רגלי השער חיים , הוצאתי מים נאמנים , וכשטמתי
בנפ׳ת אשר נתחזק כלבי הקיחת אבותי בפלפול וסברא ישרה בחסד דר מעוני , הנבתי
לי ציונים , בסמתרת הרבנים , רשעת ורקנוים , תכרתי אני הרל כאולי יתודה ,
ואב ואלף כלאיא פדר מה׳ יהודה חלוי אבי׳ דקק וטל :

Title page of "Emek Halacha" by Rabbi Zev Wolf Halevy

The rabbis were: Reb Shmuel Avigdor Tosfaa, Reb Yehuda Leyb Zalkind from Dvinsk, Reb Yitzkhak Avigdor from Vasilishok, Reb Borukh Mordkhai Lifshitz from Semiatchich and Reb Shmuel Mohilover from Gluboky. You can find more details about Reb Zev Wolf Halevy in the work: "The History of the Jews of Zhetl".

From Zhetl, Rabbi Reb Zev Wolf moved to Zabludove and died in 1859.

The Rabbi Reb Zvi – Hirsh HaKohen Dvoretzky

The rabbi Reb Zvi – Hirsh was the rabbi in Zhetl from 1850 –1891. He was the son of Reb Khaim Orliner, who descended from the family of Reb Khaim Zhaludker, the father of the Eliashberg family.

Reb Khaim Orliner had thirteen sons and seven daughters. One of them was Reb Zvi Hirsh the Zhetl rabbi. Zvi Hirsh was known as a great scholar and a clever man. They spoke of his wisdom in Zhetl for years. He died at the end of Yom Kippur in 1891 after he had been chief rabbi of Zhetl for 41 years.

The Rabbi Reb Borukh Avrom Mirsky

The rabbi Reb Borukh Avrom Mirsky was born in Mir in 1850. His father the rabbi Reb Moishe was the head of Rabbinical Academy at the Mir Yeshiva. After his father remarried the family moved to Nesviezh where Reb Borukh Avrom got married.

[Page 52]

ספר

שמעתתא דרב"א

חלק ראשון

(כולל שרת חדושים וביאורים בש"ס ובפוסקים ראשונים ואחרונים)

מאת כאאמו"ר הרב המפורסם בדורו לגאון וצדיק כש"ת מה"ו

ברוך אברהם מירסקי זצלה"ה

אבדק"ק מדוויבה וק"ק דיטל

בן הגאון ר' משה זצלה"ה. היה ר"ם איזה שנים בישיבת מיר
ואח"כ ר"ם בעיר נסוויזש בערך חמישים שנה, הרביץ תורה ברבים
והעמיד תלמידים לאלפים והרבה מגדולי תורה מישיבתו יצאו

סודר וחובא לדפוס ע"י בנו

דוד סביל מירסקי

Title page of "Shemata Deraba" by Rabbi Borukh Avrom Mirsky

In accordance with the recommendation of Reb Nokhemke from Grodno, in 1873 Reb Borukh Avrom was hired as rabbi in Parizov. He was hired as rabbi in Zhetl in 1892 and remained as chief rabbi for 20 years. He left us a manuscript of a great essay "Shemata Deraba" in two parts, which his son, Reb Tevel published. You can read about Reb Borukh Avrom Mirsky's involvement in the Hovevei Zion movement in this chronicle in the works of Rabbi Y. L Maimon and Moishe Tsinovitch.

The Rabbi Arye Mikhal Dvoretsky

The rabbi Reb Arye Mikhal Dvoretsky was rabbi in Zhetl for 30 days when in 1912 suddenly died of a heart attack. Reb Arye was the son of Reb Zvi Hirsh HaKohen Dvoretzky who was rabbi in Zhetl for over 40 years. Before Zhetl he was rabbi in Ivenitz and Stavisk.

The Rabbi Reb Zalman Saratzkin

The rabbi Reb Zalman Saratskin was chief rabbi of Zhetl from 1912 –1929. He describes his activity in Zhetl in this book.

You can also read the biography of Reb Zalman Saratzkin in the article written by his son Rabbi Elkhanan Saratzkin.

The Rabbi Reb Yitzkhak Raytzer

The rabbi Reb Yitzkhak Raytzer was the last rabbi of Zhetl. He was the chief rabbi from 1930 – 1942. Before Zhetl he was rabbi in Sayny. He died a martyr's death during the second slaughter in August 1942.

Rabbi Yitzkhak Raytzer

[Page 53]

The Great Miracle of the Author of "Machane Yehuda"

by Mordkhai V. Bernshteyn (Buenos Aires)

Translated by Janie Respitz

The book "Machane Yehuda" was published by the Shuldberg Brothers Publishing House in Warsaw in 1893. This book contains novel interpretations of venerated texts and subtle argumentation over finer points of Jewish law in three tractates: Something Profane (Secular), the Talmudic tractate Betzah, and Sukkah. The author is listed as: the Rabbi, the Gaon (Genius), the sharpest and best known of his generation, righteous and innocent in his deeds, our esteemed teacher Yehuda from the holy community of Zhetl. This book was brought to publication by his grandson. He was his grandfather on his father's side. He tells us his maternal grandfather was the holy Reb Levi Yitzkhak of Berditchev. His name is Dovid son of Yehuda Epshteyn from Zhetl.

Who was the author and when did he live?

The publisher of this book tells us in the introduction that he could not innovate any novel interpretations of venerated texts.

We have learned that the grandfather of the author, Reb Yehuda Kharif (Harif) who died more than one hundred years ago left behind Chidushei Torah. His grandson decided to publish these innovations to honour the memory of his grandfather.

Recommendations in the front of the book were written by: the Rabbi from Slonim, who writes under the name Naum Yosef, and the Zhetl rabbi Reb Borukh Avrom.

Both recommendations ask for financial support to help publish these writings. We learn from the Zhetl rabbi that the person publishing this work is not a wealthy man and it is difficult for him to carry this burden…we also see in the introduction the author's name was Reb Yudl Kharif.

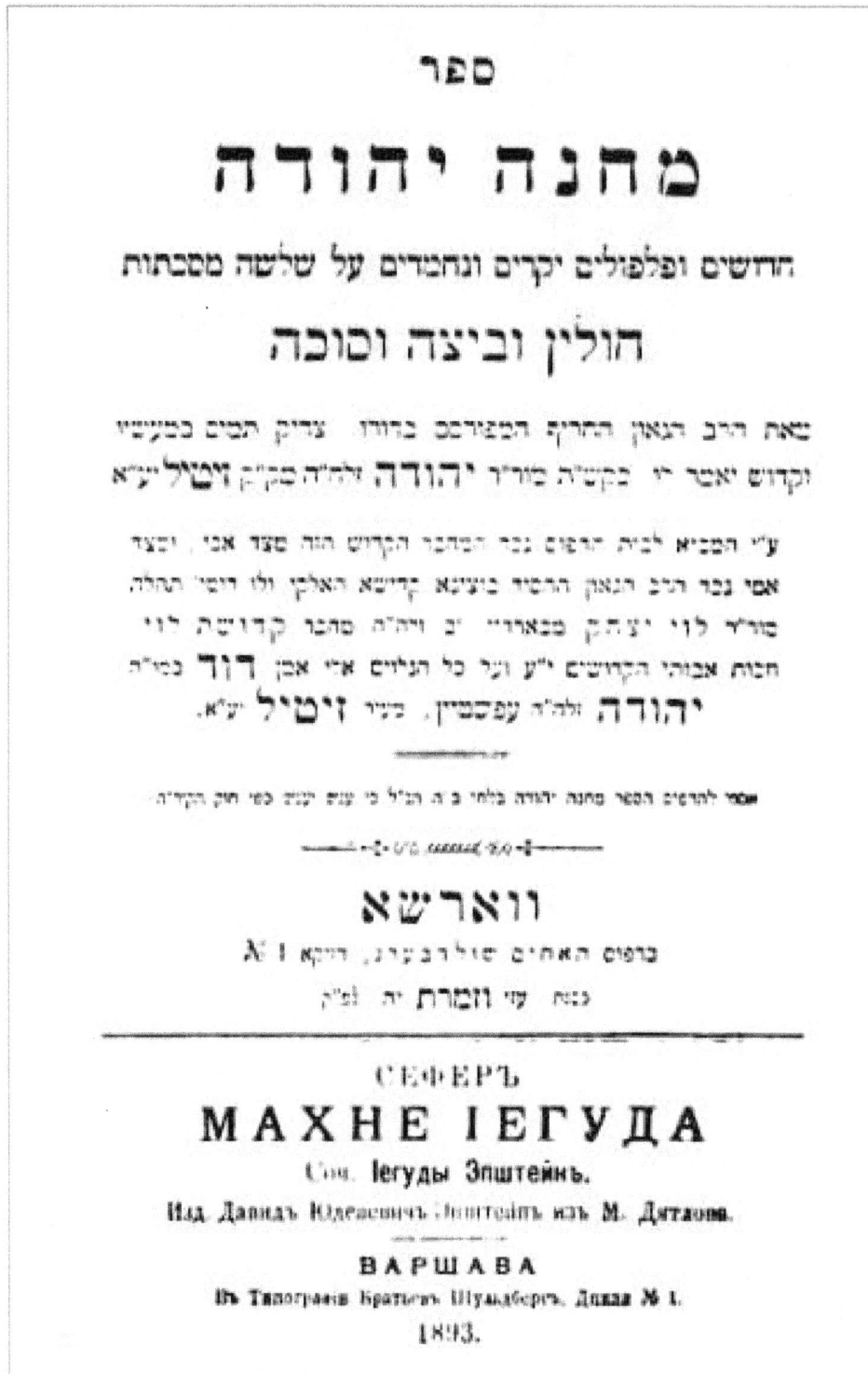

ספר

מחנה יהודה

חדושים ופלפולים יקרים ונחמדים על שלשה מסכתות

חולין וביצה וסוכה

מאת הרב הגאון החריף המפורסם בחורו צדיק תמים במעשי
וקדוש יאמר לו בקהלת מורר יהודה זללה"ה בן הרב זיטל זי"ע

ע"י המביא לבית הדפוס נכד המחבר הקדוש הוה סבד אבי ונכד
אמי נכד הרב הגאון הרסיד בעינא קדישא האלקי ולו דומי תהלה
מורר לוי יצחק מבארדי' ז"ב והה"ה סהנר קדושת לוי
חתנת אבוהי הקדושים י"ע ועל כל העדים אדי אבן דוד כמ"ה
יהודה זללה"ה עפשטין בנדי זיטיל זי"א

יאמר להדפים הספר מחנה יהודה בלחי ב"ה הג"יל כי ענת יעבד כפי חוק הקדו"ה

וווארשא

בדפוס האחים שולדבערג, רויכא No 1
גם עי וזמרת יה זצ"ק

СЕФЕРЪ

МАХНЕ IЕГУДА

Соч. Iегуды Эпштейнъ.

Изд. Давидъ Юдельевичъ Эпштейнъ изъ М. Дятлова.

ВАРШАВА

Въ Типографіи Братьевъ Шульдбергъ. Дивал № 1.

1893.

Title page of "Machane Yehuda" by Rabbi Yehuda Harif

This book contains 32 columns, 64 pages, numbered with letters and numbers. On page 62, under the title "The Story of the Miracle" the author recounts the miracle which happened to him.

We see this took place in 1783 on the 24th of Cheshvan (October) when after midnight a guest, a servant of a neighbouring nobleman, wanted to kill Reb Yehuda, whom he had allowed to spend the night.

He shot him but did not kill him. Disregarding this great danger, the author recovered and lived another 15 years after this event.

From the thanks the author expresses to those who helped publish his book we learn details about his family.

His mother's name was Golda, a granddaughter of "Kdushat Levy". When the book was published she was still alive.

His wife, Khana Miriam, the daughter of Moishe was also a granddaughter of the author. His son's name was Alter and his daughters were: Mushka, Stirke and Yehudis.

He thanks his brothers in law: Avrom Yegal from Piesk, Shimshon and his sister in law Stirke.

[Page 54]

Books by Zhetl Authors

Translated by Judy Montel

Author	Title of the Book	Printed
Rabbi R Tzvi son of R Meir HaKohen	Innovations of the Maharsha	Hanau 1717
Rabbi R Aryeh Leib Segal Horovitz	Marganita Taba (Good Pearls)	1755
Rabbi R Chaim Rappaport	Responsa of our Rabbi Chayim Kohen on the Four Sections of the Shulchan Aruch	Lemberg, 1861
Rabbi R Chaim Rappaport	Zecher Chayim [Memory of Life]	Lemberg, 1865
Rabbi R Baruch Bendit	Ner Tamid [Eternal Candle]	Nowy Dwor, 1788
Rabbi R Baruch Bendit	Ner Elohim [Candle of God]	Nowy Dwor, 1788
Rabbi R Yaakov Krantz	Kol Yaakov [The Voice of Jacob] (on the 5 scrolls)	Warsaw, 1819
Rabbi R Yaakov Krantz	Emet LeYaakov [Truth to Jacob] (Commentary on the Passover Haggadah)	Zolkiew, 1836
Rabbi R Yaakov Krantz	Mishlei Yaakov [Proverbs of Jacob]	1862
Rabbi R Yaakov Krantz	Kochav MiYaakov [A Star from Jacob]	Warsaw, 1872
Rabbi R Yaakov Krantz	Sefer HaMidot [Book of Qualities]	1862
Rabbi R Nissan	Otot LeMoadim [Signs for Holidays]	Grodno, 1798
Rabbi R Zeev Wolf HaLevi	Emek Halacha [Valley of Jewish Law]	Vilna, 1845
Rabbi R Yisrael Meir HaKohen	Chafetz Chayim on the injunctions against slander	Vilna, 1873
Rabbi R Yisrael Meir HaKohen	Shmirat Halashon [Preserving the Tongue] essays and advice how to avoid negative speech	Vilna, 1879

Rabbi R Yisrael Meir HaKohen	Machaneh Yisrael [The Camp of Israel], Commandments with instructions for those serving in the army.	Vilna, 1881
Rabbi R Yisrael Meir HaKohen	Ahavat Chessed [Loving Kindness]	Warsaw, 1888
Rabbi R Yisrael Meir HaKohen	Mishna Brura	Warsaw, 1892
Rabbi R Yisrael Meir HaKohen	Collections of Rulings, Conclusions on the Matters in Seder Kodashim [the volumes of Talmud dealing with Purity and Impurity]	Warsaw, 1899
Rabbi R Tzvi Hirsch HaKohen	Chidushei Maharsha [Innovations of Maharsha]	
Rabbi R Baruch Avraham Mirski	Shmateta DeRaba	Jerusalem
Rabbi R Aryeh Yellin	Yfat Eynayim [Of Beautiful Eyes]	Vilna
Rabbi R Noach Rabinovitz	Torah VeHaMitzvot [Torah and the Commandments]	Vilna, 1864
Rabbi R Noach Rabinovitz	Mei Noach [Waters of Noah] (Innovations on Jewish Law)	Vilna, 1881
Rabbi R Noach Rabinovitz	Toldot Noach [The History of Noah] (in three volumes)	Vilna, 1884
Rabbi R Netanel Patzavski	Meshivat Nefesh [Restores the Soul]	Berditchev, 1891
Rabbi R Netanel Patzavski	Emunat HaTchiya [Faith of Resurrection]	Berditchev, 1893
Rabbi R Yehuda Charif	Machaneh Yehuda	Warsaw, 1893
R Asher Shushan	Maaseh Shushan (Explanations and Commentaries on the Tanach)	Warsaw, 1893
R Nathan Nette HaKohen Zeishtik	Chidushei Torah [Innovations on the Torah] (Published by his son in America [in *Yiddish*])	
R Dov Moshe Namiat	Divrei Moshe [Words of Moshe]	Vilna, 1906
Rabbi R Zalmen Sorotzkin	HaDeah VeHaDibbur [Knowledge and Speech] Part I	Warsaw, 1937
Rabbi R Zalmen Sorotzkin	HaDeah VeHaDibbur [Knowledge and Speech] Part II	Jerusalem, 1948
Rabbi R Zalmen Sorotzkin	Oznayim LaTorah [The Torah has Ears] Part I	Jerusalem, 1951
Rabbi R Zalmen Sorotzkin	Oznayim LaTorah [The Torah has Ears] Part II	Jerusalem, 1953
Rabbi R Zalmen Sorotzkin	MeOznayim LeMishpat [Scales for Justice]	Jerusalem, 1955

[Page 55]

Articles About Zhetl in Encyclopedias

SŁOWNIK GEOGRAFICZNY KRÓLEWSTWA POLSKIEGO str. 556–8

Zdzięcioł al. *Dzięcioł, Dzięciołki,* w dok. *Zdzietel,* urzędownie obecnie *Diatłowo,* tako nad rzką Zdzięciołką, wpadającą o 22 w. poniżej do Niemna, pow. słonimski, w 4 okr. pol., gm. Zdzięcioł. W pięknem położeniu, przy trakcie ze Słonima do Wilna, odl. od Grodna o 212 w., od Słonima 43 w., od Wilna 133 w., od Nowogródka 35 w., od Lidy 42 w., od Dworca 14 w., od stacyi dr. żel. poleskiej Nowojelnia o 10 w., Mtko w r. 1893 miało 3233 mk. Podług innych danych było tu do 7000 mk., w tem około 400 prawosł. i 700 katol., reszta żydów, 1096 dzies. ziemi włość. Znajduje się tu cerkiew paraf., kościoł par. katol., kaplica cmentarna katol., 2 synagogi i kilka domów modlitwy żyd., szpital wiejski na sześć łóżek, utrzymywany kosztem kilku sąsiednich gmin, szpital przy kość. paraf. katol., zarząd okręgu policyjnego i gminy, st. poczt. listowa, 2 lekarzy, kilku felczerów i akuszerka, szkoła ludowa, apteka. Odbywają się tu targi tygodniowe i dwa jarmarki doroczne. Przemysł i handel pozostają w ręku żydów. Przemysłem rękodzielnym zajmuje się kilkadziesiąt osób, w tej liczbie 10 stolarzy, wyrabiających głównie posadzkę. Cały przemysł fabryczny miatka stanowią 2 młyny wodne na Zdzięciołce, piec wapienny, kilka drobnych garbarni, miododolnia, kilka zakładów wyrabiających wino z rodzenków i parę farbiarni. Starożytna ta włość hospodarska, zw. „dwór Zdzieczoło", nadaną została w r. 1498 d. 6 czerwca przez w. ks. Aleksandra kn. Konstantemu Iwanowiczowi Ostrogskiemu, hetmanowi, z prawem założenia miasta (Arch. Sławuckie, t. I, 116). Ostrogski na majętności tej zapisuje d. 5 czerw. 1499 r. dziesięcinę cerkwi sobornej w Wilnie (ibid., t. I, 212). Zygmunt I, wynagradzając Ostrogskiego za długoletnią niewolę, do której dostał się po bitwie nad Wiedroszą, hojnemi obdarzył go łaskami. Przywilejem wydanym w Mielniku 28 grud. 1507 r. potwierdził nadanie dóbr Z. przez króla Aleksandra; w 1509 r. uwalnia poddanych „zamku Zdeteł" i in. włości od opłaty „wołowszczyzny", w r. zaś 1511

raz jeszcze zatwierdza kniaziowi prawo własności wszystkich dóbr jego dziedzicznych, tak przez Aleksandra jak i przez siebie nadanych, w ich liczbie wymieniając i „dwór Zdzięcioł" (ibid., t. III, 54, 70, 87). Tenże monarcha pismem datowanem w Wilnie d. 3 lipca 1514 r. poleca Annie Bartoszowej Taborowicz, aby ks. Konstantemu nie broniła przewozu na Niemnie około Z. (ibid., t. III, 117). Po śmierci kn. Konstan. Ostrogskiego w r. 1530 pozostała po nim wdowa kn. Aleksandra Słucka wyrokiem królewskim z d. 20 marca 1531 r. przyznany ma sobie do czasu Z., zwrócić ma natomiast kn. Ilii „pasierbowi swemu", Turów i in. włości (Z. 17, k. 60, w A. J. Z. R.) Niedługo jednak cieszyła się posiadaniem Z., już bowiem 5 sierpnia t. r. nakazano jej oddać i ten majątek najstarszemu synowi nieboszczyka. Kn. Ilia d. 1 sierp. 1531 r. zanosi protest do grodu, iż ojciec jego powróciwszy z niewoli, zamiast własny swój majątek Zdzięcioł, zapisał na cerkiew majętności macierzyste kn. Ilii: Szeszoły, Świrany i Kroszty. Sprawę odłożono do dojścia do pełnoletności brata jego kn. Wasila (l. c., Z. 17, k. 98—100). Gdy rzeczony kn. Wasil miał lat 15 i pełnoletność jego ogłoszoną została, nastąpiły między rodzeństwem działy. Wyznaczeni w tym celu komisarze zjechawszy do Wilna d. 20 grud. r. 1541, Zdzięcioł, Dubno i in. przyznali kn. Wasilowi (Przeździecki, Jagiellonki, t. II 64, 269—276). W r. 1570 ks. Konstanty Wasil Ostrogski, wwda kijowski, marszałek ziemi wołyńskiej, według Paprockiego syn Konstantyna, fundował tu szpital przy kościele parafialnym, nadając mu opatrzenia po 20 złp. w gotowiźnie i 20 beczek żyta co rok, oraz po 5 wozów drzewa co tydzień. Zapewne drogą wiana Z. od Ostrogskich przeszedł do Sapiehów, którzy tu kościół parafialny w r. 1646 na nowo przebudowali. W r. 1655 podkanclerzy Kazimierz Lew Sapieha testamentem zapisuje siostrzeńcowi swemu Aleksandrowi Hilaremu Połubińskiemu, pisarzowi polnemu w. ks. lit., za usługi

oddane Rzpltej, majętność Zdzięcioł i in., w pow. słonimskim, z warunkiem wypłacenia siostrom swym i potomstwu Ogińskiej po 25000 złp. (S. 227, k. 293). Krzysztof Konstanty kn. Połubiński aktem z d. 17 sierp. 1685 r. odziedziczone po ojcu dobra: Zdzięcioł, Jawor, Wiazowice przekazał hetmanowi Sapieże, ten jednak legatu nie przyjął, owszem dokumentem spisanym w Dereczynie d. 22 września t. r. oddał takowe do równego podziału między dwie siostry, naturalne sukcesorki zmarłego Połubińskiego, starosty wołkowyskiego (Akt. Tryb. Głównego, Nr 856—7). Wskutek nastąpionego wówczas działu, Z. otrzymała Anna Marya z kn. Połubińskich, żona ks. Dominika Radziwiłła, podkancl. w. ks. lit. (Z. 144, k. 1—8). Odtąd Z. stanowił posiadłość Radziwiłłów linii szydłowieckiej żyrmuńskiej, która nie posiadała żadnej ordynacyi, ich też staraniem podniósł się w zamożności i znaczeniu. Oni to odbudowali starożytny zamek, a w r. 1738 Mikołaj Faustyn Radziwiłł sprowadził tu zakon bonifratrów, umieściwszy ich przy istniejącym z dawna szpitalu, co biskup wileński Zieńkowicz t. r. potwierdził. Wszakże bonifratrzy nie długo musieli przebywać w Z., bo w r. 1806 czytamy napomnienie biskupie nie do nich lecz do plebana, aby pobierając annuaty szpitalne, starał się ten zakład wydźwignąć z opuszczenia. Pod koniec XVIII w. ks. Radziwiłłówna, wychodząc za Stanisława Sołtana, marszałka nadw. lit., wniosła Z. w ten dom. J. U. Niemcewicz zwiedzając te strony w r. 1819, takie nam o nim pozostawił wspomnienie: „Z. zawiódł mię w nadziei oglądania w nim JW. Sołtana, za sejmu 1791 r. marszałka nadw. litew. Znalazłem atoli syna jego. Mko niewielkie, lecz czyste i porządne. Gdym wszedł do pałacu, jakimże mnie smutkiem ogarnął widok trzech portretów obok siebie wiszących: pani Sołtanowej, pani Mostowskiej i Józefa Weyssenhofa" (Podróże, str. 392). Ostatnim dziedzicem dóbr Z. był syn marszałka Adam, pułkownik wojsk pol. Po r. 1831 dobra przeszły na własność rządową. Z dawnych gmachów po-

74 A Memorial to the Jewish Community of Zhetl

[Page 56]

zostały dotąd: zamek, niegdyś obronny, dźwignięty przez ks. Ostrogskich na początku XVI w., przerobiony na pałac przez Radziwiłłów w XVII stuleciu, nosi na sobie piętno panującego naówczas rococo. Zewnętrzne mury jego zachowały do dziś swoje architektoniczne piękno: zdobią go gipsatury stylowe oraz herby ks. Radziwiłłów, czarne ordy z trzema trąbami na piersiach; wewnątrz, po przejściu na własność skarbową, zupełnie przerobiony, mieści dziś koszary wojskowe. Gdy pod koniec zeszłego wieku Z. stał się dziedzictwem Stanisława Sołtana, zamek pięknie odnowiono, zachowując starożytną jego postać. Założono tu wówczas ogród angielski, do czego pomogła i sama miejscowość. Tu i za parkiem, w zacisznem ustroniu, zw. „Chatki", pobudowano kształtne budynki, które wewnątrz ozdobił freskami sławny artysta Norblin (rysunek zamku z krótkim opisem zamieścił Tyg. Ilustr. z r. 1872, t. VII, str. 205). Cerkiew prawosł. parafialna, niewielkich rozmiarów, drewniana, założeniem swoim sięga zapewne czasów ks. Ostrogskich. Uposażenie jej stanowi, podobnie jak i świątyni katolickiej, 33 dziesięciny ziemi. Parafia prawosławna, dekanatu (błagoczynia) zdzięcielskiego, ma 3957 wiernych. Dekanat prawosławny obejmuje 12 parafii: Zdzięcioł, Dworzec, Luszniewo, Mołczadź, Nahorodowicze, Nakryszki, Nowojelnia, Ochonowo, Raudziłowo — Kozłowszczyzna, Rohotna, Wężowiec i Wysock, w ogóle 24333 dusz. Kościół katol. paraf., p. w. Wniebowzięcia N.M.P., na miejscu dawnego zbudowany z cegły w r. 1646 przez Kazimierza Lwa Sapiehę, podskarb. w. lit., a kształcie podłużnego prostokątu, 50 arsz. długi, 18 szeroki a 17 wysoki. Trzymany w stylu rococo, od frontu zdobią go dwie wspaniałe wieże, o trzech kondygnacyach, zakończone kopułą z krzyżem. Pomiędzy wieżami nad pierwszą kondygnacyą wznosi się facyata owalnego kształtu z krzyżem i zegarem. Sufit i posadzka ze zwyczajnej cegły. Nad głównemi drzwiami chór z organem o 16 głosach, biały, lakierowany, częściowo wyzłocony. W kościele jest 7 ołtarzy, z tych 3 w przezbyteryum a 4 w nawie. W wielkim ołtarzu zwraca uwagę cyborium z drzewa, snycerskiej

roboty, ślicznie rzeźbione. Po nad chrzcielnicą, w murze naprost kazalnicy, znajduje się nagrobek z blachy mosiężnej, a za nim w naczyniu serca ks. Mikołaja Faustyna i syna jego Jerzego Radziwiłłów († w 1746 i 1755 r.). Wyżej jeszcze nad tym pomnikiem jest portret Mikołaja, olejno malowany, w kształcie owalnym, w mur wprawiony i dobrze zachowany. Skarbiec tego kościoła jest ubogi, a nadto 1837 r. został okradziony. Ze srebrnych naczyń większego rozmiaru posiada 6 lichtarzy i cenną, z byłego dereczyńskiego kościoła, ślicznej roboty, monstrancyę o podwójnych promieniach, pacyfikał z drzewem krzyża św. i t. p. W r. 1743 d. 4 czerwca wszczął się straszny pożar w Z., w którym nie tylko wszystkie zabudowania plebańskie, całe mko, ale i kościół z ołtarzami, aparatami, sprzętami kościelnemi, archiwum a nawet z nieboszczykami w podziemiach do szczętu, prócz samych ścian, zgorzał. Po tej klęsce w r. 1751 z ruin został na nowo dźwignięty przez Mikołaja Faustyna Radziwiłła, przy współudziale jego żony Barbary z Zawiszów, która była szczególniejszą dobrodziejką i protektorką tego kościoła. Niewiadomo kiedy i przez kogo świątynia została konsekrowana; rocznica jednak poświęcenia obchodzi się w pierwszą niedzielę po Wniebowzięciu N. Maryi Panny (Tygod. Ilustr. z 1874 r., t. XIII, 120). Parafia katol. dekanatu słonimskiego, 8145 wiernych. Kaplice na cmentarzu w Z. i w Orlinie; dawniej też w Mirowszczyźnie, Żukowszczyźnie i Strzelance. W r. 1717 kahał „Dzięciołki" z partykularzami płacił podatku pogłównego żydowskiego 1000 złp. (Vol. leg., VI, 183). Gmina, położona w płn.-wsch. części powiatu, graniczy od płn. z gub. wileńską, od wschodu z gub. mińską, od płd.-wschodu z gm. Rohotna i Dworzec, od płd. z gm. Kozłowszczyzna, od zachodu z gm. Pacowszczyzna, obejmuje 54 miejscowości, mających 1292 dm. włośc. (obok 310 należących do innych stanów), 8307 mk. włościan, uwłaszczonych na 13746 dzies. ziemi. Nadto w obrębie gminy znajduje się 3278 dzies. większej posiadłości (1447½ roli, 485 łąk i past., 1097½ lasu, 248 nieuż.) i 307 dzies. należących do cerkwi i kościoła (213 roli). Okrąg policyjny zdzięciolski obej-

muje 5 gmin powiatu: Dworzec, Kozłowszczyzna, Pacowszczyzna, Rohotna i Zdzięcioł. Lud okolicy tutejszej, zdaniem duchowieństwa, jest moralny i pobożny, mówi przeważnie językiem białoruskim, w trzech tylko wioskach otoczonych lasami: Pogirach, Zasieci i Norcewiczach używa dotąd mowy litewskiej. Osady te sięgają jakoby czasów ks. Trojdena. Są to podług podania potomkowie Bartów, ludu litewskiego przybyłego z Prus. Prawdopodobnie są oni szczątkami Jadźwingów. Do najciekawszych miejscowości w pobliżu Z. należy niezaprzeczenie odległa o 12 w. wś Nahorodowicze, w w. XVI i XVII własność rodziny Welaminów Rutskich. Pamiętne w dziejach, że tu odbył się pierwszy zjazd kapituły unickiej po zjednoczeniu kościołów, pod przezydencyą metropolity Welamina Rutskiego w r. 1617 (ob. Stabelski, Chronologia). Cerkiewka drewniana postawiona została przez metropolitę Rutskiego, jak świadczy dokument przy niej przechowujący się. Do chwil ostatnich świątynia ta zachowała pierwotną postać, dopiero w r. 1894 przerobiona, cechę swoją dawną zatraciła. Również ciekawym zabytkiem w dworze nahorodowickim jest bardzo stara budowa murowana, jak styl włoskiego baroko wskazuje, pochodząca z XVI w. Był to kościół kalwiński, wiadomo bowiem, że ojciec metropolity Feliks († 1599 r.) był tego wyznania, syn zaś dopiero w młodości przyjął katolicyzm, nim za przyzwoleniem papieża przeszedł na obrządek słowiański. Kościołek ten obrócony na składy a w części na mieszkanie, otrzymał z czasem nazwę skarbca, pod jaką i dziś pozostaje (rysunek jego podały Kłosy z r. 1871 czy 2). Nahorodowicze w r. 1635 zostały sprzedane przez metropolitę Welamina Józefa Rutskiego Bułhakowi, potem były własnością Surynów, Tyzenhauza i Głuchowskiego, dalej w XVIII w. generała Morawskiego, ożenionego z ks. Radziwiłłówną, siostrą Karola „Panie kochanku". Gdy za długi generała dobra poszły pod eksdywizyą, Nahorodowicze kupiła starościna Łęska i następnie je odprzedała w r. 1820 Dmochowskim. Obecnym właścicielem jest Władysław Dmochowski, znany artystamalarz. W lesie nahorodowickim znajdują się mogiły, porosłe drzewami, do-

[Page 57]

tychczas niezbadane, niewiadomo z ja-
kiego czasu pochodzące. O 9 w. od
Z. majętność Strzała, miejsce urodzenia
i własność niegdyś poety Juliana Korsa-
ka, dziś Mackiewiczów. O w. 15 od Z.,
we wsi Rohotnej (ob.) Wołłowiczów,
w pobliżu dworu znajdują się szczątki
bardzo starożytnego zamku. Między
ludem okolicznym przechowuje się po-
danie, że wzięta i spożytkowana stąd
cegła powoduje śmierć biorącemu. Temu
zawdzięczyć można, że ruina ta dotrwała
aż do naszych czasów.

M. Raw. Witanowski.

Starożytna Polska — Michał Baliński.
Tymoteusz Lipiński. Warszawa 1887.
tom 4, str. 523—524.

Zdzięcioł, miasteczko w lasach
między Lidą a Słonimem, dobrze wybru-
kowane, z zamkami mieszkalnymi.
Znaczne dobra te musiały kiedyś nale-
żeć do ks. Konstantego Ostrogskiego
W-dy Kijowskiego i Marszałka ziemi
Wołyńskiej, bo on w r. 1570 fundował

szpital przy kościele parafjalnym. Z czasem stały się własnością Radziwiłłów
linji Szydłowieckiej Żyrmunskiej, która
nie posiadała żadnej ordynacji.

Przy końcu 18 wieku, Stanisław
Sołtan Marszałek N. L. przez ożenienie
z księżniczką Radziwiłłówną, stał się
dziedzicem Zdzięcioła, gdzie zamek
pięknie odnowił, zachowując starożytną
jego postawę i ogrodem angielskim
otoczył.

Geographical and Statistical Dictionary of the Russian Empire, year of 1865, p.267

Translated from Russian by Maria Krol

Zdzentsiol (Zdentsiol, Dzentsiol) a small state place of Grodno Governorate, Slonimsky Uyezd (subdivision), located 45 versts northwards from the county town, by the postal road to Vilna near Dzentsiolka river. In XVI century Ostrozhski dukes who owned the place built a fortified castle here. Later on it was owned by Radziwill family and then Saltana family. Number of residents - 602 people of both genders, 85 yards (homesteads), an orthodox church, a catholic chapel, a Jewish synagogue and 3 prayer schools. Weekly bazaars and twice-yearly fairs (on Yuriev day [St.George's Day] and Pentecost Day); in 1859 goods worth in total 2000 rub. were brought here, and sold for 1480 rub. in total.

(Balinsky, Staroz. Polsk., III, 648; Urban Settlements, part II, p.113; Bobrovsky, Grodno Governorate, part II, p.1,070, appendix, part II, p.158).

Materials for Geography and Statistics of Russia, p.1070.

Forty-five versts northwards from Slonim by postal road is located a small place named **Zdentsiol**, in which vicinities in several villages there live descendants from Prussian Bartians, who speak Lithuanian. Some people mistakenly believe them to be the remnants of Yotvingians. As is known, Bartians accepted by Traidenis (the Great Duke of Lithuania), were partly settled in Grodno, and the other part was settled in the suburbs of Slonim.

Encyclopedic Dictionary, vol.XI, 1893. - F.A. Brockhaus, I.A. Efron, p.400

Dyatlovo (Dzentselovo) - a small place in Grodno Governorate, Slonimsky Uyezd [subdivision] located in 44 versts from the county town; 3233 residents; dressing of parquet, known as "dyatlovsky".

Jewish Encyclopedia

A small town in Slonim Uezd [subdivision] of Grodno Governorate in 1897 - 3979.

Great Soviet Encyclopedia, vol.85, p.368.

Dyatlovo - an urban-type settlement, the center of Dyatlovsky area in Baranovichi region of Belorussian SSR. Located along the road 13 km westwards from Novoyelnia railway station (Baranovichi - Lida railway line). In Dyatlovo there is a sawmill, an industrial complex, several artels. As of 1952 there is a secondary school, a cultural center and a cinema. In the area there is grain and potato cultivation, animal production is developed (cattle and pigs).

[Page 58]

Zhetl in the Hebrew Press][a]

by Yitzkhak Epshteyn (Kfar Neter)

Translated by Judy Montel

The Meeting of Chovevei Zion (Lovers of Zion) in Zhetl to Commemorate the 100th Aniversary of the Death of the Vilna Ga'on

From Zhetl (Horodna Province) B"Z announces that on the evening of the third day of chol hamo'ed Succot, on the 100th Yahrzei of the Vilna Ga'on Z"tzl, the Chovevei Zion Association in the city gathered at the study hall (Beit Midrash) and held song and prayer in memory of the soul of the Ga'on, Z"tzl with great pomp and circumstance, and the attendees pledged to "Gan Shmuel" in order to plant two trees in honor of the Ga'on Rabbi Shmuel Mohilever Z"tzl and afterward the attendees said words of acclaim to the Grsh"m to the committee in Odessa, to all of the Conolists in the holy land and all of the Chovevei Zion, and many members joined the support organization.

From "HaMelitz", 1897, No. 227.

Yehoshua Aizenshtat Visits Zhetl

Zhetl (Grodno Province). It is announced that a respected visitor has arrived there, who is Mr. Yehoshua Aizenshtat, member of the HaPoel committee in Jaffa, and who was previously a resident of the city, and he will speak there about the situation of the Yishuv (Jewish settlement) in these times in the holy land and will describe to the audience the material and spiritual situation of our brothers the farmers in the Moshavot (early settlements) of the Land of Israel and its good relationship with the government and with their Arab neighbors, also he had much to say about the National Bank (Bank Le'umi) and other large undertakings that are now on the agenda in the world of the Yishuv in the holy land, from which good will result to our nation and our land.

His words made a large impression on the hearts of the people of the city, causing many to donate to Zion, and even the extreme opponents have already begun to look with a kinder eye upon the Zionist movement. And the following day in the evening, Chovevei Zion gathered around him and he spoke again and give them details of the lives of our brothers the farmers, at home and in the field, and gave them a faithful picture from the Moshava Kustina (today, Be'er Tuvia) of which one of its sons, Reb Elimelech Izraelit, is a native of this city. And after this he made a toast to the lives of all of the Chovevei Zion wherever they are, and to the lives of our brothers who are working upon the mountains of Israel, and the entire crowd responded with a trumpet-like call: Amen! Amen! And they pledged donations for the workers in Kustina.

"Hamelitz," 1898, No. 232.

Donations for those Working in Our Holy Land

Due to the terrible tragedy which happened in our city, Zhetl, on the second night of the portion of Bishalach in the women's section [of the synagogue], since twelve women were asphyxiated when they pushed one another to get out of the building (details of the tragedy were printed in Hamelitz 22) the following women whose names are mentioned [lth"p?] in the holy ark and give thanks to the merciful God that they were not in the upheaval:

M. Shifra Leah Dzhenchelski, Sarah Rachel Dunetz, Sara Dvora Wernikovsky, 36 kop each.

Elke Mirski, 30 kop. The Rebbetzin of the place, Shifra, wife of Rabbi Yehuda Levit, Solieh Rabonovitch, Leah Doba Finklstein, Hinde Miriam Izraelit, Sarah Shifra Dvoretzki, Mecha Kamenitzki, Shifra Yeletzki – 18 kop each. Elke Leah Solimianski – 10 kop. Nechama Lichter, Sarah Musha Shushan, Sarah Dvoretzki, Leah Dvoretzki, Shayna Breskin, Pruma Mirski, Yocheved Orzichovski, Rivka Aronovski, Elke Serevrovski, Bayla Levit – 9 kop each.

The money, a total of 3.91 rubles was collected by Mr. Shlomo Zalman Dunietz and Mr. Moshe Orzechovski and I received as written 5/122.

The history in the city of Zhetl: Menachem Vernikovski.

"HaMelitz," 1898, No. 44.

A Zionist Association was founded in Zhetl in 1899

In spite of vigorous objections from the extreme Haredim and the followers of the Rebbe of Slonim who are commanded to oppose Zionism, the few Chovevei Zion (Lovers of Zion) in our city have finally succeeded in founding a Zionist Association. Every Friday evening, they explain the weekly portion before a large audience which gathers each time in the old Beit Midrash (study hall). And in this and other such ways they have succeeded in promoting Zionism in our city.

Also, the "Holiday of the Maccabbees", which the Zionists celebrated in a large hall, and gave speeches and sang nationalist songs did much to spread the Zionist idea and at that same event some thirty members joined our Association.

The daughters of our city have also founded themselves a "Daughters of Zion" association, and the respectable founders are working, as much as possible, to spread Zionism among the women of our town.

"Hamelitz", 1899, No. 280.

[Page 59]

The Bernikker Magid of Zhetl Preaches in Kaidani

The preacher, teaching rabbi Bernikker from Zhetl visited Kaidani and with his excellent speeches, in which he spoke on Zionism in this city, moved the hearts of his listeners and many people joined the association of Zionists in that city.

"HaTzefira", 1900, No. 155.

The Zionist Association during the German Occupation

In the town of Zdzieciol; there is a Zionist association, whose numbers have become very numerous. During the four months of its existence the association has collected approximately 400 Mark benefiting the National Fund and has sold 120 Shekels. The association maintains a library with 223 members. The number of readers is over 123. A large number of lectures and readings about Zionism, Hebrew History, the history of Hebrew and Yiddish culture and literature. Five public gatherings have also been held, two in the study hall (Beit Midrash) and three in the theatre. Classes for adults have also been instituted.

"HaTzefira," 5678 (1917-18) Nos. 13, 14.

Reception for Rabbi Reb Baruch-Avraham Mirski

A day of celebration and joy was had by us, the congregation of Zhetl, on the 30th day of the Omer (15th Iyar, 5652 – 1892) [May 12, 1892], for the great rabbi, Reb Avraham Baruch Mirsky from Porozowa, came to dwell in honor on the rabbinical seat in our city. All of the shops were closed and bolted, each and every person left their work and business and they streamed to greet this honored guest with great pomp and circumstance. The moment he arrived everyone cried out "Welcome!" and across from them came the answer, "Hooray, hooray!" Before entering the city, the great rabbi stepped out of his carriage and walked on foot in honor of the many who had gathered, with many of the prominent citizens around him and a great crowd before them and with a celebratory clamor brought him to the old study hall (beit midrash), which was already full of people. And the rabbi went up onto the stage and gave a fine and pleasant sermon, and the content of his sermon was to awaken the feelings of our brothers, the children of Israel, who dwell in our city, and to unite and connect their hearts to their father in heaven and to love their nation. All of this with exalted ideas and holy emotion. Afterwards, the entire congregation accompanied him to the house and parted from him in peace full of good feeling. That very day our congregation received letters of greeting from the great rabbi M. Yitzchak Elchanan of Kovno, from the great rabbi R' Shmuel Mohilever of Bialystok, from the great rabbi Yosef of Slonim and from the great rabbi Yehonatan of Volkovisk.

Reported by: Eliezer Mattityahu Kantorovitch

"HaTzefira", 1892.

The Death of Rabbi R' Aryeh Michl Dvoretzki

On 26 Tevet, 5672 [January 16, 1912], our new rabbi, the Ga'on R' Aryeh Michl Dvoretzki died, less than three weeks before assuming the rabbinical seat in our town. Just two months ago we accompanied the great rabbi R' Baruch Mirski to his burial place, and again a great rabbi has died here.

In his death our nation lost one of its more excellent and beloved rabbis, for besides being a great leader and scholar, he was a pleasant man and well loved by everyone.

The deceased was born in our city Zhetl to his great father, R' Yosef Tzvi Hakohen, and served here with the rabbinical crown for over 40 years. When he was still young, he was appointed to the rabbi of Timkovitz, and later to be a rabbi in Ivintz and from there he moved to Stavisk and later was brought (after the death of Rabbi Mirski) to be a rabbi in our city. He was fifty-five years old at the time of his death.

Y. Zimilvitz

"Hazman", 1912, No. 5

The Funeral of Rabbi R' Aryeh Michl Dvoretzki

Residents of the city including several rabbis from the nearby towns participated in the funeral of the rabbi in Zhetl, 27 Tevet [January 17, 1912]. From his home he was carried to the courtyard of the synagogue. There eulogies were given by Rabbi Shmuel Rabinovitch of Zhaludok and the rabbi of Bielitz. All described the excellent traits and elevated habits of the deceased and the great loss experienced by our city in particular and our nation in general. For besides being one of the excellent rabbis of the generation, besides his great genius and greatness in Torah knowledge, he was also very involved in public works, a lover of charities, and did much to improve the lot of every poor person.

In the large study hall (Beit Midrash) a long elegy was made over him by Rabbi Zalman Sorotskin of Varnova. He was buried next to the grave of Rabbi Baruch Avraham Mirski z"l. The people of Zhetl knew to do their duty to the widow of the deceased and committed to give her, after one year, a total of 3300 rubles, beyond the salary of the rabbi for an entire year which costs a total of 1200 rubles, after deducting 80 rubles a week for a teacher.

[Page 60]

Permission was granted to the people of the city to appoint a rabbi also in the middle of the year, but on the condition that they would pay this amount to the Rebbetzin retroactively.

"Hazman," 1912 No. 7

A Dispute Regarding Choosing a Rabbi in Zhetl

The Zhetler Rabbi died and the question of the rabbinate came up in Zhetl. And when the question of the rabbinate comes up, that is where the devil dances. The devil dances in Zhetl as well and is inciting the people against one another. Some want one rabbi and others want another. Some choose for themselves and so do others. Some make haste and announce by telegraph amongst the entire diaspora of Israel from Dan to Beer-Sheva: 'So-and-so has been chosen' and others make haste and announce from one end of the world to another by the telegraph that some other person has been chosen. And I receive the two Zhetler telegrams at one time and stand in confusion, without knowing where the truth lies. And it can happen that while still speaking I receive a third telegram with the command and warning not to publicize the previous telegrams at all, because it's all baseless: there were no elections and no rabbis were chosen at all; and it happens that I receive a fourth telegram begging me to ignore the third telegram because it was sent by a person who favors the wishes of the widowed Rebbetzin, who doesn't want a new rabbi, so that the sextons (gabbays) of the community won't stop paying her board. And thus, these telegrams upset my mind frequently, and bring me into a confusion from which I am unable to extract myself.

"Hed Hazman," 1912, No. 55 – from "A View of Cities and Towns"

People from Zhetl who Donated Funds for Our Siblings, Children of Israel in Persia who were in Danger of Starvation

The Honorable R' Avraham Shlomo Namiat – 3 rubles, Mr. R' Avraham Yitzchak Levit – 1 ruble' Rabbi Ze'ev Wolf – 1 ruble.

Donations of 50 kop: Rabbi Yosef Chever Masef, Rabbi Yosef Ber Ginzburd, Tzvi Hirsh Behari, Eliyahu Me'ir Finsklstein, Yehoshua Ailperin, Avraham Yitzchak Lobenski, Aharon Zelig, Moshe son of Eidel HaLevi, Yehoshua Eizenshtat, Nissan son of R.I. (or Nissan B.R.I.), Mordechai Dvoretzki, Shlomo Levinstein.

36 kop: Gershon Katz.

35 kop: Gedalyahu.

30 kop: Neta Zeitzik, Zalman Bras, Zecharya Nissan,Noach Rabinovitch, Leib Michobedkia, Yitzchak son in law of R' Dov.

Donations around 25 kop: Chayim Dober Slutzk, Shlomo Shlomovitz, Moshe Tanchum Breski, Aharon Katz, Uri Bar David, Yitzchak Bred, Ya'akov Baruch, Yehushua Zelig HaLevi, Mendel son of Gershon, Yehushua Zelig Katz, Herz son of Menashe Shub, Avraham son of Daniel, Dober B.R.A.

Donations around 20 kop: Yisrael Dov Luski, Benyamin Chanan Schatz, Yitzchak son of R' Aharon, Ya'akov Katz.

Donations around 18 kop: The groom Ze'ev Wolf son of R' Menashe Yizraelit.

Donations around 15 kop: Chayim Ochanovski, Leib from Minsk, Meyrim Katz, Moshe Ya'akov Dvoretzki, Leib Sadow.

Donations around 10 kop: Shlomo Barsh (B.R.S.), Yoel David, Moshe Eizik, David Ber Katz, Moshe Aharon, Yitzchak Meklir.

Collected by: Yechiel Michl Berkovitz, Yosef Chever.

"HaMagid", 1872 No. 30.

Yosef Hailperin of Zhetl Educates Abandoned Children

Zhetl. (Grodno Dist.)

In our town there is a man and his name is Yehushua Hailperin, who has himself done "the act is greater than the actor," for even if he is not one who is protected by money and works hard to earn his livelihood for his large household, in spite of this he has allocated from his efforts and time to a good and beneficial thing. He saw that mischievous boys from our nation had been led by idleness and poverty to extend their hands into the purses of strangers, without differentiating between Jews and Christians, and he was zealous for his people and he persuaded the boys to leave their despicable activity and to choose a profession and a craft. For the past three years he has supervised the boys as a father would his sons, including their behavior and their moral lives and paid artisans for their tuition. In order to fund all of the expenses of this endeavor, he himself went around every week to ask for charity and with this he educated approximately twenty boys to be useful people for themselves and for human society and without shame to Judaism.

And you, my bothers, here, know to respect the enterprise of this dear man, strengthen his hands so that he will have enough to expand his activity and to cover all of the needs of this great endeavor, and to ease from him the added burden and also to strengthen his hands that they should not falter, and that he should not become disheartened. And even if our city has become impoverished due to the fires, even so it is necessary to support he who worries about the good of Jewish children and to save them from poverty and shame and to ease the future of the congregation lest they fall upon it as a burden and a disgrace: Ya'avetz

"Hamelitz," 1883 No. 15.

[Page 61]

Bikur Cholim (Visiting the Ill) In Zhetl in 1888

In the town of Zhetl, a "Chevre Lina" ["Lina" means sleeping, it was common at the time to aid the ill by having someone sleep at their home to help with their care] was established due to the efforts of the honorable citizens: R' Moshe Leib Levit and R' Zev Wolf Slutzky, to visit the sick. Announced by: Yosef Winietzki.

"Hatzfira," 1888 No. 138.

Controversy over the Doctor

Zhetl (Grodno Dist.)

For many years there has been a Jewish doctor in our town, an expert and experienced doctor and an honest man, who participates in all of the charitable works in our town and is also a member of the support association of Odessa, and he is also the doctor for the "Bikur Cholim" association that is in our town and is known to carry out the responsibilities of his task with them in good faith: responds to the ill who are poor humbly, and accepts everyone politely and for this he has been beloved and well-liked by all the people of the town.

But recently a certain man in our town who has a shop for selling medical drugs has gotten up and has joined with someone else in our town, a comrade like him, and they began spreading terrible libels about the respectable doctor and about those who head the respectable organization "Bikur Cholim," and despite what is clear and known to all the people of our town, that they were doing this only for their private benefit, they succeeded in their slyness to attract others to them, from those who always jump in to things, and they founded themselves a new "Bikur Cholim" organization, and they brought in some young doctor who barely finished his studies at the University of Warsaw a year ago. But as far as it seems, with all of his great knowledge, which he has studied, he didn't learn the simpler thing that is known to every cultured person, that it is not appropriate to settle in a small town, which in no way can support two doctors at a time, and to use all means to chase away the first doctor.

And thus, for the past three months, from the day the new doctor came to our town, the controversy and disputes have increased, and the most aggressive among us have found ample opportunity to tell tales and slander and several respectable people were already jailed and many cases were handed over to the lawyers. And they have still not stopped their activities, and their leader continues to incite and with all of this they were not content and on Shabbat, Chol HaMo'ed Sukkot that just passed, they continued to bring shame on the name of Israel by gathering disreputable people to the dwelling of the new doctor and there they opened the good treasure that is all "Mashkeh" (alcoholic drinks) and this aroused them to riot in the study hall. And during the prayers when it was time to take the Torah scrolls out of the holy ark, they all burst into the study hall and snatched the Torah scrolls and put them back in the holy ark. And they made a great noise and commotion and called for blows as well, but with the help of the police, those in prayer were able to quiet the storm to silence and the name of Israel was desecrated. M.R.

"Hamelitz," 1899 No. 280

The Situation of Institutions and Hebrew in Zhetl

Zhetl (Grodno Dist.)

In the public life of our town light and darkness are mixed together. It contains honest institutions that are run in an orderly way and governed wisely like "Linat HaTzedek," "Bikur Cholim," and others. And about two years ago a Savings and Loan Association was founded here. This latter has been growing and developing from day to day and brings great benefit to the small and medium-sized shopkeepers and grocers in particular, and to all the townspeople in general. Currently, it has about 300 members.

In contrast, the instruction of Hebrew is lacking. There are about 20 "melameds" (teachers) here and among them a few Hebrew teachers, but their situation is very run down. The degree to which the language of the past is loved in our town can be attested to by the number of Hebrew Newspapers that are received in our town: three instances. Everyone wants the Yiddish Newspapers, and amid the twenty Yiddish newspapers, in first place is "Friend" newspaper, and by reading the Yiddish papers the fathers have also done their duty in educating their daughters. There are 12 instances of Russian newspapers that are taken in our town.

There is no library in our town at all. Several years ago, there was a small one, but sadly it did not last long.

In our town, many of the young men aged 13 and up study Gemara and the rest go to general school (in other cities) or learn a craft and a minority are aimless.

Ya'akov Zimilivitz

"Hed Hazman," 1909 No. 186.

Forging Mezuzot

In the town of Zhetl, near our town of Slonim, one "sofer" (scribe), by the name of Avraham Tikachinski, invented a trick to enable the young scribes to not sit on their seats all day, not to mention the nights – to write out the parchments for mezuzot and the portions that go into tefillin, which is work that exhausts their weak bodies and pays very little. So, he brought a printing press from Vilna and thus he prints hundred and thousands of mezuzot and portions every day {page 62} without any agitation and sends them over the Atlantic Ocean. Some say: this clever man became rich from the unfit mezuzot and portions. But to his sorrow, critical eyes found him out here in our town for our scribes examined them and discovered that they were not written by hand, but by machine, and only the words "Shadai" and the words "kuzo bemuchso kuzo" – were written by hand.

Eliezer Benkstein of Slonim

In the Hebrew weekly "Hayehudi," that appeared in London, 1903, No. 35.

A Large Fire in Zhetl in 1874

A terrible event took place here, in Zhetl that is near to Slonim. In the last month of Menachem-Av a large fire burst out and spread itself over the four directions of the town and burnt two hundred and fifty houses down to the ground and three study halls of stone, that had just recently been built and the work on them finished and their cost was twelve thousand rubles, for naught did those who built them toil. Also, the old synagogue which had stood for over two hundred years with beautiful paintings and flower buds became a tumbled ruin and all of the people of our town left their homes naked, even though we worked hard to save our property and Torah scrolls and holy books and brought them to the cemetery, for we imagined that the stone wall that stands around the cemetery would protect them.

Alas, what we imagined was not to be, for where they were set, there they were buried. When the stormy wind arose with a fury, it didn't skip the cemetery either and heated it all around until the flames licked the graves themselves and the damage was close to two hundred thousand rubles. Also, a six-year-old boy was lost and despite searching for him tirelessly, he was never found. And our hearts ache about the houses of Torah learning and the various "cheders" (schools for children) where five teachers used to sit at the head of the advanced study hall to preach lessons to hundreds of boys, who had come on foot from a distance to come here and the sextons (gabba'im) in charge did not stop or tire from elevating the foundations of the Torah. Day and night they would be on guard to supervise with open eyes its income and expenses to prevent its pillars from weakening, that its character would not be diminished and so that it would not be too difficult for them to spend the amount of money necessary for this thing and they kept an eye on the teachers and on the students to increase Torah learning and glorify it. And now they are left as a bird who leaves its nest, as a scattered sheep, to this you, readers of "HaLevanon," put this to your hearts, and don't withhold your hand from feeding many souls who are hungry for bread and to help them in their straitened time. May God allow and comfort those mourning for it and fulfill the desires of their hearts and the year will end as will its curses. I speak to you with a broken and downcast heart – Shlomo Hemtzovski

"HaLevanon," Eve of Succot, [September 25] 1874 No. 7

Zhetl (Vilna District)

May our appeals be pleasantly received above to give room for our words, to report in the public gate how God judged our town with fire and put to flame all good things.

On Monday, 28 Tammuz (July 13, 1874), a fire started in the outskirts of the town and for three hours the town turned into a tumbled ruin and over two hundred homes were burned, aside from the synagogue and the study halls with their books and all of the houses that were the glory and beauty of the town went up in smoke.

And now, merciful ones, children of merciful ones, have mercy on your miserable brothers, help them with much or with a little, as far as you can bear, and send to this address to the following rabbi (the ga'on, head of the holy rabbinical court)/

Yitzchak Yaakov Perls

"HaMagid," 1874 No. 36

Fire in Zhetl in 1882

Zhetl (Grodo Dist.)

The evening of Monday (September 18), in the ten days between Rosh HaShana and Yom Kippur a fire broke out and consumed over one hundred houses and three study halls as well as shops with their merchandise were burnt. The people of the town are wandering the streets with their wives and children without an anchor or support. Therefore, I ask in the name of all those whose homes were burnt to send help rapidly whether with money or with clothing and to send to the name: Yitzchak Naftali Hirsch Kosowski of Dvoretz, Slonim District.

"HaMelitz," 28 September, 1882. No. 37

The Great Fire in Zhetl in 1883

Zhetl, 11 Shvat 5643 (January 19, 1883)

I have just received a total of 25 rubles to support those whose homes burned and as this person has been so good to us, I thought to turn to him with a request, but first of all I must describe the situation in our town, Zhetl.

Previously our town was the first in the entire district of well-known people who were learned and God-fearing, in respectable congregants and generosity of charity and loving-kindness and now it has become a tumbled ruin, for during a year and five months it has been fated to suffer fire three times, may the Merciful One save us, and the last conflagration during the ten days of repentance of this year was aggravated because it started in the middle of the night and all the inhabitants of our town have been left without any of their capital and work. Some two thousand people, naked and {page 63} destitute in the streets and the barns on cold and freezing days, which days have predominated, no fireplace to warm their flesh, no dress to protect from the terrible frost and their bones and joints knock against one another and the great tragedy is that hunger has taken hold of the town and there are many ill people and quite a few souls die every day, for our many sins.

I myself composed a letter to the Champions of Judah in Petersburg and Moscow with no response. Only in Kiev did the respectable heads of congregation the great Yona Zeitzow and Dr. Mandlstam arouse themselves and send us six hundred rubles and we quickly spent this money as frugally as possible to feed those who have felt God's anger. And now we do not have even one farthing and we have nothing with which to feed a great multitude, whose souls are wavering from hunger and cold. Therefore, I raise my eyes to the respectable publisher of "HaMelitz," please, do well with those who know shortage and scarcity in our town and please try to awaken the generous members of our nation to a large congregation in Israel, whose inhabitants are in a great misfortune, wrapped in starvation and naked in the frost, lest they die before their time, if no care is taken of them soon.

My heart is certain and ready, for my words come from a broken heart, which is depressed and shaken from what my eyes see, may they take root in the heart of one who feels the pain of his brothers, and with the feelings of his soul and the power of his pen come to help and enliven a great multitude. And may the Merciful God put his words in the mouth of his pen to work upon the hearts of our brothers, so that by his efforts the pains will be lifted. And for this may he be blessed by God in all that he turns to, be successful and merit to see the comfort of Israel, my soul blesses him, heart and soul.

Yosef Zvi-Hirsch HaKohen, standing here in the holy community of Zhetl.

And the Publisher himself added in the margin of this letter: "The words of his honor, the rabbi of Zhetl must shake the heart of anyone with a soul, for our newspaper is ready to take the average between the volunteers and between those who demand support and he hopes, that our brothers, children of Israel, will awaken to the voice of the honored rabbi, who describes the terrible catastrophe that has come upon his flock in faithful and frightening colors that shake the feelings of the heart.

The letters to Peterburg I sent to Baron Horotz P. Ginzburg, to the Minister Shmuel Poliakow and to the generous nobleman, M. Meyer Friedland and I did not get any answer from them.

"HaMelitz," 1883 No. 6

Fire in Zhetl in 1894

Zhetl (Grodno Dist.)

On Wednesday, April 6, at the third hour after midnight, a fire suddenly burst out of one of the houses in the heart of the town and some twenty houses, including shops with their merchandise, were burned to the ground. Some thirty families that at that moment had no lack and in one moment the wheel of fate upturned them and naked as the day they were born they are rolling on the dung heaps together with their young children who cry out for bread but there is none. For these unfortunates did not have time to save anything from the fire even a shoelace, and they escaped with their lives. Two nearby towns, Slonim and Navahradok, hurried to rescue their brothers and that day they sent two wagons loaded with matza, meat and wine, but this mite was not enough to satisfy the lion.

Maurice Namiat

"HaMelitz," April 13, 1894. No. 85

A Scoundrel from Zhetl is Exploiting the Fires for his Own Benefit

Today a Jewish man came to me, around fifty years of age, who has streaks of white in his hair and said to me, that he is a rabbinical arbiter in the town of Zhetl and he was sent to collect charity for that town, which had gone up in flames. And as a reference for his words he showed me a letter of request from the great rabbi of our generation, the great rabbi R' Yitzchak Elchanan shlit"a, from 8 Iyyar, 5654 (May 14, 1894) in which was written that the town of Zhetl had been totally burned down with its synagogues and our brothers the children of Israel remained naked and barefoot and destitute.

And thus, said the great rabbi, I sent the rabbi and arbiter Zvi Hersch son of rabbi Yechiel Halprin, great grandson and grandson of many generations to collect charity etc. After the signature of the Ga'on shlit"a there were in the notebook of that collector two letters in Rashi script from two scholars of the town, requesting their brothers the children of Israel to stand up to help the one collecting. And in a small notebook, wherein the donations were written, the collector showed me two letters, one from Rabbi Benizni Novogorod and the second from the rabbi of the town of Koretz, asking from their brothers the children of Israel in favor of the collector. And after I showed this collector that in "HaMelitz" No. 85 of 5654 (1894) it is reported from the town of Zhetl that only 20 houses were burned on the 6th of April and not the entire town with its synagogues etc, this man responded first, that the reporter in "HaMelitz" is a child, very young and we couldn't rely on his words, however later he admitted to me that the collection was only for himself and not for the town. I the undersigned indeed wrote these words on the letter mentioned above!

The writer of those words was to collect charity only for himself and not for the town, because in the town only around 20 houses burned – in any case, I thought it right to report this in the dear "Hamelitz." A stranger and resident.

"Hamelitz", 1895, No. 33.

[Page 64]

Twelve Women Asphyxiated in Zhetl

From Zhetl, (Grodno Dist.) we have reports of terrible tragedies that have occurred there this month: Saturday night, the portion of "Bo", while a sermon was being given there by one of the preachers, fire broke out in one of the Christian homes and the townspeople ran from the study hall to the location to offer their help. And while they were rushing to and fro part of the burning thatched roof fell on the respectable mayor, also a townsman, and the flames took hold of him, and even though they saved him from the fire and accompanied him to his home, several hours later he died from the force of the pain.

And on Monday, the portion of "Beshalach" [i.e., the following week] in the evening, many people, men and women, gathered in the study hall to hear the eulogy that the same preacher gave for the great rabbi Mahar"il Diskin [died, January 22, 1898] and the crowding was very great and to a greater degree was this so in the women's section. And there are two sections [for women]. One next to the northern wall and it is built above the corridor of the study hall from the outside – and the second – against the western wall from within the building upon beams, where one end is attached to the wall and the other end rests on a long beam that lies in a north-to-south direction. And there is one small and narrow access point from the outside through which the women can enter these two women's sections.

Suddenly, one of the beams that supported the floor of the western section broke. From the weight of its burden and from the sound of the break, there was chaos and confusion in all three areas. Many of the men hurried to escape with their lives through the entrance for they thought the ceiling was falling on them, and several broke the windows of the building and created an escape route through them.

The pandemonium grew from moment to moment, especially in the western women's section. When they saw that the floor had collapsed beneath their feet, each took strength to leave the tight space before others. In the small and narrow entry-way they fell from the tremendous crowding and blocked the way to the exit for the other women who were hurrying after them, and the steps that lead to the entryway was full of beaten and tortured women, holding on to one another and pressed together, and even women who wished to turn around and go back into the building could not do so.

After the initial fright passed, many of the men came to the aid of the women. But every idea they had to get the women out of this turmoil through the entry-way failed, so they set up ladders and climbed up the windows and the lattices of the women's section that overlooked the study hall and they pulled the women back into the building and thus they were able to bring about salvation. This tumult went on for an hour until they came up with and idea of how to take down the small wall that separated the entry-way and the corridor of the building, and when they took down the wall, many women rolled out of the space, but it was too late, for 12 women had asphyxiated.

Most of the women were young and left behind small children with fathers who are not wealthy. The outcry encompassed the entire town and every face was pained and reddened, and who can describe the loud cries and wails of the small children who had in a moment become unfortunate orphans. Besides this, one of the men also suffered a brain injury and the doctors despaired of his life. In addition, some forty women were injured and took ill. For now, the police have sealed the study hall.

"HaMelitz," Tu Beshvat [February 7], 1898, No. 21

A Flood in the Town

Zhetl

On Wednesday, second day of the new moon of Elul [August 18, 1909], the waters of the stream in the small road Pomereika overflowed due to the many rains and flooded the houses who stand on the two banks of the stream on Lisigori Street and the courtyard of the synagogue, and also the houses on "Courtyard Street," that stand close to the stream. For two hours dreadful damage was done in the town. The houses were filled with water higher than the windows and those who lived within were in great danger and they cried out for help.

Thanks to a few young people, there was no loss of life. They also saved many possessions from the houses. The force of the water destroyed the bridges, the trees planted alongside the stream were uprooted, and many planks that had been prepared for building were swept away by the current. The contents of the gardens that were close to the stream with all of their plants and fruit-laden trees were swept away. The flood lasted from about 7 until 9 in the evening and during that short time it managed to do a great deal of damage amounting to several thousand rubles. Those with cellars suffered especially, for they were filled with water and many different types of merchandise were ruined. Many people could not save their most precious possessions and escaped with their lives.

The waters also made their way into the study halls. The Chassidic study hall was filled with water up to the third step around the bima. Also, the waters burst into the "Talmud Torah" school building and did a lot of damage in the room, which is also where the collateral pledges of the "Gmilut Chassadim" [charity loan society] were located. Many objects were ruined, the cellars and low buildings are still full of water, and using special machinery, the fire department is now emptying them of water.

In total, some thirty families have suffered from the flood, amongst whom are some in abject poverty who lost the remainder of their capital, and also their houses – though not totally destroyed, but they are now unlivable without repair and therefore they need help.

Z. Zimilevitz

"Hed HaZman," 1909. No. 178.

Original footnote:

    a. Collected by Moshe Tzinovitz and Baruch Kaplinski

[Page 65]

Dates From the History of Zhetl
Translated by Janie Respitz

15th Century
1498 – Duke Konstanty Ostrogsky receives Zdietyl Estates with the rights to found a city there.
16th Century
1507 - King Zigmund I confirms the handing over the Zhetl Estates to Duke Konstanty Ostrogsky
1530 – The Zhetl Estates are given over to the widow of Hetman (Cossack chief) Konstanty Ostrogsky, Duchess Alexandra Slutzka.
1541 – The Zhetl Estates are passed down to Duke Vasil Ostrogsky.
1570 – Duke Vasil Ostrogsky builds a hospital at the church.
1580 – The first information of a Jew, Nisn, who occupies an area of 8 poles on the Zhetl marketplace.
1598 – A second bit of information about Jews, Aharon Goshkevitch from Mizevetz, Meir Levkovitch and Merl Yuditch live in Zhetl and litigate with the nobleman Yarash Zhibort.

17th Century
1627 – Zhetl together with Dvoretz is mentioned for the first time in the records of the Jewish Council of Lithuania.
1646 – Zhetl Estates are given over to the family of Duke Safyeha.
1646 – The Church in Zhetl was rebuilt by the chancellor from Slonim, Duke Casimir Leo Safyeha.
1655 – The Zhetl Esates are given over to Duke Alexander Polubinsky.
1685 – The Radziwills from the Zhidlovetz line are now in possession of the Zhetl Estates.
1670 – The great Talmudic scholar from Zhetl, Reb Arye Leyb Segal, author of "Marganita Teva" is hired as rabbi in Minsk.
1670 – The Zhetl synagogue is built.
1670 – Zhetl is independently taxed by the Council of Jews of Lithuania.

18th Century
1704 – The story is told in "Knesset Yekhezkl" by the rabbi Reb Yekhezkl Katzenelnboygn about the Zhetl leather merchant Reb Yisroel son of Yesheyahu who was murdered on a raft in Banden near Telz and Reb Yekhezkl had to inform his wife she was an Augunah (a woman who can't remarry as she has no proof of her husband's death).
1738 - Mykolai Fausten Radziwill brings Rachitov law to Zhetl.
1720 – 1729 – The rabbi Reb Khaim HaKohen Rappaport serves as chief rabbi of Zhetl.
1740 – The Preacher of Dubno, the rabbi Reb Yakov Krantz is born in Zhetl.
June 4, 1743 – a great fire breaks out in Zhetl and destroys the town.
1750 – (Approximately) the first records of the new cemetery.
1751 – The church in Zhetl is rebuilt.
1790 – Reb Nisn is now chief rabbi in ZzZhetl.

19th Century
1806 – 1813 – Reb Khaim Lifshitz is chief rabbi in Zhetl.
1831 – The Zhetl Estates which had belonged to the Saltans since the end of the 18th century were confiscated by the Czarist regime.
1836 – The rabbi Reb Moishe Avrom Eisnshtat leaves the Zhetl rabbinate.
1839 – The Chefetz Chaim, Reb Yisroel Meir HaKohen was born in Zhetl.
1840 – The first Interest Free Loan Society was founded in Zhetl.
1840 – 1850 – The rabbi Reb Zev Wolf Halevy, author of "Emek Halacha" is chief rabbi in Zhetl.
1850 -1892 – Rabbi Zvi Hirsh HaKohen Dvoretzky is chief rabbi.
1874 – 250 houses in Zhetl burn as well as the old synagogue.
1877 – The new Talmudic Society was founded.
1882 – The writer A.M. Dilan (Zhukhovsky) was born in Zhetl.
1882 – One hundred houses burn including all three Houses of Study.

1883 – A great fire breaks out in Zhetl and 2000 people remain without a roof.
1891 – A library was founded in Zhetl.
1892 – The chief rabbi is now the Parizov Rabbi, Reb Borukh Avrom Mirsky.
1894 – 20 houses burned down in Zhetl.
1898 – A horrible tragedy occurred in the women's synagogue where 12 women lost their lives.
1898 – The well known Zionist businessman, Yehushua Barzilai (Eisneshtat) came from Eretz Yisrael for a visit. His in laws lived in Zhetl.
1899 – The Zionist organization "Agudah" was founded.
1899 – The first circles of the Bund were organized.

[Page 66]

20th Century
1902 – The Volunteer Fire Department was founded.
1906 – Zhetl revolutionaries carried out an expropriation on the train at Novoliyene.
1907 – The first Savings and Loan Credit Union was founded in Zhetl with 300 members.
1909 – The Talmud Torah was built.
1909 – A flood destroyed property in the area near the Pomerayke River.
1912 – The position of Chief Rabbi was taken by the Voronov rabbi, Reb Zalman Sorotzkin.
1915 – Zhetl is occupied by the Germans.
1915 – The youth in Zhetl begin a drama club.
1917 – Two sisters, Esther and Libka Kaplinsky founded the first school in Zhetl.
1918 – An independent authority is organized and lead by Yisroel Kaplinsky.
1918 – 1920 – Zhetl goes from one regime to another.
1920 – A delegate from the Joint visits Zhetl by the name of Lev and organizes a help – action committee for the town.
1921 – A Folks Shul (school teaching secular subjects) is founded in Zhetl.
1923 – They begin building the school.
1924 – "Hechalutz" (Zionist organization) opens in Zhetl.
1924 – A Professional Union is founded.
1926 – The Interest Free Loan Society is reorganized.
1927 – The "Tarbut" organization opens a Hebrew kindergarten.
1928 – The first graduates of the Zhetl Folk Shul.
1928 – The first City Council is elected.
1929 – A "Tarbut" school is founded in Zhetl.
1930 – The Chief Rabbi in Zhetl is the rabbi Reb Ytzkhak Raytzer,
1933 – A great fire breaks out in Zhetl.
1935 – Another great fire breaks out in Zhetl.
1939 – Zhetl is occupied by the Soviets.
1941 – Zhetl is occupied by the Germans.

[Page 67]

Geographic and Climate Conditions in Zhetl

by Dr. A. Y. Braver (Jerusalem)

Translated by Janie Respitz

In a bill of divorcement, where great attention must be paid to every letter and spelling of every word, Zhetl, according to the great rabbi Reb Zalmen Saratzkin was called: "Zitl on the river Zhitklo and on the river Pomerayke and on spring sources". (Translator's note: A Jewish divorce (a get) can only be issued on a town on a river).

The name Zhetl is apparently a shortened version of the name Zdietel, taken from the Lithuanian – Polish period and fit well phonetically into the Yiddish language.

The Polish name Zdzicciol and the Russain name Dyatlovo apparently derive from the name of a forest bird whose Latin name is Picus, Russian name is Dyatel and Dzicciol in Polish. (Translator's note: Woodpecker).

In the forests around Zhetl there were two types of woodpeckers: green and black. However it is not certain the name of the town really derives from the bird. It probably had an old name that came from a language incomprehensible to the Slavs and they pronounced it to sound like the bird.

Geographic Conditions

Zhetl lies at 53° 33' to the northern geographic length and 25° 24' geographic width, east of Greenwich. It lies north of Jerusalem 21° 45' to the west 9° 41'.

Midday, sunset and the sunrise in the months Nissan – Tishrei (Approx. April – September), occur 39 minutes later than Jerusalem. In the period: Tishrei – Nissan (September – April) the days in Zhetl are shorter.

The long summer days and the long winter nights, together with climatic conditions, had an effect on the lives of Zhetl's Jews.

Two rivers flow through Zhetl: the Zhetlke River whose Polish name is: Zdzicciolka and the small river Pomerayke which flows into the Zhetlke.

Both the Zhetlke and Pomerayke are tributaries of the Nieman which flows 13 kilometres north of Zhetl. The Malchadke River also a tributary of the Nieman flows 7 kilometres to the east of Zhetl.

Zhetl is situated on the north – west end of the Navagrudke Highlands, at the spot where they descend in the direction of the Nieman valley.

Zhetl is situated 150 – 160 metres above sea level. In the region there are hills which are 200 metres above sea level. Between the hills there are valleys and flat lands with small rivers running through. Near these rivers you can find marshes and small natural ponds. There are two such ponds in Zhetl which the Zhetlke River flows through.

Zhetl's soil is sandy and muddy, mixed with stones. Fertility is low. Large areas around Zhetl are covered with evergreen trees (in sandy soil), as well as leafy trees (Ash, alder and others).

The poet Adam Mickiewicz described the landscape of the region beautifully. He came from Novogrodek which is 30 kilometres east of Zhetl and wrote the following words: "Turn me toward the forest hills and toward the green meadows".

This landscape was created by glaciers during the last ice age.

In its long journey from Scandinavia, the glacier brought along rocks, stones, sand and earth. This entire mass was left by the glacier which melted due to rise in temperature. This is how these small hills were formed that stand a few dozen metres high.

The Nieman Valley is like a crater where the melted water of the glacier flowed. In the direction of the crater valleys tributaries were formed and among those tributaries were those that flowed through Zhetl.

Given that the mountains made of glacier sand and stone blocked the path of the streams to the Neiman, marshes and wetlands developed which were not well suited for raising livestock or producing hay.

Temperature

The climate in Zhetl matches its geographic situation bordering between central Europe which is dominated by the influence of the Atlantic Ocean and Eastern Europe whose dominant influence is the Eurasian continent with its vast temperature differences winter and summer.

The average temperature of the month of January, which is considered the coldest month of the year is between 4 – 5 degrees Celsius below zero. However, the temperature would sometimes drop to 30 degrees Celsius (below zero).

[Page 68]

The warmest month is July. The average temperature in July is 19-20 degrees Celsius. However the temperature sometimes reaches 30 degrees Celsius.

If we were to compare the temperature in Zhetl to a place in Israel at the same altitude, we can be sure the difference would be greater in winter than in summer. On a hot wet July day, before the rain, one can really sweat in Zhetl, but in Zhetl the summers are much shorter.

The greatest difference someone from Israel would observe when visiting Zhetl is the amount of sunlight and moonlight. Not only is the light in Zhetl weaker, because the sun and the moon are not in the middle of the sky, but rather in its margins, and it is much cloudier.

The clear skies we see in Israel are rarely seen in Zhetl, and only in the winter.

There is another difference. In Israel, fields grow all year. In Zhetl, they grow approximately 200- 205 days a year. For 160 days a year the temperature does not lend itself to cultivation of what was planted.

Atmospheric Precipitation

The difference in the amount of precipitation (rain) between Zhetl and Jerusalem is not so big. The average rainfall in Zhetl is around 600 cm a year, and in Jerusalem it is sometimes more. The difference, just between us, is that in Zhetl it never happened that it would not rain for 10 days while Jerusalem is rainless for 7 months.

Our dry summer is the main rainy season in Zhetl. That is the blessing of that region. Rain falls in the hot summer. It is a blessing for agriculture which is the basis of the economy.

In Israel, the water evaporation is often higher than the atmospheric precipitation. In the region of Zhetl, evaporation is far less than precipitation resulting in moisture of the soil and a large amount of marshes and swamp.

Agriculture

Zhetl and its vicinity lived off primitive agriculture, from livestock and forestry.

The most important agricultural products of Zhetl is corn, (bread) potatoes (for eating, fodder and producing alcohol) and flax. Zhetl is situated in an area which produces a lot of flax for export. The buying up and exporting of flax was in Jewish hands. Cattle, sheep, horses and pigs in the Zhetl region were backward (Deficient) breeds not desirable in western markets. The businesses of fur, wool, pig hair and lumber were also in Jewish hands. The main export, lumber, sailed down the Nieman.

Livelihoods

Zhetl specialized in the manufacturing of poplar parquetry which were called Zhetl Parquet. The production did not transform into another industry and remained within the framework of handiwork.

The main source of income for Zhetl's Jews was small business with the farmers, buying their agricultural products and selling them to industry and handicraft production.

A few generations before its destruction, Zhetl was unable to support its Jews. Therefore, many Jews left Zhetl for larger local cities or across the ocean, particularly to America. Beginning at the end of the 19th century, support by American relatives played an important role in maintaining the town.

When we examine the geographic situation of the town we don't find any economic pluses which could ensure the existence of such a large Jewish community, except for the road from Slonim to Vilna which passed through Zhetl and was probably a source of income before the railroad was built and wagon drivers would stop over and spend the night in Zhetl.

Another important plus for Zhetl compared to other towns was that within a radius of tens of kilometres, the fact was, it always belonged to important Polish magnates, who had other estates throughout Poland. The protection by the nobility defended the Jews of Zhetl in town as well as on the road which served as a powerful attraction for many Jews.

Understandably, the Zhetl nobility exploited their Jews and actually the protected Jews and lessees of the Ostrogskys, Safyehas and Radziwills were never wealthy however they earned a living, taught their and grandchildren Torah, Khuppa (married them off), and good deeds.

The large palace in Zhetl is a reminder and witness of the great magnates who, to their merit, allowed the Jewish community of Zhetl to grow.

[Page 69]

Population and Occupations

by Borukh Kaplinsky (Tel Aviv)

Translated by Janie Respitz

The population in Zhetl was mixed. It was comprised of: Jews, White Russians and a small cluster of Poles. We do not have any statistics of the population on Zhetl from the 17th or 18th centuries. Our first information comes from a Slavic Geographic source which states in 1893 there were 3233 people in Zhetl, 2233 Jews comprising 70% of the general population. In later years Jews comprised 77% of the population.

The Jewish and General Population in Zhetl

Year	General Population	Jewish Population	% of Jews	Source
1893	3233	2233	70%	Slavic Geographic Source
1897	3079	3033	76.2%	Jewish Encyclopedia (In Russian)
1921	3080	2376	77.1%	Periodical Demographic / History Berlin 1928
1926	4600	3450	75%	According to A. Ivenitsky

Right after the First World War the populations of the general and Jewish communities fell. However by 1926 there were 4600 residents, 3450 Jews, (75%).

Occupations

We do not have any statistics of the occupations of the Jews in Zhetl from the previous century. From the statistics we find in the work of Avorm Ivenitsky in his "Yekapo Books" from the years 1926 -29 we learn there were 621 Jewish families according to the following trade distributions:

303	Artisans
210	Merchants and retail
33	Scribes
30	Coachmen (teamsters)
19	Professionals
12	Land Workers
9	Jewish Functionaries of Religious Life
Total:	621

According to A. Ivenitsky there were 3450 Jews in Zhetl in 1926. On average there were 5 ½ members per family. The job distribution is not exact but does reflect the proportion. We learn, almost 50% of Zhetls providers were artisans.

M.M. Lazerovitch, in his work "Zhetl and its Artisans" gives the percentage of artisans at 65%. Even if we count the scribes as artisans, the percentage according to Ivenitsky is no more than 54. Therefore we must note the distinction between merchants and artisans is not exact. Some of the butchers in Zhetl were merchants but in our statistics they feature as artisans.

From the "Statistical Information" from the cooperative credit unions of Poland we find the following table:

Membership in the Zhetl Cooperative People's Bank in the Years 1929 -1921 in Numbers and Percentages

Year	Amount of Artisans	% of Artisans	Amount of Retailers	% of Retailers	Amount of Merchants	% of Merchants	Amount of Professionals	% of Professionals
1929	107	62	63	36			3	2
1931	156	40	140	35	22	6	22	6

Year	Amount of Farmers	% of Farmers	Amount of Varia	% of Varia	Total
1929					173
1931	20	6	34	8	394

From this table we learn, in 1929 28% of Jewish providers in Zhetl participated in the bank. In 1931 63% of all providers.

In 1931 the artisans comprised 40 % of bank members and we believe that their percentage in the total amount of providers did not exceed 50.

[Page 70]

The distribution of trades among the artisans is the following:

Needle trade	81 families
Leather trade	80 families
Nourishment trade	51 families
Lumber trade	27 families
Metal trade	24 families
Building trade	22 families
Various trades	18 families
Total	303 families

As we can see, the needle and leather trades employed the largest amount of artisans, 161 in total, 53% of all artisans.

The artisans of Zhetl were well organized with a union which defended their wages and cared about their social position in town. For exact information about the artisans in Zhetl see the article "Zhetl and Zhetl's Artisans" by M.M. Lazerovitch.

Merchants and Retailers

210 families, or 35% of all providers in Zhetl worked in large or small businesses. This amount includes peddlers. Merchants and retailers comprise 41% of bank members. Apparently they had a greater need for help from the bank than artisans. Unfortunately we do not have exact statistics on line of business distribution in Zhetl. However, even without statistics we can see the majority of businessmen and merchants were concentrated in the food and clothing industries.

The statistics of A. Ivenitsky probably does not include forest merchants who made up about a dozen Zhetl families and earned an honourable living.

Scribes

Scribes held an important place in the economic life of Zhetl. The majority of them were artisans and worked for merchants and exporters in Slonim. Their Torah scrolls and Mezuzahs were exported abroad. In the weekly "Ha Yehudi" ("The Jew") which was published in London, (vol. 32, 1903) we read this work was difficult and exhausting and did not pay well. From this correspondence we learn about a scribe from Zhetl who brought a printing press from Vilna to print his Mezuzahs. He was punished by the other scribes. From the statistics of A. Ivenitsky we learn the scribes of Zhetl comprised 5% of all providers.

Coachmen

A similar number of Zhetl providers were coachmen, or as they were called, wagon drivers. For generations, wagons were the only means of transportation between Zhetl and the rest of the world. These wagons brought people and loads of goods to Novogrudek, Slonim, Baranovitch, and even Vilna. Every driver had his route. There were those who only connected our town to Lida or Slonim. This occupation was practically tenured and was passed down through inheritance.

In the 1920s buses were introduced. Some wagon drivers became partners in this new mode of transportation. Others remained in their old profession which was now confined to transportation of goods. Zhetl's shopkeepers and merchants relied on these Jewish wagon drivers to bring merchandise from other cities: Slonim, Baranovitch and Lida.

Professionals

Zhetl's youth yearned for education, but unfortunately only a few could achieve this as studying in a high school or university in Russia and post –war Poland was very expensive. Therefore the number of people from Zhetl with higher education was very small. The greatest number were high school graduates.

Zhetl imported doctors, dentists, pharmacists and teachers from large cities. According to our statistics only 3% of Zhetl's providers worked in these secular professions.

Farmers and Unskilled Workers

The percentage of farmers and unskilled workers in Zhetl is insignificant. Farmers comprised 2% of providers and unskilled workers did not even amount to 1%.

Inaccuracies

The general picture of the occupations of Zhetl's community is not exact. We are lacking statistics about business employees, forest merchants and forest employees. We are also lacking information on second or third members of families.

However the general picture is clear. About eighty percent of all Zhetl families were either merchants, storekeepers or artisans.

[Page 71]

<u>On the Verge</u>
<u>of the 20th Century</u>

The Lusky family

First row: Gitl, Meir, Gele
Second row: Our grandmother, Eliezer, unknown
Third row: Leah, Leyb, Miriam
Fourth row: Motl, Yitzkhak, Yosef

[Page 72]

On the Verge of the 20th Century

Translated by Judy Montel

On the verge of the twentieth century, the community of Zhetl still shelters under the wings of tradition that shapes the life of the town and focuses its public activity in the study halls.

There were four study halls in Zhetl, all of them built in the area known as "Schulhoif" [synagogue/school courtyard], on the banks of the small stream "Pomreika", across from the old cemetery and the fire-fighter's tower.

In the old study hall, the important people of the town gathered, the home-owners headed by Rabbi Damta. In the middle study hall – the liberal democracy, that still observes commandments but is progressive in spirit. In the new study hall, the proletariat of Zhetl gathered – those were artisans. Dozens of meters from them the chassidim had their center.

This differentiation was reflected also in the public life of the Zhetl community. From time to time, it suffered crises, which are best called by the traditional term "machloket" [Talmudic disagreements] on the basis of supporting a certain rabbi or doctor and so forth. Then the town divided into two camps, usually in the following way: home-owners on one side and artisans on the other.

On the verge of this century, new currents arrive in Zhetl. "Hibbat Zion," Zionism and the revolutionary workers movement took hold there. As a result, alongside the study hall, the Zionist prayer group (minyan) appears, that preaches nationalism, and the revolutionary cell that is fighting to change the rules of the government in Russia.

The new forces heighten the social differentiation in the town and gradually move the center of gravity away from the study hall.

However, despite differences of opinion, the Jews of Zhetl find common ground in establishing institutions for charity, mutual aid and culture. A list of institutions such as aiding the ill, "Linat HaTzededk," charity, burial society, volunteer fire-fighters demonstrate the highly developed public spirit amongst the Jews of Zhetl. Heading these institutions are sextons and committees who arrange for someone to sleep at the home of the ill, for an ice store, for inexpensive medications, for short-term charitable loans and for the means to put out fires.

In addition to the institutions extending aid there are also Torah study groups such as "Chevrat Shas" for those who study Talmud, the "'Ayn Ya'akov" society ('Ayn Ya'akov is a multi-volume collection of the story & legend material from the Talmud) as well as the Psalms society for the simple people.

However, alongside the cultural and social abundance, the economic recession is worrying. Both the public and the individual are fighting for their existence. The community's many requirements (paying the rabbi, the cantor and the ritual slaughterers) are barely covered by the taxes on the sale of yeast and meat.

And the condition of the individual is not much better. Our ancestors, the people of Zhetl, were tradesmen and artisans who depended on farmers for their livelihood. But the farmer's poverty impacted the economic state of the Jew of Zhetl.

Poverty on one hand and persecution by the government on the other, forced the youth of Zhetl to emigrate. Many went to America. A few – moved to the Land of Israel.

[Page 73]

Zhetl Fifty Years Ago

by Moishe Bitan – Bitensky (Tel Aviv)

Translated by Janie Respitz

It was the beginning of this century. I was a ten year old boy, a child from a well off home in Zhetl. This town was as similar as two drops of water to many other small secluded towns in White Russia and Lithuania.

Moishe Bitan – Bitensky

Only two or three streets are worthy of being called "streets"; the rest were narrow winding alleys. The length of the town was not more than a few kilometres and the width – half of that. The town was divided in two parts. Except for a few one story brick houses, the rest were wooden small huts with sloping roofs covered with shingles.

At the marketplace which was situated in the middle of the town there was a long row of about a dozen shops selling all sorts of goods – "catchall" goods. The busiest day was Tuesday, market day, when peasant farmers came to town from the surrounding villages. There were no sidewalks at this time in Zhetl and people walked in the middle of the street.

On market days the people mingled together with the wagons, horses and livestock which were brought to sell. Various scents flew through the air. It was a mixture of city and village, field and store. In the evening as the famers prepared to return home, it was dangerous to be out on the street due to their drunkenness which filled the streets with shouts and wild songs. This is what Zhetl looked like on a market day.

On all other days the streets were empty, there was not a lot of revenue to be had and the shops would open only out of habit.

We would travel 12 kilometres to the train station in Novoliyenie on a sandy road with Jewish wagon drivers who earned their living on this route. These were simple Jews who tried to entertain their passengers with a joke, witticism or a nice story on this difficult journey. The peasants would transport freight to the trains.

Houses of Prayer and Study in Zhetl (Bes Medresh)

The spiritual life in Zhetl was concentrated around the synagogue courtyard where three Houses of Study stood beside each other: the "old", "middle" and "new".

The first two Houses of Study were in the same building and only a wide long corridor separated the two.

The largest was the old House of Study. This is where the elite came to pray, the wealthy Jews led by the rabbi. They occupied the seats along the entire eastern wall and the remaining spots until the Bimah (platform where services were conducted), which was in the middle of the room. Anyone who did not have a regular seat would pray behind the Bimah along the western wall and near the exit door as well as the less honourable householders whose social position in town was not distinguished.

The "middle" House of Study was smaller. This is where the middle –class came to pray. They were more equal without class differentiation and everyone had his regular place. Those who prayed there were considered to be the democratic, liberal intellectuals of our town. This was also, by the way, the Zionist House of Study as the leaders of the Zionist organization prayed there: Reb Menakhem Vernikovsky of blessed memory and Reb Aron Hersh Langbart, of blessed memory.

On Shabbes Nakhamu, which was considered the Zionist Sabbath, and on all the holidays they would give passionate sermons on Zionist themes after the reading of the Torah.

Mainly artisans prayed in the third House of Study – the "new" one. Their head Gabbai (manager of the synagogue) was Yosl the house painter. They had their own Talmud society, Mishnah society and psalm society.

The Hasidic house of prayer was not far from the synagogue courtyard. The Slonim and Kaidenov Hasidim prayed there. They were few in numbers and their influence in town was not significant. Although their customs and clothing were strange to us, we all respected them, especially us kids. Their enthusiasm, song and dance left an unforgettable impression. When their Rebbe would come, or on Simkhas Torah, their house of study would be filled with Misnagdim (non- Hasidim), particularly children.

[Page 74]

I would like to mention that the butchers in Zhetl, most of which were from the same family, were all Hasidim. Normally, Hasidim everywhere were simple, ignorant folk, but it was different in Zhetl. The Hasidim in Zhetl were for the most part learned capable men. I cannot explain this phenomenon but it is necessary to explore this matter.

Rabbis, Scholars and Teachers

Outwardly, topographically and architecturally, Zhetl was similar to other towns in White Russia, however culturally and socially she stood above the rest.

The rabbis of Zhetl, dating back to the Gaon of Vilna were known as great scholars and intellectuals. Fifty years ago, the chief rabbi of Zhetl was the genius and great scholar Reb Borukh Mirsky, of blessed memory. He was a supporter of the Hovevei Zion (Lovers of Zion) and later a Zionist and had a great and positive influence on the Jewish community of Zhetl, particularly the founding of the Zionist association in Zhetl.

There were scholars among the business owners in Zhetl. Some of them became rabbis in towns near and far, after their business went under. Some became teachers in Zhetl and in other towns.

There are a few I would like to mention by name. First of all I would like to mention the great personality Reb Nosn Notteh HaKohen Zaytchik, of blessed memory. Very few of us remember him. I remember him from my youth. He was already an old man. He was extremely capable, studied with the Talmud society and was meticulous and devout.

Some years ago, in a small religious book store in Tel Aviv which sells old, rare books, I found an important book "Khadoshei Torah", written by Rabbi Nosn Notteh Zaytchik, which his son, a rabbi in America published. I bought the book and brought it home with great joy. It serves as a memorial to a generation and period in our beloved Zhetl which was and will never return.

Among the greatest scholars from Zhetl was the genius Reb Shmuel Rabinovitch, of blessed memory, the son in law of Avrom Shloimeh Zhikavchin. As a child he was recognized as a prodigy from among the best boys at the Volozhin Yeshiva. He particularly excelled with his character. He lived in Zhetl for many years, and when his family grew and he had grown sons and daughters he moved to Zholudok and became the rabbi there. Before the First World War he was, with great honour, hired as the chief rabbi of Moscow. Being enlightened and talented, he held a distinguished position as an artist in Moscow.

From among other great scholars I remember Reb Khaim Reznikovsky, of blessed memory, Reb Avrom Leyb Iliovitch, of blessed memory, (I had the privilege to study with both) and Reb Menakhem Vernikovsky, of blessed memory, the leader of the Zionist Association in Zhetl, who moved to Eretz Yisrael with the third Aliyah and passed away in Israel in 1930.

It is worthwhile to mention, scholars from Zhetl stood above the teachers from other towns with their knowledge and their status in society. In my youth, when I read about religious teachers in Hebrew and Yiddish literature, who dominated their students with a whip, I could never compare them to the teachers who taught me in Zhetl. Our teachers were kind hearted and capable. They educated the children with love and understanding and we truly loved them. I remember them until today: Reb Avrom Veynshteyn, of blessed memory, (Avreyml Etes), Yekhezkl Slonimer, of blessed memory and many others whose names I do not recall.

Without exaggerating, I can say, every second Jew in Zhetl was educated in Torah, a member of the Talmud society, or at least the Mishnah society.

In those years we did not have a large Yeshiva in Zhetl, therefore many boys from Zhetl studied away from home and wherever they were, excelled as prodigies.

Zionists and the Zionist Association in Zhetl

I have already mentioned how Jews of Zhetl excelled in community liveliness. I want to take this opportunity to recall a few facts.

All Zionist and revolutionary parties existed in Zhetl in those years, beginning with the Zionist Association and ending with S.R.T (Socialist and Revolutionary Terrorists). There were many families where each child belonged to a different party. The fathers belonged to the Zionist Association, business owners and artisans. I already mentioned Reb Menakhem Vernikovsky and Reb Aron Hersh Langbart.

I also want to mention Reb Zalmen Dunyetz (Zhame Patchrer's son, Eliyahu, who was known in Zhetl as an activist) who excelled with a lot of passion and devotion to Zionist thought and to Zionist practical work.

[Page 75]

In my life, I never met a Jew who served the Zionist movement with such devotion and love like Reb Zalmen Dunyetz. He is etched in my memory and I feel a lot of love and respect toward him. Still in the diaspora he understood the secret of Zionist accomplishments. I think he accomplished Zionist goals in every hour of his life. In his old age, Reb Zalmen Dunyetz left his family and moved to the Land of Israel where he passed away. Unfortunately I do not have any information about the last period of his life in the Land of Israel.

The Zionist Association in those years was considered part of Mizrachi although not all its members belonged to Mizrachi. However they were all religious. Its main activities took place in the House of Study. On holidays the Zionist Association had its own quorum for prayers in a side room of the "middle" House of Study or in a room in the Talmud Torah. After prayers they would deliver sermons on daily issues and Zionism. The Association would also organize parties with a bit of whisky, and if a bottle of Carmel wine happened to drop by, they were thrilled with the scent and taste of the Land of Israel and the celebration was even greater.

The Zionist Association supported the Heder Metukan, (modernized religious school) which the teacher Reb Leyzer Mates opened in Zhetl. I went to that school right after I finished my course with my first teacher, Reb Notteh, of blessed memory. I doubt if it was really a modern school because they did not teach Hebrew in Hebrew.

Revolutionaries

As already stated, our fathers belong to the Zionist Association and the children – to socialist revolutionary parties: the Bund, S. R. left (terrorists) and the right (populist). The parties in Zhetl were well organized and mutually battled each other. Their activities were illegal and their meetings took place in the surrounding forests.

From among the Zhetl revolutionaries I remember Yitzkhak Rabinovitch (Feivl from Skidl's son), an enlightened young man who was sentenced to death for revolutionary activities in St. Petersburg.

Many revolutionaries from Zhetl were sent to forced labour and many ran away to America, after the Czarist gendarmes mercilessly chased them. I believe the membership of Zhetl youth in the revolutionary movement and the difficult material situation were the main reasons that caused the mass immigration of people from Zhetl to North America.

My Last Visit

In 1936, before I immigrated to the Land of Israel I visited Zhetl after many years in order to say goodbye to my younger sister Pesia, her six children and my extended family. I was very happy to see Zhetl had developed and progressed in many areas, externally rebuilt and hard to recognize. Socially and culturally the town pulsated: schools as well as Zionist youth groups, educated and organized in parties.

Who could have imagined, six years later, the Zhetl Jewish community would be annihilated, and only remnants of survivors in Israel would carry in their hearts the holy memory of their town: Zhetl.

Fifty Years Ago

Moshe Bitan

Translated by Judy Montel

The Zionist Association included some of the home-owners and artisans, the fathers. The heads of the Association were: Reb Menachem Vernikovski and Reb Heschel Langbort. I want to mention here another community activist, who I remember particularly for his Zionist fervor and his boundless dedication to Zionist activities and ideas, who is none other than Reb Zalmen Dunetz (Zchameh Patshter) of blessed memory. I never again met a Jew with such great enthusiasm and love of Zion as Reb Zalmen Dunetz. I had great admiration for this elevated man in my childhood. In my imagination I saw in him the best of Zionism. He is engraved in my memory with feelings of love and esteem for him. He knew the secret of Zionist fulfillment while he was still in the Diaspora. It was as if he was fulfilling Zionism all of his life. In his old age, he left his family and moved to the Land of Israel alone and solitary, and here he died.

The Zionist Association in Zhetl in those days was considered a "Mizrachi" Association, even if not everyone was stamped with the official seal of that organization, but all of the members of the Association were observant Jews. The activities of the Association were concentrated between the walls of the study hall. On holidays, they had a separate "minyan" (prayer group) in a side room of the middle study hall or in one of the rooms of the "Talmud Torah" school. After the prayers, the heads of the Association would speak about current affairs. They held nice parties at which they sang Zionist songs. If by chance a bottle of Carmel wine from the Land of Israel came into their hands, it made for a merry time, as they became intoxicated with the aroma and taste of the Land of Israel.

[Page 76]

I Left Zhetl in 1900

by Yitzkhak Gvori (Tel Aviv)

Translated by Janie Respitz

I, Itzke Avrom Yakov, the teacher's son, was born in Zhetyl in 1886. When I was 14 I moved to Vilna.

Yitzkhak Gvori

My mother's name was Esther Rokhl. She was called "Bobbe" (Grandma) and was the midwife in Zhetl. I believe many of my townspeople who read these lines were held by my mother when they were born. I can only describe events that occurred until 1900, because that year, after Pesach, I left for Vilna.

Disputes Between Artisans and Business Owners

One year, those who prayed in the new House of Study, the artisans, revolted. What did they want? They also wanted to study a chapter of the Mishna every morning after prayers. They found a young man, a student in the Yeshiva, to study with them. He had to be paid; this is where the whole story begins.

The artisans from the middle (Translator's note: they probably meant new) House of Study wanted the town treasury to pay. The wealthy Jews from the old and middle Houses of Study claimed anyone who wanted to study should pay for it himself. This is how two sides were formed. One side was called the "the Rabbi's side" and the second was called "the artisans". Both sides threw pitch and sulfur at each other. But the main battle was lead by the artisans and they, in addition, did not spare the rabbi, Reb Borukh Avrom.

The Artisans Bring a Second Doctor

In the meantime they realized Dr. Hirshkop, the only Jewish doctor was siding with the rabbi. Now the burden of the struggle was carried by the doctor.

The Artisans claimed Dr. Hirshkop was not really a doctor, but a lessee, a shoemaker who does not understand any illnesses and won't visit a poor patient. In short, a second doctor was needed.

They actually brought a second doctor from Vilna. His name was Rom and the battle intensified. The artisans agitated for the new doctor and claimed he understood better than Dr. Hirshkop.

They would attack Dr. Hirshkop in the middle of the street with insults to the extent that he was afraid to leave his house.

A Fire, Epidemic and Collapse

At the height of this battle a fire was ignited in the roof of the old House of Study. At the time we did not live far from the House of Study, the second house from the fire station, behind Gershon with the saw and Yosele Mendes. One of our walls bordered the old cemetery. When we saw the House of Study burning in the middle of the night, we assumed the artisans started it. The Rabbi declared a ban on the arsonist.

Meanwhile, an epidemic of dysentery began in town. There was practically not a single house untouched. Three children git sick in our home, me, an older sister and my little 4 year old sister. The little one actually died of dysentery.

They brought doctors from Lida and Dr. Hirshkop ran with them from house to house. Once again the artisans blamed the rabbi: they said it was due to the ban he instilled.

Once in the middle of the night we heard a bang, as if a bomb fell. My father ran outside and saw the roof of the old House of Study collapsed. They explained the old wooden beams had deteriorated from rain which poured on them. Thank God this happened in the middle of the night and no one was harmed. They immediately installed new beams and supported them with iron posts.

The Tragedy in the Women's Synagogue

Another thing happened during those years. Rabbi Diskin of blessed memory died and it was decided in Zhetl to offer a eulogy. Our rabbi Reb Borukh Avrom was a weak man and could not deliver the eulogy so they asked a preacher to do it. When this preacher came to Zhetl to preach he would fill the old House of Study.

[Page 77]

This was the 7th day of the month of Shevat (Late January - early February). When the artisans heard who would be delivering the eulogy, they put down their work. Storekeepers closed their shops, women in the market extinguished their braziers and everyone went to hear the eulogy. There was such a large crowd, the floor of the women's synagogue could not bear pressure and collapsed in the middle of the eulogy.

It was dark in the House of Study and when people heard the noise of the breaking boards they did not know what was happening. There was a double floor in the women's synagogue. The under layer broke and the upper layer remained intact. Someone turned on the light to see what was going on. The dust which rose due to the breakage of the floor looked like smoke. Someone shouted:

"It's burning!"

Nu, nothing else was needed. Thus began a stampede with everyone pushing. The men left through the windows and the women ran down the stairs. However they could not open the door - this is where the tragedy occurred.

They heard the women screaming: save us! The men ran to the door of the women's synagogue which exited toward the river. The door was bolted shut and could not be opened. They put up a ladder and went in through the window.

The women pushed one another. The men began to drag them from the steps. They found many who had fainted and had scratched faces and torn out hair. The main thing was: 12 women were dead. I remember two of them: one was the wife of Moishe Aron the stagecoach driver, Dvoyre, and the second was Yisroel Dvashke's daughter.

The funerals took place the following day. They brought all 12 women to the synagogue courtyard, eulogized them and buried them in one grave.

The Jews I Remember

From the rabbis I remember the rabbi I mentioned earlier, Reb Borukh Avrom. I remember Notteh Herzl's who was an angry Jew, who taught everyone in the morning after prayers at a table full of Jews in the middle House of Study. He would shout and swear. I remember: Reb Shmuel Avrom Shloime's, who later became a rabbi in Moscow, Reb Shmuel Khaim who later became a rabbi in Deretchin, Reb Idl Gabai from the old House of Study, a pious and quiet man, Reb Moishe Ayzhe, head of the Yeshiva and Talmud Torah. When he left for the Land of Israel his place was taken by Yisroel Avrom. I also remember Reb Yonah. He was replaced by Avrom Leyb Meylekh, the teacher from the Talmud Torah. In those years my father was also a teacher in the Talmud Torah. I remember Hinda Miriam's Velvl, the old bachelor Hinda Miriam's Mitzl, and the aristocratic Hinda Miriam, Hendl the pharmacist, Dovid the beer maker, Moishe Leyb the carpenter and his son Yosele Mendes, my first teacher.

Fires

I remember the fire of 1893, three days before Pesach. It began in Hinda Miriam's attic. People said Mitzl forgot to extinguish the samovar. Hinda Miriam's house burned together with Malke Motkes' store, Notteh Herzl's brick exterior wall and Dr. Hirshkop's home. The fire later reached Berke the tanner's stalls.

I remember another fire two years later. In the middle of Pesach a fire broke out on Novoredek Street, the area where Yisroel Dvoshke and Ayzhik lived. The fire broke out at the tall Khaim Itche's. It was night and no one knew how it got to Mateh the doctor's home. A burning wall collapsed and he was burned.

I remember another episode. It was a Tuesday, market day. A few gentiles went wild, led by Kanaval (that's what they called him), and they began to beat up Jews. One of the Jews they beat up was called Kheme the butcher. He walked around with his head bandaged for a long time after. The regional police superintendent came to help the Jews who were being beaten but the peasants wanted to beat him as well. He ran to Berek the tanner's stalls and hid on the roof. Afterwards the attackers were brought to trial.

A Story About Zhetl's Scribes

One more thing I remember. There were scribes in Zhetl who would write Torah scrolls, and Mezuzahs and send them to America. The American clients found out they were deceived with printed Mezuzahs, not handwritten and they threatened they would no longer purchase these items from Zhetl. The rabbi got involved and promised he would make sure this would not happen again.

The rabbi tried to make the scribes more pious. He hired a religious teacher to come every evening to Avrom Yakov the scribe at Moteh Velvl's house to study with them. One time, in the dark vestibule, they placed a piece of wood under the teacher's feet and he fell. Then they threw a bag over his head and beat him up. They did not study again after that.

[Page 78]

My Memories of Zhetl

by Avrom Shepetnitsky (Kfar Hasidim)

Translated by Janie Respitz

It is difficult to establish when Jews settled in Zhetl. Especially because the record book was burnt in one of the fires. However it is known that in our town there were old Jewish and Christian settlements. We have witnesses who said the old military barracks and their building materials, long and wide bricks of 20X50 centimetres, and the palace which burned down in 1908 and was renovated by the Russians, are witnesses to the old settlement.

Our parents used to say that Jewish settlement in Zhetl goes back 400 years. Also both Jewish cemeteries, the old and the new are witnesses of an old Jewish settlement. I remember in 1906–07 I read on a woman's tombstone that she died in 1528. The fact is only one tombstone was legible. The others were sunken and a sign that the settlement was very old. In my work about rabbis from Zhetl I let it be known that in the book "Kneset Yekhezkl" written by Rabbi Yekhezkl Katenelnboygn from Hamburg, there is a religious question posed by an abandoned woman from Zhetl 250 years ago.

I Am Saved From the Flood

Zhetl sits on two rivers: the Pomerayke and the Zhetlke. In a divorce decree the rabbis of Zhetl would write: Here in Zhetl on the Pomerayke River.

Zhetl suffered greatly from the flooding of the Pomerayke, which runs through the middle of the town, near the Houses of Study. I remember from the years 1902 –1912 Zhetl suffered three floods.

In 1912 on a rainy day I was sitting in the middle House of Study learning with the rabbi Reb Zvi Khurgin, of blessed memory. Suddenly we were sprayed with water which poured into the House of Study from the Pomerayke. Together with the head of the Yeshiva we climbed a ladder to the women's section. After an hour the water reached the height of the windows and we sat in the women's section from 11 in the morning until 4 in the afternoon when the water receded and we were out of danger.

Village Jews

I read in a Russian journal that at the beginning of this century there were 4000 residents in Zhetl, 75% Jews. However besides this, many Jews lived in the villages around Zhetl: in Kurfish, Yavar, Fintshitch, Novin, Haleli, Shilevanke, Girnik, Volayniki, Petruki, Sirplevitch, Khvinovitch, Potzavcizne, Nakrishki, Ramonovitch, Strele, Alexandrovitch, Zhibertayshchine, Khadzhelan and Gnayinsk. There were villages where a few Jewish families lived and they even had enough Jews for a Minyan. (A quorum of 10 Jews for prayer). This was the case in Nakrishak, Rahatna and Sirataychine. There were great scholars among these village Jews like, Reb Arye from Karol, Reb Leyb from Khabad, Reb Yisroel from Hantsh (Kaplinsky), Reb Hertz Leyb Kaplinsky from Dubrike, Reb Zalmen from Repetshch, Reb Eliezer from Sirataychine, Reb Berish from Zhizhayk, and many others.

Jews in the villages would lease fields, mills and also did business in trade and ran taverns. Their material situation was satisfactory but at the beginning of this century anti Semitism in the villages increased and the village Jews began to move to Zhetl.

Zhetl was a poor town. There were no factories in Zhetl and the majority of the Jews lived off small business and trade. When the village Jews moved to Zhetl they opened small shops and earning a living became difficult.

A Story About Kopeks and 800 Ruble

Witnesses can attest to the fact that in Zhetl money (groshn) was printed for poor people, who would go from house to house. There was a Jew who would print the money and sell them to the wealthier men, five groshn for one kopek. Given that outside of Zhetl there were no customers for these groshn, this same man would buy them back from the poor at six for one kopek, making a profit.

Disregarding their difficult situation, the Jews of Zhetl were decent and respectable. The fact I will now recount will serve as an example. One of the wandering paupers hid 800 ruble between logs of wood in the anteroom of the synagogue. Sunday, when the beadle Reb Moti Nokhem, a very poor man, took some wood to heat the room, he found the money. Reb Moti Nokhem immediately returned the money to the pauper and did not request a reward for his honesty.

[Page 79]

Zhetl's Ruskies

As in every generation, every town in our region had a nickname for its residents. For example, people from Dvaretz were called intestines, people from Deretch were called bad guys – from Lida, thieves, from Mayschet – sour milk, Novorodek – chicken eaters, from Slonim – fools, from Kazlaytch – goats; Jews from Zhetl were called Katzapes (a nickname for Russians "Ruskies") as people from Zhetl excelled in bravery.

Karabke – Community Tax on Kosher Meat

Institutions in Zhetl were supported by indirect taxes or Karabke money. Two food items were taxed: meat and yeast. The meat tax was leased from the Russian government for a fee and collected for every Kosher slaughtered animal. This meat tax would pay for the rabbi, the ritual slaughterers and the cantor. The second tax on yeast would be leased from the Jewish community. These tax revenues would pay for the doctor. The yeast tax was also paid by Christians as the yeast business was run by Jews and there was nowhere else to buy yeast.

When the Jews of Zhetl had to be called to a meeting, the beadle Reb Nokhem Shloime, with his white beard would go through the streets with his sweet voice and called out:

Jews, Jews, come to the synagogue! He would repeat this many times until all of Zhetl would gather together.

The rabbi Reb Zev Wolf Halevy who was rabbi in Zhetl 100 years ago praises the Jews of Zhetl in his book "Emek Halacha" as scholars who supported him honourably. The rabbi Reb Zalmen Saratzky, in his book "Hadeah Ve HaDibur" part 2, mourns the Zhetl Jewish community which was rich with scribes and scholars.

Three Zhetl Jews, Reb Yehuda Idl Lusky of blessed memory, a great scholar who would blow the shofar in the old House of Study, Reb Dov Ber Zhizhayker and Reb Yisroel Dvashkes all immigrated to the Land of Israel at the beginning of this century.

Zhetl excelled with its scholars. Even the artisans had their own Talmud society and studied a page together every day. Besides the Talmud society there was also the Mishna society, Ein Yakov society and others.

An old shoemaker lived in Zhetl who was called the "children–maker" since he made shoes for children. Every day between afternoon and evening prayers he would go to the old House of Study and read Ein Yakov (a book of legends and parables not as difficult as Talmud).

Zhetl also had three Psalm societies. Every day and particularly Sabbath mornings they would come and recite psalms collectively. When a member of the society would die, his fellow members would come to his house and recite psalms until the funeral and after, during the thirty days of mourning they would gather three times a day to pray together.

Customs

It is necessary to note a few customs specific to Zhetl. For example, in all the towns around Zhetl they would forbid questioning a piece of evidence. In Zhetl, this would be permitted. However, in Zhetl they forbid ducks and geese with black beaks.

There was a custom in Zhetl that children did not attend their father's funeral. Before removing the corpse from his house, it would be announced by the manager of the Burial Society. After the burial a member of the Burial Society would ask forgiveness from the deceased and announce that he is freed from all societies.

The Zhetl Talmud Torah

In the early years of this century there were no schools in Zhetl. Children would learn religious studies with a Melamed (religious teacher). Russian and a bit of arithmetic would be taught by a tutor.

At the beginning of 1909 the Talmud Torah was founded in Zhetl where they would learn 8 hours a day, before and after lunch, Tanach (Bible), Gemara (commentary on the Bible) Hebrew, Russian, arithmetic and general subjects. The first directors and founders of the Talmud Torah were: Reb Menakhem Vernikovsky, Reb Zev Wolf Dvoretsky, Yisroel Moishe Ivenitsky, and Reb Yudl Podveliker. At the end of the semester the directors would examine the students and those who excelled received gifts.

The Zhetl Fire Station

Due to the large number of fires a good fire department was organized in Zhetl. Every firefighter had his assignment. The trumpeters would sound the "alarm" about the fire, others ran the pumps, and others ensured the fire would remain localized. Besides this there were horse riders. The first to arrive at the station would receive a prize of one ruble.

For a long time the chief of the fire station was the tax collector Yakovlev. He was a gentle person, a good friend of the Jews and really loved the town. He provided the fire fighters with brass helmets and would put a lot of his own money into the station. When he caught a Jew selling whisky, which was strictly forbidden at that time, he would punish him for the good of the station and cancel the protocol.

[Page 80]

Zhetl's Revolutionaries

Once, on a Tuesday, the Zhetl revolutionaries organized an attack on the tax collector's whisky business and confiscated about five thousand ruble. The same group organized in Novoliyenie an expropriation of the postal train which ran from Rovne to Vilna. This was not successful and a few of the revolutionaries were sent into exile.

I remember at a funeral of a revolutionary, his comrades carried red flags with revolutionary banners and at the same time forced the regional police superintendent and the gendarmes to keep order.

How Zhetl Was Saved From Anti – Semitism

At the time first Poles took over Zhetl, General Dombrovsky's soldiers wanted to go through the town. We knew these soldiers had carried out pogroms on the Jewish populations of Pinsk and Lida and we were afraid they would live it up in Zhetl.

Our rabbi Reb Zalmen Saratzky together with some of the wealthier men in town went to the Polish officer and in return for a nice bribe he promised to protect the town from anti Semitic soldiers. He did it the following way: he placed members of his entourage in a nearby forest and at night they shot rockets. The anti Semitic soldiers thought the rockets were being shot by Russians and they ran and took refuge in nearby villages. We later learned that they went wild in the villages and murdered a few peasants.

The Miracle of Reb Eli Delatitsher

In conclusion I want to recount a story I heard from Reb Zalmen Saratsky in the name of Reb Yisroel Ber the Zhetl gravedigger.

One day a woman from Vasilishok came to Yisroel Ber the gravedigger and told him her daughter ran off with a non – Jew. As soon as this occurred the unhappy mother went to Slonim to Reb Mordkhele, of blessed memory, to ask his advice. Reb Mordkhele advised her to go to Zhetl and pray at the grave of Reb Eli Delatitsher. While there, she should take two bricks. On one brick she should write the names of her daughter and husband, and on the second brick she should write the names of the non –Jewish boy and his father. When this is done, she must hide the bricks in the earth near the grave of Reb Eli Delatitsher.

Yisroel Ber the gravedigger helped the woman find the grave of Reb Eli Delatitsher and helped her hide the bricks as Reb Morkhele told her to do.

A few weeks later the woman returned and said her daughter left her non –Jewish man and returned home. However she can't find tranquility, does not sleep at night and suffers from terrible dreams. Once again she went to Reb Mordkhele in Slonim and he asked if she had taken anything from the grave. The woman admitted she took a small bag of earth from Reb Eli Delatitsher's grave, and kept it as a remedy.

Reb Mordkhele once again ordered her to return to Zhetl and return the bit of earth she took from the grave. The woman did as she was told and never returned to Zhetl, a sign that Reb Mordkhele's advice was helpful.

The Excellent City

by Rabbi Yitzkhak Veynshteyn (Jerusalem)

Translated by Janie Respitz

Zhetl was not your average town. It distinguished itself from all other towns with its specific character and dynamic. In Zhetl, there were individuals who were rarities in scholarship, business and the revolutionary domain.

You did not find dull types in Zhetl. Everything was dynamic. Established businessmen were great Torah scholars, really geniuses, who later held great rabbinic positions in the world, like the rabbi of Moscow Reb Shmuel Rabinovitch, the Gnitzaysk rabbi, Reb Shmuel Khaim Reznikovsky and the Meml rabbi Reb Meir Yoselevitch. While in Zhetl, they were all businessmen.

In the Yeshivas, people from Zhetl excelled in talent and scholarship as well as community work. People from Zhetl were involved in a variety of activities, not to mention in the revolutionary domain. People said that Moscow and Zhetl were the two main centres of the revolution in Russia.

My Parents

I want to recall a few people from my childhood, first and foremost, my parents.

My parents were righteous in every sense of the word. My father, of blessed memory, Avrom Etes, was a Gemara teacher. My mother's name was Ette. She was a merchant, dealt with linens and helped support the family.

[Page 81]

My father was similar to Khefetz Khaim. He excelled in guarding his tongue. On the Sabbath he said nothing except words from the Torah. In the House of study he would not utter a word. If he had to say something, he would go out into the corridor. Even at home and in the street, he spoke very little in order not to disparage Torah learning. He would never approach a group of people in the event they were speaking ill of someone.

He particularly stood out in charity and justice. He himself did not earn a lot, however he was always collecting. On Fridays, after he finished teaching his students, he would go through the town collecting donations.

Guests were always welcome in his home. There were often 3–4, even 5 guests. They would sleep on both couches, on the table, and when necessary the cupboard door would be removed and someone would sleep on it.

The boys studied all year in Yeshiva. One Friday I returned from the Mir Yeshiva and my father was not at home. I saw a man come in with a parcel under his arm. I realized he was coming from the public bath. He asked my mother, may she rest in peace, for a cup of tea. She told him she would bring it shortly. The man got angry and shouted that when a man returns from the bathhouse he must have a cup of tea. I looked at this man with amazement. That is when my father arrived. He asked the man why he was angry and after he told him my father looked at my mother and said in these words: "Ette, he's right!"

Reb Kaddish

A second episode. There was a certain Reb Kaddish in Zhetl, a great scholar, and a preacher who knew many languages. He was the teacher in the new House of Study for a long time. In his old age, after numerous family problems, he became nervous and imagined Zhaludke the pharmacist's two old sons and spinster daughter had a certain machine that gave him a toothache. He would make noises and curse the wicked and the murderers.

When things got worse, he would surround himself with boys who would recite an incantation and make him feel better. When he stood for the 18 benedictions he would simply wave his hand and we would all, as if in a choir recite the incantation with a melody.

He slept in the House of Study because he had no family. In his later years he was afraid to be in the House of Study so my parents took him in to our home. I would hear him scream in the middle of the night. My father would get out of bed, go to Reb Kaddish, recite the incantation and calm him down.

Reb Avrom Yitzkhak Labensky of Blessed Memory

There is no shortage of jokes about Reb Avrom Yitzkhak Labensky. He was a merchant with a very clever, prodigious mind. His expressions and jokes were popular.

Reb Notte Herzl's, may he rest in peace, was also a great Torah scholar, an author of a book, and the same age as Labensky. When these two would argue in the middle of the House of Study after prayers, sparks flew and the walls shook from their voices. When Reb Avrom Yitzkhak Labensky had an adversary he would shout that he is stupid. Someone asked him: "What's bothering you?" "Only I'm bothered, not him. A stupid person is like bad breath. It doesn't bother the proprietor, only those around him. The Master of the Universe should have created man with a defect and given one the choice to choose. He surely chose bad breath as others suffer from it."

Reb Avrom had a business partner, Shpiglgloz from Grodno. During a conflict with him he offered two commentaries:

Whoever wants to lose money should hire workers and not supervise them, but if he wants to lose his heart, he should sit with them.

The second: he should use glass vessels, simple glass, but when he wants to ruin his heart he should use "Shpiglgloz" (mirror glass). (Translator's note: a play on words with the man's name).

When Reb Avrom Yitzkhak Labensky died Avryml the painter, who was the beadle of the new House of Study, was, as an artisan his opponent, but he went to his funeral. People asked him:

"Reb Avrom, you're going to Labensky's funeral?"

He replied: "I don't believe he died. I must see them bury him".

They Are Obviously From Zhetl

In the year 5701 (1940) when I arrived in the Land of Israel I visited Kfar Saba. There I met a Jew from a village near Novogrudek. When he heard I was from Zhetl he told me that when wagon drivers and peddlers came from Zhetl he would serve them himself. He would not serve other wagon drivers. When my wife asked: "why do you serve the ones from Zhetl?" I replied: "After all, they are from Zhetl".

[Page 82]

Navahredok Kollel[1] in Zhetl

Translated by Judy Montel

A part of the activities of Rabbi Yoseph Yozel Horowitz to found Yeshivas and Kollels for married students in Lithuania and in White Russia and to have them learn in the Mussar method of Rabbi Yisrael Salanter, he opened a Yeshiva in Zhetl as well. Supporting him, in the founding of this Yeshiva, was the owner of a large estate near Zhetl, Reb Gershon Zoshiner, who had met him once when they travelled together by train. At Reb Yoseph Yozel's request, Reb Gershon Zoshiner built him an isolated house in his forest, so that he could learn in isolation.

The money to build the house was donated by the philanthropist Lachman of Berlin, who had been very influenced by Reb Yisrael Salanter while Reb Gershon Zoshiner took on the commitment of supplying Reb Yoseph Yozel's board.

For a very long time, nine years of asceticism, Reb Yozel lived in the forest and Reb Gershon's son in law, Reb Leib Wolf, would take books out to him in the isolated house and Reb Yoseph Yozel did not cease from memorizing and repeating his Talmudic studies and he became more and more learned from year to year.

Many great deeds and charities are told about that period in which Reb Yoseph Yozel lived in the forest. At the end of nine years, Reb Yozel was aroused to bring credit to many, and together with a group of students of Rabbi Yisrael Salanter, he began to found Kollels for excellent "avrechim", so they could learn in group and would ascend the levels of Torah and instruction. These Kollels were founded by him in Navahredok, Zhetl, Lubtsh, Shavli, Dvinsk and Lida. In each place over 10 avrechim studied who were great in Torah. They received food from a special kitchen that was established there and in addition they received 6 rubles a month in order to support their families who were usually in a different village. Reb Yoseph Yozel did not sit in a Kollel for more than a month at a time, but went from one Kollel to the next, and thus he did throughout the entire year. In the month of Elul (prior to the high holidays), all of the Kollels would gather in one place. Thus, for example, once this conference took place in Zhetl, and another time in Slonim. In the middle of the year Rabbi Yoseph Yozel would bring guests, from among the best students of Rabbi Yisrael Salanter. In particular, he often invited Reb Yitzchak Blazer of Kovno, to influence the avrechim in the Kollels in the spirit of Mussar teachings.

In Elul, 5656 (1896), all of the avreichim of the Kollels gathered in the town of Zhetl, altogether 50 avreichim, and the great Rabbi Reb Yitzchak Blazer spoke words of motivation to them daily in the afternoon between the time for Mincha (the afternoon prayer) and Ma'ariv (the evening prayer), besides the classes he gave for small groups. After the holiday of Sukkot the members of the Kollels went back to their permanent places.

Around the same time, Rabbi Yoseph Yozel founded a central Yeshiva for young men according to his Mussar method in Navahredok which is near Zhetl, that over time had hundreds of young men. Thanks to this central Yeshiva, the Mussar Yeshivas of Reb Yozel were called "Navahredok Yeshivas."

There was a time that because of the upheavals, most of the students at the Navahredok Yeshiva were transferred to Zhetl. It was after the death of Rabbi Yechiel Michl Epstein, author of "Aruch HaShulchan" (5668) [ca. 1908], when the Ga'on Avraham Aharon the Kohen Borshtein, the head of the rabbinical court of Tobrig (father of Re'uven Bareket from the central committee of the Histadrut[2]) was appointed to be a rabbi there. The man from Tobrig was among those who opposed the Mussar method and Reb Yosph Yozel feared for his Yeshiva in Navahredok. He decided to move the main branch of the Navahredok Yeshiva to Zhetl. And so he did. He gathered all the homeowners of Zhetl and told them about his plan. They paid off the debts of the Yeshiva and even committed to cover its expenses in the future. In 5669 (1909, about two-thirds of the Navahredok students were moved to Zhetl and only the oldest ones of the group, for whom there was no worry that they would be swallowed up in the disagreement in the town, stayed in Navahredok. Six months later the disagreements died down and the young men of Navahredok in the Zhetl Yeshiva returned to their original Yeshiva which carried on as it had in the past.

It must be noted that among the first young men to found the Navahredok Yeshiva was Reb Chaim Zelig of Zhetl(son in law of Rabbi Karlitz). With the increased enrollment of the Navahredok Yeshiva and Reb Yoseph Yozel's dedication to this central Yeshiva, the Kollel in Zhetl had fewer and fewer students and close to the outbreak of the First World War and it shut down.

(According to the book "Torah Institutions in Europe in their Building and Destruction," New York, 1957. Article written by Y.L. Nekritz)

Zhetl, Grodno District 29 January 1909

Last Friday our town received about seventy students from the Kollel of Navahredok, which is under the supervision of the great Rabbi, Reb Yoseph Yozel Horowitz shilt"a. The reason for this is that in Navahredok right now there are upheavals and confusions about the rabbis that very much interfere with the work and study schedule and therefore, the said Rabbi decided to move the greater part of the community from Navahredok to the town of Zhetl, which is a distance of five "parsa'ot" (each parse is approximately 4 km, so a total distance of roughly 20 km).

The people of our town received them with respect and treated them with great fondness. And to show their approval, they pressed upon his palm an additional 800 rubles cash to divide between the students. And truly our town has taken a new appearance ever since these decent visitors arrived in our town.

Zimel Zimelevitch

"Hed Hazman," No. 29, Vilna,1909.

Translator's footnotes:

1. A Kollel is a study hall for post-Yeshiva, married students, also known as "avrechim", "avrech," sing.

2.   Histadrut: Jewish Workers Union

For These Are the People of Zhetl!

by Rabbi Yitzchak Weinstein

Translated by Judy Montel

I moved to the land of Israel in 5701 (1941). On my first visit to Kfar Saba I met a Jew who had moved here from a village near Navahredok. When he heard that I was from Zhetl, he was very excited and told me that when wagon drivers and peddlers used to arrive at his rural inn he would not take particular notice of them, but when those who arrived were from Zhetl, he himself would wait on them and serve their needs. And when his wife asked him – why do you do this? He responded to her: For these are the people of Zhetl!

[Page 83]

My Home Town

by Nekhemiah Aminoach (Kfar Avraham)
(Known at home as: Zvi Nekhemiah son of Reb Noakh Hakohen Razvazky)

Translated by Janie Respitz

Through the fog I see my town Zhetl clearer and more striking. In a period of world shock and division on the right and left, I see a bubbling, revolutionary town filled with Jewishness and humanity.

This is how I see you before my eyes. As you are, lively, dynamic with the clever intelligence of your Jews who play politics and play the roles of diplomats. I see your Jews embroiled in discussions about Port Arthur and General Stesl: about the occupation of eastern Prussia and General Renentkampf; about Verdun and Feten; about the Baron de Hirsch and Argentina; about Herzl and The Jewish State; about Nakhum Sokolov and "Hatzfira"; Gershoni and General Trepov, and similar topics. I am sure there were heated discussions about the occupation of Warsaw and the Nazi generals. These dear Jews did not know that this time as well the play would be a new repetition of the old tragedy from the time of Magentz and Vermeyze.

A Flower Among the Thorns

For hundreds of years, these dear Jews were rooted in this crowded valley where Zhetl was situated, on the shores of two small rivers: Zhetlke and Pomerayke which nobody in the world ever heard of. People could barely wet their feet in these rivers. However, these rivers would overflow damaging houses, tearing out trees and bridges as it is written in the bible: "As rivers flow".

The Jews from my small town were exactly like the rivers. Small sheep suddenly turned into lions, rising to the top of revolutionary activity, disrupting and annihilating evil in their country and laying the foundation for a new order. Many young fighters and heroes from Zhetl can recount the history of the revolution in Czarist Russia in 1905–06.

In the middle of the highway, like a flower among thorns, among the gentile villages, materially poor and spiritually rich, my hometown bloomed. It was a Jewish town filled with Torah and wisdom among villages with dull, insensitive gentiles among whom there were many thieves and murderers who only looked for Jewish possessions and would become the devoted collaborators of the German murderers.

On the big highway named for Catherine the Great, between double rows of birch trees, tall trees with large branches, my town suddenly jumps out into the world, on a long narrow paved road which snaked uphill until the train station 12 kilometres away.

Floating in front of my spiritual eyes is the town as if I was actually seeing it now. I see it in past years when it was muddy and not paved. Jews trudging in the mud, through filthy streets to the House of Study to recite psalms and pray in the summer when dawn arose in the east, in autumn when it rained and on frosty wintery nights when the cold bit at your ears and nose.

Children Grew Up There

How much cleverness and how much profoundness did Jews produce in this town with the bizarre names: Zhetl, Zitl, Diatlava, Dzentzial.

Children once grew up there like weeds, wrapped in rags in summer and winter. Others were hatched as if from a golden egg that was warmed in a warming machine in order to play as chickens of pearl and fine gold…and from this they went into the world, young men and women who laid the foundation of a new society, great scholars, geniuses in Torah learning and science, writers, thinkers, people with important ideas and creators.

My town was especially rich in Yeshiva boys. Where did you not find them?! In Mir and Volozhin, in Ashishok and Slonim, in Slobodka and Radin, Maltch, Kletzk, Lida, Baranovitch and Telz. Everywhere you went you found a thin Yeshiva boy from Zhetl dressed in worn out clothes, a serious boy with smart eyes and a sharp mind, who solves complicated Talmudic questions and offers his own subtle arguments on Jewish law.

How numerous and strong were the revolutionary youth from this same small town!

[Page 84]

This was a steaming, boiling youth which demanded fairness and justice, not for themselves, but for the whole world. And today, if you want to do a spiritual appraisal of the Jewish ideals in Zhetl – ask yourself – why did my hometown gather all these strengths?

After the last total annihilation which devoured the towns and cities in Poland, Lithuania and Russia as fire destroys straw – you ask yourself astonished: was all the boiling, stormy life and colossal spiritual achievements of our parents and brothers futile?

A scene which I saw in my town is forever etched in my memory. Only today I understand that event. This scene solves for me the mystery of the futile hard effort and hard work which we dedicated to the world.

A Scene Etched in my Mind

It was a summer day in 1906. Jews were in the House of Study and were having conversations with the Master of the Universe and among themselves. Women and children sat on the earthen benches attached to the exterior of the houses and took in some fresh air after a long difficult work day. The whole town was dreamy and faint. The mystery of the past day and the unknown of the next day wrestled.

Suddenly, on the backdrop of the sunset he appeared, the man about whom we children heard so much about with excitement, wonder and admiration. He, whose name in those days was legendary. He, Khaim K. the revolutionary who the Czarist police had been searching for a very long time. He, a citizen of Zhetl who the non Jewish regime did not like. Khaim K., who according to our notion, the Jewish children, wanted to repair the world, but the evil gentiles stood in his way. On that evening, he suddenly appeared. He came from the big highway which led to the big world – to the broad colossal Czarist Russia.

He was wearing a long coat, almost to his ankles, a hat on his head. He was barefoot and his shoes were slung over his shoulder. He walked calmly yet with assurance. His lips were shut tight and his eyes looked straight into the world at large. This is how he strode through the town accompanied by two policemen.

He strode like the eternal wanderer, like the eternal revolutionary, like the eternal Jew. Like a living wandering tombstone of the Jewish unknown soldier, in a world where nations and states are born and then collapse. Where a regime disappears and a regime arises, and he, the eternal Jew, remains, demands and strides on to endless distances and breadth.

Where is that Khaim K.?

Later on he came to town, but now disappointed and broken, disappointed in himself and broken by others. He lived a quiet modest life, locked up in his four walls.

This was a totally different Khaim, a totally different person. Not the one I saw on the backdrop of the sunset. Now he was for me a Lithuanian Jew, a simple man. But the other Khaim K. was the picture of the eternally wandering Jew, who boils, demands, and warns about a new world that needs to be built – does that Khaim no longer exist? Has that self–assured young man, the proud child from my town, who distinguished himself at the downfall of the sinking world already left this world?

No, No! Never!

That young man from my hometown only changed his outer clothing. His inner being undressed and dressed again. He is still alive today in his full splendor and glory.

And we all stride along the old path, like before, accompanied by police who guard our steps. We walk behind everyone between sunrise and sunset, between day and night and we are disappointed every day in the gentiles and in ourselves, and we are broken…

My hometown Zhetl, the youth which were drawn from the old former source, are still alive, even after the non –Jews slaughtered millions. Young forces, effervescent revolutionaries which gathered in my hometown, the children who were saved from the slaughter, were brought to our old –new fatherland. No destroyer will succeed in annihilating you!

You are worthy. My hometown, Zhetl, a town from Lithuania, Russia and Poland, religion, national Zionist socialist Zhetl, should serve as a model of exile which has disappeared, in order to sprout anew with strong roots in our old – new fatherland, Israel.

[Page 85]

Zhetl Until 1905

by Zalmen Mirsky (Tel Aviv)

Translated by Janie Respitz

I would like to describe Zhetl according to the impression it left on me when I was a child between the ages of 5 –15. When I was fifteen I left Zhetl for the Land of Israel with my parents in the month of Adar (March), 1905.

The Jews of Zhetl were scholars. Even the artisans, including tailors, shoemakers and other labourers, would study a page of Gemara in the morning after prayers, between afternoon and evening prayers and the evening. They excelled in their piety, honesty and conscientiousness.

Zhetl's Jews were practical businessmen and established business relations in large cities. Among them there were many workers, scribes (who wrote Torah scrolls and Mezuzahs) and peddlers who would do business with the gentiles in nearby villages. There were also no shortages of taverns, iron works, textiles, foods and other articles.

The house where my family lived was surrounded on three sides by Christian houses. Jews and Christians lived together peacefully and I do not remember any conflicts between these two portions of the population.

Disputes

The Jews from this small town were divided in two camps: Misnagdim (Religious Jews who are not Hasidim) and Hasidim. There was no shortage of quarrels and fights because of a rabbi, a doctor and so on. I remember one case when the dispute between the two sides went so far that one side did a shameful thing. They exploded a still in a store belonging to someone from the other side and carried it to the authorities. Understandably the person was arrested and the town stewed over this abominable act.

The Rabbi Reb Borukh Avrom Mirsky

The Misnagdim had three houses of Study. The local rabbi prayed in one of them. In my time it was the rabbi Reb Borukh Avrom Mirsky, a great Talmudic scholar and a well known preacher. He was always a big hit with his sermons. On special Sabbaths the rabbi would preach and call his listeners to repentance and charity. The town beadle would accompany him from his home to the House of Study and then home again.

The rabbi mentioned above was an enlightened Jew. He knew Hebrew grammar well and was sympathetic to Zionism. My father, may he rest in peace, was one of his admirers and had great respect for him. He would defend his honour when someone offended him or when someone opposed the rabbi either on a private or a community matter.

The rabbi would organize a minyan (quorum of ten men to pray) in his house, and when he prayed the words sounded like pearls. My father and I were among those who went to the rabbi's house and belonged to the group that prayed in his minyan.

The rabbi's son Reb Tuvia Mirsky and his wife were childless. Thirty years ago they came to the Land of Israel and settled in Jerusalem.

Reb Menakhem Vernikovsky

The Misnagdim in town were for the most part Talmudic scholars, merchants, honourable business owners, town leaders. One of the was Menakhem Vernikovsky, a pharmacist, an enlightened Jew educated in Torah, knowledgeable in Hebrew grammar, a proficient Torah reader and a cantor. When Zionism began to spread through the Jewish streets, he became a supporter of the movement. Every Sabbath he would deliver a sermon in the House of Study about the weekly Torah portion and he would weave in some Zionist propaganda.

His daughters came to the Land of Israel 20 years ago. One of them, Helena married Shlomo Habibi, a talented person and a music lover. He opened a store of musical instruments and died one year ago.

The Hasidim of Zhetl

Hasidim on the contrary were simple people, however very religious Jews, and prayed with great enthusiasm. Among them there was a butcher who was their regular cantor. He prayed particularly beautifully on the High Holidays.

During my time their Rebbe (a Hasidic rabbi) was Reb Shmulke from Slonim, who in his youth was a friend of father. Reb Shmuel became a Rebbe and my father, of blessed memory, became a scribe, and later sold Torah scrolls and Mezuzahs.

[Page 86]

The Rebbe would visit Zhetl a few times a year. He was a stately Jew, who wore silk clothing, and shone like the sun. He would sit in his room secluded for meditation and would only emerge for prayer. On the Sabbath he would pray at the pulpit and read from the Torah. If I remember correctly, his reading did not move me due to his incorrect pronunciation and his strange accentuation of the words.

The Hasidim would prepare a table in honour of the Rebbe at their prayer house. They would eat, sing and push each other to be able to see the Rebbe and hear his teachings. A Sabbath like that would make a great impression on the Hasidim, as well as the other residents.

My father, of blessed memory, and I would often go on Saturdays and on the High Holidays to pray with the Hasidim. The prayers of the Misnagdim did not lure me, even though there were good prayer leaders among them like Reb Menakhem Vernikovsky. However their praying lacked the Hasidic enthusiasm and fervour.

Friday Nights in Zhetl

Friday afternoon, on the Sabbath eve, Jews would stop work early and close their shops and businesses. The town beadle, with his long broad beard, would stride through the streets before sunset calling out in his pleasant voice: "Jews – go to Shul! (Synagogue)".

All the Jews in Zhetl would gather in the Houses of Study to welcome the Sabbath. The divine presence came to rest on the Jews and on the town. A rare stillness accompanied by Sabbath songs would fill the air. Poor people and those passing through town were invited for the Sabbath meal. The Jews in town would rest and gather strength for the week and worries that lay ahead.

The Revolutionary Youth in Zhetl

The quiet religious local life saturated in spirituality and tradition lasted until the period of revolutionary excitement, when Marxist ideology won the hearts of the young generation. The youth that was raised in Heders and Yeshivas devoted all their energy to the new doctrine. It went from one extreme to the other, from piety to free thinking, from passivity to revolting and fighting capitalism. They began to agitate against employers who became bloody enemies. They did not even stop at physical actions against employers.

One Saturday evening they threw stones into our house. Another time they entered our home with revolvers in their hands and demanded in the name of the town's revolutionary committee, 400 ruble. Thanks to the intervention of my father's friends who also belonged to socialist groups, the amount was decreased in half. Once they met my father on the street and threatened him with a death sentence.

This is how the unity was disrupted in town. The Houses of Study which were always filled with people praying and learning emptied and life was emptied of content. Workers and artisans began to emigrate, some to America, others to different countries.

These general events, pogroms and revolutionary turmoil in Russia affected the spiritual and material life of our small town.

We decided to Immigrate to the Land of Israel

A feeling of despair dominated and we could not find a way to escape the situation. We decided to leave for the Land of Israel. Our plan had to be carried out secretly so no one would sense we were relinquishing our business and leaving our workers in God's hands, since they would have never allowed this to happen. So, we started a rumour that we were returning to Slonim and will continue to run our business from there. Our workers could not oppose this.

Quietly, in a stressful mood, we left Zhetl by train to Odessa. In the month of Adar (March), 1906 we arrived in Jaffa.

[Page 87]

From Everything to Very Little

by Avrom Yitzkhak Medvedsky (Montreal)

Translated by Janie Respitz

I would like to share my memories of our old home Zhetl, its past and great personalities from the last 50 – 60 years. This is written by Avrom Yitzkhak Medvedsky the son of Dovid Hirshl the furrier.

Nikolai's Soldiers

In Czarist times every town had to deliver 2 or 3 soldiers for 25 years of military service. In Zhetl, as in all other towns they would kidnap small children from poor families. The children were confined to the small Hasidic prayer house until they were taken away deep into Russia.

Wealthy women would bring them tasty food and pots of good soup. Two boys from Zhetl, Motte and Ayzhik served 25 years.

Russian Rulers

Before the First World War the police in Zhetl consisted of a regional superintendent, a constable and a few policemen. They lived in the home of puny Shayna. The jail was a wooden building near Reginiervitch.

Avrom Yitzkhak Medvedsky

The administrative office was on Novoredok Street, near the home of Pinkhas, Notteh Moishe's. In the yard there was a monument of Czar Nikolai's uncle.

Zhetl also had barracks near the palace. There were always two companies stationed there.

There were also a few Cossacks in Zhetl who lived in a small house near the fire station, where they had a telephone. There was a Russian seminary in the palace.

Revolutionaries

I remember the audacity of Zhetl youth who decided to overthrow the monarchy and its leaders in Russia. They would prepare their weapons among the dense shrubs in the cemetery. They also organized and succeeded in stopping the train in Novolienye. A few of the people who participated were arrested. Nakhman Gertsovsky was sent to Siberia. Many others ran away to America.

Leyzer Medvedsky was involved in the cultural work of the revolutionary youth. He died in an accident in Chicago.

Avrom Moishe Barishansky and Khaim Kaplinsky would walk to Slonim on foot carrying a sack of literature and eating only a piece of dry bread.

I remember when one of their comrades, Arzhekhovsky, Berl Yakhes' brother died. They buried him without the Jewish Burial Society. During the funeral the revolutionaries sang songs. The policemen wanted to drive them away, however they were not afraid. Pinye ran around town asking people to close their shops. Secular and Religious Teachers

I remember the teachers who taught Russian to Jewish children: Svetitsky, Itchke the writer, Hindke's grandfather, and Avrom Ayzhik Sokolovsky.

The teachers in the Talmud Torah were: Noyakh Ele, who taught Gemara, Khaim Itche taught Chumash (Pentateuch), Yosef Mutshnik taught Hebrew and Avrom Leyb Eliavitch.

The other teachers in town were: Yosele Mendes, a specialist in the Hebrew alphabet, Yudl Tankhum, Yisroel Khonen Pikelny, Arye the electrician, Moishe Khaim Namiyat, Ziml Zimelevitch and Yenkl Abelevitch. The good teachers were: Ginzburg, Avrom Langbart, Yisroel Zablatsky, the starch maker's son in law, and Eliezer Rozenfeld.

The administrators of the Talmud Torah were: Avrom Moishe, Reb Moishe Leyb, Meir Kovensky's son in law, and Noyekh Rozkosky. We feared the day of examination, especially when they tested us on "Mishpatim" (Judgements).

Heroes From Zhetl

There was a time, before the Bolsheviks, that there was no salt in Zhetl. That is when the militiaman went to get salt. On his way back to Zhetl from Slonim he was attacked by peasants from Mizevetz. Khaim Leyzerovitch saw the situation was bad and shot one peasant to death. The rest of the peasants ran away and he brought the salt to Zhetl.

Another heroic act was carried out by Moishe Mendl Leyzerovitch. He was standing in Shifra Leah's house looking out the window. At that moment he noticed a small girl, Basha Kaplinsky playing by the water. There was a sudden surge and she fell into the river.

[Page 88]

Moishe Mendl jumped into the water, grabbed the girl by the hair and saved her. This happened 40 years ago.

I remember another heroic act from the time of the first Germans. Near Shepsl Shushan and Elke Abes' house they built a small bridge. Yisroel, the manager of the small synagogue, Itche the butcher's brother in law, was working there. The German officer standing beside him was the chief of the fire department. The German told him to work harder. Yisroel took his pickaxe and hit the German over the head. Yisroel was arrested, sent to jail in Bialystok and we never saw him again.

Yosl the carpenter was a healthy man. When new recruits would come for military conscription they would get drunk at puny Shayna's and break window panes of Jewish homes. Once, glass fell into Yosl the carpenter's holiday noodles. He grabbed a strip of molding and beat 50 peasants. Many of the peasants got down on their knees and crossed themselves before him saying they will be good and pious.

Jews Talk

The Jews who finished praying early in the morning would gather in the marketplace and chat in small circles. If one guy's horse died, they would discuss getting him some money. They would also poke fun at Ruveh the smoker.

Saturday morning the stoop would be full at Avrom Moishe Kravitz': Khaim Shilovitsky, Avreyml Kakrysky, Aron Leyb Shvedsky, and Yoshke Bagdanovitch would be sitting together. They would peel kernels and talk about thieves from Tuken and bandits from Kurfish, have a conversation with Motele Idlak, drink a cold glass of soda water at Berl Khodzhelon's or chat with Mitzl Izraeliyet and ask him why he did not marry female Messiah.

The Big Flood

On a Tuesday in 1913 it started to pour. There was lumber beside the Pomerayke which held back the water. The river overflowed and water entered houses, at times reaching up to the windows.

Merchandise swam in the shops. Yosl the painter's wall collapsed and Shloime Nahinsker's smithy was flooded. Besides these damages there were also casualties. Matshuk, the medic's wife, drowned.

The mobilization of 1914

On Shabbat Tish B'Av 1914 when the First World War broke out, everyone who had a red card for military service had to appear in Slonim. I remember the heart rending scene of wives and children crying and young men saying goodbye to their betrothed. Wagons were filled with bags of hay for the horses and we accompanied those mobilized to Khadzhelan. In Slonim they were divided into regiments and sent to the front.

Many men from Zhetl were killed leaving behind widows: Taybe Green, Elke Berman, Indershteyn and others. Many from Zhetl were taken prisoner and later returned home: Tzale Vinarsky, Yisroel Kaplinsky, Motl Medvedsky, Shimen Feyvuzhinsky, Moishe Mendl Leyzerovitch, Dovid Grekuchiner, Dovid Yarmovsky, and Yoel Dovid Dunetz. Arl Mordkhai Kikkes was blinded in the war.

Before the First Germans

Zhetl experienced difficult times during the First World War. Warehouses were set up in the Houses of Study. They taught German in the Talmud Torah. After three o'clock we would learn Yiddish in the women's section of the synagogue, prayer and bible – with Khaim Itche. There was a shortage of food as the peasants ran away to Russia.

We would stand in line for a piece of bread straight from the oven. Yisroel Ozer handed out bread as Joseph did in Egypt.

The whole town wore wooden shoes. The head shoemakers were Berl the swindler and Leybovitch the photographer. It was most difficult for small children who had to go to school without eating and without shoes.

Zhetl's community workers founded a committee headed by Borukh Man and Berl Mirsky. They organized a soup kitchen. Feyge Mirke's Yisroel distributed the soup.

There was a shortage of wood for heating. They brought shavings from the highway where they were building bridges. Boys and girls worked on the highway which ran from Zhetl to Midzvinevitch. Sholem Krashinsky was the foreman.

Another job was: sending logs on horse drawn carts. They would let the carts go downhill on their own from the palace to Kalmen Sovitsky's. Ruven Turetsky, Berl the swindler's son was killed there.

[Page 89]

Before the First Poles

On Purim, six o'clock in the evening, Polish legionaries under the leadership of the nobleman Semoshke, began shooting from Mohilnik over to Slonim Street. They detained Motl Krashinsky who was on his way to hear the Megillah (Scroll of Esther read on Purim) but let him free when they recognized him. The organist's daughter and a Jewish man from Novoredok Street were shot. Ruven, the blacksmith's son in law was wounded in his hand. Bolsheviks were lying shot in the streets.

Participants in the Flower Day for the medical aid society

First row: Miriam Leybovitch, Masha Leybovitch, ...Savitsky, Khana Lifshitz
Second row: Avrom Langbart, ...Butkovsky, Peshke Izraelit, Grunia Vernikovsky, Unknown

The Poles claimed Jews were shooting from their windows, however the Polish priest assured the Jews were not guilty. After they denounced Ele Ivenitsky, they beat him up in Shepsl Shushan's stable. The first gendarmerie was in Krayna Khaya's house. The first Polish commander in Zhetl was Sverin from Zhibertayshtshine. The second commander Makhersky was the fire chief.

The Burial Society

The following belonged to the old burial society: Avreyml Yoshke Khaykes, Motke the harness maker, Yisroel Bom, Alter Bom, Yakov Meylekh Dvoretsky, Meir Savitsky, Leyzer Eli Slitsky, Leyzhe Feyge Mirkes, and Yenkl Borukh Kaplinsky.

The head shroud sewers were: Khana Yeshias, Soreh Leah, Motle the shoemaker's mother in law and Kahyke Yakers. They would cut pieces without a form and their work was as good as gold, especially the head covering of the corpse.

The Library

Zhetl had one of the nicest libraries. The first founders were: Shmuel Shvedsky, Artchik Alpert, and Yisroel Moishe Ivenitsky. The rumour was that the old time fanatics cursed them. Shvedsky was blinded in one eye, Alpert's feet became paralyzed and Ivenisky suffered from heart disease.

Later the youth took over their work. Among them: Itchke Leybovitch, Dovid Lifshitz, Motke Rozvasky, and Hirshl Rabinovitch. During the great fires the library burned in Yisroel the watchmaker's court yard.

Theatre

The first performance in Zhetl was "The Sale of Joseph". The main actors were: Moishe Rozvosky, and Areh Vinarsky. A few years later before the arrival of the first Germans they performed "The Sorceress" and "Grandma Yakhne" at Patyeh Dvoretzky's house on Dvoretz Street. The performers were: Noyekh Turetsky, Hindke Shak from the Lodz workers and Rokhl from Vilna. Later on fresh talent arrived in Zhetl and a good drama club was formed at the Folk – Shule (public school) and a second club at the Tarbut School.

Medical Aid Society and Spending the Night With the Sick

Zhetl had a Medical Aid society whose leaders were: Moishe Ruven Mordkovsky, Yosl the painter's son in law, Hirshl Gertzovsky and Peshke Izrealit. They would prepare ice, bladders and cupping glasses. Shmuel Shvedsky was active in the good deed to spend the night with the sick. Every night they would decide who would take a turn staying with the patients.

The Professional Union

The professional Union in Zhetl was composed of the more aware and left leaning elements of society and was founded in the early years of Poland's independence.

[Page 90]

The first meeting took place at the home of Yokhe Arzhekhovsky, next to Khaim the harness maker. The organizers were: the teacher Herman Frenkel, Berl Arzhekhovsky, and Mikhal Guzavsky, who died young of Tuberculosis, Noyekh Mnuskin, Zelda Likhter, Mina Leah Shepshelevitch, Hirshl Indershteyn, Rokhl Lidsky, Beynish Savitsky, Yenkl Namiyat, and Motke Gonshorovsky.

The first struggle was for an eight hour working day and a raise in working wages. They were also concerned with cultural work, started their own drama club and performed plays. Their locale was in the home of Moishe Khaim Namiyat. This work was managed by Mikhal Guzavsky.

The professional Union created a fund so that striking members could receive a few zlotys. Every year on the first of May the Union organized a meeting. When Mikhal Guzavsky died and many members departed, this work weakened.

The Young Pioneers

The Young Pioneer organization of which I was a member participated in the work of the Jewish National Fund, planting gardens and sending members to pioneer training camps. When I was 17 I spent 6 months on Kibbutz Shkhira, near Semyatitch. I worked at a saw mill in the Bielavezh forests. Some of our members worked in the fields of a nearby village. The leader of this Kibbutz was Menakhem Funtzik from Semyatitch.

Photo: A group of pioneers at work in preparation to immigrate to the Land of Israel 1924.

From left to right: Hirshl Rabinovitch, Yoel Tcheplovodsky, Efraim Klin, Yosef Berman, Zelik Orlinsky, Hirshl Gertzovsky.

In Zhetl we worked in Fraydl Kusiel's garden. We also cared for the garden of Meir Yoshe's, Dobe Alter.

Here are some of the members of the Young Pioneers in Zhetl: Avrom Yitzkhak Medvedsky, Shimen Berniker, Khashke Leybovitch, Shyana Leah Karpelovitch, Borukh Busel, Nokhem Broyde, Herzl Gertzovsky, Dovid Zelikovitch, Shepsl Namiyat, Elke Koyfman, Alte Busel, Leybl Lusky, and Dovid Lifshitz.

קבוצת חלוצים בזיטל בעבודה צ"ית .24.XI

Factories

There were a few factories in Zhetl. The first produced cotton. It belonged to Leybe Kaplinsky. The leather tanneries were run by Yisroel Bom and Feyve the tanner. Hirshl Aron Volfovitch and his brothers Yenkl and Avreyml produced ceramic tiles. Clay pots were made by Berl and Aryeh. Oil was produced by Avrom Levit. Kurgman was a shingle maker. The following had machines to brush wool: Hirshl Musher, Zerakh and Kalmen Levit.

Those who produced cereal grains were: Peretz Indershteyn, Feygl Dobe's and Noyekh the grain maker.

Soda water factory: Yisroel Ozer Barishansky and Berl Dvoretzky.

Cup makers: Berl and Shmuel Mirsky.

Pharmacies

The pharmacist in Zhetl was Zhbikovsky. The pharmacy stores were owned by: Menakhme Vernikovsky, Krinsky, Reb Ayzele, Kharif's son in law, Elye Yudelevitz, Berl Dvoretsky and Khaim Koyfman.

Matzah Bakeries

Right after Chanukah some Matzah bakeries would begin baking Matzah for the big cities. Feygl Meir's wife on Lipave Alley was one of the first. Frumche the glazier's wife's bakery was more respectable, meaning the wealthier would come to her to bake egg matzah. Moishke Solomon's matzah bakery was on Dvoretz Street.

Motl Krashinsky's mother in law was a kneader. I also remember Dobeh and Rokhl.

In the matzah bakeries there were water pourers, rollers and oven – men.

The following always had a matzah bakery: Yosl Yente's, Frumke Moishe Mikhl's, Moishe the tinsmith, Peretz Indershteyn and Khaim Meir Dvoretzky.

On the eve of Passover there was joy in the streets. People carried braided baskets with matzah and mortars to grind matzah meal.

[Page 91]

Prayer Leaders

I remember the prayer leaders and cantors in Zhetl who prayed tastefully: Hertz Leyb Kaplinsky, Reb Shloime Tcheplovodsky, Reb Moishe Tentzer, and Reb Yehuda Leb Khlebnik. Moishe Ayzhik would pray in the old House of Study during Saturday evening prayers and sing "You Are One".

Prayers in the new House of Study were led by Yisroel Ber the gravedigger and Moishe Rozvosky.

The following lead prayers in the small chapel: Niyameh Guzavsky, Yitzkhak Rozovsky and Hirshl the blacksmith (Reznitsky).

Cantors

I remember the great cantor and conductor who ran a good choir: Reb Eli Ber. Many Christians would come hear him pray on Yom Kippur (the Day of Atonement). He was a ritual slaughterer and a great scholar. Some of the best singers in his choir were: Moishe Rozovsky and his sons, his grandson Efroyke, the Manor, Berl Koyfman and others. In the last years the cantor in Zhetl was Yitzkhak Kogan.

Beadles (Administrators)

The administrators of the Houses of Study in Zhetl were: Motteh Nokhem's, Leyzer Mordkhai Leyserovitch, and Yehuda Leyb Khlebnik in the old House of Study. Avrom Hirshl the beadle in the new House of Study and Moishe Yehuda Savitsky in the middle House of Study.

Respectable Well Off Men

Zhetl had respectable, well off learned men who continued to study regularly: Yisroel Avreyml Sokolovsky, Yosl Tchires, Menakhem Vernikovsky, Noyekh Eli Levit, Yosele Mendes, Moishe Tentzer, Shabsai Shuahan, Shmuel Levit, Yosl Belitsky, Zhameh Dunetz, Asher, Velvl Slutsky, Khaim Yitzkhak the electrician, Noyekh Rozovsky, Yisroel Ber Epshteyn, Yehuda Leyb Khlebnik, Kuperman, Shloimeh Tcheplovodsky, Borukh Man, Zalmen Khvinevitcher, Khaim Yitzkhak the tutor, Velvel Izraelit, Feyvl, Yisroel Gonuzovitch, Yisroel Bom, Mikhal Berniker the preacher, Areh Zlate Beylke's Aronovitch, Yosl Khaim Belitsky, Avrom Hersh Langbart, Shmuel Kustin, Avrom Ayzik, Avrom Leyb Eliyovitch, Moishe Beres, Hertz Leyb Kaplinsky, Yudl the ritual slaughterer, and Ginzburg the teacher.

Hasidim

I also want to mention the Hasidim in Zhetl: Shmerl Lobensky, Motl Tules, Velvl Slutsky, Yudl the ritual slaughterer, Yenkl Abelevitch, Khaim Nakhes, Hirshl the butcher, Yisroel Zablotsky, and the old Krupnik. They were all Slonim Hasidim.

Sons and Sons in Law

I remember respectable sons of Zhetl both in religious and secular education: Yitzkhak Shimen Etes, Isar Shotzkes, Mikhl the preacher's sons, Berniker, Yishayhu Moishe Pilnik, Avrom Ivenitsky, Gdalyahu Shvedslky, Yitzkhak Leybovitch, Mikhl Rabinovitch, Noyekh Lusky, and Avrom Langbart.

Respectable sons in law in Zhetl: Moishe Tentzer, Ruven Mordkovsky, Yisroel Krokhmalnik, Borukh Lipeh Pinsky, Yosef Mutchnik, Meir Kakenske's son in law, Moishe Leyb and Avrom Hersh Langbart.

Medics and Doctors

I remember the past medics and doctors who received a lot of practice: Velvl the "old time physician" (without training), Motte the "old time physician", Berl Pagerer and Avrom Meir Lidsky. Their medical remedies included: leeches, castor oil, buckwheat leaves, cupping glasses and enemas. Those specializing in cupping were: Shloimeh Lidsky, Beyle Zelda and Tsirl Perl Berniker. The greatest specialist was the medic Artchik Green. The doctors were: Shapiro, Vafner, Vinik from Novogrudek and Yezhikovitch, who was a Pole.

After the First World War the whole town contracted typhus. The head doctor then was Shapiro. The nurse was: Peshke Izraelit. After she got married the assistant was a Christian, Vania.

Artisans

The old time artisans in Zhetl once held an important position in all town matters. They would sit at the table in the new House of Study and learn Mishna, the Code of Jewish Law or Chafetz Chaim with the maker of children's shoes. After he died they studied with Yisroel Berl the gravedigger. Those at this table were: Motke the harness maker, Velvl the carpenter, Tzaleh the blind, Moishke the shoemaker, Avrom the blacksmith, and Avrom the recluse. Hirshl the blacksmith and Noyekh the bent would study in the small chapel near the lake.

The founders of the Artisan Union in Zhetl were: Motl Medvedsky, Moish Mendl Leyzerovitch, Hirshl Benyaminovitch, and Tzela Busel. They represented the artisans at the bank, the interest free loan society, the professional union, at City Hall and in the Zhetl Jewish community.

Rural Settlements and Jews Who Lived There

I remember the rural settlements around Zhetl and the fine respectable learned Jews who lived there like: Reb Leyb Khabdkier, Yenkl Orkes' father in law. He would study day and night.

[Page 92]

Shmuel Kovensky, Moishe Aron Yezernitsky, Shimen the gusset maker, Yudl Podveliker, Zalmen Refitsher, a scholar who also performed circumcisions, Yudl Yenkl Rashkin's father, Leyzer from Orlin, Khaim from Zhibertaytch, Simkha from Vohl – Berl Rabinovitch's father, Shelubsky from Pintchet, Zalman from Khvinievitch, Epshteyn the ritual slaughterer from Levanevitch.

I will take into account the Jewish nobility who owned their own estates but were forced by the Russian authorities to sell: Avrom Shloimeh from Zhikotchin, Reveh from Azhiran and Gershon from Zazhen.

Musicians and Wedding Entertainers

I would like to mention the old time musicians and improvisers (Badkhan) who would perform at Jewish celebrations. The band consisted of Arye Levit, Khaim Levit, his son Kalmen Levit, Avrom Busel, and Pinke Mnuskin on the drum.

Avrom Moishe Medvedsky, the improvising entertainer at weddings would say: Don't cry bride, as you are filled with charm.

Moishe Rosvosky would make up rhymes: Don't make such a fuss, the in laws will pay the groom in cash.

The main matchmakers in Zhetl were: Khasheh Beyleh, a fat lady who was always smiling. Khaim Nakhes, with a red scarf around his neck. He always had a handkerchief sticking out of the back pocket of his overcoat and carried a parasol in his hand. He was tall and thin with a pointed beard. He would run quickly in order to bring everyone happiness.

Hoyf Street

Neighbours would sit on the stoops in the courtyards and share the news of Zhetl. Sometimes they would speak ill of others. The street was happy and filled with sales.

Vazke travelled every day, summer and winter to Kaplinsky. At dawn they would send lumber to sell. In the evening when he returned it was once again joyful on the street. Motl Krashinsky took in receipts from his restaurant, Yakhke Kovensky – for whisky, Henieh Leykeh Slonimsky – for kerosene. Velvl Hinde Zlate's - for a glass cover for a lamp, Golda Lrokhmalnik – for challah and bread. Eli Moishe Borukh's for a hat, Tuvia Idl for giblets and non-kosher meat, Yoshke Leyzshe's – for paint and Dovid Shepetnitsky – a store filled with gentiles from Patsutchin.

Feytche Yosl Yente's and her husband always had a lot of work, sewing blouses and caftans for gentiles. Alter Feyshes and his brother Mordkhai would pump kerosene in all the shops in town. At Avreyml Krokhmalnik's shop, gentiles would buy oil cake for cattle and oil. At Feyge Mereh Levit's they would repair cimbaloms. Khaim Yaverer would stand with a washtub filled with pickles, Bune Berkes – with good apples and pears. This was life on Hoyf Street.

I want to mention that this street had a good Jew, he did not speak badly of others, always wished others well and did not make demands from God. He kept the Sabbath, never tasted non kosher food, never stole a penny from anyone and yet, was shot by murderous hands in the garden near his house. I am talking about Dovid Hirshl the furrier (Medvedsky).

Areh Vinarsky was a good man. Never refused to give money to the poor.

I must mention Motl Leybovitch, a well off artisan. He participated in various societies and was a regular at Reb Zalmen's Saratzky's.

Old Stravinsky

I remember, and we must eternalize the name of the old land owner from Miraytchin, Stravinsky. He was beloved in Zhetl, because he provided Jews with an opportunity to earn a living. Flamuk the tailor worked for him. He also gave work to Shepsl Shushan. Every Passover he would give poor Jews wheat or flour for matzah and potatoes. A few Jews received help from him to build a house.

When they brought him from Warsaw to the Christian cemetery and lowered his coffin in the crypt where all the Stravinskys are buried, I saw Dovid Indershteyn, whose nickname was "Hindke", recite the Kaddish (Mourner's prayer).

The First Car

Who remembers the first car in Zhetl 43 years ago? It arrived with the post to Meir Kovensky, at the house where Yudl Khaim Rashkin later lived. A wagon running without horses. Well, the whole town ran to see what an automobile looked like.

The next year a hot air balloon flew over our town with a braided basket. It dropped a string which got caught in a tree and two people emerged from the basket.

The first radio was brought to town by Ostashinsky. He had a restaurant at Khane Areyml's Kayle's. Before you put on the earphones to listen to the radio for a few minutes, he would take 10 groshen. Later on a couple more radios appeared in town.

[Page 93]

Jews Living in Rural Villages and Conscripts

by Avrom Leyzerovitch (Kfar Haroeh)

Translated by Janie Respitz

I would like to describe, as much as I can remember, the Jews who lived among gentiles in rural villages around Zhetl.

During the time of Czar Nikolai there was not a village where there were no Jews. Jews lived in the villages with their whole families, sons, and daughters, daughters in law and sons in law. They married off their children there providing dowries and lodging.

Avrom Leyzerovitch

Profitable Livelihood

These people earned a good living especially if they had few expenses . They would have a potato field, their own cow who grazed in the field therefore not costing anything. They did not lack in chickens and they baked their own bread from milled corn as well as other grains. They really had everything they needed. They would also sell: milk, butter, cheese and eggs. They did not have to pay rent as everyone had their own house and a stall.

Jews in the villages lived a calm life. If they earned a ruble a week, it was enough – as the only items they had to buy in town were sugar and kerosene.

Jews in the villages were for the most part tenant farmers who leased mills, breweries, inns or fields.

The inns were situated at the entrance of the village and everyone passing through could stop to rest and have something to eat.

I would like to describe these village Jews as well as I can remember. I would like to ask forgiveness as perhaps my writing is not one hundred percent as I am not a great writer.

Reb Avrom Shloimeh Namiyat

Number one of all the rural settlements was Zhukovchizne. It was a large estate with mills, forests and a brewery. This all belonged to Reb Avrom Shloimeh Namiyat, of blessed memory. All of his employees in the village were Jews, therefore he always had a quorum,

10 men required for prayers. He would come to Zhetl with a coach pulled by three horses, as the government did not allow Jews to ride with four horses.

When Czar Nikolai put forth the edict that Jews were no longer permitted to own estates, he had to sell his property to a countess for which he received seventy thousand ruble. With this money he bought a large brick building in Vilna. He also had a house in Zhetl which in the last years belonged to Berl Rabinovitch. His son in law was Reb Yisroel Rabinovitch the Moscow rabbi.

Other Village Jews

My father Reb Khaim lived in Zhibertyachshine. I was born in this village and this is where my father married off his children.

In Yanovtchine a Jew had the lease and brought milk to Zhetl. Recently, Wolf Farfl lived there.

Dovid lived in Strele but later moved to Zhetl.

Shimen Leyb was an estate farmer in Bogudzhenke. In recent years, no Jews lived there.

The families of Meir and Shmuel Kovensky lived in Nokrishok. In 1929 Meir Kovensky immigrated to Israel.

Zvulun lived on the estate in Zielane. On the Sabbath there was a quorum at his place and Jews from Fintchitch and Kurfish would come there to pray. In his later years he left for America.

Mordkhai lived in Kurfish.

My uncle Reb Ayzik Lipe lived in Fintchitch. His wife was my mother's sister. He was a learned Jew who studied a lot. I remember he would sit all day and study Gemara. His son in law the rabbi Reb Dovid Rovensky was a preacher in Zhetl and later rabbi in Pinsk. Hi son, Reb Asher lives in Israel.

Reb Avrom, my grandfather live in Nartzevitch. He had two sons and three daughters. One daughter was my mother, the second – Reb Ayzik Lipes' wife and the third, Zalmen Shepshelevitch's wife. The last one would travel from Zhetl to Vilna. His grandchildren live in Israel.

Reb Berl lived in Khiliman where he ran the mill.

A Jewish blacksmith lived in Zashetshe.

[Page 94]

Hirshl lived in Romanovitch. His children Shayna and Eliyahu live in Petach Tikva.

Reb Yisroel Kaplinsky lived in Hantshri. He leased a mill from the nobleman Stravinsky. He sat every day and studied while his wife, Cherna Rokhl ran the mill. His son, Reb Shaul Kaplinsky was a gentle man, studied a lot and dealt in lumber. His grandchildren: Borukh Kaplinsky and Arye Zelikovitch live in Israel.

The Jewish blacksmith Moishe Zelik Bushlin who lived in Khabadki now lives in Israel.

Two Jews lived in Pager: one was a blacksmith and his son Reb Moishe lives in Israel. The second one was Berl, the old fashioned (untrained) doctor.

There was a Jewish forest merchant in Mizevetz. His daughter Shayna lived in Zhetl and from Zhetl she left for America.

Jews lived in the following villages on the road between Zhetl and Slonim : Bodonovchine, Zadvarie, Shundri and Kaladishke.

Draftees to the Polish Army, 1922

Just as I began with a wealthy man I would like to conclude with a wealthy man who had his own estate with forests and fields. His name was Berl Zhelaner. Novoyelne belonged to him. He managed his business on high standards and the gentiles were afraid of him. When it was forbidden for Jews to own estates, he sold.

Russian and Polish Edicts Against Village Jews

I calculated about 20 villages where Jews lived. However there were more villages around Zhetl where Jews lived: Petruki, Pesutzky, Zatshefitch and others.

Jews lived in these rural villages for generations and withstood many Czarist edicts and persecutions. Among others, the last edict in Novoseliene. According to this edict the Czarist government forbid Jews to live in a village if their parents had not lived there. However, despite the Czarist edicts the village population treated the Jews favourably.

The situation changed under Polish rule. The Polish government organized the peasant population against the Jews, took trade out of Jewish hands and created an atmosphere which was wired in danger.

In view of this danger, Jews began to leave the villages.

Military Conscription

in Zhetl took place after Sukkot, in the month of Cheshvan (October) when the rains begin. As at this time there were no paved highways and the road from Slonim to Zhetl had to be repaired so the district police chief and the doctor could travel comfortably. Authorities would travel by horse, which in those days was called a stage coach. They would travel from Slonim to Zadvaria and change horses there. Berke the tanner owned the coach in Zhetl. If authorities had to come from Slonim, he would supply the horse and wagons.

Recruits in Zhetl

Conscription would last for 8–10 days. During this time all the taverns and shop would close as all the recruits would steal everything. There would be 400 – 500 conscripts.

Many would be released as they were not capable of military service. However, 150 – 200 men were taken into service.

[Page 95]

Every recruit would arrive with a father, mother, brother, or sister, so that during the period of conscription there would be between 1500 – 2000 people in Zhetl, among them, many bandits and drunks. They would receive liquor for money and go through the streets looking for something to steal. The Jewish recruits were scared and were not spared beatings.

Exemptions

Now I will tell you about our Jewish brothers who were conscripted, who had no defects and were sure they would be taken into the military. They would make a list of those who would not go to the military due to a defect or would receive an exemption for which they demanded money. An exemption could happen if the conscript was an only son. That was the first exemption. Another reason for exemption was that your father was over 55 and your brother was under the age of 16. Another reason for exemption was if you had a brother in the military.

They would take money from the above mentioned guys. Those who were recruited said: they are staying home and we will go into the military, therefore they should pay.

There were also Jews who were registered in Zhetl but lived in different cities. They too had to come to Zhetl for conscription. For example, I lived in Zhibertaychshine which belonged to Zhetl, however I was registered in Polonke, and was called to conscription in Novi – Mush, near Baranovitch. I also paid taxes in Polonke.

One of the taxes Jews had to pay in the days of Czar Nikolai was for permission to light candles.

"Angels"

One received a passport where you were registered therefore many Jews were registered in Zhetl and reported for service in Zhetl. Since in those days there were no photographs, they would send "angels". Why did they call them angels? Because they would go to every conscription, today here, tomorrow somewhere else. This was their profession. Obviously, these were young men with defects and they would present themselves instead of a healthy guy and of course, they would be released from service.

Many of the Jewish recruits ran off to America in order to avoid military service.

Consequently the government gave an order that before you are taken into the army your parents must pay a 300 ruble fine. Because of this fine people had to show up. It also happened that after they were enlisted, they left for America, so the Russian government gave an order that until you take your oath the 300 ruble had to be paid, which meant only after 6 months of service, the 300 ruble fine did not have to be paid.

Draftees into the Polish Army 1928

Jewish Recruits Cause Scandals

Now let's turn to the Jewish recruits I described earlier. They would take money from those who did not serve in the army, often with beatings. They would use the money to make parties every evening.

Besides this, they would demand money from the city, but this they would not receive easily.

[Page 96]

First they would approach the town elder of Zhetl, who in my time was Avrom Patzovsky. Everyone was registered with him and he would distribute passes. He was the leader of the town.

The recruits would go to him for money, but understand, they did not receive any money from him. What would they do? Saturday morning they would lock all the prayer houses and notify everyone they could not pray. They would only leave the old House of Study open and all those wanting to pray had to go there. During prayers they interrupted the service and demanded people give them money.

My father and I, Reb Khaim, of blessed memory prayed at Avrom Patzovsky's. That morning, when all the prayer houses were locked, we went there as usual. Everyone was afraid to pray, but Avrom Patzovsky said he was not afraid of anyone.

There was turmoil in the old House of Study. Finally they said they would call upon Avrom Patzovsky. When the group of recruits found us praying they began shouting and things got out of hand.

We promised we would all go to the old House of Study and they demanded Avrom Patzovsky come as well. He did not agree and they threatened to beat him up and bring 20 more friends to take him by force to the old House of Study. Finally he agreed to go but without anyone accompanying him.

This commotion went on for two weeks. Finally, in the end everyone drafted into the army received 2–3 ruble and peace was restored.

In the last years under the Polish government people reported to the army Novoliyenie, however the custom of taking money and making parties ended.

For These Are the People of Zhetl!

Translated by Judy Montel

I wish to speak about the Jews who lived in the villages in the Zhetl area during the rule of Tsarist Russia.

There was no village in the Zhetl area without Jews. In the village they had sons and daughters who grew up there, married and sometimes were there for years, around their parent's table.

There was not much concern for livelihood. Usually, it was near at hand since the village Jews could meet most of their own needs. The cow that grazed in his meadow provided milk, butter and cheese. There were many chickens which supplied meat and eggs; frequently there was a calf for meat, potatoes and other vegetables that grew in the field. There was no rent to pay since for the most part they lived in their own homes.

Thus, the Jew of the village could live in ease and peace. If he earned one ruble a week, that was enough for him, since he only needed cash to buy sugar and kerosene.

What was the occupation of the Jew of the village? Mostly he would rent a flour mill from the landlord, or a brandy still, an inn or fields. The Inn stood at the entrance to the village and was a meeting place for the Christian villagers and a place to sleep for visitors.

The main village in the Zhetl area was Zhukovschizna. This estate included a flour mill, a brandy still and forests. All of this belonged to Reb Abraham Shlomo Namiot of blessed memory. All of his clerks on the estate were Jews, so that he could always count on a *minyan* (quorum) for prayers. To Zhetl he would travel in a carriage with three horses. After the publication of the ordinance of the Tsarist government that forbade Jews to hold property in the village, he was forced to sell his estate for 70,000 rubles. With this money he bought a large house in Vilna and in Zhetl. His son-in-law was the rabbi, Reb Shmuel Rabeinu-Beech, a rabbi in Zhaludek and later in Moscow.

In Zhbertoishchina my father, Reb Chaim lived. In this village I was born, grew up and married.

In Nortzvitz my grandfather, Reb Abraham, lived. He had two sons and three daughters. One of them, my mother, the second, the wife of Reb Aizik Lipa and the third, the wife of Reb Zalmen Shepshelevitch whose grandchildren live in Israel.

In Romnovitch lived Reb Hirschl Romnovicher; his daughter Yafa and his son Eliyahu live in Petach Tikva.

In Hanchri lived Reb Yisrael Kaplinski. He leased a flour mill from the landlord Strebinski. All of his life he studied Torah and his wife, Tcherna Rachel, ran the business. His son, Reb Sha'ul, was a student of the Torah and traded in wood. His grandsons, Baruch Kaplinski and Aryeh Zelikovitch live in Israel.

In Poger lived Reb Moshe the Blacksmith and the "Doctor" Berl the Pogerer.

Since I began with the owner of a large estate, I will also end with the owner of a large estate. That is, Reb Berl Zhloner. He owned the estate at Novoilania that included fields and forests. He ran his farm with a firm hand and frightened all of the villagers in the area. After the government ordinance was published, he too was forced to sell his estate.

Avraham Layzerovitch

[Page 98]

During the First World War

Translated by Judy Montel

On August 1, 1914, World War I broke out. Its initial events hit the Jews of Zhetl hard. The sons were conscripted into the Russian army, and the fathers were set to digging defense works. Streams of war refugees passed through the streets of Zhetl as well as the columns of the Russian army, retreating from the front. Many families fell victim to looting by the rampaging Cossacks and in more than a few houses hunger and want appeared. Because of this situation, quite a few families decided to escape to central Russia, far from the front.

In September of 1915, Zhetl was conquered by troops of victorious Germany. The fact that the town was somewhat distant from the front line allowed the German authorities to set up a civilian administration with a local police force and a local municipal government. Leib Luski OBM was appointed chairman of the city and Meyrim Epstein OBM was appointed police commander.

Although the Germans enlisted the townspeople for forced labor, in general they governed decently and Zhetl could heave a sigh of relief after the years of Tsarist rule. Creative forces that had been suppressed and functioned underground, now burst forth unbridled and openly organized public activities. Two clubs were set up in the town: the Zionist and the Dramatic-Literary, whose lectures, question and answer parties and reading rooms concentrated all of the forces that hungered for culture. The Zionist club, on which interest centered, led by Efraim Blogolovski-Hermoni also published an oral newspaper in Yiddish and in Hebrew that reflected the life of town.

However, alongside the cultural development, the poverty and deprivation the community suffered must be mentioned. In order to ease the lot of many, community leaders set up a popular kitchen that gave out 100 meals a day for free or a nominal fee. 150 families received financial aid and hundreds of refugees and forced-laborers were helped. Above all others, the children's kitchen was most notable which saved hundreds of children from hunger and stunted growth.

In November of 1917 [*sic* – this actually took place in November of 1918] the German revolution broke out and as a result German troops retreated from the conquered areas. To mark the liberation from German occupation, Zhetl organized a public celebration. However, before Zhetl had recovered from the joy of liberation it was caught up in political upheaval, groups of Bolsheviks and Polish Legionnaires came through from time to time, but neither established their rule in the town. Sometimes one group would arrive and sometimes they would leave the town and all of this was accompanied by fear, looting, searches and at times even arrests and murder. In order to escape this terrible fate and to release the town from the nightmare of the Polish Legionnaires, the community leaders, headed by Rabbi Reb Zalmen Sorotzkin and Yisrael Ozer Brishenski, used the method of mediation and giving bribes. These time-tried methods brought a temporary calm to the Zhetl community. In this period the "Jewish Republic" was also founded in Zhetl, the home rule of the Jews of Zhetl equipped with arms and defenses, as described in this volume by Efraim Hermoni.

In 1920 the Russian-Polish war broke out. The columns of retreating Poles, and afterwards the fleeing Bolsheviks and the persecution by the deserters who gathered in the forest all had an effect on the Zhetl community.

For two and a half years, Zhetl was thrown from one government to the other and as a result of the constant political changes deprivation, hunger and disease only spread. Only in the middle of 1921 did the civilian Polish government stabilize and then a new period began in the history of the Zhetl community.

[Page 99]

The First World War

Zhetl During My Rabbinate

by Rabbi Zalmen Saratzkin (Jerusalem)

Translated by Janie Respitz

I took over the position of Chief Rabbi of Zhetl in 1912. Before I discuss the events of my rabbinate, a few words about Zhetl.

Zhetl was a poor town largely because the peasants in the surrounding villages were poor. They worked a sandy soil and did not enjoy success.

Rabbi Zalmen Saratzkin

Understandably the financial situation of the villages had an effect on the Jews of Zhetl who primarily worked in retail and trade, as there were no factories in Zhetl.

Despite the poverty Zhetl excelled in Torah study and wisdom. The rest of the world referred to people from Zhetl as the Sages of Zhetl. If a Jew in Zhetl would arrive late for prayers he would not find an empty lectern even though the Houses of Study were large for such a small town. When I took over the rabbinate I was told that throughout the world there were close to 100 rabbis from Zhetl as well as great Talmudic scholars from Zhetl who were worthy of becoming rabbis.

I would like to mention a few: Reb Shmuel Rabinovitch – Rabbi of Moscow, Reb Moishe Leyb Lusky – Rabbi of Sventzian, Rabbi Shmule Khaim (I don't recall his last name) – Rabbi of Genitzesk, Reb Avrom Alpert – Rabbi in Shverzne, Reb Shabsai Alpert – Rabbi in Polonke (now in America), Reb Zelik Kaplinsky (Reb Hertz Leyb's son) – the Loykev Rabbi M. M. Lidsky – Koretz Rabbi Reb Yisroel Senderovsky (Yasha Leyb the pelt seller's son) – judge in the Jewish court in Rovno, Yakov Yankelevitch (Lyubtcher) – judge in the Jewish court of Kovel and Reb Yehoshua Lidsky – ritual slaughterer in Derevne.

From among the great scholars it is worthwhile to remember: Reb Zalmen Yoel Kaplinsky and his son Reb Avrom, Reb Avrom Leyb the teacher, Reb Aron Shatzkes, Reb Avrom the recluse, Reb Mikhl Berniker, Reb Yakov Ostrovsky (Yakov Moishe Ayzhes), Reb Yisroel Avrom Sokolovsky and his son Mordkhai (now a ritual slaughterer in Johannesburg), Reb Moishe Tentzer, Reb Noyakh Eli the teacher, Reb Shaul the teacher and his son Reb Leyb Khabadiker, Reb Feyvl Skidler, Reb Aron Hersh Langbart and Reb Moishe Gertzovsky.

Those who occupied the position of chief rabbi in Zhetl had great reputations throughout the world. I will mention a few beginning with: Reb Yosef Zvi Hirsh Dvoretzky, of blessed memory. He was a great Talmudic scholar. He was rabbi in Zhetl for 40 years. Jews of Zhetl often spoke of his intelligence and sharp mind.

Reb Zalmen Yoel Kaplinsky

After his death he was succeeded by the rabbi Reb Borukh Avrom Mirsky of blessed memory, a great scholar and among the first Hovevei Zion (Lovers of Zion), and the author of "Shmatat Deraba". However a dispute over two slaughterhouses had an effect on him and shortened his life.

After his death, in recognition of their beloved deceased Rabbi Yosef Zvi Hirsh Dvoretzky, Zhetl hired his son Reb Mikhl Arye as chief rabbi.

Rabbi Mikhl Arye Dvoretzky was only a rabbi in Zhetl for 30 days when he died of a heart attack. People said the same dispute over the two slaughter houses shortened his life as well.

Since two rabbis died as a result of this dispute I must tell you about it.

Slaughter Houses

A few years before the First World War a wealthy man from Zhetl Berl Dvoretzky built a slaughter house with the permission of the government. The butchers in Zhetl were suspicious of this slaughter house from day one. They were afraid of larger slaughter taxes, and most important, they knew they would be required to slaughter only in that slaughter house. Both slaughterhouses had its supporters and violent quarrels would break out which the rabbis could in no way appease.

In those years I was rabbi in Voronove. Zhetl invited me to eulogize the deceased Reb Mikhl Arye Dvoretsky, and right after the eulogy offered me the position of chief rabbi. I told the men that as long as there is a fight in Zhetl, I will not take on the rabbinate. These established men understood and turned to me, to Rabbi Shmuel Rabinovitch of Moscow and Rabbi Kalmen Levin of Dvoretz and asked us to solve the conflict.

[Page 100]

We remained in Zhetl for a few weeks and succeeded in bringing peace.

According to our verdict Berl Dvoretsky received compensation from the butchers and agreed to close his slaughter house. Later he opened a cotton factory in that same building. The butchers were obliged to give 10% of their slaughter house income to the Talmud Torah (religious school).

Once this conflict was solved I agreed to take the position.

A few months after my arrival in Zhetl another conflict ensued: a large portion of the population, mainly common folk, demanded another doctor in Zhetl. The only Jewish doctor, Shapiro had many opponents and they demanded a second doctor. I had to solve this dispute.

I would like to emphasize that during my time at the rabbinate in Zhetl I enjoyed a general trust which allowed me, with God's help to solve almost all disputes.

The 300th Anniversary of the Romanov House

In a similar fashion I succeed in untangling a dispute which arose in connection to the 300th Jubilee celebrations of the royal dynasty in Russia.

The year was 1913. An anniversary committee was created in Zhetl composed of the Russian Orthodox priest, the regional police superintendent and both tax collectors: Yakovlev and Pranyevitch. Yakovlev was a very honest respectable Christian with higher education and liberal tendencies. He gladly worked together with the Jewish intelligentsia in the fire station.

According to his plan, the firefighters orchestra, which was composed mainly of Jews, would be present at prayers at the Russian Orthodox Church and later play at the head of Christian procession with icons. Berl Mirsky, the head firefighter informed me of this plan.

I invited the important man Reb Menakhem Vernikovsky, a member of firefighter's administration to come to me and I asked him:

How is this possible? A Jewish orchestra in church and leading a Christian procession?

I warned him, if this takes place, I will leave town before the celebration and will not deliver a sermon in honour of the Jubilee in the House of Study. Zhetl was shocked by this news.

Reb Menakhem Vernikovsky promised me he would meet with Yakovlev and present my standpoint. A few days later Yakovlev came to me. He asked me to give my sermon in the House of Study. I thanked him and explained that if I am their rabbi they must listen to me and a Jewish orchestra is forbidden to lead a Christian procession. At first he wondered: the entire Christian intelligentsia will be present at prayers in your House of Study, so why can't the Jews be present at Christian prayers?

In place of an answer I told him the following story: in a certain city there was a liberal ruler. He allowed the publication of newspapers without censorship and meetings without restrictions.

Suddenly a state of war was declared in town and the liberal leader became strict. He instituted censorship and cancelled all freedoms. The same is with us Jews. We have been living for 1800 years in a state of war and must restrict our people otherwise folk life will be threatened. It is forbidden for us to look at your icons. However you, Russians, are not threatened by any danger and nothing will happen to you if you attend our prayers.

My example made an impression. Yakovlev promised me to cancel the Christian procession with the Jewish orchestra. He did however ask me to send a letter to my colleague, the priest. I agreed to write the letter, but I explained that it would take a long time before a rabbi will be a priest's colleague.

My conversation with Yakovlev and my letter to the priest helped. The orchestra did not play during the Christian procession, did not enter the church, and I gave a sermon in honour of the anniversary.

After the celebration Reb Menakhem Vernikovsky asked me why I didn't really want to give the sermon. I told him the following story:

Tolstoy recounts that Alexander the First did not die of a hemorrhage as described in the official sources. During his royal funeral they buried someone else and the Czar left for Siberia to lead a life of wandering and deprivation disguised as a simple man. The Czar agitated against priests and challenged them causing great upheaval. One day he was asked:

How could a believer not go to confession?

The Czar replied: if during confession I tell a lie, the sky will tremble.

[Page 101]

.If I tell the truth, the earth will tremble. Therefore, I don't go. The same is with my sermon. If I go up to the podium in the House of study and tell the truth about the Romanov House the earth will tremble. If I lie, the skies will tremble. Therefore I did not want to speak, but if I must, I have to be sure not to cause the earth or sky to tremble. Reb Menakhem Vernikovsky of blessed memory told this story to Yakovlev and even though he was a liberal, he was not happy with it.

Zhetl During the War

The First World War broke out during my third year as chief rabbi in Zhetl. Many refugees arrived in Zhetl, among whom were my wife's family. The mood was stressful. Wagon trains loaded with military dragged through Zhetl and the Russians dug trenches in the area.

During that time we had twins and one died. This greatly disturbed my wife and she left with the children and her family to Minsk. I remained in Zhetl.

After her departure Reb Yeshayahu Moishe Pilnik lived in my house. Every night the military wagons would wake us to ask directions. Reb Yeshayahu Moishe Pilnik would dress and go with them. I would go crazy until I saw him return safely.

Meanwhile I received letters from my wife asking me, with God's help to come to Minsk. However, I was busy collecting money for the Cossacks. They demanded money in return for not burning down the town. Thanks to the money we collected Zhetl was spared the fate of many other towns and cities.

I told the householders of Zhetl I would remain until the last Russian left. It was evening, then morning and I received news the last Russians were leaving. According to the agreement I should have left, but who would take me?

Coincidentally it happened, a gentile was travelling to Novoredek and I went with him.

In Minsk

The road swarmed with military wagons and Cossacks. I cannot say I felt comfortable in their company. Just think what a Cossack would do to a rabbi. While thinking about this I noticed a Russian officer. I felt a bit better. I tried to strike a conversation with him and succeeded. He told me the Russians were leaving their trenches around Zhetl and no battles will take place there. This was a great relief. I thought: if this news could reach Zhetl, the Jews would be thrilled.

Finally we arrived in Novorodek. I went to Eli Ber, the cantor's son. I rested at his home and thanks to him I got a wagon and continued on my way. On the eve of Sukkot 1915, barely alive, I arrived in Minsk.

There I found groups of refugees. Thousands of people roamed around depressed and despondent. I decided to help and began working for the refugee committee.

We would distribute 7 to 10 thousand ruble daily. We received the money from Jewish and state sources and we often had to travel to St. Petersburg to get the money for the refugee committee.

I enjoyed a general trust, even when the Bolsheviks demanded removal of the leaders of the committee, I remained at my job.

I used my stay in Minsk for broader community work. I organized a branch of Agudas Yisroel in Minsk which had around 10 thousand members. I opened a Talmud Torah and a school for girls. I also succeeded in freeing Russian rabbis from military service.

Among the 30 thousand Jewish refugees in Minsk were 300 rabbis. One fine morning they were mobilized, myself included.

That is when I went to St. Petersburg, stirred up all the Jewish businessmen and reached the Czarist Ministry of War. The Minister of War received our delegation which consisted of me and the rabbi of St. Petersburg, Rabbi Katenelnboygn. We argued:

When did you ever hear of spiritual leaders being taken to the front?

I spoke Russian fluently and with great pathos convinced him of our point of view. At first the minister wanted to evade the issue. But I stood up to him and finally he ordered the release of acting rabbis from military service but not the rabbis who were refugees. After much intervention we succeeded in releasing the refugees as well, but this happened under Kerensky's regime. Thanks to our intervention, among others, the great rabbi known by the title of his work Khazon Ish was released as well. He passed away not long ago in Israel.

During Kerensky's regime we held elections throughout Russia for a Jewish constitution. I organized all the religious Jews and in the Minsk region and we acquired 11 mandates out of 17.

[Page 102]

At the end of 1917, when Minsk was occupied by the Germans, the linen merchant Avrom Avigdor Obershteyn came from Zhetl and took me and my family home.

We Bought the Electricity Plant

During the war the Germans installed an electricity plant in Zhetl. Now that they were retreating they decided to take it with them. I called a meeting and we decided to buy it from the German county department. We collected the money, bought the plant and chose Yisroel Ozer Borishansky as manager.

The Bandit Plague

Meanwhile Russian deserters were gathering in Liftshansk Putche. We later learned there were not as many as we thought. In total around 90 men. However they spread fear as if they numbered in the thousands. They would pitilessly rob and kill peasants, Jews living in the villages and people passing through.

One day, Shmuel Kovesdky from Nokrishok brought me a letter from the bandits. In the letter they demanded Zhetl pay them 120 thousand ruble within the week. If not they threatened an attack. I immediately called a large meeting which was attended by Reb Avrom the starch maker, Reb Zhame Dunetz, Reb Moishe Tentzer, Reb Moishe Ruven Mordkovsky, Reb Yisroel Ozer Borishansky, Reb Hertz Leyb Kaplinsky, Reb Menakhem Vernikovsky, Reb Avrom Moishe Kravetz, Reb Yosl (the painter), Reb Mordkhai Leybovitch, Reb Shabsai Shushan, Reb Wolf Izraelit and many other important householders whose names I do not remember. We decided: 1) to mobilize all the Jewish retired soldiers. 2) to call for a Jewish excommunication with black candles and blowing of the shofar, and to oblige every Jew in Zhetl to pay into the community fund 10% of his cash and 6% of his merchandise.

In order to achieve this we put out a box and every Jew in Zhetl had from 8 in the morning until 8 at night to put his payment in an envelope and place it in the box. We also warned people to calculate the true amount they owed before God. We ordered poor people to throw in empty envelopes.

This act brought us a colossal amount because there was not one Jew who did not pay his share. We sent Alter Bom, Nakhman Gal and a few others with this money to buy weapons. We distributed the weapons among 300 Jewish retired soldiers and ordered the Christian Gruner, a former Russian officer with Gypsy roots, to do military exercises with our armed "army" every Tuesday and Friday.

Peasants who came to the market saw everything and informed the bandits who then sent me a second letter, where they demanded an answer to their first letter. I answered them like this:

Actually, you should all be home. The war ended a long time ago. The least you can do is go home. Anyone lacking money can come to us and we will help him with expenses.

As an answer to my letter the bandits attacked Bielitze and robbed their stores. Right after they sent us a third letter and threatened we would face the same end as Bielitze.

The Polish police liquidating a gang of robbers
active around Zhetl

[Page 103]

Also this time we were not afraid. We divided the town into four regions, placed 30 of our soldiers in each region, and they did tours of duty all night. We organized a headquarters with a telephone and were ready for battle.

We lived in this atmosphere all winter. The bandits declared a blockade on us and would not allow any agricultural products into town. We, understandably, were afraid to go to the villages to make our purchases.

Salvation came faster than we imagined. It happened like this: the Bolsheviks were nearing Zhetl, they were already in Novoredok. The Poles were stationed in Dertchin. The bandits calculated that if the Poles would be victorious they would kill them as Russians and communists. So they reached an agreement with the Bolsheviks. A political instructor went to the bandits in the forest and advised them on how to retreat.

A few days later, accompanied by Bolshevik authorities, they marched through Zhetl. They prepared a meal for them in the community and then sent them to Novoredok where they were beaten with chains and shot. This is how our story of the bandits ended and the admirable self defence of Zhetl's Jews. Immediately after our army disbanded.

The Audacious Attack of the Poles on Zhetl

It was Purim. The Bolsheviks were stationed in Zhetl. At dawn I heard violent shooting in town and right after a knock on my door. A Jewish militia told me Poles and Bolsheviks were shooting at the marketplace and the Polish commandant ordered I should come to the marketplace. If not he will order shooting in the Jewish homes.

I immediately went to the marketplace and found the Polish commandant at Wolf Dvoretsky's hotel. The commandant ordered me to get him 50 wagons and breakfast. When I asked how many men we needed to prepare breakfast for he did not respond. Later I learned there were only 12 men. They attacked suddenly, and chased out 200 Bolshevik soldiers who were staying in garrisons in Zhetl. In order not to divulge the secret of their strength, they did not answer my question about how many men needed breakfast.

Meanwhile, I sent our beadle from the old House of Study, Reb Leyzer Mordkhai to mobilize the wagons in which the Poles loaded the ammunition they captured from the Bolsheviks.

They did not eat the breakfast we prepared, and in the midst of great chaos and confusion decided to leave Zhetl. However, before they left Zhetl they ordered me to call for a prohibition and oblige Zhetl Jews to surrender the weapons that belonged to the armed Jewish defence.

I attempted to clarify the matter, but they did not want to hear my arguments and threatened me that if I didn't obey their order they would take me together with the loaded wagons. I knew very well what that meant.

I escaped their hands and went to the House of Study. Even though it was Purim, the place was empty. Jews were not praying and not eating. Meanwhile the Polish soldiers left and we breathed more freely.

When the wagon drivers returned they told us the Poles took Bolshevik prisoners with them. They released the Christians but shot all the Jews in the village of Khadzhelan.

Zhetl Without a Regime

In the meantime Zhetl was left without authorities. We lived in great fear. Who knows who will attack us next? We called a large meeting and decided to collect money for problems that were sure to arise. We also ordered everyone who had wine, whisky or weapons, to bury them. Everyone was also ordered to hand over the decided amount of cigarettes. If a soldier would ask for cigarettes, he should be sent to the rabbi.

In those days, groups of Polish soldiers would come to Zhetl every couple of days. One of these groups, due to a denunciation, arrested the daughter of Reb Shmuel Mirsky allegedly because she was a communist.

Wolf Dvoretsky explained to me she could be released through a bribe. I went to the Polish commandant. Life then did not play a role and I dared to give the commandant an envelope with money. He took it and left.

A few hours later Reb Wold Dvoretsky returned and told me the commandant was talking about releasing the girl, but he wanted me to come back.

[Page 104]

When I came to the commandant he honoured me with his moralizing as to why Jews are Bolsheviks and wanted my opinion of the Mirsky girl.

Before I had a chance to respond he explained that if I signed a document stating that she was not and will not be a Bolshevik, he would free her. I had doubts if I could commit myself to the fact that she would never be a Bolshevik, but I obliged and saved a Jewish daughter.

The Black Passover Seder

We managed to observe the first Seder in 1919. During the second Seder Polish legionnaires marched through Zhetl. They planned an attack on the Bolsheviks 12 kilometres from Zhetl. While marching through Zhetl the soldiers demanded whisky and cigarettes. Our police, who were placed on all the streets told them we do not have whisky but they can get cigarettes at the rabbi's. Understand, after this announcement, the soldiers did not allow me to conduct the Seder. A row of 100 soldiers snaked around my house. Each one received 6 cigarettes for one ruble. The price was symbolic and I wanted to emphasize that Jewish property is not arbitrary and we don't give it away for free. A cashier sat in my house and a second person distributed the cigarettes.

That night I ran out of cigarettes. I sent for more, but getting to my house was not easy. The cigarettes were passed down the row from hand to hand until I received them. From time to time a soldier rebelled – complaining – only 6 cigarettes? I would explain it would be unfair if one would receive a lot and another, nothing.

And this is how, instead of leading a Seder I spent the whole night handing out cigarettes. At dawn, the Poles ran away. On their way out they broke window panes in a few houses on Novoredok Street and shot Yenkl Ebes.

This case left a difficult impression on the town. The next morning a Polish officer came to me to ask forgiveness for this act. Of course I had to forgive, but I did give the officer a little taste of my moralizing.

We Organized a Bread Action

Until this time the record books of Zhetl were looked after by Reb Moishe Shatzkes. After he died the Jewish community council decided I should now be responsible. Controlling the record books I now ascertained that during the German occupation 350 Zhetl Jews died of stomach typhus. As you know, stomach typhus is a direct result of hunger. I then decided to alleviate hunger in Zhetl.

To achieve this goal I set up a cooperative whose goal was to distribute 4 kilograms of bread per person every week for a cheap price. I placed Yakomovitsky, the owner of the mill in Shilevonk as head of the cooperative. Together with him and Yisroel Kaplinsky, I would go to the surrounding villages to buy wheat at cheap prices, mill it into flour, and bake and distribute bread. This is how I alleviated hunger in Zhetl.

At the same time an office opened in Slonim to distribute American help for the starving population. I became friends with the manager (I don't recall his name) and began to bring goods to Zhetl: wheat flour, potatoes, rice, sugar and oil. Twice a week I would travel with the wagon drivers Hilke and Notke to Slonim and return with wagons filled with goods. With the produce I brought we opened a children's kitchen and served warm tasty food to Jewish children.

The Christians in town grew jealous and sent the priest to Slonim for produce. He did not agree to go and in the end they asked me to bring products for them as well and allow their children to enjoy our kitchen as well.

One fine morning I received news that there were two wagons of wheat flour for us in Slonim. Fetching two wagons of flour was no small feat. Firstly – where to find the required amount of money? And secondly – how do we mobilize so many carts?

Finally I collected money from Jews and Christians, organized the carts and set out for Slonim. With me were Reb Shmuel Mirsky, two militias and the priest.

It was a difficult trip. From Kazlayshchine we travelled accompanied by Polish soldiers who were shooting recklessly. When I asked the priest to calm them down he replied he was also afraid of them. We finally arrived in Slonim, devastated and exhausted.

On our return home, peasants were stealing our bags of flour. I stopped the wagons, climbed up on a cart of flour and said to the peasants in these words: I understand you are hungry and haven't seen wheat flour for a long time. But understand, this flour is for children. I ask of you, return the flour and we will, here on the field, cook a big pot of "Zatcherke" (noodles like farfel) for you. And that is what we did. The peasants returned the flour and we cooked a "Zatcherke" for everyone.

[Page 105]

We Fought for a City Council in Zhetl

When the Poles took power in Zhetl, they felt embarrassed. On one hand they wanted to show they were democratic, on the other hand they did not realize that we comprised the majority in town. They also could not count on the Christian population as they were Belorussian and a minority in Zhetl.

Therefore, in principle they were forced to nominate a city council with a Jewish majority. This Jewish majority was like a thorn in their side and they decided to incorporate Zhetl into the township. And that is what happened.

We however decided not to switch to their agenda on this decision. We went to Slonim and stated our case that we didn't want our taxes to go to the surrounding villages. We wanted our money to support our city. Our complaint was heard and Zhetl was declared an independent unit headed by a magistrate within the framework of the township. The magistrate nominated was a local Pole by the name of Yaroshevsky along with a council. We however, did not relent and explained to the authorities we would like to elect a magistrate and council and don't approve of a nomination. Our candidate for magistrate was Motl Man.

The Defamation of Motl Man

In order to discredit our candidate the Poles devised a false accusation. They found witnesses who said that during the war between the Poles and the Bolsheviks, Motl Man and two other Jews disarmed Polish legionnaires.

On the basis of this statement, Motl Man was arrested and threatened with a severe punishment. I travelled to Warsaw and with the help of Senator Mendelson from "Agudas Yisroel", I brought it to the attention of the Polish liberal Professor Kanopke and he agreed to take on Motl Man's defence. The Jewish lawyer from Vilna, Yosef Tchernikhov also agreed to participate, free of charge.

The trial took place in Slonim. Under cross examination from our defence the accusers became confused and in the end admitted this was a false accusation. Our lawyer Yosef Tchrnikhov renounced the accusers and Motl Man was freed.

I remember in his closing remarks Tchernikhov said the following:

"They say Bismarck falsified documents in order to unite Germany. For something important, everything is worth the effort. However, it is far from important and undistinguished to devise a false accusation in order to avoid the election of a Jewish magistrate. I believe, the time will come, when a Jewish president will be elected in Poland and no one defame him."

We Fought Against Grabsky's Methods

The period when Grabsky was finance minister in Poland is well known. In those years Poland wanted to choke Jewish business with taxes. There was also a little "Grabsky" in Slonim. He totally ruined Jewish business in the region and there was nothing we could do to him.

One day he came to Zhetl for an inspection. He went from store to store inspecting finances and inventories. One storekeeper was not prepared. The inspector wrote an official report. When the storekeeper, on one foot, in the presence of the inspector prepared a statement (just imagine how much merchandise he had), he rejected it due to an inaccuracy and charged him a heavy fine which he had to pay on the spot.

This was not the only case. Thousands of such cases happened all over the country and there was a huge outcry. The central merchants union in Warsaw organized a convention of all merchants in order to offer advice on the situation.

The Zhetl merchant's union lead by Yitzkhak Kaplinsky asked if I would represent them at the convention. I was the only rabbi and the only Yiddish speaker at the convention. In the presence of Polish minister of commerce and the leaders of Jewish businesses Vishnitsky and Shereshevsky I explained:

How does a rabbi come to business? The reason is in order to permit Yiddish to be spoken at a Jewish convention. Then I told a story about a Jew who came to his rabbi with an emergency.

[Page 106]

He had eaten dairy immediately after meat. The rabbi said to him:

"How can you do such a thing, young man".

The person in question replied: "Rabbi, I came to you for something completely different: I need to know if I am now considered meat or dairy?"

I want to know the same thing about my poor little store in Zhetl. Is it meat or dairy? If he did not have his list of inventory, how could he be punished for an inaccuracy? And if he had it, then why is he punished for not having it? And secondly: I understand, taxes are demanded straight from the citizen as he is evaluated, however the solution is not incumbent on a punishment. Punishment should not be demanded if it is submitted in a reclamation.

My speech made a great impression. It was immediately translated into Polish. The next morning I participated with Vishlitsky and Shershevsky in the delegation to the finance minister.

Our intervention was successful. A few months later a decree was published saying fines can not be demanded before considering the reclamation. What made us even happier was the fact that we got rid of our own little Grabsky.

We Renovated the Bathhouse

At first the bathhouse in Zhetyl belonged to the burial society. At this opportunity I will say a few words about the society. Belonging to the burial society in Zhetl was a great distinction. This honour was inherited, passed down from father to son. A Jew could not simply join. The society was known for its banquets. I believe throughout the year they would hold 7–8 banquets. I did not like this very much and once during a banquet I gave a sermon with a bit of moralizing. I will not repeat it here, but anyone interested can read in in my book "Ideas and Words", part A.

The burial society sold the bathhouse to a village Jew named Yudl from Podvelik. Besides a one time down payment, the burial society promised him at a banquet he would have to pay a yearly payment of 50 ruble and the rabbi Reb Yosef Zvi Hirsh Dvoretsky of blessed memory made a declaration prohibiting the building of a second bathhouse.

When I became chief rabbi of Zhetl, Yudl from Podvelik was already running the bathhouse. Understandably, he was not concerned with modern installations, comforts or sanitary conditions.

While I was chief rabbi I was inundated with many complaints about the sanitary conditions, but there was nothing I could do. Had there not been a prohibition I may have decided to build a new bathhouse.

A Story of Swamps

Just off the highway to Lida there was a meadow overgrown with weeds. The peasants in the area knew the meadow belonged for many generations to the Jewish community of Zhetl, and only Jews were permitted to have their horses graze there. However because of the swamps the pasture was really bad. People and animals would often sink.

In those years I became a member of YEKAPO's (a Jewish social service agency) central office in Vilna. Among other things they supported Jewish farmers. At one meeting I put this issue on the agenda. YEKAPO showed interest and decided to send engineers who worked out a plan to drain out the water through canals. Unemployed boys from Zhetl carried out this work. We achieved a few goals. Firstly, Zhetl now had a good pasture for its animals; secondly we dried up the swamps which would spread plagues; and thirdly, we provided work for the unemployed.

We Planned to Move Zhetl

During my time as chief rabbi I saw Zhetl Jews were suffering greatly from tuberculosis. The reason was clear. Zhetl is situated in a valley, on the filthy small Pomerayke River.

[Page 107]

I never understood why that spot was chosen for settlement. However the fact is I decided to look for new healthy territory to build new homes. Such land existed on the sandy hills behind Zalmen Green's house.

I decided to bring this to the attention of the Polish authorities and suggested they divide up the land into housing lots. The authorities liked my plan.

They asked us to work out the division plan. We invested a lot of money and with the help of YEKAPO worked out the plans we had agreed to supply. The authorities approved our plans but to our great disappointment decided to distribute the lots among Polish legionnaires. Only two Jews obtained lots on this property, Moishe Ruven Mordkovsky and Leyzer Mordkhai, the beadle's son. This is how this fiasco ended after we invested so much money and energy.

Directors and pupils of the Zhetl Talmud Torah 1921

We Renovated the Talmud Torah

The Zhetl Talmud Torah was situated on the bank of the Pomeryake River near the old Jewish cemetery. The old Talmud Torahs were very different from todays. Firstly, wealthier Jews would not send their children there as they believed the Talmud Torah was for poor children; secondly, very little was taught.

The situation was the same in Zhetl, although the teachers were very good. There was an excellent teacher for beginners, Yosele Mendes. He had a special method. He would teach each boy separately for half an hour resulting in great success. For the older boys the teacher was Yudl the ritual slaughterer's son in law, Yenkl. He taught the bible and succeeded at this work. In those years wealthier families would send their children to a private tutor. Those tutors in Zhetl were Reb Yisroel Khonen and Reb Noyekh Eli. They both produced great results, a generation of well prepared boys who went on to study in Yeshivas.

However the Zhetl Talmud Torah had another disadvantage. The building was sinking and was neglected. I made use of my work at the Medico Sanitorium in Bialystok and got them interested in our Talmud Torah and actually received a large sum of money from them. We also received help from the rabbi Reb Khaim Ozer Grodensky from Vilna and the Mrs Reding, formerly from Zhetl, now living in Australia. With their help it was decided to rebuild the Talmud Torah.

Since the construction cost a lot of money I decided to organize people to help with the work.

One day, during prayers, I called everyone together from all the Houses of Study and announced the poor condition of the Talmud Torah and our plan to rebuild. Actually, many of those praying came with me to help with the work.

[Page 108]

A short time later the Talmud Torah was renovated and we now had four large rooms.

Evening Courses for girls in the Talmud Torah

First row: Eliyusha Lusky, Soreh Levoranchik, Peshe Dvoretzky, Frume Shilovitsky, Yekhezkl Garber
Second row: Sonia Shilovitsky, ...Frume Gankovsky, Etl Mordkovsky, Teacher Golda, Leah Rabinovitch, Eltshe Kogan, Khane Rashkin, Soreh Mayevsky
Third row: Khaya Rokhl Senderovsky, Libe Yoslevitch, Roze Daykhovsky, Dvoyre Rashkin, Shayna Berman, Feygl Lidsky, Etl Rozenfeld, ...
Last row: Hirshl Rabetz, ...Yehushua Lisky, Krinsky, Motl Mirsky, Yudl Lusky

We also hired new teachers: Ginzburg and Eliezer Rozenfeld.

As a result of this reorganization, Reb Menakhem Vernikovsky and Reb Moishe Tentzer registered and taught many boys. I would come to test the boys. This stimulated the teachers and encouraged them to keep their teaching at a high level.

At the same time the problem arose about educating girls. There were not yet any Beys Yakov schools (religious school for girls). I decided to organize evening classes for girls in the Talmud Torah. From 4 o'clock in the afternoon until 8 o'clock in the evening 180 girls received a Jewish traditional education.

Goodbye

This is a short and partial summary of events in the communal life in Zhetl during the 18 years of my rabbinate.

I am happy that all the memories and events have found a deliverer and will reflect the suffering, the unity and the communal undertakings of the small, poor but spiritually rich Jewish community: Zhetl.

Evening School for girls at the Talmud Torah

[Page 109]

During the German Occupation [a]

by Yosef Vinyetzky of Blessed Memory

Translated by Janie Respitz

As it is known, during the German occupation the population was in great need of food. In this respect Zhetl did not lag behind other cities and towns that were occupied and it is possible they suffered more as the breadwinner of Zhetl, the German county supervisor, was the type of person who spoke a lot and did nothing. Due to these traits the local Jews crowned him with the name: "Miracle Worker".

On the first day of every month he was supposed to distribute to the local citizens' committee a set amount of rye and other products for the population that should have amounted to a half pound of bread daily per person. But instead of distributing these life sustaining goods on the first of every month he would delay it by a few days and would deduct the amount of food for the days missed claiming the people already survived those days and no longer needed those portions.

Naturally the members of the citizens' committee opposed this and they would begin to bargain with the supervisor. However, given that the amounts were previously established, he would bargain a bit.

The Spiritual Life

As a result the Jewish population was satiated with spiritual nourishment. The Jewish population had never before shown such an interest in cultural matters as during this time of hunger. The German authorities distributed for free German books, and a newspaper from Bialystok (published in German, Polish and Yiddish) which people read with great enthusiasm.

The Jewish youth opened two locales: a dramatic – literary club and a Zionist group. The members of the first one were mainly young workers. The second, besides Zionists, included almost all the wealthier residents in town. Both groups had their own libraries which were filled every evening with Jewish male and female readers who would either take home books or read there. Besides this, they held meetings, literary discussion and the like.

Most people went to the Zionist locale which was right in the middle of town. Every Friday night local intellectuals would hold lectures on many issues, but mainly on Zionism. The evenings ended with the writer of these lines reciting his own humorous poems for the audience.

Saturday night would be a checkers evening. The leaders of the Zionist group would distribute a weekly journal called ("The Friend") which contained literary articles, stories in Hebrew and Yiddish and a humour section. That section mainly reflected life during the occupation.

Due to technical issues only one copy of "The Friend" was printed and it would be read aloud to the audience. During a fire which was set by the Polish authorities, all editions of "The Friend" were burned together with the desire of the local youth for a cultural life.

Zhetl's Enlighteners and Writers

Our town produced doctors, engineers (the Namiyat brothers), authors of enlightened books, moral teachings and journalists. The following were among the enlightened: Menakhem Mendl Merlinsky, (the father in law of the Bialystok writer Peysakh Kaplan), who was a teacher in Zhetl for many years, Avrom Shalkovitch (Ben – Avigdor) – the founder of the publishing houses "Toshiah" and "Central", Yehoshua Aysnshtat – Barzilay.

I would like to mention a local writer Asher Vikhnes' (Shushan). His wife Vikhne was a woman of valour. She would run their store and their inn while he sat in the House of Study learning all day, allowing him to become very knowledgeable in bible and Hebrew grammar. In his older years he became a teacher and taught his pupils bible and grammar which he explained in an original manner. Not long before he died he published a book called "The Story of Shushan" –containing biblical explanations.

[Page 110]

Saniye the teacher (Natanel Patzovsky) in our town excelled even more with his writings. He was an exceptional teacher of young children who later in life wrote books of moral teachings, particularly dealing with the after life. He was also a preacher who travelled from town to town giving passionate sermons in Houses of Study, offering moral teachings. He would sell his books which after hearing him speak, the audience would buy enthusiastically; in many towns, artisans would form groups that would get together between afternoon and evening prayers and read his works.

His brother Mikhl Dantchik's (Patzovsky) also taught young children. He devoted himself to reading books on Kabbalah (Jewish mysticism) of which he had a large library. For many years he wrote with beautiful calligraphy handwriting, in half rounded lines, books about Kabbalah, but due to poverty they were never published.

Four Old Men

From the 4 old men in our town, Meir the Stagecoach (Orlinsky – 100 years old), Areh the carpenter (Namyiat); Noyekh Eliyahu the teacher (Levit) and Aryeh the musician (Levit), who had lots of sons, daughters, daughters in law, sons in law, grandchildren and great grandchildren, Arye the musician deserves special recognition. In his nineties besides being a musician he also worked in masonry, he built almost all the walls in Zhetl.

He also understood the so –called musician's language (as seen in Sholem Aleichem's "Stempenyu" chapter 3) which had its own unique expressions. For example: a soldier was called a "cop", and they had their own words for hat, meat, girls, brides etc...they even had their own expressions not used by others.

Editorial Board of the Zhetl Journal "The Friend" 1918

Seated from right to left: Efraim Kharmoni, Solomon Lubtchansky, Yosef Vinyetzky, A. Sideransky
Standing: M. Bender, Mikhl Rabinovitch, Nekhemieh Razovsky, Yakov Zimelevitch, Shmuel Shapiro, unknow, Shloimeh Khaim Vernikovsky

Original footnote:

     a.   This article was published by the author in "The YEKAPO Chronicle", 1926.

[Page 111]

An Appeal to Zhetl Jews in America

by Menachem Vernikovsky

Translated by Janie Respitz

Citizens of Zhetl now in America!

By chance I am now in Vilna and with the permission of our citizens' committee I am reaching out to you with this appeal:

Whomever among you has parents, children, a wife, sisters, brothers or extended family – help them!

A small portion of us have enough bread, but the rest, mainly those who earlier received their livelihood from America are suffering from outright hunger. Those who are well off – and there are very few – have to support their families that live in other cities (for example, I am one of the few who has bread but I must send it to my father in law in Vilna who is suffering from hunger).

Also try to help our charitable foundations which have been organized and are controlled by department representatives and the regional supervisor, namely the Jewish People's Kitchen which distributes more than 200 hot meals a day (one meal costs 10 fenig and the poorest receive it for free).

We also designated a weekly handout for the poor which gives financial aid every week to more than 150 households (the aid consists of 2 – 10 marks a week per household); we are also supporting many homeless people from the nearby evacuated cities: Lubitch, Karelitch and others, the Jewish Folk School (the former Talmud Torah), where more than 100 children learn bible, the holy tongue (Hebrew), commentaries, translation of the bible in Yiddish, arithmetic and other subjects, (poor children do not pay tuition). Don't forget brothers, many of you studied in this Talmud Torah.

Until now the Jewish Aid Union in Berlin helped support us with 100 marks per month. Last month we received only half that amount and do not have the means to run our foundations. Every week our donors decrease and the number of those in need increases.

Soon it will be Peysakh (Passover) which demands extra expenses. Just as we did last year, this year we will also have to supply over 60 workers in the region around our city with food as we cannot let them eat food that is not kosher for Peysakh.

Whomever among you will be called up to the Torah, to pray in the synagogue on the Sabbath should awaken the others spiritually.

I hope my words will not be lost.

You can send money to my address or to the address of the greatest businessman who does so much for our charitable foundations, Hertz Leyb Kaplinsky.

May God protect you and your families,

Your fellow countryman,

Menachem Vernikovsky

My address: (Written in Polish) Manachim Wernikovsky Kreis Zdzieciol Slonimer Str. 120

The address of H. L. Kaplinsky: (Written in Polish): Hertz Leib Kaplinski Rohotner Str. 5526

This appeal was published by Menakhem Vernikovsky in "Di Letste Nayes" (The Latest News), no. 32, issues for the year 1916, published in Vilna.

Published by: Moishe Tzinovitch

Sponsors of Zhetl's Children's Kitchen during W.W. I

Seated in the first row: Mordkhai Sokolovsky, Zvia Kovensky, Mirl from Lubitch, Eli Bensky, Khaneh Lifshitz, Soreh Rabinovitch
Seated in the second row: Yente Kaplinsky, Efraim Rabinovitch, Soreh Moindl Kaplinsky, Berl Dvoretsky, Etl Man, Dovod Savitsky, Khaneh Rozhke Roznov, Yehoshua Dvoretsky
Standing in the third row: Gdalia Shvedsky, Yisroel Binyamini, Libe Kastilansky, Khaim Kaplinsky, Henia Veynshteyn, unknown, Yitzkhak Leybovitch

[Page 112]

Only Memorial Books Have Remained

by Avrom Zak (Buenos Aires)

Translated by Janie Respitz

You have asked me to send you my memories of Zhetl, but is this at all possible after a 4–5 day visit?

I can jot down a few details about the German occupation.

I was living in Grodno at the time. In those times Grodno was somewhat of a cultural centre as we were practically cut off from Vilna and Warsaw due to social restrictions.

Together with me in Grodno was my friend Leyb Naydus, the magnificent poet who brought so much newness and beauty to Yiddish poetry. He was extremely creative during these years in Grodno, but unfortunately he died in December 1918.

Avrom Zak

In those days we were both active in the society of "Yiddish Art". This is where literary evenings and concerts took place. They also published a Yiddish newspaper and there was a library. We would give lectures in Grodno as well as in other towns in the area.

I was invited to Zhetl through a communication with the local young leadership, one of the Dvoretzky brothers. On that same tour I visited Sokolke, Skidl, Luna, Novogrudek, Iviye and Lida.

Before this I gave my lectures in Grodno at the "Yiddish Art" club.

One lecture I gave,"Yiddish the Language of our Culture" caused a heated discussion. It took three evenings until all those opponents registered had a chance to be heard. People came from all political movements, Zionists, Bundists and ordinary Jews: Hillel Issar Yanovsky, Noyakh Bas, Yosef Lipnik and others. My lecture was a bit aggressive against the fanatics who dreamt of Hebraising the diaspora and against the deniers of Yiddish and Yiddish culture. There were such people when the dream of the State of Israel was still so far away.

In Zhetl I had one or two opponents. One was a young man with fine diction whose name I don't recall. The discussion was not drastic and we had a calm conversation.

My second lecture in Zhetl was on a purely literary theme: "About Modern Yiddish Literature". (About Avrom Reyzen, Y. M. Veysenberg, Yoine Rozenfeld and others).

The lectures took place on holidays. It was Sukkot 1918, in a primitive hall, with a large audience, mostly young.

The town left an impression on me like most Lithuanian small Jewish towns. There was a sincere group of young people who longed for and wove dreams. A youth who were attached to secular and religious learning.

Where are they now, my young dreamers?

My reception was warm. The group of activists and organizers took care of me. They took me for walks through the streets in and around town. I felt as if I was in my home town, Amdur.

How similar each one was to the other, these Lithuanian Jewish towns. Similar with their streets, wooden huts, and their poverty. Even the landscape was of the same genre with no extravagant surprises.

My farewell evening left an impression on me. It took place at the end of Simkhas Torah in a private home of one of the community activists. There were many people. Food was served on a long table without a tablecloth: herring, black bread, and bottles of beer. This was during the days of the occupation where dire poverty could be felt everywhere and black bread and herring were considered a feast…

But the holiday spirit was there. The crowd sang a vast repertoire of folk songs. I particularly remember the heartfelt sadness of the melody of one song, which everyone around the long table sang:

"As the joyful festival is over and leaving us"

The next day I left Zhetl and that melody was stuck in my head.

Now, after the Holocaust, we repeat those lyrics but now in mourning. Gone are the "Joyful festivals" together with those beautiful, sincere young people, together with the poor Jewish towns, together with the Jews.

Only memorial books have remained.

[Page 113]

During the First World War

by Moishe Mirsky (Montreal)

Translated by Janie Respitz

The First World War broke out at the end of July 1914. I remember it fell on Tisha B'Av. There were red posters hanging in the streets to mobilize the reserves. The next day, which was Saturday, when families would normally go out for a stroll, they went instead to say goodbye to the young men who were being mobilized and had to leave for their meeting point in Slonim that same day.

The day evolved into a sad day. The parting of two families left a particularly difficult impression on me; Motl Medvetsky and Moishe Mendl Leyzerovitch. Their families wailed as they said goodbye. That day is difficult to forget.

A few weeks later there were already notices in town about fallen soldiers. I don't remember all the names but those which have remained in my memory are: Feytl Sokolovsky, (Itche the cripple's brother), Khatzkl Solomansky, Abbe the carpenter's son, and Shmuel whose last name I don't remember. I do remember he had a nickname. They called him Shmuel with the nasal voice.

Moishe Mirsky

Before the Evacuation of the Russian Army

In the fall of 1915 when the Russian army was already in East Prussia, near Goldob, the Germans began their offense. The attack happened quickly. The Russian authorities mobilized the Jews of Zhetl to dig trenches near the Nieman River, in Peskovtzi on the road to Slonim, in Latushi, Shundri and other places.

A terrible panic captured the town. Many Jews and Christians left their homes for central Russia. Over the next few weeks, train wagons full of refugees arrived in Zhetl. Every day there were more and more soldiers on the streets. They drove away herds of cows and horses they didn't want to leave behind for the Germans. Many refugees remained in Zhetl too afraid to travel any further. The front was nearing, they were digging hide outs, frightened of the battle.

Yom Kippur fell on the Sabbath, and the following morning, Sunday, the last remnants of the Russian army departed. The Cossacks appeared that night. They wanted to have some fun and set fire to the town. However among us there were bold Jews who knew how to handle the Russians. They managed to appease them with a bribe of a few hundred ruble. The mediators were: Yisroel Ozer Borishansky, Mayrim Epshteyn and my father Dov Mirsky. The Cossacks then tore up the bridges, set fire to the sawmill and left town. Monday morning, September 1915, Zhetl was occupied by the Germans.

The Germans Occupy Zhetl

The Germans did not treat the Jews too badly. The town commandant Kretchmer organized a civilian militia and according to the proportion of the population, the majority were Jews. The police commander then was Mayrim Epshteyn, the mayor was Leyb Lusky (Leyzhe Feyge Mirke's son) who immigrated to Argentina before the last World War and died in 1951.

Due to Germany's heavy fighting in France, in Verdun, they withdrew their main forces from the east and the front remained between Lyubich and Minsk, approximately 100 kilometres from our town. All the towns such as: Lyubich, Kareliych, and Novoyelne were forced to evacuate. Our town was the first on the front line to establish a civilian authority. The aforementioned towns belonged to the front line and their Jews moved to Zhetl.

**Leyb Lusky of blessed memory and his wife
Beyleh**

[Page 114]

Zhetyl then had ten thousand residents plus two thousand Germans, a hunting regiment and a power column who transported products twice a day in trucks from Novoyelne to the front. Food products in Zhetl were cheap because free business was forbidden and the train traffic was restricted. Therefore all the products from the big cities were very expensive and extensive smuggling began.

The Germans said the Russians allowed this to happen and accepted bribes. We obviously did sweet business with them. People from Zhetl supplied products to: Novogrudek, Slonim, Baranovitch, Bialystok and Vilna. This is why the Jews of Zhetl did not live too badly during the occupation. The youth of Zhetl organized very active, benevolent and cultural work. Two inexpensive kitchens were opened in town where food was distributed three times a day to refugees. We also founded a committee which distributed food products to the poor.

After the Resignation of Kaiser Wilhelm

At the end of 1917 news arrived in Zhetl that Kaiser Wilhelm resigned. Our town experienced stressful days. The military took over the authority and a soldier's council was formed which took away swords and epaulets from the officers.

The situation in town was very difficult a few days prior to their evacuation. I remember on a market day the Germans took out the horses to sell. The peasants began to rebel and shout that the horses belonged to them. The peasants angrily accused the Germans. A local town dweller agitated. Frightful shooting ensued. Within minutes the marketplace was empty. The dead were lying in the marketplace. Among them was the agitator, a big anti Semite whose name was Kostush Kovalevsky. There were no Jewish casualties that day.

The next day the Germans left Zhetl. The town was left for a few weeks without authorities. A self defence was organized. Later, a small group of Bolsheviks arrived.

The Bolsheviks stayed for a few months. The Polish nobility chased them out of the region. The leader of the Poles was a guy named Syemosheko who was a known anti Semite.

Zhetl members of the German administration during the First World War

Seated: Peshke Izraelit, Mikhl Rabinovitch, Hidnke Mirsky
Standing: Dovid Savitsky, Eli Bensky, Dovod Vilner…Khaim Dvoretsky…,…,…

Syemoshko first arrived with his gang in Zhetl on Purim at 6 o'clock in the morning. They gave an order forbidding anyone to go out into the street. Syemoshko himself shot a Jew on Novoredok Street. He had no idea what was going on in town and left his home to go to the synagogue to pray. This was Yakov Senderovsky, a butcher (Yenkl Ebes). Later they went to Jewish homes looking for weapons and communists in hiding. They captured a few young people (the majority managed to hide), and brought them to Shabsai Shushan's stall where they were beaten and tortured.

The well known nobleman Stravinsky lived not too far from Zhetl. A delegation of Jews went to him and Mrs. Stravinsky brought a letter to Syemoshko. She then sent her estate director together with Yisroel Ozer Borishansky with a larger sum of money and the harassment ended.

I would like to mention that in the vicinity of Zhetl there were very wealthy estates with whom Zhetl Jews carried out many business transactions. They would also, when necessary help us out with large donations. However the most respectable and honest friend was the old nobleman Stravinsky from Nokrishki.

From One Authority to Another

[Page 115]

From 1919 until 1920 we endured many problems. Our town went from one authority to another a few times, from the Poles to the Bolsheviks and back. We did not suffer under the Bolsheviks but the Poles lived it up.

Bandits arrived in Zhetl. They stole from homes and shops and beat up Jews.

A little later the Bolsheviks began their offensive on Warsaw. The Poles withdrew but continued to rob and steal from Jewish homes. When the Bolshevik military intelligence was at the entrance of the Novolyenie highway, two Polish soldiers remained at the other end of the highway near Slonim still rummaging through Jewish houses. Our youth made good use of this moment and disarmed the not yet satisfied robbers, honoured them in a fine way and let them go.

The Bolshevik army marched through our town on their way to Slonim – Bialystok, and we are again without authorities. However we were already well oriented on what to do under these circumstances. Our self defence was well organized however we were not left alone for long.

Pilsudsky organized an army in central Poland which defended Warsaw and began a great counter – offensive. In 1920 we were occupied by the Poles. The army went through. Only a city commandant remained with a sector of field gendarmes and this is when our new troubles began.

The Bandit Plague

As our region was often left without any authority, bandits would attack nearby villages at night. The attacks would take place on the Novolyenie highway where Jews from Zhetl would travel to the train and get robbed. Once during such an incident the bandits stopped the passengers but the driver managed to escape. Two Jews, Shmerl Feyvuzhinsky (the wagon driver) and Yudl Khaim Rashkin were severely wounded.

A second incident occurred when the bandits led the Jews off the highway into the Shelvanker forest, took their money and brutally attacked two girls. The money victims were: Avrom Moishe Kravetz and Yitzkhak Kaplinsky. There was another incident when they wounded Feyvl Zabitch who lives today in America.

The Jews of Zhetl reported these attacks to a higher authority. They sent in a punishment battalion headed by a certain Major Relsky. The city quickly befriended Major Relsky and he got rid of the bandits. I must say they did a masterful job and thanks to Major Relsky, within a few months our town was free of the bandit plague.

Under Polish Rule

The military authority left and was replaced with a civilian authority: a city high official and a police post. It was decided by a plebiscite if the town will be led by the township or by city hall. The Christians preferred the township since this meant they would pay less taxes. The Jews preferred a city hall. Since the Jews comprised a majority, the plebiscite decided to organize a city hall.

Due to their failure, the Christians could not rest and one of them, Francishek Reginievitch (the worst anti Semite in town) thought up a false accusation against the Jews. The victim was Motl Man (Avrom Patsovsky's grandson). In his accusation Reginievitch claimed that a few Zhetl Jews whose names he could not recall disarmed and killed a Polish soldier during their retreat. What he could confirm was that Motl Man was the leader and murderer. In addition he provided two witnesses: Leonard Burdun and Hulnitsky, the two biggest drunks in town. A few days later Motl Man was arrested and sent to jail in Bialystok where he sat for a year until his trial.

The Jews of Zhetl could not calm down. Our rabbi, Reb Zalmen Saratzkin made some noise in Warsaw, calling for legal help. They sent the best lawyers for his trial.

One thing remained: to prepare the witnesses. This is when the priest in Zhetl intervened. He was a very fine man. He invited the two Christians over and made them promise they will handle themselves honestly, will not falsely swear on the bible and will tell the truth.

Yisroel Ozer Barishansky spent a week with these two drunks at Krashinsky's restaurant. After browbeating them he touched them up with a large sum of money.

The trial took place in Slonim. For two days they guarded the witnesses so the accuser could not browbeat them. Due to lack of evidence, and thanks to the defence, Motl Man was freed.

Later he became ill from grief and aggravation, and a year later, barely forty years old he ended his life.

[Page 116]

The Jewish Republic in Zhetl

by Efraim Hermoni of blessed memory

Translated by Judy Montel

This is not a joke, not one of the republics of "Shalom Aleichem," but an actual republic, i.e., independent government, that was elected by all of the Jewish inhabitants in secret elections, according to all of the rules of democracy with an armed force at its side. This republic was established in Zhetl after the First World War in 1918. And this is how it happened!

After the German Revolution, the military arm was broken. The Germans rapidly left the occupied countries, even though their military strength was still strong and the front was still holding. Overnight, fortune changed! The German gendarme, who just yesterday was walking the streets of the town with Prussian arrogance with a large hunting dog at his side, casting fear on the Jewish and Christian townspeople, overnight became helpless.

The great flight of the Germans from the occupied areas began. The Russians, who advanced after the retreating Germans, for some reason didn't dare to conquer Zhetl and the area around it. Also, the Poles, who were advancing from another direction, stayed a certain distance from the town. Thus, in Zhetl no ruler remained. The townspeople began to feel the lack of food and other supplies. On the one hand, it was not possible to travel to the villages to buy food, because deserters from the Russian army, who hid in the forests and in the nearby villages during all the years of the war, would attack passers-by, steal their belongings and at times also their lives. Fears of deserters and thieves attacking Zhetl itself grew as well, and the situation was very bad.

The Jewish townspeople talked amongst themselves about setting up local government, but the Christians in the town would not participate. Eventually, the Jews decided to elect a municipal government without the participation of the Christians. The elections took place according to all of the rules of democracy. The campaign was mainly between the United Zionist list and the United-Israel list. The spiritual leader of the United-Israel (Achdut Yisra'el) list was the rabbi of Zhetl at that time, Rabbi Reb Zalmen Sorotzkin who now lives in Israel. Rabbi Sorotzkin later became one of the pillars of the *Agudat-Yisrael* party in Poland. Besides these two lists there was also a list of the Yidishist circles and those who opposed Zionism.

The electoral campaign was very fierce. Dozens of meetings were held with speakers from all of the lists participating. Especially notable was the success of the speakers from the veteran Zionists: Reb Menachem Vernikovski OBM and Reb Aharon Herschel Langbort OBM.

The first was, in his time, a member of "Bnei Moshe," sensitive of spirit and of elegant thought, learned in Torah and wisdom. The second was an outstanding speaker, erudite and educated. These two veteran Zionists had a decisive influence on the townspeople. From the younger generation, especially successful were the sons of the two veteran Zionists: Shlomo-Chayim Vernikovsky OBM and Avraham Langbort OBM. From among the people of "Achdut Yisra'el" the group of younger men, certified to be rabbis, students of Reb Yozel, the Mussar teacher and amongst those, Reb Yitzchak Vaynshtein, currently living in Jerusalem.

[Page 117]

The elections led to victory for the Zionist list, which received the largest number of votes proportionally. In second place came "Achdut Yisra'el" and in last place the bloc of the YIdishists and anti-Zionists.

The Zionist Yisrael Kaplinsky was elected as chairman of the municipality. Moshe Bitenski, today (mid-1950s) the director of the Burea of the Keren Kayemet in Tel Aviv, was elected as treasurer. And I, author of these columns, was elected as director of the Municipal Economy. (All of these three were not long-time residents of Zhetl, but people who had recently come to the town due to the circumstances of the time. Bitenski, who had gone through the revolution in Russia, was considered an expert at elections and therefore was elected to be the chair of the election committee.)

The municipality received control of the power station there, got it working and promised light to the townspeople. We also did the preparatory work to take over the flour mill there. But our main concern was to ensure the well-being of the townspeople by setting up a municipal militia. By buying from the retreating Germans we were able to get hot and cold munitions for it. The militia, unlike the municipality, also included several Christians. Over time, we sent messengers to the closer and more distant villages to purchase supplies for the townspeople. Every delegation had several militiamen attached to it to protect it from attacks by the deserters and thieves. Once such an attack did take place on our convoy and in the battle, one of the attackers was killed. In order to take revenge for their loss, the deserters sent us notice that they would carry out an attack on the town. This forced us to strengthen the militia even more and to arm it. At the same time, we succeeded in ensuring supplies needed by the townspeople and first and foremost the distribution of bread that we had baked from the flour we had obtained in the villages, and life began to go on its usual course.

However, the days of our government did not last long. The Red Army approached Zhetl in the meantime. As it drew nearer, the leftist circles in the Jewish community began to transfer to the Communist Party. Also, a leader appeared for the Communist Party – a Christian who had operated underground for a long time and now appeared in the open and took over leadership. He was called by all "The Chairman." Communist power continued to grow. The main sign of this was the municipal militia going over to the communists and changing its name to "Battle Company."

Then we received an announcement that an "Association of the Representatives of the Workers and Farmers" had been formed in Zhetl, and that it demanded transfer of the town's government to it.

One of the evenings, a large Communist procession marched with red flags and the "Battle Company" at its head. With songs and shots fired in the air, the procession approached the municipality. The chair of the Communist Party, accompanied by several militiamen, entered the municipality and demanded that the governing of the town be transferred into their hands.

The Chairman of the municipality, Yisrael Kaplinsky, declared in response to this demand: "We were elected by the townspeople in democratic elections, and we see ourselves as responsible for this town and no one has the right to take from us the duties that the townspeople have assigned to us. However, since we cannot withstand your armed force, therefore we surrender to you and with strong protest hand over the governing of the town."

And indeed, after the militia – our armed force – went over to the communist side, in any case the government became concentrated in their hands, even without our official surrender.

And thus the Jewish Republic in Zhetl came to an end.

From One Rule to Another

Translated by Judy Montel

It was a very interesting episode that went on for about half a year. The German occupation forces had already left Zhetl, but no other ruling force had yet appeared in the town.

The first question that came up was: Who will protect the town? This question did not just concern the Jews of the town, but also the Christian population. In the forests surrounding Zhetl, Russians had gathered who had escaped being German prisoners of war and threatened the town with attack, robbery and looting.

This situation forced us to organize a defense that over time became the ruling force in the town. It is not easy to explain how a defense force came to be organized in a small Jewish town that was headed by a Christian, who, it became clear later on, was not a lover of Israel. However, this is a fact. The defense force numbered 40-50 members and was equipped with several dozen rifles, a few hand-guns, a box of grenades, and hundreds – perhaps even thousands of bullets.

Interestingly, the defense force in Zhetl did not become a dictatorship, on the contrary, it allowed the Jews of Zhetl, according to all of the rules of democracy, to elect a town council, which is worthy of praise for the arrangements they put in place.

Everything was going nicely until the Soviet Army appeared on the horizon, planning to conquer the town. Youth who had just a day or so ago become friends, turned their backs on one another. And those who hoped to benefit from the new government raised their heads especially high.

On an uncomplicated morning, the defense was reorganized, those who were not enthusiastic about Soviet rule were removed from its ranks and it declared itself as a revolutionary force whose job it was to serve the Council of Workers, Soldiers and Farmers. Armed and singing the Marseillaise, the armed show of force marched to the city council. The town council surrendered to them and Zhetl began preparing to receive the Soviet Army.

The town did not take this change with a light heart, and confusion was especially strong amongst the Zionist youth. The revolution in the town council had raised the question for them: what next?

[Page 118]

The Transition from Ruler to Ruler
(An interesting episode from a small town in the big world)

by Nekhemiye Aminoakh
son of Reb Noyakh Ha Kohen Rozvosky (Kfar Avraham)

Translated by Janie Respitz

This was a time of chaos and fear of the next day. The town was still under the authority of a city administration which was chosen from among secret, direct, professional and free elections during the time of transition after the German occupation.

This was a very interesting episode which lasted half a year. One fine winter day the German military occupation authority left Zhetl, but no new authority appeared. A dead stillness took over the streets while we waited for a new authority.

The first question was who would be responsible for life and security in town? This was not only a question asked by the Jews, but the Christian population as well. The Germans took everything from Zhetl that could be considered a weapon. All that remained were a few rifles, revolvers and a box of hand grenades. We also worried about who would organize the authority.

Around Zhetl, in the forests were many Russian soldiers who had escaped German captivity. There were rumours spreading that these prisoners were planning to rule our town with the intention of stealing all Jewish property.

In the region around my town gentiles were never ready to risk their lives for Jews. They were more inclined to seize the opportunity to enjoy Jewish possessions. This was however in "ancient times" before Hitler poisoned the world against the Jews, who were not yet abandoned. The gentiles in our town were afraid of the Jewish population as well as the prisoners who were not a regular power, but rather a gang of thieves.

We Organized a Self – Defence

In the first days when our town became its own state, a self defence was organized which became the ruling authority of the town.

It is hard to understand how a small town, which was abandoned like a ship in a stormy sea, organized a Jewish self defence, which was led by a Christian who we later learned was not overly friendly to the Jews…

The self defence which was composed of 40 – 50 young men had around 20 rifles, a few hundred or even one thousand bullets, very few revolvers and as I mentioned earlier, a box of hand grenades. The leader of the self defence was a Christian from a nearby village. He was about 40 – 45 years old and participated in the First World War and after the Russian revolution joined the Social – Revolutionary party in Russia. His deputies were Jews from our town. At another opportunity it would be interesting to recount how the self defence governed the town.

The most important thing about the history of the self defence is the fact that it did not become a dictatorial authority in town. On the contrary, they organized a democratically elected city council which led by example.

The Soldier's Council Takes Over

Everything went well until we felt in the air that the Soviet military authority was approaching and preparing to occupy our town. Our youth who just yesterday were united and woven together with one intimate thread were suddenly strangers. It raised awareness to those who hoped and believed a new authority would be built.

The Zionists were also split. Their foreheads were wrinkled and faces clouded over and everyone waited to see what tomorrow would bring with a different thought in their heart.

One morning the self defence suddenly regrouped and excluded from their ranks everyone who did not show hope for the new authority.

Under these circumstances the local self defence transformed into a revolutionary power, which was prepared to help the new local authority which was called the "Socialist Workers – Peasants – and Soldier's Council". With rifles, grenades and revolvers, accompanied by youth and artisans who put hope in the new authority, singing the Marseillaise on a beautiful evening just after sunset, they marched demonstratively to city hall and demanded they give over authority to the council of workers, peasants and soldiers. The town council led by Yisroel Kaplinsky gave in. The authority and atmosphere in town was "Soviet" and the town readied itself to receive the new occupiers.

[Page 119]

The Mood

In general, the town embraced the new situation with a heavy heart. The Zionist youth were most disturbed. Under the German occupation they were unified as they did not partake in political work, which by the way the German authority prohibited. In this short time the Zionist youth had not yet crystalized who they were and where they were going. The upheaval that took place that evening at the doorstep of the city council posed this question to the youth: What next?

Understandably, the majority of youth in town were not well enough informed to take a stand for or against the Soviet authority. Many had material questions about the future: how will every day life normalize, will there be enough food, livelihood, bread, meat, kerosene and wood? Those who had an inclination for community life knew they must take a stand in support of the new regime.

A portion of the youth were worried, as if faced with a riddle or a mysterious event. For another group the Soviet feeling grew like yeast. Not all were so idealistic, many were focused on building their careers. Be that as it may, many awaited the new authority with fear and curiosity.

Truth be told, most of the Zionist youth were sympathetic to the new authority, where they saw the new revolutionary Russia. However there were a few who were aware and well oriented and quietly examined their own conscience and assessed the reality of what lay ahead.

This is where I enter this episode. I want to tell you about the false steps which I myself took part in. It is difficult for me to offer an assessment as to what brought about my decision to welcome the new regime with ceremony and pomp. It is interesting that those who had spoken out against Bolshevism decided the Zionist youth should partake in the ceremonies on the day the Soviet authority would officially arrive in town.

Three Opponents

Who were the active members of our town's Zionist youth who were ideologically against the Soviet regime and yet decided they should be welcomed in a friendly manner in order to be able to continue with our Zionist activity?

The three leading ideological opponents were: Khaim Ganuzovitch, the strongest opponent, who was the only one to vote against the fact that we should celebrate the dictatorial and extreme – socialist regime which must in time bring down Zionist thought and Zionist work. The second was Efraim Belagolovsky and me – the third. Before I describe what transpired I must present the three "heroes" I just mentioned.

Khaim Ganuzovitch was around twenty years old, not too tall, with a clever look with penetrating black eyes which looked at everything with doubt and a certain anger. Doubt and disdain were the best friends of the Zionist youth in our town. His ideas deviated to the right. His arguments were built more on nationalism than socialism.

He was the son of an enlightened Jew, an iron dealer, whose main concern earning a living, yet he was interested in science, new the history of Zionism, belonged to the Zionist movement in town and raised his children in this spirit.

The older son, Moishe Ganuzovitch, studied with me in the Lida Yeshiva and later became a Hebrew teacher. The younger brother Khaim, worked with their father in his shop and in my day, belonged to the right wing young Zionists in town.

Efraim Belagolovsky was actually a son in law in Zhetl. It is worthwhile at this opportunity to mention that Zhetl did not only excel with its sons, but sons in law as well. This was not only true in the days that I remember, about 50 years ago when these sons in law were old men, but my old grandfather (who was known in town as Old man Yehoshua) would tell me about many sons in law, exceptional young men, great religious scholars (like the "Beautiful Eyes", the Talmudic scholar, who later became a rabbi in Bielsk and Reb Avrom Tiktinsky – the head of the Yeshiva in Mir, Reb Shmuel Rabinovitch – chief rabbi of Moscow, and Reb Shmuel Khaim – rabbi in Genitshesk and others). There were sons in law who held important positions in Zionist or literary history (Yehoshua Barzilai – Ayznshtat).

[Page 120]

Apparently, Zhetyl had a magnetic power, or perhaps Zhetl's daughters were no less exceptional then its sons.

Efraim Belagolovsky was full of life, with a smiling face always with an affable and optimistic expression. He had grey eyes and parted lips which always seemed ready to say what he felt in his heart, helped by gestures, with a gentle, correct somewhat coquettish manner, always ready to serve others who considered themselves students of his ideas.

Belagolovsky carried with him many ideas and ideals. He was a first class speaker, on more than one occasion people gladly listened to him speak for hours. He was an expressive substantial member of the young Zionists a few years before. Although in my time the Zionist association in Zhetl was a young Zionist group without an avowed political platform, Belagolovsky always tried to give it young Zionist colours. His inclinations were toward the left, and his devotion to Zionism was undoubted.

I met him in Zhetl when I returned from Russia after the First World War in 1918. The Germans were still ruling and we began brotherly work with the local Zionist youth.

I did not have any great sympathy for the German authority. I left home in 1915 as a soldier in the Russian army and was sent to Russia. I lived out the war years in Russia and Finland and later experienced the Russian Revolution and pogroms in the Jewish towns.

In general, the Russian Revolution enchanted me, however I did not feel sympathetic to the Bolshevik regime.

Observing the first steps I already had the impression that Jewish life was declining materially and spiritually. Everything preached and declared by the Bolsheviks went against the Jewish religious and national character.

On the other hand I did not have any special inclination toward the S.D nor to the social – revolutionary justification of the revolution in Russia. Being in Russia, I lived under such circumstances that did not allow me to form my opinions concerning the national Jewish youth and while in a Russian village I helped out with the agitation of the S. R.

I must admit that other spiritual ideas influenced me which I absorbed in the "Yeshiva". I was greatly influenced by Jewish anarchism, and from the Zionists, Gordonism. I struggled with different ideas. I was filled with life, energy and spiritual power which I will not here and now dedicate to any particular opinion. The truth is my inner struggles often bothered me more than the outer circumstances, to take a clear, sure stand. I held leftist tendencies, but was drawn by an unknown fear to the right, perhaps due to religious motives.

The Zionist Deliberation

E. Belagolovsky and I spoke and called for a restricted deliberation dedicated to the ceremonies. Those who were left leaning did not invite me. However even among those present there were divided opinions.

The first to speak was Khaim Ganuzovitch, who in a nice way substantiated that we should not participate in the ceremonies. I must say his words were prophetic. He clearly foresaw everything.

E. Belagolovsky recommended we do participate. If my memory serves me correctly, Belagolovsky justified his opinion by saying this was not a central authority and if we show support they will allow us to continue our work. The other members were silent. The mood was solemn. Then I said we should go with all the splendor to this celebration and show our positive attitude toward the new authority. I remember I was motivated that the new authority should liquidate the gangs and this necessitated our support.

Our Participation in the Ceremonies

The ceremonies took place a few days later. Understandably, every group walked under their own flag. The Zionist youth carried a white and blue flag and looked like the fifth wheel on a wagon.

[Page 121]

There was no shortage of red flags. Communists, workers, soldiers and all the youth were decorated with red bows in their lapels. The entire crowd was happy, lively, contradictory to the inner fear which totally took over from the start. We wanted to believe a miracle could happen and the devil would not be as terrible as we thought. It is after all a regime whose idea is equality and fighting against injustice.

Not a lot of authorities arrived in town. A small group marched with great pomp and assembled in the marketplace. Various groups began to enter from all the streets, each under its own flag. Besides our blue and white flag, all the others were red, however even our flag was decorated with a red band. We wore blue and white bows braided with a small red ribbon in our lapels.

We were met and greeted by the chairman of the local workers and peasant's council. He was the former leader of our self defence. He spoke in the spirit of the social revolution and welcomed the authorities with mutual ideas of the S.D (Bolsheviks) and the S.R. He underlined the country awaited the new regime and expressed his gratitude to the new authorities with whom the workers and peasant's council would soon be working with in a brotherly fashion.

This gentile did not forget the Jews in his greetings to our town, some of whom, even after the victory of the new regime, did not forget the old reactionary feelings. He regretted and asked forgiveness and believed that time would heal and convince the people.

This was the content of his speech. We felt its effects immediately, like a cold wet rain that gets into your bones.

The activities of the young Zionists were interrupted. Each one of us carried two spiritual passports and thought about the future. More than one of us thought about the Land of Israel or immigration in general.

The Split

The first split among the Zionist youth happened immediately, the same day. After the ceremonies, many felt they were returning from a funeral, broken and filled with resentment. A small group led by Shloimeh Vernikovsky who was loved and respected by many in the movement, was more of a leftist and expressed resentment that from the start we did not carry the red flag or wear red bows in our lapels like all the other "Revolutionaries". They quickly organized themselves as left wing "Labour Zionists". The rest would have declared themselves right wing "Zionist Youth" but were afraid.

The New Authority Lets Itself be Felt

The new authority began to rule our town. We immediately felt its impact on our daily lives. They requisitioned businesses and merchandise. They brought in a civilian authority and chose a commandant, a Jewish guy. They brought young people into the new administration who were previously far from these influences, but now they had the nerve and audacity to rule with the power of the new authority.

The Zionist youth still attempted to work in harmony, but with heavy hearts. We tried to receive opportunities within the framework of the new authorities. This proved to be very difficult.

The workers and peasant's council which was the ruling authority became the central power, not just for Zhetl but for the surrounding villages and they admitted representatives from among the peasants. The Jews involved were not from the Zionist youth. It seems to me in general it was composed on the basis of parties and from the right, only the "Young Zionists" were able to participate.

Soon after there was a huge gathering of the Professional Union. There was practically no one from the Zionist youth who had the right to be admitted into the professional union because we were our parent's children, the native "dear children of the regime" which already ruled all matters with all its strength and let this power be felt by the members of the white and blue flag.

Zhetl was always a revolutionary town…I was the only one that received full rights as a member of the Professional Union of Land Workers, although they kept an eye on me.

With the support of the "Young Zionsts" Moishe Bitensky and I were admitted into the workers and peasant's council. However we were slowly approaching the day when remaining with the new regime would become more and more impossible.

[Page 122]

The Transition Period
(Recollections From My Childhood 1918 – 1920)

by Yitzkhal Epshteyn (Kfar Neter)

Translated by Janie Respitz

"The hoods are already here" shouted Khane Gatshikhes at the marketplace.

"What hoods, it's summer, why do we need hoods?" wondered the old man Berl Fishkes.

"Not hoods, Bolsheviks" some young guys corrected him, (Translator's note: the word for hoods in Yiddish is Bashlike which he mistook for Bolshevik), as they ran breathless from Lisagura Street toward Novoredok Street, across the street from the Red Army.

A stampede, great noise – the Bolshevik cavalry under Marshal Budyonny was chasing out the Polish Legionnaires from Ukraine and reached as far as Zhetl.

The red flag was already waving at Khaim Koyfman's house along with a large banner which read: REVCOM (Revolutionary Committee).

Meylekh Shvedsky, Hirsh Ivenitsky, Yisroel Rabinovitch and Yakov Komay stood in the middle of the marketplace and shouted three times: Hurray! Hurray! Hurray! Welcome (in Russian)! Long live the Red Army!

Meylekh Shvedsky rode through the streets of Zhetl on a white horse. He was the commissar of the town.

The girls stood by their windows and watched Meylekh Shvedsky on his horse with a dagger in his hand and head haughty. They could not take their eyes off him. Each one wanted to Meylekh to stop by her window and smile.

The Red Army passes through on their way to Warsaw!

The Bolsheviks set up their headquarters in my grandfather's house. They sat around the tables smoking cheap tobacco and the only words you heard them say were: "Lenin and Trotsky; this is what Lenin said: we will take over the world!"

Alexander Yefimke who led the Red Army into Zhetl was seriously wounded in the battle of Shtshareh. They brought him wounded to Zhetl and all the efforts made by Dr. Shapiro to save him did not help, Alexander Yefimke died from his wounds.

The commissar in Zhetl, Meylekh Shvedsky gave an order that the fire brigade should take part in the funeral.

They organized a solemn funeral. The funeral procession was led by the fire brigade orchestra. Avromcheh the blacksmith led the orchestra and Pinkeh the wagon driver accompanied them on his drum.

Next came the leaders and high officials of the fire brigade: my father Mayrim Epshteyn of blessed memory, Berl Mirsky of blessed memory, Shmuel Shvedsky of blessed memory, and other important people in town. Meylekh Shvedsky, Yakov Komay and Alter Gertzovsky carried the red flag.

Our neighbour Bunia Goldshteyn (Moishe the tinsmith's wife) comes from Zhetl "aristocracy", supported the Poles and was against the "barefoot tramps" – the Bolsheviks. She did not like the whole scene; that such a "nothing" who comes from "simple folk" like Alter Gertzovsky is leading this group and carrying the red flag. She went out on her porch and shouted:

"Nu, can you even compare? There (that means the Poles) are all the noblemen and magnates and here, among the Bolsheviks is Kikeh (Alter Gertzovsky's nickname was Kikeh). Nu Jews, tell me, can there be justice in this world?"

"Have you seen my husband? My darling Alter disappears every day" shouted Alter Gertzoksy's wife Khayke.

"Ha, you're looking for your 'darling husband'"? Answered Bunia with an ironic smile, "I saw him carrying the red flag".

For us kids, this was all one big celebration. Our teacher Yosef Mutchnik dismissed our class, it's wartime and we, the kids, are wandering the streets and talking…politics. My friend Avromke is a great supporter of Budyonny. He said that Budyonny will not only capture Warsaw quickly, but Berlin and Paris as well.

Pinkeh Kaplinsky and Motke Rozovsky think differently. And as we walked we arrived at the Talmud Torah. What a noise. Suddenly, Yudke Khlebnik jumped up on the table and shouted:

"Just what the Jews need, politics. The Poles will defeat the Bolsheviks, or the Bolsheviks will defeat the Poles, they will capture Warsaw or they will not capture Warsaw, – the main thing is the army of the Zhetl Talmud Torah, when they go to war, will defeat the Poles with the Bolsheviks together."

My friend Itche Kravitz became a businessman. He wore a Jacket with five pockets. In one pocket he had Russian Czarist imperial rubles, in the second

[Page 123]

In the third pocket – Bolshevik rubles, in the fourth pocket – dollars, and in the fifth pocket he had a small notebook and a pencil. All day he wandered through the marketplace and made deals. Everyone was jealous of him, especially the women.

"He has so many "Tollars"!"

His brother Veveh became a cantor. He wandered through the streets all day singing cantorial pieces. Veveh discovered a few things. For example, the meaning of their family name Kravitz; the Hebrew letters stand for: The Voice of the rejoicing and salvation is in the tents of the righteous.

One day I went walking in the fields with Veveh. As we walked we approached the priest's fields. Veveh went up to the peasants and began to sing, in his High Holiday voice, Unetana Tokef (Let us speak of the awesomeness, a prayer from Yom Kippur). At the same time he turned his head, lifted his hands, sighed and cried.

At first the gentiles were frightened, then they lifted their scythes and began to shout:

"What? You came here to cry?" Then they came at us with their scythes. But Veveh was not afraid, and he shouted: "Shir Hamaalot (Song of Ascent) on your backs!" this is what he would shout to the gentiles when he wanted to frighten them.

The gentiles were frightened and began to check their backs. Meanwhile we ran away.

As we were running back to town we began to hear shooting. Rafael the tailor ran while shouting to his wife:

"Soskeh, they're shooting, Soskeh they're shooting!"

"Who is shooting, where are they shooting" Veveh and I shouted. Coming toward us was Avromke and my uncle Hirsh of blessed memory, and told us Budyonny was retreating from Warsaw. Avromke became very sad. He could not imagine Budyonny retreating.

We all ran to Avromke's yard. His father Mordkhai of blessed memory advised us to talk to his worker Maxim. He said Maxim had a Jewish brain and had he had the opportunity to study, he would have become a minister.

Maxim had a thick hidden book which described the end of the world.

We all ran to Maxim so he could show us his book and tell us what was happening in the war.

Lag BaOmer festivities in Zhetl 1920

[Page 124]

This is How I Remember You, Zhetl

by Soreh Medvetzky (Buenos Aires)

Translated by Janie Respitz

One marketplace and one circle of shops
Also one fair,
From this alone lived
The businessman, artisan and every Jew.

Tailors, shoemakers, businessmen
Lived a delightful life,

Even though there was not
One single factory.

Reb Avrom and Reb Noyakh Eli
And Reb Tzalieh the blacksmith
It was an honour
To have such Jews.

Yisroel Ozer accomplished
Everything quietly,
A favour and a kind word
All with humanity.

If you were poor or sick
Or needed a bridal dress
You went straight to Etl Man
And to Peshke Izraelit.

These kind people
Never turned you down
Although they were inconvenienced
By day and by night.

When there was
A wedding in Zhetl,
Our own Reb Moishe
Would entertain with charm.

Then the music
Played with feeling
A beautiful march
Would be played.

In our town
It was very special
Our own artists
Our own music.

When we held a parade
It was very joyful
As if a king
Was about to arrive.

The orchestra played
Beautifully at the marketplace
With our own bandleader
Abrashe Levit.

Our fire brigade
With four barrels
And Kalmen Yoshe Maytchiks
As the commander.

Each and everyone
Was always prepared

As early as the
Sun appeared.

Now after such destruction
See what became of our Zhetl
This must be inscribed
In everyone's memory.

[Page 126]

Between Two World Wars

Translated by Judy Montel

During the period between the two world wars (1921-1939) the Zhetl community enjoyed great progress. While the Polish government didn't grant the Jews much favor, the freedom of association that Poland granted, as opposed to Tsarist Russia, was used in extensive public activity.

In the twenties, two modern schools were started in Zhetl. The Zionist parties founded the "Tarbut" school with Hebrew and the language of instruction and the Yidishists and anti-Zionists established the "Tzisha" school. The two schools were the axis around which all the public and political activities clustered. Although they divided the Zhetl community into two warring sides, they concentrated all constructive thinking and together moved the point of gravity away from the study hall.

Besides hundreds of graduates who acquired knowledge and modern education there, the two schools started two drama troupes, organized celebrations, balls and bazaars.

Along with the cultural and political associations, professional associations arose as well. To begin with, the tradespeople started their association, afterwards, the artisans and finally, the workers started a professional association. Each organization focused on the interests of its members, protected them from over-taxation and looked after their social and professional representation.

Charity organizations that were rebuilt after the war also increased their activity. Alongside the traditional institutions, for example: "Linat Tzedek" and Aid for the Sick, the Popular Bank was founded, the Committee for the Care of Orphans, "TOZ" and so forth.

The town's municipality improved the views, installed sidewalks, paved the streets, painted fences, took care of general cleanliness and added charm to the town.

In this period, the Zhetl community also rebuilt its economy. The tradespeople developed their shops and the artisans expanded their workshops. Of course, their livelihood was not abundant and the quality of life was modest, but compared to the period before the war, noticeable progress had been made.

The highlight of this period was the youth. In Zhetl alert and vibrant youth arose who dreamt and realized their dreams. They trained to a life of work, moved to the Land of Israel and built a bridge between the diaspora and the homeland. This interesting development, full of potential, was tragically halted with the outbreak of the Second World War.

[Page 127]

Between the Two World Wars

Cultural and Economic Life[a]

by Avrom Ivenitsky of blessed memory

Translated by Janie Respitz

Zhetl now has 4,600 inhabitants of which 75% are Jews. The Christians, with very few exceptions are White Russian land workers. The surrounding land owners are almost all Poles. The state clerks, among whom there are a significant amount of elderly, Russian clerks trying to pass themselves off as Poles, but according tot their names and accents their Polish identity is problematic. Yet they polonized quickly despite the fact it is not easy for them as they speak the provincial White Russian dialect with all the nuances of the entire Christian population.

The White Russian use the White Russian language almost exclusively in all tasks except any written communication with the authorities. That is always in Polish.

Jewish children attend the Talmud Torah, the Yiddish secular school and the Tarbut School. Zhetl's secular Yiddish elementary school goes until the 6th grade, and besides this there are Heders (traditional religious schools) which satisfy more or less the educational needs of the Jewish population. However, there are many Jewish children, mostly girls, in the local Polish public school which does not cost any money.

The high school situation is more difficult. The few children from Zhetl who have the opportunity to attend a high school in another town are almost all students in the Jewish – Polish High Schools.

The Zhetl Yiddish Elementary School

The Zhetl Yiddish secular elementary school was founded 6 years ago by the young people in Zhetl. Like all of its sister schools it has to endure cold and warm from inside and out. But the school became naturalized with us and this summer celebrated its first graduation. The graduation showed our parents that pedagogically they were not bad, however financially they had many problems.

Three years ago, the school management with their bare hands undertook the task of building their own building. Given that however, good will is not enough to build a building and from the small amount of money we received from America, we bought part of the lot. The rest of the money we raised among ourselves through small contributions.

For pennies, we erected a nice spacious ruin and laid down a floor.

When the school was founded, children came from poor houses. Now we have 120 children in all levels and it is becoming more and more popular.

From time to time the Yiddish elementary school organizes evenings of amateur shows and lectures on their own. Bringing a lecturer from Warsaw or Vilna is difficult, forget about an acting troupe, since Zhetl is too poor. If a lecturer or an acting troupe would stumble upon Zhetl, we remembered it for a long time. In the winter of 1924 Dovid Herman's studio visited Zhetl. Old and young ran to all three performances and people are still talking about it today.

The Situation in 1929

The situation of the schools in June 1929 was like this: the TZISHO School and the Talmud Torah were barely breathing and were in an unbearably difficult situation of permanent lack of funds. The amount of children (approximately 200) was the same in both schools, with very little fluctuation. Of course the difficult financial situation affects the pedagogic work.

Concerning state subsidies there is not much to talk about. The city hall, over the past year raised the subsidy for the schools to 50%, that is to say, instead of 2000 zlotys this year, both schools would receive 3000 zlotys.

The building of the Yiddish school 1925

[Page 128]

Perhaps we will be able to squeeze another few hundred zlotys from them. 1500 gulden a year, with 200 children and 4–5 teachers is a weak financial foundation.

Tuition is insignificant in the percentage of our school budget. Our town is extremely poor. They do not pay tuition and the little they do pay is never punctual. This is the reason this is the reason many teachers leave. Here we see the great expansion of the Polish Public School where 30% of Jewish children learn, mainly girls but many boys as well.

Over the last few years there have been two classes at the "Tarbut" School which exists under the label of Talmud Torah, and is not far away. There is also the Agudah's "Ezra" school which was founded under the protectorate of the former Zhetl rabbi (now in Lutzk) Zalmen Saratzkin.

There was a cultural battle between the TZISHO and Tarbut schools. And they both had trouble making ends meet. The main competition lay in: very low tuition, or no tuition at all, and the national and religious sentiments of the Talmud Torah and Tarbut schools and on the other hand, the secular approach of the TZISHO School. Meanwhile, more and more children were being sent to the Polish public school where they taught "Jewish religion" once or twice a week (not in the school, the children would go to a tutor's home).

The building of the TZISHO School was far from ready, inside and out. Summer was not too bad. In the winter they had to heat all day (if there was not a lack of wood), because the interior was not plastered and the exterior was not panelled.

The Library

The school was the most important cultural centre for Zhetl's youth. Next came the library which was founded 35 years ago. From 1905 until 1915, due to police persecutions, the library was in private hands. When the Germans arrived in 1915 the Zhetl youth took back their library which functioned normally until 1921 and served Zhetl then what the Yiddish school does now.

That is when the decline of the library began. Firstly because the new school zapped a lot of the energy from the youth, and secondly, the difficult economic crisis and the occupying regime killed the vivaciousness of Zhetl's youth.

The Public Library 1918

From right to left: Khaim Ganuzovitch, Yitzkhak Leybovitch, Eli Bensky, Shloimeh Khaim Vernikovsky

The school question remained at the forefront, and the library was pushed into the shadows, but thanks to the dedication of our librarian Mr. Yitzkhak Leybovitch, it did not fall completely by the wayside. There is now a resurging interest in the library and there is no doubt it will be revived.

Our library work now falls under the legalization of the merchants union. The book collection is not too bad. We received a small subsidy from city hall, a few hundred gulden. We hope the subsidy will increase.

Institutions

Zhetl now has a new electricity station with a diesel motor. The electricity station, although a very good one, with a very good electrical network and excellent light, squeezed city hall making it hard to breathe. This pleasure cost a bit too much. City hall suffered with loans and promissory notes from the state economic bank and so on.

[Page 129]

The hospital was transformed into an infirmary where there was a doctor five days a week. You had to pay 1 gulden per visit. We now have two infirmaries in Zhetl: a Polish one and a Jewish one. The Polish one costs 50 groshen. In the Jewish one there is a sunlamp which you can use for a minimum fee.

As in all Jewish towns and cities Zhetl has its Zionist organizations, the united Z.Z and P.Z, pioneers and a mixed professional union. All the dreams of a lecturer or organizer from Warsaw remains just a desire due to lack of money.

Participants in the concert on behalf of the philanthropic institutes 1920

**Seated in the first row: Musheh Turetsky, Shaul Rabinovitch, Melekh Shvedsky,
Avrom Levit, Aron Eliovitch, Moishe Izraelit
Second row: Rivka Breskin, Yehoshua Shushan, Mirl Zernitsky, Hirshl Aron
Volfovitch, Etl Man, Boreh Dvoretsky, Khashkeh Ganzovitch, Yakov Dvoretsky
Last row: Yehoshua Dvoretsky, Khane Malkeh Shvedsky, Moishe Mirsky,
Hindkeh Mirsky, Menakhem Kaplinsky**

The pioneers learned trades and how to work the land and little by little left for Palestine.

Among other cultural institutions we must remember the "TOZ" Society and the last arrival the "Cultural League". All these societies are active. They are comprised mainly of young people who have nothing to do, they were landless and preoccupied with many worries: "If you say, what will we eat". The desire to immigrate was very strong. Here and there people were disappearing. Whoever could was immigrating, the majority to South America.

Over the last few years many small shops have opened. The people are hopeful that the guild laws would prevent more shops to open so quickly and easily.

There is nothing to say about White Russian cultural activity. They were Polonizing easily. All the White Russian children have no choice but to attend Polish schools. They do not even wrangle over this. The few that are unhappy go unnoticed.

Zhetl continued to possess all the specific Jewish societies and institutions such as The Society to Spend the Night With the Sick, Society to Aid the Sick, The Interest Free Loan Society, The Firefighter Society, which was already 24 years old and well organized.

The Firefighter Society was created with Jewish manpower and means and until today, most of its members are Jews. In fact it is a Jewish society because besides the Jews hardly anyone is interested in it. All the inventory was bought with Jewish money.

Finally, I would like to talk about the important Jewish communal, economic institution – The Zhetl Jewish Public Bank. The bank encompasses the entire economic life in Zhetl and is involved with the Vilna Central Jewish Cooperative Public Bank.

Zhetl's shopkeepers and artisans are organized in the Merchant Union and Artisan Union. Both unions are connected with the Warsaw Central Unions and function relatively well.

What Does Zhetl Live Off?

This is the question that everyone who comes to Zhetl asks, when he is astounded by the amount of stores and small shops which like a rusty chain surround entire spacious empty – bare marketplace in the middle of the town and infest all the other streets and lanes. The first and correct reply a Zhetl Jew would give this question is:

"What does it matter, what do Jews live off? We live…"

Taking further interest in this question you will learn that Zhetl earns its living on market days when the surrounding peasant population come to shop. There are now two market days: Tuesday and Friday. The real market day however is Tuesday.

[Page 130]

All the other days of the week are just the antechamber to the market day. In one word: the entire economic – financial and to a great extent social and cultural life in Zhetl is dependent and regulated by the market day. Given that the peasants in the region were also very poor gives the market day more noise than substance.

Professionally, Zhetl looked like this:

Industrial enterprise – the steam mill and sawmill belonged to four partners.
Shopkeepers – 170. Mainly – groceries, textiles, iron, leather, haberdashery, shoes, glass, pharmacy warehouses. From these 150 were in the Merchant Union, almost all in the third and fourth category.
Beer Halls – 10; Tea Houses –10; hotels – 4; restaurants – 2; a small ceramic tile factory; a small fur dealer and peddlers all totalling 40 families. Together with the shopkeepers – 210 families.

Artisans – approximately 250 families. According to these trades:

Needle trade: seamstresses and dressmakers – 75 families; furriers – 6.
Leather trade: shoemakers – 50; cutters and stitchers of shoe leather –10; tanners – 10; saddle makers – 8;
Lumber trade: carpenters – 25; shingle makers – 2.
Metal trade: Blacksmiths – 15; locksmiths – 3; coppersmiths – 1; assistant machinist – 1; watchmaker – 2; tinsmith – 2.
Building trade: Glaziers – 10; housepainters and artistic painters – 4; whitewashers – 1; bricklayers – 3; mortar makers – 2.
Nutrition trade: Bakers – 20, butchers – 25; sausage makers – 6, soda water small factories – 2; miller (water) – 1; rolling mill (steam) – 1.
Land workers: Farming – 3; gardeners – 2; orchard keepers – 7.
Varied trades: photographers – 2; electricians – 2; coachmen – 30, barbers –4; wool brushers – 2; stocking makers (machine) – 1; potters – 3.
Specific Jewish Trades: Scribes – 30, parchment makers – 3; wig makers – 1.
Secular Professions: Doctors – 1; medics – 1; dentists – 3; teachers and religious tutors – 15.
Religious Functionaries: Rabbi – 1; cantor – 1; beadles – 3; gravediggers – 1; (the same person also inscribed tombstones).
Unskilled labourers – 5.

Before the war, even 3 years ago Zhetl was a centre for lumber. The employees (all Jewish) the so called record keepers of the lumber operations, amounted to a large percentage of the Zhetl population.

American Aid

As in the rest of Poland the "Joint" prevented many Jewish families from literal ruin during the transitional years from 1920 –1922 and helped rebuild the destroyed Zhetl.

The actual aid work of the "Joint" and from America in general began in 1920. That same year a delegate from the "Joint" visited Zhetl and left us 10,000 mark which was equivalent to 300 dollars. The delegate, Mr. Lev, enlivened the economic and communal ruin of Zhetl and connected us with Slonim as an independent point. Until then, Zhetl was isolated from "Joint" activities.

A community council was immediately formed with representatives from various movements who were given the task to distribute the funds which from then on would arrive every month in larger or smaller amounts. The money was distributed, without exception, to each of the community's institutions which were now revived.

A kitchen opened for the poor which served 200 portions daily. The town would partially cover the expenses for the food through taxation. Many also received handouts. Many helped to build workshops and stand independently on their own feet.

Every month there would be a gathering in Slonim to distribute the money from the "Joint", as well as food and clothing to the whole county. In 1922 Zhetl joined the Bialystok County with our Rabbi Sorotskin as representative. This is when the well planned rebuilding activity began in our region.

The Bialystok "Joint" distributed to three headquarters: medical and sanitation, orphans and credit. The Zhetl rabbi was elected to the presidium of Bialystok County. With the help of the "Joint" the town purchased the bathhouse from a private owner, renovated it appropriately making it a new, modern facility.

The Jewish hospital was reorganized, renovated and given modern equipment and began to function normally. An infirmary was opened at the hospital. They organized school medicine and hygiene for more than 200 children. They also built a town ice warehouse which supplied ice in the event of illness, not only for Zhetl but for the entire region, for Jews and Christians.

[Page 131]

With help from the "Joint" the Jewish hospital was legalized. There were only two legal Jewish hospitals in the 110 towns in Bialystok County: Zhetl and in Ruzhinoy, near Slonim. A sanitation commission was created which cleaned, whitewashed and disinfected the town. They burned old hay bags and distributed new ones and legalized the Society to Aid the Sick. The poor received medical help free of charge.

A county commission to care for orphans was founded in Zhetl headed by Reb Moishe Ruven Mordkovsky. The amount of war orphans adopted in Zhetl rose from 8 to 20. In actuality, they cared for many more.

With the help of the Central Credit, the aforementioned Public Bank was opened in Zhetl. The restoring and rebuilding work of the "Joint" in Poland greatly affected Zhetl.

Zhetl also received subsidies from YEKAPO which helped to ease the difficult economic situation in town. The subsidies helped to reinstate the old interest free loan society which was desperately needed.

In the last years the YEKAPO in Vilna sent aid for orphans after the decision was made to liquidate the "Joint" in Bialystok, Baranovitch and Slonim.

Thanks to YEKAPO, in 1926 an aid committee was founded to help the unemployed. They provided funds to dry out the town's swampy meadows – 2.7 acres of pasture was created for Jewish animals. On any given day there were 25 Jewish unemployed men working on this project. In order to reach their goal, the town demanded a day of work from every Jewish family.

On the 25th of August 1926 the General Secretary of YEKAPO, Mr. Moishe Shalit visited Zhetl. Among other things, he visited the Dried out swamp land expressed his joy by increasing the subsidy.

ביים גרונדשטיין אײלייגן פון "הכנסת-אורחים און מושב-זקנים.

Corner stone ceremony for the guest house and home for the aged. 1920

Private Aid

Besides the "Joint" and "YEKAPO", the Zhetl Relief Society in America helped to alleviate the economic need in Zhetl. In the years 1919–1921, 50 –60 percent of Zhetl's Jews lived off this aid. The need for help began to decrease. Today 30–35 families regularly receive help from America. From time to time, 30 percent of the town. The amounts however are not less than before.

The General Picture: Lonely and Needy

The economic situation in Zhetl compared to surrounding towns is unsatisfactory. The town has entered a normal framework and exactly as before the war, after the war Zhetl is still poor. The only difference is we now see all the possibilities to escape.

Original footnote:

  a. This list was published by the author in "Records of YEKAPO" in 1926 and completed in 1929.

[Page 132]

Zhetl and the Zhetl Craftsman

by Moishe Mendl Leyzerovitch (New York)

Translated by Janie Respitz

In 1914 I was mobilized into the Czarist army. In June of 1918 I returned to Zhetl. I lived there under German occupation for 7 months until they left the region. I experienced living under the Germans in those years. If only it did not get so much worse. Our families would still be alive.

Without Authority

When the Germans began to evacuate we felt that our true hell was just beginning. Having survived the Russian civil war and the fall of the Czarist power I anticipated we would now experience the wrath of those looking to take over. It really did not take very long. As soon as the Germans began to leave Zhetl we felt the black clouds approaching.

Zhetl was left without authorities and this was taken advantage of by various dark elements. Seeing that a horrible state of chaos would begin, Yisroel Ozer Barishansky, who was always the first to help Zhetl deal with problems, organized a committee to form a self defence led by Zhetl's firefighters. There were 120 registered firefighters who protected us from attacking gangs which were romping through the forest.

Gangs Threaten Zhetl

When the Russians left our region their armies fell to pieces. As they did not want to be taken prisoner, they hid in the forests and organized partisan groups. They built hideouts in the forests and threatened the village and city. They would capture Germans, kill them and wear their uniforms. At night they would go to the villages and terrorize the peasants and at the same time send threatening letters to the Jews of Zhetl, demanding money from those they thought were rich.

When Zhetl was without authority, rumours spread about 500 armed men who were coming to kill the Jews. The fear was great. However, this did not last long. Within a short time a company of soldiers was sent from Novoredok by the Soviets. They began to administer the town, searched Jewish homes and taking whatever they wanted.

We began to feel what we had anticipated. We began to lack essentials and long lines developed for a piece of bread. Forget about better things. They did however do one good thing for our town namely: together with the town committee they began to negotiate with the bandits. We decided on a point in Mezivetz and negotiated with them for a whole month. We promised we would send them all home and they agreed.

One fine day they entered our town armed with guns, horses and essential supplies. They brought them in as if in a parade to the marketplace. They were led in by the fire brigade orchestra. Speeches were made. Then they were taken to Novoliyenie, put on trains and sent home. A few of them ran back to the forest. Apparently they preferred forest life. This is how the story of the deserters ended.

From Authority to Authority

The Soviet military company held power from December 1918 until March 1919. I will remember that day forever because my son Areleh was born that same day, March 23rd, 1919. It was Purim. At exactly 5:00 in morning gunshots woke us from our sleep. The Poles were attacking the town and the Soviets panicked. Some lay dead in the streets while others ran away.

At night, soldiers attacked Jewish homes and took everything we had. Screams and cries were heard every minute. It continued like this until they installed a civil authority with police and a city commandant. This was in 1921.

The Situation Stabilizes

Things began to improve. The situation began to stabilize. People returned to work. Business revived followed by a few good years.

[Page 133]

Money was cheap and everyone had lots of banknotes. The business world was working in dollars. Support began to arrive from America, private and communal; providing necessities for Passover for the poor and funding for the Talmud Torah. Later the zloty stabilized at 5.25 to the dollar. That's when people realized that nothing remained of their money.

Meanwhile they began to raise taxes. The economic situation worsened. This resulted in the merchants creating a union.

At the same time an elementary school was opened and we began to work on culture elements, but we were lacking the most important thing: a bank and an interest free loan society. People were doing business, expanding workshops but there was nowhere to get credit.

This is when, due to Rabbi Saratzkin's initiative, the People's Bank was opened with branches throughout the province. Rabbi Saratzkin devoted all of his energy to this effort and opened a branch in Zhetl. The merchant's union was already in existence and therefore they were represented in the bank. They began to give loans, not that large, but enough to encourage business.

Merchants and Artisans Organize

At this time the authorities raised taxes; both on merchants and artisans. The merchants who were organized would travel to Slonim as in that district there was still a finance office. Merchants who sold books were free of appraisal, but there were very few of them.

Every year they would choose a craftsmen to present to the judiciary. Understandably the merchants were only interested in their class and the craftsmen became the scapegoats, not because the merchant wanted to, God forbid, maltreat them. But when a craftsman refused to be appraised, it was really because he did not know how to go about it. If he was a friend they would put in a good word, but the rest they would leave in God's care.

When we sensed the craftsmen were subjected to the privileges of the office craftsmen bureau and compared to the merchants they were being abused, we decided to organize the Association of Craftsmen.

Such unions already existed in Poland, however there were very few in our region and they were only in the big cities.

Our organizing committee was comprised of 10 people: 1) Alter Bom, 2) Hirshl Benyaminovitch, 3) Yitzkhak Benyaminovitch, 4) Tzaleh Busel, 5) Dovid Berkovitch, 6) Zalmen Getzovsky, 7) Yisroel Zanarotzky, 8) Ruven Nilolayevsky, 9) Moishe Mendl Leyzerovitch and 10) Khaim Velvl Eliyovitch.

We legalized the committee temporarily until an election and began to organize all the craftsmen through an announcement at the Houses of Study, which was common at that time. In the course of one day, all the craftsmen in Zhetl, which comprised 65% of the population, registered. We worked out our status and went to Novoredok, to the Starosta (Russian village elder) for a certificate. The Starosta informed us that soon our status would be worked out by the government.

Meanwhile we began to gather, call meetings, hold elections and choose a board of directors. We began to be independent and finally felt the craftsmen were a force to be reckoned within a democratic country.

[Page 134]

Before long the Starosta called us and informed us the craftsmen were recognized by the government. He then gave us a status which the craftsmen's office in Warsaw had worked out.

At the same time we were informed by the finance office that we must choose six craftsmen. We chose the six men and for the first time we were well evaluated. 70% of all the craftsmen were freed from taxes. We made a big hit with the director of the finance office and he later informed us that we should also go to the merchant's meetings. This made a good impression on all the craftsmen in Zhetl.

We appointed a secretary and a beadle. The first few weeks we worked voluntarily. Dovid Berkovitch was the secretary and I was the chairman. We were the beadles until we were able to stand on our own two feet. We immediately rented a locale where we met a couple of times a week. We later subscribed to a few newspapers and the formerly lethargic craftsman began to be more interested in communal life, reading a newspaper, meet and converse and talk his heart out.

The Committee of the Association of Craftsmen

From right to left: Alter Bom, Dvoshe Busel, Hirshl Benyaminovitch, Zalmen Gertzovsky, Malkeh Lutsky, Moishe Mendl Leyzerovitch, Soreh Breskin, Avrom Matyuk…Berl Arzhekhovsky

We Fight for a City Administration

This is how life flowed until 1926. Until that year we belonged to the township. Jews were represented only through one representative Motl Man. Understandably he had only problems. He could not do anything for the good of the town. The budget was big. Proportionally, Jews carried the burden of the taxes which the township imposed, but there was no one to shout at as the only Jew was also the spare. In the end they turned him into a communist and put him in jail. After great effort they freed him.

At this time we began a movement in town that included all the organizations, headed by Rabbi Saratzkin. We set out to create a city administration where our money could be used for the welfare of our town. The township had been taking our money to build schools in the villages. No money went to the Jewish institutions.

We began by approaching the higher ups, the Starosta and the governor. It took a few years and finally a mayor was nominated to organize a city hall. When he arrived he invited representatives from the craftsmen association as well as the merchant association. After half a year we finally had elections for a city administration.

The town was excited about the elections. It was one of the most interesting moments in our town in 1928. Jews crawled out of the woodwork to choose a city council in order to take the power away from the non – Jews and become our own bosses. This went on for approximately 3 months. Every organization wanted to be represented. In total we had to elect 12 men, 9 for the city council and 3 for the board of directors. The craftsmen association pushed harder than the other organizations as we comprised 65% of the population. I believe there were more Jewish organizations than Jews…

When we realized no good was resulting from all this we decided to call 2 representatives from each group to negotiate. According to percentage, Jews were able to send 6 councilmen to the council and 2 to the board of directors as the Jewish community in Zhetl comprised 79% of the population. After long negotiations among the Jewish organizations Zions we arrived at the following conclusion: 2 craftsmen, 2 merchants, one from the Yiddish school, one from the Tarbut School, and 2 independents.

The elections began. There was a great drive to vote. No one stayed home. The Christians hope that due to the amount of Jewish organizations the Jews would fail. However we were very well organized, brought people from their homes, and won.

The joy was indescribable. We were rid of the township, the village. We were now a town with a council and we were in charge! True the taxes were higher but we would benefit from them.

The Zhetl Fire Brigade

For example: the fire fighters. They would take money from the town to subsist. From time to time they needed new machines since after a fire machines would break and have to be repaired. They also had expenses for the annual parade. The wealthier Jews would pay for this from their pockets. However there were those who did not want to contribute. In such a case they would notify the fire fighters and would go onto the roof of such an individual and cause 10 times more in damages than the amount he had to pay.

[Page 135]

I must add that the firefighters orchestra which had a great reputation in the entire region was the crowning jewel of our town. When there were large parades in Baranovitch, Slonim and Lida they would invite the Zhetl orchestra to play. When Yosef Pilsudsky, the Marshal of Poland passed through Noviliyenie, the provincial governor invited the Zhetl orchestra with the firefighter section to play. I was at that parade for Marshal Pilsudsky. When Pilsudsky walked by he said we played very well and shook our leader's hand. Our town derived a lot of pleasure from this event.

President Moshtzizky also came to our town. He too was received by our fire brigade and its orchestra.

In difficult times the fire brigade would save us from our problems. They extinguished fires that burned and wanted to burn. Such an institution could not subsist on its own. After the emergence of city hall its situation improved.

City Hall Develops the Town

The budget of city hall was big enough but not much bigger than the township budget. As a result, all the money remained in town. The council would decide what subsidies each administrative body would receive: the Talmud Torah, the Yiddish School, the Tarbut School, and the Fire Brigade. They also placed the electricity station in their administration. We had a special fund for accidents, or if we had to take someone to Vilna, and also for the public school which was open to everyone. Over the next few years city hall built school buildings, rebuilt the streets, tore out large stones from the cobblestone pavement and built sidewalks.

In 1933 and 1935 big fires broke out where more than half of Zhetl burnt down. However, after the fires we planned new streets. Someone from Zhetl who left and returned for a visit would have gotten lost.

The sanitary conditions were satisfactory. Public places like hair salons, bakeries, cafes and restaurants were painted. Every corner smelled good. The sanitation supervision was strict. There was inspection every month and a fine of 10 zlotys for any transgressions.

The streets were clean and the market was moved to the outskirts of town. The sides of the sidewalks were whitewashed and garbage was nowhere to be found. The houses were all surrounded by fences painted the same colour and there were garbage cans in the courtyards with a sewer for dirty water. The toilets were provided with concrete and were cleaned by the city. Trees were planted along the streets and the market place became a place to take a walk.

Transportation was lively. Every few hours a bus would pass through town taking people all over the country.

The town developed in other areas as well. A fine young intelligentsia was developing. We would organize beautiful celebrations on Lag Ba Omer and after exams thousands of children would march through town like angels accompanied by the orchestra. All of this began when city hall became ours.

My Activities as Councilman

I served as a councilman from the first day in 1928 until 1939. There were three elections and I was elected in all three because I devoted my whole life to communal work. I would spend three months a year doing communal work. I would tear myself away from my job and neglect my own family. I would put down my work and run to city hall in order to provide answers for everyone. This one could not afford to pay for a chimney, another for a sign, property taxes or local taxes. Someone else was sick and had to be taken to Vilna. I had influence over the mayor as an older councilman and I would always get my way.

My goal was to get the backward craftsman on his feet. I must say that this was also successful for us. We put so much into the craftsmen society, that when the governor had to make plans he invited me personally as a representative of the craftsmen.

We established a normal life for the artisans. Whenever we knocked on a door it was always opened for us. This was for us a great achievement.

I worked as chairman and organized the Craftsmen Association from 1921 until 1939, however with the arrival of the Soviets the last chapter of Zhetl institutions came to an end.

[Page 136]

The Ban in Zhetl

by Rabbi Elkhanan Saratzkin (Jerusalem)

Translated by Janie Respitz

The uniqueness of Zhetl that set it apart from the surrounding cities and towns lies in the well functioning communal life which embraced all the religious, cultural, economic and political issues. For example, the organized Jewish community owned the electricity station which it took over from the Germans during the First World War.

Zhetl also possessed its own food cooperative, the only Jewish cooperative in the region, which provided food for the entire population after the first war; a bank and an interest free loan society, its own pasture for its horses and cows on land which they were involved for years in lawsuits with the peasants who claimed the land belonged to them because how could Jews have their own land?

The Jewish community held a distinct position on the issue: should Zhetl have a rural administration or a city hall.

The Power of a Ban

The Jewish community council was not elected and was composed of leaders from all social classes: merchants and craftsmen, Talmudic scholars and simple Jews with the rabbi at the head who enjoyed great authority, often more effective than the state laws.

There was great discipline on all sides. Every decision made by the community council, which in Zhetl was referred to as "the city", was carried out even if it went against the financial interests of the individual or the group at large. A sort of "Jewish State" ruled Zhetl whose army and police were "bans" or "prohibitions" which were announced by the beadle (the rabbi's personal assistant) in the old House of Study on the Sabbath after the reading of the Torah. The bans had the charming power to stop each dispute and obligated everyone, religious or non-observant, rich or poor, with no exception to obey. The power of these bans was as effective as the state laws.

This is how the Zhetl Jewish community council took care of its poor, making sure they would have inexpensive products for Passover especially eggs, an important product for the holiday. Two weeks before Passover a "prohibition" was declared forbidding the export of eggs from town until after the holiday. Although the sale of eggs was an important component of the income of many peddlers, the prohibition was respected and thanks to this the prices fell and the population had affordable eggs for the holiday.

Through a "prohibition" on the sale of yeast, the budget was secured for religious needs such as rent for the rabbi and other functionaries of Jewish communal life. Not one baker or merchant used any yeast except the yeast provided by the Jewish community, which was very expensive.

The Ban on Illegal Distilleries

During the German occupation, 1917-1918 there was great hunger in our town and in the surrounding area. Dozens of Jews died from hunger and epidemics. The shortage of flour and rye greatly increased due to the amount of illegal distilleries in town and the surrounding area where they distilled whisky from rye because the state stopped the production of hard liquor and the prices rose. Rye which was meant for bread ended up in whisky which was sold by peasants and bandits who were rampant in the forests around Zhetl and attacked village Jews and travellers on the road. Besides this, grain merchants exported their goods out of town and the hunger situation increased by the day.

In order to liquidate the illegal distilleries and the export of rye the use of the "ban" as a weapon was implemented in our town as well as in nearby towns like Novoleniye and Dvoretz. The "ban" was solemnly declared by my father, may he be blessed with many years, in the old House of Study in the presence of the surrounding rabbis. The solemn sermon which my father, may he be blessed with many years, delivered was published in his book "The Idea and the Word" vol. 1. He emphasized that those who were criminally transforming bread into whisky, with harmful objectives, were stimulating and encouraging bandits to spill blood, attack and steal often the whisky producers themselves.

The "ban" was effective and the illegal distilleries and the rye export were stopped. However one baker and grain merchant transgressed the "ban" and as it was proven through witnesses, exported about 60 kilos of rye from town. This story caused a lot of excitement in town.

[Page 137]

He was called to the House of Study and admitted to his crime. On the spot, a personal ban on him was proclaimed, people were forbidden to do business with him, buy from him. The crowd immediately distanced themselves from him and he left the House of Study. No one crossed his threshold. Even Christians stopped buying from him when they learned of the ban that was placed on him…

That same night (Saturday night) this merchant became very ill with smallpox. Two days later his family went to the rabbi asking for forgiveness and mercy and to lift the ban. They had to pay a large fine and promise he would never do such a thing again. The ban was lifted.

The Ban for the Good of the Self Defence

The second time a "ban" was declared in Zhetl was during the days of the Jewish "Republic", after the Germans left and about half a year before the Soviets would arrive. The Jewish council organized the well known self defence which was composed of all militarily capable men. In order to organize and buy weapons they needed large sums of money. The Jewish council decided to tax every Jew a percentage of their income.

In order to prevent abuses and arguments it was decided to threaten a "ban" which would obligate everyone to give the correct percentage. So that no one had to know the exact earnings of another, it was decided to place a box in the rabbi's house where everyone had to drop off their money. The power of the "ban" was so great, the entire amount was collected. This was the best proof that everyone paid the correct amount.

A Story About a Robbery

Another interesting incident involving a "ban", which shocked the whole town, occurred just before the outbreak of the First World War. One morning the town was shocked to learn of a robbery which emptied the dry goods store of Khienke Kohen in the marketplace. The owner of the shop went from being a prosperous woman to a pauper.

The entire police force was brought in as well as a detective from another town to search for evidence, but to no avail. When the police investigation ended without results the Jewish community council decided to declare a "ban" on the thieves, and anyone with any information about them.

A few days later, one of the wealthiest women in town came to the rabbi late one evening and told him, her brother, a respected young man, acted stupidly…he committed the robbery and now is scared and remorseful and would like to return the goods. However he would like a promise that this would remain a secret and the police will not be informed. He received the promise from the rabbi and a few nights later all the stolen goods were dropped off beside the store.

The entire town was spinning. No one knew what made the thieves return the stolen goods. The police were particularly interested. After long investigations and demands the police came to the conclusion that the rabbi knew something about it and the superintendent demanded the rabbi tell him who the thief was.

The rabbi categorically refused to tell him, straining the relationship between himself and the police superintendent. The superintendent threatened to bring the rabbi to trial for hiding the identity of the thief, a crime which carried a harsh punishment. My father consulted with an important lawyer in Vilna and for a moment even considered leaving Zhetl for America in order not to have to break the promise he made to the thief.

After long negotiations the superintendent agreed to tone down the incident and not bring the rabbi to trial. The incident has remained a secret until today and will remain a secret until all involved are no longer among the living.

Let these lines serve as witness to the picture of our unforgettable and beloved town Zhetl, its customs, activists, shopkeepers and craftsmen who excelled in responsibility and communal discipline and together cultivated this holy community.

[Page 138]

The Great Fires

by Soreh Epshteyn – Shoer (Natanya)

Translated by Janie Respitz

Life flowed calmly in Zhetl

From my earliest memories until I left Zhetl there were no remarkable changes to the life of our town.

I do not remember the effect of the First World War on Zhetl. Perhaps that is why I remember a calm, beautiful town, enveloped in summer in green and in winter, covered in white snow.

The Jewish community with its communal activists energetically founded institutions, schools and organizations which flourished filling our hearts with joy.

Often a neighbour would come visit my mother and quietly and seriously whisper to her. It was then I understood: someone was in need of help, a poor family, a poor bride, or a sick person who needed someone to spend the night.

Soreh Epshteyn Shoer

I would see deep sorrow on my mother's face which would evolve into a strong desire to help. And help she did!

Practical signs of help could be found in father's cupboard and in the drawer of his desk. In his cupboard his firefighter uniform hung festively with his helmet. In his drawer there was his shiny trumpet and other items that were part of his uniform.

As children, we were not allowed to approach these items. We could only look at them with respect. Until today they have remained sacred in my memory.

The fire brigade was always ready to fulfill its task: sometimes a traditional ball, sometimes a fire drill, and most importantly, to extinguish a fire, to battle the flames, to sacrifice themselves for Jewish possessions and property.

Fires! How often would you visit our town, how often were we terrified by the sound of the alarm which began at the electrical station and ended at Leybe Kaplinsky's sawmill.

Everyone is running chasing and sighing. Tears and cries fill the air. In this strained atmosphere the firefighters appear and the crowd breathes easier.

The fire brigade was the pride of our town because they not only extinguished the flames but the despair as well and the desperation of the burning families.

The work was hard, even more so with primitive means. They harnessed the horses and loaded the wagons with buckets which they filled with water in the lakes. The horses would often bolt, especially at night when the fire was blinding.

My father served as chief of the fire brigade for many years. He would never exploit this position, rather he would serve as an example for others who followed his orders. He would drag water and be the first in the fire to extinguish and save lives.

Unfortunately there were many fires but luckily, localized. Sometimes a portion of a house, at times an entire house or a barn or a stall.

For us kids, it was always an event. We would run to see the fire…

The Fire of 1933

In the years prior to my departure from Zhetl there were two great fires. In the first more than 200 houses burned. This was in June 1933.

At the time I was in Novogrudek preparing for final high school exams.

Suddenly an alarm.

A fire! Who? Where? – Zhetl was burning! They were calling for help!

My Zhetl! How do we go home? I say "we" because Henie Gertsovsky was with me in Novogrudek. We were lucky; the chief of the Novogrudek fire brigade was our Christian history teacher. Knowing we were from Zhetl he took us in his fire truck to Zhetl.

We were on the highway heading home; Henie and I cling to each other, the fear is oppressive, the anxiety is hastening, we would like to be in Zhetl already!

How often we would travel home on this highway, happy and joyful, returning for holidays or vacation.

[Page 139]

We are wondering where the fire is. It is hard to imagine from 30 kilometres away.

We continue to travel. We are already at the Nvoleniyie River. Crossing the bridge we are on the Maltchadke. We go up Holelier Mountain. We arrive at Leybe Kaplinsky's sawmill.

I can now affirm: Novoredker Street, where we lived, was not burning…the natural, egotistical feeling is calmed.

But what do I see? Is the mountain burning? No! It was Khaim Koyfman's two storied house; at the time Zhetl did not have higher houses.

We jumped down quickly from the truck. It's getting dark.

I run into my house, it's empty. There's no one there. With one glance I look around my beloved home, how nice it is, how loving; something is stuck in my throat, my eyes become moist…the house has recently been renovated, good that it was not burning…

The Fire Rages

And in the street? The fire rages. The main task of the firefighters is to localize the fire and not allow it to spread.

The left side of the marketplace, coming from Novoredker Street is one big fire. Red flames are tearing to the sky, crackling, the ceilings are breaking, and it looks like a big hell fell from the sky in order to destroy the town. This fire is nothing like previous fires when a house burned, a barn or a stall. Then, we, the children stood curiously, looked at the fire, counted the beams which fell one after the other; the eye concentrated on one small area.

But now the fire was raging without boundaries, excessively!

My little sister Libeleh runs by. A frightened crying little girl. My mother is beside her, and as always, worried. Father has disappeared somewhere. She is searching for him at the fire, watching for him…

My dear, poor father! You were active and encouraging at so many fires. Like a hero you ruled at every difficult situation – now you are sick, weak and tired. You are no longer allowed to react like in the past. The symptoms of your disease already exist, but you my dear do not know about it…now you are standing on the side, without your uniform – it's hanging in the cupboard. But thanks to your years of experience you are giving practical advice and from time to time a command: "Now here! From this side of the street!"

You stand at the corner of Khane Gotshikhes' house at the entrance of Synagogue Street. You don't want to allow the fire to spread, and you succeed!

The fire glows in your sick eyes as you slowly extinguish it with your bold glance.

Night. There are still flames which are being extinguished. Here and there are glowing black wet burned out ruins.

Mayrim Epshteyn

We accompany our tired, soaked from sweat, teacher to our home. Mother gives him a warm cup of milk, however he asks for vodka. "Well so be it" said mother, "if he wants vodka I'll give him vodka"!

The next day in class he told everyone that thanks to his pupil's mother he did not die in Zhetl, neither from thirst or hunger.

It was good for those who after the fire were able to return home.

But those whose homes burned had to find a place to spend the night and a place to stay until they found something.

Of course many friends took them in. Dr. Kru and his wife were among the victims. We gave them a room in our house.

A New Fire

Slowly Zhetl began to rebuild. Two years later we were startled by a heartrending siren.

It was Saturday before dawn. The fire started in the marketplace. We quickly left our warm beds and ran like shooting arrows toward the marketplace.

I run through the street, people are packing, the fire cannot be trusted. I ran to my aunt Leyke Daikhovsky. She is also packing. I grab a bundle and run to Fantchik's lake.

At the bridge there are a lot of people with lots of bundles. It is noisy. Everyone wants to protect their bit of poverty, although we hope the fire will not reach the bridge.

I put down the bundle and returned. I was now at Khaya Tules' yard.

"Quick!" I shouted, "Give me a bundle!" they threw me a bundle and I felt as if the fire was hitting my back. I took the same road, but now I could not return. The bridge on the Pomeraike River was burning making the firefighters' work more difficult.

[Page 140]

The marketplace after the fire of 1933

The marketplace after the fire of 1933: a view from the sky

I run through the rabbi's street and jump to Anna Shapiro's. I help her pack. Who knows if the fire will reach here?

Anna is sadly quite stunned. Among the goods she gives me to save is a full salt shaker. I run with the bundle and I am very careful; making sure the salt, God forbid, does not spill…

This time the fire destroyed our beautiful Manor Street. Black ruins stood on the spot where warm homes once stood.

I did not see the houses that were rebuilt. That autumn I left Zhetl. I hoped I would one day visit. I never imagined that I was leaving forever.

I never returned to you, my beloved Zhetl. Not because I was not attracted to you, not because I forgot you. That would have been unappreciative of me…

There are two large communal graves in Zhetl; one at the entrance of town the other where you exit. You were destroyed, my Zhetl, and I do not want to see you like that.

I will always carry you in my heart, like you once were.

The National Democrats (Endecja) Rage

by Moishe Mirsky (Montreal)

Translated by Janie Respitz

After Hitler, may his name be blotted out, came to power, fascism began to spread throughout Europe. It did not take long before anti Semitic waves were infesting Poland, first in the larger cities, later in the small towns. Zhetl did not escape this.

Hooligans arrived in town and organized Christian gatherings and agitated not to buy from Jews and told them to open their own cooperatives. At first the fascism was veiled, but by 1938 –39 it was without restraint. The hooligans came on market days, preached to the peasants and hung placards which read:

"Do not support business that lies in Jewish hands, don't buy from Jews, just from your own".

They would also picket Jewish businesses. If a Christian would walk out of a Jewish store they would attach a sign to his back which read: "Christian traitor".

They hung signs on Christian businesses which said: "Christian Business".

There would often be clashes between picketers and Jews which would result in accusations against the Jews for insulting the Polish state.

Once, on a Tuesday at the beginning of 1939, the entire town, including the church wall was plastered with anti Semitic slogans. The Polish priest noticed this early in the morning as he was setting out to the village. He called his congregants and asked them to remove the placards. The following Sunday, in his sermon he called the peasants to order and warned them against being influenced by hooligan adventurists.

Notwithstanding that the priest was beloved by the whole Christian population, his speech was not very effective. The Hitler instructors had a better understanding of this business and their speeches made a bigger impression on the peasants.

[Page 141]

Political Parties

Pioneers at Harvest in Zhetl 1919

[Page 142]

Political Parties in Zhetl

Translated by Judy Montel

Zhetl was aware of what was happening in the Jewish communities of Russia and Poland. And indeed, it also had all of the political parties: Zionist, anti-Zionist, Socialist and civilian, that had been finding adherents in the Jewish public from the second half of the nineteenth century. Until this period, Zhetl was a religious and traditionally observant town, which was characterized by the division into Chassidim and *Mitnagdim*, home-owners and artisans, those who studied and simple people.

In the second half of the nineteeth century, the *Haskala* [Jewish enlightenment movement] arrived in Zhetl and soon afterwards, the *Hibat Zion* [early Zionist] movement. The head and very first lover of Zion in Zhetl was Reb Yehushua Eizenshtat-Barzilai. He lived in Zhetl for 16 years (1871-1887) and moved to the land of Israel from here. In the Zionist world he was well-known as one of the founders of "Bnei Moshe" and one of the heads of the "Land of Israel Office" in Jaffa. In around 1898 he visited Zhetl and with his speeches attracted many adherents to the Zionist idea. As a result of this visit, and thanks to the support of Rabbi Reb Baruch Avraham Mirski, who had been the rabbi of Zhetl since 1892, the Zionist Association was founded in 1899. It was headed by Reb Menachem Vernikovski, Reb Shlomo Zalmen Dunetz and Reb Aharon Hersch Langbort.

The Association included the more progressive fathers, all of them religiously observant. Their activities concentrated in the middle study hall and in the Talmud Torah school and was expressed by selling "shekels", shares in "Bank Ha'Otzar", collecting monies for the Keren Kayemet and explaining the Zionist idea.

In the same years the first buds of the socialist and revolutionary movement could be seen in Zhetl. Those were years of expansion for the socialist forces, which strove to change the rules of government in Russia. Following the change in the rules of government, the Jewish socialists also hoped for a solution to the Jewish question.

Two socialist parties started in Zhetl: The Bund, and the S.R. Their members were organized in small groups, and would gather in private homes, while their larger meetings would take place in the forests around the town. Their activities concentrated on distributing written and spoken propaganda, in which they argued for an 8-hour work day and for social benefits. Occasionally they would organize demonstrations and attacks on government institutions or on the railway.

At the head of the Bund in Zhetl were Chayim Kaplinski, Avraham Moshe Brishensky, Yehoshua Obsievitz and others. At the head of the S.R. David Nedlshtein and Ilya Dovkovski were notable. As the waves of the revolution in Russia calmed, there was a certain slackening among the socialist parties in Zhetl.

Until the outbreak of World War I, Zhetl was characterized by the following division: the sons tended towards the anti-Zionist socialism, the progressive fathers – toward Zionism, while most of the people were faithful to tradition. The traditionally faithful were gathered by the Rabbi, Reb Zalmen Sorotzkin, in "Agudath Israel."

With the outbreak of the first world war, the situation changed. Starting in 1915, the Zionists, headed by the young Efra'im Blogolovski, opened the Zionist club, which gathered to it a large portion of the youth of Zhetl. When World War I was over, factional differentiation appeared in the Zhetl Zionism as well as the hegemony of the youth.

From the twenties and up to 1939, all of the important Zionist parties existed in Zhetl: The General Zionists, "Po'alei Zion" (Zionist Workers), "HaShomer HaTza'ir" (The Young Guard), The Revisionists and the Mizrachi.

In the beginning of the twenties, the advantage was held initially by the anti-Zionist circles, thanks to their energy and excellent organization, but beginning in the second half of the twenties, the advantage passed to the Zionists, who made their impression on all matters going on in the town, and who created joint frameworks such as: the Tarbut school, the Keren Kayemet Committee, the Keren HaYesod Committee, the Shekel Committee, and so on.

The equal side to all of the parties in Zhetl: their activity was great and decisive in deepening national and social awareness. With the Soviet invasion in 1939, they all disappeared from the horizon and the only ruler became the Communist Party. At first, the Zhetl communists were active in it, but before very long they were pushed aside and their places were taken by emissaries of the party from outside of Zhetl. The German invasion put an end to this party as well.

[Page 143]

Hovevei Zion (Lovers of Zion) and the Zionist Movement[1]

by Borukh Kaplinsky (Tel Aviv)

Translated by Janie Respitz

In the second half of the 19th century Zhetl was still an orthodox and extremely religious town. However enlightenment leanings began to slowly seep in. We don't know how large the circle of enlighteners was. We also don't know exactly who they were. However we can surmise that one of these enlightened Zhetl Jews was Yehoshua Heilpern.

From a correspondence in the newspaper "Hameilitz" (vol. 15, 1883) we learn that he arranged for 20 neglected boys to be trained by Zhetl craftsmen. He paid for them to learn a trade.

In this correspondence we read: "he noticed these neglected, poor boys were turning to crime. Worrying for their future he convinced them to leave their dirty work and learn a trade".

As we know, work and productivity are the foundations of the Jewish enlightenment. Without a doubt, Yehoshua Heilpern was one of Zhetl's enlightened Jews.

It is also clear that the author of this correspondence who uses the pseudonym Yevetz was also an enlightened Jew.

There were enlightened Jews from Zhetl who wrote for the Hebrew press: Yitzkhak Yakov Perles ("The Preacher"), Shloime Hemtzovsky ("The Lebanon"), Mayrim Namiyat ("Hameilitz") and two Zhetl writers: A. Ben Avigdor and Menakhem Mendl Merlinsky, who later became very famous.

We know a lot more about members of the Hovevei Zion, who were probably recruited from the enlightened circles.

Zhetl's Hovevei Zion members were merchants, store owners and craftsmen from the middle and older generations. They had to fight the orthodox and Slonim Hasidim who did not look favourably upon Zionism.

Yitzkhak Gibori (Khabravitsky) who left Zhetl in 1900 tells us that some established men in town came to his father and said: "Reb Avrom Yakov, your son is running around with the "little Zionists".

Reb Avrom Yakov replied: "may he never run around with anything worse".

This was a typical conversation. He claimed when the movement took its first steps in Zhetl, it already had a bit of prestige and its followers were referred to as "little Zionists".

The atmosphere changed a bit with the arrival of Rabbi Borukh Avrom Mirsky in 1892, but I'll talk about that a little later. Now, a few words on this topic: who were the members of the Hovevei Zion in Zhetl.

Reb Yehoshua Eisneshtat – Barzilai

One of the first members of the Hovevei Zion in Zhetl was Reb Yehoshua Eisenshtat, later known by the name of Barzilai. Together with Ahad Ha'am he was one of the founders of B'nei Moshe, a director of the Eretz Yisrael office in Jaffa and participated in the founding of the Centre for Artisans in Eretz Yisrael. He was also among the founders of a girl's school in Jaffa and helped the Biluim in Gdera and was among the early founders of Rechovot, Be'er Tuvia, Metula, and Mishmar Hayarden.

Reb Yehoshua Eisenshtat – Barzilai was born in Klezk in 1855. In 1871 he married Taybeh the daughter of a Zhetl merchant Reb Leyzer Fraydkes. His daughter Shifra was born in Zhetl in 1880.

Yehoshua Barzilai lived in Zhetl for 16 years. He ran large businesses. He dealt in lumber with a businessman from Grodno named Ahkenazi, eggs, leased the bathhouse, and was very successful. Besides all this he was very active in communal life. He was one of the founders and the breath of life of the Hovevei Zion in Zhetl. In a list published in "Ha Magid" (vol. 30, 1872) the names of about a dozen Jews from Zhetl appear who donated money to aid Persian Jews who were, at the time, suffering from hunger. Among those donating was Yehoshua Eisneshtat who gave 50 kopeks for this cause.

In 1887 Yehoshua Barzilai immigrated from Zhetl to Eretz Yisrael. Eleven years later, in 1898 he returned to Zhetl for a visit and gave a lecture in the House of Study which was written up in "Ha Meilitz" (vol. 232, 1898). His lecture about farmers on the Moshavot and the Anglo – Palestine Bank made a great impression. Many Jews in Zhetl decided to become involved in the Zionist movement. Even the extreme opponents began to show more compassion toward the Zionists.

During a party of the Hovevei Zion in Zhetl, Yehoshua Barzilai told them about a colonist from Zhetl in Kastina, Elimeylekh Izraelit. After the party the Jews of Zhetl donated money for the workers in Kastina.

[Page 144]

Reb Menakhem Vernikovsky

Another son in law of Zhetl was Reb Menakhem Vernikovsky from Slonim who married Soreh Dvoyreh Zeltzer from Zhetl. He became a central figure in the Hovevei Zion and Zionist movements in Zhetl until he emigrated in 1925.

Reb Menakhem Vernikovsky was the representative in Zhetl for the Odessa Society to Support Agriculture and Artisans in Syria and Eretz Yisrael ("HaMeilitz" vol. 4, 1898). In a letter from the Odessa Committee to Menakhem Vernikovsky dated October 29, 1897, we learn that the Czarist Minister of the Interior granted permission to the Odessa Committee to elect 67 representatives throughout Russia who had the right to collect membership fees. Reb Menakhem Vernikovsky was appointed, in this letter, as the representative from Zhetl. Membership dues amounted to a minimum of 5 rubles a year.

From this letter we learn Zhetl was an important Zionist centre, one of 67 in the Russian Empire and Reb Menakhem Vernikovsky was one of the most important Zionists in the country.

Many Zionist meetings took place in his home. In later years he displayed a lot of compassion and understanding for Labour Zionists although he himself was a religious Zionist.

Reb Shloime Zalmen Dunyetz

Reb Shloime Zalmen Dunyetz played a very important role in the Zhetl Hovevei Zion. His life, especially his Zionist activity and his emigration to Eretz Yisrael is described in our book by his grandson Mordkhai Dunyetz.

Reb Aharon Hersh Langbart

Reb Aharon Hersh Langbart, the father of the representative of the Jewish National Fund Reb Avrom Langbart was one of the most passionate preachers of Zionist thought in Zhetl.

Other Members in the Zionist Movement

Other members of the Zionist movement in Zhetl were: Eliezer Matisyahu Kantorovitch, who published often in "Hatzfira", Ziml Zimelevitch and Yakov Zimelevitch who complained in an article in "Ad Hazman" in 1909 that Zhetl only subscribes to three Hebrew newspapers, when there are 20 subscriptions to Yiddish papers and 12 Russian. Other members of the Zionist organization were Meir Mirsky, Yoine Leyb Khlebnikov, ("Hameilitz" vol. 46, 1902), Moishe Arzikhovsky, Noyekh Rozvasky, Aharon Alpert and others.

The Rabbi Reb Borukh Avrom Mirsky

As mentioned, Hovevei Zion in Zhetl received a lot of help from the rabbi and Hovevei Zion member Reb Borukh Avrom Mirsky. His Zionist activity is described in this book by Rabbi Y. L. Maimon and Moishe Tzinovitch. Thanks to him and Yehoshua Eisenshtat there were often Hovevei Zion gatherings in Zhetl.

The 100th Anniversary of the Death of the Vilna Gaon

We read about this gathering in "Hameilitz (Vol. 227, 1897). It was during the week of Sukkot, 1897, marking the 100th anniversary of the death of the Vilna Gaon, the Hovevei Zion members gathered in the House of Study and organized a celebration through prayer. At his event it was decided to plant two trees in Shmuel Garden in the name of Rabbi Shmuel Mohilover and greetings were sent to Rabbi Shmuel Mohilover, to the Odessa Committee, and to all the colonists in Eretz Yisrael and to all members of the Hovevei Zion around the world.

The Founding of the Zionist Association

Meetings such as this would often occur however there was still no organized Zionist Association in Zhetl. Only in 1899 was a Zionist Association founded in Zhetl. We learn this from "Hameilitz" (vol. 280, 1899). The correspondent of this information who hid behind the initial M.R. tells us, "in spite of the opposition of the Slonim Hasidim and the extreme religious, the Hovevei Zion in Zhetl finally succeeded in organizing an association".

From this article we can surmise that the Hovevei Zion in Zhetl was still very small and despite the help of Zhetl's rabbi they still had to battle the religious circles in town.

Daughters of Zion

At the same time the Zionist Association was founded in Zhetl, an association of Daughters of Zion was also founded. Unfortunately we do not know the names of the members in this organization, but we learn from the aforementioned article, the founders attempted to spread Zionism among the women in Zhetl.

The Enlightened Activity

The enlightened activity of the Zhetl's Hovevei Zion was concentrated in a few places: at the middle House of Study, at the Talmud Torah, and at Menakhem Vernikovsky's house.

The middle House of Study in Zhetl was considered to be the progressive, Zionist House of Study.

On holidays the Zionist Association would pray in a side room. Sometimes they would organize their prayers in a room in the Talmud Torah. After prayers, Reb Menakhem Vernikovsky or Reb Aharon Hersh Langbart would deliver a passionate speech dedicated to Zionism.

The Hovevei Zion would organize special celebrations on the Sabbath Nakhamu and on Chanukah. Sabbath Nakhamu was considered to be the Zionist Sabbath. After reading the Torah the Zhetl preachers would propagate Zionist thought. Similar celebrations would take place on Chanukah. From the article in "Hameilitz" written in 1899 we learn that year the celebrations took place in a hall with Zionist speeches and songs and 30 new members joined.

Friday nights the Hovevei Zion members would gather in the old House of Study, learn the Torah portion of the week and share their love for Eretz Yisrael.

The Hovevei Zion would often organize parties with a bottle of Carmel wine and the singing of Zionist songs. (See Moshe Bitan – "Zhetl Fifty Years Ago").

[Page 145]

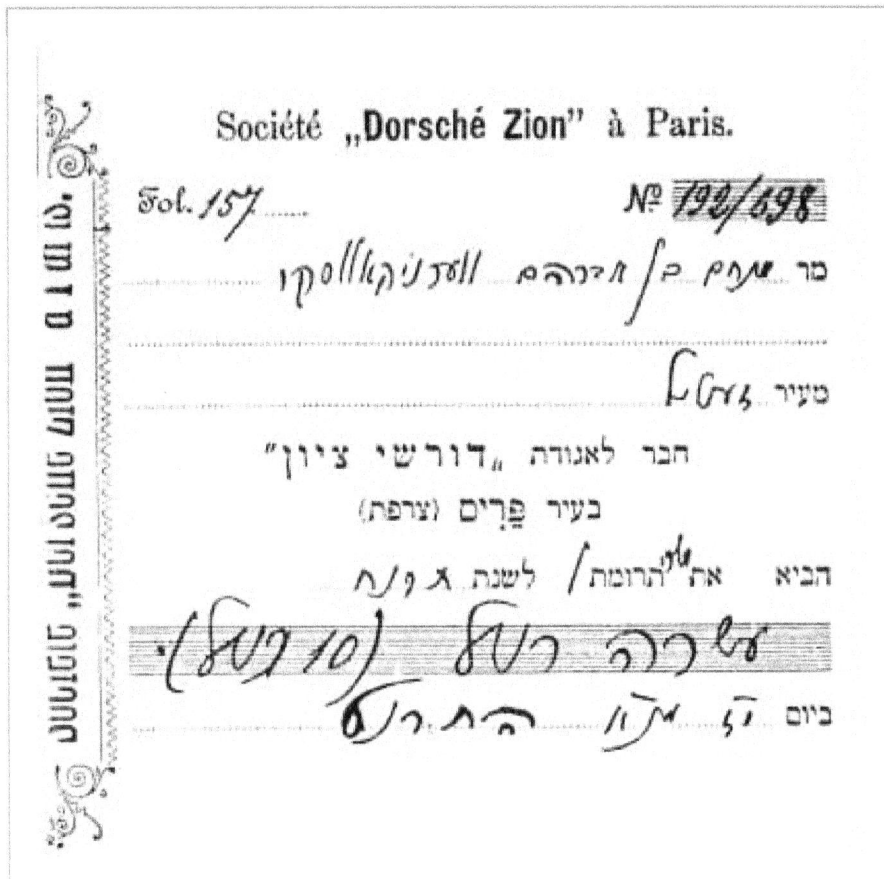

Menakhem Vernikovsky's membership card to "Preachers of Zion", (Dorshei Zion) Paris

Practical Work

What comprised the practical work of the Hovevei Zion and Zionists?

One of the most important tasks was to collect membership fees for the Odessa Committee. Of no less importance was the task to recruit members for Zionist colonization societies. One such society was the "Dorshei Zion" (The Preachers of Zion) in Paris. The branch of "Dorshei Zion" in our region was situated in Minsk with members from all the towns and cities in the area. The task of the association was to buy land in Eretz Yisrael for its members. In order to realize this, every member had to pay yearly dues. After a certain amount of years every member received a kushan (a certificate of registration on immovables) for a piece of land according to his yearly contribution.

According to financial receipts which are in our possession, Reb Menakhem Vernikovsky was a member of "Dorshei Zion" from 1893 until 1902. In 1893 he paid 100 francs in membership dues, in 1898, 20 ruble and in 1899, 10 ruble.

From a letter written by the secretary of "Dorshei Zion" in Minsk to Reb Menakhem Vernikovsky we learn that members of the society did not pay their due regularly therefore the association could not send its delegate to Eretz Yisrael.

Besides Reb Menakhem Vernikovsky the are also other Hovevei Zion members from Zhetl who belonged to "Dorshei Zion" but unfortunately no records have remained.

H. CAHN & C⁰, BANQUIERS

34, Boulevard Bonne-Nouvelle et 1, Rue d'Hauteville

Capital 4,000,000 de Francs

Nᵒ 698   Francs 100

REÇU de la Société DORCHÉ-ZION I. la somme de CENT-FRANCS.

Paris, le   13 Octobre 1893
H. CAHN & Cᵒ

M. Vanikoosky

A receipt from the Dorshei zion Society, October 13, 1893

[Page 146]

Later, with the emergence of Zionism, the former members of Hovevei Zion and the present political Zionist begin to sell shares from the Colonial Bank, collect money for the Jewish National Fund and sell shekels.

Ideology

We do not have any material on the ideological orientation of Zhetl's Hovevi Zion. We can however surmise the orientation of the Zhetl's Zionist Association from an appeal which was published in "Hameilitz" (Vol. 46, 1902).This appeal was signed by dozens of Zionist associations in Russia, including Zhetl with its five leaders: Menakhem Vernikovsky, Ziml Zimelevitch, Eliezer Matisyahu Katorovitch, Meir Mirsky and Yoine Leyb Khlebnikov.

It was emphasized in this appeal that the undersigned have nothing against the democratic wing, to the contrary, they value the young energy in Zionism. However, the proclamations of a few members of the wing forced them to publish this appeal.

The appeal protests against Dr. Chaim Weitzman who invited secretaries to a gathering of young Zionists. Two from the "exile language" but not one from the "Zion language". Dr. Weitzman's proposal was not well received, therefore the appeal was gratifying. It stressed that the hostess (Hebrew) had the honour to sit at the presidium beside "maid" (Yiddish).

The appeal was also aimed against one of the "youth" who proposed that they only observe the Jewish laws which are appropriate for our times and only celebrate holidays which possess a national character.

The appeal stresses that each individual can fulfill any good deed he wishes and Zionism, as an organization cannot divide our Torah and culture into military companies as this can be used against Zionism in general.

The appeal protested against the young (Abramovitch) who claimed Zionism was a solution only for our economic and cultural needs.

Finally the appeal protests against Dr. Motzkin who suggested forgetting our past.

From the unanimity of Zhetl's Zionists concerning this appeal we learn they are progressive and value the young. (The appeal ends with these words: Peace for Israel and our youth). Understandably they could not force every individual to fulfill all the commandments, however at the same time they stood firm with both feet on the subject of our long tradition.

We have very little information about the activity of the Zionist association from 1902 –1915. We have gathered more information from the period 1915 – 1918 during the German occupation.

During the German Occupation

In his article entitled "Zhetl During the German Occupation" Yosef Vinyetsky describes the activity of the Zionist club. The club has its own locale, a library, organizes gatherings, checkers evenings and a weekly newspaper called "Ha Chaver" ("The Friend"), written in Hebrew and Yiddish.

The breath of life behind the Zionist club was Efraim Belagolovsky.

Performance of Zhetl Zionists "Scenes of Farmers in Eretz Yisrael", Tu B'Shvat 1918

His activism is described in this book by Nekhemieh Aminoakh. E. Belagolovsky's greatest achievement was attracting Zhetl's youth to the Zionist association. Until this time those active in the movement were established men from the middle and older generations. Although Belagolovsky was part of the Zionist youth, he tried to make sure the association in Zhetl would maintain a general character.

Efraim Belagolovsky was not satisfied with his Zionist work in Zhetl. He helped organize the Zionist movements in surrounding cities and towns.

In "Ha Tzfira" (Vol. 13–14, 1918) we read the Zhetl Zionist Association collected 400 mark for the national fund and distributed 120 shekel. There is a list which tells us there was a library with 123 readers, lectures, meetings and courses for adults.

[Page 147]

Young Zionists in Zhetl

At the end of the German occupation a Zionist youth group was organized in Zhetl. Its members were: Ayge Izraelit, Pesieh Izraelit, Mordkhai Bender, Khayeh Batchkovsky, Shloime Khaim Vernikovsky, Yakov Zaltsman, Yakov Zimelevitch, Avrom Langbart, Shloime Lubtchansky, Yitzkhak Leybovitch, D. Maslovata, Bezalel Mashkovsky, Namiyat, Avrom Sideransky, Mayrim Epshteyn, Feygl Epshteyn, Yishayahu Moishe Pilnik, Khaye Soreh Kastilansky, Mikhal Rabinovitch, Alte Rabinovitch, Mikhl Roznov, Khane Malke Shvedsky.

There are two tendencies within the youth movement: right and left.

In 1918 a split occurred among the Young Zionists in Zhetl. A group of comrades, led by Shloime Khaim Vernikovsky decided to join the left wing "Poalei Zion" (Labour Zionists).

This group had 30 members. According to a photograph we have from that time, here is a list of the "Poalei Zion" members in alphabetical order: (the Hebrew alphabet)

Avrom Ivenitsky, A. Bensky, Rivka Breskin, M. Bender, Y. Bunimovsky, Sh. Ostashinsky, A. Gershovsky, Shloime Khaim Vernikovsky, Alter Zernitsky, Yitzkhak Leybovitch, Tz. Maslovata, Mayrim Epshteyn, V. Savitsky, A. Sideransky, Wolf Farfl, Soreh Kastilansky, Khaim Mikhl Roznov, and Khane Malke Shvedsky.

The "Poalei Zion" group in Zhetl organized "Ha Chalutz" (The Pioneer), and performed plays about the life of the workers in Eretz Yisrael and devoted themselves to the public library.

Shloime Khaim Vernikovsky's funeral

In 1920 Shloime Khaim Vernikovsky died. He was in his early twenties. His death came as a shock to the Poalei Zion group in Zhetl.

After his death the group radicalized. This was as a result of the split in the international Poale Zion movement to the left and right. The radicalization also played a role among Zhetl's youth during the Polish – Bolshevik war.

As a result of both processes a portion of Zhetl's members of Poalei Zion left the party and joined the Yiddishist and anti – Zionist wing of Zhetl. A portion of former "Poalei Zion" members together with the leaders of the literary – drama circle became founders of the Zhetl Yiddish school.

Shloime Khaim Vernikovsky

Young Mizrachi (Religious Zionists)

By 1918 there was an active group of Young Mizrachi in Zhetl numbering around 15 members. Among them were: Shmuel Dunyetz, Ben–Zion Peskovsky, Mordkhai Sokolovsky, Mordkhai Senderovsky, Ruven Kantesbrot and others.

Goodbye

As mentioned, Zionism in Zhetl up until the First World War was of a religious nature. During the First World War there were two substantial changes in Zhetl's Zionism. 1) Many young people got involved and 2) differentiation in Zhetl's Zionist movement. The movement lost its unity, religious character and three new groups were cultivated: 1) the Young Zionist, 2) Young Mizrachi and 3) the Polaei Zion.

All these groups cultivated the foundation for the emergence of Zionist political parties in Zhetl after the war.

Originally, in the years right after the war the communal initiative in Zhetl lay within anti –Zionist circles. However, slowly the Zionist camp began to organize and by the mid – 1920s they became the dominating force on Zhetl's Jewish streets.

The history of Zhetl Zionism after the First World War is described in our book by these friends: Yosef Berman, Yakov Indershteyn, Eliezer Namiyat, Dvoyre Gordaysky, Avrom Alpert and others.

Translator's note:

1. The Hovevei Zion movement was the precursor to political Zionism.

[Page 148]

Zhetl's Revolutionaries

by Moishe Mirsky (Montreal)

Translated by Janie Respitz

In Czarist times two revolutionary parties existed in Zhetl: the S.R (Social Revolutionaries) and the "Bund". The main leader of the "Bund" was Khaim Kaplinsky who due to his political activity spent many years in Siberia. In later years he was among the builders of the Yiddish School and today he and his wife live in Poland.

In 1906 an expropriation of the post train was carried out at the station in Novoliyenie. The group that carried out this attack was comprised of nine Russians and three Jewish guys from our town: Shmuel Zhelianier, Eliyahu Rabinovitch (the son of the Moscow rabbi), and Dovid Nodlshteyn, the lead organizer of this group.

Due to a provocation this expropriation failed. Police forces were notified in three towns: Lida, Baranovitch and Slonim. They blocked all the roads around the town and one day after the expropriation all those who participated were captured at the Nieman River.

Dovid Nodlshteyn was not with the group at the Nieman but a few days later he was, incidentally, arrested.

This was a Sunday during a Catholic holiday procession. Dovid Nodlshteyn lived in the garrett at the home of the Krigel family. This house was next door to the church. People stood on the stoop of the house watching the parade, including children who noticed something was sticking out of the attic. When they took it down they were shocked to find a few revolvers and two bombs.

Khaim and Rivka Kaplinsky

They immediately notified the police who searched the house and arrested Nodlshteyn as a political suspect, but not as leader of the attack. However, during the investigation a friend betrayed him and he was accused of leading the expropriation.

The trial took place a year later in Grodno against those who participated in the attack. Eliyahu and Shmuel Rabinovitch were released due to lack of evidence. They were found with the group but they did not take part in the attack. Their job was to wait by the river and take the attackers across to the other side. At the trial they said they were coincidentally at the Nieman River fishing and suddenly the attackers came with weapons and forced them to take them across the river. This is why they were released.

Dovid Nodlshteyn, the organizer, was sentenced to twelve years in prison. He languished in a Moscow jail until 1917 when he was released by the revolution.

I still remember an interesting evening in 1919 during the occupation of the Bolsheviks. Dovid Nodlshteyn was visiting Zhetl. The Literary – Drama Society organized a reception for him. Over a cozy cup of tea, he told us of his experiences during ten years in a Moscow jail.

I also remember the expropriation of the state treasury which took place on the streets of St. Petersburg. The attack was partially successful, that is to say, they took the money but paid for it with two human lives. During the shooting two revolutionaries were wounded. They were captured and later sentenced to death. One of the victims was from Zhetl, Yitzkhak Rabinovitch, the son of Feyvl.

"Katsapes" (A pejorative word for Russians)

In Noyekh Prilutsky's folkore collection, where all the nicknames of Jewish towns in Poland are listed, our town Zhetl is recorded with the nickname "Katsapes". I will explain here how our town got such an unsuitable name.

[Page 149]

Zhetl was considered one of the most cultural and important Jewish towns in the region. Jews lived in unity – really like one family. Everybody enjoyed each other's celebrations and empathized with their sorrows.

I remember still in Czarist times when conscription took place in our town. Non Jewish boys would come to our town from the surrounding area. Understandably, there was no lack of anti–Semitism at that time. They would get drunk and let loose on a Jewish beard, throw stones at Jewish windows and grab something from a Jewish shop without paying.

As our Jews hated to be pushed around they "honoured" these gentile boys until they finally respected the Zhetl Jews.

Friends of our local gentile boys would go work in larger cities and always threaten the city Jews: remember our guys will come from Odessa and settle accounts with you.

I would like to recall an event: four nice young guys came for conscription (I even remember they came from the village Pager). At the train station in Novoliynie they went to the buffet, had a couple of drinks and beat up a few Zhetl Jews. They also bragged that when they came to town they would "honour" the rest of the Jews.

A special courier on a bicycle came to town and informed us. As one should, ten Zhetl boys, headed by Leyb Dorevsky, were waiting on the highway to "honour" the gentile boys, as they deserved. Two of the guys spent time in the hospital and the rest avoided the Jews.

This is how Zhetl youth defended the honour of our Jews, therefore I would call them heroes and not "Katsapes".

Attacks

Translated by Judy Montel

Close to Zhetl, next to the station at Novoilanya, an attack was carried out against the mail train in 1906. The attackers meant to steal the treasury chest for the S.R. revolutionary party. Nine Russian revolutionaries took part in the attack as well as three young men from Zhetl: Shmuel Rabinowitz, Eliyahu Rabinowitz (son of Rabbi Reb Shmuel from Moscow) and David Nedlshtein.

The attack failed and the attackers were caught near the Neman River. However, the head of the group, David Nedlshtein was caught in totally different circumstances. It was on Sunday, during the Catholic procession in honor of the Christian holiday. The children of Zhetl, who were watching the procession, came across a suspicious package in the attic of David Nedlshtein's home in which there were hand guns and bombs.

The police, who were called to the place, arrested David Nedlshtein who was later sentenced to 12 years imprisonment. David Nedlshtein was only released from prison in 1917 by the forces of the revolution, but Eliyahu and Shmuel Rabinowitz were released immediately from lack of evidence.

At the trial that took place against the two of them in Grodno, they claimed that they happened to be in the area of the Neman in order to go fishing, and suddenly the attackers surprised them and forced to cross the Neman, however, they had no connection to the attack and the attackers. To their joy, the court accepted this claim.

In 1919, David Nedlshtein arrived in Zhetl as a visitor. In a party in his honor that was organized by the literary-drama club, he told of his suffering in the Moscow jail.

I also remember an attack on the treasury chest in the streets of Peterburg. The attack succeeded, the chest was stolen, however two of the participants in the attack were injured. One of them was Yitzchak Rabinowitz, son of Reb Feivel Skidler, who was caught and sentenced to death.

[Page 150]

Memories of the "Bund"

by Yekhiel Kuznietzky (Tel Aviv)

Translated by Janie Respitz

The "Bund" was founded in Zhetl around 1902.

The organizers were:

Avrom Moishe Borishansky, Alter Bom, Bene Blokh (Notke the teacher's son), Yosl Khemes, Yitzkhak Levit, Nakhman Shmuel Moishe's, Mayrim Epshteyn, Yekhiel Kuznetzky, Leyzer Rabinovitch, Shloime Pilnik and others.

Yekhiel Kuznietzky

As I remember the founding took place in Oleshnik on the Novolienye highway. Smaller meetings would take place at the home of Pinkhas the shoemaker. Our liaison officer to the committee in Slonim was Khaim Kaplinsky who would go back and forth by foot in order to provide us with revolutionary literature.

The goal of our political party was to carry out educational work between the workers and youth and fight for a shorter work day. I would like to recall here some of the actions our party carried out.

A Proclamation Not to Take Any Russian Money

It was 1904. We received proclamations from Slonim calling on us not to take

[Page 151]

Memories of the Zhetl S.R. (Socialist Revolutionaries)

by H. Lubchansky – Khabibi (Tel Aviv)

Translated by Janie Respitz

Under the influence of my uncle Yitzkhak Asher Vernikovsky I joined the S.R. as a young girl. As everywhere else, we were organized into groups of ten. The leader of our group was Gele Bom.

We would meet, most of the time, at Dovid Goldshteyn's, in the attic (of Krigl's house), where we would read and explain chapters from socialism and Marxism. We would print appeals on a hectograph and hang them in the streets and often send them to nearby towns. I was one of the liaisons and would often go to Dvoretz and Slonim with printed material.

My Mother is Not Happy

I would keep the typewriter, printing materials and weapon parts in our home. Because of this there were often searches. My mother was not overjoyed. She claimed that if my father had stopped us we would not have joined the revolutionary movement. But father did not stop us. Despite the fact he was a passionate Zionist he was sympathetic to the revolutionary movement, especially the S.R.

Larger meetings were held in Oleshnik, on the way to Novolenyie. On Saturdays, especially in the summer, we would sit on the ground in Oleshnik and have passionate discussions. Representatives from other parties, Bundists and Zionists, would often participate at these meetings. People would often come to these meetings to give lectures, from the central office and even from Moscow.

Tuesday, from time to time after the market day, we would gather at Yosl the house painter's tea house. At four o'clock, when the peasants went home we would sit in the packed tea house and listen to lectures from the central office or from neighbouring towns which called on us to perform revolutionary acts against the Czarist regime.

During such meetings, our comrades would stand armed on the street to guard us and ensure the police would not come. I remember at one meeting a fire broke out and everyone ran away.

Zhetl's party comrades would not attend these meetings. Due to security reasons they would go to other towns while comrades from other towns would come to us.

The leaders of the Zhetl S.R. were Elye Zabkovsky and Hirshl the pious man's son. Elye Zabkovsky did not play an important role only in Zhetl but in the entire region as well. In 1905–06 he was sentenced to forced labour and served his time in Moscow. He was given amnesty in 1917.

We Disrupt a Zionist Speaker

We would often go to the House of Study and disrupt a Zionist speaker. Such an incident would naturally end with a commotion, until the superintendent of the police would arrive and chase away both sides.

After such meetings there would be arrests. We would always find a solution with the Zhetl police. For a few rubles we would free our comrade.

The first strike in Zhetl was organized against Avrom Yakov Tikachinsky. He was a ritual scribe and employed many writers. We demanded money from him, if I'm not mistaken, 2000 ruble. It is worthwhile to mention, his own son, a Bundist, instigated the action against his father.

At Our Home

There was a very different atmosphere in my father's home. He often hosted Zionist meetings and celebrations. In the interim days of Passover and Sukkot, all the Zionists would come to us, give donations and receive receipts for the Jewish National Fund or buy stocks at the Anglo – Palestine bank where Zhetl Jews would buy on credit. At these gatherings there would often be a report given by Reb Zalmen Dunetz who would travel throughout the province collection money for the Zionist cause.

[Page 152]

The Zhetl Worker After the First World War

by Dov Arzhekhovsky (Akko)

Translated by Janie Respitz

After the First World War when the last boots of the German occupiers left Poland and White Russia a civil war broke out between the Polish nobility and the not yet well organized Red Army. Zhetl remained under the control of newly emerging Polish power.

Dov Arzhekhovsky

Later, when the life of the Jewish population began to normalize, Zhetl's youth began to feel something was missing. They began to search for what the four war years brutally took from them.

A group of young people among whom were: Yoel Tcheplovodsky, of blessed memory, Mote Turetsky, of blessed memory, Noyakh Mnuskin, of blessed memory, Mikhal Guzovsky, of blessed memory, Shmuel Mnuskin (now in Israel) and Berl Arzhekhovsky (now in Israel), began to talk about opening a corner for the youth where they would be able to spend their free time. They decided to establish a cultural group called "The Youth Society in Zhetl". To achieve this goal they needed a locale which Zhetl did not possess at that time.

A founding meeting was called in the home of Yokhe Arzhekhovsky. Those gathered declared the goal of the organization. All gathered, except the girls had the right to join the Youth Society. Boys signed up from all levels of Zhetl youth no matter their parentage, which in those days played an important role on the Jewish street.

The registered members ranged from 15 –18 years old. It was decided at the founding meeting that everyone had to pay monthly membership dues, which would go toward renting a locale as well as buying newspapers and books.

We rented space in the home of Yokhe Arzhekhovsky, which had a room where we held our meetings as well as a reading room. In those years we did not have our own cultural forces as the majority of us were boys who did not even finish our studies at the Talmud Torah due to the World War.

The older youth as well were not well organized so there was really no one to turn to for cultural help.

Then, one of the older youth approached us whose name was Noyakh Mikulitsky (Moishe Dovid the stagecoach driver's grandson). He left the Yeshiva and became a teacher in Zhetl. He offered to help us, voluntarily, in the form of readings and lectures for our standing members.

We also turned to the municipal library in Zhetl, which had been in existence from before the war to help us obtain books for our reading room.

The board of the directors of the library under the directorship of Yitzkhak Leybovitch, accommodated us with books.

At one meeting a suggestion was made to allow girls to join, but the majority voted against in order not to create chaos among those who were not yet culturally developed.

After a certain amount of time, when the youth had become a bit more mature and aware, a suggestion was brought to the general meeting to create a drama circle within the Youth Society. In order to present performances, they needed girls. This is when the suggestion to allow girls re–emerged and this time was accepted. The first two female members were Khaya Dvoyre Sovitsky (Khaim Velvl the tailor's daughter – today in Argentina), and Khaya Soreh Grande (who perished in the ghetto).

The Youth Society existed from the beginning of 1922 until the end of 1924. New winds began to blow through Poland. Political parties were being founded such as the "Bund", the communist party and the Zionist organization. Each member, according to his convictions, decided on a party causing the Youth Society to disband.

The Professional Union in Zhetl

After the undoing of the Youth Society, we began to hear rumours, that in the surrounding towns like Slonim and Baranovitch professional unions were being organized. Zhetl's young workers began to think about organizing and establishing a professional union in town.

[Page 153]

Two delegates of youth workers were sent to Baranovitch which was then the centre of White Russia. The members were: Noyakh Mnuskin, of blessed memory and Mikhal Guzovsky, of blessed memory. They had to become informed and bring instructions back on how to organize a professional union. These members brought the necessary material as well as the address of the Central Professional Union in Warsaw at 17 Brotzke Street. As there was no locale a founding meeting of all workers was held in the small forest near Zhetl, behind the cemetery.

It was the spring of 1924. The organizers of the general meeting were: Mikhal Guzovsky of blessed memory, Noyakh Mnuskin of blessed memory, Shmuel Mnuskin (now in Israel), Mote Turetzky of blessed memory, Khaim Sovitzky (now in America) and Berl Arzhekhovsky (now in Israel). At that meeting it was decided to turn to the central office in Warsaw in order to legalize a professional union in Zhetl, because without their permission it would not be possible to hold these gatherings. At the same time a temporary board of directors was elected composed of those mentioned above in order to begin the work.

The temporary board turned to the central office in Warsaw at 17 Brotzke Street. When permission was received from Warsaw to create a union a second meeting was called of all Zhetl workers in order to announce the legalization and register new members.

At the general meeting it was decided to tax all members in order to rent a locale, without which no work could get done. The administration took the money and rented a locale in the home of Moishe Khaim the teacher (in the synagogue courtyard). The administration began to recruit members and organize trade sections.

The needle section consisted of: tailors, seamstresses and hat makers. The leather section: cobblers, stitchers and saddle makers. The building section: carpenters, blacksmiths and locksmiths. They also organized the labourers at Leybe Kaplinsky's sawmill, which was made up mainly of Christians. It was difficult to organize the Christian workers who came from the villages. Work for them was not a matter of life and death, and because of them, the Christian village workers, strikes often broke out in workshops which opposed salary increases.

There were approximately 100 – 120 members of the professional union in Zhetl.

We Join the Central Bund

In the early years of the Polish democracy the centre of the professional union in Warsaw at 17 Brotzke Street was under the influence of the communist party. Until 1925– 26 the Polish authorities tolerated this situation. However, in the years when angry winds began to blow in Poland they began to harass the professional union and put some of the leadership in jail. Also the provincial unions which had joined the communist central began suffering from harassment, Zhetl included.

The situation reached the point that the central office of the professional union in Warsaw at 17 Brotzke Street had to liquidate and joined the Bund, which in the eyes of the Polish authorities was "kosher". This unification took place according to the conditions of the Bund. Automatically, the professional union in Zhetl also joined the Bund at 1 Tlomatcki Street.

The professional union in Zhetl did not preside over political activity. However, outside the framework of the union, each member took part in political activities according to his own convictions.

As long as our union in Zhetl was connected to the communist central, the communists had the main influence. Later, the situation changed.

We Are On Strike

The first strike in Zhetl broke out at the end of 1924 in the leather trade; the stitchers. When the bosses, after long negotiations did not want to concede to the striking workers, a solidarity strike broke out among the cobblers which were a strong section of the leather trade.

After, when the negotiations with the craftsmen's union did not produce results, the administration of the professional union decided to open their own workshops, produce shoes and sell them at the market at competitive prices. To achieve this goal Zhetl's professional union required a stitcher from Baranovitch. Workshops were set up and the shoes they produced were sold at the market for competitive prices. This broke the stubbornness of the bosses and they conceded to the striking workers. I must mention, strikes would normally break out before the Christian holidays when all the workshops had enough workers.

[Page 154]

The second big strike broke out in the spring of 1925 among the tailors. Here too, the bosses, under the direction of the craftsmen's union were stubborn, and used Christian strike breakers for whom work was not a matter of life and death.

Once, when the workers from the professional union wanted to take down a Christian strike breaker from Y. L's workshop, the boss threw a hot iron at them.

A second incident took place at Aharon Yoselevitch's workshop. When the striking workers wanted to take down a Christian strike breaker, and he resisted, he was badly beaten by the workers.

Photo: Members of the dramatic society of the seamstress union.

Name of the play: "Itzikl Wants to Get Married".

Seated in the first row: Herman Frenkel, Khaim Leybovitch. Second row: Moishe Lisagusrky, Nokhem Bryder, Shimen Levaranchik, Blond Noishe (Indershteyn), Ruven Krugman. Third row: Beyle Mnuskin, ...Fourth row standing: Yokhe Zernitsky, Zelda Likhter, Alter Gertzovsky, Sorke Novogrudsky,...., Sayne Leah Karpelovitch,....,Kalmen Sholkovitch, ...Meir Mankovitch.

We must be thankful that the commander of police was a leftist and sided with the workers. He was satisfied with a warning that this should not happen again. Finally, after long negotiations with the craftsmen union, the strike in the needle trade was liquidated. The professional union in Zhetl also organized its own drama circle and with their own resources, directed by Herman Frenkel of blessed memory, carried out performances and review evenings.

This is how Zhetl's workers lived and fought for their existence until the outbreak of the Second World War in 1939.

We are Striking

Translated by Judy Montel

In the first years after the first World War, there was a professional union in Zhetl that was a branch of the center in Warsaw, that was under communist influence. However, over time, the communist center in Warsaw was dismantled and we became a branch of the professional union that was influenced by the Bund.

The first strike in Zhetl after World War I broke out at the end of 1924 in the workshops of the stitchers. After these did not agree to the demands of the workers, a sympathy-strike broke out also in the cobblers' workshops.

The exhausting negotiations with the Artisans Union were not successful and then the committee of the professional union in Zhetl decided to open his own workshop, and to manufacture shoes and to compete with the stitchers and cobblers. In order to accomplish this decision, a stitcher was invited from Baranovitch and started manufacturing cheap shoes and this softened the stubbornness of the artisans. By the way, I wish to note that we would mostly declare a strike before the holidays of the Christians, when all of the workshops were working at full capacity.

The second strike broke out in the spring of 1925 in the tailors' workshops. They, guided by the artisans union, remained incalcitrant and ordered Christian strike-breakers who worked for very little since the work was not a matter of livelihood for them, and they usually also worked in agriculture.

[Page 155]

The HeChalutz (The Pioneer)

by Yosef Berman (Tel Aviv)

Translated by Janie Respitz

We were a group of young Zionists, almost all the same age. Many of us were idlers, while others worked in their parents' shops. But we all dedicated a lot of time to Zionist work.

Yosef Berman

Our small group headed by Avrom Langbart belonged to the most active Zionist movement in town. Besides us there were many Zionist activists in town, but they were older, they had families, business and worries about earning a living. We however, were young, unmarried and unemployed.

Our first Zionist work was to collect money for the Jewish National Fund, the Jewish Agency and other Zionist funds. We were devoted to this work with heart and soul.

A bit of time passed and suddenly our lives changed. This was approximately 1924.

One Friday in the summer I received an invitation to come that evening to the home of Menakhem Vernikovsky. It was emphasized in the invitation that this meeting was urgent and secret. This made me very curious. I wanted to learn the secret sooner than later. However, there was nothing I could do except be patient and wait until the evening.

The Founding Meeting

As soon as my father returned from synagogue I ate quickly and left for Menakhem Vernikovsky's. When I arrived I saw old friends as well as some new faces. I soon learned the purpose of this secret meeting. They confided in me that a member from the central office of HeChalutz came from Warsaw with the intention of starting a branch in Zhetl. Our duty was to be first pioneers, the founders and spreaders of this idea. Avrom Bialopolsky from the central office came to explain the tasks and goals of HeChalutz in general and particularly our task in Zhetl.

This took me and the other members by surprise. I was overjoyed. We had waited a long time for this moment. Now we were happy that we lived to see the minute where we could realize our dream.

The meeting took place in secret as we were not registered with the authorities. Our group had 30 members. We went down to Menakhem Vernikovsky's cellar to be sure we would not be discovered.

It was dark in the cellar but we did not want to turn on a light on the Sabbath in the presence of Menakhem Vernikovsky, so we sat in the dark until late at night and listened to A. Bialopolsky's lecture.

I Decided to Become a Pioneer

A. Bialopolsky explained he had the authority from the central office to create a branch of HeChalutz in Zhetl.

He explained the tasks of HeChalutz: Physical training and pioneer training. When someone joins HeChalutz he is not asked which political party he belongs to as HeChalutz is apolitical, however it is affiliated with the Histadrut Haovdim (Worker's Union). The first condition to receive a certificate from HeChalutz was to participate in a training camp for 6 months to a year. To achieve this goal training centres were established.

He spoke at length until late into the night. He told us about life in the Land of Israel, about the Kibbutzim, the working class, and emphasized that our task was to prepare the youth here in the diaspora to go and settle on a kibbutz and not in a city.

However, given that not everyone was capable of the hard work of drying out swamps required on a kibbutz, longer training would be demanded to prepare our members in the diaspora to be good pioneers in the Land of Israel. He ended with these words:

"Friends, you will have to leave your work, your parents, and your home, become pioneers, travel to the Land of Israel and with your own strength build the new country for yourselves and future generations".

[Page 156]

It was dark and quiet in the cellar. Everyone was dreamy and did not speak a single word, but everyone felt deep in the hearts that these were the words of a prophet who came to bring the message of the redemption of the land and it was up to us to realize this dream.

At that moment I felt I must be one of the redeemers and I decided to be a pioneer. All of our friends made the same decision.

We knew we were taking on a difficult obligation, but at the same time we understood, if not us, no one.

It was decided that the next afternoon we would gather again. In the middle of the night we all sang Hatikva and separated.

The First Organizational Steps

The next morning our group held a meeting with A. Bialopolsky. A temporary council was elected with three members until the general meeting would be held. The council consisted of: 1) Yoel Tcheplovodsky – chairman, 2) Efraim Klin – secretary, 3) Hirshl Gertzovsky – treasurer.

According to instructions we received from the central office of HeChalutz, each of us who joined HeCHalutz had to fill out a requisition and provide a biography. We did not accept anyone who opposed Zionism. Those confirmed by the council were accepted as candidates for a period of 6 months. Candidates who were active in the organization and fulfilled all obligations were accepted by the general assembly to join as members.

It was a Saturday afternoon (I don't remember the exact date), when HeChalutz in Zhetl was founded. Later, together with HeChalutz HaTzair (The Young Pioneer) numbered 150 members. Some of them are living today in Israel on a Kibbutz, Moshav or in a city.

When HeChalutz was founded the group had 11 members: 1) Zelig Orlinsky, 2)Shmaya Broyda, 3) Yosef Berman, 4) Dvoyre Gorodaysky, 5) Yoel Tcheplovodsky, 6) Nimke Leybovitch, 7) Zvi Lusky, 8) Yisroel Senderovsky, 9) Efraim Klin, 10) Mordkhai Rozovsky, 11) Zvi Rabinovitch.

Everyone in town soon learned about the HeChalutz organization. We began to receive dozens of requests from young people who wanted to be pioneers.

According to instructions you had to be between 18 –26 years old to join. We had so many requests, we were able to choose the best.

At first we did our work at the home of Zelig Orlinsky, illegally. One evening the police showed up at Orlinsky's to carry out a search. It appeared to be a denunciation by an opponent. Luckily, they only found 2–3 members. They did not find any of our material. From that time on we hid everything.

Finally, we rented a locale at Yosl Gertzovsky's, in the name of the Zionist organization. It was a small but very comfortable room.

[Page 157]

In order to pay rent we charged our members a monthly fee. We were independent.

As the amount of requests grew we were forced to stop taking new members. The members we deemed appropriate were invited to a meeting as well as to an exam. Every evening you could see the council sitting in the small room, calling in members to take the exam which scared them.

The council grew from 3 to 5 members. Zelig Orlinsky and I joined. After a few months HeChalutz had over 100 members.

The HeChalutz became very popular. We managed to accomplish a lot for the pioneers and Zionism. Through us, the Zionists in town received fresh young energy, well disciplined people who were enthusiastic and devoted to the cause.

We brought some of the Land of Israel life into almost every Jewish home. We were well respected and our work was held in high esteem.

The Zhetl Pioneers 1925

From right to left, first row: Dovid Lifshitz, Mordkhai Rozovsky
Second row: Hirshl Rabinovitch, Shmaya Broyda…Mikhle Savitzky, Dvoyre
Gorodaysky, Sonia Shalkovitch, Arye Cohen
Third row: Khaye Soreh Abelevitch, Afraim Klin, Fraydl Levit, Khaim Itzikovitch
Standing: Yisroel Senderovsky, Yudl Belsky…Yosef Berman, Yoel Tcheplovodsky,
Hirshl Lusky, …Zelig Orlinsky, Yitzkhak Belsky,…Avrom Guzovsky
Standing in the last row: Antzl Sokolovsky, Yosef Leyzerovitch, Mulke Mnuskin, Avrom
Leyserovitch, Hirshl Gertzovsky

We Become Workers

We had previously been known in town as idlers, however, thanks to HeCHalutz, we became workers. We did all the work in town, hard and easy. The unskilled among us did unskilled labour. 75% of our wages went to the National Pioneer Fund to help poor pioneers with travel expenses to the Land of Israel and to create training facilities.

When the folk – school in Zhetl needed workers to build a building our secretary Yitzkhak Leybovitch asked us to send a set amount of workers every day. We took on this work with enthusiasm, worked quickly, got paid well and were praised.

We also worked in the tannery and turned the wheel to grind bark.

Later on we organized a carpentry shop with Mulke Mnuskin as head worker.

The central office of HeChalutz helped us by sending a member to work in the carpentry shop who also helped us with our cultural work. Later, we lived to see the moment of sending members from Zhetl to the Land of Israel. That was the ultimate goal of HeChalutz.

At the Training Camp

We received from the central office of HeChalutz a circular with declarations for candidates who wanted to leave for 6 months of training camp in various locations in Poland. We were all prepared to go and awaited the moment impatiently. We knew this brought us closer to the Land of Israel.

We certified a long list of members and sent it to Warsaw. It did not take long for us to receive a notice to leave for the training camp. It was fated that Yoel Tcheplovodsky and I would go together to a place near Volkovisk, to a well established Jew. Such training establishments temporarily received 20 members. Those who were involved longer, went to training camp sooner and received a certificate to go to the Land of Israel sooner.

The Young Pioneers in Zhetl 1927

First row seated: Rokhl Berman, Eliezer Namiyat, Hinde Senderovsky, Dovid Lifshitz,
SOreh Sokolovsky, Moishe Orlinsky, Mereh Skrabun
Second row standing: Elke Koyfman, Avrom Yitzkhak Medvedsky, Sahyne Leah
Karpelovitch, Borukh Busel, Khane Obershteyn, Khashke Leybovitch, Leah...
Last row standing: Rokhl Shelubsky, Mosihe Aron Robetz, Shepsl Namiyat, Libe
Yoselevitch, Dovid Zelikovitch, Herzl Gertzovsky, Alte Berniker, Shimen Berniker

[Page 158]

The youth in town were jealous of us. Before our departure they organized a farewell evening with representatives from all the Zionist organizations. The entire HeChalutz as well as regular Jews accompanied us to the highway which leads to Novoyelnie singing Hatikva and Tekhezakna. (Anthems of the Zionist movement).

A little later there were confirmations for new members to go to training camps for 6 months. We spent the entire summer there. We worked in the fields, learned Hebrew and studied about life in the Land of Israel. We returned home for Sukkot and waited for our certificates. It did not take long for us to receive the certificates. Members prepared the necessary papers needed and a few had the honour to go to the Land of Israel and enjoy the new, very difficult but interesting life. These were the first to emigrate:

1) Zelig Orlinsky, 2) Efraim Klin, 3) Shmaya Broyda, 4) Arye Cohen, 5) Zvi Lusky, 6) Henye Piekelny, 7) Shayne Leah Karpelevitch, 8) Shaul Kovensky, of blessed memory, 9) Khasieh Leybovitch, 10) Leybovitch, 11) Miriam Lushtzky, 12) Soreh Shalkovitch, 13) Mulke Mnuskin.

They all live in different parts of the country. I also received a certificate, but due to military service I remained in Poland.

The Zhetl Pioneers 1934

With honour and respect I would like to mention the Zionists who helped the HeCHalutz in Zhetl.

1) Menakhem Vernikovsky, of blessed memory, 2) Zalmen Dunetz of blessed memory, 3) Avrom Langbart of blessed memory, 4) Moishe Ruven Mordkovsky of blessed memory, 5) Mendl Mirsky of blessed memory, 6) Shaul Kaplinsky of blessed memory, 7) Bezalel Mashkovsky of blessed memory, 8) Feyvl Epshteyn of blessed memory, 9) Noyakh Mikulitsky of blessed memory, 10) Aron Zvi Langbart of blessed memory.

Our Influence on Zhetl

Until the founding of HeChalutz in Zhetl, Zionism did not penetrate within the masses. In our town for example, they knew Menakhme Vernikovsky the pharmacist was a Zionist and Zhame the postman (Zalmen Dunetz) and a few other Jews were "crazy" for Zionism. But they knew very little about Zionism.

Thanks to HeChalutz which became a mass movement, Zionism spread and penetrated into every Jewish home and every Jewish heart.

It was clear, that in a house, if a son or daughter was a pioneer, the parents, as a matter of course, as well as brothers, sisters, acquaintances and friends, and even neighbours became Zionist supporters.

Later, when the pioneers left for the Land of Israel, our influence was strengthened in all circles in town who benefited from Zionism.

I was one of the founders of HeChalutz and was of the few who sacrificed his youth for the Land of Israel.

The HeChalutz existed in Zhetl for about 10 years. Some members were sent to the Land of Israel, some remained in Zhetl and got married but remained good Zionists and never lost hope to one day have the honour to be in the Land of Israel. However, they did not live to realize this dream as they were killed in Zhetl at the hands of the murderers. May these lines serve as a tombstone over the grave of our friends and particularly my best childhood friend Yoel Tcheplovodsky of blessed memory.

May their memories serve as a blessing!

[Page 159]

Poalei Zion (Labour Zionists) – Z.S (Zionist Socialists)

by Eliezer Namiyat (Kiryat Chaim)

Translated by Janie Respitz

Cruel fate dictated that all who stood at the cradle of the Poalei Zion party in Zhetl would be killed, and I, who joined the party a bit later, had to write its history. I made a great effort trying to remember some details of our activities.

The Founding of the Party

The party was founded in 1926 according to the initiative of Alter Dvoretzky and Yudl Bielsky. The first to join the party were: Hirshl Rabinovitch, Mereh Rabinovitch, Shaul Kovensky, Pinkhas Kaplinsky, Borukh Busel, Motke Razvosky and many others. A while later some younger people joined: Me, Dovid Zelikovitch, Shepsl Namiyat, Moishe Aron Robetz and many others from "HeChalutz" and "HeChalutz HaTzair".

The party and its youth developed intensive activity, most important, among the working youth who were by that time organized in anti Zionist parties like the "Bund" and the communists.

Farewell evening for Nokhem Broyde when he left for the Land of Israel, 1931

From right to left: Yudl Bielksy, Nokhem Broyde, Soreh Sokolovsky, Dovid Zelikovitch, Malke Lusky, Leybl Lusky, Yente Rivka Gal

Our appearance in the political arena in Zhetl had a different character. Firstly our scope was wider. We recruited over one hundred members into the party and the youth wing. Secondly we felt we were on a mission which the town required. We were the only socialist Zionist factor. We filled a gap which had existed. Even later, when the "HaShomer HaTzair" was unfolding their very successful activities, they could not play the same role we filled as they were mainly an educational factor and not a socialist Zionist factor.

The Political Activities of the Party

In the beginning we would meet in the small forest on the road to Baranovitch. We called it the Freedom Forest. Later, we rented a locale at Hirshl Kovensky's (the Romanovitch). This made it possible for us to carry out systematic activities. Our events had a good reputation in town. For example the Borokhov Academy which took place every year on the anniversary of Borokhov's death, with participation of the teachers from the Yiddish school led by Herman Frenkl.

Herman Frenkl was ideologically very close to us. With his enterprising spirit he drew in almost the entire Yiddish school into our circle, even anti Zionists liked Leybl Frenkl and Alter Fersky.

Besides this we received great support from the party in Slonim. The members Khatzkl Rabinovitch and V. Romanovsky from Slonim would visit us often.

Two separate political actions which the Poalei Zion in Zhetl executed are deeply engraved in my memory. Our participation in the elections for city council, really insolent on our part, because on the Jewish street there were two strong blocs: the Zionist bloc headed by the committee from the Tarbut School, and the second, an anti Zionist bloc led by those active in the Yiddish Folk School.

[Page 160]

Poalei Zion in Zhetl

From right to left – first row: Libe Shatzky, Pinke Kaplinsky, Mireh Epshteyn, Mikhle Sholkovitch, Asneh Zatzefitsky, Motke Rozvosky, Zelda Shelubsky
Second row: Binyomin Mnuskin, Libe Yoselevitch, Khaye Busel, Notte Izbornitsky, Mereh Rabinovitch, Dovod Zelikovitch, Nekhameh Belaus, Moishe Orlinsky, Libe Koyfman, Etteh Lusky
Third row: Henie Namiyat, Yekhil Yoselevitch, Frume Sholkovitch, Leybl Lusky, Rivka Dvoretzky, Avrom Yitzkhak Medvetzky, Kayla Rozovsky, Borukh Busel
Last row: Rivka Senderovsky, Zvia Krugman, Risheh Senderovsky, Minye Berman, Fraydl Green, Avrom....

It was clear to us that as a third power we had no chance to succeed, and yet we presented our own list, ignoring the fact the majority of us did not have the right to vote, and we did not have money or candidates. Our list had two candidates: Alter Dvoretzky and Kalmen Busel. It was hard to believe, when the results came in, and the votes were counted, we were lacking 8 votes for a mandate.

The second communal action we took, if I am not mistaken in 1931, during the last democratic Sejm in Poland, we presented a bloc made up of the "Bund", independent socialists (Dr. Kruk) and the Poalei Zion – Z.S.

At that time we did not have a locale. The "Bund" invited us to create a common election committee, however our members received this suggestion coldly.

Firstly, the list on scale did not have a chance for a mandate, and if yes, for the "Bund" and not for us. That's when it was decided to delegate me and Dovid Zelikovitch to the election committee. In the end only I remained on the committee.

I remember the night, when we went out to hang posters. Me, Moishe Indershteyn (the blond) and if I am not mistaken Sholem Lisogursky as well. We hung posters all over town, even on the House of Study.

The "Bund" did not believe this list would attract votes. The evening before the election the teacher Brandes asked me:

"How many votes will we get?" When I estimated one hundred, he laughed.

"We are at most a minority" he said. He estimated the Bund 30 votes and the Poalei Zionists, 20. The biggest surprise was at two o'clock in the morning the teacher Marayn came out and announced we received 153 votes. 80% were from our members and supporters.

Poalei Zion in Zhetl 1931

From right to left – first row: Moishe Orlinsky, Rokhl Shelubsky, Nokhem Bryde, Henia Namiyat, Motke Rozovsky, Leyzer Namiyat, Dobeh Lusky, Shepls Haydukovsky, Dovid Zelikovitch, Shepls Namiyat
Second row: Mikhle Shalkovitch, Libe Yoselevitch
Third row: Nishke Dvoretzky, Yosef Shelubsky, Shmuel Zakrysky, Kayle Rozovsky, Yente Rivka Gal, Noyakh Alpert, Malke Lusky, Borukh Busel, Henie Green
Standing: Leybl Lusky, Etl Belsky

The Poalei Zion and the Yiddish Folk School

Regarding our activities for the Yiddish school there were differences of opinion within our party. For example, Hirshl Rabinovitch, Pinke Kaplinsky, Mereh Rabinovitch and Motke Rozvosky and other members did not feel badly in the folk school. Opposing members were: Dovid Zelikovitch, Nokhem Broyde, Borukh Busel, me and others who could not bare to breathe the anti Zionist air which the board members: Avrom Moishe Barishansky and Shike Avseyevitch planted in every corner of the school. Later we decided to make an effort to recruit graduates from the Yiddish school. The first graduates we recruited were: Malke Lusky, Yente Rivka Gal and Nekhama Bielsky.

[Page 161]

Later we succeeded in receiving the entire graduating class. I did this with the help of my sister and her friends as well as Hirshl Rabinovitch and Mirele Epshteyn.

After a few meetings with them we absorbed all the graduates with a few exceptions. This is how we broke the Chinese wall of Zionist hatred which existed in the Yiddish school.

At that time we had a teacher by the name of Marayn. We already had restricted relations with the school and decided to open our own pavilion at their bazar with our own slogans. We negotiated with the school administration for a long time until they promised our slogans would be valued. However, the "Bund" did not honour this agreement.

The Committee of League of Workers in Eretz Yisrael 1932

Seated: Khane Obershteyn, Yitzkhak Rabinovitch, Yitzkhak Leyzerovitch, Nekhama Belaus
Standing: Moishe Orlinsky, Khaim Yoselevitch, Dovid Zelikovitch

After the bazar opened they tore down our Zionist slogans. After short negotiations we took back our pavilion and with that almost disrupted the entire bazaar. Later we gave away our goods to the Jewish National Fund's bazaar.

Our Activities for HeChalutz

After this, when the older Zionists were not successful, the "HeChalutz" educated our members and the graduates of "HaShomer HaTzair". I must say, as a compliment to us, some of our members went to the Zionist training camp and then left for the Land of Israel. The well off youth of "HaShomer Hatzair" did not go to training camp except for Yosl Dvoretzky, Feygl Dvoretzky and Yakov Indershteyn.

The League of Workers in the Land of Israel and the Party

As soon as the League was created I became its secretary from the first day. We worked systematically in town. We recruited many members and collected membership dues. We had a very good treasurer, Itche Rabinovitch. He would prepare a balance just like in a large bank. We would often bring in speakers, Funt and later Morgnshtern. Their visits were always a happening in town.

Our Activities for the Jewish National Fund

We always participated actively in the daily work of the Jewish National Fund like emptying collection boxes, organizing bazaars, flower days and other activities. We were also always represented on the council.

Our Professional Activities

The only professional union which existed in Zhetl was the Needle Union. This union obviously belonged to the Central Union of Clothing Workers.

Despite this, we belonged to the union. Our representative in their administration was Shaul Kovensky. After Shaul left for the Land of Israel I joined the administration and participated in their work as long as the union existed. The tailor's strike and later the solidarity strike of all other trades was organized in our locale with our active participation.

Ideological Questions

To begin with, all of our active members considered the works of Ber Borokhov holy, just as a pious Jew would revere the Code of Jewish Law. We read them many times and constantly discussed them.

As time passed two groups, if that's what we could call them, with two positions, were educated by us. The first was mainly composed of Yudl Bielsky and Dovid Zelikovitch. In political life they supported the Social Democrats. For Yudl Bielsky, the German Social Democrats were his guides. At the previously mentioned Sejm elections he did not vote for our bloc but rather for P.P.S. That is how much he was enamoured by the Social Democrats.

On the other side we had members like: Hirshl Rabinovitch, Pinke Kaplinsky, Motke Rozovsky, me, and many others who were not charmed by the Social Democratic ideology of the party.

[Page 162]

We stood close to the left "Poalei Zion". Only their inactivity in the building of the Land of Israel bothered us.

There were also differences of opinion concerning our participation in the Zionist Congress. There were in our party, those who opposed participating in the Zionist Congress. So it happened, at the election of the 16th Zionist Congress, all our members with the right to vote did not want to sit at the ballot box. I then received authorization from the party to sit at the ballot box, however I was in the minority and the commission rejected it. However, thanks to the intervention of Eliezer Rozenfeld and Shaul Kaplinsky who vouched for me, I remained at the ballot box. There were other differences of opinion such as our position on the Socialist International and Soviet Russia.

The Last May Day Celebrations

This was in 1934. The chief of police was changed in Novogrudek and we attempted to receive permission for a May 1st academy. In those days I was spending more time in Novogrudek than in Zhetl. I went to the chief of police every day until I got permission.

Given that it had been a few years since we had received permission to openly celebrate May 1st, we decided this time to make an impressive celebration with an orchestra in the movie house.

At the opening I spoke about anti Semitism in Poland and about the fascist process which was taking place. Then the orchestra played the International. Suddenly, I noticed the "Pshadovnik" disappeared. Meanwhile, Dovid Zelikovitch began to speak. The "Pshadovnik" returned and announced that since we played the International he had to leave our meeting. (Translator's note: I could not find the meaning of "Pshadovnik").

Borukh Busel was responsible for our relations with the authorities that evening. The police arrested him and beat him because of what I said about fascism in Poland. In the end we were sentenced and paid a fine.

Participants in the Flower Day for the Pioneer's Fund

Seated in the first row: Sonia Sholkovitch, Shaul Kovensky of blessed memory, Libe Zhukhovitzky
Second row: Miriam Kontesbrat, Yisroel Goldberg, Mereh Dvoretsky, Dvoyre Gordaysky, Fraydl Lvenbuk, Nokhem Broide, Fruma Sholkevitch
Standing: Borukh Bisel, Zavl Mankovitch, Shepsl Namiyat, Herzl Gertzoksky

That May 1st has remained in our memory. We did not sleep that night. We wanted to know what happened to Borukh Busel but the police would not let us in to see him.

*

I have brought a few facts about the diversified activity which the "Poalei Zion" Zionist Socialists and its youth group "Freyheyt" (Freedom) carried out in Zhetl.

[Page 163]

Hashomer Hatzair[1]

by Yakov Indershteyn, Kibbutz Eilon

Translated by Janie Respitz

1926 was a year of renewal in Zionist activity in Zhetl and it would not be an exaggeration to say this year brought radical changes which decided and defined the activities of the national movement in town during the following years.

The most obvious expression of these manifestations was the emergence of two important institutions which were busy educating the young generation and with their existence ensured the flood of fresh blood in Zionist activity – meaning the "Tarbut" School and the "Hashaomer Hatzair" organization which were founded in the same year. Here we will speak about "Hashomer Hatzair".

It is known throughout the world the "Hashomer Hatzair" attracted masses of Jewish intellectual youth from well –off origins. The organization appeared in the Jewish public as a revolt of the youth against the hardened lifestyle of their parents.

HaShomer Hatzair in Zhetl 1928

The youngsters went out to the fields and forests with their scout's wandering sticks. Wanting to protect what they called "youth culture", the "Hashomer Hatzair" demanded self accomplishment of every member.

This was expressed in emigration to the Land of Israel and life on Kibbutz. This is how the "Hashomer Hatzair" crystalized as an educational organization which embraces children from a young age and teaches them self accomplishment in order to crystalize the pioneer who was suitable for the needs of the land.

In our towns the idea of "Hashomer Hatzair" did not take its original form. Firstly, our human material was simple and we did not have the leader type who could have provided the above mentioned educational tasks. Therefore, the "Hashomer Hatzair" in our towns had only an outward resemblance to the organizations in the larger cities. Above all we imitated the outward form, the Land of Israel song, the scout uniform, the style, but the development of the individual, his individual education was inadequate. Here we must look for the reason why so few members of the Zhetl branch of "Hashomer Hatzair" live in Kibbutzim. (Most Zhetl Jews in the Land of Israel live off the Kibbutz).

If the Zhetl branch did not belong to the outstanding organizations of the movement in Poland,

[Page 164]

The Alizim Group of Hashomer Hatzair 1928

From right to left: Leyzer Lusky, Khaim Yoselevitch, Berl Senderovsky, Moishe Breskin
Second row: Hirsh Berman, Yitzkhak Leyzerovitch, Moishe Levit, Kalmen Shalkovitch
Standing: Boreh Krigel, Moishe Breskin, Yisroel Goldberg, Shloime Kravetz, Aharon Butkovsky, Moteh Zakraysky

It did fulfill the utmost important tasks in communal life.

It is sufficient to mention the activities of "Hashomer Hatzair" for The Jewish National Fund, for the "Tarbut" School, for the drama club or the activities in the League for Workers in the Land of Israel, in "Hechalutz" and many other areas.

However, the most important thing the "Hashomer Hatzair" gave our town was a corner of the Land of Israel in Zhetl. A corner ruled by the song of the Land of Israel and the Hebrew word. This corner attracted and enticed the youth. Through this branch of "Hashomer Hatzair" the youth that went to the Polish school connected to Jewish history, the geography of the Land of Israel and crystalized their national and socialist world philosophy with a strong emphasis on self accomplishment.

It can be said that the majority of Zhetl's youth participated in Zhetl's "Hashomer Hatzair" organization during its 13 year existence. "Something" appealed to everyone, "something" from the special "Shomer" style whose expression was – simplicity, open heartedness, and hatred of phraseology.

The "Hashomer Hatzair" in Zhetl respected friends and opponents. They valued general Zionists despite the fact that they did not like their leftist stance and devotion to the League of Workers in the Land of Israel. They showed respect to the "Bund" and the communists despite the fact they were seen as "bourgeois" and "nationalistic". The specific "Shomer" style roused respect especially in its goal toward self accomplishment.

Those brought up in "Hashomer Hatzair" were not ashamed of their movement, even during the bitter days when the town was under the boot of the Nazi animals.

I am not competent to write about this tragic period, but it is enough to mention the first leaders of our branch of "Hashomer Hatzair" Hirshl Kaplinsky of blessed memory, who stood at the head of the partisan movement; Yisroel Busel, of blessed memory who excelled with his technical ideas in the partisan's sabotage activities, and many many others.

The writer of these lines left for Zionist training camp in 1933. From then on he would come to Zhetl only for short visits until his immigration to the Land of Israel; this is why he had no idea about the activities of "Hashomer Hatzair" in our town during the last years. However, having known the organization for many years I can say:

The "Hashomer Hatzair" during its 13 years of existence in Zhetl brought a refreshing spirit to the provincial ideas of our town's youth. It raised the value of Jewish young lives in their own eyes, straightened their backs and helped them fulfill their tasks in Jewish communal life in Zhetl in the 1920s and 30s.

Hashomer Hatzair in Zhetl 1932

[Page 165]

Revisionists and Betar in Zhetl

by Avrom Alpert, Hadera

Translated by Janie Respitz

On an autumn evening in 1929 we gathered at the home of Khaim Lemkin. He was living with Frumka the baker. We were a group of boys penetrated with national thoughts and in no way could we feel complete with moderate Zionism and the unnatural pairing of Zionism and socialism. We decided to create a division of the Zionist – Maximalist movement of Ze'ev Jabotinsky which does not recognize dualism and fights for the primacy of Zionism and the blue and white flag.

The main organizer of the movement in Zhetl was Mitye Lusky who was at the time studying at the Vilna University and was a member of the movement.

As I remember, the following partook in the founding meeting: Khaim Lemkin, Moishe Bitensky, Khaim Meir Epshteyn, Dvoyre Garadaysky, Yakov Indershteyn, Antzl Skolevsky, Yidl Lusky, Leyb Zhukhovitzky, Avrom Alpert, Shloime Levenbuk, and others. Those gathered also decided to create a branch of Betar and chose Shloime Levenbuk as commander. After he left for the Land of Israel he was replaced by Yidl Lusky.

As in all branches, there were three ranks in the Zhetl branch. Rank "A" which consisted of the youngest until the age of 14 was led by Moishe Alpert. Many youngsters from Zhetl completed Rank "A" under Moishe Alpert's direction.

During its ten year existence (from 1929 – 1939) the Revisionist organization and Betar carried out diversified work in all spheres of political and communal activity. They raised sons who were faithful to land and nation, and who while in the movement learned Zionist monism, and understood they must learn to put their own lives in danger.

Nordia football (soccer) team in Zhetl 1939

Betar committee in Zhetl 1931

Seated from right to left: Yidl Lusky, Raya Khabibi, Mania Romanovsky, Khaim Lemkin
Standing: Yisroel Raytzer, Leybl Zhukhovitsky, Avrom Vernik, Borukh Kaplinsky, Veveh Kravetz, Zavl Mankovitch, Shloime Levenbuk

This doctrine reverberated among the members of Betar when the Germans occupied Zhetl. The members of Betar who joined the partisans were: Yoineh Medvetsky, Eliezer Vinarsky, Peysakh Finkelshteyn, and others.

We also organized a sports club called "Nordia", participated in summer colonies and founded a training camp at Khaytche Levit's house.

Both movements, Tzhar (Revisionsits) and Betar excelled in their work for the Tel Chai Fund as well as cultural – literary activities led by one of our members B. Kaplinsky. We often organized literary trials. For example: the trial of Bontche Shveyg.

(*Translator's note:* Bontche the Silent, a character in a story by Y. L. Peretz).

I remember in 1939 under the Soviet regime, our branch worked secretly for the illegal escape, directed by the Baranovitch branch, smuggling people to Lithuania and Romania. The N.K.V.D found out and arrested two members from Lida. This is when our work in Zhetl stopped. Members who wanted to escape remained and were killed in Zhetl.

This is how we carried out our work until Hitler's occupation.

[Page 166]

Agudas Yisroel[1]

by Yisroel Karpl, Ra'anana

Translated by Janie Respitz

Wanting to eternalize the memory of our beloved town Zhetl I feel it is my obligation to describe what until now has not been described, namely: the founding of the Agudas Yisroel in Zhetl.

The movement began here with the distribution of the Aguda newspaper "Dos Yiddishe Togblat" (The Jewish Daily).The first subscribers to the newspaper were the respected business owner Reb Hertz Leyb Kaplinsky of blessed memory, Reb Moishe Tentzer of blessed memory, the cantor Reb Yitzkhak Kogan and Reb Avrom Goldberg ("The Tiller") may God avenge his death.

Among those who distributed the newspaper were: Yehoshua Abba Busel, today in America, Yisroel Meir Rozovsky, Yitzkhak Akhanovsky, as well as Alter Senderovsky, may God avenge his death.

The main activists were the older Yeshiva boys returning from Aguda's pioneer training camps. This is when we ordered propaganda material from the central office of Agudas Yisroel in Warsaw with posters which we nailed to the walls of all the Houses of Study. We also distributed charity boxes to collect money for the Settlement Fund which Zhetl's Jews contributed to.

At this time, the well known preacher Rabbi Naftali Rafaelovitch, may God avenge his death, was in Zhetl. He later died a martyr's death during the war.

Sending off party for I.E. Pikelny on his way to the Land of Israel in 1934

He violated a German ban. It was ordered that an entire congregation would be killed if they would not betray a culprit.

Rabbi Rafaelovitch, may God avenge his death, was asked by the head of the Yeshiva, to remind all the religious Jews during his sermon in the old House of Study that they must organize. In a packed House of Study the founding of Agudas Yisroel took place with many signing the declaration.

The strengthening of the Agudas Yisroel's activities brought about opposition in Zionist circles. Threats were made saying those belonging to Agudas YIsroel would not receive certificates from the local Land of Israel committee for travel to the Land of Israel. However, Agudas Yisreol already had an agreement with the agent that with their payment to the Settlement Fund they had the same rights to emigrate and the division of Agudas Yisroel in the Land of Israel would take care of all the formalities. Such announcements were published in Agudas' newspaper "Togblat" and were plastered on all the walls of the Houses of Study.

This had appropriate reverberations. A committee for the Settlement Fund was created in Zhetl led by the head of the Yeshiva. Money was raised for the fund with yearly declarations and promissory notes to achieve their goal.

The writer of these lines was one of the participants in the various activities of Agudas Yisroel and was even punished for it when he did not receive an honour in the middle House of Study where the manager Yenkl Borukh Kaplinsky, may God avenge his death, was a passionate Zionist.

This is how the Agudas Yisroel slowly penetrated into the region and into our town Zhetl.

The last few years before the war a Beys Yakov School was also founded. That happened thanks to the initiative of a dear simple Jew, Avrom Goldberg and the teacher Rokhl Ginzburg, the daughter of Rabbi Hillel Ginzburg from Radon, the son in law of the "Chafetz Chaim" of blessed memory, who was devoted to education.

This is how religious Zhetl lived until its rich pulsating life was annihilated by the cannibals of the 20th century.

Land, land, do not cover my blood!

Translator's footnote:

1. Orthodox Religious Movement

[Page 167]

The Bund

by Sholem Lisogursky, Montreal

Translated by Janie Respitz

It is known that the Bund and other revolutionary parties played an active role in Zhetl in the years 1904–05. They wrote a nice chapter in the general and Jewish revolutionary worker's movement.

However, my memory does not go that far back as to be able to provide details of the movement in its early years.

Sholem Lisogursky

I know only one thing. Despite its success, the Bund in Zhetl did not manage to leave behind deep roots from which a movement could grow. In short, it can be characterized like this: it played a significant role, but disappeared, not leaving behind any traces of a party, except for a few splinters, in other words, a few, not well organized individuals like: Khaim Kaplinsky, Avrom Moishe Barishansky, Yehoshua Avsyevitch who did not lead and Bundist activities.

The Founding

In the cold winter nights of 1926, Rokhl Yezyernitsky, Yosele Mendes' granddaughter, had the idea to organize Zhetl's working youth in a new organization called "Youth – Bund – Future". Although another organization was not lacking in Zhetl. They thought and did.

According to her initiative, with help from the Bitne Yeshiva boy Moteh Velvl, later a functionary in the central committee of the Bund in Warsaw, and Matvei Bernshteyn, "Youth – Bund – Future" was created in Zhetl.

The founding meeting took place at the home of Noyakh the twisted, namely Rokhl Yezyernitsky's step father.

The following members were present at the founding meeting: Abba Vanyshteyn, Rokhl Yezyernitsky, Yitzkhak Lisogursky, Risha Sovitsky and others who I don't remember.

The agenda was short: constitute and continue with our work. A presidium was elected with the following members: Yitzkhak Lisogursky – chairman, Rokhl Yezyernitsky – secretary, Abba Vaynshteyn – treasurer. It was also decided to begin a recruiting campaign.

After the founding meeting everyone threw themselves into the work with their youthful energy in order to recruit new members of which I was the first "victim".

The organization grew very quickly. A little later, Binyomin Kaplinsky joined the organization and would become the spiritual leader of the Bundist party in Zhetl.

Later on Eliezer and Mania Shapiro joined. In short, the organization already numbered in the dozens and ran diversified cultural and educational programs for youth.

This was a new worry for the police. They had no idea what type of creature the "Bund" was. They assumed we were like the communists and began to persecute the "Bund" and all its organizations including: "Youth – Bund – Future", "SKIF", and the "Cultural League". The police were the first to arrive at all announced and unannounced lectures, checker's evenings and other events. This would often result in the arrest of a few members who they assumed were the leaders and speakers.

After some intervention they would always release those detained.

Education in a Leftist – Marxist Spirit

The "Bund" in Zhetl raised a Marxist, aware youth which we could be proud of today. Unfortunately, very few have survived. It is worthwhile to mention the suspicions of the police were not far from the truth.

The Zhetl "Bund" was educated in a spirit of leftist – Marxism and did not always fit within the limits of the "Bund" program.

I remember when a certain functionary from the Central Committee of the "Bund" said the "Bund" in Zhetl was a faction.

Opposing the Second International

Another episode is important to mention as it characterizes the mood which ruled the party in Zhetl.

[Page 168]

In 1931 when the "Bund" was discussing joining the Second International, the Zhetl "Bund" protested in writing. The leader of the Central Committee, H. Erlich felt it was necessary to respond in the Bundist organ "Naye – Folkstzeitung" (New People's Newspaper) with these words: "Before me lies a letter that is larger than the town from which it was sent. The letter is filled with shouts of anguish, protest and rebellion!"

When the "Bund", after long discussions joined the Second International, the party as well as the youth organization in Zhetl split.

However, the "Bund" in Zhetl continued to exist and run activities until 1939 when the Red Army arrived in Zhetl. This is where the rich in content chapter of the "Bund" ended in Zhetl.

Founders of the Bund in Zhetl in 1926

Seated: Risha Sovitsky, Mordkhai Bernshteyn, Rokhl Yezyernitsky
Standing: Shimshon Novogrudsky, Yitzkhak Lisogursky, Shimen Levoronchik, Abba Vaynshteyn

Personalities

Talking about the "Bund" in Zhetl we cannot forget to mention a few honest personalities who are no longer alive, for example: Binyomin Kaplinsky. He was a rare individual, a brilliant intellectual; perhaps one of the few in Zhetl. He did not have a personal life. He gave his entire being, talent, energy and young life to the idea.

Rokhl Yezyernitsky – the founder of the "Bund" in Zhetl, had an unsettled nature, full of life, energy and combativeness. She was always searching for the truth, and by the way, never found it. In 1928 she left for America and a few years later came back to visit Zhetl. She returned to America and after a few years returned to Zhetl. She then moved to Baranovitch and live there until the Nazi occupation. She was taken to a forced labour camp "Kaldichev". Here too she was restless and with a few others organized an escape from the camp. This action was successful but unfortunately some of them were captured by the Germans, she was among them. They were all tortured to death.

Abba Vaynshteyn (the Palisade) was very handsome and honest. He was devoted to the party in Zhetl. He lived in a difficult economic situation and got the proletarian disease, tuberculosis, and died a natural death in the summer of 1931.

His funeral which was organized by the "Bund" was the first of its kind in Zhetl.

Malkeh Mayevsky was a very interesting type filled with promising talents, one of the most devoted activists in the "Bund" in Zhetl. She died in her own bed in 1935, in her blossoming youth.

Eliyusha Shapiro was raised in comfort, far from the Jewish spirit. After his father died the family was in a difficult financial situation and this is what probably brought him to the Jewish socialist worker's movement. While still a student at the Polish high school he became an active member in the Bund youth organization.

Later, as his awareness grew together with his revolutionary temperament he no longer found his place in the "Bund" and together with many others threw himself into the work of the underground revolutionary movement.

At the beginning of 1933 he was arrested and after a year in jail he was released. After his release from jail he proceeded with his medical studies but he still was dissatisfied. He struggled on two fronts until a third front opened for him.

This was 1936 when Franco's fascists attacked the Spanish republic. His fighting character did not allow him to sit quietly. He tried every way possible and finally made it to the Spanish front and fell in a courageous battle against Spanish and international fascism.

Everything I have written here is based solely on my memory. Therefore, I ask everyone who reads this to forgive me for any inaccuracies.

[Page 169]

The First Jewish National Fund Bazaar

by Lize Kaplinsky (Tel Aviv)

Translated by Janie Respitz

Chanukah 1930 the Zionist activist Avrom Langbart called a meeting in the building of the Tarbut School. He explained to all the women gathered that in all other towns and cities they have organized bazaars for the Jewish National Fund and we must create a women's committee and begin this important work. As the first commissioner of the Jewish National Fund bazaar I feel it necessary to mention a few people who were very active in the work for the Jewish National Fund: Dvoyre Gorodaysky, Soreh Kaplinsky, Asneh Gertsovsky and Yoel Tcheplavodsky. They were among the first founders and carried out this work year after year. More activists joined in later years but unfortunately I do not recall their names.

Every member of the bazaar committee took it upon himself to work a street. He would go from house to house explaining the importance of the Jewish National Fund. The youth in Zhetl were always enthusiastic about Zionist work and now their main job was to collect goods. The collection lasted from Chanukah until Passover. During the winter evenings, girls in Zhetl would do handwork which was sold at good prices at the bazaar. Many business owners in Zhetl gave us antiques.

On the first interim day of Passover we brought all donated items together in the movie house in Lobenske's gate. The opening took place that evening. The entire town participated in this celebration. For this celebration we invited the song director from the Hebrew high school, Bernholtz, who greatly impressed the audience with a beautiful performance. Avrom Langbart gave a beautiful speech. After all the speeches the well known Zionist activist Feyvl Epshteyn cut the ceremonial ribbon of the bazar exhibit.

With great interest the crowd began to buy the items. Everyone felt an obligation to buy. The event was very successful. Everyone was excited. It felt like a holiday. This lasted throughout the interim days of Passover.

We also organized a lottery. The women's committee bought inexpensive items and the children, with outstretched hands, attacked the lottery like bees. There was such a rush, all we saw were children's little hands outstretched with money.

The youth also had a great time. They would dance and grab something to eat. We used this opportunity to ask the parents of the children who attended the Tarbut School to donate food for the buffet. This is how we arranged a free kosher buffet for Passover.

As you can see we raised money for the Jewish National Fund in various ways, as we sang and danced. We ended with the singing of Hatikva as dawn broke.

The treasurer of the bazaar was Feyvl Epshteyn. Every year he would send large sums to the Jewish National Fund central office and we would receive many thank you letters which unfortunately were lost in the ghetto.

This small town Zhetl, had lots of energy to collect money for national causes. Now the town has been completely silenced and only graves have remained from the holy, exuberant, Jewish Zhetl.

Contributors to the JNF in 1924

From right to left: Polkeh Leybovitch, Efraim Klin, Binyomin Leybovitch
Second row: Yisroel Kogan, Leyb Kohen, Zelik Orlinsky, Hirshl Rabinovitch, Mordkhai Rozovsky

[Page 170]

The Last Jewish National Fund Bazaar

by Sarah Gal – Begin (Jerusalem)

Translated by Janie Respitz

Every year, during the interim days of Passover, all of Zhetl would spin. From early in the morning until midnight they would hustle and bustle for the Jewish National Fund bazaar in the Tarbut School. Children would "swindle" a few pennies from their parents for the lottery with the hope of winning something although the lottery was 2/3 empty in order to bring in more money.

Every evening they would dance until dawn. The Yiddishists could not control themselves and they too would come dance and pay the few zlotys toward this "unblessed cause"…the Polish intelligentsia would also come. They hated the Jews, but they did enjoy having a good time dancing with a Jewish girl. They would mainly buy things at inflated prices. The bazaar ended with the singing of Hatikvah which everyone listened to with respect, even the Yiddishists and Poles.

The bazaar began very differently in 1938. We did not know if we should even prepare.

JNF Committee 1932

From right to left: Yoel Tcheplovodsky, Avrom Langbart, Soreh Kaplinsky
Standing: Dovid Zelikovitch, Libe Zhukhovsky, Yitzkhak Rabinovitch, Levit, the teacher Hadassah Bril, Mayrim Lusky

This time the normal quarrels between the Hashomer Hatzair and the Poalei Zion about their booths did not take place as there was already the smell of gunpowder in the air. Poland was at war with Czechoslovakia. The following Zhetl young men had been mobilized: Zvi Kaplinsky and Zvi Eliyahu Rayzhes. All night wagons went to register at the township. The mood was oppressive.

At a meeting of the Jewish National Fund's board of directors which took place at Avrom Langbart's, they decided to organize a bazaar and not break the tradition. The following belonged to the board of directors at that time: Avrom Langbart, Yoel Tcheplovodsky, Yosef Khlebnik, Leybke Mnuskin, Hillel Borishansky, and Soreh Gal.

The principal of the Tarbut School, Pergamenik, was also invited to the meeting. He participated in all Zionist events in town and was loved by the youth.

We approached the work with great energy. We worked all night at Mariashke Senderovsky's and sent the school graduates to collect for the lottery. We wanted to make up for lost time as we awaited news from the front. The walls of the hall echoed with song in order to chase away the heavy mood.

Feyvl Epshteyn's large samovar stood ready as it did every year but without enthusiasm.

Yet, the bazaar opened with a parade for the victory of the Poles who had captured Shlonsky – Tchechisnksy.

All those mobilized came on furlough. No one was missing. Therefore the opening of the bazaar was joyful like every other year.

The bazaar was our saviour. It helped improve the mood in town. We enjoyed ourselves more than in other years and we made more money than ever.

Our joy disappeared very quickly. However, no one would imagine that this would be the last Jewish National Fund bazaar in Zhetl.

Everything was silenced forever. Zhetl was orphaned of her dear residents.

Only the few survivors who are spread throughout the world will eternalize the history of Zhetl for future generations.

[Page 171]

Communal Life in Zhetl
(Taken from newspaper extracts)

Collected by Soreh Gal– Begin

Translated by Janie Respitz

The First Jewish National Fund bazaar in Zhetl

Thanks to the initiative of the "JNF Brigade" a women's committee was organized in Zhetl to hold a bazaar in the first interim days of Passover to raise money for the Jewish National Fund. Mrs. Lize Kaplinsky has been chosen commissioner of the bazaar. "Haynt" ("Today"), 17.4.1930, "From All Around Poland".

Tuesday, the first interim day of Passover, the opening of the bazaar took place in the large hall of the new cinema. This was the first bazaar organized by this especially appointed women's committee.

The commissioner of the bazaar was Mrs. Lize Kaplinsky. The bazaar occupied three rooms. Particularly impressive was the handwork section.

During the four days in which the bazaar took place every last item was sold. The baazar was visited by practically the entire Jewish population and some of the Polish population. "Haynt" ("Today") 6.5.1930, "From All Around Poland".

Party of the sponsors of the Keren Hayesod (Jewish Agency Foundation Fund), 1938

From right to left seated: Yehoshua Lusky, Yoel Tcheplovodsky, Feyvl Epshteyn, Shaul Kaplinsky, Yisroel Pergamenik, Lize Kaplinsky, Gotesdiner, Khaim Levit, Avrom Langbart
Standing: Frida Beshkin, Feygl Dvoretsky, Yakov Borukh Kaplinsky, Yakov Indershteyn, Dovid Zelikovitch, Leybl Mnuskin, Tzalia Mashkovsky, Mordkhai Abaranak, Henie Gertzovsky, Nakhman Gal, Nokhem Shoykhet, Mire Volfosky, Henie Rashkin, Libe Likhter, Tzile Zernitsky, Rivka Grin, Eliezer Rozenfeld. Standing last two: Henie Shalkovitch, Yudis Berman

Commemorative Gathering for Herzl in Zhetl

Thanks to an initiative of the Jewish National Fund committee, a commemorative gathering was organized on the 20th of Tammuz in memory of Dr. Herzl. "Hyant" ("Today") 5.8.1930 "From All around Poland".

An Event for the Keren Hayesod (The Jewish Agency) in Zhetl

The general secretary of The Jewish Agency, Dr. Shapiro, came to Zhetl. He gave a lecture on Saturday in the old House of Study. The masses who came to hear him were very excited. Many thanks to the energetic participation of the following members: Eliezer Rozenfeld, Yerukham Izraelit, Shaul Kaplinsky, Nakhman Gal, Khaim Levit, Zvi Gertzovsky, Yosef Butkovsky, Yoel Tcheplovodsky, Zaydl Ovzarovitch and Yosef Berman. The event was a great success. "Haynt" ("Today") 21.7. 1930, "From All Around Poland".

A Meeting of the League of Workers in the Land of Israel

A general meeting for the League of Workers in the Land of Israel took place here. The following were elected to the new board of directors: Yitzkhak Kohen – chairman; Yitzkhak Rabinovitch – treasurer; members:

[Page 172]

Golda Leybovitch, Rivka Tinkovitsky, Yitzkhak Leyzerovitch and Dovid Zelikovitch. "Haynt" ("Today") 2.6.1931, "From All Around Poland".

The Second Jewish National Fund Bazaar in Zhetl

Sunday, the second interim day of Passover, in a packed hall in a celebratory atmosphere, the second Jewish National Fund bazaar opened in Zhetl with the participation of the delegate Mrs. Leah Virdovitch from the Land of Israel. Mrs. Lize Kaplinsky opened the evening in the name of the women's committee and handed over the chair to Avrom Langbart who delivered an informative speech. He welcomed the many local organizations and institutions. After reading many telegrams with greetings, the next word was given to our guest Mrs. Leah Virdovitch who movingly described Jewish life in the Land of Israel. After the orchestra played "Hatikva" Mrs. Virdovitch was given the honour of cutting the ribbon. The celebratory closing of the bazaar took place when Passover ended. Disregarding the crisis, the bazaar, thanks to Mrs. Virdovitch was a colossal, moral success. The money raised, according to the Zhetl's proportions, exceeded all expectations. "Haynt" ("Today"), 30.4.1931, "From All Around Poland".

About "TOZ" Activities in Zhelt (Translator's note: TOZ is the Polish acronym for the Society for Safeguarding the Health of the Jewish Population).

On the 1st of February, the Local "TOZ" board of directors organized a dance in the Tarbut School to raise money to feed Jewish school children in Zhetl. With a bit of support from the "TOZ" central office in Warsaw and a minimal subsidy from the local city hall, the local "TOZ" division feeds around 400 children in Zhetl's Jewish elementary schools. More than fifty percent of these children receive their food at no cost. The remainder pay 5 groschen. Recently the food distribution suffered from a lack of funds and had to stop this service. The dance evening to raise money for feeding the children had warm resounding reverberations through the entire local population and raised proportionally, a good amount. "TOZ" board of directors, "Haynt" ("Today"), 17.2.1936.

The Cleaning Campaign of "TOZ"

As in all other towns and cities "TOZ" ran a cleaning campaign.

The campaign began with an assembly with speeches by: Dr. Vinik and the teachers from "Tarbut" and "Tzisho" schools. Over a period of one month, a sanitation patrol went through the town to become familiar with the sanitary conditions of the Zhetl population.

The campaign ended with an impressive procession from all the schools through the streets of town.

"Moment", May 30th, 1938.

The General Protest Strike in Zhetl

Tuesday, on the 17th of the month, all the workshops were controlled by the strike committee. All the workshops were on strike including the Matzah bakeries. On Tuesday at 10 o'clock, in the locale of the professional union a "Moscow" took place in which workers from all affiliations participated. The "Moscow" ended with the singing of the "International". "Dos Naye Vort" ("The New Word"), 22.3.1936.

The Situation of the Zhetl Library

Four years ago, when Zhetl experienced a fire epidemic, the large public library with more than 4000 books went up in smoke, except for hundreds of volumes in Hebrew and Polish. With great effort, we succeeded in reopening the library.

It is already a year that due to various reasons, the library is locked again. It is therefore just and fair on the part of the higher intelligentsia in town to take interest in the cultural situation of Zhetl's youth.

"Moment", June 24th, 1938.

Interest Free Loans

One of the most important institutions here in our town is without a doubt, the Interest Free Loan fund. In these bitter present times the fallen shopkeeper and the artisan have no other institution to turn to for help.

[Page 173]

With the participation of all the members, an annual meeting took place recently in the House of Study, which was opened by A. Langbart. The following board of directors was confirmed: Chairman – A.H. Langbart. Vice chairman – D. Shepetnitsky. Treasurer – Nakhman Gal. Board members: Moishe Vinakur, Z. Bernshteyn, Busel, Lidsky, Peskovsky and Benyaminovitch. "Moment". June 30th, 1938.

Rabbi Zalmen Saratzkin Takes Over the Rabbinate in Lutzk

At this time, our beloved rabbi, the esteemed genius Rabbi Saratzkin, may he live long, left to take over the rabbinate in Lutzk.

For a long time other cities tried to take away our rabbi. We always resisted and many times succeeded to convince him to remain in our town.

This past year the Jewish community in Ostrov invited our rabbi, may he live long, to take over their rabbinate. Meanwhile however, the government annulled the regulations of elected rabbis in Congress Poland, and as the communities were at the end of their cadence, the government no longer allowed the election of new rabbis (meaning, until a new Jewish community council was elected). The situation now made it impossible for our rabbi to take the position on Ostrov.

The strong will and unanimous decision of the entire Jewish community of Ostrov outweighed the official difficulties and they asked our rabbi for a deadline to find an exception. Our rabbi accommodated their request and gave them a deadline of half a year (Until just before Purim).

Their intervention did not bring any positive results and our rabbi extended the deadline. This was a great loss for Ostrov and a big win for us.

Meanwhile, Lutzk invited our rabbi to take over the rabbinate in their town, and immediately to that end he received an official appointment. (Lutzk had a new Jewish community council). They did not receive valid approval from our rabbi as long as the deadline with Ostrov had not been reached. This week ended with no results for Osatrov to hire our rabbi. Therefore, our rabbi, may he live long, gave his agreement to Lutzk and has left for Lutzk to take over this rabbinic position.

Our esteemed rabbi has not left us for good. He will remain in Lutzk until after Shavuot due to the previously arranged visit of the state president in Lutzk. The he will return to Zhetl and remain until the end of the summer. However, the mood is very stressful and it is hard to get used to the idea that our beloved rabbi, may he live a long life, will be leaving us. With Ostrov we had a grain of hope that at the last minute we would succeed in keeping him, but now our chances are weak. Until it is an actual fact, we still want to hope! Z. Leybovitch "Dos Vort" (The Word"), vol. 245, 13.6.1929.

The Campaign for the Council of Yeshivas in Zhetl

Due to the initiative of our rabbi, the esteemed genius Reb Yitzkhak Raytzer, may he live long, the esteemed genius Reb Zvi Khurgin, Z. Leybovitch and Sh. Rabinovitch, the work of the Council of Yeshivas strengthened. They carried out the "Harkat Tevet"(Evacuation) with great success. Those who participated in the evacuation were: Rabbi Mayrim Berniker, Reb Yakov the ritual inspector of kosher meat, Reb Yitzkhak the cantor and ritual inspector, Reb D. Izraelit, Reb Y. L. Khlebnik and others.

I strongly wish that other Orthodox activists of our town would take into consideration the terrible situation of the Yeshivas and undertake this work actively. "Dos Vort" ("The Word"), vol. 332, 20.2.1931.

In our town, thanks to the initiative of our local rabbi, Rabbi Yitzkhak Raytzer, may he live long, and the esteemed Rabbi Khurgin may he live long, the work for the Council of Yeshivas was reorganized.

Since the last district conference in Baranovitch, we carried out the last evacuation over the last months, which was very successful. We also successfully carried out in our town the event of Torah portion Yitro, thanks to the rich in content and influential speech which the local rabbi, may he live long, gave on the Sabbath, before the reading of the Torah, to a packed House of Study, encouraging the crowd to take an active role in the enterprising work for the good of the Council of Yeshivas in general and event of Shabbat Yitro specifically.

[Page 174]

He also explained the importance of Torah learning in general and especially these days, when ignorant people are frolicking in the Jewish street and we see the sad results this has brought about and therefore we cannot dismiss the strength of Torah. The speech left a great impression, calling for great excitement in the holy work of strengthening Torah study. The crowd responded warmly with donations to the Council of Yeshivas.

In the name of the Council we would like to express gratitude to our local rabbi, may he live long, for his successful activity for the good of strengthening Torah, and thanks also to the managers of the Houses of Study who helped carry out these events.

It is our deep wish that the community activists, who until now did not partake in this work, will take into consideration the situation of the Yeshivas and help with this work. "Dos Vort" ("The Word"), vol. 337, 27.3.1931.

Last Sabbath, the Polonker rabbi, the esteemed Reb Shabsai Alpert, may he live long, visited our town. Saturday afternoon this important rabbi gave a rich impactful sermon to a full House of Study about the importance of strengthening Torah study in this day and age.

This sermon left a great impression on the crowd, arousing great excitement for the holy work of strengthening Torah study and especially for the good of the situation of the Council of Yeshivas.

Immediately after the holy Sabbath, at the home of our revered rabbi, a meeting took place of the most important wealthy men with the participation of the Polonker rabbi, may he live long, on what means were needed to strengthen the work of the Council of Yeshivas. Thanks to his influence and his devotion and self participation together with the most important members of the Council like: Moishe Tentzer, Yoineh Leyb Khlebnik, Aron – Zvi Langbart, Yitzkhak Kaplinsky, Shmerl Markus, Yiroel Elkhanan Pikelny, Yitzkhak Ari Kogan the cantor, Shaul Shalkovitch, Meir Yehuda Shifmanovitch and Khaim Kantarovitch, they succeeded in raising a lot of money.

In the name of the entire town, and specifically the local council, we would like to express our heartfelt thanks to the Polonker Rabbi, may he live long, for his beautiful and thoughtful sermon with which he instilled in us spiritual pleasure. "Dos Vort" ("The Word"), vol. 417, 7.10. 1932.

The Apolitical Unification of "Akhdes" (Jewish Worker's Association)

To Zhetl's Jews!

Sunday, elections will take place for our Jewish community council.

Remember Jews, these are not elections for the Sejm (Polish parliament), or city hall, where everyone supports the party or organization which defends his economic interests. No! This is a Jewish religious community council, which must concern itself with how we live according to the laws of the Torah and we must ensure we have our Houses of Study, rabbis, ritual slaughterers, ritual baths, places of learning for our children in a Jewish traditional spirit, hospitals, orphanages with kosher kitchens and other Jewish philanthropic institutions.

Until now we handled our own spirituality; now through a decree we must entrust a special committee which we will now choose.

But to whom will we entrust our spirit? Our holy Torah for which our ancestors spilled rivers of blood? To whom will we pass on the education of the next generation? – To those who do not themselves attend a House of Study, who have a program to disturb our entire tradition and who will, God forbid, ruin the Torah and tear our children away from the ancient Jewish tradition?

If you place our Jewish community in the hands of those parties whose leaders in the big cities have already proclaimed the program of past Hellenists: A) Not to learn Torah, B) Not to circumcise their sons, C) Not to keep the Sabbath, should we entrust our souls to them? No! The election to the Jewish community council is not a class struggle, rather a fight for the religious character of Jewish public life.

Everyone, who within him still has a spark of Jewishness, will certainly stand in our ranks and give his voice to the list of five who still pray at the House of Study, Jews who have a firm desire to defend our traditional positions, Jews, who will take into account the difficult economic situation of our town not encumbering it with big taxes, Jews, who live with us, suffer with us and feel with us.

Therefore, Sunday, June 24th, every Jew votes! No one is permitted to stay home, and you must vote for the list of "Akhdes" 5.

The election bureau of "Akhdes".

[Page 176]

Institutions in Zhetl

Translated by Judy Montel

The Zhetl community was not a sovereign state, but it did establish all of the institutions that a municipality and government are required to establish. These institutions encompassed all of the areas of life in the town from health to education and culture. One after another we will list the most important institutions.

In the medical field, the Zhetl community opened a hospital, a clinic and the traditional organizations: Aiding the Ill, Visiting the Sick and "Linat Tzedek" (sleeping at the homes of the ill to care for them overnight). These institutions ensured medical help, medical supplies and medical instruments, a supply of ice in the summer and arranged for overnight care in the home of the sick person so that the members of the family could regain their strength.

After the Second World War, [almost certainly they meant the First World War, likely an error that escaped the editors in the original] a modern medical institution was established in Zhetl called TOZ that established summer camps for children, arranged for nutritional supplements for those without means, hygiene, treating infectious diseases and health education. This magnificent medical enterprise was established with very little means, without budgets and with the support of voluntary community leaders.

In order to grant credit without interest, a Charitable Association was established back in the middle of the nineteenth century. In the Twenties of the 20th century a Cooperative Credit Bank was opened that operated on commercial principles.

Zhetl also did not lag in the field of education. For the youngest children the Talmud Torah school and private "cheders" were established. For older boys a "Yeshiva Ketana" was opened. A large Yeshiva also operated in Zhetl for short period.

In the Twenties, two modern schools opened in Zhetl. One where the language of instruction was Hebrew and one where the language of instruction was Yiddish. The two schools did much to increase modern education in Jewish Zhetl.

In the cultural arena, Zhetl established classes for Torah study such as "The Veteran Sha"s Group" and "The Young Sha"s Group." The Veteran Sha"s group was exemplary as membership in it was conditional upon having wide-ranging knowledge in the Talmud. In addition to those, there were other groups devoted to the study of *Mishnayot, 'Ayn Ya'akov*, and for the reciting of Psalms. Modern Zhetl established classes for adult education such as: The Popular University founded by the Yiddish school, two drama troupes, a municipal library and libraries at the schools.

In the social realm, the Committee for Orphans was established that took care of feeding and educating orphans, Care of the Aged, Hospitality and Support for Brides, that arranged for the daughters of poor families to have what they needed before their marriage. During World War I two kitchens were established that distributed meals to those without means.

In order to prevent fires, a Volunteer Fire Department was established in Zhetl in 1902, that also organized a band that enhanced every celebration in Zhetl.

Who can list or count all of the philanthropic institutions with which Zhetl was blessed, not counting those connected to professional and political organizations. Who can appreciate the initiative and the energy that were invested by a battalion of community activists and volunteers who took the trouble and labored and did not relent in order to support all of those institutions.

Keep in mind: Zhetl was not spoiled with budgets. All of the institutions we listed were supported by donations, tithes and appeals. In the later years some new sources of income were added: balls, stage-plays, flower days and help from former townspeople who had emigrated to America. With these internal resources, the Zhetl community organized a network of praiseworthy institutions.

[Page 175]

Institutions

Eighteenth Anniversary of the Foundation of the Zhetl Volunteer Fire Brigade

[Page 176][blank][Page 177]

Societies and Institutions

by Baruch Kaplinski

Translated by Janie Respitz

Great rabbis always held the position of chief rabbi in Zhetl. This indicated Zhetl was considered a great centre of Torah study. One of the most important Torah institutions in Zhetl was the Talmud Society. Besides this old society there was also a new one which demanded less scholarship from its members.

Other societies in Zhetl were: the Mishna Society, a few Psalm societies, the Ein Yakov Society, a small Yeshiva and in 1909 the Talmud Torah was built.

In a correspondence from 1909 in "Hed Hazman" (Vol. 186) Yakov Zimelevitch tells us that in Zhetl there were 20 religious teachers and a few Hebrew teachers.

The Burial Society

All the Jewish philanthropic and social institutions existed in Zhetl. The oldest was the Burial Society. Unfortunately their record books have been lost, but there is no doubt it has existed since Zhetl became a town about 400 years ago.

We learn from A. Ivenitsky the Jewish cemetery in Zhetl was opened around 1750. Understandably, the Burial Society was already in existence. It also existed when Zhetl used the old cemetery.

We do not know when the old cemetery was opened, however it probably is as old as Jewish settlement in Zhetl and the Burial Society is the oldest institution in Zhetl.

The Burial Society was also the most important institution. Many important men made an effort to join the society. Firstly, because burying the dead is considered a good deed and secondly, the Burial Society determined the place and cost of burial, two things that played an important role for our parents.

The Burial Society also had a lot of property. Until the First World War they owned the bathhouse. All of this gave them a lot of importance and the Burial Society in Zhetl had a say in all communal matters.

Membership in the Burial Society was inherited and was shared with managers and members of the society. In the last years the managers of the Burial Society were: Yisroel Bom, his son Alter, Yakov Meylekh Dvoreztky, Leyzer Eliyahu Slutzky, Meir Sovitsky, Motek the harness maker and others. In his article "Zhetl Duirng my Rabbinate", Rabbi Z. Sarotzky describes the virtues and drawbacks of the Zhetl's Burial Society.

Overnight Justice and Visiting the Sick

From an article in "Hatzfira" (vo. 138, 1888) we learn that in 1888 two wealthy men, Reb Moishe Leyb Levit and Reb Zev Volf Slutzky founded Overnight Justice and Visiting the Sick Societies. (Translator's note: Overnight Justice was a society which organized people to spend the night with the infirmed).

In a correspondence from Zhetl in "Hed Hazman" (Vol. 186, 1909) these institutions are highly praised. During the German occupation, Overnight Justice stopped its activities and only resumed in 1923 as recounted by the article by Henie Rozenblut from Ra'anana.

The Interest Free Loan Society

The second most important institution in Zhetl was the Interest Free Loan Society. It was founded 100 years ago. One of its founders was Rabbi Zev Volf Halevi who also signed the first protocol in the record book of the society. Apparently, over time the Interest Free Loan Society came to nought and was reinstated in 1923 thanks to the initiative of Rabbi Zalmen Saratzky.

The Fire Brigade

One of the most important Zhetl institutions was the fire brigade which they called "Pozharne" (Fire in Russian).

Zhetl suffered greatly from fires. The wooden houses fell victim to every spark. There were many fires in Zhetl but we do not have a lot of information about them.

The first piece of information we have about a big fire dates from June 4th, 1743. Among other things that burned down was the Zhetl church which was built in 1646 by Duke Casimir Leo Sofia. The church was rebuilt eight years later.

[Page 178]

In 1874 a second large fire broke out in Zhetl burning down 250 houses, all three Houses of Study which were soon after rebuilt at a cost of 12 thousand ruble. The old synagogue also burned in this fire which had been standing for 200 years, all the Heders (Religious schools) and the Yeshiva where 100 boys from other towns studied. The damage was assessed at 200 thousand ruble. A six year old boy was killed in this fire. ("Halevanon" vol. 7, 1874).

In 1883 another fire broke out in Zhetl where 2000 people were left without a roof over their heads. ("Hameilitz" Vo. 6, 1883). The Zhetl rabbi, Reb Yosef Zvi Hirsh Hakohen Dvoretzky wrote in a correspondence that in 17 months Zhetl burned three times.

The third fire was the worst. The homeless suffered from hunger and there were deaths every day. In order to help those who lost everything in the fire, the rich man from Kiev Yoyne Zitzov and Dr. Mandelshtam sent 600 ruble. Alexander Tzederboym, the editor of "Hameilitz" sent 25 ruble.

On April 6th 1894 another fire broke out where 20 houses burned down and 30 families were left without a roof. Mayrim Namiyat informed people about the fire in "Hameilitz" Vol. 85, in April 1894, and wrote that the Jewish communities of Slonim and Novogudek sent two wagons filled with food for the fire victims.

The frequent fires which caused suffering and hunger encouraged the Jews of Zhetl to think about defending themselves against the fires. This is when it was decided to establish a fire brigade.

This happened on August 5th 1902. The founders were: Mayrim Epshteyn, Motl Man, Khaim Koyfman, Menakhem Vernikovsky, Leyzer Eliyahu Slutzky and the brothers Kalmen and Hirshl – Meir Sovitzky.

The Zhetl fire brigade was composed mainly of Jews but the commander was usually a Christian. The first commander of the fire brigade was the tax collector Yakovlev. During the German occupation the commander was a German officer. Under Polish rule the following served as commanders: Makhersky, Yaroshevsky and Kiatkovsky.

The role of the Zhetl fire brigade during the First World War was told to us by our rabbi Reb Zalmen Saratzky and Dov Azhekhovsky. In their works we find information about the primitive equipment and their participation in the defence of Zhetl against Cossacks and bandits and about their yearly celebration on August 5th.

On this day people did not go to work, all the stores were closed and all of Zhetl partook in the celebrations.

This is the best indication that the fire brigade was respected by the entire population.

The Zhetl fire brigade was known and respected throughout the region. In all regional conferences the Zhetl fire brigade held an honourable position.

However, despite the well organized fire brigade, they were unable to extinguish the two big fires of 1933 and 1935.

The fire brigade also had an orchestra. This orchestra had a great reputation. During state celebrations on May 8th and November 11th, or on Lag B'omer, the highlight of the celebration would be the orchestra. It was the same at every party and dance. The main attraction was the orchestra. We can find detailed information about the Zhetl orchestra in the articles by F. Zabitch and Moishe Mendl Leyzerovitch.

Floods

Zhetl also suffered from floods. In the spring the small river Pomerayke could not contain the waters of the melting snow and it would overflow. The floods caused the most damage to Lisagura and the Synagogue courtyard.

Zimel Zimelovitch describes this in a correspondence in "Hed Hazman", vol. 178, 1909. The houses near the Pomerayke were flooded until their windows, the bridges were destroyed, trees were pulled out with their roots and merchandise swam through the streets. This correspondence estimated the damage of the flood at a few thousand ruble.

A second flood in 1913 is told to us by Avrom Yitzkhak Medvetsky. On a Tuesday in 1913 a storm caused a flood where a woman was killed, houses were drowned and merchandise swam through the streets.

[Page 179]

Volunteer Firefighters

by Dov Arzhekhovsky (Akko)

Translated by Janie Respitz

The volunteer firefighter organization held an esteemed place in the communal life of Zhetl Jews. They united the entire Jewish population without differentiating between rich and poor.

The Origin of the Fire Brigade

The anarchy which ruled in Czarist Russia and the powerlessness of the state organs which had no sense of responsibility for the population forced the Jews of Zhetl to look for ways to fight the enemies of humanity: diseases, fires and similar cases.

Zhetl, a town of 4 thousand souls, under the leadership of the following distinguished citizens: Mayrim Epshteyn, Motl Man, Khaim Koyfman, Menakhem Vernikovsky, Leyzer Eliyahu Slitzky and the brothers Kalmen and Hirshl – Meir Savitzky, organized, around 1902 the volunteer firefighter organization.

The firefighter community consisted of volunteer youth, 90 percent Jews.

The firefighting equipment in those days was very primitive: two hand pumps to bring water to the fire, and one hand machine to draw water from the river as there were not yet any motors. The water was brought to the fire in pails carried on two wheels.

The Zhetl firefighters played an important role in the First World War. In 1915 during the Cossack retreat, which sowed death and fear, and in 1918–1919 when General Haller's army staged a pogrom on Zhetl, our firefighters stood guard.

The firefighters also organized an orchestra under the direction of Kalmen Levit (who we called Arye's Kalmen). Until the First World War the firefighters organized entertainment at the city garden and at the hospital with the participation of the orchestra. The entertainment program consisted of dancing and other attractions such as swinging and fireworks. They also organized sports competitions with prizes like climbing a post or sack races.

A Festive Holiday

Every year the management together with the entire population of town would organize a celebration for the firefighters. This would take place every summer in August.

It was a joyful day in Zhetl. The stores would close, the streets would be decorated with fir trees. Everyone was in a celebratory mood. The happiest were the students from the Heder and Talmud Torah as on that day they did not have to learn.

The holiday began by raising the flag on the tower which was built in the synagogue courtyard in 1909 by Christian workers and Jewish carpenters to observe fires. At six o'clock in the morning the trumpet sounded to begin the festivities. The second signal was given at 10 o'clock in the morning. This is when the firefighters had to assemble at the tower.

From there, accompanied by the orchestra they would march to the Christian chief Yakovlev who was a good friend of the Jews. They would take the firefighter flag from him and carry it with pomp.

Then, the firefighters would march in closed rows to perform their prayers, each according to his own religion. After prayers the firefighters marched through the streets accompanied by the orchestra. At one o'clock a lunch was organized for the firefighters by the people in town. After lunch there was entertainment and competitions, horse and bicycle races.

The firefighters also held an esteemed position under Polish rule.

This continued until the outbreak of the Second World War when the animal Hitler dug his nails into European Jewry and Zhetl's Jews were not spared this fate.

[Page 180]

Our Fire Brigade Orchestra

by Philip Zabitz (New York)

Translated by Janie Respitz

My fondest recollections from my old home are of the Fire Brigade orchestra. How many pleasant hours did I spend, sitting on a summer evening in Palatz Park listening to the sweet melodies of the Fire Brigade orchestra? The sounds would pour over the green, moonlit quiet park, echoing in the darkness of the starry summer night.

Zhetl Fire Brigade Orchestra, 1933

From right to left – first row: Avreyml Mnuskin, Leyb Zelikovitch, Yosef Busel, Peysakh Feyvuzhinsky, Khaim Savitsky
Second row: Avrom Rashkin, Meir Alpert, Romanovsky (a Christian), Khaim Leybovitch, Eli Busel, Pinkhas Mayevsky, Motke Rozovsky
Standing: Gershon Rashkin, Khaim Belaus, Berl Goldberg, Khaim Yosef Goldshteyn, Pinkhas Grin, Yosef Leyzerovitch, Avrom Leyzerovitch, Hirshl Volpovsky

It seemed the whole atmosphere was filled with sweet heavenly sounds. The tones would harmoniously mix and enchant the young hearts of couples walking through the green, moonlit Palatz Park.

We cannot say the Zhetl fire musicians were great artists. However, when the whole band would come together and play a march or a waltz, there was something to listen to.

Let's take for example Khaimke the Bandit. Don't think he was really a bandit standing on the road with an ax attacking travellers. No, he was simply stubborn and would get angry, and his anger was dangerous. He was no great player, and therefore, when he would take his strange instrument in hand, which was an old trombone, he would start to moan: es –tra –di – ra– ta– tra– ta– and it sounded really nice.

The Third Tenor

Or take Abramtche, who was, may he forgive me, hardly a musician, but the "Puk – puK" would come out so sweetly. At times it was so quiet you could barely hear it, and I believe, Abramtche himself also did not have the great honour to hear the sweet tones emerging from his instrument.

[Page 181]

As the legend goes, his instrument dates back to the days of King Sobieske. The fact is, at a parade, no matter how much you shined the instrument, it would remain its former colours: green, yellow and moldy. No one knew what Abramtche's instrument was called. Some simply called it a "bugle", others called it a "horn", but Abramtche called it the "third tenor". Why the third and not the fourth, or second? No one knows the correct answer. However, when you listen to Abramtche talk about his wonderful instrument, it sounds like it stems from great pedigree. In the days of Peter the Great the same "third tenor" was called the "first baritone" and played an important role in the king's regiment. Counts and barons would dance to the sounds of this present "third tenor" and former "first baritone". People would be amazed by the divine tones that emerged from this aristocratic "first baritone".

But this all took place many years ago. Today his instrument is called the "third tenor" and is old, weak, and barely sighs a weak "puk –puk". And in this hoarse "puk–puk" one can feel the longing for the good years that have passed, when counts and barons danced to its sweet tones and it held high position in the king's regiment.

The Clinette

Lifshitz was an expert on his long black instrument. He would simply display wonders on his dark black pole. When Lifshitz would play his long black fife, which in our town was called "Clinette", and his long thin fingers would fly over the white buttons of his long instrument, people would stand amazed, with gaping mouths simply absorbing every note of his fife.

I remember a melody our fire brigade orchestra played where the "Clinette" would often have a solo. This is where the "Clinette" showed what it could do. The long black fife would emerge with a language, like a plea: "Help you stubborn mule that you are! Why are you bothering with the futile to no avail?" And suddenly, the same instrument would fall into a type of laughter, as it appeared everything around, the table and chairs, the walls and the shelves, everything was laughing with the black long "Clinette". This is how Lifshitz would enchant his audience with his magical long pole which in our town was called "Clinette".

However there was something strange in Lifshitz's playing: his tongue and fingers seemed to always be at war. There was a terrible hatred between his tongue and fingers. Therefore, a fiery battle would ensue. When his tongue did "didl – didl", his long fingers would ironically mimic with a "lidl – lidl". Lifshitz would fly into a rage and from great agitation he would become red as a beet and swell up like a turkey and froth at the mouth while his long fingers would fly over the white brass buttons with such fervour and outrage that it seemed that he would destroy his "Clinette", which would bring an end to this wonder, this art and the fire brigade orchestra. It would also be the end of Lifshitz. But this was only an illusion. In fact, Lifshitz truly loved his instrument which brought him honour and a lot of pleasure.

The Quiet Player

There was nothing impressive about Simkha's musical activity in the fire brigade orchestra. Firstly, what kind of instrument was this, the size of a copper ladle which when he brought to his lips and raised his head toward the sky, he played so quietly it was difficult to distinguish if his horn was playing a march or a waltz. He played so quietly, not because he could not God forbid play, but because he believed that if he was going to play in the street, he should play quietly so that no one could hear him. He complained that something was lacking in our orchestra, but he never said what that something was, either because he himself did not know or he did not want to divulge the secret…

The Bass

The most "independent" player in our orchestra was Moishe Taneh (Whisky). His "independence" was based on the fact that when the entire orchestra was seated, he stood with his gramophone around his neck. The instrument he played was called "bass". This bass was as big as the Jewish diaspora. When this strange large "bass" would let out a wild roar: "Tam – Tam – Tra – Ta – Tam", the entire town would tremble. Small children would be awakened from their sleep and cry, old people would wash their hands and say the blessing over thunder without even noticing the sky was clear and starry. Such fear would befall the town when they heard this strange large wild "bass".

[Page 182]

Pinkeh the Drummer

However the real place of honour in our fire brigade orchestra belonged to no other than Pinkeh the drummer. We would lead through the air with his giant kettle drum, which looked like a boiler from hell where they burn and roast sinning souls in the after world. From under the kettle drum you were able to see a small piece of Pinkeh with a piece of wood in his hand with which he would bang to the beat on this large Turkish drum: Tzum – tsum – tum – tum.

Pinkeh received a lot of praise for his beautiful, pleasant playing. It was not for nothing that his Turkish drum looked bigger and sounded stronger and lovelier than all the other instruments in the band.

Pinkeh understood fully the important role he played in the orchestra and therefore, at every possible opportunity he would boast that without him there would be no music in our fire brigade. So, whenever there was even a small celebration at the fire station, they would slip Pinkeh the first and largest glass. Pinkeh would not wait for an invitation and would pour one glass after another without stopping. His eyes would become small and red and he would speak with half words, making it hard to understand what he was saying. He would stop drinking when he would fall asleep with a full glass in his hand…

Pinkeh would come to play a bit hungover and this would add a bit of charm. He had such a nature, that when he began to play he would immediately close his eyes and nod his head as if saying "yes". With each bang on his big drum his head would nod: "Yes, Boom Tzoom – Yes".

One thing I could never understand. Why did Pinkeh play with his eyes closed? Was it because he wanted to show the others that while they buried their noses in their black musical notes, he could show off and play without notes, or was it that he fell asleep? What was strange, when the conductor would raise his stick as a sign to end, and the whole orchestra would stop playing, there would always be two more sleepy bangs from Pinkeh's drum: "Boom Tzoom".

Trumpet Blood

It was interesting when the whole orchestra would gather for a rehearsal.

[Page 183]

They would rehearse no matter what and everyone learned their portion perfectly. This is good, no? But this is where the problem lay. The two main instruments, the clarinet and the coronet did not get along. There was great hatred and jealousy between these two solo instruments and all due to competition and begrudging. The clarinet got annoyed when a small solo was written for the coronet and not for him causing the coronet to be angry with his constant competitor. Very often these little wars would end ugly.

For example I remember the following episode: one beautiful summer evening the conductor called the orchestra together for a rehearsal. They rehearsed the fantasy "Under the Light of the Moon". In this fantasy, there is a lot for the coronet to play. The coronet played the solo accompanied by the entire orchestra, one with an "es – tra –di – ra –ta" one with a "puk – puk" with sparks at the climax. The coronet solo was played so sweetly it seemed he wasn't playing but rather speaking with these words: "see here, big cudgels that you are, you cannot play anything more than "es – tra– di –ra– ta" or "puk –puk". And I, such a little one, play so sweetly and tastefully. And all those who are standing at their windows came to hear my sweet playing and not your "didl – lidl". This is probably the coronet sermon this solo instrument put forth.

The Fire Brigade 1921

And it appears the clarinet understood the broad hint, who the coronet meant with this "didl – lidl". Well, what more did they need. When the coronet ended his boastful sermon, out jumped the heated, angry clarinet. The long narrow fingers began to jump over the brass white buttons. The squealing began which was deafening. Tones flew like braggarts. Understandably the coronet did not remain a debtor and shot back trumpet sounds. This would not be such a bad idea, but who cared if these two aristocratic solo instruments turned up their noses?

However, here a normal thing happened. As in every war, two sides emerge: supporters and opponents. This is exactly what occurred. The altos together with the tenors took the side of the coronet while the flutes and clarinets, of course sided with the clarinet. The giant bass and Pinkeh's kettle drum caused more trouble with their "Boom Tzoom", "Trata –ta– ta" Boommmmm…

Immediately the altos sent machine gun fire in opposition to the "puk–puk" and "Tra –ri –ra– ta– ta". This got the flutes squealing. The noise and commotion were terrible. Every bang in the kettle drum and every explosion from the gigantic bass shook the town. It went so far that no one remembered which side they were on…

A real rampage. Trumpet blood spilled like water. The war would have ended in an ugly way had the conductor not come up with an idea. Seeing the wild, unruly trumpets with the bloodthirsty altos he gave his first command:

"Piano, piano, pianissimo"! This did nothing. They paid no attention to him. The bloodthirsty trumpets were embroiled in their bloody battle, and his "piano – pianissimo" would help as much as cupping a corpse.

Now the field marshal gave his last command. He lifted the stick with which he commands high in the air, as if it was a white flag signaling that the war must come to an end.

And a remarkable thing happened: as soon as the unruly trumpets, which had just been involved in a bloody battle saw the stick raised, they all stopped playing and were silent. However, from Pinkeh's kettle drum we heard two more bangs: Boom – Tzoom…

String orchestra conducted by P. Zabitz. 1921

....., Dovid Savitsky, Eliyahu Busel, two sisters Shayne Raynes, P. Zabitz, ..., Moishe Mendl Leyzerovitch, Yitzkhak Benyaminovitch, Lize Kaplinsky, Yasinsky (a Christian form Zielani).

[Page 184]

The Drama Club

by Hindke Mirsky (Montreal)

Translated by Janie Respitz

Winter 1915–16. The First World War was in full force. Once the Cossacks left our town we breathed a bit easier. Although hunger was great, we looked for spiritual nourishment.

A group of young people began to think about how we could rebuild the cultural life in town while providing for a soup kitchen for the refugees and our needy in Zhetl.

We decided to create a theatre. The first initiators were: Yehoshua Ovseyevitch, Yisroel Moishe Ivenitsky, Alter Gertzovsky, Shloime Khaim Vernikovsky, Yehuda Vinitzky, Motl Levit, Moishe Mirsky, Motl Man, Yosef Senderovsky, Mayrim Epshteyn, Yisreol Ber Rabinovitch, Gdalyahu Shvedsky, Noyakh Turetzky. The directors of the club were the Lis brothers, refugees from Lodz.

We Perform "The Sorceress"

Noyakh Turetzky suggested we perform "The Sorceress" by Avrom Goldfadn. Solomon Lubtchansky, Menakhem Vernikovsky and Yisroel Moishe Ivenitsky auditioned the actors. They had to define each role. It was particularly difficult to decide who will play the lead role of Mirele. She had to be a young pretty girl and she had to have a nice singing voice.

They auditioned a few candidates but no one had all three qualities. Finally, they gave the role to the 15 year old Hinde Zanaratzky (today Mirsky), after much quarreling as all the actresses wanted the lead role. Fortunately they found the talented Hinde Zanaratsky who could sing and recite beautifully.

Hindke Mirsky

Finally rehearsals began. With great diligence we learned our lines by heart and learned the songs under the direction of the Zhetl musicians: Solomon Lubtchansky, Hirshl Aron Volpovsky, and Avrom Hirshl Levit. Later we rented a hall at Patye's on Dvoretzer Street, built a stage and prepared for our premiere.

The performance was a great success. Those who excelled were: Noyakh Turetzky as "Bobe Yakhe", Simkha Robetz as "Hotzmakh", Avrom Moishe Barishansky as "the butcher", and Hindke Zanaratzky as "Mirele". The actors were often assailed by the town's children who called them "Sorceress" and "Hotzmakh" and the songs from the play were sung by all.

We performed for a month. Every performance was well attended. Even our occupiers, the Germans, came to see the performances. I even remember the Germans, among whom were high ranking officers, would sing all week the song: "Buy little Germans, little sticks and little whips…"

These performances brought in a lot of money. Everyone worked hard toward one goal namely: to support the soup kitchen, a Jewish library and a Literary –Dramatic society.

We Buy Our Own House

In 1916 a decision was made by the Literary – Dramatic Society to buy our own house. The society already had 150 members. It did take long before we bought the house of Itche Bere the carpenter. The house was totally renovated with a performance hall and room for the library.

With time, the house turned into a cultural centre where the entire cultural life of our town was concentrated. This is where readings, discussion and literary trials took place. The lecturers were: Yudl Ivenitsky, Avrom Langbart, Avrom Ivenitsky, Libke and Esther Kaplinsky, Gdalyahu Shvedsky and others. We often invited lecturers from other cities like Leyb Naydus, Avrom Zak and Yakov Pat.

Our second performance took place in our own locale. We put on the play "The Yeshiva Boy" with Shaul Funt playing the lead role. This play was also very successful.

[Page 185]

In time we performed the entire repertoire of Y. Gordin. In "Khasia the Orphan Girl" and in "The Slaughter" they following excelled: Feyvl Kuznyetsky, Libke Kaplinsky, Hindke Zanaratsky (Mirsky), Avrom Moishe Barishansky, Alter Gertzovsky, Kahyke Ovseyevitch and others whose names I do not recall.

We Open a Yiddish School

In 1917, with the outbreak of the revolution the work of our drama club came to an end. Zhetl experienced a terrible time of bandit attacks and changes in authority.

In 1919–20 when the situation stabilized a bit, the same group of activists decided to open a Yiddish school. We sold the house of the drama club and rented a school locale at Berl Mirsky's where we opened the first class.

The first teacher in the school, Liberman, truly brought in freshness and vitality to the cultural life in Zhetl. He began to organize lectures and readings.

The school was completely supported by the drama club. As we no longer had our own locale, we performed at the palace, in the public school and even the firing range behind the church.

The second teacher at the school was Herman Frenkel who came from Lodz. He was a good teacher and also a good organizer and director. We performed operettas like "Khantche in America", "Song of Songs", "The Americans" and "The Fake Widower".

We Build a School and Perform Theatre

Now the aspirations of the school activists increased. We decided to build our own school building with a performance hall. For the library, which already had 1500 books, we rented space at Mitzl's. Yitzkhak Leybovitch was the secretary of the school as well as treasurer of the library. Meanwhile, one of our most dedicated workers, Shloime Khaim Vernikovsky died. His funeral was organized by those active in the library and the drama club.

We bought a place for the school at Tcherne the miller's in the lane. We put up the walls but we were lacking a lot of money to complete the building. The American Relief Fund sent us money but it was not enough to finish the building. The drama club quickly prepared a new operetta "The Romanian Wedding", with song, dance and costumes.

There still was no floor or roof in the school building however, on Shavuot 1923, we performed on a hastily built stage for a full house. With the few hundred zlotys we made from this performance we were able to complete construction of the school.

Interest in the school grew every day. The seventh grade organized their own mandolin orchestra directed by Feyvl Zabitz and later by Eliyahu Busel. Teachers that came from various cities and towns brought us news.

Under the direction of Herman Frenkel we performed the repertoires of the playwrights Yakov Gordin, Leon Kobrin, Peretz Hirshbein as well as translations of world classics.

In 1936 the building of the Yiddish school went up in smoke. Once again we were forced to rent a place for the school at Yosef the barber's on the second floor near the cinema. We built a stage there as well and continued to perform. We presented Nomberg's "The Family", "The Fake Widower" and other plays.

It did not take long before we built a new building for the school, bigger and nicer than the first. We now had better possibilities and conditions for the work of the drama club. Lize Kovensky, now in Zhetl, had performed in Grodno. She settled in Zhetl and brought great enthusiasm to our club. She played leading roles in "The Thieves" by Bimko and Theresa in "Theresa Raquin" by Zola as well as others.

Actors in the performance of "The Villager" 1921

From right to left seated: Lyuba Leybovitch, Khaim Itzkovitch, the teacher Leah, P. Zabitz, Peshe Reznik
Standing: Zabitz, Khaim Ganuzovitch, ….., Soreh Bayle Ostoshinsky, ….., Yakov Dvoretzky, Soreh Novogrudsky, Yitzkhak Leybovitch, Feyvl
Kuzniyetsky, Eli Bensky, Hinde Mirsky, Breskin, Moishe Mirsky, Avrom Moishe Barishansky, ….., Yisroel Ber Rabinovitch

[Page 186]

We did not tire of performing a new play almost every month. With great success we performed "The Days of Our Lives" by Andreyev, "The Father" by Strindberg and "Motke the Thief" by Sholem Asch.

All of these performances brought in money to help support the school and the library. In the performance of "The Inspector" by Gogol, Alter Persky was excellent in the role of Khlistakov. He was also very good in his roles in "The Gold–Digger" as well as "It's Hard to be a Jew" by Sholem Aleichem.

We crowned our drama club with the name "Arvy" (Artistic Corner) in the school and library. Our performances had a great reputation in the entire region around Zhetl. We felt our contribution to the cultural life in Zhetl was no small thing. Thanks to us, the Yiddish school was able to develop and do its work. The same can be said about the Yiddish library.

Our Club Splits

With the emergence of the Tarbut School the forces in our drama club were divided. Many of our actors left "Arvy" and organized a separate drama club at the Tarbut School. Among them were the talented Avrom Langbart (murdered in 1941), Khaya Ovseyevitch, Khaya Dvoyre Savitsky, Leyb Beshkin, Yoel Tcheplovodsky, Hirshl Kaplinsky and others. Particularly successful was the play "The Duke" directed by Avrom Langbart. The performances directed by the Tarbut teacher Nokhem Shoykhet were also very successful.

Now there were two drama clubs in Zhetl which rarely competed against each other. For example, the play "Herzele the Illustrious" was performed the same evening by both groups. One in the hall of the Yiddish school and the other in the hall at Tarbut…both performances were well attended and the whole town was confused…

No More Theatre

This is how we performed theatre and enriched the spiritual life of Zhetl's Jews. But, the 17th of September 1939 wiped out all political parties, movements and organizations. The Soviets brought their order with them. Both drama clubs united and played Yiddish theatre under the Soviet regime.

At the Olympiad of All Nationalities in 1940 we performed the "Gold Digger" by Sholem Aleichem and won first place in artistic performance.

However, this too did not last long. The invasion of Hitler's hordes tore apart the chain of Zhetl's cultural life forever. The Yiddish school was turned into a jail, the Tarbut School served as a hospital in the ghetto and on the 6th of August 1942 Jewish Zhetl with its blossoming and exuberant life was silenced forever.

Participants in the performance of "The Romanian Wedding",
performed by the drama club of the Yiddish school in 1926

[Page 187]

Medical and Social Institutions

by Dr. Avrom Alpert (Ramat Gan)

Translated by Janie Respitz

I know very little about medical help in Zhetl before the First World War. I could not learn a lot from speaking to people who lived in Zhetl at that time. They did tell me that until the First World War Zhetl had a doctor, sometimes two. This would happen when the Jewish community was divided in two due to disputes over communal matters. There were no lack of arguments on the Jewish street. In a dispute, the doctor, a central figure in town, would support one side. The other side would declare a boycott on him and bring in a second doctor. Y. Gibor, who left Zhetl fifty years ago recounted the following story. In a dispute between the artisans and wealthy men led by the rabbi broke out. The doctor at the time, Hirshkop, fought on the side of the artisans. The wealthier men plotted against him and brought Dr. Ram from Vilna with great propaganda.

The main medical help was received by unqualified or half qualified people, medics who received their training in the army.

A Russian doctor, Ivanov, worked at the hospital on Lisagure Street, then, Dr. Shapiro of blessed memory and the medic Velvl, on Novoredker Street.

The Russian authorities supported the hospital which was used mainly by peasants from the surrounding villages. Jews would go there very seldom.

As for trained midwives or nurses, there is nothing to talk about. Grandmothers took care of this. By the way, during the First World War there were no Jewish doctors in Zhetl. Dr. Shapiro was mobilized by the Russians at the beginning of the war and medical help was given by military doctors from the local garrison. The very sick were brought to neighbouring, larger cities.

Dr. Shapiro and His Family

In 1918 Dr. Shapiro and his family returned from Russia. His wife Aneh was a trained midwife and assisted her husband with his work. For many years, Dr. Shapiro, of blessed memory, was the only Jewish doctor in Zhetl. He was not well liked by the Jewish population because of his use of the Russian language. By the way he was not accessible and could not get used to living among the Jewish masses. People would often joke about him repeating his medical demands in a Yiddish mixed with Russian expressions.

He worked very hard in order to run a modest house while at the same time educating his daughter Mania, and son Ilyusha, of blessed memory, who were both medical students. His daughter Mania lives in Russia and works as a neurologist. His son, after high school became a communist activist. In 1937 he quit his studies at the university, left Poland and through France arrived in Spain in order to join the liberation struggle of the Spanish people. As it has been told, he was the editor for the front newspaper of the International Brigade, and for active propaganda. He was killed in battle. Far from his small hometown of Zhetl, his bones were scattered in the land of the Pyrenees in a battle for freedom against the Fascist hordes of General Franco.

His father, Dr. Shapiro, fell victim to his hard work. It can be said he died at his post. His health was affected by his hard work. While he was visiting a very sick patient, he dropped dead of a heart attack.

Dr. Shapiro did not leave an inheritance for his wife Aneh and two children who were still studying. Life was difficult for them.

Medics

During Dr. Shapiro's time there were a few medics working in Zhetl. We must mention Velvl the Medic from Novoredker Street. Women said he was an expert in children's diseases. He died very old (I think his family name was Savitsky).

Another medic we must mention is Berl, who was an expert in all sorts of wounds.

[Page 188]

He was the main specialist in Zhetl. The peasants respected him and every Tuesday there was a lineup of wagons with sick people outside his house.

Besides them there was the medic Aron Grin, Zalmen the blacksmith's son. He was a trained medic with a lot of experience which he received at the Jewish hospital in Vilna. He had a huge practice with Jews and Christians. People said he really understood the illnesses. He also took great interest in the volunteer fire company and served as chairman for many years. He was killed together with his family in the second big slaughter in 1942.

Doctors

After Dr. Shapiro died many different doctors came to Zhetl. First, Dr. Kivelevitch, who besides his medical work, was involved with social medicine. He was active on the board of "TOZ" (Society For Safeguarding the Health of the Jewish Population) in Zhetl.

Dr. Vapner also worked as a doctor for a few years. I do not know his fate after he left Zhetl.

Dr. Kru worked during the few years before the war. He was a partisan in the Nolibaker Forest and remained in Russia as a devoted communist.

Dr. Vinik from Novogrudok worked in Zhetl before the war. During the Soviet occupation he worked as director of the birthing department in the hospital. Dr. Vinik was killed in Zhetl during the second slaughter. He had a chance to survive: however he did not want to leave his sister.

At the same time, Dr. Fraydzan, a refugee from Mezritch also worked in Zhetl. He was killed in Novogrudok after the liquidation of the Zhetl ghetto.

Before the Soviets, Dr. Kagan practiced in Zhetl. He was a well known community activist, and was also active in the Poalei Zion movement in Baranovitch. He was killed trying to escape from the workshops in Novogrudok through a tunnel which they dug for this purpose. He did not manage to escape because he limped. While they were shooting he became disoriented and returned to the workshops.

Doctors Born in Zhetl

From the doctors born in Zhetl I would like to mention my cousin, Noyakh Alpert, of blessed memory. He spent the difficult years of the German occupation in Mezritch, worked as a doctor with great success and survived many military operations which took place there. He was killed with his wife and child in the last extermination operation in Mezritch. We were told he and his wife were hidden by a Christian who turned them over to the Germans.

The writer of these lines is one of the few from Zhetl (4 in total) who graduated medical school right before the outbreak of the war, survived the difficult years of the German occupation in the ghettos of Vasilishok, Shtushin, then sent to a labour camp in Lide. Together with my wife and small son, we escaped from the camp in 1943 and joined the partisans, first in the region of Lide near the Nieman, and from July 1943 until liberation in 1944 I was sent to the Bulak brigade where I served as brigade doctor until we were liberated by the Red Army. In 1945 I left Russia and wandered throughout Europe with a longer stop in Italy. With the large immigration current in 1949, I arrived in Israel with my family.

Nurses

From among the medical personnel that worked in Zhetl I would like to mention Peshke Langbart. She was not a trained nurse however she carried out her work with perfection. She dedicated a lot of time to communal work, particularly the Zhetl Orphan Committee. She was called the mother of the orphans. She was the wife of the well known Zionist activist Avrom Langbart.

From among the younger nurses I have to mention Shifra Dunetz, a graduate of the "TOZ" Nursing School in Vilna. She was a trained nurse and worked for the Soviets in the Zhetl hospital. She was killed with the first 120 after she was handed over to the Germans for her socialist convictions.

From the Zhetl midwives I would like to mention Raykhl from Lisagure Street and Aneh Shapiro who died before the German occupation. From the younger generation we must remember Dvoyre Rashkin who graduated from the Warsaw State Midwife School and later worked in Zhetl. She survived the partisans and now lives in Australia. Hindke Mirsky also worked as a nurse during the Soviet occupation and later in the forest.

[Page 189]

Dentists

From among the dentists in Zhetl I want to mention the Kuperman sisters, who worked until the last days and died after the last slaughter. After the First World War many dentists worked in Zhetl, among them were Lotvin, who actually was an assistant, but knew the work very well and attracted the largest number of patients. A large number of tooth technicians also fixed teeth. Among the technicians were: Nakhman Breskin, who is now in America, Avrom Rashkin who was killed as a partisan in an ambush in the village Savitch, Mayrim Lusky, who lives in Israel, Yosef Levit who was killed in one of the slaughters in Zhetl.

I want to make special mention of the Zhetl dentist Gdalyahu Shvedsky who was active in the community, was one of the most important workers in Zhetl's "TOZ", and an active member of the Zhetl Secular Yiddish School. He was killed in Oygustov where he had been living during the last years.

Druggists

I would also like to mention the pharmacists and half pharmacists, meaning those who worked in the pharmacy stores. They learned how to prepare medications and would give medical advice and even make diagnoses.

The pharmacy, as far as I remember, was owned by Christians, however the pharmacists were Jews. Belonging to the older group of druggists were: Reb Menakhem Vernikovsky, of blessed memory, a well known Zionist from the early Hovevei Zion (Lovers of Zion). He died in Israel. Khaim Koyfman and his son Berl, Hendl Dvoretsky, Yudelevitch, Hinde Mirsky, Mania Rabinovitch, Pesia Levit and others.

"TOZ"

The most important social medicine institution in Zhetl belonged to the "TOZ" division in Zhetl.

"TOZ" in Zhetl was first organized by the Yiddishists, meaning those communal activists from the Yiddish Secular School like: Etl Ovseyevitch, Lize Kovensky, Yehoshua Lusky, Yosef Senderovsky, Khayke Ovseyevitch, Herman Frenkel and Khane Malke Shvedsky. After the Zionists revolted, they chose a new board of directors including the following: Aron Alpert – chairman, Volf Farfl – vice chairman, Dr. Y. Kivelevitch, Berl Dvoretsky, Dvoyre Gorodaysky, Rivke Lusky, Etl Ovseyevitch and Gdalyahu Shvedsky. Dr. Kru and Dr. Vinil were also very active in "TOZ".

The activities of "TOZ" were diverse. They ran summer camps in Novyelnia and half summer camps in Zhetl. The prophylactic work consisted of: healing various parasite diseases, especially diseases in children's hair. Children with this disease would be sent to Bialystok for x–rays.

Besides this, "Toz" looked after children who suffered from tuberculosis and would send them to the tuberculosis sanatorium in Novoyelnia. They would manage the sanitary condition of poor houses and provide a warm meal in school for poor children.

Doctors would visit the schools and examine the children in order to discover parasites and especially tuberculosis.

"TOZ" summer camp in Novoyelnia 1929

[Page 190]

Sponsors of the medical aid society 1918

First row: Khaye Busel. Nekhama Roznov, Babel Lusky, Mushe Levit, Leah Kovesnky, Grunie Vernikovsky, Khane Lifshitz
Second row: Mendl Mirsky, Avrom Langbart, Leyb Lusky, Peshke Izraelit. Yisroel Moishe Ivenitsky, unknown, Yehoshua Lusky
Third row: Soreh Libe Shatzky, Minke Zayontchek, Mirl Lusky, Shayndl Butkovsky, Zvia Kovensky, Yudis Mirsky, Rivke Rayzl Vaynshteyn
Fourth row: Khaye Belsky, Soreh Rabinovitch, Libe Belsky, Etl Vilner, Mashe Leybovitch, Mayte Savitsky. Mere Savitsky

Institutions and Activists

It is worthwhile to mention the blessed activity of the Medical Aid Society in Zhetl. They mainly worked in healing the sick poor. Dr. Shapiro would receive them at the hospital on Lisagure Street and the Medical Aid Society would pay. They would also receive medication free of charge as well as physiotherapy, quartz radio therapy and the like.

Among the volunteers in the Medical Aid Society were: Moishe Ruven Mordkovsky the well known Zionist activist in Zhetl. It is worthwhile dedicating an entire chapter to him. Avrom Moishe Barishansky, Rivke Lusky, Yoel Tcheplovodsky, Avrom Savitsky (now living in Israel), Yehoshua Lusky, Leyb Lusky the former mayor, Avrom and Pesiye Langbart, Khaim Itzkovitch now in Israel and many others.

Among others it is worthwhile to mention those active in the Society to Spend the Night with the Sick: Shmuel Shvedsky, Aron the shoe leather cutter, Avrom Savitsky and Moishe Ruven Mordkovsky.

The Orphan Committee worked energetically. Its main activist was Peshke Langbart. She supplied clothing and made sure to find places for children in the orphanage.

[Page 191]

In Zhetl there were many institutions which helped in an emergency and provided the first steps in the direction of prophylactic medicine. In the photographs of the Medical Aid Society and Society to Spend the Night with the Sick that we published here, the activists, the ones I mentioned and did not mention, of all the institutions will be remembered eternally. Let their heartfelt and varied communal work sanctify their names. Honour their memory!

The Committee of the Medical Aid Society 1922

From right to left: Mordkhai Sokolovsky, Mosihe Ruven Mordkovsky, Mahse Leybovitch, Avrom Savitsky, Philip Zabitz

Participants in the Flower Day on behalf of the Medical Aid Society 1923

Seated: Dentist A. Barukhin, M.Sh. Glikman, Lyuba Leybovitch
Standing: A. Savitsky, Yakov Pilnik, Sh. Kalmanovsky, Sh. Vilensky, A. Smayevsky, V. Eliyovitch

Chanukah party of the Society to Spend the Night with the Sick, 1933

From right to left seated: Khineke Lusky, Khaya Bielitzky, Frume Shalkovitch, Moishe Ruven Mordkovsky, Zelik Berman, Yisroel Ozer Barishansky, Yiosroel Elkahanan Piekelny, Yosef the painter, Yakov Abelevitch
Standing: Sholem Reznitsky, Soreh Rabinovitch, Noyakh Mikulitsky, Sonia Shilovitsky, Tzfira Raytzer, Yokhe Mordkovsky, Shmuel Shvedsky, Aron Kontzevik, Leyzer Eli Slutsky, Khanie

[Page 192]

The Society to Spend the Night
with the Sick and the Medical Aid Society

by Henie Piekelny – Rozenblum (Ra'anana)

Translated by Janie Respitz

Our town Zhetl was a state unto itself. The concern for social aid, health and even self defence was found among devoted community activists who benefited from general sympathy.

As we know, Jews of Zhetl excelled in helping the needy and lived by the biblical passage which states Jews are responsible for one another.

Before the First World War Zhetl had a Society to Spend the Night with the Sick, a Medical Aid Society and an Interest Free Loan Society. One of the most devoted activists in these institutions was my father, Reb Yisroel Elkhanan Piekelny, of blessed memory. He was responsible for the town ice cellar and the Interest Free Loan Society.

Often, they would wake him in the middle of the night requesting ice for a sick person who had a fever. My father, of blessed memory, would fulfill this good deed with devotion and a smile so that they would not think, God forbid, it was an effort for him.

A totally different type of work was the Interest Free Loan Society. Not only did they have to worry about distributing money, they also had to make sure the fund would grow its credit possibilities. In order to achieve this they would collect usury as well as income from payment for honours to come up to the Torah. A portion of the collected money went to the Medical Aid Society and supplementary nourishment for the needy.

The Society to Spend the Night with the Sick played an important role in Zhetl. In those years Zhetl did not have a hospital. Patients would remain at home, often for a long time which would exhaust the family. The society would send someone to spend the night with the patient so the family members could get some rest.

Almost all of Zhetl signed up. This institution was run by a committee divided into the following functions: a chairman, secretary and those responsible for certain streets. A family in need would approach the chairman who would bring the request to those responsible for the streets. The person responsible for that particular street would send someone to spend the night according to a list.

Around 11–12 at night they would check if the person was on duty. If not, they would go to his house and pull him out of bed.

The Society to Spend the Night with the Sick had a warehouse and supplies. According to orders from the doctor the patient would receive what he needed and return them once he recovered.

This is how they worked all year long with great devotion, day and night, visiting the sick and the needy

At the beginning of the German occupation in 1915 the social aid activity was stopped. In 1923, when life in town normalized it was decided to renew the activities of the Society to Spend the Night with the Sick. Two women, one of whom was Bayle Tentzer went through the town to enlist members for the Society to Spend the Night with the Sick and the Medical Aid Society.

By that time I was busy organizing the "Young Pioneer" organization. The women approached me to organize the institution because the previous activists were either too old or sick.

I accepted this task and wanted to express appreciation for the previous workers.

I did this work alone for about a year and a half without any help. I would distribute the night shifts and with my study books under my arm, go around and check.

Participants in the Flower Day on behalf of the Medical Aid Society 1926

From right to left – seated in the first row: Yoel Tcheplovodsky, Khaye Dvoyre Savitsky, Leybl Mirsky
Second row seated: Sime Shapiro, Mania Rabinovitch, Karpelovitch, Avrom Savitsky, Rokhl Obershteyn, Senderovsky, Dina Shilovitsky
Standing: Hirshl Belaus, Henie Piekelny, Yakov Pilnik

[Page 193]

If I did not find the one who was supposed to be on duty sitting with the patient, I would remain for the rest of the night. This is how I continued with this sacred work and made sure no patient would be left alone.

Tired from the burden and responsibility I turned to Moishe Ruven Mordkovsky of blessed memory for help. One evening we organized a general meeting in the old House of Study. I gave a report of the work and suggested we form a committee of 18 people. My suggestion was accepted. Among others chosen for the committee were: Moishe Ruven Mordkovsky – chairman, me as secretary, Yenkl Yudl the son of the ritual slaughterer, Yisroel Ozer Barishansky, Shmuel Shvedsky, Avrom Alpert, Noyakh Mikulitsky, my sister Badaneh and others.

The newly elected committee approached the work with great zeal. We would often organize parties for the volunteers in the Society to Spend the Night with the Sick and Yenkle Yudl, the ritual slaughterer's son would entertain everyone with his beautiful voice. On the Sabbath of VeYikhye, we would host a reception for all the residents of Zhetl, which made everyone happy.

It is hard to imagine the unity and the friendship that existed among these workers.

Going away party for Khaya Savitsky 1930

Seated: Aron Kontzevik, Shmuel Shvedsky, Sonia Shalkovitch, Khaya Savitsky, Elke Khaya Dzhenchelsky, Moishe Ruven Mordkovsky, Volf Leybovitch
Standing: Noyakh Mikulitsky, Soreh Rabinovitch, Avrom Savitsky, Sholem Reznitsky

Going away party for Henie Piekelny 1926 at the Society to Spend the Night with the Sick and the Medical Aid Society

From right to left: – seated in the first row: Berl Dvoretsky, Avrom Moishe Barishansky, Shmuel Shvedsky, Henie Piekelny, Moishe Ruven Mordkovsky, Gershon Zhukhovitsky, Aron Kontzevik
Standing in the second row: Khaya Savitsky, Mordkhai Sokolovsky, Shifra Savitsky, Yoel Tcheplovodsky, B. Piekelny, Hirshl Bielaus, Rivka Lusky
Standing in the last row: Yakov Pilnik, Elke Dzhenchelsky, Avrom Savitsky, Soreh....

All members were ready to be called upon day or night. We would even have someone stay with a contagious patient.

The devotion of the committee was contagious. I, the youngest of the group devoted myself to this work and received great satisfaction.

In 1926 I was preparing to immigrate to the Land of Israel. I will never forget the farewell banquet they prepared for me. We enjoyed the evening at the home of Yisroel Ozer Barishansky and we were all photographed. Yenkl Yudl the ritual slaughterer's son did not want to be photographed, but he entertained us all.

That evening was very enjoyable. It was so hard to leave! No one imagined we would never see each other again.

The tragedy that took away our best friends that worked to help Zhetl's needy Jews was horrific.

[Page 194]

The Orphans Committee

by Shifra Medvedsky, Montreal

Translated by Janie Respitz

The founders of the Zhetl Orphans Committee were: Moishe Ruven Mordkovsky, and Peshke Langbart. They both devoted heart and soul to this work and sacredly fulfilled their obligations.

Shifra Medvedsky

The orphans would go to Moishe Ruven as if to a father and he would answer everyone with a smile. His mother – in law would stand at a distance grumbling and wringing her hands because her son in law was neglecting his livelihood and was busy with charity work. His wife however, was loving and kind like him.

His life in general was heartache, illness and troubles. After many months laid up in bed, he died young of lung disease. The town mourned him.

After his death, Peshke Langbart took over this work. I remember they had to send a few orphans to the Land of Israel and there was not enough money.

Peshke Langbart

They approached their families for a contribution and organized a performance at "Tarbut" with a nice buffet, and collected the necessary funds. Peshke was happy the task was accomplished. This is how she managed to provide the orphans with clothes and shoes.

I saw this all as a child and promised that when I grew up I would also work toward this sacred goal. And that is what happened. I got to know Peshke through the "Tarbut" drama club and the bazaars for the Jewish National Fund.

Once, during a meeting of the drama club, Peshke asked me to come to her house because the Orphans Committee together with "Tarbut" were organizing an evening and they needed help. When I arrived at Peshke's I met: Khaye Bielitzky, Fruma and Sonia Shilovitsky, Etl Rozenfeld, Nekhame Goldberg, Bobtche Beshkin and other women. We had to decide what type of ball we were going to organize and what it should be called. Since it was autumn we decided to name it: "The Autumn Ball".

The hall had to be decorated with yellow leaves. Peshke called together all of her daughter Khasia's friends and of few other girls and we went to the forest to collect bags full of leaves.

At the "Tarbut" school we sewed the leaves into garlands. Hirshl Kaplinsky, a devoted volunteer for "Tarbut" hung the wreaths from wall to wall.

The hall was beautifully decorated and the ball was one of the nicest ever in Zhetl and raised a lot of money. The orchestra gave us a discount and Peshke was thrilled. I don't remember the exact year, but I think this was the last ball in Zhetl. When the Russians came, everything faded away.

During the German occupation I hardly ever saw Peshke. Her husband was taken with the first 120 victims. After she escaped from Zhetl I saw her in Dvoretz. She was broken like the rest of us.

———————

Social Women's Aid

by Soreh Gal – Begin, Jerusalem

Translated by Janie Respitz

Zhetl was known throughout the region for its social institutions. Among others, an important place was held by Social Women's Aid whose important task was to help poor pregnant women, brides and all those in need. The following belonged to the committee: Dvoyre Senderovsky, Mertche Gal and Bayle Tentzer.

For a minimal salary, Bashe Drayzl Karpelovitch would go around town collecting monthly dues from the women. Every year at Dvoyre Senderovsky's house and our house, we would make jam for poor pregnant women. Our neighbours Rokhl the blacksmith's wife and Henie the painter would participate in this good deed helping to stir the jam so God forbid, it wouldn't burn.

The community leader was Khayke Zernitzky. She would reach every poor corner. She would gather items and distribute them among the poor children at the Talmud Torah. She knew when a child was born, and which poor girl lacked a trousseau. When a tragedy occurred she would send out a few women to help out as quickly as possible.

Year in and year out the cellars were filled, then emptied. The fund as well. Every year the list of those in need changed but the committee remained the same.

Many did not know about this quiet sacred work however those in need felt the help as well as the activism.

This small society of women's aid was wiped out with all the other institutions.

[Page 195]

The Popular Bank

by Arye Zelikovitch

Translated by Janie Respitz

The Zhetl Popular Bank was founded in 1923. Before the bank was founded Zhetl had an Interest Free Loan Society that gave out small loans to craftsmen and small businesses. However, larger business owners did not have a financial institution which could finance their businesses which were based on promissory notes and open credit.

Rabbi Zalmen Saratzky who was involved in every aspect of communal life was also involved in creating a bank in Zhetl.

Due to his initiative a general meeting was called with all the businessmen and merchants and they decided to found a Cooperative Popular Bank. Besides the rabbi the founding members were: Yitzkhak Kaplinsky, Shmuel Kustin, Yisroel Ozer Barishansky, Meir Kovensky and others.

The capital of the bank was based on fees of up to 10% of the certified loan, deposits and a loan from the "Joint" in Warsaw. With this capital the bank began its activity with great success.

The first director, secretary and bookkeeper of the bank was Khaim Kaplinsky. He devoted himself completely to this work. He could be seen after working hours sitting in the bank reviewing the books.

Within two years the volume of work grew and it became necessary to increase personnel. This is when they hired Reb Yeshayahu Moishe Pilnik as a cashier. He excelled in his habits, and was honest and kind.

Arye Zelikovitch

After a few years of existence the bank grew to 600 members. Merchants, small businessmen and craftsmen began to carry out their financial operations through the bank. This is where they bought their promissory notes, received credit and deposited their savings.

With the broadening of operations and membership the bank decided to move to a new location and hire more people. They rented space at A. Lusky's at the marketplace. After, since Khaim Kaplinsky left his job at the bank, he was replaced by Yerukham Izraelit from Novoredok. Yitzkhak Kaplinsky who had until this time been active in administration of the bank was elected director and I, the writer of these lines was chosen as clerk. A year later we hired another employee, Basia Rabinovitch. By 1928 there were 6 people working at the bank including the beadle Movshovitch.

From 1927 – 1933 the amount of members grew and the maximum loan received by a member was up to one thousand zlotys.

The bank became one of the most useful and popular institutions in Zhetl. It helped the Jewish merchant and craftsman in their difficult struggle to earn a living.

Besides the administration the general meeting also elected a bank council. The active members were: Khaim Ganuzovitch, Meir Kovensky, Khaim Levit, Alter Bom, Moishe Mendl Leyzerovitch, Yehoshua Shusahn, The Barishansky brothers and tens of others whose names I do not recall, but they devoted a lot of energy and time to the development of the bank.

I worked at the bank for 6 years until one fine day, about 20 years ago, I left my job and immigrated to the Land of Israel.

These memories are fresh, as if they occurred yesterday. All the clients and members of the bank with whom I had daily contact stand before my eyes. It hurts my heart and I cannot find comfort knowing that this institution which was built over many years with so much devotion, was, within a few days, together with its activists, so cruelly murdered.

[Page 196]

Balances of the Zhetl Cooperative Popular Bank

*According to statistics from the Union of Credit Cooperatives

Translated by Janie Respitz

Balance December 12, 1929 Active

Treasury	4981 zlotys
Rent	70 zlotys
Securities and payments to other institutions	1000 zlotys
Promissory loans	56827 zlotys
Moveable property	360 zlotys
Various accounts	445 zlotys
Administrative costs	3250 zlotys
Interest rates, provisional installments	3043 zlotys
Collector documents	10490 zlotys
General balance total	80466 zlotys

Passive

Payments	8188 zlotys
Reserve fund	650 zlotys
Deposits and operating accounts	42706 zlotys
Debts to Central Cooperative	12500 zlotys
Other accounts	171 zlotys
Rates and postage of loans	4793 zlotys
Provisions from other operations	968 zlotys
Various debts	10490 zlotys
General balance total	80466 zlotys

Information

Amount of loans	320 zlotys
Sum of loans	175766 zlotys
Average rate of loans	549 zlotys
Received deposit documents	1397 zlotys
A total of	**214010 zlotys**

In the office of the Interest Free Loan Society 1939

Among the clients standing: Khaim Berl Izbornitsky, Shayne Levit, Esther Busel, Soreh Fin, Dvoyre Tinlovirsky, Aron Vinarsky
In the background: Khaye Movshovitch. In the office: Nakhman Gal, Yakov Obershteyn, Hirshl Busel, Malke Lusky

Balance December 31, 1931

Active

Treasury	1474 zlotys
Rent	162 zlotys
Securities and payments to other institutions	6250 zlotys
Habitual promissory loans	56879 zlotys
Deposits	9281 zlotys
Other credits	797 zlotys
Immoveable properties	5451 zlotys
Moveable properties	1476 zlotys
Various accounts	2996 zlotys
Administrative and organizational expenses	13178 zlotys
Rate provisions	9878 zlotys
Losses from the previous year	164 zlotys
Documents of debts	26673 zlotys
General balance total	134659 zlotys

Passive

Payments	19257 zlotys
Reserve Fund	5693 zlotys
Special funds	329 zlotys
Deposits and running accounts	39361 zlotys
Debts in the central cooperative	20786 zlotys
Other accounts	1730 zlotys
Percentage and postage of loans	14374 zlotys
Provisions of other operations	6223 zlotys
Various deposits	26906 zlotys
General balance total	134659 zlotys

Information

Amount of loans	442 zlotys
Total	164496 zlotys
Average rate of loans	372 zlotys
Discounts	67986 zlotys
General balance total	49236 zlotys

[Page 197]

The Interest Free Loan Society

by Soreh Gal – Begin, Jerusalem

Translated by Janie Respitz

During the First World War Zhetl was not on the front lines and was not destroyed like Karelich, Lyubitch, Shieluv and other towns. However, it did suffer from offensives, counter– offensives and bandits who robbed. When life normalized after the war the residents of Zhetl who even before the war were not the richest, had to struggle to earn a living.

Once, after a conversation between the teacher Aron Hershl Langbart and his student Nakhman Gal, the plan was born to create an Interest Free Loan Fund. In order to realize this plan they turned to people from Zhetl now living in America for help.

Jews from Zhetl in America embraced this request warmly and sent the first 500 dollars. Aron Hershl Langbart and Nakhman Gal called a general meeting in the old House of Study and suggested the creation of an Interest Free Loan Fund. Those gathered warmly accepted the idea and decided to ask for dues at a minimum of one zloty.

By the second meeting the foundation stone was laid. A board of directors was chosen and this new institution was registered with the government. This was Chanukah 1926.

At the beginning the aid that was given was between 30 – 50 zlotys. With time, the fund grew as did the aid. This is thanks to the regular weekly payments of 50 groschen paid by the members and the yearly support from America. In later years, every member was able to receive a loan of up to 200 zlotys. He only had to provide two endorsers.

In the early years the fund was open to clients twice a week, later, three times a week. In urgent cases, they went to Nakhman Gal's home and he would take care of everything. The secretary of the Interest Free Loan Fund was Malke Lusky.

The annual meeting took place every year on Chanukah. After giving the report they would elect a new board.

The Interest Free Loan Fund was the tree that with its branches supported and with its fruit fed hundreds of families in Zhetl.

"TOZ" in Zhetl[1]

Translated by Janie Respitz

At the end of 1923, thanks to the initiative of the teacher Akiva Baksht a group of Zhetl's Yiddishist activists came together to found a division of "TOZ" in Zhetl. The first board of directors elected at the meeting at the home of Shmerke Lobensky was comprised of the following: Gdalyahu Shvedsky – chairman, Hindke Mirsky, Etl Ovseyevitch, Herman and Khane Malke Frenkel and Lize Kovensky.

Within a few years, Zionist activists joined the "TOZ" board like: Aron Alpert, Dvoyre Gorodaysky, Hirshl Kaplinsky, Khane Obershteyn, Khaye Ovsyevitch and others.

One of the most important accomplishments of "TOZ" was the summer camp in Novayelenia and the half summer camp in Zhetl.

Banquet for the sponsors of TOZ 1938

First row: Moishe Mirsky, Eydele Farfl, Yitzkhak Leybovitch, Feygl Epshteyn, Shlime Daykhovsky, ….., Khasie Kaplinsky, Hirshl Kaplinsky, Etl Ovsyevitch
Second row: Hindke Mirsky, Fraydl Mnuskin

After the fire in 1933 over 100 poor and weak children went to the summer camp in Novayelenia.

The second most important activity of "TOZ" in Zhetl was devoted to feeding 400 school children. Over 50% of the children received this food for free. The rest paid 5 groshn.

The sanitation action played an important role as well. Sanitation patrols would check hygiene conditions. "TOZ" would also distribute linens and cod –liver oil to needy and sick children.

The revenue of "TOZ" came from traditional Zhetl ventures: membership dues, flower days, dances, aid from the "TOZ" central office and a small subsidy from Zhetl city hall.

Translators' footnote:

1.   "TOZ" is the Polish acronym for the Society for Safeguarding the Health of the Jewish People

[Page 198]

Remember!

by Moishe Man, Buenos Aires

Translated by Janie Respitz

After the European destruction one often heard the expression: "Continuation" meaning we should continue with the lives we lived in the old home, because the greatest art in the world is the art of knowing how to live. Our parents possessed this art. In the poorest of times they lived a rich spiritual life and lived by the words: Love thy neighbour as you love yourself!

Moishe Man

Despite the greatest suffering which everyone experienced, they were always ready to help another as much as they could. How many institutions did they support with their weak forces? There was the Tarbut School, the craftsmen's union, a merchant's union, and more and more. Who is even capable of counting all the institutions, unions and political parties.

We also had a beautiful library under the direction of Yitzkhak Leybovitch. How devoted was he to this library, how difficult it was to collect a few books not to mention a wagon load of wood needed in the winter to heat the room. If anyone in Zhetl read a book it was thanks to Yitzkhak Leybovitch.

There was a Yiddish school where many children from the poorest families went. Every year Jewish intellectuals graduated proficient in Yiddish and world literature.

We maintained an Interest Free Loan Fund, with which every loan saved a small businessman or a craftsman.

The Society to Visit the Sick made sure that God forbid, no poor person would lack a doctor or prescription.

The Society to Spend the Night with the Sick, so the family could rest.

There was a Society to Save the Fallen offering loans at low interest, and the poorest of the poor who had to be helped discreetly. Remember all these institutions.

Tradesmen Committee

From right to left – first row: Avrom Zobelinsky, Yitzkhak Kaplinsky, Leyb Lusky, Yakov Borukh Kaplinsky, Morkhai Lusky
Second row standing: Zaydke Rzvosky, Avrom Savitsky, Yitzkhak Moishe Gafanovitch, Avrom Moishe Barishansky, Mordkhai Mishkin, Asher Levit, Bezalel Moshkovsky, Khaim Mikhl Roznov

[Page 199]

Schools

המחזור הראשון של בי"הס תרבות ביזשל א' הלוז תרצ"ד

The first graduates of Tarbut School 1934

[Page 200]

The Schools

Translated by Judy Montel

Two periods must be noted in the development of education in Zhetl. In the first period, up to the 1920s, education in Zhetl was traditional. Poor children learned in the Talmud Torah, which was a public institution and was supported by the rabbi, while the wealthier students learned in the private "cheders". Among the *melamdim* (teachers) in the latter period one must mention Reb Yoseli Mendes, Reb Noach Eli and Reb Ya'akov the Shochet. Young boys continued their studies in the small Yeshiva under the direction of the rabbi Reb Tzvi Churgin, while the teens left to gain Torah in the famous yeshivas of Poland and Lithuania.

General studies such as Russian and mathematics were learned from several private teachers. A few also were able to gain a high school education in the cities near Zhetl.

During the 1920s a change took place in the educational system in Zhetl. In 1921, the YIddishist and anti-Zionist circles established a Yiddish school named for Shalom Aleichem, and in 1927, the nationalist circles established a kindergarten that turned into the Tarbut school named for Chayim Nachman Bialik.

Both schools were modern, taught their students a general and Jewish education and became centers of culture and public initiative in the town.

The schools had to fight hard for their existence. Tuition did not cover expenses, municipal support was miniscule and therefore both schools needed side income from balls, plays, lotteries and bazaars. The considerable help received from former Zhetl residents in America must be noted as they kept the schools running and helped to construct their buildings.

A considerable portion of the children of Zhetl, particularly the girls, received their education at the government Polish school while they completed their Hebrew education at evening classes.

This was the face of education in Zhetl up to 1939. That year Zhetl passed to the rule of Soviet Russia which cancelled the public schools and instead established government Soviet schools. In June of 1941 those school came to an end as well and Zhetl approached its tragic end.

[Page 201]

The Talmud Torah

by Alexander Ziskind Silverman, Toronto

Translated by Janie Respitz

The Talmud Torah was situated not far from the Houses of study. The building had four classrooms and a kitchen. Two grades studied in each room, a younger one and an older one.

The teacher of the youngest class was Reb Avrom Yakov. He taught the Pentateuch with Rashi and the beginning of Gomorrah (commentary).

The second teacher's name was Reb Meylekh. He taught Gomorrah to his younger students, beginning where Reb Avrom Yakov left off. He taught the older students Gomorrah with annotations to the Talmud.

The third teacher was Reb Yoine who taught Gomorrah and Talmudic interpretations. His students were able to learn a page of Gomorrah on their own.

The fourth teacher was Reb Shmuel Khaim. He taught the same as Reb Yoine with some additional biblical passages.

Friday evening and Saturday evening the important men in town would come listen to and test the students. Those who regularly came to listen were: Reb Arye the first manager of the old House of Study as well as the Talmud Torah. The second listener was Reb Menakhem the pharmacist. Often, the fourth teacher Reb Shmuel Khaim would come listen to students from other classes. However, the other rabbis would not come to his class, firstly because the boys were old and you had to be a great scholar in order to listen to them, and besides this we must note, Reb Shmuel Khaim came from great pedigree, a son in law of a wealthy grain merchant and it was not befitting for the rabbis of the younger classes to test his students.

Very often an argument would take place between the listeners and the class teacher and they would forget they came to hear the students and not themselves. It was mainly Reb Yoine who would argue with the listeners. We, the students would be happy with such disputes as the listeners would forget about us.

The Students

Most of the students in the Talmud Torah were from Zhetl. However, there were some students who came from surrounding towns. The students from other towns would eat their meals at the homes of the important, well off families. Some of the poor children would also eat their meals with these families. It would sometimes happen that some children would not receive a meal so the Talmud Torah had a kitchen where women cooked food they collected from wealthier homes and gladly helped this cause.

I remember an Incident

I remember a humorous incident that happened to one of our rabbis. As usual, students do not like to silence complaints about their teachers. This is what happened: a few of Rabbi Meylekh's students were angry with him and decided to pull a prank. On a moonlit night, they gathered in the yard of the Talmud Torah, removed the window pane and climbed into Reb Meylekh's classroom. They took his chair, turned it over and poured tar on it and put it back in its place. They left the room and replaced the window pane and agreed to remain silent about it, and they did.

The next morning, when Reb Meylekh came to his class he sat on his chair of course not knowing what the guys did.

His second class meanwhile was reviewing their afternoon lesson. At that moment they became rowdy and the rabbi decided to go see what they were up to. He wanted to get up from his chair, but could not. He tried once, twice, until he stood up with the chair. With great difficulty, we managed to tear the chair off the rabbi.

We could not control ourselves and burst out laughing. Nothing else was needed. The rabbi grabbed a stick and not knowing anything about Freud's theory of self responsibility, he began to ask the students who did this. We stuck to our agreement and remained silent. The rabbi began to beat a boy that he suspected pulled this prank. This boy, and the rest of us ran into the street and the rabbi followed us with his stick. We continued to run until we arrived at the home of Reb Arye. When Reb Arye saw us running and being chased by Reb Meylekh and his stick he called out:

"Feh, it is not nice for a rabbi to chase
[Page 202]
his students with a stick, even if they deserve a beating. This is how we were saved from the rabbis stick. Who knows, maybe a son of the boy that was saved was one of the brave Zhetl partisan fighters?

My Uncle Reb Yoine

Reb Yoine was a sickly man. He suffered a lot and he would often leave his class and go to a certain place for long periods of time. Meanwhile the students would be mischievous. What more do you need! Our voices and shouts would irritate the other teachers and they would tell the managers of the Talmud Torah that Reb Yoine was not supervising his students. They did not consider the fact that he was a weak man. This resulted in Reb Yoine leaving his job as teacher at the Talmud Torah and he began to teach a class at the Middle House of Study for a small group of chosen students.

I remember an incident which shows Reb Yoine's honesty. As mentioned, my uncle Reb Yoine began to teach a class at the Middle House of Study. One day, during his lesson the manager of the House of Study came to check where these students were from: from Zhetl or elsewhere. If the students were not from Zhetl they would have to pay to use the space. When the manager began to question the students he also came to me. My uncle Reb Yoine said that he did not know what to say about me. He cannot say I am not from Zhetl because my ancestors were from Zhetl. But he cannot say I am from Zhetl because my father, in order to earn a living, was in another town. The manager decided that I was from Zhetl as well as most of the other students and the House of Study did not have to charge us any money.

I remember another episode in connection to the Talmud Torah. One Friday afternoon, my uncle Reb Yoine sent me to one of the managers, Reb Efraim to fetch his rent which amounted to three rubles a week. When I arrived at the manager who had a large store I asked him for my uncle's rent so he can buy what he needs for the Sabbath. After he heard me, he left the store and left me waiting. I waited and waited until I couldn't wait any longer. I asked him again and that is when he gave me the three rubles.

It was already late in the afternoon when I brought my uncle his money. Understandably, it was now too late to buy anything for the Sabbath.

My uncle Reb Yoine said: "Reb Efraim does not give me his own money, but money from the town, so why such a fuss?

Also this attitude led to my uncle Reb Yoine's departure from the Talmud Torah and teaching a class at the Middle House of Study.

I would like to include a song we heard from Reb Yehoshua Barzilay during his visit to Zhetl in 1898.

[Page 203]

The History of the Yiddish School[1]

by Binyomin Kaplinsky of blessed memory

Translated by Janie Respitz

I

Zhetl is a poor town in the Novogrudek Township, 150 kilometres from Vilna, 15 kilometres from the train station (Novoyelnia), and has in total barely 4000 residents, 70 percent Jews, the rest being Poles and White Russians.

There are no factories or enterprises in town which could employ a large amount of Jewish workers. The only large enterprise in town, which incidentally belongs to a Jew, employs few Jews.

The majority of the Jewish population are craftsmen (the majority: shoemakers, carpenters and tailors), and merchants. A large number of merchants deal in agricultural products from the surrounding village population. Zhetl was known as a town of religious scribes. Young people from Zhetl would write Torah scrolls and Mezuzahs that were sent to America. This earned them a fine living. Over the past few years this trade has fallen and the former scribes live in dire need. Zhetl is known in the region for being a developed cultural town and before the war had a reputation with its revolutionary movement. The scribes who worked for merchants laid the foundation of the revolutionary movement in 1905.

At this time there were a couple of factories in Zhetl with 50 workers and already in 1899 there were circles of the "Bund". In 1904–05 the socialist revolutionaries were gaining ground and even today stories are told about the great discussions and meetings that took place in the forest behind the town which would last for days and both sides would bring forces from other towns. The majority of the youth during those years of reactionary activity left for America and from there helped build the Yiddish school in Zhetl.

Those who took part in the movement in 1904–05 and remained in Zhetl were community activists in various institutions. They were the founders and builders of the Yiddish school which they support until today.

II

The actual history of the school in Zhetl begins in 1917. This is when the so–called "Literary – Dramatic Society" was founded by people who graduated from the school in 1905.

During its short existence the Literary – Dramatic Society succeeded in running rich and varied activities: there were many lectures and readings, they founded a library, and the drama club performed theatre in Yiddish for the first time in Zhetl. The Literary – Dramatic Society bought its own building which over time was sold. Thanks to this society the prestige of Yiddish and Yiddish literature grew. They brought the Yiddish poet Leyb Naydus to Zhetl for a few weeks and he held readings. There was such an exciting atmosphere toward Yiddish in town that the teachers Esther and Libke Kaplinsky, with the permission of the German occupation authorities, opened their own school and had to use Yiddish as an auxiliary language to German.

The above mentioned teachers had previously worked at the German Military School, which was headed by a teacher in military uniform. The foreign pedagogical language and military discipline created a revulsion among the children to the school. Later, when these teachers founded their own school, their use of Yiddish attracted the students as well as support from the Literary – Dramatic Society.

At the end of 1918 when the Germans left Zhetl and the surrounding region, the school was closed and the Literary – Dramatic Society was forced to cease its activities.

The authority changed every day. Hunger and typhus epidemics were rampant and did not allow parents to think about their children's education. The children ran around tattered, isolated, filling the streets and experiencing all the horrors.

[Page 204]

In 1919 when the Poles gained authority those active in the Literary – Dramatic Society came together and decided to open a school in Zhetl. They themselves were not sure what type of school this would be. The old way was no longer appropriate, of this they were certain.

In an abandoned building in "Patiye's brick building" a school was opened. They took the benches from the Literary – Dramatic Society. The school resembled a modernized religious school with Hebrew taking priority. There were 2–3 classes. The first teachers were A. Ivenitsky, Esther and Libke Kaplinsky, Zimelevitch and others. In 1920 when the Bolsheviks entered Zhetl, the school was closed.

By the end of 1920 a group of initiators gathered in the library. They were: Ovseyevitch, Barishansky, G. Shvedsky, M. Leyserovitch, Y. Sendrovsky (deceased), Y. Gertzovsky, Y.B. Rabinovitch, A. Ivenitsky and M. Rabinovitch and they decided once again to open a school, however with a firm foundation and clearer direction. There was a rumour in town that in Bialystok there was a school organization that supported Yiddish schools. We wrote to them asking for help. An instructor came from Bialystok who was sure there already was a school in Zhetl. She refused to help due to lack of funds. She claimed her organization can only help schools that already exist. She advised us to open a school and then she could get us some help. We took a loan of 1500 marks from the library fund and borrowed 10, 000 marks from our supporters and Shvedksy went in the spring of 1921 to Vilna to find teachers. Right after Passover our first foreign teacher arrived in Zhetl, Liberman, and the first grade of today's 7 grade Sholem Aleichem School was opened in Zhetl.

III

The school opened with 15 students. Within the first 2 months the amount rose to 30 including 5 boys. The school was divided in two grades and 2 new teachers were hired: the teacher Ganzovitch for Hebrew and a female teacher Berlinerbloy for Polish. They also hired a secretary who was in fact the administrator Y.B Rabinovitch. A few "experts" from town came to Liberman's first few classes and could not imagine how he could teach everything in Yiddish. The school had 10 –15 volunteers but not all were active. From the beginning, the orthodox fought bitterly against the school and even opened up classes in the Talmud Torah for girls so they would not attend the Yiddish school. A heated discussion arose among the board of directors of the school as to which direction the school should take. There were differences of opinion. The following wanted the school to have a Yiddish secular character: Barishansky, Ovseyevitch, Shvedsky, D. Vilner, Y. Senderovsky, Rabinovitch.

The committee, teachers and pupils in the Yiddish School 1922

[Page 205]

Opposing them there was a minority who could not separate themselves from the old tradition. The minority lost. The school joined TSISHO and received 30,000 marks and later, regular subsidies. The board of directors wrote to Zhetl Jews in America about the school and asked for financial support. The board held a meeting every Saturday afternoon at the school (this tradition continues until today), to deal with actual questions about school life. At this opportunity they would discuss important world events (this tradition also continues today). At first tuition covered 40 % of the budget and including the monies the school received from the central organization there was a deficit of barely 30% which had to be covered by the board. For this purpose they organized lotteries, concerts, performances and entertainment which brought in earnings. Our American friends pulled through and the school subsists.

The school was not just a learning institution for children. It also became an educational institution for the parents and volunteers who had a scant notion about a modern Yiddish school. Many parents believed that walking with your children in a field or forest was a waste of time, and the study of nature was useless. Once at a board meeting it was suggested the school buy anatomy pictures, – thanks to the insight of one of the board members, the purchase was made.

It is worthwhile to add, the school was opened completely without a charter. In 1922 we elicited a charter in the name of the deceased board member Man, and in 1928 the division of YISHO was legalized in Zhetl and took on its name.

The school began to grow as did the need for an appropriate location. It was clear to the board that if they wanted the school to exist, it needed its own building. This way, they would no longer have to worry about rent and the school would have a firm foundation under it.

The appeal for help was warmly received by Zhetl Jews in America who created a committee to support the school headed by the tireless Max Handelson, who provided the other volunteers with courage and hope to continue with this work. The slogan for the school to have its own building was divulged at a banquet at the home of D. Vilner celebrating the first anniversary of the school. Everyone present donated on the spot for the planned building. The board strove to build the building on a public lot. Where does one find an appropriate place? One lot is too low, the other, too small, another, "a sacred place" where it would be forbidden to build such a "non kosher" thing like a Yiddish secular school. Thanks to the help of our American friends the issue was solved and the school bought its own lot. In 1922, Leyzer Rabinovitch arrived in Zhetl as the representative from America, bringing support for Zhetl's institutions. Rabinovitch, who ran away from Zhetl in 1905 clearly remembered the rabbi's stick at the Talmud Torah where he went. He showed interest in the education of Zhetl's children in general, and specifically, our school. He's interested in a school where the child receives knowledge and an education without beatings and fear of the teacher. He realized that the school must exist and needed to have its own building. A bitter struggle ensued with the other Zhetl institutions but in the end the school was victorious and received 200 dollars with which we bought a lot.

The board sent a delegate to TSISHO in Warsaw and received 100 dollars for the building. A representative from YEKAPO, M. Shalit also came to Zhetl at this time. He succeeded in receiving a subsidy for our building from the YEKAPO central office in the amount of 100 dollars. In 1923 construction began and within 3–4 years it was ready.

A special building committee was created. Various fundraisers were organized in Zhetl as well as in surrounding cities and towns. The drama club performed and all proceeds went to the building. We received lumber at a discounted price from Zhetl lumber merchants. Our board member Man, did not forget about Zhetl Jews living in other cities and they responded warmly. They also took out loans which were later paid back through ticket sales of performances at the school. Our American friends supported the construction the entire time and finally, with everyone's effort, the building was built.

[Page 206]

IV

Meanwhile the school grew and developed. Every year a grade was added and we were forced to rent a larger space. The number of teachers also increased. In 1922 an instructor by the name of Poliak came from the central office to offer instruction in school work. The school was in regular contact with TSISHO which was sending regular support. A children's library was founded at the school and the prestige of the school was continuing to grow. On Chanukah, the end of the school year and at every other opportunity, the teachers organized children's evenings which were well received in town. Every children's evening was a celebration for the children and their parents. Everyone came dressed up to see the little ones move freely on the stage, singing and playing.

The board, teachers and pupils in the Yiddish School 1928

The amount of children attending the Talmud Torah was shrinking. Girls completely stopped attending the Talmud Torah and the boys began to visit our school. Our school organized open meetings and gatherings where with their own forces (teachers and board members) and with the help of instructors from Warsaw, advocated for the Yiddish secular system.

In 1925, a meeting was organized in the House of Study with the participation of Sh. Gilinsky from Warsaw. The orthodox barricaded in an attempt to disrupt the meeting. However we gently advised that the foolish outbursts from the teachers of the Talmud Torah would only bring more prestige to our school. Influenced by our school, the children from the Talmud Torah began to demand vacation, and they organized a few strikes until their demands were met.

According to its position and convictions of the board, the school was progressive and enlightened. The portion of volunteers who felt more connected to traditional Judaism slowly moved away from it: some earlier, some later. The atmosphere in town however, where there was not a large working class, was middle class, petty bourgeois. The school, wanting to gain the confidence of the parents so they would send their children to the school, had to adapt. In order to achieve this, in the first few years of the school's existence there was a quorum and on Saturday and the Jewish holidays they would pray and the school had income from these religious obligations and vows. On Sukkot, the janitor of the school, Pinye, would run around to the parents of the children with his own Etrog asking them to bless his Etrog. Pinye the janitor must be included in the history of the school. He worked at the school from its founding, for 15 years, and felt he was the boss. Board members and teachers change or move away. He has remained. One thing he could absolutely never learn: how to tell time. The teachers had to make a special board showing where the big hand and little hand of the clock had to be for him to ring the bell for recess.

The level of the school also rose gradually. In 1925 the school organized an exhibit of the children's work. Representatives of the government would come. The teacher Ekshteyn would greet the crowd in Polish and dwell upon the demands of full equal rights for the Yiddish School.

[Page 207]

In 1925 they began teaching German and in the sixth grade part of the Polish program was passed on to seventh grade. The school also had a very fine choir. In 1926 the first graduation ceremony took place. Together with the teachers, the graduating class took a trip to Vilna where they spent a whole week.

1926–27 was a year of feverish construction. They could no longer learn in the rented space due to overcrowding and our own building was not yet completed. Although the building was still without a floor, we began to use it in 1926 as a source of income. A temporary stage was built and the drama club performed. The school's drama club now had a name, "Arvy", which stood for artistic corner (Vinkl). The name was given by an amateur actress who came from Grodno, L. Garber – Kovensky. The first production in the new building, "A Romanian Wedding" brought in an income of 1000 gulden. They were now organizing performances and balls in the building and the proceeds went to the building. The firefighter's orchestra played these school events for free.

Although they were still not learning in the school, the dedication of the new building took place in December 1926. Representatives from all of Zhetl's institutions were present. A large sum of money was collected especially for small ovens. Finally, in 1927, one grade of the school began to learn in the building. The children marched festively through the town and were warmly greeted by all. At the beginning of the next school year, the school finally went into the new building which was built with everyone's effort.

V

As we entered the new building the school began to blossom. The entire school lot was 70 metres long and 30 metres wide: and the building, which was 22 metres long and 12 metres wide became the centre of all cultural work in town. The children spent their free time in the walled schoolyard. The school had a permanent stage and was built according to the corridor system. When there was a large event, they would remove the plywood walls of the rooms and create the largest theatrical hall in town. Travelling troupes would rent it for performances. The hall was used intensively: for example, from May 1926 until September 1928, 248 different cultural events took place.

The school grew to seven grades and because of this there was no graduation in 1927, but only in 1928 with 16 graduates.

Those active in the school were also active in communal life, in city elections, Jewish community elections, everywhere we went, we were a force to deal with. From 1927 until today the school received subsidies from city hall. The school has representation on city council, the Jewish communal council and all the economic organizations take us into account. When elections to the Popular Bank and Interest Free Loan Society take place, the voice of our school movement plays a distinguished role.

The school tried to organize evening courses for workers, and in 1927 the children organized a mandolin orchestra with more than 20 instruments. A special music teacher was hired and within a short time the orchestra lit up all the school celebrations.

The school library continued to grow, and under the direction of the teacher Baksht, who had a certain weakness for the library, there were more than 1000 books by 1929. The school succeeded in bringing together the working youth in town. In 1928 a sports club was founded which was later legalized by "TOZ" (which was also founded in Zhetl as a school initiative). They would exercise in their green and white uniforms and add prestige to the school. For a time there was a cycling section of the sports club, and until today the former tourers remember with love their instructor, the teacher Herman Frenkel, who made them work hard.

The number of children in the school increases and reaches 250. Besides this, we opened a kindergarten and hired a special kindergarten teacher. Materials in school were not bad. The tuition flowed in regularly, our American friends sent a larger sum every year and the performances brought in profit. There was a so–called "Mother's Committee" that helped plan all the events. They would arrange for all the props that were needed and the energetic Khane Malke would get as much done alone as ten others together.

The fast growth of the school did not allow its opponents to rest, the orthodox as well as the "enlightened" Zionists, who in the early years hoped the school would go in their direction.

[Page 208]

Both understood that the Talmud Torah would never compete with our school which continued to develop and needed something new to attract a crowd. In 1927 the Tarbut School opened in Zhetl, where Torah and heretics were brought together, where they taught girls Mishna and on breaks you could find pupils eating pork. These were the same managers of the Talmud Torah, the same franchisees, but the sign is different, new. The Zionists began to group around "Tarbut" and with demagogic baiting they instilled fear in the provincial parents. They also started a drama club at "Tarbut" which competed against our school and both clubs performed the same play on the same night.

In 1930 we celebrated the tenth anniversary of our school. The celebrations which lasted a few days took place at the end of the school year, and besides the representatives from the surrounding towns, it was also attended by Senator Dr. Tzemakh Shabad from Vilna whose attendance added great importance and prestige to our celebration. Saturday night there was a festive children's evening and Dr. Shabad arrived in the middle.

The String Orchestra of the Yiddish School 1929

First row: Dobeh Lusky, Miriam Epshteyn
Second row: Libe Koyfman, Malke Mayevsky, Luba Sahtsky, Mikhle Shalkovitch,Rivka Breskin, Yudis Mayevsky, Khaye Alpert
Third row: Khaye Rokhl Karpelevitch, Yokhe Bulansky, Rokhl Berman, Shayne Sokolovsky, Eliyahu Busel, Sonieh Shilovitsky, Shifra Dunetz, Malke Grosh, Rivke Mirsky, Yekhil Yoselevitch
Fourth row: Aron Gertzovsky, Shifra Fridnberg, Rokhl Rabinovitch, Malke Lusky, Soreh Breskin, Yente Rivka Gal, Hinde Barishansky, Nekhame Belaus, Moishe Lisagursky

Dr. Shabad was impressed with the performance. He didn't believe he would see something so good in Zhetl. There was also a parade where the children in the sports club, led by the late Leyb Frenkel, went to the market place and then to the synagogue plaza and performed various gymnastics exercises. Jews who would have never entered our "non kosher" walls came to our school to hear Dr.

Shabad. His name itself was an attraction. Later, Dr. Shabad shared with his readers of the "Vilna Tog" his impressions of our anniversary celebrations and placed Zhetl as an example for other towns.

In honour of our anniversary we published a special newspaper which we called "Our School", with articles and dissertations about the history of the school written by L. Frenkel, Barishansky, Brandes, Moreyn, Y.B Rabinovitch, and others. In the paper there were greeting s from A.Golomb in the name of the Yiddish Teacher's Seminary and notices of the deaths of two board members, M. Man and Y. Senderovsky.

[Page 209]

Most of the copies of this paper were sent to our supporters in America.

By the 10th anniversary the board of directors was comprised of: Yehoshua Ovseyevitch, Avrom Moishe Barishansky, Hirsh Busel, Alter Gertzovsky, Khaim Ganzovitch, Asher Levit, Yehoshua Lusky, Mashke Mirsky, Avrom Savitsky, Simkha Rabetz, Khaim Mikhl Raznov and Gdalye Shvedsky.

VI

The anniversary celebration gave the volunteers courage and energy to carry on their work in difficult bitter times which were already being felt in the air with the crushing repressions. The school was among the first to feel the consequences of the difficult economic crisis in the land. Parents did not have the means to pay tuition. Some removed their children from the school and sent them to public school. When a father asks, what is the priority, to provide a child with bread or tuition, it is hard to give him advice. The wealthier were attracted to "Tarbut". The board did not take this casually, so besides publicity work they looked for new sources of income to help cover their losses. To achieve this they organized the first school bazaar in 1931 where items were sold, mostly gifts from graduates and friends of the school. The first bazaar raised a lot of money and from then on, the school has organized a bazaar every year.

The same year the school ran broad cultural activities in town. They organized a Popular University which offered lectures twice a week in the winter on various literary, natural science and communal topics. The teachers headed the lecture roster along with other cultural forces in town. The Popular University was very well attended and even brought in an income of a few hundred gulden.

The school was the first to feel the period of reaction which was beginning throughout the country. There were a series of attacks from all sides on the school. Even the greatest optimists felt everything was lost. "Tarbut" wanted their subsidy increased at our loss. We did not allow this to happen. The parents of our students were mobilized, contributed to the debate and the attacking criticism was rebuffed.

The board of directors which ran the Popular University was not pleased with the authorities, and when the new school laws came into being in 1932, it was one of the first victims.

When the new school year began we had to look for a new board.

Members of the board also suffered…some lost their source of income and suffered in other ways because they belonged to the school. Due to many reasons the financial situation of the school was very bad. Teachers were barely paid for 8 months and no help came from the central office as they were facing the same problems. During the school year of 1932–33 conflicts existed at the school, even teacher's strikes which demanded they be paid minimum wage.

The board remained devoted to the school during these difficult times. More than one was haunted by the thought: "What next?

Sixth and seventh grades of the Yiddish School, 1928

First row seated: Mikhle Shalkovitch, Yudis Mayevsky, Nekhame Senderovsky, Shmuel Kaplinsky, Yosef Senderovsky, Dobeh Lusky, Henia Namiyat, Malke Mayevsky
Second row seated: Eliyahu Busel, teachers Shaykov, Olshteyn, Blyuma Markus, Herman Frenkel, Esther Bruk, Akiva Baksht, Fania Batsheykov
Third row standing: Yehoshua Lusky, Rivka Mirsky, Zlateh Patzovsky, Shifra Fridnberg, Khaye Alpert, Leah Rabinovitch, Yekhie Yoselevitch
Fourth row standing: Shifra Dunetz, Libeh Koyfman, Sonieh Shilovitsky, Nekhame N+Belaus, Khaye Vilner, Minye Berman, Rokhl Berman
Fifth row standing: Feygl Stukolsky, Rozeh Daykhovsky, Hinde Barishansky, Dina Man

[Page 210]

How much longer can we suffer? How will we be able to sustain the school so it doesn't collapse in this time of crisis when a black cloud is about to destroy us?" It was then decided to expand the board and attract active elements. Some parents co–opted the board. The recent ones believed the school must adapt more to the town and its ambience, to the other parents and offer more Hebrew, this would make the foundation of the school more solid and make it easier for us to compete with "Tarbut". They tried to steer the school in that direction but their wishes were not fulfilled.

During the school year of 1933–34 practically an entire pedagogical council was hired. The newly arrived teachers began to fortify everything that was shaken up during the difficult years of crisis. The nominal wages of the teachers were agreed upon and what the board promised was paid. The number of teachers was reduced to 4, who worked 7 hours a day, besides the extra curricular work like the drama club, library, cooperative etc… The students were now those who left a few years earlier. The most difficult years of the school were 1933–34 when the Zionists prospered and "Tarbut" had the strength of certificates. Our school responded with stronger publicity work. In 1935 the school was visited by the chairman of TSISHO, Sh. Kazdan, who became aware of our situation, held an open meeting as well as a separate meeting with graduates and school activists.

The children's evenings continued with great success, especially those with a social tendency. The parents and the entire town had changed, becoming more progressive. If at one time we feared just saying the word "socialism" within the walls of our school not to frighten the fathers, it was now a natural thing which no longer frightened the majority of the parents. The school won a lot in content.

VII

Friday, the 21st of February 1936, around 7 o'clock in the evening an alarm suddenly sounded in town: The school was burning! Although Zhetl was used to fires, at that moment we did not want to believe this was happening. We ran closer to the school and saw smoke and flames coming from the locked building. Those gathered ripped off the doors and windows and began to save what they could. However, the fire quickly seized the dry walls of the building and they only succeeded to save the secretariat and a portion of the library. The entire town gathered around the burning building. The cries of the children were horrible, in the glow of the flames which they wanted to extinguish with their tears. In view of this tragedy we were able to see how our school was deeply rooted in the town and how much it was surrounded with love and devotion. Thus, the desire to correct this injustice and rebuild the school was strengthened.

While the spot where the school stood was still smoldering with remnants of the building, the board gathered at the home of Ovsyevitch and decided to get to work. It was decided, the next day, Saturday, all the parents would be invited to a meeting at the cinema.

Practically the whole town came to this parent's meeting. When Barishansky spoke about what the building meant to the town he could not hold back tears and cried together with most of those present. It was decided to rebuild right away. The atmosphere at the meeting was such that even our opponents promised to donate.

Two urgent questions faced the board: should they try to rent a place so the school could continue to function normally and the children would not run around without supervision, and then raise funds to rebuild the building. The Polish public school allowed the older grades to study there in the afternoon. Besides this, we rented a place for a few classes and took a few rooms in the Jewish communal building. It is worthwhile mentioning, the Jewish communal building wanted to remove our classes with force and when the children were learning, the police had to intervene.

On Sunday, 2 days after the fire, a consultation took place at the home of Barishansky where, from among invited sympathizers, a building committee was constituted. On the spot an assessment was made for over 500 gulden. It was decided to carry out a campaign throughout the country, beginning in Zhetl with a public appeal to help rebuild our building.

The appeal to help our school was published in the newspapers "Folkszteytung", "Vilner Tog", and the American "Forverts".

[Page 211]

The board immediately sent Ivenitsky and Barishansky to Vilna to try and get something for our school. Although at the time Vilna was running its own campaign for their own school chaired by A. Rozental, it was decided they would help in our campaign. Ivenitsky remained in Vilna for a few weeks to carry our campaign. The Vilna press warmly supported our campaign. The family of the late Dr. Shabad showed interest in our campaign, the school children gave some money and within a short time we raised almost 1000 gulden in Vilna.

The work in Zhetl did not stand still. Young and old were assessed and paid in installments. Building began. The first money we received from the insurance company (the whole amount came to 4000 gulden) went to buy lumber and the work went quickly. Whoever did not have cash, paid with work. The wagon drivers provided their horses for free and on the Sabbath, when they did not work and the young people had free time, they became the wagon drivers and brought the lumber from the sawmill to the building.

The board's goal was to have the building ready for the new school year and worked with great speed to achieve this. The money received from the central office was not sufficient because we had to pay the teachers at the time when the income of the school was significantly reduced. The danger was we would have to stop work due to lack of funds. Representatives from our school went to neighbouring cities such as Novogrudek, Lida and Baranovitch to carry out campaigns for our building. In order to inform the central office of the situation of our school a delegation consisting of A.M Barishansky and B. Kaplinsky went to Warsaw. B. Kaplinsky remained in Warsaw for quite a while and with the active help of M. Bornshteyn, Todres and others, carried out a campaign for our building. Practically all the Warsaw professional unions contributed including the artist's union and other institutions. There was also a meeting of individuals in Warsaw which resulted in raising over 500 gulden. During this campaign a photograph of our building was published in "Folksteytung".

Ivenitsky carried out a campaign for our building throughout the township of Novogrudek as well as through Polesia and Volhynia. Donations came in for our building from all corners of Poland from former teachers, graduates and friends. The call for help went beyond the borders of Poland. We received 5 pounds for the committee to support Yiddish secular schools in South Africa. Our American friends founded a committee which held a lottery and sent over 200 dollars for our building. A group of our graduates sent donations from Cuba as well.

By the end of the school year the building was ready, except for the roof and it was decided the graduation ceremony should take place there. A temporary stage was built and we prepared for the celebration. It rained cats and dogs all day and the children along with the teachers and volunteers continued to watch the sky. By evening, the sky cleared and the ceremony which was dedicated to the 60th birthday of Avrom Reyzn took place under a starry sky.

The tempo of work did not slow during summer vacation. The board was in debt, borrowed and at the beginning of the school year a portion of the building was complete: no ovens for heating, but nevertheless, ready.

The dedication ceremony for the new school building took place on September 12th, 1936. It was bigger and much nicer than the previous building. The building was 30 metres long and 15 metres wide and had a permanent theatre which could seat 500 people and 6 spacious rooms.

Dr. Veinreikh (Weinreich) came from Vilna as a representative from YIVO. Guests came from the surrounding towns and cities. A special car came from Novorudek as well as representatives for the schools in Slonim and Zholudek. The hall was full to capacity. Kh. Ivenitsky opened the celebrations in the name of the board. He greeted all the guests, friends and builders. We received greetings from TSISHO from Y. Aronovitch, from YIVO from Dr. Weinreich, from our school supporter's in Novogrudek from the lawyer Gumener and from the Zholudek school from their teacher Voltchkovsky. There were also greeting from Zhetl's institutions (The Bund, "Cultural League", Clothing Union, Builders Union, Craftsmen Union, the Popular Bank and others). Every institution and individual donated certain amounts to complete the building. At our celebration we received 28 telegrams with written greetings.

[Page 212]

There was also a celebratory renewal of our school flag funded by graduates.

Dr. Weinreich later wrote about his impressions of our celebration in the "Forverts" giving our friends in America regards from their hometown.

Those who planned the celebration were proud of their work. They really did a colossal job. Up until the dedication of the building, the cost was 11,000 gulden and all was made possible thanks to the energy of the volunteers who managed to transform the warm feelings our school enjoyed from the public into actual deeds.

It is worthwhile to stress that the school did not receive a penny from the state, the communal authority nor the Jewish community.

VIII

The School entered its own building but the volunteers could not rest: half the building was without a floor and ceiling, winter was approaching and there were still no ovens. We could not raise any more money in Zhetl – almost 2000 gulden for our town was a colossal amount. The board delegated Ovsyevitch to go to Warsaw to bring cheques from the central office in the amount of 500 gulden with which we bought the first three small ovens.

Over the next two years the construction of all the rooms was completed. However, the walls looked naked (by 1930 only two rooms were painted), the roof was not yet complete, there were no double windows. The travelling performers said our hall was excellent but lacked comfortable seats. For 4000 gulden we can eliminate all these defects…

The board was now composed of Ovsyevitch, Ivenitsky (chairman), A.M. Barishansky, Busel, Binyaminovitch, Isar Gertzovsky, Kh, Ganzovitch, M. Mirsky, B. Kaplinsky, Kh. Roznov. Graduate representatives were: Z. Patzovsky and Y. Indikhshteyn. The secretary of the school was Y. Khlebnik.

The largest amount of school volunteers were parents of the school children, or parents of graduates. To replace those who lost interest in grey school activity, the board co–opted new members which they perceived to be diligent and hard working.

One of the most important and vital branches of the school is the "ARVY". Beginning in 1917, when they first performed Goldfadn's "The Sorceress" until very recently they have provided hundreds of amateur performances.

Original footnote:

    a.   The author wrote this work in 1939 and it was published in "Shul Vegn" (School Paths). Due to the outbreak of the war, the second part was not published. We are publishing it here verbatim without any changes because it reflects the events from an important part of Zhetl's population. We also avoided stylistic and orthographic changes in the text.

How Can I Grasp This?

by Avrom Savitsky

Translated by Janie Respitz

How can I grasp this, how can I understand,
My town of Zhetl is cleansed of Jews.
In the peaceful nest, where my cradle stood
My parents are no longer present.
My friends and acquaintances, youthful as lions
Have you all perished? How can I believe this?
How did death not fear you,
The giants that you were?
Your arms of steel, your hearts, which burn
Your gait and stance, as if forged from bronze.
Only a bit of ash remains, which the wind has carried,
There is not even a tombstone to cry at, wail,
For your unlived years,
For your children who were never born.
For your celebrations you could not enjoy,
Tears of joy, which mothers could not shed.
But your testament will remain forever,
Distances, oceans will not grind them up.
I hear my mother's voice, my father's,
I hear your voices, dear guys.
When I eat, when I sleep,
As long as I live,
And I will pass on to my children,
That you did not fall in battle,
With guns in the trenches to achieve more power.
No!!! You fell with the souls of heroes,
With a tired bodyv And only because
You were born Jews.

[Page 213]

We Are Building a Yiddish School

by Moishe Mirsky (Montreal)

Translated by Janie Respitz

During the First World War a Literary – Dramatic Society was founded in Zhetl and it did not have any political allegiance. Its goal was the cultural revival of the town. Its founders were: Gdalyahu Shvedsky, Avrom Moishe Barishansky, Shloime Khaim Vernikovsky, Yudl Vinitsky, Yisroel Ber Rabinovitch, Yosef Senderovsky, Yehoshua Oseyevitch, Motl Levit, Yisroel Moishe Vinitsky, Motl Man and Moishe Mirsky. The drama club was organized under the leadership of the Lis brothers from Lodz. They also ran various cultural activities including lectures by visiting lecturers. I remember a few by name: Avrom Zak, Leyb Naydus (Grodno) and Yakov Pat.

After the war in 1920 the Literary – Dramatic Society decided to open a Yiddish secular school with Yiddish as the language of instruction. This decision led to a split in the society. A group of Zionists left and opened their own locale. The leader of this group was Shloime Khaim Vernikovsky, the son of Menakhem Vernikovsky (the pharmacist).

Shloime Khaim was considered to be one of the most talented young men in town. He devoted all his youthful passion and energy to Zionist work, however his life was short. He developed inflammation of his lungs and died at the young age of 24. His untimely death had a huge impact on all those involved in the Literary – Dramatic Society. He was an intimate friend to all from our early days in Heder. May his memory be a blessing!

We opened the first class of the Yiddish school. The first teacher was Lieberman from Vilna. He won the trust of the parents in Zhetl with his modern teaching techniques.

The school continues to grow day by day. We hired a teacher and opened a preparatory class. A few years later we hired Herman Frenkel (from Lodz) who brought a lot of life into our town.

It is difficult today to describe the bitter and obviously distinguished struggle that ensued between the two administrations to recruit students to both schools. This ambitious cultural struggle instilled a lot of content for the youth and the school directors.

The Literary – Dramatic Society transformed into a school organization and joins the drama club without the central Yiddish school organization. At the time the drama club had 40 members. The director was Herman Frenkel, and the technical director was Moishe Mirsky. The drama club existed until the last World War. It performed almost the entire Yiddish repertoire and carried the financial burden of the Yiddish school.

In 1922, Leyzer Rabinovitch (Feyvl's son) came to Zhetl on a visit from America with his family. He brought 500 dollars from the American Zhetl Relief Fund for the Yiddish school. This is when it was decided to build our own building. The board appointed a building committee with the following members: Avrom Moishe Barishansky, Khaim Ganzovitch, Yosef Senderovsky, Moishe Mirsky and Yitzkhak Leybovitch.

The school board of directors received nice gifts from the neighbouring noble estates.

**The board members and teachers of the Yiddish School
at a going away party in honour of Y. and M. Dvoretzky**

First row: Asher Levit, Hirshl Busel
Second row: Khaim Mikhl Roznov, Gdalye Shvedsky, Avrom Savitzky, Mayta Savitzky, Yakov Dvoretzky, Esther Leah Busel, Avrom Moishe Barishansky, Yehoshua Ovseyevitch
Third row: Khaim Ganzovitch, Alter Gertzovsky, Gitte Zaks, Dovid Moreyn, Leybl Frenkel, Yehoshua Lusky, Moishe Mirsky, Simkha Robetz, Mrs. Brandes and the teacher Brandes

[Page 214]

The nobleman Stravinsky from Nakrishki sent twenty five giant beams for the school building.

In time, two magnificent buildings were erected in Zhetl. One housed the 7 grades of the "Tarbut" School named in honour of Khaim Nakhman Bialik, the other, the 7 grades of the Yiddish School named in honour of Sholem Aleichem. The schools also had kindergartens. I will not mention the names of the teachers from the "Tarbut" School because I do not remember them. I remember the names of the teachers from the Yiddish School since I sat on the board.

The Yiddish School went into its own building in 1926. The teachers at the time were: Herman Frenkel, Akiva Baksht, Leyzer Olshteyn, Gitte Zaks, Blumeh Markus and Fanieh Botchaykova. The first kindergarten teacher was: Leah Berniker.

Leah was a great pedagogue and she won over the parents with her devotion to the small children. She built up the kindergarten to 150 children. Leah Berniker was also very successful with her children's presentations. She lived in Zhetl for a few years and today she lives in Montreal, Canada.

The building of the Yiddish School also had a theatre which seated 400, a wonderful stage and even a section for the musicians. This was the largest and nicest hall in the region. Thanks to this the best troupes came to Zhetl from all around Poland including: Avrom Morevsky, Samberg, Yona Turkov and Diana Blumenfeld, "Azalzel" form Lodz, Dzhigan and Shumakher, Godik, Ella Lilis and Dovid Herman and his studio. The last one spent a few weeks in Zhetl with his troupe. This was in 1920 before he left for America. The Jews of Zhetl were great theatre lovers with eyes and ears open to everything that had a connection to theatre.

The Yiddish schools in Poland were not subsidized by the government and had to support themselves. Part of the budget was covered by tuition. A negligible subsidy was given by the city. Most of the budget was subsidized by performances and the central office.

Our board struggled to keep the school running, but thanks to their devotion and stubborn work the school existed until the last World War.

Tenth Anniversary Party of the
drama club by the Yiddish School in 1927

[Page 215]

The Tarbut School

by Dvoyre Gorodaysky–Shkolnik (Kfar–Saba)

Translated by Janie Respitz

The Tarbut School began to organize in Zhetl in 1927. Its first founders were: Reb Hertz Leyb Kaplinsky, Feyvl Epshteyn, Shaul Kaplinsky, Khaim Levit, Tzaliye Moshakovsky, Dovid Senderovsky, Dvoyre Gorodaysky, Yerukham Izrealit and Yoel Tcheplovodsky.

Dvoyre Gorodaysky

I remember the first meeting of the school board of directors on Sabbath Nakhamu at Feyvl Epshteyn's home. We decided to begin with a kindergarten and in time, transform into a school. In order to realize our plan we needed a location, inventory and a kindergarten teacher. Feyvl Epshteyn went to Vilna, hired a teacher, Rozeh, and rented a room at Itche the butcher's. We raised money for inventory from all possible sources.

Feyvl Epshteyn

Feyvl Epshteyn gave the first 100 zlotys, Hertz Leyb Kaplinsky–300 zlotys. The remaining money we took to the bank and bought chairs and tables. In truth we had a poor inventory however it allowed us to open the kindergarten.

But we were still missing one thing: children. In order to solve this problem we went from house to house to mobilize children. We did not take into consideration the age of the child or ability to pay tuition. We took big and small children by the hand and led them to the kindergarten. I remember carrying out this task with Hirshl Kaplinsky and we succeeded in recruiting 35 children. For a beginning, this was a lot and encouraging.

The second year we rented a larger space at Haynke Breskin's. We rented two rooms and invited Berta Tchapnik from Grodno to be a kindergarten teacher. During the school year we succeeded in recruiting 70 children and we broadened our circle of volunteers. Among others involved in the school were: Yosef Kalmen Butkovsky and Leybl Beshkin. The kindergarten teacher Tchapnik did all the preparations in order to open the first grade of the Hebrew school.

We rented space at Yosef the barber's for grade one. We then turned to the central office of "Tarbut" and they sent the following teachers: Golda Finkel, Shleymke Goldinberg, and Bas–Sheva Beshkin.

Budget

The Tarbut School fought all its years for a flowing budget and even more for an investment budget. Nothing was too difficult for us when it came to raising money for the school. Besides tuition we raised money through performances, the drama club, Sukkot bazar, dances and other sources. Important entries in our budget were: the subsidy from city council, help from America and besides this there was a group of patrons who would often open their wallets to fill a gap in the budget. Two such patrons were: Reb Hertz Leyb Kaplinsky and Feyvl Epshteyn. They gave from their own pockets what was lacking from other budget entries. The profits of the drama club played an important role in our budget.

The Drama Club

The drama club at the Tarbut School was founded in 1930 by Leybl Beshkin. The decorator was Avrom Matyuk. As I remember the first performances were: "Hertzele the Illustrious", "Soreh Shayndl From Hehupetz" and "The Jewish King".

Kindergarten of the Tarbut School
1935

[Page 216]

The performances took place in our school rooms at Yosef the barber's.

Participants in the drama club were: Khaya Urseyevitch, Soreh Abelevitch, Fraydl Berman, Bas -Sheva Beshkin, Yosef Kalmen Butkovsky, Shloime Goldinberg, Hirshl Gertzovsky, Yoel Tcheplovodsky, Avrom Langbart, Hadasa Leybovitch, Shloime Levenbuk, Dvoyre Savitsky and others.

The entire time we rivalled the drama club at the Yiddish school. We tried to hide the plays we planned to perform from them, but as if out of spite, they always found out.

The board, teachers and pupils of the Tarbut School 1928

Standing in the last row: Avrom Lngbart, Yitzkhak Krashinsky, Shaul Kaplinsky, Hertz–Leyb Kaplinsky, Moishe Ruven Mordkovsky, Yitzkhak Moishe Gafanovitch, Yisroel Ozer Barishansky

It is possible they saw which books we borrowed from the library, yet for a long time we had another suspicion. We suspected our friend Fraydl Berman, then Levit, whose sister, Peshe Levit was in the drama club of the Yiddish School, got the secret from her. Later it appeared the opposite was true. Peshe would repeat her lines of her role in her sleep and Fraydl would then know what the Yiddish drama club was rehearsing.

Angry tongues would wag and say the members of the Yiddish drama club would stand under our window, listen to our rehearsals and learn what we were planning to perform. As soon as they found out what we were doing, they would begin to rehearse the same play. This is how Zhetl would enjoy the same play in two separate locations.

The following would often happen. We would hang up a notice that we would be performing one play or another, and a half hour later the drama club of the Yiddish School would hang up a notice that they were performing the same show.

Most of the plays were very successful. However it did happen, that we did all the preparations, the artists were already made up, the stage was decorated, but there were barely 50 people in the audience. Nervously we would run from the box office to the hall and from the hall outside, sometimes to our opponents in order to see how they were doing.

Sometimes our show would end successfully but with the cash box half empty.

The Building

We made a big effort to build a building for our school. We worked hard to collect money from wherever we could. We began with a five dollar appeal. To achieve this we drew a "dollarubke" on a piece of paper and asked the photographer Dovid Leybovitch to photograph it and copy it.

[Page 217]

Then we sold these photographs for 5 dollars and this is how we began the fund to buy the lot behind Yudl Khaim Rashkin's house. The board members of the school borrowed from the interest free loan society in their own names and later the school paid them back. It often happened that the board members would pay the debt out of their own pockets.

A second source of income was American help as well as the Tarbut central office in Warsaw. Besides this, we assessed the craftsmen. One gave us a door, another a window. Others donated labour. If I am not mistaken we also received a large gift from the nobleman Stravisnky in the form of wooden beams.

This is how we assembled wall after wall until we had a five room place with an office.

Yisroel Fergamenik

When we had a celebration we would take down the walls of the rooms and create a large hall.

The dedication of the building was organized with great fanfare with the participation of director Bernholtz from Lida and inspector Eynshteyn from Warsaw.

The first graduation from the Tarbut School took place in 1934. There were 5 graduates in total. I figure, all told the school graduated approximately 200 children, mostly boys.

Actors in the performance of "Hertzele", 1927

First row: Khaye Abelevitch, Yekhiel Turetsky, Mayshke Levit, Hadasa Leybovitch.
Second row: Khanie, Yoel Tcheplovidsky, Fraydl Berman, Feyvl Epshteyn, Avrom Langbart, Rivke Breskin, Shaul Kaplinsky, Yitzkhak Krashinsky, Soreh Turetsky.
Third row: Gershon Rashkin, Khaye Ovseyevitch, Rokhl Rabinovitch, Soreh Libe Breskin, Hirshl Gertzovsky, Khaye Dvoyre Savitzky, Yosef Berman, Dvoyre Gorodaysky, Yisroel Senderovsky.
Fourth row: Hirshl Kaplinsky, Khane Obershteyn, Yitzkhak Leyzerovitch, Shaynke Mnuskin, Leyb Zelikovitch, Pinkhas Mayevsky. Last row: Yosef Leyzerovitch, Zelik Gertzovsky, Moishe Ruven Mordkovsky, Avrom Matyuk, Avrom Aron Breskin, Leyb Mnuskin.

[Page 218]

Stamp of the Tarbut School

Teachers

It is hard for me to remember all the teachers at the Tarbut School. Please forgive me if I have simply forgotten a few names. I remember these teachers: Hadasa Bril, Shloime Goldenberg, Khaim and Etl Vilensky, the teacher Kakiel, Naftali Blukh, Tchertches, Borukh Kaplinsky, Yisroel Fergamenik, and Nokhem Shoykhet.

The teachers put a lot of energy and strength into the school. Disregarding the difficult financial situation, they brought the school to a high level.

The board, teachers and pupils of the Tarbut School, 1939

Tarbut School

by D. Gorodieski-Shkolnik

Translated by Judy Montel

The Tarbut school in Zhetl began to be organized in 1927. At the founding meeting at the home of Shraga Epstein we decided to open, for now, just a kindergarten, and over time turn it into a school. In order to accomplish our goal, we needed a kindergarten teacher, an apartment and equipment. Shraga Epstein invited a kindergarten teacher from Vilna, her name was Rosa. We rented the apartment in the home of Reb Yitzchak the butcher and the equipment we obtained with donations from Reb Herz Leib Kaplinski (a total of 300 zloty) and from Shraga Epstein (a total of 100 zloty). We borrowed the rest of the money from a local bank

However, we were missing the main thing. To remedy this, we went from house to house and registered children. We did not pay attention to the age of the children or to their ability to pay tuition. We took from whatever we could find. And we succeeded. Tzvi Kaplinski and I registered 35 children. It was a good beginning.

For the second year, we rented a larger place already in the home of Shayna Mirsky and to run the kindergarten we invited the teacher Berta Chapnik from Grodno. During this year the number of children rose to 70 and we also succeeded in widening the circle of community activists connected to the school. And then we found the right hour to open the Tarbut school.

[Page 219]

Memoirs of a Student

by Soreh Epshteyn – Shoar (Natanya)

Translated by Janie Respitz

The grasses grow evenly in the field,
A child must be happy, rich or poor;
The sun sends us all its blessing and shine,
We are happy to be Jewish children!"

This was the first song we sang on the first day of school. This was also the first day in the history of the Yiddish School in Zhetl, 1921.

I was among the first pupils. Until then I had not attended any school. The majority of the children in Zhetl, until this time, received their education from private teachers. I remember, as if in a dream, the well known teachers in town that would come to our house: Mutshnik, Bender and others.

The first two classes of the newly founded school were in the home of Berl Mirsky, on Hoyf Street across from the post office. The place was not suitable, it was crowded and uncomfortable. Within a short time we moved to a second place in a small street past the synagogue, at the Christian Kavalevsky's and then to Senderovsky's brick building at the marketplace.

Here we finally felt at home. Firstly, we occupied the second floor, the rooms were bigger and it was possible to organize evenings and performances for larger audiences.

With the growth in the amount of pupils (every year a new grade was added) the administration could not have all the pupils learning in the morning. Some had to learn in the afternoon.

Fall and winter, when the days were short we returned home with lanterns. We would walk slowly, not rushing.

Tuesday evenings were especially interesting after the market day in town. We would accompany the last village wagons as they left town. In the winter we would jump on the back of the farmer's sleighs; if he was a nice gentile, we would ride for a bit, if he was mean, he would yell at us and threaten us with his whip…

Often we would stop in a yard, mostly at Khaye Sorke Alpert's, and in the garden build a snowman. We would strictly guard him and after each thaw we would fix him using the light of our lanterns.

Near our school, Reyzele lived in an attic room. She had a small candy store. When we headed home in the evening we jumped into Reyzele's shop and bought a snack.

The main thing was, she would often give us snacks on "credit". She was the first to teach us about debts…

However, this inn was also not suitable for a school. We did not have a yard and we would sow the vegetable garden at Dorogavn's on Novoredker Street.

We would bring wheelbarrows filled with manure, fertilize the garden and quickly return to our lessons at school.

Gradually a request was made: to build our own school building, more comfortable with a suitable yard.

At the time, when the school moved into Senderovsky's brick building at the marketplace, people began to "make noise" in town.

The attention turned to the big brick building in the middle of the marketplace which "ruled" over the whole area. This was my grandfather Feyvl's building.

How many pleasant recollections I have in connection to that house!

In those days a guest from America was a rare phenomenon. And now, my uncle, Leyzer Rabinovitch, is coming for a visit. The town was spinning. They cleaned, whitewashed the gutters, threw yellow sand in the yards and decorated the streets more than usual.

The big day arrived!

Delegations from various institutions began to approach the brick building. Among them was a delegation of school children. My uncle Leyzer brought some money with him. Some of the money he donated himself but most of it was collected from American Jews to build a building for the Yiddish school.

[Page 220]

**The pupils from the Yiddish School say
farewell to their teacher P. Zabitz, 1922**

Understandably, it took some time, but finally the plan was realized.

They chose a nice lot on the corner of Novoredker Street which led to Tcherne the miller and there, with great celebration, they laid the cornerstone of the school. The joy was great, indescribable. The Tarbut School did not yet exist in Zhetl and the Yiddish School was the first Jewish educational institution in Zhetl.

Slowly, slowly the school was built. Large, comfortable bright rooms, a large place to play and a garden.

There was a special stage where school children performed as well as theatrical performances for adults.

The small street became alive with loud, happy children's voices.

Unfortunately I did not go to the new school because by then I was studying at the Polish public school.

However, I loved the Yiddish School very much because I remembered the difficult times when it struggled for existence.

It was a joy to see how it slowly grew and became a beautiful, splendid school which was capable of educating all the children who longed for it.

The Polish Public School, 1928

[Page 222]

Rabbis

Translated by Judy Montel

The town of Zhetl was founded in the year 1498, but the year in which the Jewish community in Zhetl was founded is shrouded in mystery. It stands to reason that over the years the few tenants, artisans and tradespeople organized themselves into a Jewish community and hired themselves a rabbi.

The first rabbi of the Zhetl community that we know of is Reb Chaim HaKohen Rapaport (1720-1729), who had been the rabbi of Lemberg and participated in the debate with the Franciscans that took place under the auspices of the Catholic clergy. It makes sense that the father of the Maggid of Dubnow, Rabbi Ze'ev Kranz served as the rabbi of Zhetl.

During the years 1840-1850, Reb Zeev Wolf HaLevi, author of the book "Emek Halacha" sat on the throne of the rabbinate in Zhetl.

In the past century, the following has held the crown of the rabbinate in Zhetl: Rabbi Reb Tzvi Hirsch Dvoretzki (1850-1891), Rabbi Reb Baruch Avraham Mirski (1892-1912), the only one of the rabbis of Zhetl who was a Zionist activist, Rabbi Reb Zalmen Sorotzkin (1912-1929), currently one of the great rabbis of Jerusalem and the last rabbi of the community of Zhetl: Rabbi Yitzchak Reitzer (1930-1942)/

The cradle of many rabbis stood in Zhetl, rabbis who became famous in the Jewish world and served as rabbis all over Russia and Poland. We will list some of them here: Reb Aryeh Leib Segal, author of "Marganita Taba", who was elected in 1696 as the rabbi of Minsk, Reb Tzvi Hirsch HaKohen, author of "Chidushei Maharsh"a", who lived at the end of the 17th and beginning of the 18" centuries/ In 1740, Reb Ya'akov Kranz was born in Zhetl who became famous as the Maggid of Dubnow, in 1839, Reb Yisrael Me'ir HaKohen was born in Zhetl, who became known as the Chofetz Chayim. Zhetl was the dwelling place of the Rabbi Reb Aryeh Yellin, author of "With Beautiful Eyes," who died in 1886. In Zhetl, Rabbi Reb Shmuel Rabinowitz lived, the rabbi of Moscow, who died in 1924.

The rabbis of Zhetl ran the spiritual leadership of the town for generations, and if they also had organizational talents, they managed its practical matters as well. From here came our ancestors' extra vigilance in choosing a rabbi. They were very concerned that the rabbis of Zhetl should be great in Torah and in leadership. And indeed, the community of Zhetl can be proud of its rabbis.

[Page 221]

Rabbis

The Rabbi Gaon (Genius) Reb Meir HaKohen Writer of Hakhafetz Khaim born in Zhetl in 1839

[Page 222][blank][Page 223]

The Rabbi Reb Yakov Krantz – The Dubner Preacher
1740 – 1804

Excerpts from a larger essay published in "Goldene Kayt", vo. 19, Tel Aviv 1954 (PP. 39-60)

Translated by Janie Respitz

The rabbi Reb Yakov Krantz is known in the world as the Preacher of Dubno. He was born in Zhetl in 1740 to his father Rabbi Zev Krantz and his mother Hinde, the daughter of the rabbi of Kobrin, Reb Nokhem.

Reb Yakov distinguished himself with outstanding talents. As a child he already memorized many tractates of the Talmud. The preacher of Mezeritch recounted how Reb Yakov learned the entire tractate of Chulin by heart.

At age 18 he arrived in Mezeritch. His sermons, which were filled with parables, quickly made him famous and they invited this young man from Zhetl to become the town preacher. He remained in Mezeritch as preacher for two years, then went to Zhulkove and from there spent 18 years in Dubno.

Great rabbis and simple people would come hear his sermons. He was especially loved by the Gaon of Vilna, Reb Eliyahu. When the Vilna Gaon got sick in 1790 he invited Reb Yakov Krantz to come to him to preach.

The Vilna Gaon once asked him: "how is it possible to always find an appropriate parable for every passage?" Reb Yakov replied with a parable:

Once a man went to a village and saw a practice shooting target with holes only in the middle. When he asked the shooter how it is possible to shoot only in the centre he replied: first I shoot, then I draw the circle. I am the same. First I understand the object of the parable, then I apply it.

In 1795 the Vilna Gaon invited him a second time. On his way he stopped in Vlodove and became the town preacher. After a year in Vlodove he spent two years in Khelm and finally became the preacher of Zamosc.

In Zamosc Reb Yakov Krantz ran a Yeshiva and would explain the most difficult Talmudic passages with a parable. He easily explained what other great rabbis and scholars could not.

His piety was without boundaries. He would wake up in the middle of the night, recite the midnight prayer, study until dawn and then immerse himself in a ritual bath. From dawn until evening prayers he would be wrapped in a prayer shawl and phylacteries. As he prayed, he did not move a hand or a foot. He stood before God like a slave before his master. After the morning prayers he would study until lunch and only then take something to eat. After lunch he would return to the House of Study and teach the Yeshiva boys.

In the midst of teaching he would begin to cry and recite psalms. After he died, the beadle of the House of Study said Reb Yakov Krantz would ask him to inform him of every sick person or tragic incident in town. Seeing as Zamosc was a big city with many troubles, he would cry every day and pray for the sick and unfortunate.

His entire life, from age 18 on, he was awake half the night and every Monday and Thursday he would fast.

He prepared his book "Sefer Hamidot" for publication on his own. His other books were published by his son Reb Yitzkhak Krantz and his student Reb Berish Flam (Kol Yakov, Kokhav Mi Yakov, Emes L'Yakov).

Rabbi Yakov Krantz died on the 17th of Tevet 1804 and was buried in Zamosc. The inscription on his tombstone states he was a famous preacher, well known throughout the world, there was no one like him before and won't be another after. (According to Yakov Dov Mandelboym from Sefer Zamosc).

Y.Y. Trunk Writes About The Preacher of Dubno

The Preacher of Dubno travelled around preaching to Jewish communities in Russia, Poland, the Austro – Hungarian Empire and Germany. While in Berlin, the well known Moshe (Moses) Mendelsohn came to hear him and called him the "Jewish Aesop". This comparison is incorrect. The Preacher of Dubno was not a "fable writer" and he never took his parables from the lives of animals.

The simple audience felt uplifted by the preacher's parables. He saw symbols of a moral way of life in daily scenes of Jewish life.

Even after his death, Jews would come en masse to synagogues to hear his parables which other preachers told in his name.

His parables did not only uplift the simple folk. The folksy piety of his words and his understanding of humanity as seen in his stories about Jewish life, was seen as the highest thinking of the Jewish intellect by great rabbis of his generation.

[Page 224]

A Discussion with the Vilna Gaon

The Vilna Gaon who was considered the greatest rabbinical authority of his day really liked the Preacher of Dubno and considered their meetings to be of great spiritual pleasure.

There is a story told about a meeting of these two great personalities of that time.

As is known, the Vilna Gaon rarely left his house. He would sit all day in his room, with the shudders closed even during the day and study Torah day and night.

When the Preacher of Dubno arrived and saw the Gaon's leadership, how he separated himself from the world and did not leave his home, he said to him:

It's no big trick to be the Vilna Gaon, when you sit closed in your room studying Torah. Going out into the street, seeing the world, meeting people, doing business and being the Gaon, now that's tricky.

The Vilna Gaon answered him abruptly – I'm not a magician!

If the Preacher of Dubno, due to his travelling around to Jewish communities, did not manage to come to the Gaon in Vilna, the greatest Talmudic authority wrote him letters, which are touched with modesty and longing for the folksy righteous man and his stories about Jewish life.

Although the Preacher of Dubno was extremely popular throughout the Jewish world, he wrote very little. It seems he felt the pen stood as a barrier between him and the simple Jew for whom his heart burned with humility and love.

When the Preacher of Dubno stood at the podium, wrapped in his prayer shawl talking to Jews, he did not fear the fires of hell. He comforted the Jews and tried to steer them on the path to justice. He behaved like a holy ascetic and demanded of himself the strictest discipline. He demanded a lot less from others.

The Preacher Celebrates the Exile

A folk tale is told about the Preacher of Dubno which also characterizes his lifestyle.

Once on a Sabbath the Preacher of Dubno stood in front of the congregation and gave a sermon. The synagogue was packed with everyone swallowing every word. The Preacher's mouth spewed pearls of wisdom, bright thoughts. The Preacher of Dubno raised himself to the divine chariot in the heavens and to the golden chairs of the righteous. Suddenly he heard an accusation against him from the ministering angels. He searched for his deeds and felt he was nearing the golden chairs of the righteous, he descended from his actual rank. In order to correct his ascent, the Preacher of Dubno took it upon himself to celebrate the exile.

The Preacher of Dubno disappeared for a couple of years among the large nameless masses of poor Jews and wandered throughout the Jewish world as a simple poor man. Together with other poor Jews, he walked from town to town, torn, with a stick in hand and a pack on his back. He slept in poorhouses, took coins from well off Jews and on the Sabbath, together with the other poor people, ate at Jewish prosperous homes. He hid his popular and beloved name from everyone.

In this bitter community among the simple poor people he cleansed himself spiritually. He became engrossed and uplifted in his love of the Jews and his new life experiences helped him create new stories.

I will quote one of his parables.

A Parable About a Deaf Man with a Cripple

A lame man and a deaf man who went from house to house begging together formed a partnership. The lame man sat on the deaf man's shoulders. They went together from house to house begging.

One day they came to a house where a wedding was taking place. The lame man heard the musicians playing. He felt like dancing. But how can he dance when he only has one leg? The poor deaf man could not hear the music.

"Dance a bit, jump a bit, I'm happy" shouted the lame man to the deaf man.

The deaf man could not hear the lame man nor the music. What did the lame man do? He took a bottle of whisky out of his pocket and gave the deaf man a sip. The deaf man tasted the whisky, began to feel happy and started to dance. The lame man gave him another sip, and then another and the deaf man began dancing with all he had. The lame man, who was sitting on the deaf man's shoulders was bobbing up and down. This is how they both danced. The lame man because of the music and the deaf man, from the whisky.

How much irony of the essence of a person lies in this simple story. We can not demand too much from a person. We must love him in his weakness. This is the content of the Preacher of Dubno's sermons.

[Page 225]

Why Didn't the Preacher Write Down His Stories?

Jews say: they once asked the Preacher of Dubno why he does not write an essay on Torah, the Prophets or interpretations which would contain his preaching. This is what the other preachers do. He said: I'll answer you with a parable. A rich man was marrying off his child. Many guests came to the celebratory meal, rich and poor Jews. They ate and drank and were very happy. The difference was this: the invited rich man sits at the table, eats the fine food and drinks the liquor according to a certain order. First he eats the fish, then he takes a bit of whisky. Then he eats the soup with noodles, meat and vegetable stew and ends with a glass of wine. The poor man stands on the side and quickly eats people's leftovers. The poor man sadly, cannot follow an order. He mixes the fish with the soup, meat with the herring, hot and cold to make sure he eats everything thrown at him.

The same is with me. The great Gaon of Vilna always sits at his holy table studying Torah. He can enjoy the wisdom and insight which, as if possible grants him order. But me, a Jew who wanders from town to town – I have to be satisfied with what is thrown at me from time to time. Here falls an interpretation of a passage on Khabkuk, and soon after a parable on the words between Balak and Blemen, or an interpretation of the story of Noah. I must take all these things in haste, and without order take note and prepare to continue in my way.

Rabbi Yisroel Meir Hakohen – The Khafetz Khaim
1839–1933

by Rabbi Moishe Meir Yashar

Translated by Janie Respitz

Rabbi Yisreol Meir Hakohen was born in Zhetl in 1839. His father Arye – Zev died young and he moved with his mother to Vilna. At 17 –18 years of age he married in Radin in the Vilna region.

After his wedding he spent his whole life learning and his wife supported the family running a store.

He wrote many holy books. His best known work which made him famous was his book on moral instruction called "Khafetz Khaim" (the Desire for Life) (Vilna 1873), published anonymously. The name of the book became the name of the author. Among his other known books are "Shmiras Haloshen", "Mishneh Brurua", a collection of laws from The Code of Jewish Law (Shulkhan Arukh) which included telling Jewish soldiers how to observe Judaism during military service.

Immersed in moral instruction, the Khafetz Khaim strove to spread virtues and strengthen religion through Yiddish. Besides his preaching, he had some of his books published with Yiddish translations under the Hebrew text. One that stands out is "Sefer Nidkhai Yisrael" which is one of the most important new religious literary works in Yiddish; the writer wrote on the cover page: "due to the request from many people, for this to be a useful book accessible to everyone, we translated it into simple Yiddish, so everyone can look at the important matters about our holy faith, which must be known and observed by every Jew, especially those who live in far away places. We also discuss here necessary laws and many other issues every Jew should know."

His other books translated into Yiddish deal with women's modesty, immersions etc…

He received help with these Yiddish translations from Bentzion Alps and his son in law Hirsh Levinson who was the head of the Yeshiva in Radin for 36 years until his death. The communal activism of the Khefetz Khaim is connected to this Yeshiva which he founded and used his name to make it renown and collected the money it needed to exist. In recent years the name Khefetz Khaim is remembered together with greatest geniuses who influenced generations with their greatness.

From the Lexicon of Yiddish Literature, Press and Philology of Zalmen Reyzn, vol. 2, 1930, Vilna.

The Childhood of Khafetz Khaim

In Zhetl, Grodno province, (Polish Lithuania), on the 11th day of the month of Shevat (1839) a child was born to Reb Arye Zev Hakohen and Mrs. Dobrusheh. Reb Arye Zev was not a wealthy shopkeeper. He came from a respected family, he was an important man and a great scholar. In his youth he studied at the famous Volozhyn Yeshiva, probably after the time of the esteemed Reb Khaim of blessed memory.

As a young man Reb Arye Zev studied in Vilna at Reb Khaim Parnas' house of study. In order to earn a living, he tutored a few rich boys. He would send a portion of his earnings home to his family.

[Page 226]

His wife Dobrushe was a very pious, quiet, modest woman. In honour of the Sabbath she would light many candles and observed the Sabbath with the utmost care. If there was a wire border around town which indicated an area which one was permitted to carry objects on the Sabbath, she would not even carry a key. She would spend her day reading the weekly portion and commentaries. She would not let her prayer book, supplications or psalms out of her hands.

She was Reb Arye Zev's second wife, a sister to the first. She was 14 years old when they married in 1833. Reb Arye Zev's first wife, Miriam left him with three children, a daughter Reyzl and two sons: Reb Moishe and Reb Aron. Reb Aron was 18 years old when his aunt gave birth after her wedding to her only son.

Reb Arye Zev's young wife was very happy seeing her prayers were answered and she was blessed with a beautiful little boy whose beautiful little face shone with heavenly light.

Oy, how she wished the holy temple would already be rebuilt. Then she would consecrate the son she prayed for to the Almighty as Khana did with her son Shmuel. Her son is even more prestigious, he is a Kohen and Shmuel was only a Levi! Whatever happens, her son would study Torah. Torah is the best merchandise! This is the only treasure that has remained since the destruction. When you study Torah you can reach the heights of the High Priest.

As she was thinking these thoughts she looked at her child. It seemed to her that when he smiled at her, she saw in his bright eyes a promise her hopes would be realized.

His circumcision took place on the 18th of Shevat. The rabbi came as well as all the important men in town. When they heard he was being named Yisroel Meir, (Yisroel =Israel, Meir = Light) everyone blessed the parents and said this child will grow up to be a light upon the Jewish people.

"Amen!" answered his mother with a trembling heart and tears in her eyes.

His Youth

The Name Yisroel Meir in reality reached its full meaning, as the child grew up to be a true light of Israel, the illuminator of his people.

He recounted, when he was a small boy his father took him to Vilna, took him to an acquaintance, a great rabbi, so the rabbi could test his knowledge of Talmud. After listening to him the great rabbi pinched his cheek and said: "Yes, you are a good little boy, be careful my dear child, do not lose your name".

He remembered these words his whole life. His parents felt proud and the small Yisroel Meir made them happy, because from childhood they recognized his prodigious talents. He was soon known as one of the best children in town. He stood out with his diligence and enthusiasm to learn. His diligence can be seen from a story his father told, that when they were in Vilna his beloved Yisroel Meir fell asleep while studying. His father carried him sleeping to the bedroom and put him to bed. He was astounded later to see his son studying and repeating what he had taught him that morning.

His Honesty

From childhood on he was admired for his exceptional naivety and honesty. Once, when he was a child playing at the marketplace with other children a fruit dealer dropped a basket of apples. The little brats happily grabbed the apples as did the little Yisroel Meir.

Later, when his father finished teaching him the phrases from the bible "Thou shalt not steal" and "Thou shalt not covet" he asked his mother for a kopeck to buy fruit. He took the kopeck, went to the market and bought apples from the same lady. After he paid, he threw the apples back in her bushel and ran away.

Another story was about a poor water carrier in town. He was a simple man and not very smart. School boys would tease him and pull pranks on him. In the winter when he would leave empty buckets near the well, these brats would fill them with water so they would freeze during the night. At dawn, when the water carrier would come to draw water he had to work hard to break the ice in the buckets. He would become irritated and curse.

When the young Yisroel Meir learned of this, he would go, unnoticed by the other boys, and empty the buckets so that the poor water carrier would not have problems in the morning, and without too much effort, fill his buckets and earn his bread.

[Page 227]

After His Father's Death

When the boy was ten years old, he became an orphan. His father who had studied in Vilna in Reb Khaim Nakhman Paranas' House of Study died at age 47 during a cholera epidemic. As he lay on his deathbed his only worry was who would educate his son in Judaism and raise him to study Torah and perform good deeds.

His father's death did not weaken the steady ascent of this young boy thanks to his noble, righteous mother.

Like a true woman of valour, she carried the burden of earning a living and kept a watchful eye on her child. His brother Reb Aron, of blessed memory also did a lot for him. He was a great scholar and personally taught his little brother. He also contributed financially to his successful education and the Khafetz Khaim always remembered this.

The small Yisroel Meir ascended in his Torah studies and did good deeds. Meanwhile, his widowed mother remarried Reb Shimon, a well established man from Radin. Her second husband committed himself to support her child. However, he was rarely at home. He was already studying in Vilna, the Jerusalem of Lithuania, which from then on he considered his second home after Radin.

An Excerpt from "The Life and Works of Khafetz Khaim", by Rabbi Moishe Meir Yashar, New York.

My Meetings with the Khafetz Khaim

by Shabbtai Mayevsky (B'nai B'rak)

Translated by Janie Respitz

As it is known, the world–renowned genius and righteous man, Reb Yisreol Meir Hakohen from Radin, of blessed memory, was born in Zhetl. He published his first book "Kahfetz Khaim" at age 18. It is based on a line in the Book of Psalm "He who wants to live, should not speak badly of anyone".

The book which was published anonymously made a great impact on the world, not only due to its content and great scholarship (there was no shortage of great scholars in those days), but because of its theme which was new to rabbinic literature. No one had written on the topic of slander and gossip before.

The Khafetz Khaim practiced what he preached. He lived his life as he instructed others to do. Those who knew him claimed he never said a bad word about anyone, therefore, deserving of his name.

The Khafetz Khaim wrote about 30 books. I want to mention only one: The Love for Justice. As the previous book, this too was new to the religious Jewish world because of its theme: disinterested act of charity. The book discusses the good deed of giving charity.

There were many biographies written about Khafetz Khaim. In the framework of my few words I would like to recount my meetings with him.

In 1927 I was studying at the Yeshiva in Ayshishok, 12 kilometres from Radin. On the 10th of Shevat, a day we did not study because it is a fast day, a group of us walked to Radin to meet the Khafetz Khaim.

We arrived in Radin frozen and went straight to his house. He made an incredible impression on me. A small Jew with a snow white beard, a high black cap the type old men in Zhetl would wear, his face radiant like the sun. He was by then in his eighties and could barely walk. He snuck into another room and began to drag a chair. His son in law saw this and asked:

"Rabbi, why are you dragging that chair?"

He replied: "the boys are tired, they should rest".

My second visit to the Khafetz Khaim was when my father of blessed memory got sick and was hospitalized in Vilna. I went to the Khafetz Khaim to ask for a blessing. When I approached him and put forth my request he did not answer but began to cry like a small child. A few days later, my father of blessed memory died.

I believe it is worthwhile that everyone from Zhetl living all over the world should know this great man and lover of the people of Israel was born in Zhetl.

[Page 228]

The Wise Men of Zhetl

by Moshe Tzinovitz, Tel Aviv

Translated by Judy Montel

Rabbi Reb Tzvi Hirsch son of Reb Me'ir HaKohen

The author of Torah studies, Rabbi Reb Tzvi Hirsch son of Reb Me'ir HaKohen of Zhetl lived 250 years ago [i.e. early 1700s]. He published a book called "Chidushei Maharsh"a" on the Rashi commentary to the Five Books of Moses. In this book he collected all of the innovations of the Maharsh"a and with this helped explained every problematic passage in the commentary of Rashi.

In the title page of his book, he is described as "a Torah champion from the holy community of Zhetl in the country of Lithuania." His preface to the book contains valuable historical material about the history of Israel in Lithuania during the days of the northern war that took place between Sweden, Poland and Russia.

Because of persecution, many Jews, including writers on matters of Torah, were forced to travel to Jewish communities in western Europe, especially to Germany, to earn money and also in order to print their books at one of the Hebrew presses.

The author of Zhetl writes: "For I saw excellent people, all of them holy, take to their feet, a large congregation of Israel, each one left their place, expelled and abandoned, some from one place, some from another. Because of the great want and robbery, that is growing in the country of Poland, the sheep have scattered, with no shepherd, as foxes amid ruins and brave people and sin-fearing and wise – in sorrow, destitute and weeping.

Oh to the eyes that see this! The sons of Zion who are excellent in Halacha, how have they been considered no more than a clay bowl at the top of every street? The spirit of my stomach tortures me and my heart shrinks in my chest like a small coin in a large vessel."

The author tells us of his troubles and travels from the time he left his home and abandoned his inheritance and with his wife and members of his household left the country, spent time in various towns, until he found a place to settle in Manheim in Germany.

There, "the lord, the officer, the elevated and generous champion crowned by a good reputation," Reb Avraham Zedenheim, noticed him. Reb Zedenheim had a reputation as great as the great ones who are glorified, and he found a refuge with him for a time and was supported generously by him, so that he could recover from the illnesses he had suffered in the 'wandering' lands, far from his birthplace and former influence.

A short time later, Rabbi, Reb Tzvi Hirsch moved to the Jewish community of Hanoi [Hanau am Main]. There he finds succor and support from the blessed Officer Falk who gave him room and board and in this town he was given the opportunity, in 1717, to print his book "Chidushei Maharsh"a" [Innovations of the Maharsh"a].

His excellent book was given "Haskamot" [recommendations] from the great rabbis of the time: Rabbi Reb Yechezkel Katzenelenboigen, the head of the rabbinical court of Altona-Hamburg-Wandsbeck, who had previously been the rabbi of Zhetl and knew the author from this, his birth town; the Haskama of the rabbinical judge and head of the yeshiva in Frankfurt, Reb Shmuel Shatin, Reb David, head of the rabbinical court in Manheim and Reb Moshe, head of the rabbinical court of Hanoi.

In this book, the author of Zhetl brings the commentaries on Rashi; from what he heard from his mentor, the best of the wise men, whose name was known and glorified by many, the elevated champion and wondrous rabbi of Torah learning, Reb. Aryeh Leib Katz, who was secure in his seat in the holy community of Zhetl in the country of Lithuania.

Apparently, Reb Tzvi Hirsch stayed in one of the German communities like other Torah authors, and certainly worked there as an educator.

Rabbi Reb Yoseph David

Rabbi Reb Yoseph David was born in Zhetl in approximately 1767 to his honorable father, Reb Tzvi, who was a scholar and a great tradesman. At a young age he was famed for his talents, his diligence and his righteousness. He married the daughter of Rabbi Reb Moshe Eisenshtat of Keltsk.

After his marriage he settled in Zhetl, sat in the tent of the Torah and was a loyal student of his mother's father, Reb Chaim, head of the rabbinical court there. As the rabbi aged, his grandson, Reb Yoseph David helped him in all matter of deciding matters of religion and law.

The elderly rabbi as well as the leaders of the Zhetl community thought that Rabbi Yoseph David would take his grandfather's place in the town's rabbinate. However meanwhile, in 1793, he was appointed as a rabbi in Mir, there he labored for 53 years and became known as one of the great rabbis of Lithuania.

Reb Yoseph David would torture his soul with fasting, study all day in holiness and purity. He was tall, taller than most people and had an honorable appearance. When he sat in judgement, the litigants were in fear of him. He preserved his words with holiness and purity and whatever he expressed verbally, for good or, heaven forbid, for bad, took place.

His second son, Reb Moshe Avraham, was the rabbi of Zhetl. Reb Yoseph David died aged 78 in 1846.

Rabbi Reb Avraham Elyakim

Rabbi Reb Elyakim was born in Zhetl in 1797. He was a supervisor in the Volozhin Yeshiva. He died in 1865 in Volozhin. In "Magid" (No. 25, 1865) he was described as follows:

Fourth day of Chol HaMo'ed Pesach, the great, honorable, elderly rabbi, Rabbi Elyakim aged 68. For over 40 years he worked at the Yeshiva and it's been over twenty years since Reb Itzeleh made him a supervisor.

Reb Elyakim knew the great Rabbi Akiva Eiger and his son, Reb Shlomo well. Reb Elyakim was awake all day and at night he also sat in the Yeshiva and would study Torah. He was one of the few who remembered Reb Chayim, founder of the Yeshiva.

Rabbi Reb Yitzchak Yehoshua of Karlitz

Rabbi Reb Yitzchak Yehoshua of Karlitz was the head of a yeshiva in Slonim and later on in Zhetl. He was one of the great Torah scholars 120 years ago. Some of his students were: Reb Chaim Leib Tiktinski, head of the Mir Yeshiva and the son of his brother-in-law, Rabbi Mordechai Gimple Yaffe – head of the rabbinical court of Rozhnoi. Towards the end of his life Reb Yitzchak Yehoshua was a teacher-arbiter at Mir and that's where he died.

Rabbi Reb Yitzchak left many manuscripts, but all were burnt except for his book "Beit Yisra'el" on the Passover Haggadah, which was published in Minsk in 1836. This book was reprinted in 1838 by one of his descendants, Rabbi Reb Shimon Heilprin a rabbinical decisor in Vilna and in Jerusalem. Encouraging the publisher to print the book was the great rabbi Reb Avraham Yitzchak HaKohen Kook, who was a relative of the author.

Rabbi Reb Aryeh Yellin

Rabbi Reb Aryeh Yellin lived several years in Zhetl in the house of his father-in-law, Reb Moshe Pinchas.

This famous rabbi was born in Skidel which is near Grodno. For a number of years, he learned in Volozhin.

[Page 229]

From Zhetl he was accepted as a rabbi in the town of Yeshinovki near Bialystok. In Yeshinovka he wrote his book "Mitzpe Aryeh" and "Kol Aryeh."

From Yeshinovki he was accepted as a rabbi in Bielsk. In this town he wrote his great book "Yefe Einayim," in which he demonstrated a deep knowledge of the Babylonian and Jerusalem Talmuds. This work of his was attached to the new edition of the Babylonian Talmud that was published by the Romm Press, and it drew much attention in the world of Torah scholarship and was considered one of the precious pearls in Talmudic literature.

He was a great leader of Torah and his gaze was always on the literature of the written and oral Torah. He died in 1886.

Rabbi Reb David Moshe Namiot

Rabbi Reb David Moshe Namiot was born in Zhetl to his father, Reb Yechiel Michel. He was the fourth generation (great grandson) to Rabbi Reb Eliezer Namiot, the rabbi of Zhetl. Rabbi Reb David Moshe Namiot studied in the yeshiva of Rabbi Reb Chaim Ozer Grodzhinski.

In 1906 he published his book "Divrei Moshe," which contains new citations and references in the Babylonian Talmud. Rabbi Reb Chaim Ozer wrote in his preface to the book about its author: "He studied with great diligence in my tent here, and I knew very well that a blessing dwelled in him, a new vessel, full of ancient [tradition]."

Two Zhetl Residents – married students at the Brodsky Kollel

In 5646 (1885-6) a special Kollel was established at the Volozhin Yeshiva to support ten excellent married students, who would receive financial support to maintain their families until they were qualified to be rabbis and great Torah scholars in one of the Jewish communities. These married students were called "Avreichim of the Brodsky Kollel," since the lord Yisrael Brodsky from Kiev dedicated an endowment for this purpose.

Among the excellent ten students were two from Zhetl. Rabbi Reb Tzvi Shachor, the grandson of the great Rabbi, Reb Yoseph David, the head of the rabbinical court of Mir. Rabbi Reb Shmuel Tzvi Shachor lived in Zhetl. The second student: Rabbi Reb Shalom Eliezer son of Reb Nachum Yisrael Rogozin of Zhetl.

Rabbi Reb Tzvi Yoseph HaKohen Rizikov of Zhetl[1]

Rabbi Reb Tzvi Yosef HaKohen Rizikov of Zhetl was one of the great Torah scholars of his time. He was the head of the Slonim yeshiva. All of his life he didn't not stop learning Torah. He was well-versed in the Talmud and its commentaries which he had committed to memory. All of his actions and way of life were holy. He had excellent characteristics, hated honor, made do with little and had no desire for wealth. He never wanted to be a rabbi. In spite of this, great places wanted to have his honor dwell among them, yet he did not want to relent for a moment from studying Torah.

Rabbi Reb Tzvi Yoseph did want to write down his innovations. He considered that a waste of time. He also did not conduct rabbinical correspondences, and only gave an answer when asked directly.

For 18 years he served as the head of the Sovalk (Suwalki) Yeshiva. He elevated the yeshiva until people arrived there from distant places to study with him.

Rabbi Reb Tzvi Yoseph HaKohen died in Sovalk on the 11 of Nissan, 5672 (March 29, 1912) at the age of 71. He was eulogized by famous rabbis. The rabbi of the town, Reb Moshe Luria said: "If the Holy Temple existed, the deceased could have served there as a high priest."

Rabbi Reb Menachem HaKohen Rizikov

Rabbi Reb Menachem HaKohen Rizikov was born in Zhetl in 5628 (1862) [this is a typographical error. 5628 would be 1868, but elsewhere he is reported to have been born in 1866], to his father, Rabbi Reb Tzvi Yoseph HaKohen, head of the yeshivas of Slonim and Suwalki. Rabbi Reb Menachem served as the rabbi of Kazan in Russia and the rabbi of Brooklyn in the United States. His books are: "Tiferet Menachem," "Divrei Menachem," "Sha'arei Zevach," and "From the Torah of Tzvi Yoseph," in two parts. His last book was published in New York in 5686 [1926].

Rabbi Reb Moshe Eliezer Gavrinovski of Zhetl

In the case of the great, sharp, amazing, knowledgeable, generous and incredible rabbi, Reb Moshe Eliezer, Torah and greatness were united in one place. He was known in the regions of Lithuania as "Reb Moshe Eliezer Mastilevitzer. He was born in Zhetl in 5609 (1849) to his father the extraordinary philanthropist and doer of good deeds, Reb Moshe Eliezer, who died before his son was entered into the covenant of our father Abraham and was named for him.

The orphan, Reb Moshe Eliezer, was educated with his father's father, the governor and philanthropist, Naftali Hertz Gvorin in Slonim. (Reb Naftali Herz's mother was the daughter of Reb Chaim Orliner HaKohen of Orlin, which is next to Zhetl, who had 13 sons who were great in Israel, one of them the rabbi of Zhetl – Rabbi Reb Yosph Tzvi HaKohen.)

Reb Moshe Eliezer learned Torah in the yeshiva of Zhetl with the sharp rabbi, Reb Shlomo. His excellent talents were very much appreciated by Rabbi Eizel Charif, head of the rabbinical court of Slonim. Afterwards he learned in the "Kloiz" [small study hall] of the Gr"a [the Vilna Ga'on] in Vilna, was a particular student of the teacher there, Rabbi Yoseph Sakovitz. In the year 5629-5630 [approx. 1869-70] he was mentored in his Torah study by the great rabbis, Rabbi Yisrael Salanter and Rabbi Yechezkel Landau. Already then, he was a highly respected home-owner in Vilna, after he married the daughter of the famous lord and he studied in wealth and honor.

He managed the estate Mastilevitz near Keltzk. In 5664 [1904] he came to America and founded with his sons a large business for medicines and grew wealthy there. Also in America, in Brooklyn, he continued to do holy work, much charity and did much in general and community matters. Among his many manuscripts we find many Torah innovations in all of the subjects of the Talmud, on which he debated with the great scholars of his time.

Rabbi Reb Noach Rabinowitz

Rabbi Reb Noach Rabinowitz was born in Zhetl in 5598 (1838). When still in his youth he was notable for his elevated talents. At the age of 13 he had memorized the orders of Nezikin and Nashim [of the Talmud].

At the Volozhin Yeshiva he was one of the most beloved students of the great Rabbi Reb Yoseph Dov HaLevi Soloveichik and adopted his study method for himself. When Reb Yoseph Dov was accepted as a rabbi in Slutzk, he took with him his student Reb Noach who worked as his assistant. In 1860, Reb Noach Rabinowitz was invited to occupy the seat of the rabbinate in Turets. He excelled in this position and gave wondrous sermons. In 1872 he was accepted as the rabbi of Silev [Vselyub] near Novogrudek.

Reb Noach Rabinowitz was one of the few rabbis who associated with the *Hibat Tzion* [Lovers of Zion] movement and in his public appearances he advocated for the settling of the Land of Israel.

In 1890 he was accepted as the rabbi of Shadowa [Seduva, Lithuania] and he ran the community there until his death in 1901.

Reb Noach Rabinowitz was one of the rabbis who didn't content themselves with their spiritual role, but who also did community work. He founded charity organizations and was always ready to help every sufferer.

He wrote the books: "Mei No'ach," "Toldot No'ach," and "Sefer HaTorah VeHaMitzvot."

Translator's Note:

1.   In searching online for Rabbi Tzvi Yoseph I found that he was also listed with the last name Reznik, while his son, mentioned below, had the last name Rizikov.

[Page 230]

Rabbi Reb Baruch Avraham Mirsky OBM
1840-1912

by Rabbi Y.L. Maimon (Jerusalem)

Translated by Judy Montel

Because I was a member of the editorial board of "HaPisga," I was fortunate enough to come in contact with a number of great rabbis, first by an exchange of letters, and afterwards with some of them in person. Among these rabbis I feel obligated to mention here one of the greatest of the rabbis, who I first met in the home of "Hapisga's" editor, Rabbi Trivush, and afterwards we became friends and worked together to forward building the land, and this is: the Ga'on, the Tzaddik, Rabbi Baruch Avraham Mirsky of blessed memory.

His History

Rabbi Reb Baruch Avraham Mirsky was born in the town of Mir, on the holiday of Shavu'ot, in 5600 [1840]. His father, Rabbi Moshe, was one of the great leaders of that generation, the head of the Yeshiva of Mir. Rabbi Baruch Avraham's mother died when he was still very young, when he was two years old. His father later married a second wife from the town of Nesvizh [Nyasvizh, Belarus] and settled there. Here he founded a large yeshiva for the study of Torah and excellent students came from the entire area to study Torah with him. Over time, his son Rabbi Baruch Avraham also was educated in this yeshiva and became well known as an "ilui" [exceptional].

When he was sixteen, he married – the daughter of one of the wealthy people of Nesvizh and on his wedding day he gave a sermon and amazed the great scholars of the town with his sharpness and profundity. And among those scholars was also the great Rabbi Shmuel Avigdor Tosfa'a who was then the rabbi of Nesvizh.

After his wedding he continued to learn Torah from the greats of that generation: his uncle, Rabbi Tevli of Minsk, Rabbi Avraham Shmuel of Rasayn (author of "Amudei Ha'Esh" [Pillars of Fire]) and Rabbi Avraham Shimon Traub, the rabbi of Keidan (author of "Chidushim veBi'urim" [Innovations and Explanations] for the book "Halachot Gdolot" [Great Laws]).

In 5629 [1869] he was appointed to be head of the yeshiva in Nesvizh and his classes in Talmud and in Jewish Law that he would give to his sharp students (and of whom there were later national leaders) were suffused with sharpness and erudition in a wondrous fashion. In 5633 [1873] the rabbinical seat in Porozowa became vacant, and because of the efforts of the great and holy rabbi Nachum of Grodno, who respected and liked Rabbi Baruch Avraham very much – the latter was accepted as a rabbi and head of the rabbinical court there. In 5652 [1892] he became the rabbi in the town of Zhetl and served there for over twenty years, until he died.

Opinions of Great Torah Scholars

This great rabbi was excellent and well known, including among the greater rabbis of the generation, as a tremendous scholar. Once, when he was in Brisk in Lithuania, he visited the home of the tremendous leader, Rabbi Chayim Soloveitchik, and as they were in the midst of the typical conversation of Torah-scholars, Rabbi Baruch Avraham told him of some explanation to words of the Rambam [Maimonides]. From great astonishment over the truth of this explanation, Rabbi Chayim called his friend, Rabbi Simcha Zelig and said to him: "Come, listen, how the rabbi of Zhetl learns Rambam and explains him."

Rabbi Baruch Avraham Mirsky left several books on various tractates in the Talmud, a valuable book on the commentary of the Ramban [Nachmanides] on the Torah and also the book "Shmatteta DeRaba", questions and answers and negotiations in matters of Halacha [Jewish Law] with the great Torah scholars of his generation, but most of his books and innovations were lost in the Diaspora, during the days of the previous, terrible world war, and only his book "Shmatteta DeRaba", which had been typeset ready to print, was miraculously saved and it can be found in the hands of his son, Reb Tevel Mirsky who lives in our holy city of Jerusalem (and was printed with the help of the "Mossad HaRav Kook" Press).

Our teacher the great rabbi and tzaddik Rabbi Avraham Yitzchak HaKohen Kook, the first chief rabbi of the land of Israel, was very desirable of seeing one of Rabbi Baruch Avraham's books published. He didn't have a chance to meet him in person, but once he saw a pamphlet of his with his Torah innovations, and from that he learned his study method.

The Rabbi's Humility

He was modest by nature, and at the same time, dedicated to study Torah and teach it. His persistence and dedication are evidenced by this fact: while he was the rabbi in the city of Porozowa, a man came to him from the surrounding area along with his daughter, who was ill and suffered from mental illness, and asked him to arouse heavenly mercy on her with his prayers, so that the Healer of all Flesh would send her a complete healing amid the rest of the ill people of Israel. The rabbi, with his great humility, refused to fill the request of this man. He did not want people coming from other towns to trouble him with such matters. But the unhappy father would not let it rest. Every day, morning and evening, when the Rabbi would walk to the synagogue to pray – he would run after him and ask him to mention his daughter's name in his prayers. According to him, many of his acquaintances had told him that his daughter could be saved only by the rabbi of Porozowa. The rabbi wept and begged his fellow townspeople to try to calm the heart of the sad father and to tell him honestly, that their rabbi did not get involved in such matters. To the question of his congregation: "What does it matter to the rabbi if he promises this unhappy father to request mercy for his daughter that she should be healed and enlivened?" the rabbi answered innocently:

"With all of my heart and soul I want to calm the heart of this poor father, but I fear that if his daughter should coincidentally heal from her illness, people will consider me a miracle worker, and from near and far, sufferers, each one with their troubles, will badger me with their requests and will stop me from the study of Torah, and for this my heart fails (later on, it became known that he had been advised to travel to the Admo"r [Chassidic rabbi] of Porisov, and the troubled father confused Porisov with Porozowa).

Rabbi Baruch Avraham was also well-known among all of the great scholars of his generation for his love and his affection and his longing for the Land of Israel. In a letter by the great & righteous Rabbi Ya'akov Moshe Charla"p of blessed memory, to the writer of these lines, he wrote among other things: "The innovations of the great scholar, our teacher Rabbi Baruch Avraham Z"tl [may his righteous memory be for a blessing], head of the rabbinical court of the holy community of Zhetl – are a wonder. In any topic that he deals with he is a rising spring, a flowing spring, he travels around the depths of the sea of the Talmud and the "Poskim" [scholars of Talmudic law], dives into deep waters and brings up precious pearls. He is known for his great affection, for he was devoted with his whole soul to the holy love, the love of our holy land, and was one of the activists and those who loved it, and for this reason, the holy light of the holy air was upon him."

[Page 231]

And indeed, these words were very faithful. Although all his life he never left off studying Torah, he did and acted much in our communities in support of the love of Zion and Zionism. Already in his younger days he would from time to time correspond with Rabbi Natan Friedland on the matter of the Land of Israel, and later, also with the great scholars Rabbi Shmuel Mohilever, Rabbi Mordechai Gimpl Yaffe, and also with Rabbi Yechiel Michl Piness.

In 5646 [1886], when the thought arose to several of the leaders of Hovevei Zion who were in Russia, headed by lion of the group, the great scholar Rabbi Shmuel Mohilever, to make efforts to purchase the land of the Arbel which is in the lower Galilee, an ancient historical site, that even now contain remnants of an ancient synagogue from centuries ago – Rabbi Baruch Avraham participated in this deal and invested all of his funds in this purchase. And when his friends, acquaintances and those who respected him asked him: why is he so interested in the purchase of the land of the Arbel in particular? He replied to them with a small smile:

"The whole practical idea of settling the land of Israel slowly and with our own powers as preparation for our future redemption reached us from the valley of the Arbel, and as it is written in the Jerusalem Talmud, tractate Brachot (page 1, side 1): "Rabbi Chiya, Rabba and Rabbi Shimon ben Halafta were walking in the valley of the Arbel at dawn and saw the morning star break forth, Rabbi Chiya said to Rabbi Shimon ben Halafta: thus is the redemption of Israel, at first it's little by little, the more it progresses, the greater it becomes" and from this," Rabbi Baruch Avraham concluded his words, "the valley of the Arbel is worthy of being redeemed from the hands of foreigners."

And indeed, despite the fact that this entire purchase was not successful and Rabbi Baruch Avraham lost all of his money in this deal, his love for the land of Israel did not cease nor did his longings for it diminish. The rabbi of Zhetl also took part in the controversy over the Shmitta* permit in the settlements of the holy land and among his writings, which to our sorrow have been lost, there was one pamphlet that dealt with this ruling in which he came to the conclusion – to permit

*[Shmitta is the seventh year in which the Torah forbids working the land of Israel].

With the sunrise of political Zionism, he was one of the first of the Jewish leaders to give it his hand and heart, and with the death of Rabbi Shmuel Mohilever, when prosecutors of Zionism were increasing amid a well-known circle of the ultra-orthodox, he answered the request of the Zionist activists in Bialystok (who knew that Rabbi Baruch Avraham was well respected in the eyes of the generations Torah leaders), and despite his weakness and fragile health he traveled to Kovno and met there with the great Rabbi Tzvi Hirsch Rabinowitz (son of the great rabbi Yitzchak Elchana), and suggested to him a complete program of joint work with all of the various streams of Zionism to further the building of the land.

Rabbi Tzvi Hirsch agreed to this program and signed it, and also confirmed it with his own seal. Afterwards, he travelled to Lodz and to Brisk, met with the great rabbis, Rabbi Eliyahu Chayim Maizel and Rabbi Chayim Soloveitchik, and they hesitated whether to lend their hands to Zionism, going back and forth on the matter, unable to take a decision.

Meanwhile, well-known forces intervened, and with their influence the scales were tipped to the negative, a fact that sorrowed that righteous man all of his life, but he stayed faithful to Zionism.

Before the second [Zionist] congress, he participated in the preliminary Zionist conference that took place in Warsaw at the time, and he was also one of the first who helped to found the Mizrachi Histadrut. [Union]

It is worth noting, that while the well-known rabbis who were opposed to Zionism used their opposition to forbid the use of the "etorgim" [citrons, used in the Succot holiday] of Gan Shmuel [i.e., grown in the land of Israel] for a variety of halachic reasons, he came out with a long response, full of sharpness and erudition, to cancel all of the claims from a halachic perspective, and this is written in his book: "Shmatteta DeRaba".

When the Keren Kayemet Le'Yisrael was founded to redeem the land, and its "Golden Book" was opened, he was one of the first of the rabbis who registered his son Me'ir in the "Golden Book," who died before his father, and when he himself died (12 Cheshvan, 5673) [September 23, 1912], those who respected and admired that great and righteous man knew to fulfil his desire and registered him as well in the golden book of the Keren Kayemet.

[Taken from the book "Sarei HaMe'a", Leaders of the Century].

Rabbi Borukh Avrom Mirsky the Lover of Zion

by Moishe Tzinovitch (Tel Aviv)

Translated by Janie Respitz

When the idea of Love of Zion began to spread among rabbis and enlighteners in Russia, Rabbi Borukh Avrom Mirsky was among the first to join the movement. While still the rabbi in Parizov (Volkovisk Region) he began to propagate among the town's Jews to help the colonists in the Land of Israel and organized a society to buy land and immigrate.

Rabbi Borukh Avrom Mirsky was in regular contact with the Bialystok rabbi, Rabbi Shmuel Mohilover, receiving from him news about everything that was happening in the Land of Israel, which he would weave into his sermons which were filled with love for the Jewish land. He ended every sermon with a quote from the Talmud expressing his love for the Land of Israel.

With the appearance of Dr. Herzl, he espouses political Zionism. This step attracted the attention of the Jewish national and religious social fabric in Russia. Rabbi Sh. Y. Rabinovitch from Sopotzkin, one of the Zionists in the country wrote about it: "The esteemed rabbi so well known throughout Lithuania, has dedicated his heart and soul to the idea of Zionism." "Hameilitz" 1899.

[Page 232]

[This is the Hebrew text of Rabbi Nissenboim's article in "HaMelitz" of 1898, Nos. 218, 239 regarding Rabbi Mirsky's relationship with Zionism]

Translated by Judy Montel

"The Rabbi Zhetl is one of the first Lovers of Zion and one of the great rabbis of our time. He has knocked on the doors of many rabbis to turn their hearts to Zion and its settlement and has done much work in this area. His son is a diligent laborer in one of the villages [in the land of Israel] and writes his father letters full of fierce love for our country and for working its soil. The father weeps many tears over these letters and a terrible doubt awakens in his heart lest the farmers are not following the path of the Torah as the Jews of Zhetl do and lest also his son may leave the straight path. And this doubt, which leeches the blood from his heart, which burns with the fire of religion, is not able to be assuaged by our letters written in the spirit of the religion nor by the testimony of faithful people, for the farmers of Ekron, for instance, do not fall in their Judaism from the Jews of Zhetl. And the rabbi aforementioned worked with all of his strength to pull the great rabbis to the camp of the Lovers of Zion that they may inspire the towns in the land of our ancestors with their spirit. Whoever has seen the tears of this rabbi, at the times when he asked for mercy from the Zionists on our Torah and our religion, who has heard his words which come from the heart, a heart full of the love of Torah and affection for Zion, saw and felt that before him a righteous, holy man was standing whose mouth and heart are equal and who speaks the truth that is in his heart."

We learn from this article that Reb Borukh Avrom Mirsky's son lives in one of the colonies in the Land of Israel however the rabbi sheds a lot of tears as he fears, God forbid, his son is not keeping all the Jewish laws and fulfilling all the required good deeds. However, he tries to interest rabbis with the idea of Love of Zion and wants them to use their religious spirituality to influence the new colonies.

Rabbi Borukh Avrom Mirsky participated in a meeting of rabbis before the second Zionist congress which took place in Warsaw in 1898. At that meeting he opposed the suggestion of the rabbi from Poltov, Rabbi Eliyah Akiva Rabinovitch, to create a committee of rabbis that would oversee the Kashrut of Zionism.

I would like to underline the moderate attitude the anti–Zionist rabbis had for Reb Borukh Avrom. They knew his Zionism was for the glory of God.

The Rabbi Reb Shmuel Rabinovitch
Resident of Zhetl and Rabbi of Moscow

by Moishe Tzinuvitz

Translated by Janie Respitz

Rabbi Shmuel Rabinovitch was the grandson of the Gaon and Cabbalist Reb Eliyahu, the rabbi in Slobodke and Kalish.

Rabbi Shmuel Rabinovitch married the daughter of the renowned wealthy man from Zhetl, Reb Shloime Namiyat. For years he lived in Zhetl at his father in law's Reb Shloime, and would study in the House of Study every day. After his father-in-law lost his wealth, Reb Shmuel became the rabbi in Zholudek.

In 1911 he was appointed as rabbi in Moscow, replacing the deceased Rabbi Eliyahu Yerukham Veysbrum. At that time Moscow chose a special commission to elect an appropriate rabbi. The commission searched throughout Russia and they chose Reb Shmuel Rabinovitch. Since Reb Shmuel did not have a permit to live in Moscow, he was officially hired as an assistant to the Kazyon rabbi, Rabbi Yakov Maza and that is how he received the right to reside in Moscow.

During the First World War Jews were permitted to live in Moscow. Of course, Jews exercised that right. Reb Shmuel Rabinovitch's house was open to all. The Jews kept him so busy he simply had no time to eat or rest. However, he always found time to answer everyone and gladly arbitrated on various religious themes.

Under the Bolshevik regime he suffered from hunger and destitution. His face swelled up, he lost all his strength and suffered from a neurological disease. He would often sit and study all night until dawn. His household would beg him to rest, but he would study without a break.

Reb Shmuel Rabinovitch was a great scholar. He had great insight and was extremely talented at explaining. In addition he was modest and hated greed. He could have lived in comfort and luxury as he was the chief rabbi of such a wealthy community as Moscow, however he lived in poverty, often dire.

In 1922 his friends suggested they sell Etrogim to the wealthy Jews in order to alleviate his poverty. Reb Shmuel rejected the suggestion.

He was very active on the Moscow Jewish communal council and his opinions were respected.

Although he was not a big talker, his few words had a persuasive influence.

Reb Shmuel Rabinovitch passed away in the month of Elul in 1924. His death announcement in "Izvestsia" did not mention he was chief rabbi of Moscow. The announcement said that Shmuel Rabinovitch who lived here and there died, and his acquaintances are invited to attend his funeral.

There were many commentaries written after his death. It was stressed everywhere that he was the last rabbi of the Jewish community of Moscow.

[Page 233]

The Life Journey of Rabbi Zalmen Saratzkin

by Rabbi Elkhanan Saratzkin (Jerusalem)

Translated by Janie Respitz

Rabbi Zalmen Saratzkin was born in 1880 in the town Kharine, Mohilev province, the youngest son of the local rabbi Reb Bentzion of blessed memory. All his brothers were rabbis and his sisters married rabbis. The family stems from great rabbinic pedigree from the renowned Shklov rabbi Reb Yisroel, author of "The Light of Israel".

Rabbi Zalmen Saratzkin studied in the Yeshivas of Slobodke and Volozhyn and was known to be an assiduous and sharp student. In 1905 he married the daughter of the world renowned head of the Telz Yeshiva the esteemed Rabbi Eliezer Gordon. Within a short time he perfected his secular studies and was a candidate to enter university in Pernov (Kurland) together with the renowned Dr. N.Y. Shteynberg who later served as Minister of Justice in the Kerensky government.

After his father in law died in 1910 he became rabbi in Voronove where he opened a Yeshiva for young boys. He became well known as a great speaker and was active in the community and was offered the position of official state rabbi in Slonim. He turned down the post as he did not want to leave the rabbinate in the actual meaning of the word, though the Slonim Jewish community wanted to appoint him as one competent in deciding matters of rabbinic law and city preacher.

At this time the Zhetl rabbi, Reb Ari Dvoretzky of blessed memory, died. He was invited to give the eulogy for the deceased rabbi. As a result of this visit to Zhetl he was invited to become rabbi of Zhetl and he did in 1912.

In Minsk

In 1915 when the Germans were close to our town and there was a danger he would be taken "hostage" by the Russians. He left Zhetl with the retreating Russian army after he did all he could to prevent the Russians from staging a pogrom in town. He left with the last group of Russian soldiers and settled in Minsk. Here he headed the committee to help the tens of thousands of refugees and became very well known for his communal work.

After the outbreak of the revolution he headed the Agudas Yisroel party in White Russia and was chosen as a deputy to the All Russian Jewish Conference (The Jewish National Council). He headed the rabbinic delegation to St. Petersburg which demanded rabbis be exempt from military service just as the spiritual leaders of other religions. He travelled to St. Petersburg 12 times until they achieved this goal.

He then was chosen, secretly, as head rabbi of Irkutsk, the capital of Siberia where many Jews settled during the war. He turned down this high paying post not wanting to leave the Pale of Settlement, and waited for the first opportunity to return to Zhetl. The opportunity was found when the Germans captured Minsk. He returned to hungry Zhetl.

Returning to Zhetl

He began his work helping the needy population through intervening with the German authorities to provide the town with produce and food supply.

When the Polish legionnaires marched into Zhetl he went under a hail of bullets to the military commander and negotiated that if the legionnaires won't rob the town he would provide the soldiers with food and cigarettes.

After the military left town he began to rebuild the ruins and improve the economic situation. He founded a bank, an interest free loan society, a food cooperative, rebuilt and expanded the building of the Talmud Torah, opened a school for girls, (the first religious girl's school in the region), repaired the bathhouse and the shelter for poor travellers and helped to reopen the Yeshiva.

At this time he was invited by the rabbi in Kovno, in the name of Agudas Yisroel in Lithuania, to take on the position of Minister of Jewish Affairs in the Lithuanian government, however, due to various reasons he did not accept this offer.

Communal Activity on a National Scale

Representing the institutions in Zhetl he travelled to many conferences and meetings and took on a leading role. He was chosen as chairman of the Society for Caring for Orphans in Bialystok (which Zhetl then belonged to), chairman of the Sanitation – Medical Organization of The Joint and chairman of Cooperative Banks. Later he spent many years as a member of the Council of Cooperatives in Poland and would travel almost every month to meetings in Warsaw where he played an active role. For a while he was chairman of the Central Cooperative Bank in Vilna.

[Page 234]

He also participated in all rabbinic meetings in Poland and became known for his speeches. He was chosen for the highest positions in rabbinic organizations taking a place of honour. He was known as the confidant of "Khaftez Khaim" and Reb Khaim Ozer Grodshensky who were the rabbinic leaders in Poland.

He was one of the founders of the "Council of Yeshivas" in Vilna and played an active role in its activity until he left in 1940. He was one of the leaders of the religious school organization "Khorev", the central organization of the Talmud Torahs and religious schools in the region. He took part in the World Congress of Religious Jews in Vienna in 1923 and made a great impression with his speeches which were marked with logic and rhetorical power.

In 1928 he was a candidate for the Sejm (Polish parliament) on the Agudas Yisroel ticket. He received a lot of votes, but due to a split in Jewish votes, no Jews were elected.

In 1929 he was elected head rabbi of Lutzk, a community which had more than 30 thousand Jews and was a big administrative and political centre where almost one hundred towns and cities from Volhynia Township were concentrated.

Zhetl could not "compete" against a Jewish community as large as Lutzk as they did when their rabbi was offered chief rabbi positions in towns like Ayshishok, Semiytitch and Ostrov – Mazavietzk and they were able to influence him to remain at his post. Now they had to give up their struggle.

In Lutzk

In Lutzk, as his work was broader and more diversified, he quickly became known as a complete rabbinic personality who was respected by Jews and Christians, in and outside the city. He was recognized as the religious and political leader of Volhynian Jewry. Rabbis consulted with him on all religious questions, sending him their questions and answers and communities would seek his advice when electing rabbis or ritual slaughterers and about Jewish politics in the country.

He stood at the helm of rabbinic delegations to the Polish government and presented the demands of religious Jews in Poland, like the organization of Jewish communities, and rights for a religious school system. He took part in the large, famous rabbinic delegation to the Polish premier Prof. Bartel, together with the Khafetz Khaim and other prominent rabbinic personalities. He was chosen by the government as a member and later chairman of the "State Rabbinic Collegium" which confirmed the election of rabbis and rabbinic judges throughout Poland after they were chosen by their communities. After the decision of the Rabbinic Collegium the Ministry of Education would confirm the election and the rabbi could take on his position.

When the sad, famous regional law emerged prohibiting ritual slaughter, he worked tirelessly in order to have it repealed and was elected chairman of the committee to defend ritual slaughter in Poland. He spent months in Warsaw organizing the political struggle against this edict which reached its culmination with a strike of the entire Jewish population of Poland who did not eat meat for 17 days in a protest against this law.

In 1937 he participated in the congress Agudas Yisroel in Marienbad which then discussed dividing the Land of Israel into Jewish and Arab states. He read for the Religious World Congress the famous resolution which stated Jews were not permitted a piece of the Land of Israel. He was then chosen as a member of the Council of Torah Scholars and at the same time a member of the international executive of Agudas Yisroel. The speech he gave as an introduction to the resolution became famous throughout the world and reverberated in the circles of the mandate commission of the British government.

That same year his first book "Idea and Talk" was published. It was a collection of articles and sermons on actual problems. It made a great impression in the rabbinic world and was quickly sold out. The book was published again in 1946 in London and will soon appear in its third edition in Jerusalem.

In The Land of Israel

[Page 235]

After the fall of the Polish state and its division between Soviet Russia and Hitler's Germany, Lutzk was in Russian hands. At first it seemed possible to continue Jewish communal activity under the Soviet regime in religious and educational fields and various circles exerted pressure on him to remain to continue with his work. But soon it became clear that this was an illusion. The Soviet authority quickly began to liquidate all Jewish institutions and from a good friend who had contacts in the NKVD he learned he was a candidate to be arrested. He ran away to Vilna which was independent and after many transformations, made it to the Land of Israel in 1940.

In the Land of Israel he founded a "Council of Yeshivas" based on the one in Vilna which was a union of all the Yeshivas in the Land Of Israel, and headed it until today. The Council of Yeshivas, under his direction, has grown into a powerful institution with a budget of almost one million pounds a year, with almost one hundred Yeshivas and learning institutions and thousands of students.

The Envoy for Religious Jewry

He quickly occupied a respected place in religious and political life in the Land of Israel. For a while he held the position of chairman of Agudas Yisroel in the Land of Israel. He was also a member on many aid committees for refugees that arrived during the Second World War.

In 1946 he visited England for the Council of Yeshivas. He went to the largest cities giving talks that were well received by English Jews. He was offered an important rabbinic position, but he turned it down. He did not want to leave the Land of Israel. In 1948 he published the second volume of "Ideas and Talk" which dealt with Jewish holidays and eulogized the great destruction of European Jewry, particularly those Jewish communities where he served as rabbi, Zhetl included.

The same year he flew to New York in order to organize aid for the Yeshivas in besieged Jerusalem. He participated in a few conferences bringing the call of Torah Jews in Israel and organized an appeal for support of Yeshivas in this difficult period of war. While in New York he participated in the Agudas Yisroel Congress where it was decided they would participate in the provisional Israeli government.

When he returned to Israel in 1950 he was chosen as a substitute chairman of the "Council of Torah Scholars" and after the death of the eminent Rabbi Isar Zalmen Meltzer of blessed memory, he was elected chairman.

In 1951 the first part of his large work on the Book of Genesis was published called "Ears to the Torah" which places him in first rank of rabbinic authors of today. He received the Rabbi Kook Prize from the Tel Aviv city council for the best book published that year.

With the introduction of the state educational system the Agudas Yisroel decided to maintain its independence from the educational network. He now is heading the "The Non – Partisan Independent Education of Agudas Yisroel" and accepts the position of chairman of the board of directors and manages a network of schools for boys and girls with more than 25 thousand pupils.

In 1953 he published a second volume of "Ears to the Torah" and in 1955 "the Scales of Justice" which includes questions and answers from his forty years of rabbinic activity. This book was also received in the rabbinic world as a great contribution in the field of Jewish law.

Today, Rabbi Zalmen Saratzkin is one of the greatest rabbinic authorities in the world and remains in contact with all the rabbinic institutions in the world who consult with him on all aspects of religious Jewish life.

His children: Rabbi Elkhanan Saratzkin was the rabbi in Zholudek until the outbreak of the Second World War. He was sent to Siberia, freed in Moscow in 1944 where he worked in the Jewish division of "Committee of Polish Patriots" in Russia. In 1946 he returned to Poland and was elected chairman of Agudas Yisroel and member of the Council of Jewish Communities in Poland. In 1947 he emigrated to the Land of Israel and worked in the administration of The Council of Yeshivas and is a member of the International Council of Agudas Yisroel in Jerusalem.

Rabbi Eliezer is the executive director of the Telz Yeshiva in Cleveland; Rabbi Borukh is head of the Telz Yeshiva in Cleveland; Rabbi Yisroel is head of a Yeshiva in Petach Tikva, and Reb Bentzion is the head clerk in "PIKA" in Haifa. His daughter Temeh, may God avenge her murderer, perished in the Warsaw ghetto together with her husband and child.

[Page 236]

Rabbi Zvi Hirsh Khurgin of Blessed Memory

by Yosef Eliyahu Piekelny – Pniel (Kfar Haroeh)

Translated by Janie Respitz

Among the personalities who distinguished themselves in our town and was respected by all social classes was Rabbi Zvi Hirsh Khurgin, of blessed memory, or as he was called "Head of the Yeshiva".

The writer of these lines had the privilege to live in his time and benefit from this luminary. I must stress that besides his modesty and not wanting to distinguish himself, his personality placed a stamp on the spiritual life of our town.

I do not remember when he came to us, no one really took interest. His life with us was self evident, as if he had always been with us. He was attached to all of us, big and small.

Since I can remember, there was a Yeshiva in Zhetl and the boys would sit in the House of Study with the Head of the Yeshiva. The head of the Yeshiva would either give the boys a lesson or he would sit at his lectern absorbed in the Talmud and commentaries and the entire House of Study would echo with the voices.

The Yeshiva boys found the head of the Yeshiva's home to be the warmest and dearest place. He took interest in everyone personally. The boys did not feel like they were in a private home but rather continuing their studies in the House of Study.

On holidays his house was filled with guests and students who would come from different Yeshivas. To his great joy there were no boundaries, everyone was welcome and he showed interest in everyone. He would ask about their learning, their situation and progress while his wife would cook delicious food and prepare a holiday feast where each one would demonstrate what he knew.

The room where the head of the Yeshiva taught was filled with sacred books and he had a Torah in a special holy ark. Often, a quorum would be organized in his home. He would begin prayers exactly on time. Regularly, at the exact same time every day, you could see him going to pray even though he lived far from the House of Study.

Disregarding the fact that his economic situation was difficult, he never complained. He also did not demand a special position in town. He took upon the job of teacher and educator and he would often substitute for the rabbi in his duties. He was always ready to give to charity.

Everyone knew you could find the nicest Etrog and four species at the head of the Yeshiva's as he was a great Lover of Zion.

Everyone knew his hands were clean and he could be trusted. People would deposit their money with him as well as dowries for poor girls. The truth – this was his main motto, and with great devotion and self sacrifice he protected the religious character of our town.

One Friday night when Jews were already in synagogue for evening prayers someone told him that some people are still working in a certain workshop in town. He quickly stopped praying and ran there. He turned over the table with the work tools and did not budge from the spot until they closed the workshop. His handling of the situation made a great impact in town.

Another incident worthwhile recounting: he made a deal with the pharmacist, his former student, that he would only give out medication on the Sabbath in the event of a life threatening emergency. In order to ensure this, he gave up his Sabbath nap and sat in the pharmacy (of course with a sacred book) to prevent the pharmacist from desecrating the Sabbath.

The majority of his students were youngsters from our town who finished their studies at the Talmud Torah and under his influence continued studying at the Yeshiva. Many of these boys went on to study in large Yeshivas.

In Polish Lithuania, where the majority of Yeshivas were concentrated, there was not one that did not have a student from Zhetl. The majority of them excelled in learning and in time became rabbis, ritual slaughterers or just well established Jews who held a respected place in society.

I have spoken here about a personality from our town who had many virtues.

In memory of all the communal leaders, I have described the great personality of our teacher and rabbi, Rabbi Zvi Hirsh Khurgin who perished in horrific circumstances together with all the other Jews of Zhetl in the big slaughter of 1942.

[Page 237]

Communal Leaders and Men of the People

Reb Hertz Leyb Kaplinsky

Reb Menakhem Vernikovsky

[Page 238]

Communal Leaders and Activists

Translated by Judy Montel

Who can count and who number the communal activists of Zhetl, who faithfully dealt with the needs of the community, became tired, went hungry, worked and didn't stop, from morning until night, and all of this for no reward.

Among them were activists in philanthropic organizations in the traditional fashion, and there were a young group of public servants in political and public organizations. Both groups dedicated all of their strength and souls to ease the suffering of their fellows and to bring progress to the life of the town.

In the cover page of this section two salient community activists of Zhetl: Reb Hertz Leib Kaplinski, a man of noble virtues, learned in Torah, a grandfather who knew how to do community work alongside his sons and grandsons, and Reb Menachem Vernikovski, who both preached and fulfilled Zionism, active in the Talmud Torah school and friend of the Socialist Zionists.

And how could we not mention Reb Yisrael Ozer Brishenski, from the younger generation. Worn and thin, desperately poor in his personal life, he was rich in activity and wealthy in projects for the good of the many. He risked his life but stood tall to protect the town in times of trouble and hardship. Who can be compared to him? Who is his equal?

May we be forgiven for not succeeding in putting on paper the glorious names and magnificent deeds of ALL of the activists of Zhetl. May our efforts bear witness that we greatly desired to memorialized their holy characters

We have also unfurled a wide canvas of social characters who were simple, honest, modest, unambitious, but how wonderful were their figures! In memory of all of these, may we say: may their names be amplified and sanctified.

[Page 239]

Reb Avrom Patzovsky – The Elder (Starosta) of Zhetl

by Moishe Man (Buenos Aires)

Translated by Janie Respitz

Reb Avrom Patzovsky was born in Zhetl in 1835. Already at a young age he was known as a very gifted and intelligent young man. He knew Russian which in those years was rare for a Jewish boy from a small provincial town. He also had great success in business but he was never a rich man. In addition he was very generous and with an open hand supported the needy.

I will recount a few episodes which will describe the personality of the "The Zhetl Starosta" (town elder, an official civic position) as we used to call him.

It was 1905 at the height of the revolution. One morning they arrested a Jewish revolutionary. The same day, one of the town's Jews died. The revolutionaries decided to inform the Russian authorities that an innocent man was arrested, as the deceased was the one who committed the offense against the Russian government…They proposed they return the arrested man to Zhetl and the Starosta, Reb Avrom Patzovsky confirmed this was the truth. The organizer of the plan was Mayrim Epshteyn, or as we called him Mayrim Mashkes.

When they came to Avrom Patzovsky with the plan he trembled with fear. If the Russian authorities learned God forbid we tried fooling them, he would be sent to a forced labour camp in Siberia. He did not give an answer right away as he wanted to examine the possibility of realizing this plan.

He went to the regional police superintendent. They greeted each other warmly and had a long discussion until the police brought the arrested revolutionary. When Reb Avrom Patzovsky saw him he said he was a good friend and was innocent…it was the deceased that was involved in revolutionary work.

Reb Avrom Patzovsky prevailed in having this man immediately freed. When he got home he called Mayrin Epshteyn over, gave him 100 ruble and asked him to escort the revolutionary out of town.

He did many favours for the Jews of Zhetl as the Starosta, especially when it came to military conscription. Thanks to him many youngsters were exempt from serving the Czarist regime.

I remember an episode involving my grandfather. He had a relative named Mania Mnuskin. In 1905 she was active in the revolutionary movement. Thanks to my grandfather she escaped arrest because he sent her and her fiancé to Germany.

One day in Berlin she went to the market to buy food, carrying a linen handbag. She was noticed by a policeman who suspected her of carrying a bomb in her bag. When he asked her what was in the bag she did not want to answer so he brought her to the police station.

With great caution experts opened her bag and to their great disappointment found pumpkin seeds. She was accused of deceiving the German police and they sent her out of the country. She notified my grandfather in a telegram and asked for his help. He sent her money and told her to go to Switzerland.

Just before the First World War my grandfather was very old and had difficulties carrying out the tasks of the Starosta. He recruited my brother Motl to help him with his work.

Before the Germans entered Zhetl my grandfather burned a lot of papers except for the most important which he gave to Motl.

On the 15th day of Sivan in 1918 my grandfather died at the age of 83.

The family of Avrom Patzovsky

First row: Khaim Hershl Man, Moishe Man
Second row: Reb Avrom Patzovsky, Malke Patzovsky, Soreh Man
Third row: Dien Man, Etl Man, Motl Man, Dvoyreh Man

[Page 240]

Reb Hertz – Leyb Kaplinsky of blessed memory

by Yudis Ostrovsky (Tel Aviv)

Translated by Janie Respitz

Reb Hertz Leyb Kaplinsky was born in the village Dubrovke near Zhetl in 1860. His parents were Yisroel Hillel and Rokhl Leah.

When remembering Zhetl, the persona of Hersh Leyb Kaplinsky emerges. I don't think there was one institution in Zhetl he was not involved with. Unfortunately I cannot provide exact details of his activity because I left Zhetl in 1915. I returned in 1922 and left again in 1923.

In 1928 I visited Zhetl for the last time. By this time there was a Tarbut School. The entire burden of the school was carried by Reb Hertz – Leyb of blessed memory.

When we say the most important part of a person is kindness, Reb Hertz Leyb of blessed memory is a true example. He sacrificed everything for the community at large with his whole being and he and his family suffered from his communal activities.

Knowing him as a man of high morals, we must say, he counted his family as a part of him and included them in his communal work.

In his old age when he was physically weak he would draw water from the well to make it easier for their servant. His daughter would reprimand him saying: "why is the servant different from you, that you can do this and not her"? He demanded the Christian servant eat with everyone at the table and not alone in the kitchen as was common.

We can of course find in Reb Hertz Leyb's personality even kinder, gentler characteristics but everyone remembers the features that are close to his own heart.

Reb Shmuel Kustin of blessed memory

Reb Shmuel Kustin was born in Deretchin in 1890 to Eliyahu and Khane Kustin. In his youth he studied at the Yeshivas in Mir and Volozhin. In 1914 he withdrew to Russia. In 1919 he returned to Poland and settled in Zhetl. He opened a shoe business and in 1921 was elected head of the Jewish communal council. He held this position until the first slaughter in 1942.

As head of the Jewish communal council he excelled with tact and patience and was considered a peacemaker. In his communal work he often faced personal insults but he always reacted calmly and with dignity.

As an educated Jew he would read the "Ein Yakov" to the craftsmen every Friday evening in the new House of Study. He was also sympathetic to Zionism, supporting the funds and the Tarbut School.

Besides his communal activity he was active in the merchant union, the Popular Bank, and the Interest Free Loan Society. He played a leading role in all the institutions and worried about the poor and needy Jews. Although he was closer to orthodox Judaism, he found a common language with all the groups in Zhetl gaining respect from all.

As chairman of the Judenrat he did a lot to ease the destitution in the ghetto. He was killed with all the Zhetl martyrs in the first slaughter in 1942.

Reb Menakhem Vernikovsky of blessed memory

Reb Menakhem Vernilovsky was born in Slonim in 1862 to Avrom Yosef and Khane Feygl Vernikovsky. In his youth he joined the Hovevei Zion (Lovers of Zion) and later became a member of Ahad Ha'am's B'nei Moshe, and later, a Herzlian Zionist. He was a great Talmudic scholar as well as an enlightener, orthodox yet progressive.

After he married Soreh Dvoyre Zeltzer he move to Zhetl and opened a shoe business and a drug store.

In 1905 the Zhetl shoemakers, fearing competition from his shoe business, shot into his house with the intention of frightening him to ruin his business. Fortunately there were no casualties.

A second attack on his house was carried out by Zhetl revolutionaries. They surrounded his house, forced themselves in and split his head. The doctor who came to help was not allowed in. This attack was a revenge against his extensive Zionist activity.

Before the First World War all the Zionist meetings took place in his cellar. He was the permanent chairman of all Zionist youth meetings.

To begin with, all his children immigrated to the Land of Israel, and then in 1925 he emigrated as well. By then he was sick and exhausted but did not turn down any communal work. He would go to the old people's home and synagogue of the artisan's centre and give lessons in Talmud.

On the 20th day of Elul in 1930, he died in Tel Aviv.

[Page 241]

Reb Shlomo Zalmen Dunetz, of blessed memory

by Mordecai Dunetz (Flint, Michigan – America)

Translated by Janie Respitz

Reb Zhame was one of the most colourful characters in Zhetl. He was called "Zhame the postman" because for years he administered the mail in Zhetl.

Mordecai Dunetz

Everyone, old and young knew him. There was not one institution in Zhetl where he did not help out.

A. Ivenitsky wrote about him in the "YEKAPO Book": "Zhame was a tall Jew, well built with a greyish – black beard and smiling, lively black eyes which looked out from under thick eyebrows. He was among the first Hovevei Zion and then later the first member of Mizrachi in Zhetl. He was a true passionate fanatical supporter of Mizrachi and settlement in Eretz Yisrael. He grasped all favourable news about Eretz Yisrael and dispersed it among opponents as well as those who were indifferent. By nature he was a truly good, simple man and a passionately devoted Jew".

My grandmother Soreh Rokhl of blessed memory, had a small grocery store for many years. She worked from morning until late in the evening. She supported my grandfather Reb Zhame…he was rarely home as he was busy with communal matters. After working ten years at the Zhetl post office they dismissed him. He took this well as he now saw the opportunity to devote all his time to communal activity. In a letter to his son Yudl in America he wrote the following from Jerusalem:

…I assume you remember I worked at the post office in Zhetl for more than ten years. When the time came and Rabbi Avrom Namiyat of blessed memory, told me the post office no longer needed a manager, and he would give me three months to find another job, I told your mother, may she live long, she cried, but I took the money, tossed it into the charity box of Reb Meir Ba'al Nes and said: "This is all for the good". As you can see, the Almighty took pity on us and we have survived over 40 years.

If I would have remained in Zhetl or Novoliyenie at the post office, like your mother may she live long wanted, I would not have come to Eretz Yisrael forty years ago for approximately ten months and I would not have been able to do all I have for the Jewish people and the Land of Israel. I also could not have been a well respected man in Zhetl for over twenty years and do what I did for the town in general and specifically for the Houses of Study. I also would not be in Jerusalem today, may the holy city be built and maintained soon in our day, Amen.

I wish my children, grandchildren and all of our good friends will live out their hundred and twenty years as I have lived until today. Let us hope to God that He will provide for us until our last days, as our sages said: "Whoever lives well will be provided for. Every man should know that all that happens to him is God's will."

His devotion to the welfare of others went as far as self sacrifice. He would leave his wife and children for months on end to collect money for Yeshivas. He was a regular visitor to Reb Shmuel Mohilever in Bialystok, the chief rabbi in Moscow, Dr. Chlenov and others. Reb Zhame was a close friend of the founder of Mizrachi, Rabbi Yitzkhak Raynes from Lida.

Seventy years ago he decided to leave Zhetl for Eretz Yisrael. After wandering for many months by foot he arrived in Odessa where he boarded a ship. While in Odessa he saw Jews desecrating the Sabbath in public. He would stop young people in the street and strongly reprimand them. They would insult him but Reb Zhame took it all in with love and hoped perhaps they would listen.

After a ten month visit in Eretz Yisrael he returned to exile in order to devote his time and energy to building a national home. He infected the youth with his fanatic love and enthusiasm for Eretz Yisrael. He considered collecting money for the Jewish National Fund as holy work.

I was told that once Reb Zhame came to a meeting at the Yiddish school. All he needed to see was a Jewish map of "Palestine"…Reb Zhame created a scandal as to why they used a non Jewish name for our land.

[Page 242]

They took the map off the wall and promised they would change the name to "Eretz Yisrael".

Avrom Ivenitsky, of blessed memory, recounted the following episode: the opponents would often provoke Zhame with unfavourable news about Eretz Yisrael. However, Zhame would take the opportunity to take revenge in his own way.

Once, an opponent, the Zhetl businessman Dovid Shaykes approached him with a venomous smile and announced that Delfiner liquidated his silk factory in Eretz Yisrael. Zhame looked at him bitterly and turned away.

One morning Dovid Shaykes was awakened by a loud noise on his window. Neither dead nor alive he went to the window and ran into a laughing radiant Zhame who shouted in his face:

-Ha! Dudkeh, I wish you apoplexy in your bones! What do you say now?
Dovid stood there confused.
-What?!

-What?! You don't know?! Look how he's pretending!

-What is it? Talk!!!

-Delfiner reopened his silk factory!

-Phooey on you, you crazy Jew! – said Dovid as he spit and returned to bed wishing Zhame bad dreams…

Skeptics and progressive elements in Zhetl, who in those years were very involved in the revolutionary movement often made fun of Reb Zhame's arguments in favour of a national home in Eretz Yisrael. However they loved to have heated discussions with him and were amazed by his stubbornness and passion. Reb Zhame used all his strength to spread the ideas of Hibat Zion (Love of Zion) and later Mizrachi (Religious Zionist) movement. He expressed his love of Hebrew in a letter to his son's children in America:
…I ask my grandchildren to write me greetings in any language they can. If in Hebrew, of course that is good, and if in jargon (Yiddish), also good. Ask your parents to teach you Hebrew. I am sure there are teachers and courses in New York where you can learn Hebrew. The Almighty will also help and with God's will, when you get older, you will see and feel how good it is to know Hebrew. I am sure that if God forbid you will not learn Hebrew you will regret you did not learn it as children. I hope you will do what I write to you"… (October 31, 1927).
According to Jews in Zhetl, Reb Zhame was considered to be not only a Zionist activist but also a scholar and a good leader of prayers. His heartfelt praying was renowned in Zhetl. He united the enlightened and orthodox within himself. His life's task was to observe the 613 mitzvot (good deeds) and his love of Jewish customs reached a level of fanatic perfection. Reprimanding strangers for not living according to Jewish law was for him a holy mission, especially when it involved his own family.

When his son Yudl, in America wrote to him with pride about his son's Bar Mitzvah, Reb Zhame was not impressed and replied to him with fatherly anger:

…what you wrote, that you invited friends on October 28th to celebrate your son's Bar Mitzvah is only for American patriots… the 28th of October is not the date of your son's Bar Mitzvah. You yourself wrote that on the Saturday when your son became a Bar Mitzvah he was called up to the Torah, and he made a speech as he properly should. After prayers, they came to your home to make Kiddush (the blessing on the wine). You also said a few words and everyone celebrated. If you would have, on that same Sabbath made a festive third Sabbath meal and after Havdalah (the ceremony ending Sabbath and bringing in the new week) an evening meal marking the end of the Sabbath with music, and it would have cost you a hundred times more than what you did on October 28th, your mother, may she live long and I and all of our friends would be so happy for you as this is what a "Mitzvah Feast" is all about. You should not even look at the fact if you can or cannot afford a "Mitzvah Feast". The Almighty gives many times over.

If you wanted to make a party for good friends, you could have invited them for Chanukah which is a national holiday and we recited Hallel during prayers, but not the 28th of October!!!(1925).

Reb Zhame was never satisfied with short letters. His letters were always filled with quotes from the Torah, lessons in morality, longing for Zion and filled with chronicles of daily life in Zhetl.

At age seventy he still wrote letters with a beautiful handwriting. His letters were like pearls, clear and distinct as if he was writing an important document. He never forgot to attach a stamp from the Jewish National Fund on the top of the page and filled the paper until the very last line. The family therefore preserved Reb Zhame's letters and kept them for many years as a family treasure.

Communal life in Zhetl was an integral part of him and it is no surprise this was always expressed in his letters.

Here is an excerpt from a letter Reb Zhame wrote to his son when he was in Scotland on his way to America.

[Page 243]

…you must keep your promise that you will live as you did at home and obey everything I write to you. For that reason I am writing to you now, so that you will, for the sake of God, observe the Sabbath, pray and the correct time when everyone prays, and do everything in a Jewish manner, and God give you health and luck in all you do".

…I will send you, God willing, a book of Zionist songs with musical note, if you need. I will send the "Haynt" newspaper by mail. I assume they read "Haynt" in Glasgow as they do in Russia.

Reb Moishe Novogrudsky from Siratavchine died and they took 300 ruble from his inheritors for burial, one hundred ruble for the burial society, one hundred ruble for the Talmud Torah and one hundred ruble for a medical clinic.

When they went to dig the grave, Reb Ber Dvoretsky from Khadzielan and a few others, asked the young guys not to purify the corpse before burial. They took the board upon which the body of the deceased is placed for purification and locked it in the shed of the fire house. This lasted a few hours, until they gave another hundred ruble to build a clinic.

…Reb Yishayahu, the painter's son, who was a reservist at the Minsk quarantine station, had already come to Zhetl. There was a strike in Novoredok and the following people from Zhetl were arrested: Moishe Shatzkes, Reb Noyakh Eli's son and Leybe the peddler's son. Others were let go.

This week the tax collector left for Aziad. The young Manifalshchikh left for Kobrin.

For the past two weeks they have already been baking Matzah in Zhetl in eight matzah bakeries. The ten thousand military reservists that were in Slonim were "sent off to war". (Zhetl, 1905).

Here is an excerpt from another letter which describes the life story of one of Zhetl's important citizens, Reb Borukh Mirsky.
…did you know Reb Borukh Mirsky, of blessed memory? He worked with poplar and was very poor. When he would go to Vilna to sell poplar he would borrow a coat from me. When he came from Plesk to Zhetl, he rented our house. We had two workbenches in our house. He would work on one and working on the second was Reb Mordkhai Feyvl Yarmovsky of blessed memory, with whom we lived in Sefianovitch's house. There was a kiln where wooden boards were placed to dry in what is now the small house.
Reb Borukh Mirsky of blessed memory was a Slonim Hasid.

Reb Shloime Zalman Dunetz and his son Shmuel of blessed memory

His Rebbe, Reb Avrom said he should give him 5 kopeks for Eretz Yisrael for every poplar he sold. This would bring him success. Reb Borukh obeyed and had great success.

Reb Borukh of blessed memory had a brother in law, a great scholar, God fearing and trustworthy, who would lend him money for materials.

Reb Borukh of blessed memory also had two daughters. When he had to find a match for his older daughter he paid six hundred ruble and chose a Jew, a scholar, Reb Zalmen Yoel Kaplinsky and in addition provided room and board for a few years. People in town said Reb Borukh took the dowry from his business. He also rented a large dwelling with a large garden where he made a kiln. His business was successful because he gave his Rebbe five kopeks for Eretz Yisrael from every poplar he sold.

A few years passed and Reb Borukh had to make a match for his younger daughter. This time he gave one thousand ruble for a dowry and a few years of room and board, and chose a scholar who was also an enlightened man, Reb Avrom Kravchik. He studied to be a ritual slaughterer but he threw it all away and left for America.

Reb Borukh of blessed memory bought a house for 6-8 hundred ruble, married off two sons, left his business for his children and moved to Eretz Yisrael. There, his wife got sick so they returned to Zhetl. He left 800 ruble for a guest house and old people's home. People say the Reb Borukh also left hundreds of ruble to the Rebbe for Eretz Yisrael and a Torah for the Hasidic House of Study".

Reb Zhame's constant dream was to settle and live out his years in Eretz Yisrael. The land of his forefathers beckoned. His life in exile was filled with longing and in no way did he want to find his eternal rest there. However, for a Jew, a family man, aged seventy, this was not an easy trip to undertake.

[Page 244]

His wife, Soreh Rokhl did not even want to consider giving up her small shop where she had spent practically her entire life, and leave for Eretz Yisrael. In Zhetl she had her family, friends and village customers who called her Sorkeh. They were for her like members of her family, and they will surely not come to Eretz Yisrael…so why should she join him?…her answer was therefore: No! She did not want to suddenly tear herself away from her home soil in which she was so deeply rooted.

This was no answer for Reb Zhame. He stubbornly claimed that his life would not be a life if he could not live out his last years in the holy land. This was his life's goal and nothing would stop him from reaching it. His younger son Shmuel had left to Eretz Yisrael as a pioneer a few years before. This only strengthened his decision.

After long discussions with his stubborn wife and family he prevailed. It was a difficult yet important step but old Zhame's love for Eretz Yisrael outweighed all his personal feelings for his wife and family.

All of Zhetl came out on the first day of Chanukah 1926 to say goodbye to the old beloved Zhame the postman. He blessed the second candle with a radiant face and got into the car that was taking him to the train station in Novoliyenie. Reb Zhame was finally on his way to Eretz Yisrael – the land of his dreams and aspirations.

He settled in Jerusalem. The economic situation was very difficult. A man of his age could not even think about earning a living. He had to resolve himself to accept support from family in Zhetl. However there too the situation was not good and they could not send money too often. Reb Zhame never complained about his poverty as the joy of living in Eretz Yisrael was more important than everything else.

His greatest joy was to walk from settlement to settlement in the Jezreel Valley in order to see with his own eyes the settlement of Zion.

With special enthusiasm he would go to the market on the 15th of Shevat in order to buy fruits from the Land of Israel. For him it was a privilege sent from heaven to be able to breathe the air of the holy land in his older years.

Reb Zhame began to suffer from loneliness. His son Shmuel who worked in Petach Tikva and saw rarely, could not help him much as for weeks he had been unemployed. So Reb Zhame decided to move to an old people's home where he could be together with people of his age.

But here he discovered a whole strand of difficulties. The old people's homes in Jerusalem were very small and in order to get in you had to pay a lot of money. Reb Zhame wrote home asking for money. Others that promised him help were the former chief rabbi of Eretz Yisrael, Rabbi Kook, and a townsman from Zhetl Rabbi Tevel Mirsky.

With great difficulty the family collected the money and sent it to Jerusalem. This is the report Reb Zhame sent home providing an account of what he did with the money:

…I gave the beadles of the old people's home 40 pounds, the burial society for a plot on the Mt. of Olives – 3 pounds, a burial shroud – 1 pound, a tombstone – 1 pound, digging and covering the grave a half pound. Carrying and other expenses – 2 pounds. In total 7 pounds. 10 pounds had to be paid to the old people's home. This was paid by Tevel Mirsky with a promissory note. In total I need 70 dollars more in cash".

Thank God I have lived to see Jerusalem, the holy city.

Reb Zhame lived in the old people's home for four years where with other Jews, he studied a page of Talmud every day, and was involved in discussions. With quiet steps he approached the final days of his life.

In a letter to the family, his son Shmuel from Petach Tikva reported on Reb Zhame's death:

On the 13th day of Kislev 1933 I received a letter from Jerusalem that father is very sick. I was there by three o'clock that afternoon. I found him very weak. He was no longer speaking and almost gone. I gave him my hand. I don't remember if he gave me his hand or I took it myself.

He had a very difficult night and the following morning at 11:45 he died.

The funeral took place at 4 o'clock that afternoon. Rabbi Tevel Mirsky delivered a moving eulogy.

This is how one of the most interesting and beloved characters of Zhetl Jewry lived, and died at the age of 76.

[Page 245]

Reb Yisroel Ozer Barishansky of blessed memory

by Avrom Ivenitzky of blessed memory

Translated by Janie Respitz

Yisroel Ozer Barishansky, was actually called Sroyleyzer. This name, until a few years ago, embodied all of Zhetl, more accurately, the power of communal Zhetl in every aspect.

Yisroel Ozer Barishansky

Small, thin and lively, with dark blue nearsighted eyes, with a trimmed yellowish grey beard and hair – Sroyleyzer, in the horrible days, right after the German occupation, when Zhetl was surrounded on all sides by terrifying forest bandits, from pitiless hunger and deprivation: in the horrible days, when every few weeks the authority would change; today, Poles, tomorrow, Bolsheviks; when soldier's debauchery terrified Jewish Zhetl; when everyone feared for their lives, for all the possessed, in those days, Sroyleyzer was the only one who ran from one powerful representative to another with requests, brought bribes, joked with the hooligans and saved more than one Jew, more than one Jewish family from destruction.

He was well known by the Poles and the Bolsheviks. They would listen attentively to what this young assistant rabbi said, because Sroyleyzer was no fool. They knew, what he promised, was sacred.

In those days Sroyleyzer would run through the streets of Zhetl, where you would rarely see a Jew, knock on closed shutters, awaken, encourage, demand, shout, bring news, and most importantly, calm everyone down. During the terrifying days and nights, when one power left and all of Zhetl waited fearfully for the next soldiers to arrive; when all of Jewish Zhetl would bury themselves wherever they found a hole, dazed and trembling, listening to the banging of the window panes and the desperate cries for help – in those days and nights Sroyleyzer was the only one who was not afraid, but ran from one commandant to another, organized a procession of soldiers at the rabbi's house where they were given cigarettes and tea; where there were negotiations with the commandant – in those terrifying transition days Sroyleyzer was literally the saviour - angel of the town.

However the chapter about Sroyleyzer does not begin during these days. Back in the good old days there was not an institution or Jewish communal society where he was not the initiator or the most active member. He brought liveliness and gusto wherever he went. He received a few slaps when he bought the hospital from the Russian government and turned it into a Jewish hospital. During various disputes, quarrels with a rabbi, a doctor or an institute, he would often be berated but he would not get excited. He would shout, make noise, tell his opponent exactly what he thought and go on his way.

Without Sroyleyzer there would not have been a Talmud Torah, bathhouse, old people's home or Jewish hospital in Zhetl. In the bitter years of hunger, 1919 -1922, when Zhetl ran the American kitchen for children, the adult kitchen of the "Joint", when they would distribute money, clothing, underwear, shoes, that is when you would see Sroyleyzer running through the streets of Zhetl, disheveled, tattered, with one torn old shoe and one woman's cloth shoe, with an open scolding mouth, surrounded by a group of noisy, shouting, crying, wailing women – each with her own complaints and demands to the "committee", to Sroyleyzer…

Sroyleyzer now has a second wife and small children and lives off his post at the electric company. This is how it has been these past few years. Until now no one knew how he earned a living and when Sroyelyzer did something for himself. But no one ever suspected him of dishonesty, or abuse of communal funds which he would often have in disorder. Nobody claimed this. In Zhetl, everyone knows that Sroyleyzer is absolutely honest.

Let us Perpetuate his Deeds

It is the obligation of everyone from Zhetl to perpetuate one of the most remarkable Jews of our time. I don't think such Jews are born every day, I mean: Yisroel Ozer Barishansky, or as we used to call him "Podrabinek" (assistant to the rabbi). This is a person who gave everything to the town and did not take anything for himself.

[Page 246]

This went so far that he was pauper his entire life. He was a man that always worried about the poor while his wife and children did not have enough food or clothing. A person who experienced all the dangers during the war in order to save the town. If Zhetl was not destroyed during the Russian – German and Bolshevik – Polish war, it is thanks to Yisroel Ozer.

The Poles came into Zhetl for the first time in 1919. Later, they came and went. The officers would always stay with us. A few days before Passover a company of soldiers arrived preparing to attack Novogrudek. The population was not allowed to go out in the street after 8:00 p.m.

It was the first night of Passover. There were two officers staying with us, one was a Jew from Galicia. In the middle of the night there was a knock on our door. We ran to open. It was Yisreol Ozer.

"How is it possible for you to be here? You are risking your life". Yisroel Ozer shouted that we must wake up the officers because the town was being robbed. We woke up the Jewish officer and told him. He immediately got dressed, sounded the alarm, assembled the soldiers and saved the town.

The next morning Yisroel Ozer was there with a pair of black boots. We called in the officer, he tried on the boots, but they would not get on his feet and he had to leave for Novolenyia that evening. Yisroel Ozer ran to bring Herzl the shoemaker, he took measurements and by evening brought a pair of finished yellow boots. No one but Yisroel Ozer could accomplish this.

He did not earn a living. In his thirties he became a baker. My sister Dina would go to him specially to buy bread because he was Yisroel Ozer. One day she went to him as he was kneading rolls for market day. She spoke to him and asked: "Tell me, are you at least making some money from this?"

He replied: "Listen Dinakeh, if at my age I have to knead rolls and birds and have to think on which side the bird should hold its head, can I earn a living?"

If Yisroel Ozer had two pairs of shoes he would take away one pair and give it to someone who did not have any shoes.

Let's collect more facts about Yisroel Ozer, and because during his life he never earned a living, let us at least perpetuate his good deeds.

The Two Brothers

by Moishe Mirsky (Man)

Translated by Janie Respitz

I would live to remember the two Barishansky brothers in Zhetl. The older one, Yisroel Ozer "Podrabinek" was a smart Jew with a lot of energy which he devoted for the good of others, while he remained a very poor man. He belonged to all the societies in town, was a regular guest of the rabbi, knew everyone in town, and knew what was cooking in everyone's pot. In addition he had great influence on people and helped to solve personal and municipal conflicts. He would help the town in all hazardous and serious instances.

When someone falsely accused Motl Man and the false Christian witnesses had to be gratified, the mediator was Yisroel Ozer. After the First World War, during the Polish Bolshevik conflict, they were beating, torturing and shooting Jews. Yisroel Ozer would, with large sums of money, have all the decrees annulled.

His brother, Avrom Moishe, belonged to the youth wing of the "Bund" and was one of the founders of the Literary – Dramatic Society and later, the Yiddish School. He was involved throughout his life in world politics. In the morning at the marketplace there were two circles. One group was vigorously discussing municipal matters, and Yisroel Ozer had the last word. The second group relentlessly discussed world politics with Avrom Moishe in the centre. People in town would ask:

"What's all the noise at the marketplace"?

They would answer: "These are the discussions of the Barishansky brothers. One is guiding the town, the other, the world".

[Page 247]

My Grandfather Reb Yisroel Elkhanan Piekelni
of blessed memory

by Leah Rozenblum (Raanana)

Translated by Janie Respitz

A tall, thin figure in a black, long caftan, his face pale from age and suffering, his beard, white, his forehead wrinkled and his blue eyes looked out from their deep sockets. His steps, proud and slow. This is how my grandfather appeared to me when I was a small child. My grandfather was old and weak, but he did not lose his intellect until he died.

Every morning, before praying he would wash from a small jug of water which my grandmother prepared beside his bed as he did not want to begin his day before he performed the ritual hand washing. Then, quietly on tip toe, he would get out of bed, God forbid wake anyone, and leave for prayers. He would pray for a long time and return late for breakfast. When my mother would ask: why do you come so late from synagogue he would reply: Let the children eat first, I don't need to eat so much anymore.

When we came home from school he would greet us with his bright blue eyes and a smile on his lips and ask us in Hebrew:

"What did you children learn today in school? Which Torah portion? Perhaps also a little Rashi?" if he liked our answers he would smile and say a blessing.

We loved our grandfather and our love for him was expressed through respect to the holiness which hovered over him. Since I remember, he was dressed in black, studied from holy texts, at times the Pentateuch with 43 commentators, sometimes a thick prayer book filled with prayers for the entire year (the pages were yellow and wrinkled from so much use). Often he would look into the Talmud with the commentaries. When grandfather read, a sweet melody would fill the house. His melody would take me to a higher spiritual world. I would see before my eyes Bialik's student as he swayed at the lectern and studied: Oy, said Rabba, Oy said Abay. Then my grandfather turned his pious eyes toward heaven and gestured with his thumb. How pious he appeared at that moment!

My grandfather would seldom pray at home. If he felt he was disturbing anyone, he would go straight to the synagogue. He never wanted to make things difficult for our household. He never asked anyone to bring him anything, he would get it himself, even though his feet did not serve him well.

Friday, on the Sabbath eve when there was so much work to do, he would prepare the candle sticks, set up the prayer books and come to the kitchen to ask if he could help us with anything. When we told him he should go eat and we did not need any help he would say:

"Today is the beginning of the Sabbath, there is no time to eat, hurry children". When he said "children" he meant all of us including our grandmother, of blessed memory.

I will always wonder about the relationship between my grandfather and grandmother. They both showed one another respect and love. They were always quiet and smiled at one another.

My grandmother died suddenly, and my grandfather soon after. After her Shiva he would sit in the synagogue for many hours and come home late. My mother would send food to the synagogue and we would barely convince him to taste something. He was tormented by deep sadness. Not long after he became ill, stopped walking and remained bed ridden until his death.

The corner where my grandfather's bed stood was holy to us. We never heard him complain about his health. He would hum his melody and we would lovingly feed him. He would always ask if we had already eaten and although he said yes, he would always leave over something for us.

I will never forget the white pillow where my grandfather laid his head which was covered with a black skull cap. His depleted body was covered with a white blanket and the colour of his face and beard merged with the whiteness of the bed linens.

A sadness poured from that corner when my grandfather fell into eternal sleep. His large prayer book sat on the shelf dishonoured and not consoled, however his melody soared through the house reminding us that our grandfather had passed away.

[Page 248]

Characters and Facts

by Moishe Man (Buenos Aires)

Translated by Janie Respitz

There were three well known sons in law in Zhetl: Reb Avrom Shloime Zhikovshchiner's son in law, Reb Shmuel Rabinovitch.

Reb Eliyahu Meir's son in law from Dvoretzer Street, Reb Shmuel Khaim.

And Reb Borukh Man, Avrom Patzovske's son in law.

These three Talmudic scholars would sit all day and study.

The first of the three sons in law was a rabbi in Moscow, the second, Reb Shmuel Khaim was the rabbi in Aginitshisk (Russia).

The third, Reb Borukh Man, was wanted as rabbi in Kiev. Besides his Talmudic scholarship he was also an enlightened Jew and a bible expert. If anyone wanted to brag about their biblical knowledge he would refer to Reb Borukh Man. At the time he was the best devotee of the Hebrew language in Zhetl and also knew Russian and German perfectly. During the German occupation he served as secretary of the town committee.

As mentioned he was an enlightened Jew and did not want to become a rabbi. He became a lumber surveyor. Thanks to his honesty, he had a good reputation. He was well trusted and earned a good living, however it was difficult work, in the heat of summer standing bent over rafts and measuring the lumber.

On the 18th day of Av it will be 35 years since he died. On that day, even though it was war time, and the Sabbath, everyone learned of his death.

Reb Yisroel Avrom Sokolovsky was a great scholar. He was Reb Arye's son in law. He served as a religious judge in Lodz for three years and then returned to Zhetl. At this time the rabbi in Zhetl was Reb Borukh Avrom, an old man. Reb Yisroel Sokolovsky would give a Talmud lesson every day and displayed expertise and insight.

Reb Leyb Khabadkier was so respected, the old nobleman Stravinsky did not allow him to leave town and did not charge him to lease his mill so that he could sit and study in peace.

Reb Noyekh Eli was a Gemara teacher in Zhetl for 75 years. His knowledge was so vast that when he lost his sight in his old age he would sit at the platform where services were led in the synagogue and mumble along with Rabbi Yitzkhak Raytzer. When the rabbi would glance at the text he realized Reb Noyekh Eli, now blind, knew the whole Gemara by heart.

The old cantor's name was Reb Eli Ber Kamenetzky. I believe, today, in America and in Israel there are many Jews who remember how he prayed. He was a ritual slaughterer, a great scholar and very devout. He would answer all questions pertaining to Jewish law himself except those dealing with what was permitted or forbidden.

The last cantor was Reb Yitzkhak Kagan. He had a unique, beautiful voice.

There were also many in Zhetl who read from the Torah: Reb Hertz Leyb Kaplinsky, in the old House of Study. In the small prayer house, Reb Itche Razvosky. Reb Khaim Leyzerovitch the Zhibertaychiner lived on our street. He would read from the Torah on the High Holidays. I remember on Purim when he read the Megillah he would bring a tin sheath. Later, he led morning services at the old House of Study.

It is worthwhile remembering Hirschl the blacksmith. He led services in the small prayer house. He was a very honest man. He became blind in his old age but would still walk alone to the prayer house every morning and evening.

The following can be included among the great scholars of that time: Reb Moishe Tentzer, Reb Menakhem Vernikovsky, and Reb Hertz Leyb Kaplinsky. It is worthwhile mentioning Reb Yisroel Ber Epshteyn the gravedigger. He taught "Ein Yakov" at the new House of Study to a large group.

The manager of the old House of Study was Khaim Itche. People said he had many pockets and in each one was the money from a different society.

Beadles: Nokhem Shloime in the middle House of Study, a tall fat man with a long beard. Friday evening he would call on everyone to come to synagogue. He would direct his face to the sky and cry out three times with a melody: To synagogue, to synagogue, to synagogue!

The manager for the old House of Study was Moteh Nokhem Dubkovsky. Later it was Yisroel Mordkhai Leyzerovitch, a tailor and an honest, warm hearted Jew. Everyone loved him. The last years, Yoyneh Leyb Khlebnik was the manager of the old House of Study.

For years, the manager of the middle House of Study was Moishe Yehuda, for a short time Asher Lusky and finally, Shaul the tutor.

[Page 249]

The Burial Society in Zhetl, like everywhere was comprised of two parts: managers and volunteers. The managers were the illustrious respected men and the volunteers would take care of the corpse.

For many years the managers of the Burial Society were: Reb Yisroel Bom, Reb Shmuel Mirsky and Reb Moishe Tentzer. Reb Berl Mirsky was one of the most active volunteers.

Hirshke Khayke's was a small man who lived on Novoredker Street. He would never go further than 5 kilometres from town because God forbid, if someone died, he would not be there to give him a proper Jewish burial.

It was very difficult to join the Burial Society as membership was inherited. A new member had to be extremely devout. The butchers had to pay a tax on every piece they slaughtered. The tax collector would give a portion of the tax to the Jewish community and a large amount to the government.

For a time, the tax collector in town was Yakov Meylekh Dvoretzky. Later it was Avrom Moishe. He also supervised kashrut in the Talmud Torah.

There was also a tax on yeast. Besides the tax collector, no one was permitted to sell yeast. After the First World War the revenue of this tax went to the rabbi to pay his salary. Yeast in Zhetl was very expensive.

Until the yeast was transferred to the rabbi, the yeast tax collector was Yisroel Bom and after, Shmuel Shvedsky.

The Society to Spend the Night with the Sick and the Society to Visit the Sick were under one administration in Zhetl. Members of the society would spend the night with every sick person. The moral and physical help they offered the patient and the household should not be underestimated. Besides this, if someone needed material help, he would receive it.

I remember Moishe Ruven Mordkovsky ran these societies for many years. It is superfluous to emphasize that these were the only institutions without political overtones.

In 1896–1897 a well known preacher would come and the entire town would go hear him. One time, when he came to Zhetl, the old House of Study was packed. In the middle of his sermon a plank of wood on the floor of the women's section broke. There was a huge commotion. 12 women were trampled on and suffocated. My mother miraculously survived.

Reb Avrom the Recluse by Efraim Pasaf (New York)

Broad shouldered, not very tall with a four cornered, not very long beard, woven with white – silver hair, a full face with happy bright eyes, always with a smile on his lips. A heavy step but agile. His clothes, always clean and tidy, were composed of a long black caftan with ritual fringes hanging out. This is the portrait of Reb Avrom the Recluse, of blessed memory or how we called him, Reb Nokhem Shloime's son in law.

We would always see him in the same corner of the middle House of Study where he would sit in front of a big book and study. He would arrive at dawn as the day would break, prayed with the first quorum and then he would finish saying all the selections from scripture and psalms. After, he would sit and study until one o'clock when he would go home to eat. Two hours later he would return to the same House of Study, the same spot at his large lectern and continue studying until late at night.

He was a reserved man. He only spoke when necessary, when he needed something. On the Sabbath he would be completely silent. If children would enter the House of Study he would not let them leave before they recited a chapter of psalms. When he prayed he would stand straight as if before an elder, without swaying or rocking, just praying quietly from his heart.

The outside world on the other side of the House of Study never interested him. He had no business with anyone. His world was Talmud and the House of Study. He was not a great scholar however his perseverance was outstanding.

Everyone in town liked him. They had the utmost respect for him because he was a simple man, almost a legendary persona.

Older men recounted that before he was Nokhem Shloime's son in law he was an ordinary carpenter, who barely knew how to pray. But because his wife's first husband had been a prodigy, he decided to dedicate his life to Torah. People said he would sit all night and study with his feet in a basin of cold water to prevent him from falling asleep. He was not embarrassed to go up to a Yeshiva student and ask to study with him.

This is one of the most modest personalities of my small town of Zhetl who has remained etched in my memory.

Reb Moishe Ruven Markovsky of blessed memory

A very simple Jew, a house painter, Moishe Ruveh, as he was called in Zhetl was the only one who was totally devoted to orphans and gave them all his time and energy. He chaired the orphan committee and the Aid to the Sick Society. A day did not go by when Moishe Ruveh did not visit the orphans who were under his guardianship, to check how they were living, learning and working. He also worried about their physical and moral education. His devotion, which was truly sincere was successfully rewarded. He was popular in town and fittingly respected.

Reb Yosef Mutchnik of blessed memory

Shloime Mutchnik (Tel Aviv)

My father, Yosef Mutchnik was born in Navaredok in 1874. His parents were Avrom and Khane. His father was head of the Yeshiva in Navaredok.

My father received a religious and secular education. At first he went to Heder, later, he attended Yeshivas among which, the famous Slobodke Yeshiva.

At the age of 18 he began to study Hebrew on his own and later became a Hebrew teacher.

He got married in Zhetl to Menukha Alpert, the daughter of Berl Alpert (Berl the harness maker).

In Zhetl he taught at the Talmud Torah which was rebuilt in 1909. My father taught all grades Hebrew, grammar and Jewish History. He was the first teacher in Zhetl to promote the Hebrew language. He organized performances to raise money to support the school. At the same time, he ran a private school.

My father was one of the founders of the Zionist organization and helped spread Zionist thought in Zhetl. He was a diligent worker and a good pedagogue. He died in the Polish – Soviet war.

Reb Yosef Vinetzky according to Avrom Ivenitsky

Yosef Vinetsky, the author of the article "During the German Occupation" which is published in this book, died in 1929 just over the age of 60. He was one of the most remarkable people from Zhetl. His last years, he lived off an inheritance from his sister in America. Because of this inheritance, in his older years, with the help of dictionaries, he corresponded with lawyers in English and handled it all himself.

Until he received this inheritance he supported himself writing administrative requests, addresses and the like. He translated Krilov into Yiddish. He showed his work to literary experts and even travelled to Warsaw to the writers union. However, his translation was never published.

In general he was distinct, original and not dependent on material things.

He was also known in Zhetl for his great love of the clarinet. He played the clarinet for twenty five years. Up until his death you could hear him play every evening at the marketplace where he lived in his own brick house. He was also known for his love of bicycles.

He was a long time volunteer with the Zhetl fire brigade and knew a lot about Zhetl.

Reb Shaul Kaplinsky of blessed memory

Borukh Kaplinsky (Tel Aviv)

Reb Shaul Kaplinsky was born in 1882 in the village Hantshri near Zhetl. His father leased a mill in the village from the Polish nobleman Stravinsky. He was a learned man and spent all his years learning.

**Reb Shaul Kaplinsky of blessed
memory**

His wife Tcherne Rokhl ran the mill.

Reb Shaul Kaplinsky received the foundations of a Jewish religious education at first in Zhetl with the best teachers, and then in Navaredok at the Yeshiva.

The Jewish enlightenment leanings on the street and the revolutionary struggle had a great influence on his development. Slowly, he began to look at enlightenment books and revolutionary proclamations and, influenced by them, left the Yeshiva when he was 22.

He was hired to work for a rich German Jewish forestry firm called Pupko and worked there until his marriage to Lize Mazovietsky in 1912.

After his wedding he was independent and worked in the forest industry.

With the outbreak of the First World War he lost his assets, which remained stuck in the Nieman and were confiscated by the Germans.

During the First World War

[Page 251]

he played an active role in communal life in Zhetl. He was one of the most active volunteers in the soup kitchen and one of the founders of the Yiddish school in Zhetl. He made great efforts to increase the amount of Hebrew taught in the Yiddish school but when he saw he wasn't making any progress among the Yiddishist teachers, he resigned from the board of the school.

Together with Hertz Leyb Kaplinsky, Feyvl Epshteyn and others, he founded a Hebrew kindergarten in 1927 and then the Tarbut School in 1929.

For ten years he was active in the Tarbut Hebrew School, especially their building campaign.

In 1935 he was chosen as chairman of the Zionist organization in Zhetl. He was also active in all the fund raising for Keren Hayesod (the Jewish Agency) often neglecting his own personal business.

Thanks to his deep Jewish erudition, logic and business sense, he was a sought out arbitrator for complicated controversies in Zhetl.

With the arrival of the Soviets he moved away from communal work and worked in the forest industry.

During the German occupation he was chosen to sit on the Judenrat and dedicated all his energy and devotion to the Zhetl ghetto. During the first slaughter on April 30th, 1942, he was killed at the hands of the criminals.

Reb Mendl Mirsky of blessed memory

Ruven Mirsky (Ramat Hasharon)

My father, Mendl Mirsky, was born in Zhetl in 1881 to Yosl (Yosele Mende's) and Rivka. Like all boys in Zhetl he went to Heder and then to Yeshiva. He got married in 1904.

He was a ritual scribe by profession. His works were exported to America.

During the First World War he was active in the "Poalei Zion" (the Labour Zionist Movement). I remember during those years many Zionist evenings and parties took place in our home. After the First World War he joined the General Zionist Organization and was a passionate supporter of Yitzkhak Greenboym.

His entire life he was very active in Zionist fundraising. Until he immigrated to the Land of Israel in 1937 he was chairman of the Jewish Agency in Zhetl and treasurer for all the Zionist funds. The money raised would be sent from our house to Warsaw. All the young pioneers in Zhetl would come to him before they left to receive permission from the Zionist organization.

He loved the Land of Israel and raised us, his children to love the land.

My father was not a talker. He was not gifted with this talent, so for that reason he became a devoted active volunteer.

In 1937 he immigrated to the Land of Israel and settled in a middle income Moshav, Beit Yania, near Kfar Vitkin. At age 56 he became a pioneer and began to build a farm in the arid area near Kfar Vitkin.

The orchard we received from the community was in bad shape and did not provide any income. My father accepted everything with love. Just the fact he was living in the Land of Israel was a great emotional experience.

The difficult work affected him greatly and he died at the age of 58.

In our town everyone knew my father, but here in the Land of Israel, he was unknown. Only a few individuals came to his funeral. There was not even a death announcement.

His death was just like his life: modest.

His children in the Land of Israel are: Ruven Mirsky, a farmer in Ramat Hasharon, Mordkhai Mirsky, a farmer in Beit Yanai and Khaya Hararit in Ramat Gan.

Reb Avrom Langbart of blessed memory

Yitzkhak Rabinovitch (Haifa)

There were many devoted volunteers in Zhetl who devoted a lot of time to communal work. One of them was Avrom Langbart. He was the son of Aron Langbart who was devoted to the Hovevei Zion and among the first political Zionist activists in Zhetl.

His son Avrom, from an early age was also a Zionist. For many years he was a teacher at the Talmud Torah and later at the Tarbut School. For a while he was the chairman of the Zionist Organization and a long serving member on the Jewish Community Council. He was especially dedicated to the Jewish National Fund.

Reb Avrom Langbart

Every year he would be elected unanimously by the Zionist parties as the representative of the Jewish National Fund in Zhetl. He held this position until the Soviet occupation. I would like to stress that in his work for the Jewish National Fund, Avrom Langbart attempted to avoid friction and with tact and moderation carried out this work. He was held in high esteem by all parties.

[Page 252]

His house was always open for Zionist meetings and consultations. With great faith and pathos he encouraged and awoke members for the sacred work of the Jewish National Fund. He was always so happy when he received a report about a successful campaign.

Avrom Langbart was also considered one of the best speakers in Zhetl. He used this talent to popularize Zionist thought in Zhetl.

Our Jewish National Fund committee was the first in Poland to organize a yearly bazar for the Jewish National Fund during the interim days of Passover. The bazar raised a lot of money. This accomplishment was publicized by the Warsaw JNF central office and circulated to all local committees. I believe the great success of the bazars in Zhetl is largely due to the efforts of Avrom Langbart. His wife Pesieh helped him a lot in his communal work.

Reb Avrom Gal of blessed memory

Sarah Gal (Jerusalem)

Avrom Nakhman Gal was born in Zhetl in 1884. He studied at the Slonim Yeshiva and married Mertche Levit in Zhetl. He later moved to Russia. Until the revolution he lived with his family Yevpotoria and worked there as a teacher.

In Yevpotoria he was known as a communal activist. Before the Bolsheviks he worked as a manager of all the kitchens in Yevpotoria.

He was arrested for his Zionist activity. When he was freed due to his Polish citizenship, he returned home. Despite his poor health, it was not hard for him to continue his communal work. He sat on the board of the Yiddish school until it fell under the influence of the Bundists.

He was the founder of the Interest Free Loan Society in Zhetl. Every person in need received help and he took joy in their happiness. He lived among the masses and died among the masses.

Noyekh Mikulitzky of blessed memory

Khaim Lusky (Natanya)

Noyekh Mikulitzky was born in 1901 to Yitzkhak and Esther – Hinde. His father died when he was four years old and he moved with his mother and sister Peshe to Zhetl.

Noyekh went to Heder and Yeshiva. In 1920 he left the Yeshiva and began to study secular subjects, particularly Hebrew literature. In the years 1922–23 he began to give private lessons in the spirit of the modern Hebrew schools which did not yet exist in Zhetl.

Noyekh was one of the most active volunteers in in "Hechalutz Hatzair" (The Young Pioneer), "Hechalutz", the General Zionist Organization, The Jewish National Fund and others. Between the years 1924–1929 there was not any Zionist work in Zhetl that Noyekh was not involved with. The pioneers of the Fourth Aliya particularly remember his activity.

His room was the centre of Zionist activity in Zhetl. This is where all the appeals, placards and plans were made for all the public Zionist events. Noyekh was also one of the founders of the "Tarbut" School in Zhetl. Besides Zionist activity he devoted a lot of time to social work. He spent many years as secretary of the Society to Spend the Night With the Sick.

In 1929 he moved to Novoyelnie where he continued his work until 1932, then returned to Zhetl. Noyekh then joined the Revisionist Movement where he remained active until 1935 when he married and moved to Lida.

The Second World War brought him to Zhetl. During the first slaughter he was among those allowed to remain alive but he refused to be separated from his family and was killed with them.

Yehuda Lusky of blessed memory

Khaim Lusky (Natanya)

Yehuda Lusky, or as we called him in Zhetl Idl, was born in July 1911 to Pinkhas and Esther – Hinde Lusky. He studied in Heder, at the Talmud Torah and in Yeshiva.

In 1928 he left the Yeshiva to help his sick parents.

In 1929 he joined Betar, the youth movement of the Revisionists.

As long as the Revisionists were part of the Zionist organization, Idl was active in their work for the National fund.

When the Germans entered Zhetl he was elected to the Judenrat and together with Alter Dvoretzky helped the partisans who left for the forests.

Before the first slaughter when they arrested the Judenrat, Alter Dvoretzky consulted with Idl about escaping to the forest. However, they decided to remain in Zhetl and not cause panic among the population.

[Page 253]

That same night when they came to arrest them, Alter Dvoretzky managed to escape and Idl tried to hide at home, however, with the help of other members of the Judenrat, the Germans found him and arrested him. He was killed after he was tortured for a long time.

Yehoshua Ovseyevitch of blessed memory

Moishe Man (Buenos Aires)

Yehoshua Ovseyevitch, or as he we called him, Shikeh Ovseyevitch, was born in Zhetl in 1892. His father Nekhemiah was a well dressed Jew with a trimmed beard and was a strict and honest man. His mother Sokheh was a smart and serious woman. Besides Shikeh there were three more brothers and one sister in the family.

All the children received a Jewish religious education. The oldest son, Yitzkhak, was stunned in the North American army in the years 1914–1918 by an artillery shot. Nevertheless, he returned to Zhetl and sat studying day and night in the House of Study.

Yehoshua did not become a ritual scribe like many young men in Zhetl from good homes at that time. He moved to a wealthy rural Jewish community where he worked as a teacher. In those days he joined the Bund and worked with Beynish Mikhalevitch.

I personally do not remember him as a member of the Bund, but rather a sympathizer.

Right after the First World War he was one of the founders of the Yiddish School in Zhetl.

The Yiddish school in Zhetl experienced difficult years: they did not have a program or a financial base and fought for their existence.

Yehoshua devoted himself to help the school through these difficult times. As a member of the Immigration Society which helped send immigrants to America, he often had to be in Warsaw. While in Warsaw, Shike would try to seek help for the school.

In 1939, when I was already in Argentina I received a letter from him. He wrote to me. He said as my brother in law, he was satisfied with his wife's writing to us, but now, he was writing to me as a delegate of the Yiddish school. He pointed out that since the majority of the children in the school came from poor families it would be only fair for Zhetl Jews in Argentina to support it.

Although Shikeh was a non believer and a socialist his whole life, when his mother died he said the mourners prayer three times a day.

He was killed with all the Zhetl martyrs in 1942.

Alter Gertzovsky of blessed memory

Shmuel Mnuskin (Kfar Saba)

Alter Gertzovsky held an important place in Zhetl's Jewish communal life. We used to call him Alter Mordkhai Kikke's.

His father was a poor bookbinder. There was always great poverty in their home since bookbinding was not a profitable business. The poverty greatly influenced Alter's view of the world.

He participated actively in the revolutions of 1905 and 1917. He was one of the first builders of the Zhetl Professional Union, the drama club and the Yiddish School. When they had to raise money for an important cause, Alter was influential: when someone needed help, they turned to Alter. Not because Alter could give money, rather because he could arrange for it. He was connected to all the charitable institutions like the Interest Free Loan Society, the Popular Bank and others where everyone knew, if Alter was the intermediary, they would not be refused.

He was of medium height, thin with a pale face, beautiful eyes and always smiling. This is how I remember him. When he was around, everything seemed happier. He infected everyone with his humour.

Alter brought pleasure to so many of Zhetl's workers and craftsmen when he performed on stage. He always played comic roles. His jokes and witticisms had everyone rolling with laughter. He was filled with original ideas and plans.

Motl Man of blessed memory

Moishe Man

After the death of Avrom Patzovsky, my brother Motl Man took over the supervision of the town documents which remained in our house. When immigration increased abroad at the beginning of the 20th century, Motl helped the wandering Jews who did not have documentation. Motl made them documents risking his own life.

[Page 254]

He helped many small town Jews during the First World War. Being the chief of the fire brigade he convinced the Bolsheviks, and later the Poles, not to take the firefighters into the army so they could remain and serve the city. For this purpose he went to Slonim many times with Mendl Solomiyansky through dangerous and risky roads. However, he could not include his own brother, Khaim Hershl, in the fire brigade and he had to run away to Lithuania to avoid military service.

He was a person who lived in great poverty but he was always ready to help another however possible. He knew the entire code of law by heart, better than any average lawyer, however he did not attempt to use this to improve his financial situation.

In 1925 he was elected as magistrate in the township. At the time there was no magistrate in Zhetl. The Christians could not accept the idea that a Jew would be the head of the town. Therefore, with the help of the postmaster, Regiyevich, they denounced him to the Polish authorities.

Motl was immediately arrested and one day later sent to prison in Slonim. Thanks to a huge outcry by the population and intervention, Motl was later freed on bail. Later at his trial he was acquitted. This took a toll on his health and he died on the second day of Passover, 1928.

The entire town attended his funeral. He was eulogized as a devoted, beloved communal activist. Zhetl honoured his memory for a long time.

Reb Yakov Obershteyn of blessed memory

Moishe Man (Buenos Aires)

When remembering the activists in Zhetl it is necessary to mention Reb Yakov Obershteyn, or as we used to call him Yenkl Avrom Avigdor's. He was a fine man, always smiling and with a warm Jewish heart.

Who does not remember, on a winter Sabbath after evening prayers, how he would go onto to the Bimah (where prayers were led from), bang the table and with his hoarse voice, in a traditional religious melody sing a sad psalm. He had the tenure as the manager of Psalm Society at the new House of Study.

I would like to present a few facts about his activities.

For a long time the new House of Study did not pay their insurance as they did not have the funds. During the second fire in 1935 the new House of Study burned down. Obviously, everyone in town was sure they would not be able to rebuild.

That is when Yenkl Obershteyn appeared and announced he had paid the insurance from his own pocket, but nobody knew.

At that time I was living in Slonim and was very friendly with the lecturers at the insurance company and I intervened on this issue. However, since Yenkl Obershteyn paid the insurance in his own name, I suggested they form a building committee to rebuild the House of Study and he should receive the entire amount, I don't remember exactly how much, but I think it was 18,000 zloty.

In 1938, before I left for Argentina I returned home to say goodbye. I went to pray that evening in the newly rebuilt House of study and said goodbye to that place forever.

The last years before the Second World War, anti Semitism was raging. This had a particularly difficult impact on those who bought to resell, those who travelled to the villages for business and the wagon drivers. If one of them would have an accident and lose a horse there was not enough money to buy another horse and the family would be left without bread.

Yenkl Avrom Avigdor's created a type of insurance fund. Every Jew who had a horse paid 1 zloty a week. This served as a fund to purchase a new horse.

One had to live in other towns then in order to appreciate the importance of this fund.

Yenkl Obershteyn was also one of the most active volunteers of the Society to Aid the Sick, one of the most important institutions in the poor small Jewish towns in Poland at that time.

I would also like to mention his life partner Peshke Sokhe's. She was a lovely woman. Her house was almost like a guest house. In the last years when they lived a bit better it was understood that anyone who was hungry, would get something to eat.

[Page 255]

In My Father's House

by Binyomin Kaplinsky of blessed memory

Translated by Janie Respitz

My father came from Smorgon. However he spent little time in his hometown. He spent his youth at the Yeshiva in Bialystok.

He came to Zhetl in 1898 as an administrative deportee. It did not take long before all the young workers in town were inspired by him to join the revolutionary movement.

My father was one of the first pioneers of the "Bund". He joined the movement in the 1890s while he was studying at the Yeshiva where he received his rabbinic ordination.

He was arrested for the first time in Bialystok in 1897. Later he sat in a Warsaw prison where, by the way, he learned a lot.

Binyomin Kaplinsky of blessed memory

He was also sent to Eastern Siberia for 5 years. During the Russian – Japanese war he was sent to Archangel then freed from there in 1905 during the revolution.

In 1907, after the suppression of the revolutionary wave, he worked in Berditchev where he was sentenced to a year in jail and sat out his punishment in Kiev. Later, he worked in other cities including Vilna.

Educated in a Yeshiva he achieved a lot through self education. Besides Russian he knew German and a little French and English. He had a lot of information about natural science and geography. Teachers who would meet him were amazed by his knowledge.

My father is a man who hates hypocrisy and loves the truth. He was known for this in our town and in the surrounding region. I sometimes have a strong desire to be as rectilinear and sincere in relations with people as he is.

My father is not religious and never goes to pray at the House of Study. There were years in town when he was the only one who did not go to pray on Yom Kippur? Four or five years ago, older and younger people gathered around me to ask if: does your father fast on Yom Kippur?

Since the war my father is not active in the movement although he is still interested. He subscribes to and regularly reads the party press, however the burden of our home and the present conditions do not allow him. He regrets this very much. He said the lion has remained but his nails have been filed so he cannot scratch.

Until the war my father was a teacher. He would give "Urok" the Russian word for lessons. In 1912–1913 he was a teacher at the Talmud Torah.

My father is exceptionally reserved and very modest. He hates outward decorations in his personal and communal life.

During the German occupation, my father was practically the only one who knew German. Since his Russian classes were cancelled he began writing requests in German.

The surrounding Christians knew him as an honest man and he quickly became known in the region. I remember how our house was always filled with farmers. They would often spend the night awaiting their turn.

The first request my father wrote was an accusation by a farmer of a German gendarme who illegally took his cow. My father would also write letters for women to their husbands who were in prison camps in Germany and those in exile mainly in the sawmills in Haynavke.

The farmers and their wives did not pay my father for his writing. However they would bring, hidden in their bosom, a few pounds of rye, a few eggs, or grain. All of this was better than money. Someone else may have made a lot of money from this however my father did not want to build his fortune on someone else's misfortune and was satisfied with whatever they gave him.

During the German occupation the Jewish soup kitchen was founded in Zhetl. This was one of the most important institutions in town. My father was one of the most active volunteers and devoted a lot of his free time to the kitchen.

There were tours of duty in the kitchen to cook and distribute the food. By the way, there was a rule that the food had to be eaten there.

The suffering in town in those years was indescribable. There were times the kitchen handed out 700 – 800 meals a day.

[Page 256]

The meetings of the kitchen volunteers would take place at our house. The board would meet every Saturday.

The volunteers, except for a few married men, were young boys and girls who would fill our home with laughter. Every year they would have a party for the volunteers where they would have fun all night.

The culminating point of the kitchen was in 1916–1917. Later, many of the volunteers left and many of the needy returned to their hometowns.

I would often go with my father to observe the facility where he introduced a novelty – to cook on steam. First they would heat stones and then pour water to create steam.

There was order in the kitchen and the apparatus worked exceedingly well.

After the evacuation of the Germans we experienced years of hunger and unrest. I was 7 when the Poles entered Zhetl for the first time. Everyone ran to see the new rulers. (Poland – a state, socks – a garment, and Zhetl – a catastrophe).

The Poles came to us in search of weapons, but in actuality, they took whatever they could. People would say they looked in dressers and drawers for hidden Bolsheviks.

My father would often oppose the arbitrariness. Once he was told the soldiers wanted to take a wagon full of grain which was designated for the soup kitchen. My father ran and opposed them. He told them the grain was for the poor and he will absolutely not give it away. He risked his life with this resistance because according to the Poles, a person's life was worthless, but he did it anyway. They did not touch the grain.

The writing of requests which was his main source of income during the German occupation came to nought when the power switched hands. The material situation in our home was not the best. Father was hired as a secretary at city hall.

The boycott of Jewish workers and employees was not apparent to us at the time. Here in Zhetl for example, there was a Jewish letter carrier, the mayor was a Christian from our town. The authorities in city hall were from the military led by a commandant who was in principle a drunk and a trouble maker.

My father did not hold this position in city hall for long. City hall was soon liquidated and my father returned to giving private lessons, mainly Polish language. Later, in 1923–1924 when the Popular Bank was founded, my father worked there as a bookkeeper. He worked in the bank for 5–6 years. Then he worked as an employee at the sawmill.

In 1923 we bought our own home with original conditions. My father's brother in America wrote and told us to buy a house and he would help. Our luck was favourable. An inexpensive house presented itself for $500 and the sale took place. Good friends were persuaded and lent us money. My uncle's money never came through. We were left with a house which until today, 11 years after the purchase we still owe almost the entire amount.

My mother, who is very skillful, runs around for days borrowing from the Interest Free Loan Society, because if we would borrow the money at interest we would not sustain ourselves for a month.

No one in our house smokes. We spend the bare minimum on clothes. I don't remember the last time my father had a suit made. Our material situation was such that we managed to sustain ourselves. If it would have been possible to save on rent for 10 years, the debt on our house would have been paid off long ago.

My father ran an account of the household. Every expense, even the smallest was recorded. Every expenditure was weighed and measured.

My mother was exceptionally overworked. She would spend days and weeks running around town borrowing from the Interest Free Loan Society. She borrowed from shopkeepers who could only loan for a few days so she had to change loans often. She would often return home crying, troubled and humiliated from asking for favours. Sometimes she would cry so hard and talk about selling the house to cover our debts. There were times when she fell in the street running over the footbridges to get a loan.

On more than one occasion I wanted to run away from home seeing the anguish and suffering of my mother when she would return home exhausted, worn out and crying bitterly. I choked on every morsel of food I ate at home.

There are homes where the parents argue, but not in ours. Only my mother often reproached my father for his exaggerated honesty. I will always side with my father.

According to "My Life's Description" – Zhetl, June 1934.

[Page 257]

Niameh Kaplinsky the Bundist and Cultural Activist

by Rishe Kaplinsky – Kovensky (Ramat – Gan)

Translated by Janie Respitz

The survivors from Zhetl remember Niameh Kaplinsky the Yiddish cultural activist and freedom fighter whose life ended in Soviet exile.

His name embodies the period of the awakening of Yiddish cultural and social life in the small Jewish towns. Already at the age of 14 he began his cultural and socialist activity. At that young age he was arrested for the first time for organizing the May Day demonstrations for the "Bund".

Niameh graduated from the Folkshul (The Yiddish elementary school). As it was not possible for him to continue his studies he continued to learn and read on his own. This is how he obtained a secular education, studied foreign languages, and studied the works of Marx and Engels and other social science books.

With his bubbly personality, he threw himself into political and communal work. He was one of the founders and leaders of "Tsukunft" (Future) and later the Socialist Children's Society "SKIF". Niameh later organized the "Cultural League" as well as the library where he worked for many years as librarian. As director of the library he had a great influence on the readers with whom he would have long discussions about the books they read.

The young Niameh knew nothing about a private life. He devoted his time and energy to the Bund and cultural communal work: he led groups, worked in "SKIF", in "Tsukungt", in the "Cultural League" and gave lectures to members of the party. He also gave lessons to young illiterates who he taught to read and write.

Besides all this he was busy with cultural work, collected folklore for "YIVO" and was rewarded by them for his work: "The Biography of a Youth".

After graduating from the Folkshul, Niameh threw himself into working for the school with heart and soul. He worked for many years as the school secretary and was a member of the board of directors until the police noticed his activities and took away his moral certificate. They never discovered any illegal acts. They just took away his right to be secretary of the school.

However, Niameh was not lacking communal work. He was one of the organizers of the Professional Union which was also involved in cultural work.

Niameh was the main speaker at the May 1st gathering of Jewish and Polish Workers. There was not any political or cultural communal work that Niameh refused to do. He carried and sold the newspaper "Di Folkstzeytung" and the Polish Workers newspaper which he distributed to the surrounding villages. He would often go in rain and snow and enjoyed every success in recruiting a new subscriber for the socialist press.

Every May 1st they would search our home and after the search Niameh had to report to the police twice a day.

In 1937, after the 1st of May, 17 Bundists and communists were arrested including Niameh. The locales of the "Bund" and the Professional Union were closed. Some of the members were released after a short time, but Niameh and one of his friends remained in jail. They were put on trial for anti – state agitation. Disregarding all the efforts of the prosecutor, the court did not find any proof of illegal activity and freed the accused…the prosecutor appealed the verdict and Niameh remained in jail. Thanks to the defense by the lawyer Emanuel Sherer, the Court of Appeal in Vilna released him.

While Niameh sat in jail, his young friends tried to continue his cultural, political and Bundist activities. They contacted the central committee of the party and the Bundist teacher Miss Goldman and consulted with her on how to continue with this work in Zhetl.

After, when the Zhetl police declared the "Bund" illegal, the illegal organization was created. The young members of "SKIF" divided into groups of three and ten. Each was responsible for three members which he would have to bring to the circles.

[Page 258]

They would prepare discussions according to instructions from the central committee. They would gather in private homes, read the papers together and discuss political questions. Every week another member would prepare a political review of the week.

After 3 months Niameh was released from jail and disregarding his weak health, returned to his work. He would regularly come to the decided meeting place which was different every time. Once at Rivka Dzhenchelsky's, another time at Khane Orlinsky's or at Asneh Gertzovsky's in the attic. In all these places they would hold clandestine meetings, organize lectures with the participation of guests like Zheleznikov and Abrashe Blum.

From 1937 until the outbreak of the war the "Bund" in Zhetl was illegal, but the work led by Niameh was not interrupted. They illegally carried out elections to the Congress Against Anti–Semitism which was later banned by the Polish authorities. Niameh was elected as the delegate from Zhetl.

When the war broke out Bundist activity ceased in Zhetl. Niameh received work under Soviet rule in the municipal hospital situated in the old palace. The Jewish population needed him to continue to participate in its communal and cultural life. However, the new authorities persecuted and arrested Bundists as criminals. None of the local communists denounced Niameh because officially the Bund did not exist and there was not one ideological opponent who did not love Niameh.

The members of the newly created town council consulted with Niameh on various problems. Our father asked him not to mix into Jewish communal issues until the situation stabilized. The truth is, Niameh no longer was involved in broader communal activity as all his energy was focused on his new position at the hospital. He worked there as a bookkeeper but actually managed the whole administration.

This lasted until March 5th 1940 when the militia entered our home searching for weapons. The search was short. Of course they did not find weapons. But, they did arrest Niameh and he never returned home.

As he was arrested in the Zhetl Township, the militia, who were Niameh's acquaintances, permitted those close to him to visit, even late in the evening. One day, Niameh had a bad toothache. They permitted Ella Kuperman to come to him in the middle of the night to ease his pain. He told her they wanted to force him to sign that he was a counter revolutionary and he was never persecuted by the Polish authorities. He responded to them that he would never sign such a document.

Family members ran to "RAIKOM" (the Organization of the Communist Party in Soviet Union). The doctors and other staff who worked with him also made an effort. Ana Shapiro, Christians and communists offered to pledge for him and asked for his release. Nothing helped. After seven days they came to our house and ordered us to pack up all our things in an hour. They deported us to Russia.

In Russia, at the beginning of May 1941 we received the first postcard from Sukhobezvadne, Gorky region. He wrote that he loves onions and biscuits and asked us to send clothes because his were torn. In addition he mentioned he was learning a new trade, braiding slippers, in exchange for his old specialty, clearing snow off the planks. On one page of the letter he wrote the number of the paragraph which dealt with his accusation. This paragraph spoke about political activity against the Soviet regime and he was sentenced to 5 years in a camp.

After receiving such a letter we began to send him parcels including the last things we had knowing he was weak and would not be able to handle the conditions in the camp.

Finally he wrote: "Hold up dear brother and sister, I am making an effort to live". These were his last words.

After amnesty was granted to the Poles who were arrested we waited for his release. Many arrested Poles returned from the camps and exile. Niameh did not return.

We continued to write demanding his return. After many appeals over a period of two years we received a short notice: "Died May 12th 1941" and 60 ruble for the food and items sent.

This is how a person died, who never thought about himself, did not have a personal life as he lived for society. He believed strongly in the ideal of justice and socialism and deeply loved the Jewish people and Jewish traditions.

Let these memories serve as a monument on his unknown grave.

[Page 259]

Neighbours, Friends, Teachers and Acquaintances

by Yitzkhak Epshteyn (Kfar Neter)

Translated by Janie Respitz

Gitl Leyzer the Glazier

Leyzer the glazier's street was specifically a Jewish street. If one would get lost there, he would have to first of all, pass through Vevke Alpert's fence and almost always meet his friend Dovid Senderovsky carrying on a dispute about socialism, democracy or the social revolution. Who knows how long these disputes would have lasted if Vevke's wife, Khaya Sorke the seamstress had not come out onto the porch to put an end to the revolution.

Continuing on our way we would pass Areh the carpenter's house. A bit further on is where Shaul the teacher lived. A bunch of little ones sat around his table and their lesson filled the street with song. Across from Shaul the teacher was Leyzer Elye's house. The head of the Zhetl Yeshiva lived there.

When the head of the Yeshiva would cross the street on his way to pray at the middle House of Study, where the manager was Avrom Moishe Kravietz, all the residents on the street would tremble. His tall body and fiery black eyes made a huge impression on me as a child. I looked at the head of the Yeshiva as if he was the high priest going to perform prayers at the Zhetl "Holy Temple".

At the end of the street in the shadows of the trees, the well bubbled up. Here, Tcherne's River, the Zhetleke, divided this street from the rest of the world.

On the other side of the river there was a different world, non–Jewish. From a distance we could see the house of the Polish priest.

Here at the border between the Jewish and Gentile worlds, at the river where frogs would constantly croak, stood the small hut belonging to Leyzer the glazier and his wife Gitl of blessed memory.

Threads of love connected our house to Gitl's house. My father Mayrim, of blessed memory always said that Gitl is the truest, cleanest soul with no match in the world. Father would often go to Gitl's house to hear kind words.

Saturday morning, a winter day. Outside is snowing and stormy. My father said to me:

"Come my child, let's go to Gitl".

The snow is scraping under our feet. The street was silent. The trees are covered in snow. We fall into Gitl's house and love and warmth embrace us.

Good Shabbes! Good Shabbes!

Gitl's face is glowing with joy.

"Leyzer! Mayrim is here" she says to her husband who is standing behind the oven.

Leyzer sits at the table and begins to tell us about his experiences in various villages where he made windows for the farmers.

"In the village Danilovitch, the bridge was broken and my horse almost broke his foot. In Krutchilovitch, the Gentile Vasilyuk gave me a sack of potatoes for glazing half a window. Dear Gentiles! When they see me from a distance they shout: "Our Leyzerko". But he told us the Gentiles in Zashetch, were bandits. "They even took away the footbridge so I would not be able to cross the river".

Gitl brought tripe and dumplings with goose fat to the table. My father tasted a dumpling and closes his eyes from sheer delight.

"This tastes like heaven" he said, "it simply melts in your mouth".

Leyzer the Glazier's Wife Gitl Recounts

Gitl's face beams with joy. She and my father have been friends since childhood. Gitl would tell me how my father would play in her parent's yard.

Once, on a market day, a wild ox got loose from his rope. There was panic among the Jews and Gentiles. People began to run over and under the wagons. The ox grabbed a Gentile with his horns, lifted him up high and threw him on the ground. Lifted him again and again, thump on the ground, until the Gentile turned into a pile of bones with his entrails pouring onto the ox's horns as he ran from Yoshek Leyzhe's house to Khienke Malka Motke's, passing Avrom Moishe Kravietz's, Khane – Gatshikhe's, until Berl Khadzelaner's and Velvl Hinde Mayrim's house.

There was a terrifying stampede in Zhetl. Jews were shouting: "Here O Israel!"

Christians were crossing themselves. Candles were lit at Yosef Zashetcher's, and people began to recite psalms in the House of Study…

[Page 260]

But the wild ox kept on running with the bloodied head and ran into Gitl's yard, where my father was playing in the sand. Gitl ran out and started to shout:

"God in Heaven, show us a miracle: let the virtues of our Mother Rachel protect us!"

And a miracle happened: the wild ox, running at great speed, jumped over my father and ran away…

Father looked out the window.

"Soon" said Leyzer, "The frost will end. It is almost the end of the month of Shvat. In Adar the sun is higher and after the stork will come".

A calmness covered the house surrounded by a world covered in snow. And here, at the banks of the little river, stands a small house, where Gitl's warm, humane heart beats.

Suddenly Gitl sighs. It has been a long time since she had received a letter from her son Hirshl, who is in Russia. God knows if he is alive. Leyzer also sighs.

"The Gentile gets smarter" he says to my father. "One day when I arrived in Pagier, Seredo the farmer said to me: "I will no longer have you make my windows for my panes. I will travel to Baranovitch and buy ready made panes.

Shadows creep into the house. The Sabbath is almost over. My father also sighs, as the Sabbath is departing…tomorrow he must travel to Zheludok to buy leather.

The shadows grow larger…you can hear a quiet murmur from the oven. Gitl recites "God of Abraham".

Vevke Khaye Sorke's Husband

Vevke Khaye Sorke's of blessed memory, or Vevke Alpert of blessed memory, was one of the freedom fighters from the fifth year (Translator's note: the fifth year is 1905). His wife, Khaye Sorke the seamstress would sit at her sewing machine day and night cutting clothes for the village women in Moldutch, Zazhetche, and Pagier. Vevke would run the household as Khaye Sorke never had enough time.

In his free time Vevke would write Mezuzahs with his friend Hirshl Velvl while they argued about socialism. On the Sabbath in the summer Vevke would sit on his porch and read the "Folkstzeytung" out loud. The neighbours would stand near his porch and listen to the news as Vevke explained everything calmly and slowly.

In the summer, together with Hirshl Velvl, Vevke would rent an orchard from the nobleman Bukhvaytz in Yanovtchizne. They would place a large covered wagon in the middle of the orchard and when the apples and pears were ripe they would sleep in the orchard. Later, Vevke took a new partner, Yoshe Kalmen's (Yosef Sovitsky).

On the Sabbath, guests would come visit the orchard and taste the various fruits.

In his free time, Vevke's old friends would come to visit and the wagon would ring out with songs such as this:

> Oh, good friend, when I die
> Carry the red flag to my grave…
> The red flag with red colours
> Sprayed with the blood of the working man.
> And then in my grave I will listen
> And hear my song – my freedom song
> And tears will flow
> For the enslaved Christian and Jew.

This is how the summertime passed in the fruit garden of Vevke Khaye Sorke's.

The House of Leybe Kaplinsky

Leybe Kaplinsky of blessed memory was the biggest lumber dealer in Zhetl. He came from an old family of lumber dealers from Dershave. His house was on Novoredker Street, surrounded by a beautiful painted fence. Wealth and magnificence oozed from his house.

There were always guests sitting in his large reception room, especially lumber people who all had the mystery of pine trees floating on their faces with happy worry free smiles.

The men from the fragrant forests, where the peasants would cut down pine trees would be transported by Berl the tiller of blessed memory. Shaul Kaplinsky of blessed memory, Khaim Hershl Shatzkes of blessed memory, Leyzer of blessed memory, Volfe Frfl of blessed memory, Motke Belitzki of blessed memory, Yisroel Yenkl Kaplinsky of blessed memory as well as Shmuel Shvedsky of blessed memory, who was not a lumber merchant, but the head of the Zhetl fire brigade, sat, played cards, ate goose fat cracklings and drank tea.

My father, Mayrim Epshteyn of blessed memory and the chief of the Zhetl fire brigade and former fighter in the fifth year sat with his friends from the fifth year, with Shvedsky, Yosef Mushes and Grisha Kheves.

In the fifth year a strike broke out among the Gentiles in Yatzuk and they refused to take the cut trees to the sawmill. My father then went to Yatzuki, penetrated the strikers, and from then on the peasants brought the cut trees regularly

[Page 261]

Leybl Kaplinsky requested we sing:

"There in the forest daisies grow…

You are looking for daisies and I found the most beautiful daisy in the forest".

As a child I would often go to the Kaplinsky's to play. Leybe Kaplinsky would grab me onto his lap, pinch my cheeks and say with greatness:

"You will be a hero, just like your father!"

I would jump off excited and run to the street. Here, another world was revealed to me. There were small poor houses. This is where Hirshl Haydukovsky, Borukh the glazier and Molokhvsky and their families lived.

I ran further. Here was the house of Moishe Izik Lusky, here were the gypsies and beside the gypsies was the house of Alter Zamotchik, the grain dealer. And here was our garden, the tannery and Lusky's house.

This was the end of Novoredker Street. From a distance you can see the white birch trees which extend the length of Kvatere until Novoredok. The story told in Zhetl was the birch trees were planted by the Czarina Catherine the Great when she took over Poland.

The road with the birch trees goes all the way from Zhetl to St. Petersburg…

I ran to the birch trees with wild joy. The road stretches very far. From one side the meadows grow green and on the other side, the Zhelon forest.

My soul struggles with the infinite distances, to the wild force of nature, and instinctively I sing:

"Volga Volga"!

As I run along the road I see non Jewish wagons taking wooden boards to Kaplinsky's sawmill. The peasants remove their hats and say good morning, and one says to the other: "do you know who that is? He is Mayrim Epshteyn's son, the friend of our merchant Kaplinsky.

I run into the Kurpesh forest and pick the blue spring flowers. Who could have imagined then that at the spot where I felt so happy there would be a mass grave where my dear mother of blessed memory and other Zhetl martyrs would find their cruel death.

Our Neighbours

Khoniye the butcher was our neighbour. He and his brother Avrom Senderovsky were Hasidim who would travel to the Slonim Rebbe. Their father, the old Meir Senderovsky would always receive the Rebbe when he came to Zhetl.

Friday nights you could hear Meir's voice throughout the yard singing Hasidic melodies.

Khoniye would spend the entire week travelling through the villages buying calves and sheep and bringing them to his brother Avrom.

On Saturdays, after the evening prayers, Khoniye would run to the new House of Study, stand in a corner and recite psalms. This is how he would pour his heart out, asking God for a good new week.

Yosl the bricklayer (Lozovsky) was highly respected on the noble estates for his fine work. He and his wife Mayteh live with us in our house.

Across from us was the house of Moishe Tentzer. When Moishe Tentzer would leave his house to go to the House of Study, he appeared to me as the High Priest in the holy Temple. He walked so majestically and kingly.

The second house was the bakery and it belonged to Moishe the tinsmith. He used to be a tinsmith, but later became a baker. That's why they called him "Moishe the tinsmith".

The third house across from our yard belonged to Eleh the carpenter (Itzkovitch) and his wife Mushka. Before the war, Eleh Itzkovitch left for the Land of Israel and settled in Petach Tikva.

My Grandfather's House

My grandfather's house, or as well called it "The Brick House" was across from the Zhetl Church in the half circle of the walls which surrounded the marketplace.

My grandfather, Feyvl Rabinovitch, of blessed memory, known in Zhetl as Feyvl from Skidel was a pious Jew who served God with his entire soul.

During the first German occupation when most of Zhetl's Jews were starving, my grandfather was the only one who supported the poor population.

My grandfather would come to us to collect food. In the middle of the night he would knock on the door of a house in need and quietly place a bit of sugar and bread on the table, wish the sick a full recovery and as he left, warned them not to tell anyone about his visit.

[Page 262]

At that time, Shaul the religious teacher and his family lived in dire need. Thanks to my grandfather they managed to get through this difficult time.

My grandfather's older son (not counting those who lived in other cities) was a socialist. His friends were: Meylekh Shvedsky, Borekh Dvoretsky, Yisroel Ber Rabinovitch, Shloime Khaim Vernikovsky. His younger son, Efraim was a Zionist and his friends were: Artchik Goldshteyn, and Shmuel Izraelit.

My grandfather's eldest daughter, my mother Feygl of blessed memory, was the most educated and well read in the family. My mother was able to quote excerpts from the Russian classical writers such as: Tolstoy, Lermontov, Pushkin, Gorky, Chekhov and others. My mother's friends were: the white Peshke, Aneh Shapiro, Geleh Komai, Merl Izraelit who now lives in Israel and Etl Ovseyevitch.

In 1905 Zhetl revolutionaries threw a bomb at the Czar's train between stations in Navaliyenie and Yatzuki. As a result of this assassination attempt, grandfather's eldest son Leyzer of blessed memory had to run away to America.

His younger son, Itche, who was active in the revolutionary movement in Zhetl and Grodno shot two Czarist ministers in broad daylight in St. Petersburg. He escaped and went into hiding. He was eventually caught and was sentenced to death by hanging. His sentence was carried out in St. Petersburg on June 6th, 1906.

Itche's tragic death greatly affected my grandfather. His tall lanky body became bent and his beard, completely grey.

In the evenings my grandfather would study a page of Talmud with Moishe Tentzer of blessed memory and Vevl Hinde Mayrim's of blessed memory. When they finished my grandmother, Frumeh Simeh would serve them hot tea with a sugar cube.

Two large white cats would always lie at grandfather's feet and when he finished learning he would pour them a plate of soup with crumbled pieces of bread. He would pet the cats and say: "Take pity on God's creatures".

As a child, grandfather's youngest son, Hirshl of blessed memory, would come over and call me over to my grandfather to hear him recite a biblical chapter. A new world would be revealed to me when I would sit at grandfather's table and listen to the passages from his mouth. A world of rabbis from the first two centuries C.E. walking in the gardens of the Creator.

When grandfather came to us and entered the orchard, a holiness swept over the garden. My mother would ask me to pick a few

pears and grandfather would make a blessing. All the kids would stand and look at grandfather in awe not able to say a word.

Our House

Our house was on Novoredker Street, the house of Mayrim Epshteyn (or Mayrim Mashke's).

We had a museum of albums, photographs and pictures of revolutionaries from the fifth year. As a child I would spend hours looking at these pictures.

This one is my uncle looking down at me, Itche Rabinovitch who was killed on the gallows in St. Petersburg. In the picture his cape is thrown over his shoulder. A second picture: Dovid Nodlshteyn, one of those involved in the attempted assassination on the train in Novoliyenie.

A third picture: the fire brigade in Zhetl. The founders of the brigade in 1902: my father, Borukh Mirsky, Shmuel Shvedsky and Khabash are standing beside the Zhetl shed wearing shiny helmets on their heads. On the left is the Zhetl orchestra with Avromtche the blacksmith (Avrom Busel) at the head.

The fourth picture: the leader of the Zhetl Poalei Zion: Shloime Khaim Verenikovsky.

The regular visitors to our home that I remember from my childhood were:

Borukh Mirsky of blessed memory, one of the founders of the Zhetl fire brigade. He lived on Slonimer Street. His orchard was the nicest in all of Zhetl. He would always tell my father how many more trees he needed to plant and how well the orchard was blooming that year.

Yosef Lusky of blessed memory (or Yoshke Leyzhe's) would come often to my father. They would go for walks and reminisce about their childhood.

Shaul Kaplinsky of blessed memory would also come to us. He would go with my father to Mendl the scribe of blessed memory (Mendl Mirsky) where they would organize events for the Jewish Agency and the Jewish National Fund. It was established that every Chanukah an evening for the Jewish Agency would take place at Mendl Mirsky's house, and on Purim, an evening for the Jewish National Fund at our house.

My father loved nature. His goal was to educate others to love nature as well. He loved to go out walking on a cold winter night when the snow was crisp under his feet and the moon shone in the cold sky. He would drag boys from their homes and go sliding on the lake, and then go marching through the snowy fields. Father would recount his memories from his heroic youth, from the fifth year. We would listen to these stories with bated breath.

[Page 263]

Working the land was foreign to the Jewish population of Zhetl. Plowing, cutting, sowing and planting was the work of the gentiles. However, my father was a different type of Jew.

At the end of Novoredker Street, we had a small field surrounded by Gypsy huts. Father put all his energy and love of nature into that field. At dawn he could be seen going with his scythe to the meadow and driving a wagon of hay. Just before his death he managed to plant a few fruit trees.

In time Zhetl educated a few to work the land like Kalmen Sovitsky, Zalmen Grin, Mordkhai Alpert, Zalmen Shepshelevitch and Leybke Lusky.

However, father got sick and after a few years of being ill he died on a quiet Friday afternoon. Avrom Ivenitsky said a few words at his open grave.

This is how the life of Mayrim Epshteyn ended.

My Teachers

The main teacher of Zhetl youth was Yosef Muchnik of blessed memory. He was the most knowledgeable in Hebrew, bible and Jewish history.

There were seven of us that studied with him: me and my friend Avreymke, Yisroel Polansky, Mayrim Yakomovitsky, Veveh Kravietz, Noyekh Alpert and Itche Kravietz.

I quickly learned to write stories in Hebrew. Our teacher Muchnik liked my writing and would always give me a "five".

My mother would take my notebook and go to experts with my work. A good Hebraist in those years was Avrom Ivenitsky.

Another Hebrew teacher was Moishe Ganzovitch, my uncle Khaim's brother.

The third Hebrew teacher was: Bender, who died recently in Israel (Herzliya).

I would go with Avreymke to him to learn. Bender, the teacher, with a smile would explain Bialik's poems to us or teach us a chapter of the bible.

He would also tell stories about Zhetl's heroes. How the Zhetl hero, the deaf Hirsh, would split open the heads of Gentiles with an iron crow bar on market days.

The fourth teacher was: Bielski, Gutke the baker's son.

My Hebrew education stopped with these teachers when I began learning Russian.

Libkeh Shvedsky, Hertz Leyb's daughter, was my first Russian teacher.

Her sister, Esther Ivenitsky was also my Russian teacher. She lived with her husband, Avrom Ivenitsky, in her father, Hertz Leyb Kaplinsky of blessed memory's house.

Khaim Kaplinsky, the veteran of the Bundist movement in Zhetl, who spent many years in exile in Siberia and now lives in Lodz was also my Russian teacher.

Khaim Kaplinsky lived in the house of the Christian Lubetsky on Lipover Street. He collected butterflies. He had a large board with many varieties of butterflies hanging on his wall. In the middle of class, if he would see a butterfly flying in the yard, he would grab his cap and run outside. When the butterfly would land on the ground, Khaim Kaplinsky would swiftly cover him with his cap. He would come back into the room happily and pin the butterfly to the wall.

I ended my Russian period with Khaim Kaplinsky and began my Polish period.

My Polish teacher was Namiyat who lived with his grandfather Oreh the carpenter. My Polish period ended with Namiyat and then I began my Yiddish.

The Yiddish school was then situated on Lisagura Street near Kovolevsky's house, across from Hirshl Aron's Tzegelnieh.

Our teacher Lieberman came to Zhetl from deep Lithuania. He lived with Aron the tailor. I used to go there for private Yiddish lessons. Yudl Bielski or as we used to call him Yudl Halubek studied with me. He was shot by the Germans.

The Romantic Years in Zhetl

Our classes ended in the evening. My friend Avreymke and I would go to the orchard. I would climb a tree, shake it, and soft ripe pears would fall to the ground. As we bit into them our eyes would close from great pleasure: the taste of paradise! These were the famous "Tzitrinke" or "Tzukravke" pears that grew on the big tree in our orchard. As we ate the pears the juice ran down our chins.

[Page 264]

It was getting late. Avreymke had to go home, far, far away near the cemetery.

Every night I take Avreymke home. I gather some courage and tell Avreymke I am not afraid even though my heart pounds from fright as we approach the cemetery.

We hold hands and begin to walk…We enter the marketplace, pass the circle stores, walk through the narrow Mitzl's alley or Khienke Malke Motke's alley, past solid Shiye's house and past the new, middle and old Houses of Study.

Here is the Talmud Torah. We cross the footbridge over the Pomerayke. Avreymche Busel's house, Khaim Kaplinsky's yard, Hertz Leyb's house, Bushlin's smithy and Shaul the carpenter's workshop.

We are now in the heart of Lisogura. The wind is blowing from the green meadow and we breathe freely.

Tall poplar trees are rustling over our heads as we approach Kalmen Hirshl Maytchik's house. This is where his kingdom begins, this is where he rules with his strong hand and with his son.

We continue to go further. From a distance we can already see the cemetery. On the hill stands the small house of Yisroel Ber the gravedigger. We are overcome with fear. Instinctively, we grab each other. We arrive at Grayevsky's house and right beside him, under the shade of a big tree is where my friend Avreymke lives.

This was the time of Poland's liberation where from every corner, from every tree and blade of grass you heard the words of Mickiewcz, Slovatsky and Sienkevitch.

As we plod through the Lisagura mud we would recite the words of those poets in a loud voice. We were so engrossed in our recitation, we would fall into the mud or remain standing by a broken fence.

Avremke's house was covered in straw and a stall was attached to the house. In the yard there was a barn from which emanated the scent of fresh hay. An old tree stood in the middle of the yard which spread its branches over the entire house.

When Avreymke would enter the house, sit down near the stove and begin to tell Sienkevtich's story "Fire and Sword", it seemed to be that the Tatars had surrounded the yard, waved their swords, and facing them would be Zoglobo shouting: "Hurrah!"

Avreymke's father, Mordkhai of blessed memory would come sit with us and tell one of his stories.

"Listen children, to what happened to me in Russia. When I served in the Czarist army I wanted to swim in the river. We took off our clothes and jumped into the water. However, I fell into a whirlpool which pulled me into a chasm. I lost all my strength. Having experienced all the wars in Russia I thought to myself, this is where I will die? In this small river? Will I survive to see my wife and children? I don't remember what happened next. A strong hand grabbed me by my hair, lifted me high and threw me on the ground.

When I finally opened my eyes, Vasil was standing beside me with a kind smile. Vasil saved my life. Yes children, the Russians are good people and I will never forget Vasil.

This is how Mordkhai, Avreymke's father, concluded his story.

They brought hot lentils to the table. I ate the lentils and black rye bread with a great appetite.

Suddenly the door opened and Maxim entered. He was a tall peasant with kind eyes who often helped Mordkhai work in the fields.

The small kerosene lamp lit the walls with a pale glow. The tree in the yard rustled. Avreymke and I began again to recite excerpts from poems by Mickiewcz as well as "Eugene Onegin" by Pushkin. It seemed to me I was in a world of heroes and dreams, of gods and goddesses.

In the corner, Avreymke's sister Khayke was reciting a poem:

"We will break the iron wall"…

The night stretched on and we continued to talk and tell stories.

These were the most beautiful years of my life, the time of youthful romantic charm.

[Page 265]

Communal Activists and Public Figures

by Yitzkhak Epshteyn (Kfar Neter)

Translated by Janie Respitz

Avrom Ivenitsky of blessed memory

Avrom Ivenitsky was a romantic with a big soul. At night he would walk and recite excerpts from the writings of the Russian writer Lermontov.

He loved nature and sports. Even in the winter he would swim in the Zhetl Lake.

Friday nights he would give lectures. He also wrote a book: "When Paths Cross", where he described his experiences as a Russian prisoner of war. He also wrote the history of Zhetl.

Avrom Ivenitsky worked for a short time at Zhetl city hall and like Herman Frenkel, had to put up with the chicanery and persecutions from the authorities. He taught for a longer time in the Yiddish school.

Herman Frenkel of blessed memory

Herman Frenkel was not born in Zhetl.

Herman Frenkel of blessed memory

He came to Zhetl from Lodz. There was an expression in Zhetl which said even a strong swimmer can drown. This means that Herman Frenkel swam for so long until he "drowned" in Zhetl and married Shmuel Shvedsky's daughter: – Khane Malka.

Khane Malka had a bubbly personality full of energy and courage. She called her husband: "Frenkel".

"Mr. Frenkel, come eat, Mr. Frenkel, how are you feeling, Mr. Frenkel, when are you giving your lecture"?

Herman Frenkel was one of the best teachers in the Yiddish school. In general he was very smart, loved people and had an exceptionally sharp memory. He knew his way around all questions. The youth loved him very much. In our free time we would besiege Shvedsky's "porch" just to be able to hear a few good, clever words from Frenkel.

He worked for a short time at Zhetl city hall, but they soon realized he was smarter than them and was unwilling to flatter the nobility. They actually fired him and he was left without a source of income.

Frenkel had a huge soul. He would often repeat the words of Y. L. Peretz:

"As long as it takes for love and peace to arrive – the fruit will be spoiled. Time is not a dream".

He was not very successful as a bookkeeper for the Soviets. He saw this was not the path toward love and peace. His heart suffered.

Herman Frenkel, the large soul, could not bear the Soviet regime. I was disappointed and one bright morning died at work of a heart attack.

His wife Khane Malka organized his funeral and made an effort for it to be impressive. My uncle Mikhl Rabinovitch delivered the eulogy at his grave.

Khaim Ganuzovitch of blessed memory

> Little flowers, garlands, drawn on the frosted windows,
> And the wind howls up the chimney.
> All is good now, beside the happy fire in our house,
> Until the kerosene in the little lamp flickers out,
> Until the clock angrily mumbles: It's late!
> It is time to lie in the soft warm beds.

My uncle Khaim Ganuzovitch would always recite this immortal poem by Mani Leyb in the long winter evening hours, when he would sit with Khaim Vernikovsky (Emeti) and Mikhl Rabinovitch at the Zhetl "Solkes" (attics) and dream about a nicer, better life.

We called attics "Solkes" in Zhetl. In these attics, my uncle Khaim Ganuzovitch and Shloime Khaim Vernikovsky, founded the Poalei Zion (Labour Zionist movement) in Zhetl. Khaim Ganuzovitch was one of the most active members of the movement.

After Shloime Khaim's death, Khaim Ganuzovitch, Moishe Mirsky and Yehoshua Ovseyevitch took over the administration of the Yiddish Folkshul.

[Page 266]

Khaim worked for a long time at the Zhetl bank. His intelligence and devotion earned him many supporters and friends.

Khaim Ganuzovitch was killed with the first 120 victims.

Velvl Izraelit's House

Velvl Izraelit's brick house was in the marketplace in the same row as Shvedsky and my grandfather's houses.

Velvel Izraelit was one of the most respected older established men in Zhetl. His house was one of the nicest and was called by his wife's name: Velvl Hinde Mayrim's house.

In the evenings Velvl Izraelit would sit in the House of Study and learn a page of Talmud with my grandfather Feyvl Rabinovitch and Reb Moishe Tentzer.

On the Sabbath after prayers, Reb Moishe Tentzer would go home with Velvl and his wife Hinde Mayrims.

When Velvl Izraelit died his children came from all corners of Poland. His eldest son Shloime came from Latvia.

Khaim from Zhibertaychin of blessed memory

Saturday morning, the dew sparkles on the grass. The trees sway quietly and from among the shrubs, the nightingale sings.

From a distance you can see the estate Zhiberaychin which belonged to the nobleman Damayko (whose pedigree stems from Polish aristocracy and is mentioned in the epic poem "Pan Tadeusz").

The Zhibertaychin estate is dipped in green. An alley of white birch trees leads to the palace and at the entrance to the estate stands a large oak tree.

I am a shepherd! I bring our well known horses to pasture, the "bay horse" together with all the shepherds – on the green fields doused with dew. Suddenly, the tall slender figure of Khaim Zhibertaychin (Khaim Leyzerovitch) sneaks out of the estate.

A tall slender Jew, with a white patriarchal beard, dressed in his Sabbath best.

His three grandsons: Yitzkhak, Yekhezkl, and Asher hold his hands as they stride toward Zhetl.

They walk quicker, faster because today is The Great Sabbath. Rabbi Saratzkin will speak today in the old House of Study. They pass me but I hide among the bushes so they will not see that I am bringing the horse to pasture on that Sabbath morning.

Aharon Alpert of blessed memory

Who in Zhetl did not know the high balcony belonging to Archik Efraim Hirshl on Novoredker Street? His business did well, beginning with nuts and ending with haberdashery.

Archik's feet were paralyzed when he was young. His children: Disheh (who lives in America) and Yentl would help push his chair from his house to work and back.

Archik was an old fighter from the fifth year. He would sit on his porch and people would gather to ask advice or pose political questions.

Yisroel Asher Mayevsky of blessed memory

A cold winter morning. The snow scrapes under the feet. It is Tuesday, market day in Zhetl. The farmers' sleighs arrive at the marketplace and line up in a row. The female farmers climb down from their sleighs covered in fur pelts with garlands of dried mushrooms. The scent of the mushrooms permeates the marketplace.

Yisroel Asher Mayevsky

These are the famous mushrooms, ceps that grow in the Akhanov, Batchkevitch and Orlin forests.

Yisreol Asher stands at the end of Khane Gatshik's house. He is the mushroom merchant and an expert in this field. The farmers go to him with their mushrooms and he examines the merchandise.

After the transactions, when the farmers leave, he examines the marketplace. His eyes look far off into the distance. He sees the rain falling in Batchkevitch forest, the earth gives off steam, the smell of fresh pitch enters your bones, and the last rays of sunshine shines through the tops of lanky pine trees. Black and red berries sprout out of the moss together with the mushrooms, the famous ceps, the same ceps from which he earns his living. Yisroel Asher lets out a sigh:

It's hard to earn a living these days, the boycott against the Jews is strengthening and the farmers are selling their merchandise to the Polish cooperatives.

He smokes a cigarette and walks nervously among the sleighs looking for fresh goods.

[Page 267]

Tcherne the Miller of blessed memory

Tcherne the miller's mill stood at the edge of town on the street that was called Tcherne the Miller's Street. It was a purely non Jewish street. Except for the few Jewish families like Meir the tailor, Isar Serebrovsky, the old Mukovozhnik and Yokhe Bulansky, the street was inhabited by Christians.

The big mill stood surrounded by tall willows.

On the other side of the Zhetlke were green meadows. If you left the narrow streets of Zhetl toward Tcherne's mill you could breathe more freely. The cool scent from the lake, the pleasant scent from the blossoming willows, the hum of the water wheel, the green meadows on the other side of the river, the monotone croaking of the frogs all helped a person to relax.

Tcherne the miller ran the mill on her own. Her husband died long ago. She was a heroic woman and carried all the burdens and difficulties on her shoulders.

When Tcherne the miller allowed the boat to be tied there with great joy. Groups of friends would row far over the still waters until the priest's bridge serenading on violins and guitars.

On Saturday mornings, Tcherne the miller would go out for a walk. She would sit in the boat and her children would row far, far over the still waters. Tcherne would sit like a queen, her large figure with broad shoulders would protrude from the row boat as she looked with great pleasure at her mill from the river.

In a boat on Tcherne the miller's lake

[Page 268]

Lost Talents

by Soreh Epshteyn – Shoar (Natanya)

Translated by Janie Respitz

With the publication of this "Zhetl" book I feel it necessary to eternalize my close family members who excelled as stage actors.

My Aunt Khashke

So many years have passed. I barely remember her. As a child I would run to her rehearsals, my hand in hers, so she would not lose me, God forbid…

She played all roles, tragic and comic, and always well.

I saw her often on stage and I will never forget when she played the role of "Mirele Efros". She was a hero in acting, in life and also in death…

At the first mass slaughter, Khashke stood at the mass grave with her two small daughters and son.

Her little boy Fyevele cried. He was afraid of the Hitler dogs and their guns, and she, Khashke, calmed him.

"Don't cry my child, it doesn't hurt…" only a great mother can offer such comfort.

My Cousin Soreleh

Her daughter Soreleh was very talented. Her main talent was acting. In all her performances she gave her very best bringing great enthusiasm to the spectator. The school inspector noticed her and showed interest in her talent.

As I have mentioned, Soreleh was beside her mother at the first slaughter.

"Let down your blonde braids," Kahshke said to her. She saw how beautiful her daughter was. Maybe they would not have the heart to kill her.

As it was fated, Soreleh and her older sister Fridaleh remained alive for a few more months, until they sent them back. Perhaps it was their fate to lie in the same mass grave with their mother and brother.

My Uncle Mikhl

He was a teacher in Gutke's house, an autodidact, taught children and studied on his own, and finally became a teacher and educator in Sofia Markovna's high school in Vilna. He was known as an important pedagogic force while at the same time endowed with dramatic talents and especially excelled as a director.

The Yiddish press in Vilna always gave his productions great reviews.

His special talent was recounting stories and episodes from the town, exciting his audience. This was an art.

My poor uncle Mikhl, if you succeeded to be saved from the Hitler dogs, why was your fate so cruel?

In far off cold Russia, you had to watch as your wife and young daughter die of hunger and destitution. That is when your kind heart collapsed…

My Sister Mirele

She grew up to be beautiful and talented. Her face was like a Madonna (this is how she also characterized uncle Mikhl). A nice voice, perfect pitch, the tones of the mandolin would quickly guide her small feet to a fast dance.

She would often perform in the school shows and delight the audience.

I see her playing the role of Hagar (who Abraham sent into the desert with her son Ishmael), where she asks pity from God: "A drop of water, a drop of dew" she said with such feeling and a tremble in her voice that it made the audience cry.

As a student at the teacher's seminary in Vilna she continued to perform on stage.

Here in Israel, I have received a few clippings from the Vilna press where she is mentioned as "the Rising Star – Mireh Epshteyn"!

This is all that remains… I keep it as a sacred memory.

*

Many years have passed. Life goes on, old wounds harden, sharp pains dull. Life's daily struggles dull the delicate feelings.

However, whenever I see a theatrical performance and I breathe once again the theatrical art of my old home, memories of my acting family awaken anew; I see them alive, moving, singing, dancing and stretching out their tender hands to me. I am happy to be with them again.

Poor, spirited souls, you will continue to live forever in my memory, I will never forget you!

[Page 269]

Public Figures

byShabsai Mayevsky (B'nei B'rak)

Translated by Janie Respitz

What Jew does not know there are 36 disguised righteous men in the world? Outwardly, they leave an impression of a simple man, but in fact they are secretly extremely righteous and when nobody sees them they devote themselves to concealed important things.

One of these 36 men had to be the beadle of the new House of Study Reb Binyomin Hirshl.

He was a simple man not incredibly smart and quite an unlucky person. Since he could not earn a living managing the House of Study, he would buy and sell bottles and always lost money. The story I will now tell you about him made me realize that he was not merely a simple man, but in fact one of the 36.

During the First World War the Germans took Jews for forced labour building highways. Hungry and barefoot, Jews would sneak away from the highway and come to Zhetl. The German's gave an order that anyone who will let a stranger into his home will be punished by death. Since Jews would not dare allow these men into their homes, they would go to the House of Study. The Germans learned of this and warned the managers they would be held responsible if strangers were found in the prayer houses. The managers were frightened and did not permit these foreign Jews to enter.

This is when the unfortunate found a saviour in the person of Reb Binyomin Hirshl, the beadle of the new House of Study. He took these people into his small house, then went from house to house collecting bread, and let the Jews stay until they recovered. Then he would collect some money for them and send them off.

Shabsai Mayevsky

One fact I remember. Right after the war the postman brought a letter from America from one of the men saved by Binyomin Hirshl the beadle.

The letter writer said he was among those that Binyomin Hershl took into his home. Since he was swollen from hunger, he remained for a long time, until he was healthy. Then he left for America. From that day on, he sent a few dollars every year.

Here in the Land of Israel, I once met a man in Petach Tikva. When he heard I was from Zhetl he called me over: "one of the 36 secretly righteous men lived in Zhetl". Then he proceeded to tell me the aforementioned story that happened to his brother who today lives in America.

When I would enter the House of Study late at night and see Binyomin Hirshl light the fire in the oven and then lie on a bench and wait for the wood to burn I would think: "is he really in fact one of the 36"?

Moishe Ruven Mordkofsky of blessed memory

Moishe Ruven of blessed memory was very well respected in Zhetl. He was a devoted Zionist and a volunteer in many institutions. I would like to emphasize what he did as father of the orphans.

I remember a family in Zhetl by the name of Bransker. They were apparently refugees that came from the city Bransk. Both parents died young and left a house with small orphans. Moishe Ruven arranged for them to eat in peoples' homes, looked after them and arranged for them to go to Heder. The children also ate in our home.

Moishe Ruven would often come to the Talmud Torah to see if the children were coming to school and how they were learning. When he found out the boy did not go to school he would come to our house, wait for him to finish eating and then approach him, sometimes with kindness and sometimes with anger, just like a real father, until he prevailed upon him to return to school.

I believe if one would point out that this man was among the 36 secret righteous men, Moishe Ruven would be welcomed into their "society".

Reb Mordkhai Rabinovitch of blessed memory

Saturday evening, after evening prayers Jews from all over town would stream to the "Hasidarniye" for the thirds Sabbath meal.

[Page 270]

Jews would delight in the melodies of their Sabbath songs which would be sung by Reb Yakov the ritual slaughterer and other Hasidim.

One of the Hasidim who had remained in my memory is Reb Mordkhai Rabinovitch, or as we called him Motl Tulye's.

When the Rebbe would come to Zhetl for the Sabbath, he would stay with him. On Tuesdays, market day, you could find him in the Hasidic prayer house reciting psalms. When I would see him on a market day reciting psalms so sweetly, I thought, if King David would come by, he would enjoy listening.

Yisroel Berl the Gravedigger

In Zhetl, we rarely referred to someone by his first name. Practically everyone had a second name.

There were however individuals who were only known by their first names. Yisroel Ber belonged to that group. If someone in Zhetl said Yisroel Berl, everyone knew you meant Yisroel Berl the gravedigger. There were two reasons. Firstly, there was no one else in Zhetl with that name and secondly due to his special occupation.

Everyone in Zhetl knew that sooner or later Berl would take care of them. This is why his name evoked fear in young and of course, the elderly. If someone wanted to tell how he had faced danger he would say: "I could have been lying in Yisroel Ber's garden".

One day, Hilkeh the clown, an old happy Jew who loved to tell jokes came to Yisroel Ber and said:

"Yisroel Berl, what do you say, do I have time to make a few more pairs of boots"?

Yisroel Ber immediately replied: "you can't die in old boots"?

One thing that differentiated Yisroel Berl from other gravediggers was that he was a Talmudic scholar. It was rare that a gravedigger was learned, but Yisroel Ber was.

Yisroel Ber was my religious tutor when I was a child.

A group of boys studied with him. He was devoted to his teaching with heart and soul. He did not waste any energy or time. His explanations of the Talmud were great. If he had to leave class early for a funeral, the next day's lesson would be longer to make up what we missed.

Thanks to his devotion, I still remember all 57 pages of Talmud he taught me until today.

As it is known, Yisroel Berl's father, Reb Khaim Meir was also a gravedigger in Zhetl. Everyone wondered how such a simple man offered his children such a good education. Yisroel Ber once told us what his father said to his children:

"Either you learn Torah, or I'll bury you". His children chose the first option. They were all Talmudic scholars.

Let these lines serve as a remembrance for my teacher, Reb Yisroel Ber of blessed memory.

May his soul be eternally bound!

The Zhetl Yeshiva and the Yeshiva Boys

In my time the Zhetl Yeshiva was under the leadership of Reb Hirsh Khurgin of blessed memory. Boys came to study from other towns and the small Yudl Meir would go from house to house collecting food for them. Boys from Zhetl who graduated from the Talmud Torah also studied there.

Boys from Zhetl had a good reputation in other Yeshivas due to their numbers and cleverness. You could find boys from Zhetl in the following Yeshivas: Mir, Radn, Volozhyn, Kletzk, Kamemnietz, Grodno, Baranovitch, Slonim, Navaredok and Ayshishok. Some studied for a few years and then went into business or found a job. A few continued studying until they became rabbis, ritual slaughterers or heads of Yeshivas. In many cities and towns throughout Poland and abroad you could find rabbis, ritual slaughterers and other functionaries of Jewish religious and communal life who came from Zhetl.

A large number of Yeshiva boys were murdered by Hitler, may his name be blotted out, together with the other Zhetl martyrs and some managed to come to the Land of Israel and other countries. May these lines serve as a remembrance candle for my friends who spent their best youthful years with me in the Yeshiva, but did not live to see the prophecy come true: May you find refuge on the Mount of Zion.

[Page 271]

The Tailor from Zhetl

by Yakov Indershteyn (Kibbutz Eylon)

Translated by Janie Respitz

If not for the noise of the children playing on the road. If not for the people in work clothes shoving one another curiously around the postal bag which just arrived from the city; if not for the questioning glances of people from their verandas, Berke would have sworn he was dreaming.

It is really like a dream. Here is a man on a verdant sunny winter day going to the road to meet the night bus. He walks slowly and feels his little daughter's hand in his and thinks: a ship has arrived with illegal immigrants. The newspapers say they will be freed today. Perhaps today the group of youth will arrive, the group our kibbutz has been waiting for, for so long. If so, it is worthwhile to walk to the road to meet the bus. It was a custom of Berke's to greet the new arrivals. It's nice to approach a new person, who looks at everything nervously with questioning eyes and the shyness of a greenhorn. It is great to go up to such an individual, look him in the eyes and say:

"Shalom, my friend"!

Berke loves to do this.

Since the ships began to reappear at the port, since the day when the kibbutz decorated their gate with flags and flowers and a large white banner which reads "and our children will return home", Berke started a tradition of taking his little daughter on the "good deed walk", to greet the new immigrants. He wanted her to get used to waiting for the arrivals!

Berke went to the bus and…what happened?

"Father"?

His father, Shleymke the tailor, wearing his cap that cast a shadow on his pale boney face, stared at his son with his black eyes.

"Berke, my son! Is this not like in a dream?

Father's cap was old and wrinkled. It had lost its shape. It was the type of cap worn by craftsmen in Zhetl. Father's hat was usually a dark grey colour, but not always because sometimes it was made from scraps left over from suits that Shleymke the tailor would make for Passover or Sukkot.

It is worthwhile to mention something else: on hot days, father would wear a cap made of white fabric together with a white alpaca jacket. This was his seasonal outfit on hot summer days. Clearly, we are talking here about the Sabbath or between afternoon and evening prayers during the week.

On those evenings Father would walk through the streets of town. Sometimes he would stop to watch the firefighters practice, sometimes he would mix with the crowd at the marketplace who were waiting for the bus which was coming from the train station, to see people coming from the outside world.

Here, on the bench near the hotel, sits the "fallen" nobleman Lisovsky, who lost everything he had in a card game. He only has one pleasure in life, playing with his aristocratic dog.

"Rex! I said no Rex!"…Ah, hello tailor!

This is how Lisovsky combines reprimanding his dog with greeting Shleymke the tailor. Since Lisovsky had been excluded from Christian aristocratic society which consisted of the judge, police commander, postmaster and neighbouring noblemen, since he became a bitter pauper, he has been living at Hotel Europa. True the Rabinovitchs are Jews, but you could reach an agreement with them about rent.

The same was with clothes. Clearly, you could not compare Shleymke the tailor to the big city tailors who sewed clothing for the nobility. His Polish was also not great. However, Shleymke had a great virtue. Although his work was fine, he didn't kill himself to make money. Lisovsky respected this trait and he liked him. Whenever he saw him, before my father had a chance to say a word about the money he owed, Lisovsky would say good morning:

[Page 272]

"How's it going tailor? Are you well? Quiet Rex! Quiet!"

The last words were for his "aristocratic" dog, who snuggles up to the nobleman and tries to lick his fat cheek. Heder boys, apprentices and other curious people stop to see this wise dog who understands the nobleman's Polish. Father removes his light cap and smiles at the nobleman:

"Good morning" he says in Polish.

The nobleman does not stop caressing his dog which awakens a sense of pity in Shleymke for this poor man:

"What else does he have left in life besides this dog"?

He turns his head and suddenly sees how the shadows on the cobblestones at the marketplace are stretched out, the domes on the church under the thin crosses shine with a pale redness reflecting the sunset fire, which was ignited far off over the priest's roof, until Tcherne the miller's lake. Delayed peasant wagons head home slowly over the cobblestones. The horses then bolted due to the noise of the oncoming bus.

Father stood there a while longer looking at people with dusty shoes who were bringing secrets from the outside world in tightly tied suitcases. It appears that it is only the head of the Jewish community returning from a mediation session with the Starosta (Government official) and Shushan the dry goods merchant returning from Lodz where he bought a bit of merchandise. A woman disembarks. She was returning from visiting doctors in Vilna, and finally the "amiable" guest, the executor of the taxes who comes every week to extract the last pennies from the town's Jews.

All of a sudden father feels an emptiness around him which makes him sad.

What was he waiting around for?

He's had enough of the dirty bus and the dressed up driver Feyvele with his jodhpurs and shiny black boots. He must think the town has forgotten about his importance, this wagon driver! Simple being…Shleymke the tailor smiles to himself.

With arms folded behind his back my father walked down Synagogue Street. Here it is one of two things, either, in the middle of the synagogue courtyard a large circle of craftsmen have gathered and are listening to Eli the pavers stories and talking politics, or they are listening to the sweet voice of a wandering preacher pouring out of the packed House of Study.

The topics discussed in the courtyard change quickly. Khaim Meir already finished his exaggerated stories from the Caucuses, and they already talked about matters of the Dumas: about Pilsudski who beat up his deputy in the Brisk prison; about new bandits roaming around the forest. This is how the conversation rolls until they talk about town issues, about the election for the Society to Aid the Poor and the scandal at the bank.

Around them, common folk are pushing as not to miss a word, especially because in the middle stands the clown and heretic, Eli the paver. When Eli begins to rail against everyone and laughs at the whole world, Shmaya the shoemaker loses his patience and says:

"Tell me Elyieh, What will you do in the world to come when they ask why you don't have a beard? What will you say? Huh? Elinkeh!" Shmaya the shoemaker looked around with a victorious smile.

"What do you mean" said Eliyeh, "I will answer: this is how it is. I was born without a beard and died without a beard!" The crowd laughed but Shmaya would not give up.

"But then they will say to you, you were born without teeth, why did you return with teeth?" Eliyeh quickly replied:

"I'll tell them: what do you want from me? Go yell at my teeth!"

The crowd burst out laughing. The pious Jews ran for evening prayers.

A summer Sabbath

The whole family was in bed enjoying a Sabbath nap.

Good Sabbath! Get up lazy bones, even the rabbi and his son in law left for prayers! This is how Shloime the tailor ran into the house after praying with the first quorum. My father was used to praying at dawn, summer and winter. The House of Study was packed with tailors, shoemakers, wagon drivers, all hard working Jews who worked hard to eke out a living until late at night.

Chanukah at dawn. The House of Study is heated and every corner is lit. All the lamps are burning. A Chanukah menorah stands on the window sill with all its candles lit. A group of craftsmen stand around all wrapped in prayer shawls. The orphan boy who sleeps in the House of Study yawns. Father's cap is still wet from the snowstorm that whipped his face as he walked the House of Study.

[Page 273]

"So guys, what are you waiting for? It's already daylight outside!" said Moishe – Zelik the peddler. During the day Moishe – Zelik walks from one village to the next selling colourful kerchiefs, needles and all sorts of pins to the gentiles.

Borukh the shoemaker who had not finished reciting his psalm of the day grumbled:

"You never have any time! What's your hurry Moishe Zelik"?

Motke the saddlemaker bangs his lectern. He wants to give the cantor a sign to begin prayers, but suddenly he is uncertain: maybe it really is too early? Motke turns to the window, wipes the wet pane with his hand, covers his face with both hands and touches the cold pane with his nose. Motke sees the disheveled branches of the pear trees at the old cemetery have already emerged from the wintery, night sky, he turns his head to the crowd and bangs his lectern. As the cantor begins the room fills with the mumbling of prayers, the naïve prayer of Jewish craftsmen.

Father stands at his lectern which is covered with a damp fur and on that, his prayer book. The little boy Berke sees clearly how his father is really enjoying praying today.

Years later, when Berke will walk through the small Jewish towns with a saw in his hand, sawing and chopping wood, working hard in the sawmills together with other pioneers who are preparing for the work in the Land of Israel, as he walks over fields with spring flowers under his feet somewhere in a secluded corner in far off Galilee, he will carry, on his thirty year old shoulders the heavy burden of so many destroyed Jewish town. Berke will preserve in his memory that Chanukah morning, the picture of his father the tailor, wrapped in his prayer shawl, enjoying his praying with the craftsmen in the warm, lit House of Study. He will then remember the biblical passage: When stars sing together in the morning…

My father would not only pray early in the morning on weekdays. Out of habit he would wake up early on the Sabbath too and go pray with the first quorum. Then he returns home and says "Good Shabbos" and wakes everyone up:

"Wake up already boys! Tell your mother she has slept enough. It is a beautiful summer day, delightful!"

He loosens the tie he wore in honour of praying, opens the top button of his Sabbath shirt. He quickly takes a bite of the Sabbath challah while glancing at the headlines of Friday's newspaper (which his oldest son brought home Friday evening).

After looking at the headlines he pushes the newspaper aside. There will be time for this later. He puts on his white alpaca jacket, looks at himself in his large tailor's mirror to check that his cap is not crooked and shouts at the boys, the idlers.

"My boys only know about books, they don't even think about praying. Even the gentiles cross themselves, but my boys… ah!

His raised hand falls in despair. He angrily opens the door and walks out of the house.

Berke, still lying in bed, smiles and puts his book aside. He stretches and enjoys a big yawn. He knows his father's refrain, an old song which he hears every Sabbath, and he knows the anger will not last long.

He knows where his father has gone. Every Saturday after praying he takes a walk through town to hear the news of the week. Later, he walks down the gentile streets to the highway. My father, the tailor, is very curious to see what the fields look like on both sides of the highway.

Berke, the kibbutznik in the Galilee preserves another memory:

A sunny Sabbath morning. A white path winds through the fields of loose corn stalks, like waves over the ocean. A man is walking slowly along the path, accompanied by his shadow. Both hands behind his back with his eyes wandering back and forth.

This is my father, Shleymke the tailor, with his white cap and alpaca jacket. This is his "traditional" walk, checking out the fields...

My father wears a cap like all the other craftsmen in Zhetl. It is no wonder that even today, on a winter day at dusk in a village in the Galilee, Berke sees before his eyes his father's head with that cap!

It's almost certain, this is how his father would arrive.

[Page 274]

But he did not come. Where did you ever hear about fathers who arrive these days at dusk?

Does that mean that everything told about father's arrival was a dream? Perhaps not a dream but a hallucination born of sleepless nights?

Shleymke the tailor will not be coming to his son in the Land of Israel. Such a pity. A craftsman like him is hard to find. He probably would not have engaged in this work on the kibbutz as our clothes are very simple.

However, if you knew how difficult it was for Shleymke the tailor to sit idle, you would understand how a whole field of work would have opened for him. How passionately he would have sewn winter coats for us, long and short, and not necessarily from new fabric. He was a master at using used clothes to make something new...

And just coats? You think, God forbid, that he would not be able to sew shorts or blouses? If that's what you think, you are making a big mistake!

Friday mornings, all his work from the week is finished and delivered to the customers, the wealthy men in town, and everything on credit. He did not have a groshn for the Sabbath. My mother's grief could tear your heart out, but what was she to do?

At such a time, as if miraculously, a gentile would come in with a piece of linen requesting a few shirts for Sunday. That is when his sewing machine would sing the nicest folk songs, just like father! The gentile sees how quickly the shirts are being made so he pays for the shirts in advance.

My mother would then run to the store to buy something for the Sabbath, and who now can be compared to us?

What do you have to say now? Of course he would have sewn shirts and blouses for us.

You ask, would have he sewn for the children? And I ask you: what would he not sew for them? They would all be treated as if they were his own grandchildren! He would invent various styles of coats and all types of suits for them. He was a great master of children's clothing.

A pity my friends, that we did not have the honour to greet Shleymke the tailor in the Land of Israel. He never even saw his grandchildren. He left this world exactly when Berke's daughter was born.

No, the Germans did not slaughter him. They did slaughter mother and the children in the big slaughter in town. Since my father was a craftsman, the enemy sent him to a camp for craftsmen in a neighbouring town. Did you hear how tens of Jews escaped from that camp? If not, it's a pity, because it is not a usual case.

When father arrived in the forest he did not have a gun so the partisans did not take him in. Young men worked tirelessly to find guns. For someone my father's age this was too difficult.

Shleymke the tailor met gentile acquaintances and tried to talk to them. When would he meet them? Winter nights he would knock on the windows of huts of his former customers. Often the peasant would chase him away. Others would threaten to set their dogs on him. But one man lent him an ax to build a "dugout" deep in the forest, another gave him his son's old rags which Shleymke the tailor repurposed and earned a piece of bread for him and his youngest son who was saved together with his father.

My father sewed without a sewing machine, with his ten fingers. He pushed the needle into used thick cloth, sewed and clothed entire villages just like in the good old days. During the day he worked in his dugout and at night he went to the peasant's huts looking for work and bread.

However, my father did not live to come to the Land of Israel. He is not alive. A few rumours reached us. They said he died from typhus as did his little boy. Others said he was killed by an enemy's bullet during the big raid in Lipitchansky forest.

As for Berke, he still goes every day to meet the bus as he did before. His brother Avreyml who served in the Red Army has survived! He can never be sure that he won't arrive on any given day. If not today, he can come tomorrow, and if not he himself, perhaps a letter from him. When Avreyml will arrive, Berke will fling his arms around his neck and both brothers will cry and bemoan the fact that their father did not have the honour to arrive on the bus at dusk on a winter day in a village in the Galilee.

[Page 275]

Zaydke

by Yakov Indershteyn (Kibbutz Eylon)

Translated by Janie Respitz

Good Sabbath!

Good Sabbath!

Shshsh! They are banging on the table!

Ah, Zaydke? We'll soon hear some news.

And Zaydke, with his long black beard looks down at the crowd with scary eyes and shouts:

"I am informing everyone that by Wednesday we have to pay a fourth installment of the business tax. By Thursday we will have to pay a fine with interest except for "bribes".

Be quiet! I am informing everyone that on Thursday there will be baths for women, and Friday, the eve of Rosh Hashanah, a steam bath! Once finished, Zaydke steps down from the platform where prayers are led from, arrogant.

When boys misbehave during prayers, playing with nuts and making noise, who quietens them with fiery slaps?

Zaydke, of course.

If there is going to be a fair on Thursday, how do we inform the gentiles? Zaydke stands in the middle of the marketplace on a wagon, bangs two pieces of wood together and shouts in Russian:

"Come hear people, I have news for you!

When Gentiles in their Sunday baggy panties and white linen blouses hear Zaydke's voice they come running from Centre Street, dragging their barefoot kids in long underwear. Village boys in caps with shiny visors, worn like tough guys on the side, wearing riding breeches tucked into shiny boots, with their girlfriends, dressed up in colourful dresses gathered at the waist, with fired red makeup on their cheeks, run faster to hear Zaydke's news.

When Zaydke sees the large crowd he begins to rant:

People, bring your pigs, your mares and stallions, your chickens and hens, Thursday, there will be a fair!

Bring potatoes and rye, cows and goats, Thursday, there will be a big fair!

Aha! Zaydke! A demon in your father's father! (A curse with humour).

They wipe their whiskers, send their wives to buy a challah, a gift for the children that stayed at home in the village. Then they harness their horse, time to go home!

At Maysheke the Ox's, the door opens quickly and a tall Jews with a black beard enters, carrying under his arm an old rubbed out briefcase. (Translator's note: Mayshke is called an ox, which can also mean a fool)

Good morning Reb Moishe.

Mayshke the Ox with wire glasses on the tip of his nose, in his shoemaker's apron and cotton jacket answers him:

Good morning and a good year. Oh Zaydke, a new paper? Apparently a new problem?

Mayshke the Ox forgets to talk in rhyme, his habit since he became a master of ceremonies at weddings, and begins to talk, like everyone else. The reason for his excitement was Zaydke's note demanding taxes which says we must pay. Zaydke takes out the paper and says:

"You have ten days to pay. This is for the sign, the blackboard with the shoe. Sign here and give me five groshn for bringing it.

The neighbour's son signed in Polish and Maysheke the Ox makes three exes (XXX) and scratches his neck.

"From where do you think I have five groshn…"

"Never mind," said Zaydke as he quickly turned to leave. It was obvious he was not happy. "You'll pay me next time. Have a good one!"

Zyadke wanted to be paid for everything. Even a tax notice! If anyone thinks Zaydke lives only off these five groshn, he's mistaken. The city administration pays him every month to deliver notices and hang announcements. But when Zaydke delivers a notice, don't be selfish, give him something for his efforts.

What? Is he any worse than Romanovsky the postman. He gets money from anyone he delivers a letter to even though the post office pays him every month!

It's true that Zaydke's notices bring trouble. But it is not his fault, he would be happy to deliver good news as he complained about this to his relative, Tuvyie Idl, the butcher at the house where all the butchers gather in the evening with large bloody pelts.

Zaydke has other jobs on the side. He walks through town with an alarm clock and sells lottery tickets. It only costs 10 groshn a ticket and you could win a new alarm clock. Tailors and shoemakers buy these tickets for their children and try their luck. Meanwhile, Zaydke earns a few groshn.

[Page 276]

* * *

Lately, Zaydkeh has become active in the community. He goes every Friday to the craftsmen's homes and calls out: "Five groshn for apples!" in order to understand this next exploit I must share a bit of history.

Every Friday evening Shmuel Kustin, the head of the Jewish community reads from the Pentateuch in the new House of Study. He talks in a weak feminine voice and explains the portion of the week. The word Khazal (all of our sages) flies from his mouth. Khazal said this, Khazal asked that, Khazal here, Khazal there.

Out on the street it is bitterly cold. In the House of Study the stove is hot. Jews are sitting around, craftsmen, peddlers, tired from the whole week, their hands spread out on their lecterns. With their heads in their hands, they sleep. From time to time Zaydke's voice wakes them up:

"Get out fellows, I'll slap you silly!"

This is how Zaydke received a group of school boys, frozen from skating who rushed into the House of Study to warm up. It doesn't take long before Shmuel Kustin lulls the craftsmen back to sleep.

This is what occurred every Friday evening. However, near me is the 20th century, and it is impossible that the 20th century would avoid Zhetl, just as it is impossible that the tax inspector would not come to control the tickets of the Zhetl craftsmen and shopkeepers.

The 20th century descended on Zhetl with talking movies, political party meetings and candy stores open on the Sabbath. However going to the movies costs money. Jews stand on the other side of the wall and hear a hoarse voice talking in English, French or other languages, who the hell knows what. On Friday evenings, men and women listen and thoroughly enjoy pictures that are talking on the other side of the wall.

The second exploit of the 20th century were lectures and meetings. Precisely on Friday evenings the speakers came and gave passionate speeches, for free. The Jews of Zhetl took their wives and children and went to listen. Ay, it's cold in the classrooms of the Yiddish school and Tarbut School. Who doesn't allow them to sit in their coats? But when the crowds gather, it warms up, Jews take a nap just like during Shmuel Kustin's talks in the warm House of Study. Other shameless people sit in the beer house cracking nuts and listen to Hirshl Meir's stories about the war.

Is it a wonder that the heated House of Study began to empty Friday evenings? Shmuel Kusitn was disappointed that he could longer delight people with his talks.

But our Zaydke did not lose his head. He went through town collecting five groshn, and for one zloty he bought a few baskets of frozen apples and shouted from the platform where prayers were led, during prayers, that during the reading of the Pentateuch he will distribute apples. And that is what happened. It became a custom, every Friday evening, after reading the Pentateuch, Zaydke distributed apples. Older Jews made a blessing, took a bite then put the apple in their pockets to bring to their grandchildren.

True the House of Study is not full like it used to be in the good old days, but Shmuel Kustin no longer talks to the walls and people still take naps during his talks.

Is this not thanks Zaydke's praiseworthy action?

The Last Badkhn
(Entertaining Rhymester at Jewish Weddings)

by Yakov Indershteyn (Kibbutz Eylon)

Translated by Janie Respitz

Among those who prayed in the old House of Study were the rabbi, scholars and community big shots with their sons in law. Those who prayed in the new House of Study were craftsmen, peddlers and small shopkeepers.

Where was it the happiest on Simchas Torah? Of course, in the new House of Study! Mayshke the Ox led services, or as we called him when he got old, Reb Moishe.

When a group of kids saw that Mayshke turned his black cap with the visor backward, and started to jump around carrying the Torah, they really felt it was Simchas Torah all over the world! Everyone loved to crowd around Mayshke and hear his rhymes.

Mayshke does not only talk in rhyme on Simchas Torah, but always, when he is in a good mood. Don't forget that Mayshke the Ox is a Badkhn, although this is only a side job.

[Page 277]

His main job was a shoemaker. A type of holiday coat.

The story goes that when the old Badkhn Avrom Moishe died, Mayshke the Ox went to his widow and bought the large book of rhymes the old Badkhn made up and collected over the years. In order to get used to his new job, Mayshke began to speak in rhyme:

Soreh Leah my love

You are the jewel in my crown.

Perhaps you know,

Where's my whetstone?

This is how he talks to his wife who rummages through the pots. When he got used to speaking in rhyme, it became his language and he didn't even realize he was rhyming.

*

A few weeks before Passover Mayshke dismantled the wall between his kitchen and workshop and built a Matzah oven. This was a time when everybody thought himself a big shot. They could not even spin shoemaker's thread, but they made strikes and unions: older workers from the Matzah bakeries got together, organized a strike, and went around to all the matzah bakeries and took away their rolling pins.

One o'clock in the morning, just before the first oven was lit, we heard wild cries at the rabbi's on the street where Mayshke lived. Curious heads peeked out from the double windows.

"What's going on?"

You can hear Mayshke screaming:

"They beat me up, they should suffer from stomach pains!"

People asked from all sides: "Who did this Reb Moishe, who?"

He answered:

Alter and Berl Yokehs, cursing them, in rhyme…

It was a surprise when during a wedding, Mayshke raised his head high, faced the in laws with his grey beard: brought his pointer finger to his thumb, closed his eyes and hummed;

The bride's sister Taybele,

Came to see her sister become a Vaybele. (Wife). ٭

Wishing everyone a good week,

Musicians! Begin the hum…

Pick up your instruments,

Show us some fun.

As he says these last words he opens his eyes, winks at Avreymche the blacksmith, a sign for him to play his fiddle. Khaim Aryeh begins to blow sideways into his flute and Aryeh the drummer, the old musician, bangs his drum as the dancing begins! What a delight!

* * *

Lately, Mayshke the Ox hardly ever performs. People are making quieter weddings. The political parties confuse us and brides and grooms are embarrassed to make a huge fanfare.

But Mayshke preys on his talent. I heard that he once approached a group of young Zionists, boys in shorts who sing all night and don't let their neighbours sleep, and asked them why don't they put on a show? He was ready to rehearse "The Sale of Joseph" with them. He once staged this at the Talmud Torah and the whole town came. He said they loved it.

Turns out the boys showed no interest in his suggestion. Nothing came of it. Mayshke, or as we called him in his later years, Reb Moishe, had to be satisfied with his old profession, fixing shoes. Once in a while he would hum a melody from the play "The Sale of Joseph".

"The old father Jacob with his twelve sons,

Would travel there and back"!

In the middle of singing he would remember the boys who made fun of this little theatre piece. Mayshke became angry, threw down the old shoe, put on his coat and cotton cap and went to the new House of Study to hear Yisroel Ber read beautiful Talmudic commentaries. Meanwhile, he remembered that not so long ago, on Simchas Torah, he stood in the middle of the House of Study and sang with everyone:

"There is no God like our God,

Let us thank our Master!…

[Page 278]

The Shiluvsky Family from Haleli

by Moishe Mirsky (Montreal)

Translated by Janie Respitz

The family of Khaim Shiluvsky, known as Khaim from Haleli lived in the village of Haleli which was 5 kilometres from Zhetl. They were well off people who owned the water mill.

Zhetl suffered economically under German occupation during the First World War. Destitution and hunger snuck into many homes. Even wealthier people who had enough money to buy bread faced difficulties due to the edicts of the occupiers.

The Shiluvsky family was not indifferent to the suffering many of the homes in town experienced.

Khaim Shiluvsky and his wife Nekhama of blessed memory could not rest. They would come to town every day to inquire who was suffering, who lacked bread, making every effort not to embarrass anyone, God forbid. With a warm heart and open hand they helped all those in need especially those who had been well off and lost everything.

Khaim and Nekhama Shiluvsky

This modest, kind charity was not easy to do. It was against the law and doing so could face harsh punishment from the Germans, may their names be blocked out.

Mrs. Shiluvsky was a quiet fine woman. Her modesty and humility helped her diplomatically to distribute bread to the hungry. If the family in need was not at home, she would leave bread and potatoes for them.

Their kindness was well known in the region. Everyone knew you did not leave the Shiluvsky's house hungry.

Later on, during the Polish – Bolshevik war life was very difficult and people began wandering from town to town. The roads were filled with refugees and the Shiluvsky's house was transformed into a charitable kitchen. Day and night pots of soup were made and bread was baked. People came to eat and received a care package for their journey.

The war also caused other problems for the Shiluvskys. Bands of robbers would often visit at night, taking what they could often accompanied by beatings.

The Shiluvsky family was convinced there was no place for Jews in Haleli or anywhere in Poland. Therefore they sold all they had, left Poland and settled in Canada. This is how they saved themselves and their children who in the meantime married and live in Montreal.

The horrible experiences and the terrifying news they heard about Jews in Poland took a toll on Mrs. Shiluvsky's health. She died on November 8th 1942 leaving her husband, Reb Khaim, four married daughters, two married sons and by then, eight grandchildren.

Today, there are, spare the evil eye, seventeen grandchildren of which some are married.

My Mother Leah Hinde Merim's of Blessed Memory

by Miriam Izraelit – Davidovsky (Givatayim)

Translated by Janie Respitz

In Zhetl my mother was called Leah Hinde Merim's. She was born in Vilna in 1866. She married in Zhetl in 1885 and lived there for 46 years.

My mother's maiden name was Kuhel. Her father, Yehoshua Kuhel was a well educated man and a successful merchant. My mother comes from a very fine family which included the Iserlins, Levin – Epshteyns and Shapiros.

My mother of blessed memory was one of the most important women in Zhetl. She was energetic, smart, beautiful and progressive. She always tried to help other people as much as she possibly could. She never differentiated between rich and poor. She treated everyone with respect. She had a personal account for the Interest Free Loan Society and never refused those in need.

My mother of blessed memory also served as the manager of women during childbirth and the Society to Aid the Sick. She made sure someone spent the night with sick people, often sending her own children.

She would often visit the Yeshiva and bring boys home to eat. Every Friday she would make sure the poor had a challah and food for the Sabbath.

She died on Chanukah 1931. Honour her memory!

[Page 279]

Efraim Belagolovsky – Kharmoni of blessed memory

by Nekhemia Aminoakh (Kfar Avraham)

Translated by Janie Respitz

Efraim son of Khaim Belagolovsky was born in 1890 in Lodz. Until the age of 13 he studied in a Yeshiva. In 1906 he joined "The Young Zionists" in Lodz. From 1908–1912 he was elected onto the council of "The Young Zionists" in Lodz and was an active member of "The Society of Lovers of Hebrew". Efraim Belagolovsky describes this period in his writings which he had left for us.

"On Saturday morning when my friend Nakhman Rozin of blessed memory and I were standing in synagogue speaking Hebrew, a tall young man came up to us and asked:

"These boys speak Hebrew and I don't know them?" This was Yekutiel Davidovitch (Today Ezroni, a Hebrew teacher in Tel Aviv).

He took us to the illegal "Mizrachi" school which was in an alcove, under the roof on Vskhodnia Street. Neighbouring "Mizrachi" was the "Young Zionist" association. The members of "Mizrachi" were predominantly Hasidim who were chased out of their prayer houses for the sin of Zionism. These Hasidic religious Zionists provided protection in their synagogue to the secular, young Zionists.

At age thirteen I worked as an assistant in a store and I worked from 8 in the morning until 11 at night. Socialism was extremely attractive. However, I was not satisfied with my nationalist feelings I had felt from childhood. From all the Jewish socialist parties, I felt most comfortable with the "Poalei Zion" (Labour Zionists).

My friends and I did not see the national question through the eyes of Borokhov. The national question for us was not any less important than the socialist one. We knew that when the social question would be answered, the world would still be faced with the national question.

Also with the socialist question we were closer to the S.R (Social Revolutionaries) than the S.D (Social Democrats). I was also a member of the professional union of the P.S.D."

In 1913 Efraim Belagolovsky organized the Zionist youth in Kastrama. During the German occupation from 1915–1916 he led the Zionist association in Zhetl. He visited cities close to Zhetl to help organize Zionist activity. In those years his thoughts were clear, and he expressed himself succinctly in writing which he used as a source of income.

It is clear why Efraim Belagolvsky organized the General Zionist association in Zhetl. If there had not been a German occupation he would have organized the "Young Zionists". But at that time in Zhetl it was impossible to crystalize the image of the association. Zionist aspirations demanded broader and less clarity in the party sense. This way, all Zionist youth from the various political leanings could join the same club.

In 1918 he was a member of the board of "Young Zionists" in Bialystok and a member of the Zionist Centre and the "Young Zionists" Centre in southern Lithuania.

In 1920 he participated in the second conference of "Young Zionists" in Warsaw and was elected to the "Young Zionists" Centre in Poland. He participated as a delegate in the Fourth Zionist Conference in Poland.

From 1920 –1926 Efraim Belagolovsky worked as secretary and as an instructor for the "Young Zionists" Centre in Lithuania. In 1926 he immigrated to the Land of Israel where he was a member of Mapai and worked as a bookkeeper for the construction company "Solel Boneh".

E. Belagolovsky participated in many international conferences. He was a delegate to the 12th, 13th and 14th Zionist Congresses, The International Conference of the "Young Zionists" and ORT in Danzig and the Conference for Lending Cooperation for European Jewry.

After his death his friends in Israel wrote:

Efraim Kharmoni (Belegolovsky) was the symbol of a socialist personality. Honest in every sense of the word. Always worked for the poor masses. Everywhere he worked he acquired good friends and a good reputation.

[Page 280]

Zhetl Writers

Collected by M. Dunetz

Translated by Janie Respitz

Menakhem Mendl Merlinsky

Menakhem Mendl Merlinsky was born in Zhetl in 1853. As a young boy he studied in the Yeshiva of the esteemed rabbi Rabbi Yitzkahk Bar Asher. He excelled with his knowledge and mastery of Talmud. He was self taught in Hebrew and grammar and soon became proficient in Hebrew literature.

He married at age 17. He was very poor and supported himself giving Hebrew lessons in wealthy homes. He studied Russian and German and mastered both languages perfectly.

In 1876 he began to write for "HaTzfira" on science and literary topics, including the articles "The History of the City of Bombay and its Inhabitants", "Mount Ararat", "Mount Etna" and others. In 1886 he opened a Hebrew school in Bialystok. His works were also published in "Magid Mishna" and "Hakol".

Menakhem Mendl Merlinsky was one of the great Jewish enlighteners of his generation. His son in law was the well known Bialystok man of letters, Peysakh Kaplan.

A. Ben – Avigdor (Avrom Leyb Shalkovitch) 1866 – 1921

Although A. Ben – Avigdor was born in the neighbouring town of Zheludok, he can be considered a Zhetler. As a young child he moved with his family to Zhetl. His father was Avigdor the untrained old time physician. Ben – Avigdor studied and was raised in Zhetl and this is where he took his first literary steps.

In 1889 his first article was published in "HaMeilitz". In 1892 he began to publish the large collection "Sifrei Agura" (Penny Dreadfuls – cheap serialized stories). He was one of the founders of "Akhyasaf" and "Toshiya" publishing houses. In 1905 he helped found the Vilna newspaper "HaZman" (The Time).

He fought for Herzlian Zionism and was a supporter of Herzl's Uganda Plan. In Warsaw he was the founder of The Hebrew Writer's Union, which he chaired for many years.

A. M. Dilan

A.M. Dilan was born in Zhetl in 1882 to old Jewish aristocracy. His name in Zhetl was A. Zhukhovitsksy. As a writer he used the name: Dilan.

In 1904 he left for America. In 1910 he debuted in an anthology called "Literature" and since then published poems in various periodicals and journals like: "Dos Naye Lebn" (The New Life), "Shriftn" (Writings), "Di Feder" (The Feather), "Der Onhayb" (The Beginning), "London Renaissance", "Tzukunft" (The Future), and others. He published in book form a collection of poems called "Gele Bleter" (Yellow Leaves) (Published by "America", New York, 1919), illustrated with drawings by Z. Maod which is one of the most magnificent works of Yiddish literature.

All of Dilan's poems are penetrated with deep melancholy and present human fear and suffering, despair and death. He died in New York.

Avrom Ivenitsky

Avrom Ivenitsky was born in Zhetl to his parents Dov – Ber and Dishe. After experiencing the First World War he married Esther Kaplinsky, the daughter of the honourable Zhetl businessman, Hertz Leyb Kaplinsky.

He worked for a short time as a teacher in Zhetl and then as vice – mayor. He participated in various literary works. He was the author of the book "When Roads Cross", a diary of a Jewish prisoner of war, published by the Union of Yiddish Writers and Journalists in Vilna, 1924.

[Page 281]

Memories

Ahuza Street

[Page 282]

Memories

Translated by Judy Montel

The memories are abundant and overflow their banks. Events, celebrations, anecdotes and catch-phrases – how can we forget them? And therefore, we will recount, just a bit, quoting those involved:

Avraham Ivenitzki OBM told: Reb Zalmen Dunetz was known for his love of the land of Israel. Once Reb David Shaykes, a well-known home-owner in Zhetl teased him with the sad news item about Delfiner who closed the silk factory in the land of Israel. A few days later, before dawn, Reb David Shaykes was awoken by loud knocks on the panes of his window. There stood Reb Zalmen.

- What do you say, Dudkeh, has the wind reached your bones?

- What happened!

- Don't you know?

- How should I know?

- Why Delfiner has reopened his factory.

- Tfu, you crazy fellow, for this you need to wake me so early in the morning?

Moshe Mirski recounts: When you reached the market in the morning you encountered two gatherings. In one crowd, they discussed the matters of the town, and here the chief speaker was Reb Yisrael Ozer Brishenski. In the second crowd a fierce argument was taking place about world politics, and here the chief speaker was his brother, Reb Avraham Moshe Brishenski. If a passerby asked about the tumult and shouts, it was explained to them: "Here the two Brishenski brothers are arguing. One runs the affairs of the town and the other the affairs of the world."

Rabbi Reb Yitzchak Vainstein recounted: Our home was always full of guests, of course, not in order to receive any reward. From lack of places, mother would lay them on the couch, on the table and sometimes on the doors which had been removed from their hinges. Once when I came home from the yeshiva in Mir, I saw a guest entering with a package under his armpit. According to the look on his face, I understood that he was returning from the bath-house. He had only just walked in when he began to complain to my mother:

- Can it be, a person returns from the bath-house and doesn't find a hot cup of tea?

I was shocked by the guest's words. For we were hosting him not in order to receive any compensation. Meanwhile, father came back. After he heard the guest's complaint he turned to my mother with these words:

- Ette, he's right!

Sarah Gol recounts: from the tiny little villages around us: from Belitsa, Dvoretz and Kovlovshchyna people would come to see a play in Zhetl, or to enjoy a dance party. After they returned home they would speak of Zhetl's glories and conclude: Long live the big city!

[Page 283]

Why Does our Heart Cry so Much?

by Borukh Kaplinsky (Tel Aviv)

Translated by Janie Respitz

Between Slonim and Novogrudek, surrounded by forests, lay our town Zhetl. We were born in its houses and played in its yards. This is where we were raised. Some went to Yosele Mendes' Heder and some studied with Noyekh Eli the tutor, some attended the Talmud Torah at Yudl the ritual slaughterer and some went to the Yiddish school where they were taught by Lieberman and Frenkel. The younger ones went to the Tarbut Hebrew School where they were taught by Kokiel, Blokh and Vilensky.

Here in Zhetl we were mature and learned a chapter of Zionism. Some through Hashomer Hatzair and others in the Poalei Zion, some in Hechalutz Hatzair and others in the Revisionist Betar.

Here is where we took our first steps into communal life: the board of the Jewish National Fund, the board of the Tarbut School, TOZ Jewish Welfare Organization and Child Protection.

In Zhetl we also vegetated without a future. In this regard, we were all the same, no differences. Yosele Mendes' students and the Yiddish school pupils, the Jewish National Fund volunteers and the TOZ activists.

We immigrated to the Land of Israel from this town. Some with a certificate in the 1930s and others with a number tattooed on their arm in the 1940s, some from the Lipichansk partisans, and others from Siberia.

The town of Zhetl ceased to exist 14 years ago, destroyed by the terrible enemy down to its foundation.

From far away, from Tel Aviv in the State of Israel, I often want to remember Zhetl, our birthplace, and together with you, remember our fathers and mothers, relatives and friends, neighbours and acquaintances, those who went like sheep to the slaughter and those who fought like lions in the forests.

Who Came?

When you travelled home to Zhetl from Novolenyie, from a distance, many kilometres away from Zhetl, you saw the spires of the Catholic Church. That cross did not set the tone in Zhetl. It did not decide the character of the town. The tone in Zhetl was set in the synagogue courtyard with the three Houses of Study and the four cornered marketplace with its circle of shops.

You can be convinced of this as soon as soon as you get off the bus at the marketplace. People from town would immediately surround you to check your pulse: Who are you? Are you a Tarbut person or do you belong to the Yiddish School? If you were a Tarbut person they would take you to Berl Rabinovitch's hotel and the door would not close. All the Tarbut people would come by led by the old man Hertz Leyb Kaplinsky.

Zhetl's Communal Activists

The old Hertz Leyb stands before my eyes, a Talmudic scholar and a good spirit, religious yet tolerant, a grandfather who found a common language with his grandchildren. I see his stately appearance and his white beard. He walks straight and doesn't even lean on his cane, sits down, clears his throat, rubs his bald spot and begins a philosophical conversation.

After him my father arrives, Shaul Kaplinsky, educated in Torah and a devoted Zionist, knowledgeable in Hebrew and a communal activist. For many years he served as chairman of the Zionist Organization in Zhetl. He built the Tarbut School and was active in the National Fund. Feyvl Epshteyn arrived with him, the youngest of the group, a devoted Zionist, and enlightened Jew ready to help reach all Zionist goals.

Of course I remember Khaim Levit, the chairman of the merchant's union, energetic, impulsive and bubbling with initiative. He calls meetings, travels to Novoredok to repeal edicts and is the breath of life of the Zionist pack in Zhetl.

This picture would not be complete if I did not mention Yisroel Ozer Barishansky, a small man, detached, but with a warm Jewish heart, a shrewd brain and a sharp tongue. He built the electricity station in Zhetl and received all the women's curses every time there was a power failure. He built the Talmud Torah and helped build the Tarbut School. He was the landlord of the bathhouse, ritual bath and hospital, and took care of poor women in childbirth, unfortunate widows, and the very sick who had be taken to Vilna. He was the one who initiated a delay in reading the Torah as a protest over the rise of the price of yeast and ritual slaughter. He was the one who went from house to house with a red handkerchief to collect money for a wagon driver with a lame horse.

[Page 284]

It would be an injustice if we would not mention the following community leaders: Tzale Mashkovsky, Dovid Senderovsky, and Ruven Mordkovsky. They devoted a lot of time and energy to Zionism, Tarbut and the funds.

You could meet all of the at Berl Rabinovitch's hotel if a Tarbut volunteer or a Zionist activist arrived in town.

If an activist from the Yiddish Folk School arrived the following would visit him in the hotel: Avrom Moishe Barishansky, Shike Ovseyevitch, Khaim Ganuzovitch, Khaim Mikhl Roznov and all the other Yiddishists.

For years they were our political opponents. We fought each other, tormented each other but all idealistically. Each one of us believed in our cause. Although we headed down different paths we were united with one goal: to improve our lives.

Today we can say with assuredness that our Zionist path was the correct one. I would like to stress that there were areas where the Yiddishists surpassed us.

They were the pioneers of stage theatre in Zhetl as well as the pioneers of a secular school.

It would often happen that both sides would be greatly disappointed: the guest arriving in Zhetl would not be from Tarbut or a Yiddishist. He would simply be a voyageur from a Lodz stocking factory.

Two Revolutionary Forces

However neither this nor any other failure managed to cool the heated positions on both sides. On the contrary. For example the Tarbut School organized a successful bazar for the Jewish National Fund with the participation of the director of the Hebrew School in Lida, Bernholtz at the same time as the Yiddish school staged a successful performance of "Mirele Efros": the Yiddish school activists built a building near Tcherne the miller, and the Tarbut people built another building, no smaller, near Yudl Khaim Rashkin's house.

This is how Zhetl ran. Two rival forces fought over grabbing more positions.

No sign of these struggles have remained. The cruel Hitler boots annihilated everything, not respecting any child or elderly person. All that remains from Zhetl is a bundle of memories. Therefore we want to keep these memories eternally so they can serve as a memorial for what was and will never return.

Friday Evenings

Sunken in my memory, in front of my eyes are the youngsters from Zhetl. It is Friday evening after supper. The streets are filled with groups making noise and shouting. I remember them as if it was today with their ringing little voices, cracking nuts and drinking soda water at Yosl Gertzovsky's or Khaya Leah Katz'.

Right after that I see them sitting on balconies, laughing, joking or walking down the highway toward the palace.

This is what Zhetl's youth were like: if someone learned a new dance, all of Zhetl would dance. Sometimes there would be soccer mania and all the boys would kick the ball around at the horse market.

Later on, when the political parties heated up all the boys and girls in Zhetl would dance the Hora and carry on discussions in their locales. Later their bubbly moods brought them to Klesov and Shkahriya where they chopped wood and drew water in preparation to immigrate to the Land of Israel. Those who did not make it excelled in Lipichansk forest where they fought like lions in order to take revenge for the lives of their brothers and sisters.

The Sabbath in Zhetl

Do you remember the Sabbath in Zhetl? The dust from the swept streets still hangs in the air but the stores have been closed for a while. Soon the lights are lit. There's a holiday feeling. People dressed up in their Sabbath best walk slowly to greet the Sabbath queen. From the small prayer house you can hear the hoarse voice of Hirshl the blacksmith. Yudl the ritual slaughterer leads prayers in the Hasidic prayer house.

A little later night falls. The Sabbath queen soars over the Zhetl houses. Each family sings the Sabbath songs. Soon you can hear the clattering of spoons, forks, plates and bowls. Zhetl is eating Sabbath supper. Soon you can see those who have finished eating. They are strolling, eating sunflower seeds and drinking soda water.

Neighbours gather on stoops and balconies telling stories like this: "What more do you need, I'll tell you a better story". The conversation is mixed with the laughter of children and teens. They walk in groups to the palace or on Novoredok Street. I can still hear their laughter ringing in my ears. I hear it now fresh and lively.

[Page 285]

Now I ask myself, how was that laughter so cruelly silenced?

Saturday morning. The House of study is full. Our grandmothers and mothers are praying in the women's section. When the Torah reading begins, Yisroel Ozer jumps out of the corner, bangs his lectern and demands a delay in the reading as a protest.

On this Sabbath he's agitating against the butchers who don't want to pay the tax on kosher meat. A week earlier he demanded the community agree to a 5 groshn price rise on yeast in order to raise the salary of the rabbi. Another time he went against the doctor who billed the sick poor.

At first the crowd listens calmly, but then reacts either for or against Yisroel Ozer. Sometimes, people got upset, raised a hand and shouted curses.

A little later. The congregation reaches the closing eighteen benedictions, but Yisroel Ozer is still standing in the anteroom. He's ranting excitedly.

After the Cholent (Sabbath Stew)

After the Cholent the meetings begin. Both at the Tarbut School and the Yidddish Folkshul. At the Talmud Torah the managers and the commission discuss the salary of the doctor. The Zhetl community activists sit all around town bickering and losing their tempers, shouting and ranting, often until the third Sabbath meal.

Mutual Aid

Zhetl would never forgive me if I did not mention the Mutual Aid and communal institutions. They were primitive but they had very good intentions!

Do you remember the old people's home and its founder Yisroel Ozer Barishansky? The Society to Visit the Sick and Aid to the Sick? Do you remember the Societies to Spend the Night with the Sick, Upholding the Fallen, Supporting Poor Brides? Do you not see before your eyes the men and women who collected money in red handkerchiefs for poor brides, orphans and lamenters?

And on the other hand Zhetl can be proud of its modern institutions, such as the TOZ Welfare Agency, The People's Bank, YEKOPO (Jewish Relief for War Victims) and the Merchant's and Craftsmen's Unions.

Who could possibly list all the institutions created in Zhetl to help the poor, sick and needy?

Why?

I can see Zhetl's communal activists before my eyes and it would be a sin not to pass down these stories to our children and children's children in Israel. Our children have nothing to be ashamed about, our Israeli Sabras and half Sabras compared to the children in Zhetl. Also our school and institutions in Israel have nothing to be ashamed about in comparison to Zhetl's schools. We have more than one Tarbut School and more than one Folkshul and no fewer devoted communal activists. However my heart gnaws and longs for Zhetl and can't be consoled: why was such a colourful and intensive life so pitilessly eradicated?

We will live out our years with this wound and a stranger will never understand why hearts cry so much in silence.

Greetings From Zhetl

A letter from Zhetl. Regards from the old home. Fresh and lively, dated October 10th, 1956, 14 years after the destruction of Zhetl. On this day the greetings were still in Zhetl. An experienced hand of a postal worker quickly stenciled the stamp: Diatlovo Gradnienskaya Oblast. And then carelessly, a second stamp: Diatlovo Baranovitzkaya Oblast. The postal worker did not understand that by then Zhetl was practically ridden of Jews, but we, Zhetl's former sons want to know exactly: which Oblast (Province) after all? And the main thing: why did he confuse us? We are sure he did not imagine how his postal stamp would cause such a shiver for Zhetl Jews all over the world. For them it is a loving greeting, although scant.

[Page 286]

Once There Was a Town...

by Mordechai Dunetz, Flint – United States

Translated by Janie Respitz

Between White Russian forests and fields, by the quiet flowing waters of the Nieman and Satshare, lay a small town.

The town lived and breathed, pulsated and squirmed, generations of Jews wove the thread of their ancestors which took them far from the depths of our ancient past.

Rabbis, enlightened Jews, functionaries of religious and communal life and ritual slaughterers, craftsmen and merchants were born there, lived quietly and died quietly. Their places were taken by their inheritors who continued to pull at the ancient thread.

The House of Study and Hasidic Prayer House, the poorhouse and the anteroom of the synagogue, the bathhouse and the slaughterhouse, the small shops and market were filled to their essence.

They mourned on the Tisha B'Av, danced – Simchat Torah and did business every Tuesday and Friday.

Wagon drivers from dusty sandy roads, shoemakers from three cornered low tables, carpenters with burning scents, and grocery merchants would all with a stately appearance, go out with their prayer shawls under their arms through the Jewish streets on the Sabbath, praise God for the past and pray for a good new week.

Hostels and inns would receive guests, brokers and matchmakers would count their "revenues".

Between school terms the boys from Mir and Volozhyn, Kletzk and Rodin, would come to rest at their father's table and gather strength for the next term.

* * *

The 80s of the previous century

New winds began to blow through Jewish cities and towns. Winds of enlightenment and renaissance.

Among the first supporters of the Hovevei Zion (Lovers of Zion) were grocers, shoemakers and tailors from the small town: Zhetl.

They threw themselves into this holy work with burning enthusiasm feeling the responsibility of the hour which was arriving.

Zionist circles, books and newspapers, congresses and meetings became the content of their lives, the atmosphere they breathed. Young people left their parents, their warm homes and set out on the long journey which would take them to their destination: Zion!

Difficult years arrived for the Jewish communities in this region. Years of invasion and siege.

Thousands of Jewish sons fell in the battlefields of the First World War. Thousands of Jewish boys gave their lives on the sacrificial alter, as they battled against tyranny, slavery and for national freedom.

The small town of Zhetl can also write a heroic page in the history of the First World War.

* * *

A standstill on all fronts. Tired, with vestiges of blood and dust, these young heroes return from the front to a wife and child, parents.

Life continues. Things appear to be normal again.

It is a time of progress. There is a thirst for life and knowledge among these trench heroes. They turn to the pen and book in an attempt to make up for the four years lost at war.

The youth prepare themselves for their greatest mission – to become the builders of our new land.

A small town is after all a corner of light and knowledge, a centre of Torah study and wisdom, a gushing source of singing, happy youthful joy. A school and a Heder, a "Tsisho" school and a "Tarbut" school have hundreds of children within their walls, forming the character of the new generation.

* * *

The town is quiet at dawn…

Everything around is wrapped in a deep sleep. Only the trees and grasses, which grow densely around the small low houses with moss covered roofs, rustle quietly. The small lake which distills its waters on the large wheel of the collapsed little mill allows its noise to be heard far off in the small narrow streets.

Somewhere in a corner an old Jew appears as he heads in the direction of the House of Study Street.

A small non – Jewish shepherd drives the hungry cows out of every Jewish stall, gathers them all together and leads them to the field.

A peasant's wagon rides over the cobblestone street waking the sleeping inhabitants.

[Page 287]

The town was quiet at dawn.

Suddenly!…The soil shook under our feet.

The foundation of this old Jewish settlement was shaking. However the building stood strong. We must firmly hang on to the roots of the birth town of the Chafetz Chaim and the preacher of Dubnov.

Echoes of canon shots and bombs got young and old up on their feet. Sulfur, gunpowder and blood filled the air of the small town.

Three at a time were thrown into the dark wagon. A loud bang forced them to look at the round marketplace for the last time, which on that day was filled with Jews with yellow patches on their clothes.

The first 120 Jews, the leaders of the community, left their small, old town, wives and children, the future they dreamed about, never to return.

Days of suffering and humiliations. Discouraged, depressed, you could hear the steps of people over the bloodied stones of the small town's streets.

With heads bent from toil and despair they return to the ghetto.

A quiet spring morning over the valley where Zhetl is situated.

The inhabitants of the ghetto are resting after work. Also resting are the blood thirsty drunken vampires after their noisy rampage.

Like a heap of meat covered with rags shining with the six cornered yellow patch, stands the Zhetl ancestral community. Bloodied spears hold the masses in a motionless, frozen state. Brows furrowed. Lips are bitten. And the screams are suppressed before they are even released.

The old cemetery is too small to receive everyone at once.

Behind the town, in the thick forest, a group of ten, one beside the other. Squeezed together are mothers and daughters, fathers and sons.

Little Khaiml clings to his mother's breast, hiding his small emaciated body from the whip.

"I want to continue living, after all, my name is Khaim (which means life)!"

The poisonous bullet passed through his mother's breast into his jerking little body which was quickly tossed into the mass grave.

The Seder Night

by Mashe Rozovsky – Shvartzman

Translated by Janie Respitz

Zhetl was a small town, but her streets were beautiful and bright. Life and learning gushed from its source. I see before my eyes scenes of Friday nights, Saturdays and holidays. Children are running around happy and dressed up. Jews go to pray, some in the old House of Study, some in the new one, some to the small prayer house and others in the Hasidic prayer house. A spiritual pleasure swept through every house. More than anything, I remember my father's Kiddush (prayer over the wine) and his Sabbath songs. I will never hear them again. Everything is gone.

I remember the eve of Passover. The preparations for the holiday. Everyone ran around, flew by, cleaning and washing. No small thing! The holiday of spring, Passover is coming. Everything is white and bright. Every corner is sparkling whiteness.

We prepare for the Seder. My mother, aunt and sisters are busy in the kitchen, sweating and talking. Suddenly the door opens and my father and brothers return from prayers with a broad: Good Yontev! (Happy holiday).

A wave of joy and warmth embraced me. Soon we will sit down at the table for the Seder and I will hear my father's beautiful Kiddush. The air in the house is filled with love and joy. The mood is great.

My father puts on his white long linen coat, spreads out on two white pillows and waits for my mother and aunt to come from the kitchen. Meanwhile my father turns the pages of his prayer book to find the Kiddush for the holiday.

There is a dead silence in the house. Father takes his wine cup in hand and begins to sing his resounding Kiddush. After him, my brothers recite the Kiddush and we read the Haggadah. I, just a small child, begin to fall asleep. I can barely wait for the Matzah balls and after I eat them I fall into a sweet sleep.

These happy childhood years are ingrained in my memory like a beautiful dream. The town, the street, my parent's house, our warm home, are all the things I remember with love and longing.

[Page 288]

A Week in Zhetl

by Sarah Gal – Begin (Jerusalem)

Translated by Janie Respitz

All the towns in our region looked the same. The marketplace in the centre, sometimes with a river, sometimes without. Every town had its matchmaker, a badkhn (a rhymester who entertained at weddings and other celebrations), a crazy person and a "Shabbes goy" a gentile who did things for the Jews which they were forbidden to do on the Sabbath. Strangers who read about Zhetl will recognize their own towns.

A week in Zhetl is a reflection of an entire year.

Sarah Gal – Begin

Sundays:

Clang clang! Bells ring on both sides of town from the Orthodox Church and the Catholic Church. The streets are filled with wagons. Every farmer pulled up at his Jew's house and every nobleman, at his "Moshke" (a humble Jew without status).

The nobleman stops amiably. His "Moshke" greets him with a warm good morning (in Polish) and helps the coachman unharness the horses. The nobleman rests for a bit in his Jew's house, like a boss.

Young Christian boys and girls come out of Church, the girls wearing colourful dresses with colourful ribbons carrying bouquets of flowers. They walk through the streets chewing on sunflower seeds. This was their greatest entertainment: strolling through town.

For Jews, Sunday was not an easy day. They could not do business openly as the businesses were closed. The police: Badovsky, Botok, Kaspshak and Motchok ran around like poisoned mice making official reports. Children stood guard to tell their parents when they saw the police coming. However, if you gave one of these policemen a bribe he would pretend he didn't see and Jews could continue doing business with their doors half open.

The best business was done at the taverns or beer houses, especially at the old Abdzhirak's and his son Sholem.

When a farmer would meet his friend he would ask him:

"How are you? Let's have a drink". No matter how much water they put in the whisky, the farmers got drunk.

The day passed quickly. In the evening the farmer's wives would harness the horses and take their drunk husbands home. All was quiet. Here and there you could see a wagon with a bell who was delayed in his return home. Women storekeepers tallied up their sales, men went to evening prayers and teenagers gathered in the fire brigade's orchard where the orchestra played dance music and we, the little ones watched through the slats in the fence.

Mondays:

The following morning, very early, Jews swept up the garbage on the streets from the previous day. They would have gladly had dirt everyday, but unfortunately they had to wait until Tuesday. On Mondays the women did not work in the stores in order to organize their households. The men would gather in a shop and take care of communal matters.

On a quiet day they paid attention to the small things like Leah the Baby walking in the streets, knitting socks and talking to someone about a betrothal all at the same time, or Baylke and Khaim Meir selling currants, or the loafers from the organizations would go to the post office to pick up the mail, since there really wasn't anything else to do. The only noise would come from the children running home from school and fighting. This is when people would say: Thank God it was a good day.

Tuesdays:

People waited for Tuesdays like one waits for the Messiah. From 4 o'clock in the morning the farmers would begin to arrive to grab a spot at the marketplace. Each farmer brought something to sell, cows, pigs or a horse. Their wagons were filled with lots of fruits and vegetables.

Across from Sonia Yosef Mushe's was a large scale. This was the regular spot of the grain dealer.

The middle of the marketplace, across from Rabinovitsh's hotel, was the regular spot of the flax and linen businesses headed by Ziamke the Vilner.

The saddle makers were bit further down and the following leather dealers were concentrated around the circle of shops: the Breskin brothers, Alter Bom, Yakov Meylekh Dvoretsky, Hirshl Butkovsky and at the end Eliezer Eliyau Slutsky. They would display their goods on tables at the edge of the circle of stores, near the sidewalk.

[Page 289]

They would compete against each other and pull the farmers away from the others. On the opposite edge of the circle of stores were Khienke – Malke Motke's daughters and beside them, Bashke the tinsmith competing against Khane – Esther the glazier.

Higher up on the steps near Avrom Moishe the old clothes dealer was Babel Goldshteyn and other saleswomen all ready to sell to a customer.

Not far from the Krigl, near the church, Musher stood with his three daughters selling old clothes.

The furriers would stand near Mikhal Roznov, all ready for the market to open.

The farmers began to unload the grain from their wagons and plead:

"Weigh honestly". So that the farmer would believe he's not being deceived he would be given half a zloty for every pood (16 kilos) of rye. By nature, the farmer is a thief. He would steal a few half zlotys and then receive payment for his rye according to how many half zlotys he had in his hand.

After his sale the farmer would go shopping in the stores.

A female farmer walked into a store with a bunch of children and began to try on clothes. Lots of haggling back and forth.

The area around the furriers was always busy. What gentile does not need a hat? The furriers attracted the farmers with their jokes. They would often, intentionally switch things around. They would place a small hat on a large head and say:

"It will stretch", and then place a hat that was too big and say: "it's perfect", because trying things on wasted a lot of time.

The cattle market was behind the church in the empty lot near the pharmacy .The farmers would tie the cows to their wagons, throw down a bit of hay so they would stand still, lift the carriage shaft to create more space and wait for customers.

Then a bunch of butchers arrive, headed by Kalmen the butcher. They spread out among the wagons, each one examined a cow or a calf and asked the same question: (In Russian)

"Uncle, how much for this cow?" They would immediately make an offer 20–30 zlotys cheaper, of course without reaching an agreement. The butchers would then walk away from the farmers, tell one another what they saw at what price and how much they offered. Then each butcher would go to another farmer and offer the same price.

In the course of bargaining the butcher would mention Vodka. When the farmer heard the word Vodka, and was tired of standing around, he would clap his hands and the sale was made.

In the evening all the butchers would gather at Tuvyie the butcher's house, sit around the long table on the long benches, still in their blood stained clothes from the slaughterhouse, and tell about the miracles that took place at the market.

There was another market in town: the horse market. All week this was the sports field. This is where the "TOZ" would play football (soccer), the cyclists would exercise and the youth organizations would hold tournaments.

However on Tuesdays, horses stood there. The farmers would buy and sell and the wagon drivers would exchange their nags for better ones.

There was unity among the horse dealers. They would go examine the horses together.

The Chashmonaim football (soccer) team, 1925

Seated: Mayrim Lusky, Moishe Levit, Avrom Rashkin
Second row: Hirshl Kaplinsky, Mordkhai Zakarysky, Veve Kravets, Leyb Zelikovitch
Last row: Noyekh Alpert, Pinkhas Mayevsky, Mikhl Kivelevitch, Yishayahu…., Avrom Alpert

[Page 290]

One would hold the horse while the other would look into its mouth. One would whip the horse from behind, giving the horse courage to run, while a fourth would hold the reins and run about 100 metres with the horse. If they were pleased with the horse they would begin to bargain over the price.

Market days were also visible on the side streets. The greatest merchant on our street was Yoel Dovid Dunetz who competed with Khaim Levit.

A large group of farmers would come to Slonim Street. They would come from Khadielan, Yurevitch, Mizevetz, Mirayshchine and Nakrishok. The first thing they did was go to Hirshl the blacksmith to sharpen their sickles and scythes.

"How are you Sorke" the gentile would say to my aunt Soreh – Rokhl as he stretched out one hand and with the other put something secretly into his pocket.

It was more difficult in the winter. Shopkeepers would stand all day with their hands congealed with kerosene and herring lacquer and they would run to the fire pot every free moment.

Tuesday was considered a lucky day. The majority of weddings took place on Tuesdays. Everyone would forget how tired they were. They would get all dressed up, be comparable to the in laws, dance to the beat of Arye the potter's drum and hear a few of Mayshke the Ox's jokes.

Wednesdays:

After the excitement of Tuesday, Wednesdays were the calm after the storm. At dawn we could hear the whistling of the shepherds taking the cows out to pasture.

In the summer we would not see a gentile all day and we had to in some way, pass the time.

Every street had its clown or someone to make fun of. On Novorodok Street the Khlebnik boys would converge on Mitzl, the eldest, and try to talk him into a betrothal with every girl that walked by on the street, although they were all older and single. In the marketplace there would be a circle around Ruven the Smoker and on Hoyf Street people would be entertained by Gershon the Smoker.

On Wednesdays during the winter there was more traffic in town. Farmers were free from field work and were busy chopping wood or coming to the record keepers of the lumber operation who worked in the offices.

When a farmer would steal a tree from a nobleman, he would chop it into firewood and sell it in town.

Maytchke Khane Gatchikhe's profited the most from these farmers. They would come to him to warm up and from the window keep and eye on their horses. Meanwhile they would buy herring and a piece of bread and drink a glass of tea. As usual, Maychke would be stingy with the sugar.

One gentile would say: "Maytchik, it is not sweet". "It will be sweet," replied Maytchke.

"Maytchik, it's still not sweet," he swore.

"You probably stirred it too much," Said Maytchke.

For kids, Wednesday was the best day. We could barely wait until four o'clock when we would run to the library in Yisroel the watchmaker's yard. Half of Zhetl's children were already standing beside the door at three o'clock waiting for Itchke Leybovitch or Motke Rozovsky.

"Motke, I want Jan Kristof" someone shouted from a corner.

"You are too young for that book," answered Motke.

"Motke, I want Crime and Punishment" a girl with a squeaky voice shouted. I ordered it three weeks ago".

Then Motke would ask the children to tell everyone, in short, what they read. He found each one an appropriate book for their age. He had a lot of patience for children.

Wednesdays, late in the evening the marketplace was filled with wagon drivers who brought Mikhal Sovitsky bags of salt, bottles of kerosene and herring from Novolenie. Yoshke the wagon driver distributed more than the rest. He was a specific wagon driver. He had broad healthy shoulders, and a leather belt with a brass buckle which he had from his days as a soldier in Nikolai's army. With his jokes and lexicon, no other wagon driver could be compared to him.

Standing beside his wagon beside Mikhl's store he was always searching for a receipt. Never remembering which pants pocket he put it in he would complain:

"When my Malke puts it away I can never find it".

[Page 291]

Thursdays:

Thursdays were shopping days for women. Beginning at dawn women would start to prepare for the Sabbath. In order to buy everything, you had to go through the whole town.

The women would begin at the marketplace to buy their fish from Yakov Shimen the tinsmith and Tzalie Vinarsky. They would attack the tubs searching for the largest fish.

"Touching costs money," Yakov Shimen said with his hoarse voice. In saying this he meant don't kill the fish.

Women stood in the streets with full baskets.

"Reb Meir, Reb Meir, bring me sixty eggs," one women said as she caught Meir in the street.

On the way home they would go to Gershon the Smoker to buy flour to make dumplings. His flour had the best reputation.

"Good morning Gershon, how are you today?"

"All's good as long as I can earn a living" he answered with his speech impediment.

All the butcher shops were filled with women, but fuller than the rest was Tuvyie Idl the butcher's. You could not even fit a pin into his store. A woman came running, out of breath shouting from a distance that she had no time to wait.

"Tuvyie Idl, if you have a stomach, save it for me".

Thursday afternoons the peddlers would return from the villages where they exchanged soap, soda and chicory for eggs and rags.

By evening every house smelled of oil challah and rolls. The scent poured out like a fine perfume.

Later, women went with their children and bundles under their arms to the bathhouse. Yakhne, the bathhouse attendant greeted each woman with a friendly good evening, especially the women who gave her the biggest tips.

Fridays:

Friday at dawn while God still slept the women were on their feet. Smoke snaked out of every chimney. They cooked hastily and placed things in the oven. By seven o'clock in the morning everything was ready.

On Fridays there was a smaller market, with hopes for large earnings. Daughters would help their mothers clean the house, wash the floors, clean the brass candlesticks with sand or wash the smaller children's hair.

By Friday afternoon, the Sabbath was ready. The table was covered with a white tablecloth. The challahs were covered with an embroidered cover across from the candlesticks and candles which were ready to be blessed. The only thing they waited for now was the whistle from the Liesopilnie sawmill.

"Thank God, the Sabbath has arrived" our mothers would say as they sighed heavily.

The town now had a holiday appearance. Candles were burning in every window. Men walked to synagogue dressed up with their children. Everything looked different, the candles, those walking, as if they had thrown off the yoke of the difficult week. Women would sit on the porches and balconies and gossip a bit. But in order to clear the conscience they would say: "May God punish me for what I'm saying".

Girls would walk to and fro, not too far from their houses because their fathers would soon be returning from prayers.

"Good Sabbath!" father would say as he entered the house and all the children would respond in chorus: "Good Sabbath!"

Father walks back and forth singing his Sabbath song "Sholem Aleichem…" The children sit at the table with their cute little faces in their hands waiting calmly, as if they owed their souls to God.

"Yom Hashishi, on the sixth day, (the beginning of the Kiddush, the blessing on the wine) could be heard from every house and everyone sang in symphony.

Friday after supper, all the organizations were full. You could also hear people singing, especially the Revisionists.

A little further on at Leah the Queen's street, in Krupnik's house, the Bundists met. They sang:

"England promised Palestine to the Jews,

The little Zionists run around happily".

The professional union was situated in the small house behind the bathhouse. Through the half opened window you could see the picture of Karl Marx with these words:

"Proletariat of all nations, unite". There, Niame Kaplinsky, with a kerosene lamp, would give a lecture on historical materialism.

Late at night, when a couple in love would return from the Slonim highway, one could hear singing and dancing from Felix's house, on Khazrish Street, the locale of Hashomer Hatzair.

[Page 292]

On Friday nights a little more was permitted because tomorrow is Saturday, the Sabbath, and we can sleep in.

Saturdays:

Saturday morning our mothers would take the pitcher of chicory off the ceramic tile and bring their husbands a glass of chicory and a roll so he does not have to wash. Men were careful not to take, God forbid, superfluous bites before praying. They took their prayer shawls under their arms and left for synagogue.

After prayers the women would hurry home and the men would walk slowly, step by step with their hands behind their backs chatting about town issues or general politics. On the street they would meet the children carrying the pots of Cholent (Sabbath stew). After eating the Cholent one could hear Sabbath songs coming from every house.

On our street you could hear Itche the butcher singing Tsur Mishelo" with his grandchildren, and Hirshl the blacksmith singing "Ribon Haolam" even louder. After singing, they would say the blessing after the meal and go to sleep. A Saturday afternoon nap is such a pleasure.

After the evening prayers you could hear "Hamavdil" from every house, the prayer to end the Sabbath and welcome the new week. Little boys would hold the candle and help with the singing.

"A good week, a good week!" and women would respond: "a good week, a healthy week and lucky week".

Jews would come from the surrounding towns like Bielitze, Dvoretz, and Kazlaytchine to attend theatre or a ball and as they would leave Zhetl they would say to one another:

"Long live this city!"

Tuesday

Translated by Judy Montel

In Zhetl, Tuesday was yearned for the way one yearns for the Messiah. From four in the morning farmers began arriving with wagons loaded with all good things and would find a place in the market.

Next to Sonya Yosef Moshess a large scale was set up. Here is where the grain dealers congregated.

In the middle of the market, next to the inn of Berel Rabinovitz, the flax dealers gathered headed by the dealer Zimka of Vilna.

A distance away the shoemakers set up, and at the "Rad-Kramen" (shopping center) the leather dealers displayed their goods. Each of them praised his wares and drew in customers.

Next to the shop of Michael Raznov the hatmakers sold their wares. They drew a lot of attention. For which of the farmers doesn't need a hat? Their jokes also aroused the curiosity of the farmers.

The hatmakers turned things upside down, for a large head they'd offer a small hat and explain "don't worry, the hat will stretch." In contrast, for a small head they'd offer a large hat and persuade the farmer: "this is exactly right, the correct size." All of this because they didn't have enough time to measure and fit each one.

Behind the Catholic church, on an empty lot, across from the pharmacy, was the cattle market. The farmers would tie the cows to the wagons there, give them a handful of hay and wait for a buyer.

And here comes a group of butchers headed by Kalman the butcher. They spread among the farmers, checking, feeling and asking:

"Aha, how much do you want for your cow?" The negotiations are exhausting and agreement is reached only when they offer the farmer a zloty (Polish currency) for brandy, then the farmer relents. He's sick of bargaining, he scratches his head, afterward shakes the hand of the butcher and the negotiations have ended.

In the evening the butchers gather in the home of Tuvia Idel the butcher. Their clothes still smell of blood from the slaughterhouse, they each sit around the long table and talk about the wonders of the market.

In the town there was one more market: the horse market. Most of the week it was a sports field and there were many games of football [soccer] there and people practiced riding bicycles there. But not on Tuesday. That day was a day of buying, selling and trading horses.

The stablemen were united. They always showed up as a cohesive bunch. One held the horse, a second checked his teeth, a third whipped him and made him run and the rest watched. Only after checking and examining did the bargaining start.

Tuesday in Zhetl was considered a day that was entirely lucky. On this day they would hold weddings and other happy events. The traders of Zhetl would rest only a little bit from the work of the demanding day and they quickly got dressed and decorated in their holiday clothing. Thus, they prepared to be in-laws, to dance to the sound of the music of Aryeh the Potter [sic but I think it's a typo and was meant to be the Fiddler, a difference of one letter, trans.] and to enjoy the jokes of Moshe the Badchan at the weddings of their loved ones.

[Page 293]

My Home

by Rivka Valdman (Paris)

Translated by Janie Respitz

Winter. In the morning children were already running to school. They would cut through Mayontek's alley, go into a good bakery and buy a cake, pudding or a roll.

The small street still appeared to be asleep with the houses squeezed together. From under shared roofs, squinted eyes peeked out of the small windows and winked at one another with weak flames.

A melody emerged from a small little window which seemed to be growing out from the ground. This was Mayontek preparing to lead services somewhere for the holidays. This was acceptable. There were towns smaller than Zhetl that did not have their own cantors. He sat in his shoemaker workshop lost in a melody and to the beat of his song pulled the thread through the patches on the shoe. He sewed with large nails and hammered the patches into the shoes. The hammering accompanied by his singing carried through the streets, reaching as far as the Houses of Study.

On the other street the children met Avrom the recluse. He sat in the synagogue day and night and studied. Sometimes during the day he would tear himself away from studying when the women would come to exorcise the evil eye. He would calm a frightened mother, eat a piece of bread, and a hard boiled egg and return to his studying. He did not need anything else.

In the mornings he performed a good deed. He ran through the street to the well. A naïve smile covered his face. He said good morning to every child, felt embarrassed and lowered his eyes.

He went from the House of Study to the well at the Pomerayke River near Leyzer the butcher's. He remained standing there beside the footbridge. To every woman and child who came to draw water he put out his hand and said:

"Allow me. I will pull out the bucket" he mumbled quietly.

The children ran further. You could already hear the shouts from the marketplace. Jews who went to pray with the first morning quorum quietly winked at each other and said:

Bunye's sons are whispering already…

And this is how it actually was. The Barishansky brothers fell upon a handcart filled with wood that a farmer had brought to town. The farmer barely made it to town. The road was difficult to travel with wheels or sleighs.

The younger brother, the already grey haired Avrom Moishe, shouted so loudly the whole town heard him. It did not bother him that people came running out of their houses.

"Yisroel Ozer, you will not buy that wood, even if you explode. You can die here. This time you will not succeed. There is not a piece of wood in the Yiddish Folk School the children are sitting in their coats".

"That's what I'm talking about" his older brother Yisroel Ozer shouted even louder. "The children in the Hebrew Tarbut School are also freezing. I am after all the older brother. So what if you saw this gentile first? I have been hanging around here since dark".

Now they were both shouting at the same time. One louder than the other. Avrom Moishe cursed his brother. People started to gather around. The circle grew and people began to take sides. Who knows how this would have ended if Yosl Khemes had not appeared.

"Where did you get hold of this?" Yosl Khemes the ritual scribe happily recounted:

"I could not sleep. I got up in the middle of the night and started to work. I wrote a page but my eyes began to hurt. I tried to bring the paper closer to the lamp but it did not help. I wanted to write more, but it wasn't going well, so I went out on Slonim Street. It was very cold in the school. The children are freezing. We must do something!"

"We must do something," repeated Avrom Moishe shouting loudly as usual and looked at the wood with joy.

The bell rang for the first recess. When the cart of wood was brought to the school the children ran out to the street, surrounded the farmer, and tried to get close to the horse. They were excited with the wood, the horse and the cold…

"It's not cold!" they shouted, and without their coats on, began to chase one another.

[Page 294]

The teachers stood on the porch and called the kids to come inside, they shouldn't God forbid catch a cold. It was so noisy the children could not hear them. Then they realized they could ring the bell. Recess was cut short.

"Come study! You must come study!"

It was quiet around the school. In the stillness you could clearly hear the voice of the teacher Leybl Frenkel. He was reading "If Not Higher" by Yitzkhal Leybush Peretz. A song from the Hebrew Tarbut School could be heard from the marketplace: "Little boy come to the window, a beautiful bird flew by".

This all poured out in chorus together with the Talmud melody coming from the Yeshiva.

Late at night Avrom the recluse walked home from the House of Study. In the streets you could still hear echoes of the last songs sung by the teenagers who walked through town like flocks of birds.

Soon all was quiet. Only Shneour the night watchman walked through the marketplace guarding the circle shops. He walked with heavy steps. He held a lantern in one hand and a thick stick in the other. He soon became bored and was chilled to the bone. He banged his stick on a metal sign which echoed through the entire marketplace.

"Let the entire town know that Shneour is guarding the circle of stores. He is not being paid for nothing…"

A person appeared on the sidewalk near the houses. Maybe someone from the Society to Spend the Night with the Sick was going to spend the night with a patient?

"Who's there?" asked Shneour, bored with nothing to do.

"It's me, Tzalie!"

Tzalie the barber, the clown, already thought of a prank.

How many pranks did he already pull?

He already woke up Leyzer the butcher in the middle of the night and informed him that his mother in law died as he stood in the corner laughing watching Leyzer run around for no reason.

Sitting beside his barber shop, he told a woman farmer who came to town to see a doctor to come into his shop first for a haircut in preparation for the doctor. When she finally took off her fifth "petticoat" he explained his mistake. She needed a doctor and he is only a barber. He explained he did not properly hear what she was looking for…

Tzalie was not lazy. One summer night he secluded himself in the new cemetery and lay there in a white shroud until late at night. When the teens calmly lay on the ground beside their horses, Tzalie crept out from behind the graves and slowly trudged toward them.

The next day Tzalie told everyone how the kids abandoned their horses and ran recklessly to town.

Now, he quietly approached Reb Avrom's house and saw through the window how he sat by the light of a candle and studied. Tzalie quietly climbed up on to the roof and shouted down the chimney:

"Avrom! Avrom!

"I'm here" replied Avrom (in biblical Hebrew as if responding to God's calling), in a quiet frightened voice. Tzalie could not believe it.

Reb Avrom stood there, pale with his eyes closed. He raised his trembling hands in the air as his lips quivered.

Tzalie was overcome with fear.

"Are there still miracles? Is this the Abraham I learnt about in Heder?"

Tzalie did a lot of thinking that night. He decided he should not pull pranks on such religious people as in the end, he's the fool.

Zhetl's scribes supported the revolution with the same passion Avrom had for religion. With the same fervent belief Jews prayed in the Houses of Study and Yenkl the Hasid danced in the Hasidic prayer house. With this passion they built the Yiddish School, the Tarbut School and the library.

Friday nights, while the Sabbath candles burned in all the windows, the teenagers went behind the town, to the Novogrudek highway.

Saturday nights, when the first stars appeared in the sky and the Havdalah prayers were said to end the Sabbath and begin the new week, there was singing on the Slonim highway. Boys and girls, set free from school, would gather in the political party locales and sing out their longing and faith.

These songs carried over the fields and gardens, back to town where their grandmothers were murmuring: "God of Abraham", the prayer to usher in the new week.

This is how I see you, my small town of Zhetl.

This is how you have remained alive in me.

[Page 295]

Friday at the Marketplace

by Khaya Alpert (Kvutzat Hasharon)

Translated by Janie Respitz

A quiet summer morning. The sunrise is in a hurry, it's Friday in town.

Zhetl's Jews still have to earn a little, but God forbid not to be late for candle lighting or receiving the Sabbath with honour.

At Maytchik the baker's you can already smell the fresh Challahs and the tempting sweet smell of the rye bread. You can see Maytchik's mother standing with her hunched back, her kerchief over her eyes and her clothes covered in flour. When you look at her you realize she also works.

She looks into the street, maybe she'll catch a bargain, a wagon full of birch wood from the gentile farmer. She's always rushing, but today the holy Sabbath will arrive and she will be able to rest her weary bones.

A little later. Avrom Moishe slowly opens his middle door. With a bright proud look he greets this summer Friday morning. He thinks:

"Perhaps today I'll have a customer for the two coats that Khaya Sorke sewed." At this time he can't seem to get rid of them. Later, he takes his prayer shawl and goes to the House of Study.

A little further on, Feytche's son stands with his hands in his pockets and looks out onto the street. There are already a few gentile women shopping in Khienke's store.

In the circle of stores. Dovid and Mariashke opened their store and first thing in the morning they were already jealous that Khienke already had customers. What could they do?

Mikhl, with his greasy pants, a newly rich man, runs with enthusiasm to open his shop. A rich man has luck.

Ida Leybke's children run to sell leather, but unfortunately, in the summer, the earnings are weak. The gentiles walk barefoot. The daughters, thank God are all ready to be married, we need a lot for dowries, but here are no prospects.

Arkin the iron dealer, bent over, skinny, with his glasses on his nose, walks without any enthusiasm to his iron shop, even though it is the season for his products. But he has no luck. On top of this he is a man burdened with many children.

Libitchke opens her store with ease. A broad fat woman with hanging fat cheeks and eyes looking greedily for sales. Her husband Zaydl, with his eye glasses, is short and thin (he is writing a Torah scroll) looks like he is her servant. She is never lacking customers in her store.

The stock exchange is always on Hendl's stoop. The gentiles from nearby villages sit there and wait for work.

Slowly all the stores open and the daily struggle for existence begins. All the tables are set up and the wagons arrive from Slonimer, Novoredker and Hoyfisher Streets.

Today is a bit of a holiday. Its' noisy and everyone is shouting: "Come on in!" It seems that all the voices are shouting together: "May God grant us livelihood".

Slowly the market place is filled with the smell of the Sabbath fish. The sun begins to set and the Gentiles leave. The marketplace is empty.

Jews sweep the streets for the Sabbath and lock up their shops. They hurry home, some with their "Haynt" newspaper under their arms, others with "Moment". They will forget about the bleak weak.

The circle of shops is covered with darkness and the other side of the street the balconies are filled with the Divine Presence of the Holy Sabbath. Sabbath candles are flickering from every corner. Reb Moishe Tentzer with his beautiful beard hurries to the synagogue, Yisroel Ozer catches up to him to chat before prayers begin. The blond Kalmen, Yosele Mendes and Reb Avrom the Pious all go to the House of study, and they all pray together for good health and subsistence.

It is quiet in town. It is a Friday night of those Jewish Fridays which will never return.

[Page 296]

Slonimer Street

by Sarah Gal – Begin

Translated by Janie Respitz

The first Jews in Zhetl settled on Slonimer Street, the road which led to Slonim. This Jewish settlement began like all others with a Jewish steward of an estate, an innkeeper, a lessee, a shopkeeper and a blacksmith.

Over the years the street grew and almost one third of the street was inhabited by the Krakhmolnikes (Starch makers) family. The great grandfather of the Krakhmolnikes leased the estate and one of his children opened the first starch factory in Zhetl, which was passed down through inheritance from one generation to another.

In time, more Jews arrived, the settlement grew and they began to think about a House of Study.

The first House of Study, which by the way existed until the last days was the place of worship. From a distance, from the other side of the lake, it looked old and tired, bent over, as if it were about to collapse. The established men from Slonimer Street protected it like a precious piece of jewelry. Every year they repaired the old walls, inside and out, just like you dress up a beloved old grandmother.

Although over time the residents of Slonimer Street changed, people married and left the street, sons in law came and went, they still protected this house of worship.

Slonimer Street stretched from Shushnen far far until Khadzhelaner Road almost until Glovotzken. It was the liveliest street in town. Everyone in Zhetl had to go through the street every day because all the following institutions were situated there: city hall, the electrical company, the post office, the court house, the public school in which 50% of the children were Jewish, as well as the locales of the Poalei Zion (Labour Zionists) and Hashomer Hatzair (Zionist youth group).

In the evenings the street was filled with teens who would go out walking to the palace or the Slonimer Highway.

Fantchik's bridge divided the street from the town, therefore giving it the character of one large family which began with the Busel sisters and ended with Mordekhai Payshes (Dvoretzky).

The street functioned as a large collective. Neighbours shared their problems and celebrations. People looked after each other as if they all had one mother. However the focal point of the street was at Hirshl the Blacksmith's.

Everyone loved Hirshl the Blacksmith. His word was as certain as his scythe and sickle.

"Hirshl said" was enough for everyone. (His word was good enough for the gentile farmers as well)

When the Gentile's asked: Hirshko, how are you doing? He responded in Russian: All's good thanks to Bokh Batko, Father in Heaven.

On Fridays there was a lot of traffic at Hirshl's. Women would come to put their Cholent (Sabbath stew) in his large oven.

It was quiet on Slonimer Street. You didn't hear the banging of the anvil. It was the Sabbath eve. Hirshl the blacksmith returns from the bathhouse dressed for the Sabbath and fills all the charity boxes, without counting how much he is putting in. You can soon hear the sweet melody of the Sabbath songs.

At the beginning of the new month Hirshl would bless the moon. Before the High Holidays you can hear Hirshl get up every night for prayers of repentance.

Fate took revenge on him. The sparks of iron burnt the light from his eyes. Yet Hirshl the Blacksmith continued in his ways, as before, with faith and belief and these Russian words on his lips: Bokh Batko.

This was Hirshl the Blacksmith from Slonimer Street, which 15 years ago pulsated vigorously with life. All that has remained today is a page of memories.

[Page 297]

Memoirs

by Yehudit Ostrovsky (Tel – Aviv)

Translated by Janie Respitz

In 1928 I left Zhetl for good. I remember they organized a farewell evening for me where I read my work: "The Small Town in the Big World".

Parts of Zhetl are alive before my eyes. I see the synagogue courtyard across from the old cemetery and the firefighter's tower. The synagogue yard experienced many celebrations as well as sadness. All of Zhetl's brides and grooms stood under the wedding canopy there accompanied by joyful musicians. This was also the place where coffins stood accompanied by the wailing of widows, orphans and the heart wrenching mournful prayers.

I remember the sad High Holiday melodies and the happy Hasidic dances on Simchat Torah. The beautiful voice of our cantor Eliyahu Ber left a deep impression on me. He prayed so gently but cruelly slaughtered chickens.

I cannot forget the firefighter's orchestra. They played every Sunday, beginning in Berl Mirsky's garden, then in the hospital garden on Lisogure Street. Zhetlers would gladly attend these concerts and pay for a ticket of admission.

Reb Arye the musician stands before my eyes with his fiddle. His brother Berl plays with him, also the fiddle: his sons Kalmen and Khaim on other instruments. Two other people played in Arye's band but I don't remember their names. One played an instrument they called a Bandura and the other banged a drum. Their playing always impressed me.

I must recount an episode. When I was a child I loved to dance. A woman from Vilna taught me how to dance the "Kakbuk". Reb Arye the musician did not have the musical notes for this dance. My friend and I went to his house, sang the song and danced and he wrote out the music.

If I'm already talking about dances and musicians I must mention the happy and joking Reb Avrom Moishe the Badkhen. (Rhymester and entertainer), who worked all year as a hat maker, but would entertain and make everyone happy at weddings. I can still hear his voice. He would call out the wedding gifts from the bride's side and the groom's side as he clanged together the silver spoons and forks making a deafening sound.

I remember those delivering gifts on Purim on trays covered with clothes. The boys carrying them would hope that whoever removed a gift from the tray would replace it with something of the same value. The Purim performers would run after them shouting:

"Today is Purim, tomorrow its over, give me a groschen and throw me out!"

When the excitement of Purim was over they began to build the Matzah bakeries. For an entire month in Zhetl they baked Matzah for their own use as well as export.

I also remember market days in Zhetl. This was on Tuesdays. Wagons, horses, farmers and goods were displayed in the length and breadth of the marketplace. It was noisy and impossible to get past the wagons and farmers.

If I'm talking about the peasants I have to mention a horrible murder the peasants carried out Reb Leyb Khabadkier's daughter and her little girl. This incident shocked Zhetl and until today, I cannot forget it.

All these memories awaken in my heart feelings of sadness and longing. I often just want to look at Zhetl, our beloved town but then I quickly remember its soil has soaked up so much Jewish blood.

[Page 298]

The Famous Zhetl

by Shmuel Rabinovitch (Herzliya)

Translated by Janie Respitz

The organization of Zhetl Jews in Israel did a very good deed and made a great effort in putting together this memorial book to remember the martyrs from Zhetl. Let this be a memorial for future generations so they can learn what happened to the Jewish community of Zhetl which excelled in its Jewish way of life, love of the people of Israel and love of Zion: with its rabbis and scholars, community activists and volunteers, with its Houses of Study, learning and charity institutions.

Zhetl was well known in the Jewish world thanks to its great righteous men, spiritual leaders who were born and raised in this small town. Among others we must mention: The Preacher of Dubno, who was born and raised in Zhetl 200 years ago. The great righteous man, the Chafetz Chaim who was also born and raised in Zhetl around 150 years ago.

Besides them, great men sat as chief rabbis in Zhetl who were renowned in the Jewish world. It is worthwhile to mention the rabbi Reb Borukh Avrom Mirsky of blessed memory who fifty years ago supported the rebirth of Jewish life in the Land of Israel.

Among the rabbis who lived in our days – Rabbi Zalmen Saratzkin who lives now in Jerusalem: the last rabbi of the Jewish community of Zhetl, Rabbi Yitzkhak Raytzer who died a martyrs death at the hands of the Nazis, may their names be obliterated. Rabbi Tzvi Khurgin was head of the yeshiva and a great teacher.

Zhetl was well known and had a great reputation because of the youth who graduated from the Talmud Torah and went on to Yeshiva under the administration of Rabbi Tzvi Khurgin of blessed memory. They continued their education and became rabbis in Israel.

Among others it is worthwhile mentioning Rabbi Elkhanan Saratzkin who became a rabbi in Zholudek and lives today in Jerusalem, Rabbi Yisroel Senerovsky, son of Yasha –Leyb and Soreh Rivka who became the rabbi in a large Volhyn community; and Rabbi Yitzkhak Markus son of Shmuel Lobensky who was rabbi in Smorgon and others. All these names will help our children appreciate the holy elders of past generations.

The Jews of Zhetl were kosher, naïve people. They were always preoccupied with their businesses and worked hard. Some were in business, others in trades, but when it came time for evening prayers the Hoses of Study were with busy Jews.

The majority of Zhetl Jews were not satisfied with praying. They continued to study Talmud and take time to read a chapter from Ein Yakov (Talmudic commentary). All the tables were occupied by Jews who came to listen to the daily teachings of Reb Moishe Tentzer, Reb Aron Hershl Langbart, Reb Moishe Beres and others.

There were artisans who worked hard all day and in the evening would come to the House of Study to learn with others.

Besides the four Houses of Study in the Synagogue courtyard, the old House of Study, the new and the middle, and the Hasidic house of worship there were two other quorums. One on Novoredker Street which was called: Meir Moishe Kalmen's quorum and the second, the small prayer house on Slonimer Street near Fantchik's mill. All the Jews of Zhetl would go to these places of worship immersed in worry about existence. Here they would forget all of their worries and unite with God.

I remember them, these dear Jews. I see them going to the sacrificial altar with a heartfelt, soulful melody of psalms. With the pleasant songs of the people of Israel on their lips, they fell into graves which they themselves dug.

[Page 299]

Impressions

by Lize Rozvosky of blessed memory

Translated by Janie Respitz

I would like to give a small review of our small town Zhetl. Disregarding that I was not born there, when I talk about my town, I mean Zhetl. When I arrived with my husband, Berl Moishe Rozvosky in Russia in 1920 I warned him that I would not live in a small town.

The First Meeting

We arrived from Baronovitch. That day was a Polish holiday and the Zhetl musicians, Khaim Levit, Hirshl Aron Volfovitch with the commandant Mirensky were invited to Baronovitch. We met them on their return to Zhetl.

It was a happy journey. When we arrived in Novolenyie, Pinkeh the wagon driver was waiting for us with his beautiful coach.

Finally we were able to see the first building in Zhetl: Leybe Kaplinsky's saw mill. When we arrived in town we stopped at the marketplace.

Lize Rozvosky of blessed memory

There were shops on both sides and behind them there was a large white church with a bell on top. I remember a short, stout woman came up to us, with dark intelligent eyes and introduced herself as Libetchke Mosieh Bere's and invited me to shop at her store. Then a tall man approached, Maytchke Khane Gatshikhe's the baker. He looked into the wagon looking for a cheap bag of flour. A fat man came out of the coffee house across the way and welcomed us warmly:

"What's doing in the big cities?"

Then a woman came up to me and whispered in my ear that she is called Big Sonia.

I liked the small town expressions and pronunciations and how they received me and we remained in Zhetl.

Our Companions in Zhetl

My husband introduced me to a fine social network, not lagging behind as I had imagined. These were people with a desire to see films, go to the theatre, read books and acquire knowledge. With time I forgot I was in a small secluded town in White Russia called: Zhetl.

On Holidays we would get together to sing and have a good time. I remember Simkhas Torah. We were a group of 20 friends, Motl Vilkovsky, a lively guy, Notte Moishe Lusky, Hirshl Busel and Lize, Isar Gertzovksy and Roze, Khaim Levit and Alter Zernitsky.

I was then living at Yosl the painter's near the Pomerayke and Hoyf Street. We enjoyed a drink as Jews do on Simkhas Torah and spent the whole day singing, reading and reciting. For me it was new to see Jews enjoying themselves so freely. I really felt connected to Zhetl and forgot about the big city.

The Yiddish Folkshul in Zhetl

Now I will tell you a bit about the Yiddish Folkshul in Zhetl. It had a difficult existence and was not supported by the state. They had to support themselves. The majority of the children came from worker's families but thanks to the devotion of the parents and the board, the school managed to crawl out of its difficult situation.

Regardless of its difficulties the school invited the best teachers: Gite Zaks, Stul, Olitzky, Hornshteyn, Feygl Goldman, Libke Yerukhomovitch and together we bore the yoke. The school was on a higher level than other schools in the surrounding towns. The children were well educated and devoted to the school with heart and soul.

I remember an incident when the school burned. It was a Friday evening in 1935. All the children cried like babies. Khaya Mera ran into the fire to save some books. When asked what she was doing she replied:

"If the school does not exist, my life is worthless". There were many children who felt like this. The school was like a second mother for them and often even more because they felt a lot freer at school than at home;

[Page 300]

The Hasidic Rebbe in our Home

by Rachel Rabinovitch (Tel Aviv)

Translated by Janie Respitz

We received the news that the Slonim Rebbe was coming to town. There was a great commotion among the Hasidim. There was great joy. And as usual the Rebbe will stay at our house. Although this was a lot of work for my mother, my father gladly accepted this honour.

The Rebbe and his assistant arrive on Thursday. The Hasidim met them in their car and they came to us.

The Rebbe is dressed in his long black coat, fur round hat and white socks. He enters our home happily, greets everyone warmly and blesses every child individually. He does not look at the women and he goes into the room prepared for him while his assistant watches over him like a hawk.

My mother starts working, preparing various delicacies, a few types of Kugl (pudding), fish, meat, Cholent (the Sabbath stew), kishke (stuffed sausage) and cuts up the leg of the animal. The Rebbe is ready to help but mother tells him everything is already prepared.

When the Rebbe returns to his room there is already a long line of men who want to see him. Some are waiting to be blessed by the holy Rebbe, others are seeking advice. Not everyone manages to come due to lack of time. It is Friday and they must prepare to receive the Sabbath.

When the Sabbath is ready: the Rebbe, his assistant, my father and some other honourable Hasidim go to the Hasidic synagogue. Everyone in the street is curious to see the Rebbe. A few succeed in seeing him on the street while those who are late run to the footbridges and stare, like at a miracle.

Later they return from synagogue singing and dancing. The Rebbe sings the Sabbath song "Sholem Aleichem Malachei Hashalom" with his sweet voice, and they sit down at the tables. The Rebbe at the head recites the Kiddush (the blessing on the wine), says all the blessings and the Hasidim repeat after him.

It takes a bit of time before they begin to eat. The Rebbe hands out the kugl with his hands. The table is long and the Rebbe cannot reach everyone. He hands it from one to another and says:

"Yenkl give Berl, Berl give Motl, Motl give Khaim" and so on.

I stand by the side and observe. I then pushed my way quietly to my father and whispered in his ear not to eat the kugl as it is not hygienic, since everyone had touched it. The Rebbe heard my secret and said to me angrily:

"Go away already, go, it's none of your business!"

My father saw my embarrassment and quietly assured me he was not eating it. Embarrassed, I moved away from the table.

The Rebbe and the Hasidim continue to eat with great appetites. All the while they sing Sabbath songs and enjoy themselves.

Meanwhile there is a throng of kids. One tells the other that the Hasidic Rebbe is at Motl Tules' house. They came to see this wonder, how the Rebbe and his Hasidim rejoice, and there really was something to see.

At our house you can see two worlds. The Rebbe and his Hasidim and the town's youth.

The house becomes very crowded and the courtyard is filled with the curious. They climb up in the park so they can watch and listen to the singing and dancing.

Among the large crowd I see my teacher Herman Frenkel. He is angry with me because I did not tell him the Rebbe was at our house. He told me he had great sentiment for the Rebbe and all the ceremonies. He comes from a Hasidic home. This is all very familiar and reminds him of home. He watches with great interest, tells me a few stories about his home and remains among the last guests.

Saturday, time to go to synagogue. The street, from the Hasidic synagogue until our house is filled with people. Everyone is curious to watch the Rebbe and Hasidim come from synagogue.

The tables were prepared with all good things. They sit around the table eating and drinking until dark when they have to say the evening prayers.

For the rest of the town, this is entertainment. Everyone spent the entire Sabbath hanging around the courtyard under the windows, swallowing the curious Hasidic melodies.

[Page 301]

Customs

by Mordechai Dunetz, Flint – United States

Translated by Janie Respitz

The Small Prayer House at Lake Pontchiks

Compared to the "aristocratic" Houses of Study in the synagogue courtyard, Zhetl's small prayer house was modest and unassuming. This was because of its location and its congregation.

The small, half collapsed little house stood on the shore of Lake Pontchiks behind the large stable belonging to Shepsl Vikhnes Zayezd. The ceiling was so low, Asher the Prisadnik (Deputy) could reach it with his elbows.

The women's section was in the beadle's room. During the week this was his cobbler's workshop. His last and pieces of leather were strewn all over the room. Behind a thin curtain was the cobbler's bedroom. There were always a few children playing on the bed whose little voices could be heard during prayers.

Up high on the little wall, which separated the cobbler's room from the prayer house, there was a small window. Through this window the women were able to hear the reading of the Torah, look down at their husbands when they were called up to the Torah and toss candies, peanuts and nuts at a bridegroom.

During the summer a cool wind would blow in through the little window from the lake. In the evening the frogs would ribbit along with the prayers.

During the eighteen benedictions we would run outside and compete in throwing stones into the river.

In the winter, the boys would sneak out of the prayer house and go sliding on the ice.

The Worshipers

Those who worshipped at the small prayer house lived on Slonimer Street, Lipover Lane and a few on Hoyf Street. They were:

Dovid Avromches, Mordkhai – Eli Kalbshteyn, the peddlers: Yoshke "Makhesron" and his sons, the blacksmiths: Hirshl, Sholem – his son, Artchik the blacksmith and Ayzl the blacksmith. The grocers: Mayrim Mnuskin, Zalmen Mirsky, Nakhman Mertches. The dry goods merchants: Yoel Dovid Soreh Rokhe's, Khaim Yudl the blond and Kalmen the starch maker. The carpenters: Khaim Leyzer Levit, Yosl the carpenter and his sons (Kaplan), Yisroel the rat (Kaplinsky). The wagon drivers: Khaim Dovid the baby (Medvetzky) and his sons, Yoshke the wagon driver (Gankovsky), Hilke the wagon driver (Shalkovitch). The butchers: Itche the butcher (Razovsky), Shloime Khaim Goldshteyn and his sons, as well as a few shoemakers, tailors and bakers.

For these poor labourers and small businessmen the prayer house was not only a place to pray but also a place where neighbours would gather three times a day to talk about day to day tasks as well as world politics.

Reb Hirsh Gives Me a Sniff of Tobacco

On the Sabbath in the winter, between afternoon and evening prayers, Jews would sit around the small oven, place their hands on the warm bricks and listen to a lesson on the Ethics of Our Fathers. At dusk, when shadows filled the prayer house, Hirshl the blacksmith would recite psalms. His voice penetrated with sweetness and piety which could move even the hardened hearts of the wagon drivers, blacksmiths and peddlers.

Reb Hirsh recited psalms his whole life. When a spark from his anvil blinded him, he recited the psalms by heart.

The other boys and I loved to go to Reb Hirsh and ask him for a sniff of tobacco. He would offer us some snuff with a smile on his lips and pitch black beard. We really enjoyed when he let us close his bone tobacco box with the wooden cover and leather string.

Nakhman Mertche's – the Manager of the Prayer House

Nakman Mertche's was the manager of the prayer house for many years. On the Sabbath he stood by the table and handed out honours. During the week he was the cashier and bookkeeper of this small synagogue.

He came to Zhetl from Crimea, from the city Yevpatorai. He presented himself as a scholar. His stories from Yevpatoria enchanted everyone, myself included, as they were vividly exotic.

I also love to listen to his memories of Mendele, Bialik and other Yiddish writers he met while in Odessa…

A pinch on my cheek from him for explaining a story from the Pentateuch well was for me a great compliment.

[Page 302]

Itche the Butcher – the Crying Torah Reader

Our prayer house did not have a cantor, however, there were Torah readers who when they led prayers, could make stones cry… When Itche the butcher would rise to sing Kol Nidre on Yom Kippur everyone in the packed prayer house knew they would not leave with dry eyes.

His bitter deep wailing moved all the worshippers deep in their hearts and brought everyone into the atmosphere of "today the world stands as at birth". The kids stood trembling beside our fathers and with our slender notions and rich fantasies ascended together with Reb Itche the butcher tearing through the heights to reach God's verdict.

The large candles in the sand pots dripped their milk, the women's cries from their section and Reb Itche's tears all came together in one big heart wrenching, imploring wail which cut through the dark night of Kol Nidre with a resounding echo over the still waters of the lake.

Asher the "Prisadnik" [1] from "Upwards Street"

Asher the "Prisadnik" was also known in town as a good Torah reader. He was tall with a long grey beard and walked proudly, more like a Russian aristocrat than a Jewish peddler. He lived at the edge of town on the Slonim highway in a small house next to Shmuel Nakrishker.

All week he would stand on the road which goes from Khadielan, Hiritch and Yatzevich and buys up chickens, eggs flax and dried mushrooms from the farmers.

He was a learned Jew. At dusk he would study a page of Mishna with other Jews in the House of Study.

All year long he prayed at the middle House of Study but on holidays he would lead prayers in the small prayer house. His lyrical voice and sweet interpretation of the prayers excited the worshippers instilling in them a sense of great spiritual pleasure. Reb Asher's praying brought a light breeze into the prayer house with scents of fir and oak trees among which he lived for years, up there on "Upward Street" on the Slonim highway…

Khayke the Patroness of the Sabbath

She was an institution in her own right. They called her White Khayke. Her personal life was lonely but she found comfort and pleasure in helping the poor and needy. She was the provider of Challah for the Sabbath for those who did not have the few groshen (pennies) to buy flour and yeast.

She was devoted to this charity work with a special love. For her, it was a holy mission to ensure, God forbid, no Sabbath would be desecrated due to lack of Challah.

The women in Zhetl knew on Thursday nights when they made their dough they must take into account a few Challahs for Khaye.

Every Friday morning, winter and summer she would walk around carrying a large basket. For us kids, this was the announcement the Sabbath was arriving. We always waited for her as we took great pleasure in putting our little hands into the basket with the warm Challahs. Her thanks and heartfelt blessings filled us with pride and made us feel we earned a portion of her good deed of helping the poor fulfill the Sabbath requirement of blessing the Challah.

No one in town knew how many families enjoyed Khayke's challahs. We did know however, that as long as Khayke could carry that basket, it would be filled and the poor would not have to violate the Sabbath.

Sabbath Eve

Although Friday was a market day in Zhetl, and Jews were very busy with "receipts", there was still a strong feeling the Sabbath was approaching.

Housewives were busy preparing for the Sabbath with all the details. Just as dawn was breaking you could already smell the Sabbath delicacies.

Women had to hurry to prepare for the Sabbath as they also had to help their husbands in the shops. Around nine o'clock in the morning, in most Jewish homes, the table was covered with a tablecloth and warm challahs and baked goods were placed on the tables. They were "good enough for the king to eat"…

Guests for the Sabbath

Tired and half asleep the wagon drivers returned home from their long trips from Slonim, Baranovitch and Lida, urging on their thin mares who dragged the heavy loads for Zhetl's shopkeepers, shoemakers and tailors.

Wagons filled with poor people would arrive in town to "work" the houses before the Sabbath. Entire families would besiege the town sending their members from house to house begging for alms.

[Page 303]

The Jews of Zhetl had a reputation in the region for being kind hearted and gave alms generously. To that end there was a special "Hotel", a part of the old people's home that was called the "poorhouse". In that community house which was located behind the hospital on Lisagura Street, the wandering poor had their headquarters where they could spend the night. However the place was too small to accommodate the great influx of "guests" so the rest had to sleep on the benches in the Houses of Study.

Friday after evening prayers they would stand in the anteroom with pleading eyes and watch the householders walk by, hoping they would bring them home as guests. The Jews of Zhetl were happy to fulfill the good deed of hosting guests.

The Bathhouse Gentile Announces the Sabbath

Candles were lit after the resounding signal the bathhouse gentile sounded from the bathhouse on Hoyf Street. Later, the mission to announce the Sabbath was given to the gentile who was the custodian of Kaplinsky's steam mill.

There were two signals given. The first was to close the stores, the second – to bless the Sabbath candles. Peasants who arrived late knew that after the first signal they could not even buy a pack of matches.

There were however shopkeepers who did not hear or pretended no to hear the first signal. But when Reb Avrom appeared on the street with his patriarchal stature and Sabbath clothes, everybody showed him respect and closed their shops accompanied by Reb Avrom's call: Jews, it's the Sabbath!!!

The Neighbour's Potato Cholent (Sabbath Stew)

Cholent was cooked in the houses in Zhetl that had large ovens, or in the bakeries that heated their ovens on Fridays especially for this purpose. From all the neighbouring houses you could see women, men and youngsters carrying large clay pots with their names written on the lids. Bakers charged a certain amount to heat the cholent however Zhetl's matrons would do it for others for free as a good deed.

The first pots would be placed on the top of the oven. Late comers had to find a spot near the oven door. Often the names would rub off due to the heat.

The following day, Saturday after prayers, women would run with rags in their hands to bring the steaming good smelling cholent home to their Sabbath table. Often the barley cholent would be transformed into a potato…Then neighbours would begin running from house to house in search of their barley cholent, before it was enjoyed in a neighbours' house.

Sabbath After the Kugl (Pudding)

After the cholent the Jews of Zhetl liked to fulfill the good deed of enjoying the Sabbath. They would lie down to nap for a couple of hours and enjoy a good rest.

The streets were empty and calm. The peasants did not come to town since everything was closed and locked. A peaceful stillness ruled the town, the true Sabbath rest.

In the last few years, Asna Gertzovsky, Shike Berl's soda stand and Mordechai Kikes' cafeteria operated behind closed doors. This is where the more progressive element, those who did not want to barricade after the cholent would gather to play billiards, read a newspaper, or merely joke around and peel dried kernels.

Yosl Gertzovsky was a religious Jew and did not want to take money on the Sabbath. Therefore he devised a "borrow board" where he had a list of his customers. Beside each name he placed a nail where he hung a note with the amount the customer spent for a glass of water with syrup, chocolate or ice cream. You could also play billiards on credit and pay the few groshen Tuesday after the market day…

When the first star appeared in the sky and people were in the Houses of Study praying, the lamps were lit in the Jewish houses. Through the dark windows you could hear the sounds of "God of Abraham" and "Hamavdil" (prayers to end the Sabbath and begin the new week). People removed their Sabbath clothes and returned once again to the difficult yoke of the weekday with a prayer in their hearts that God will grant them a good, healthy new week…

Translator's note:

1. Prisadnik means deputy in Russian. This was his nickname but no explanation is provided.

[Page 304]

My Small Jewish Town

by Pesieh Mayevsky (Petach Tikva)

Translated by Janie Respitz

My town is no longer, no remnant of you charm,
Your past magnificence has disappeared.
You wail over graves of destroyed worlds;
Death is spread over your mountains and valleys.

The stones of the bridge, your sandy paths,
Oh, my town, your houses and streets,
They accompanied my father on his last journey,
And washed themselves clean with his blood.

Your dew on the meadows that glimmered
And sparkled with the red sunrise,
Like it lit my mother's feet
While leading her to her death.

The clear river, which greeted me
With the happy murmur and pure springs,
On that last day in the darkness
Threw my sister's blood on their desires.

The familiar forest on the outskirts of town,
Which rocked me with a quiet song; –
Took away my brother's last cries
On the path of his bloody walk.
Underway, my last suffering in exile,
At the end of the sandy roads and paths,
I take your graves, my destroyed town,
Your suffering and grief will remain in my heart.

The Folklore of Zhetl

The Dzyatlava Folklore

by Baruch Kaplinski

Translated by Yocheved Klausner

Edited by Yael Chaver

The Dzyatlava folklore was rich, but very little of it has been kept in our memory. Yet, even in the few memories that did remain we can discover the wisdom, the sharpness of mind and the sense of humor of our ancestors.

A special kind of humor was expressed in the nicknames. Very few families in the shtetl were called by their official names; almost every Dzyatlaver had a nickname, characteristic of his qualities, his weaknesses and the way the members of the community felt about him or her. The nicknames were taken from the animal or the inanimate world, here are a few of them: Moishe *the rooster*, Eli *the goose*, David *the turkey*, Israel *the bird* and David *the cat*. Here are a few nicknames of another nature: Motl–Leib *the whip lasher*, Arie *the Klezmer*, Nathan *the minister*, Leizer *the bomb* and Ahre'le *the porridge–pot*.

The Jews residing in the neighboring shtetls were also "privileged" with nicknames: The Lida people were called *the Lida drunkards*, the Bielice people – *the Bielice thieves*, the Slonim Jews were referred to as *the stupid people of Slonim*. So were the Kozloszchina people called *goats* and the Dworetz people guts (maybe they liked to eat a lot). The Meitchet people were nicknamed "*white*." Jews of Dzyatlava also had a nickname – they were called *the hooligans*. Why? Nobody knows.

A few words about the Dzyatlava sayings and proverbs: they were taken from daily life. When a

Dzyatlaver wanted to say that something was impossible, he said "when nails bloom," or "when the cat will fly and lay eggs."

When he wanted to stress the ridiculous, he would say "he looks like a cat in an apron," to describe a very small quantity he said "it will be enough for him like a piece of cake for a horse." A daily laborer would be like "a crow jumping from pig to pig." These are just a few examples of the cleverness of the Dzyatlava people.

As we said, the Dzyatlava folklore was not preserved, but the little that survived is worth researching.

Reuven Chayatowitz, a common type

The water carrier

[Page 306]

The Dzyatlava Nicknames

Adapted by Baruch Kaplinski

Translated by Yocheved Klausner

Edited by Yael Chaver

In our Lithuanian and Belarus shtetlach, many Jews were not called by their name and surname, but by a nickname. The surname was no more than a formal nuisance, for the "benefit" of the authorities.

In the synagogue, and in the cemetery, a Jew was called by his first name and the name of his father. However, for the daily life and business, it sounded somewhat "heavy" to call a neighbor, for example, R'Yitzhak ben R'Yakov, and since there were many Yitzhaks and Yakovs, people began to distinguish between them by their qualities and weaknesses, by their occupations or by their social status. In most cases, the evaluation of the people was satirical and biting, and we must say that our ancestors in the Lithuanian shtetlach were blessed with a sharp sense of humor.

If a Jew liked *tzimes* [a sweet dish made of carrots], the popular dish was attached to his name right away, and he was called *Moishe the tzimes*. I remember in our shtetl there was a very clever Jew, so he was called *Mordechai Eli the fox*, but less clever people were called: the calf, the goat, the ox, etc.

Often the nickname was fitted to the occupation, and so many Jews in our shtetl carried the names of their means of livelihood: *Avraham the Starch–man, Arie the Klezmer, Noah the Old–clothes–dealer, Mote–Leib the Whip–lasher* and so on. Other nicknames stressed the character of the people, and so we had: *Yashe the strict, Yankel the liar, Shmuel the organized one, Yidel the slow one*. The "general wisdom" matched the nickname with a characteristic trait of the person. Very often, a physical feature was the reason behind the nickname, and so the following nicknames were created in Dzyatlava: *Hinde the Big, Shlomo the Colt, the Crumb*. Sometimes the *color* of the hair was the reason of the nickname: one very fine and respected lady was called *Peshke the Black*, and another very honored Jew – *Yidel the Yellow*.

Nicknames are a folk–creation. In the synagogue, the people at the *Mizrach* [the seats at the East Wall, reserved for the most honored in the shul] very seldom had nicknames, nor did they participate in their popular creation. But in the "market circles", on Shabat after the prayers, during the long winter nights, the *Amcha* [simple folks] expressed their biting sense of humor by inventing appropriate nicknames. It is worth stressing the fact that nicknames were often inherited, sometimes from grandfather to grandson, and so passed from generation to generation.

Our friends Sara Avseyewitz, Pesia Mayevski and Mordechai Dunyetz collected about one hundred and fifty Dzyatlava nicknames and we tried to arrange them by subject. Nicknames from the animal world

Here are a few examples:

Reuven the hen, Moishe'ke the *kogut*[1], Eli the duck, David the turkey, Lea the little chicken, Israel the bird, Pinye the beetle, Khane the partridge, Yosl the swallow (would fly like a swallow), David the kitten, Israel the mouse, Yosef the dog (or the fool), the goat, Rachel the calf, Khaye the cow, Mechl the he–goat, Hilye the wild boar, Moishe'ke the ox, Efraim the colt (he liked horses), Boruch the mare, Aharon–Leizer the animal, Mordechai–Eli the fox, Moishe the swan, Itche the herring (was very thin). We have here an entire zoological park – all the animals, birds and fowl, which Dzyatlava Jews knew and attached to people.

This section translated by Yael Chaver

Nicknames by occupation

Leib the Mayor, Moishe the doctor, Zhame the postman, Noah the rags–dealer, Avreml the starch dealer, Arye the Klezmer, The cobbler, Alter the estate–owner (he was a very poor man), Ayzhik the constable, Mote–Leib the whip–lasher, Berl the spinner (would spin winnings at the lottery), Yosl the painter, Pinye the groats–soup, the children–maker (he made children's shoes), the poor–man (was rich but always complained that he was poor…).

Nicknames by personal qualities

Of the collected nicknames, 19 represent human qualities: Yechiel the demon (a capable man), Devor'ke the Cossack (an *Eshet Chayil* ["woman of valor"]), Shiye the severe (was stubborn), Yankel the liar, Itchke the bomb, Shmuel the practical, Yudel slow (was speaking slowly), Chana the new one, Zelik the butter, Tewwel the scoundrel, Motel the worthless, Shifra the gourmand, Sonia the big, Shmuel speaker through the nose, Zlote the fat, Herzl the tiny, Yosl the clown.

[Page 307]

Nicknames by personalities

Some Jews of Dzyatlava liked to discuss world politics; these were nicknamed Chamberlain; Benes; Halifax. Other nicknames were: Mordechai the Kaiser (he handled himself with dignity); Note the minister; Niomke the Haman; the god (?as the best tailor); the Angel of Death (he was as thin as Death); Shepsl the philosopher; Petlura.

Now, many years later, it is difficult to establish under what conditions a Jew was nicknamed Haman. As far as I remember, that person was a fine man.

Nicknames by other nationalities

Shmuel the Pole; the Turk; Alter the gypsy; Khane the gentile girl; Dovid the gentile.

Nicknames by hair color

Peshke the black; Yudel the yellow.

Nicknames by articles of clothing

Rokhl–Leah the trousers (she wore long pants, which were visible under her skirt); Keyle the *kaftan*; Moishke the silk underpants.

Nicknames by kinds of food

Moishe–Aaron the round loaf; Hirshl the little apple; Hertzl the chicken fat; Meir the raw pancake; Khayim the bread roll; Avreml the tea essence.

Nicknames by objects

Reuve the barrel; Itche the pot of *kasha*; Berl the wagon shaft; Avreml the goblet; Pinke the drum; Alte the radio; Sholem the smithy; Efroyke the cradle.

Nicknames by family relationships

Alter the mother; Itche the little son; Rishe the grandmother.

Nicknames by natural forces

Yankl the thunder; Khayim the earth (he would often curse, "I'll see you in the ground.")

Nicknames by place of residence

The *kleyzlnik* (he lived in the *kloyz* [small synagogue]); Sonia from the tavern; Yoysef from Zarzecze.

Various nicknames

Meir dandelion; Yankl Khananya; Shimen the gadget; Yosl the rural policeman; Rokhl the eyeglasses; Shiye the proposed match; Moishke the scum; Arl the *vulinke*; Hertzl the *drishtsh*; Moishe the doctor; Khayim–Leyb the shirt; Yudel *skridlav*; Dovid *mukhasran*; Mulye the idol; Yisroel the *pasekh*; Khanye the mucus; Yehoshue the *hayduk* [highway robber?]; Henekh the young lady; Khaye the pit.

The nicknames we have listed in our work are only a fraction of all the Dzyatlava nicknames. But they are characteristic of the popular creativity of our parents in the Lithuanian–Belorussian *shtetls*, remarkably pointed and sharp. We ask forgiveness of those townspeople whose nicknames we have listed. In no way did we want to offend them. Our mission was to delineate Dzyatlava with all its quirks, as it was and as we remember it.

Mirke

Folk types

Translator's footnote:

   1.   I could not find *kogut* in any dictionary (Yiddish, Russian, Polish) or in the Yiddish thesaurus. The closest I found is Russian "kogot" which translates as "claw, talon", which didn't seem to be the name of any animal.

[Page 308]

Dzyatlava folklore

by Avraham Iventzki, may his memory be for a blessing

Translated by Yocheved Klausner

Edited by Yael Chaver

Nicknames were extremely common in Dzyatlava. Following are a few:

Moshke the child–maker: a cobbler, who made only childrens' shoes. By the way, he was blessed with many children.
Hersh the beard: a simple Jew, a painter with a long, broad, gray beard.
Zeydke the mother. Yosl the fisher [or pee–er]
Hertzl the grandmother,because he often mentioned his grandmother.
Hertzl the little girl: because he was bashful
Arele the pot *kasha.* Leyzer the bomb.
Khayim the ox.
Berl chicken–fat.
Khayim–Leyzer the hole: when he was called to the Torah in synagogue as a bridegroom, his bride asked from the women's section whether he could see her through the hole, to which he replied "yes."
The idle government supplier.

The ox.
The *cholent* pot.
The filthy wagon–greaser
King David
The barley–soup.
Vove with the mustaches
The snout
Shimen the billy–goat
The chicken
Moyshe the billy–goat.
The *klish* [?]
David the turkey
The wagon–shaft.
The badgers.
The fatty woman.
The *skuralapes* [?]
Khane the new

Nicknames derived from surrounding towns

Lida folks.
Bielice thieves
Slonim fools
Kaulaishtshin goats.
Dworetz stuffed derma.
Meitchet sour milk.

Folk proverbs

"He is Shmaya–makes–a–living" – he buys everything.
"Guests at his wedding are the kids' Hertzl, the brat's Yosl" –i.e., low–class folk.
"Poor man, sip chicken broth."
"Kiss Abe the yellow, you'll want more."
"He too is not one of the two for a three kopeck/ruble coin/note." [??]
"Here's a lazy person for you."
"[…] busy all over again"
"He is a poor man with a sack full of stains."
"A story without end, a pitcher without a lid" [*rhymes in the original*]
"Lived it up as though in Odessa, slept as though in Kaulaishtshin.
"Lost as though in a goose hole."
"May you explode like a mountain."
"But he too is not Yoshke the fool." [*possibly alluding to Jesus, who was often referred to by the nickname "Yoshke"*]
"A cat flew over the roof and laid an egg."
"When nails bloom."
"It means as much to him as a sweet cake does to a horse."
"He is as smart as a fish scale among people."
"He looks like a cat in an apron."
"For me, that's like a leap from Holovli to Zelva"–[*names of two villages in the Dzyatlava environs*].
"He looks like a king commanding a battalion [*a Biblical term for God*], like a dog among nettles."
"Kiss a bear under his tail."
"An employee is like a crow who jumps from one pig to another."
"Don't worry, you'll hold on till the new potato crop."
"A *yeshiva* student is like a potato, you can make him into anything."

Curses

"[May you be buried] with your head in the ground, with your feet in the church."

Sayings

Several Belorussian folk–sayings were commonly used in Dzyatlava, and thanks to their popularity can be included in Yiddish folklore. Here are some:[*I could not locate these sayings in the original*]

Zavali darahu – a person who reserves a spot, doesn't use it himself and prevents others from using it.

Svaya sherimyazhka nye tshazhka: one's own *shereminke* is not hard.

Harsh pamiar (worse than death): no mind to lose.

Nye dai bokh muzhiku fanat bit.

Maya dyela tyelitsha – fadyeu da u khliyev: my business is calf–like: after eating – into the barn. This phrase is applied to an uncouth person, who is indifferent to everything.

Local expressions

"*s'iz tut mir vey*" instead of "*s'tut mir vey*" – it hurts me. [*This is an inversion of the Yiddish syntax used for this expression*]

Izdzhek: mockery

Iron–smart: very smart.

Bizkl: a diminutive of biz, until.

Kanaste: young girl, young woman.

"Friday afternoon, inkwell": a fool.

Customs

On Simchas–Toyre the cantor chants *Ein Ke–Eloheynu* in Yiddish, and the community repeats it in the original Hebrew. On the eve of Yom–Kippur and Hoshana–Rabba, it was the custom to eat small cakes steeped in honey (according to *Pinkes–Yekapa*).

[Page 309]

Under the Soviet Regime

Translated by Janie Respitz

The drama Club during Soviet occupation

First row: the second – Pesie Mayevsky
Second row: Sholem Bas, Yoine Brestovitsky, Hinde Mirsky, Lazovsky, Khashke Ganuzovitch, Moishe Mirsky, unknown
Third row: Yosef Indershteyn, Peysakh Rozov, Alter Gertzovsky, Noyekh Mnuskin, Etl Ovseyevitch, Yudke Khlebnik, Leybl Beshkin

[Page 310]

Under Soviet Rule

Translated by Judy Montel

The period of Soviet rule in Zhetl was very short, only from September, 1939 until June of 1941, however in this short time decisive change took place. Zhetl shed its form and put on a new one.

The public and economic structure that had existed for centuries – was cancelled. All of the political parties and the institutions – left the stage. The veteran activists from the left and the right abandoned their positions. In their stead a young guard of communists arrived. Under their influence, Zhetl began marching towards complete Sovietization.

It was not easy to adjust to the economic revolution. The merchants were deprived of their livelihood and the artisans were commanded to organize into cooperatives and guilds. Goods vanished from the market and demand exceeded supply. The farmers refused to sell the fruits of their labor and the days of bartering returned. As a result of this, the currency lost its value.

Zhetl suffered no less under the yoke of the social revolution. The "Tarbut" school became a Belorussian school. The mutual aid organizations were dissolved. The rest day of the sabbath ceased. Freely held public opinion was throttled and Zhetl began to organize its life according to Soviet commands. And yet, all of this was like gold compared to what awaited the town in the fateful year: 1942.

[Page 311]

Under the Soviet Regime

by Efraim Shepshelevitch (Bat Yam)

Translated by Janie Respitz

Beginning in 1938 there was great tension in the world. Fascist Germany with the human glutton Hitler, may his name be obliterated, wired all of Europe. Disregarding that Poland felt they were pals with the Germans, they were also frightened.

In 1939 a partial mobilization was called. Young men from Zhetl were also mobilized and the situation was tense.

Zhetl politicians would offer their hypotheses. The main speakers were Berl Dvoretsky, Avrom – Moishe Barishansky, Artchik Green, Khaim Mikhl Roznov, Khaim Levit, and others. The majority believed that the western states would not permit an open war with Poland.

This illusion was disrupted on September 1st. The German thieves crossed the long border and called up, with all their power, the Polish army. The air force, marked with the Swastika, flew very low and shot at towns, villages, suburbs, trains and buses. There was great fear to travel on the roads, but remaining in town was also scary.

Efraim Shepshelevitch

My Return Home

On the morning of September 5th I left Vilna by bus and arrived in Zhetl in the evening. They were waiting for me at home impatiently. My mother could not sleep and waited for me to get off every bus. When I finally arrived home safely, there was great joy.

The joy was short lived as the mood in town was stressful. People were walking around confused and sad knowing full well what tomorrow will bring. Our father comforted us by saying: "whatever happens will happen to all of us, as long as our family remains together". And with these words he wiped a tear from his eye.

When you met someone on the street the first question was: "So what's new? What are they writing in the newspapers? What did the last communique let us know?"

These communiques were not at all happy. German tanks invaded Poland and had reached Warsaw. Every hour felt like a day, and every day, an eternity. We did not sleep at night and during the day we were as if in a dream.

The Soviets Free Us

Suddenly a rumour began to spread that the Soviets crossed the border and were planning to free White Russia and Ukraine. We could not believe this. Most of Zhetl's Jews were happy with this news, because under the Soviets our lives were secure.

The communists in Zhetl were particularly excited with this news and began to prepare Zhetl to be freed from the Polish aristocratic yoke even before the Soviet tanks marched into town.

On September 16th the Polish police left town and for about 48 hours we were left without any legal authority. The communists in Zhetl issued a manifesto to the population in which they asked for calm and for people to follow their orders. By then the Soviet army was near Novoredok.

Suddenly we learned a group of Polish police were coming from the Slonim highway. A few communists met them, disarmed and arrested them. A barn served as the jail and they were guarded by Jewish boys.

When the Polish police realized the guards were not armed they tried to run away. They shot into the fire truck so we could not go after them and ran to the Lida highway. A few boys chased them. Araon Leyzer Novogrudsky was wounded in this action.

The noblemen around Zhetl ran away on time but the communists paid a few visits to their estates taking furniture, paintings and other items.

On the nights of September 17th and 18th people in Zhetl were confined to their homes. On the morning of the 18th everyone left their homes waiting for the Red Army. Everyone was now an expertand began to describe what a Red army soldier looks like as well as the commanders and the tanks. Small and big, young and old, stood in the marketplace and looked in the direction of Novoredker Street.

[Page 312]

Suddenly there was a deafening noise. A large black tank appeared in the marketplace followed by another. The applause could be heard throughout the town. People began to give kisses of joy and threw flowers at the tanks.

The army arrived at night. They flowed in like a river, with cars, motorcycles, trucks, armoured cars, tanks, a motorized division and horse drawn machine guns. Many of the Red Army soldiers thanked us with smiles for the applause, but some sat with pensive faces, not looking at anyone. They must have been missing their wives and children, family and relatives who they left at home and perhaps they also were thinking if they will ever see light again.

The New Order

A short time later about ten party officials arrived and began to organize things in the Soviet style. They confiscated a few large homes in the marketplace. The party secretary moved into Rabinovitch's brick house. Hendl's house was renovated and unrecognizable. This was now the party club. Other houses were inhabited by various institutions that ended in "com", "yuz" and "targ". The entire Soviet was in Shikeh Dvoretsky's house. The N.K.V.D and passport division were set up in Motl Krashinsky's house on Hoyf Street. Zabelinsky's house became a produce store but of course, there was no merchandise.

I remember very well when they brought sugar, once in a blue moon, and people lined up in the evening. They stood all night in the cold and rain only to find out in the morning it would not be distributed that day.

"Why?" everyone asked in despair.

"We received an order" was the answer.

Some went home but others did not want to believe it and remained to guard the door. When they finally did distribute food only the privileged and those with fists received any.

There were some who were agile and received food two or three times while others received nothing.

The Zloty now had the same value as the ruble. No new goods were brought to the stores, old things were set aside and sold against other goods. We were living in times of antiquity. The farmers who could not buy anything for money demanded goods in exchange for their produce and paid the craftsmen with rye, eggs, meat and the like.

Many Zhetl Jews lost their livelihoods and looked for a way to earn a zloty. Craftsmen organized cooperatives and shopkeepers tried to find work in warehouses or other workplaces.

Since Novoredok was no longer the regional capital, my father was no longer "Avreymke the Starosta (Village Elder), or as others referred to him "Mr. Provincial Governor". There was no longer any reason to go to Novoredok.

The Raikom proposed, any one who wants to, should work the soil. A few Zhetl Jews began to do this work. My father also received a few hectares of land and we worked with our own hands.

We Went to Soviet Schools

The youth, who were not yet worried about earning a living and did not want to know where their parent's found money to buy bread, eagerly went to study.

The Soviets believed their school curriculum was at a higher level than the Polish and they placed students two levels below. The seventh graders were now in fifth grade.

The Soviets opened three schools. In the building that had housed the Yiddish Folkshul, they taught with Yiddish as the language of instruction. In the "Tarbut" School and the Public School the language of instruction was White Russian. They also opened evening courses for adults.

The first year, the majority of Jewish children attended the Yiddish school. The second year some students switched to the Russian School.

Only three Jewish teachers taught in the Russian School: Yisroel Pergomenik, Muliye Zablotsky, and another from Vastochny whose name I do not remember. The school year passed quickly and everyone was making plans for the following year.

We had the idea to learn the material of the eighth grade on our own in order to save a year. But as the expression goes: "Man plans, and God laughs". Hitler did not allow us to realize our plans.

[Page 313]

The Tailor's Cooperative

by Lize Rozvosky

Translated by Janie Respitz

In 1939 when the Soviets arrived in Zhetl we were persuaded to create a cooperative. This was difficult because tailors who had worked independently for years in their own workshops found it hard to adjust to these changes.

These specialists began to call meetings, made a big commotion but could not create a system. Then, a few people, more audacious, put together a list, and personally went to each house.

First we went to Khaye – Soreh the seamstress. Truth be told, she was the goddess of all the surrounding villages and ran a prominent workshop. She could not comprehend the idea of leaving everything, and in her old age, join a cooperative. When we explained to her they would suppress her no matter what, she had no choice but to sign onto our list. It can be said that we broke down walls.

When Hinde Zamoshchik and Dvoshke Haydukovsky saw Khaye – Soreh's name on the list they wiped their lips and said: "Well, so be it. It is what it is".

After the list was compiled they gave us a two story brick house on Slonimer Street, where the Pole Bogulitch once lived. We brought all of our work tools to the cooperative and hung a large sign on the street: "Women's and Men's Tailor Cooperative in Zhetl".

However, this is when the main commotion began: to which category does one belong, who will be the leader and who will be the cutters. In one word, it was cheerful.

After long discussions it was decided Itchke Lisagursky would be the chairman. Itchke Benyaminovitch or "The God" as he was called, would be the manager and Hirshl his brother, the cutter.

This issue was more difficult with the women, but finally they chose two cutters: one for old clothes and the second for new orders. The bookkeeper was Yente Rivke Gal and the treasurer was Itke Berkovitch.

With luck we were accepted by the whole town and began to work diligently. After we had been working for a month, no one actually thought how we would be paid.

A few people thought this was an opportunity to relax after so many years of hard work. Others thought, who would know, and who do we have to report to?

The mood changed at the end of the month when salaries had to be paid. This is when we saw there were different salaries. For example, Nekhame Breskin was earning more than Krayne Mokolovsky, and Krayne more than Khaye Busel. We ran to Itke the treasurer and let out our anger on her.

"What is this, Itke "Thunder" (that's what we called her). Why did I earn so little"?

She would pathetically ask: "Why is it my fault you've been played?"

The same thing happened with the men, let them be well. You could not compare Shaul Yoselevitch with his long feet and big hands, who ran a piece of merchandise through his machine, pressed it with the iron and it was ready. Ruvke Meir's, "The raw potato pancake" had to sweat a lot to catch up to him.

Later it was clear to all they had to get used to the conditions at the cooperative. But now new problems arose, namely working on the Sabbath and holidays, even on Yom Kippur. This was difficult for Zhetl's Jews who were not used to this. Of course we came to the cooperative, but we did not work.

Our boss was a Russian Jew, Gershman, the first secretary of the Raikom party. He understood the issue and came especially on the Sabbath.

When people saw him coming they ran to their machines. Everyone would grab something in his hand. In the evening when we barely lived to see going home a speaker would descend on us, usually Mikhal Rabinovitch.

He would stand and speak, like a passionate patriot, and when everyone noticed he entered a state of ecstasy we would quietly hold our laughter, pushing each other away, until he was left standing there alone.

[Page 314]

During the Years of Soviet Rule

Translated by Judy Montel

The Germans advance at incredible speed. After just a few weeks they are already fighting in the outskirts of Volkovisk The danger is drawing near our town, but we don't yet realize its severity.

On September 17th in the morning, we heard on the radio that the Soviet Army had crossed the border and it was drawing near to Zhetl. The Polish police stations are abandoned. The policemen fled without taking their families. The city is left with no government and the population is terrified, lest the Germans conquer Zhetl first.

On September 18th at 5 pm, the first Soviet tanks arrived in Zhetl. A large crowd gathered in the market square who greeted them with loud cheering. Soviet soldiers got out of the vehicles and started conversations with the townspeople. They were interested in knowing about our lives and told us about their lives in Russia; these conversations later became the material for jokes about life in Russia.

During the first weeks of Soviet rule no change was noticeable in the commerce of the town. The stores were full of customers and there were plenty of goods.

After a few weeks, the representatives of the central government arrived in Zhetl and began to organize the governmental offices. These officials made many changes in the town. They nationalized the large shops and in a short time liquidated private commerce. At the same time, they nationalized large homes and forced their owners to leave them.

Merchants and shopkeepers began to look for work, something that involved many difficulties, even though Russia did not suffer from a lack of work, but for traders and their children, it was not easy to manage at a laboring job. The children of wealthy families did not get jobs in offices and in government institutions and they were sent to work in forests and in camps, which were run with strict military discipline.

Many Poles were exiled to Siberia, but the Jews were not affected, with the exception of the family of Chaim Kaplinski. This was the only Jewish family that was condemned by the Soviets to exile in Siberia, apparently because of their activity in the Bund party during the period of Polish rule. Later on, the "Tarbut" school teacher, Nachum Shochat was also exiled to Siberia.

At the government's initiative, two hospitals and three schools were established in Zhetl. The languages of instruction in the schools were: Russian, Belorussian and Yiddish. In addition, they established a library, a reading room and a municipal park.

Over time, the authorities agreed to allow people from Zhetl to visit cities in central Russia and life resumed its course.

Only in the spring of 1941 did it become apparent that the political situation was unstable. This was also evidenced by the train traffic. In addition to the cars full of grain and agricultural produce that Russia was sending to Germany in accordance with the agreement from 1939, one could also see cars full of ammunition. Russia gathered them on the border for any trouble that might come. We felt that war was fast approaching.

At a club next to the Catholic church, we would gather to listen to the radio. France was conquered… the Balkans were in danger… now it was clear to us that Hitler (may his name be erased) would try to execute his plan of conquering the Ukraine and White Russia, but none of us imagined that the war was so close.

June 21st was a regular nice day. The sun sent its rays and woke the inhabitants of Zhetl up from their deep sleep, but they still didn't know that the war had already broken out. When the news spread of the war, it shocked the town.

The authorities announced a general enlistment. Hundreds of men were enlisted from Zhetl and the surrounding villages who were gathered in the municipal park. All day they registered the enlistees, sorted them, and didn't let them leave the park. The following day the enlistees were driven to the train station in Novoyelnya, but they were too late, the train was already destroyed and didn't run. The enlistees felt the embarrassment and left one at a time.

The non-Jewish population in Zhetl, who did not hide their joy at the failure of the Soviets and openly showed their sympathy for the German army, followed the released enlistees with cries of contempt.

A no less depressing impression was made in the town with the arrival of the first of the injured from Dvoretz. The Soviets had built a large airfield in Dvoretz and the Germans had succeeded, already on the first day of their war, to destroy its facilities and to cause loss of life. Heavy mourning descended on Zhetl with the appearance of the first of the injured from Dvoretz.

Embarrassment also spread amongst the Soviet ruling circles in Zhetl. Loaded automobiles left Zhetl and drove the bureaucrats of the Soviet government eastwards, but the leaders of the communist party calmed the inhabitants and demanded that they stay in place. Later we found out that they already had evacuation orders but they hid them from the civilian population. Eventually, the heads of the communist party fled and abandoned Zhetl and its Jews to the German army that was drawing near the town.

The Jewish youth in Zhetl that had become connected to the Soviet authorities and were active in it, packed their things and fled with the Soviet government. A few of them were able to successfully cross the border and reach Russia, but many of them returned and several were also hurt on the way.

[[Page 315]]

Zhetl on the Verge of Destruction

**Alter Dvoretsky of blessed memory.
The heroic organizer of the underground movement
in Zhetl.**

**Hirsh Kaplinsky of blessed memory. The heroic
commander of the Zhetl partisans in the forest.**

[Page 316]

On the Verge of the Destruction

Translated by Judy Montel

Two dates sealed the fate of the community of Zhetl. The first date: June 20th, 1941, a bitter day, on which the Nazis conquered Zhetl. And the second date: August 6, 1942, on which the final and horrendous slaughter of the Jews of Zhetl took place.

Between these two dates, the Jews of Zhetl experienced a period of 13 months of torture which brought them systematically nearer to their staggering catastrophe. We will make note of several of the horrific events to the eternal shame of the human animals who butchered our dear ones, members of the holy community of Zhetl.

14 July 1941. On this day the Nazis published the Yellow Patch command according to which the Jews of Zhetl were ordered to attach a yellow patch to their chests and backs. The intention of the command was to depress the spirits of the Jews of Zhetl and to prepare them for their physical liquidation.

15 July 1941. On this day the first six Jews of Zhetl were executed for the crime of communist activity. This was the first murder, a sign of further ills, that terrified the Zhetl community.

23 July 1941. On this day 120 of the dear people of Zhetl were taken for labor, but were in actuality shot two days later in the forest near the barracks in Novogrudok. The intention of this murder was to liquidate the respectable people of the town and thus prevent the organization of any future uprising.

28 November 1941. On this day, Zhetl was relieved of its gold, its money and all of its wealth. At the command of the Germans, the Jews of Zhetl turned over their assets that they had saved over many years.

15 December 1941. On this day, 400 Jews of Zhetl were sent to a labor camp in Dvoretz. The Jews of Zhetl struggled mightily for their existence in Dvoretz, until they were wiped out by the Nazis.

All of these events suppressed the spirit of the Jews of Zhetl, but were as nothing compared to what awaited them, and which did not tarry long in coming. On 22 February 1942 the Jews of Zhetl were ordered to abandon their homes, their property and to move to a closed area called a Ghetto. Crowded, shut in and isolated, plagued by hunger, fear and illness, the Jews of Zhetl in the ghetto drew near their tragic end.

From the darkness of this destruction two phenomena look at us that disperse the clouds of the holocaust and they are our comfort in our great catastrophe. The first phenomenon: the organization of dozens of young men in the Zhetl ghetto headed by the lawyer Alter Dvoretzki, whose photo looks out at us from the title page of this section. This group stored arms and planned a rebellion in the Zhetl ghetto. And the second phenomenon: The activities of the Judenrat, or Jewish Council in Zhetl, which included the faithful communal activists of the town and that eased somewhat the terrible suffering. Yet this suffering appeared, later, as a paradise compared to the catastrophe that overtook our town.

On 30 April 1942 the Jews of Zhetl were congregated in the area of the old cemetery and a thousand of them were led as sheep to the slaughter in the Kurfisch Forest.

On 6 August 1942 the Jews of Zhetl were congregated in the market and in the nearby buildings and two thousand of them were executed in the new cemetery. After these two slaughters, the end had come for the 450-year-old community of Zhetl.

T.N.Tz.B.H.

[May Their Souls Be Bound in the Bond of Life]

[Page 317]

Under the Yoke of the Germans

by Azriel Shilovitsky (New York)

(*became Irving Shiloff upon immigration to US*)

Translated by Janie Respitz

On a beautiful bright summer day news spread that war broke out between Germany and Russia. Immediately we saw groups of people gathering in circles, whispering and listening to the news.

The joy of the Christian population, which was not delighted with Soviet rule was unimaginable. Their happiness which only grew on the first days of the war confused Soviet officials who captured trucks and began to flee eastward.

A sorrowful impression was made when they brought the first wounded from Dvoretz, where the Soviets had built a military airfield. The Germans bombed the airfield on the first day which resulted in many casualties.

Immediately, on the first day they began to mobilize the population into the Soviet army. A few hundred boys were mobilized. The mood in town was black. Mothers cried for their sons, and wives for their husbands.

Panic

Worst of all was the news that the Germans broke through the front and were moving forward. This news confused everyone even more. Young men, who had not as of yet been mobilized, began to think about running away to Russia. This was the atmosphere in Zhetl from the first day of the war. Of course, no one slept that night.

The next day the atmosphere was stressful. Rumours were spreading that the Germans would be dropping troops that could be expected at any minute. The Soviets authorities began to prepare to escape despite the false information they were spreading saying that their army staved off the Germans.

The following day, the Soviets packed up trucks with belongings and people and left Zhetl. Jews who had been hired by the Soviet authority left with them.

That evening will stay in my memory forever, since such a scene is difficult to describe with words.

The Jewish population became a flock of sheep among wolves, which can destroy them at any moment.

Those mobilized were concentrated in the priest's garden, but slowly they went home as they were not sent anywhere. On their way home the Christians accompanied them with mocking songs which stabbed and wounded their Jewish hearts.

Fear

On Wednesday the 25th of June German planes swooped down over Zhetl wanting to bomb Kaplinsky's sawmill but hit a non–Jewish home and killed a Christian woman.

From that day on we began to smell gunpowder. We heard gunshots coming from everywhere. The troops were shooting. People were afraid to stay in town as they felt something was going to happen. Whoever had Christian acquaintances, went to stay with them in the villages in order to "wait it out". Some feared fire, others a battle and the result was, people packed up their valuables and left for the villages. The poor remained and waited at home.

The town was without authorities until the 27th of June 1941. During that time the Christians robbed the Soviet warehouses of furniture, flour and sugar. They dragged things out all day and night.

During these days parachutists were landing around Zhetl. They came straight into town to the Jewish homes and collected eggs, 2 for each man. They went civilly accompanied by a non – Jewish town dweller who pointed out the Jewish homes.

What we awaited arrived. Friday evening a Soviet military truck left Slonim. The troops were dropped off at the cemetery and shot. The truck was from an outpost of the retreating Soviet army.

The truck drove off and it became quieter. The army which followed the truck stopped and spent the night near Bodzhelan on the road to Slonim. The following day, Saturday, when they tried to tear through the town, a large battle broke out.

The scene was horrifying. Hulnik's house on Slonim Street was set on fire by an artillery shell. People thought the whole town was burning. Everyone carried their belongings out of their houses and suddenly a German plane appeared and began to shoot the unprotected civilian population assembling outside their homes. This increased the panic. Luckily it began to rain and the fire was contained.

[Page 318]

The terrible battle lasted all night. The entire town lay on the ground. Pious Jews wrapped in prayer shawls prayed to God that the battle would not stop, but to the contrary, continue providing the Germans would not enter. That night a German tossed an artillery shell into the home of Khaim Elye Meir's who lived on the corner of the marketplace and Novogrudker Street, killing Khaim and his son. These were the first two sacrifices Zhetl brought to the German alter.

A few days after the battle there were robberies. Peasants robbed warehouses and Jewish homes.

Troubles

The next day, Sunday, the shooting became weaker. The Germans immediately took 50 Jews hostage. They explained, in the event a German would be killed in Zhetl, all 50 Jews would be shot. Among the 50 Jews was the future Zhetl hero, the lawyer Alter Dvoretsky.

That evening they took another 30 Jews to cut hay for the Germans. That was their first job. The next day they released the hostages and the hay – people. But in their homes everyone was crying as they were sure they would be shot.

At first, the Germans did not treat the Jews too badly. It was explained that they were front soldiers but soon the civil authority would arrive, the S.S and S.D. and then we would have to worry.

And that is what happened. Two weeks later the German army left. During that time individual soldiers went to Jewish homes collecting eggs, soap, and here and there stole a few things. No greater horrors occurred.

One fine morning a field commander showed up and according to a list the Christians prepared, arrested 6 Jews who were ostensibly hired by the Soviets, took them to Novoleniyie and shot them. These Jews were: Etl Ovseyevitch and her daughter Dina, Alter Gertzovsky (Mordkhai Kikes), Shimen Levaronchik, Avrom Guzovsky and Yudl Bielsky.

This murder left a difficult impression. From then on they began to hide. Every time a truck filled with Germans arrived in town all the men would hide. Some in cellars, others in attics, while others lay in gardens until they left.

The First 120 Victims

This is how they played a game of cat and mouse with us until July 22 nd, 1941. On the 23 rd of July an S.S detachment arrived in Zhetl from Novogrudek and ordered all Jewish men between the ages of 16 and 60 must come to the marketplace.

Not knowing what awaited them, the Jews gathered at the marketplace, beside City Hall which was then within the parochial wall. The S.S stood in the middle and the Jews stood all around. Then they read names from a list prepared by the Christians of all the Jewish intelligentsia, took them to the side and later took them to Novogrudek and shot them. Among them were the rabbi and Alter Dvoretsky, but they were both ransomed at the last minute.

The rest, approximately 500 Jews were forced to walk through the streets singing Hasidic melodies and "Hatikva" while being filmed by the Germans.

A few days later the same murderers returned. Who ever did not actually see them could never imagine the murderous German cynicism. When we asked where the men were they claimed they were working and took gold, suits and boots ostensibly to give them, but at that time they were all already in the after world.

Prophecies

Sad days arrived. Jews would gather and discuss among themselves how this all will end. There were optimists who believed redemption would soon come, while others saw reality with open eyes.

What was interesting were the prophecies told in the name of various rabbis. At first they said the war would last 7 weeks. When it did not end after 7 weeks they extended it to 21 weeks. With time they kept extending the terms of the German defeat and our redemption.

However all these discussions took place in order for us to thoroughly enjoy smelling salts and fool ourselves as the Germans were advancing and we did not see any signs of salvation.

[Page 319]

A particularly difficult experience was on Yom Kippur under the German occupation. Of course they did not allow us to go to the House of Study to pray. Everyone prayed at home which made it even more oppressive. During the Festival of Sukkot a truck filled with Germans arrived in Zhetl to mobilize horses. As always, when a German truck arrived in town, you would not see a Jew on the street. In Zhetl there was a depressed Yeshiva boy, Yakov – Noyakh, Shayne – Raynes' son. As always, he went out walking on the street. The German's were angry that everyone else was hiding, so they grabbed him and shot him. Zhetl offered yet another sacrifice on the German altar.

Fresh Edicts

The following day an announcement was made that a permanent headquarters was coming to Zhetl. Everyone understood these would be our hangmen. They set up their headquarters at Motl's (the Abdzhirok) on the corner of Slonim and Hoyf Streets. They immediately began to order blankets, furniture and other items from the Jews.

On the 1st of October 1941 not a single Jew went out on the street. That evening news spread that headquarters ordered a list of Jews. We only imagined what this list meant.

One edict after the other was thrown at us. One demanded we send 4 glaziers to work. The second demanded 15 carpenters and finally we received an order from a higher authority that Jews had to give up all their gold, silver, copper and all other metals. This did not bother anyone as we had resigned our assets long before.

First thing in the morning on November 28th 1941 we began to hand over our gold. Everything went normally until 10 o'clock. Jews brought their possessions and the Germans took them. However the Germans did not want things to go so smoothly. When it was Mrs. Libe Gertzovsky's turn, the Germans accused her of hiding two gold rings in her pocket. Willing to instill fear in everyone with this prank, they took Mrs. Gertzovsky to the middle of the street and shot her in front of everyone. This event shook up everyone.

After this murder we clearly saw our lives had no value. We began to understand we had to finally think about taking our fate into our own hands.

Meanwhile a rumour was spreading that Jews who were working would receive certificates that would be taken into account during a slaughter. Of course Jews began to chase after certificates. Some became forest workers, while others combined various small factories of shoe polish and brushes. Some were prepared to pay a lot of money for a certificate. However the fact was that this was a German trick to delude and mislead.

On the 15th of December 1941 an order was given to send 400 men to work at the airfield in Dvoretz. We thought this too was a trick, but this time the men were actually brought to Dvoretz to work.

After that edict, another one was issued on December 25th forcing Jews to hand over all the furs they possessed.

The next day you saw Jews walking around with collars torn off their coats.

We were shocked by this following event. A few days after this order the town was shaken up by an action against the Gypsies. At night they surrounded them, brought them to the marketplace and in the morning, shot them.

After that event the Jewish population was convinced the same fate awaited them. From January 1st 1942 rumours began to circulate they would soon create a ghetto in Zhetl.

Ghetto

On February 22nd 1942 we received an order saying all Jews in Zhetl must move to the ghetto which they made on Lisagura and part of Slonim Street until Shushne.

Even before this game, an order with various edicts was given to the Jews. For example: wearing yellow patches and not walking on the sidewalk. The yellow patch in the form of a Star of David on the back and on the left breast humiliated and broke everyone, despite the fact the more intelligent and courageous Jews like Alter Dvoretsky claimed to the contrary, it should be an honour for us and was the first to put on the yellow patch.

The same day the Judenrat was formed comprised of the following: Chairman – Shmuel Kustin. Members: Hirshl Benyaminovitch; Alter Dvoretsky; Yehuda Lusky; Moishe Mendl Leyzerovitch; Eliyahu Novolensky; Dovid Senderovsky; Feyvl Epshteyn; Shaul Kaplinsky; Rabbi Yitzkhak Raytzer; and Berl Rabinovitch.

The Judenrat was directed by the clever and talented Alter Dvoretsky to whom we must show gratitude for his proud accomplishments for Zhetl Jewry.

[Page 320]

Hunger

by Pesie Mayevsky (Petach Tikva)

Translated by Janie Respitz

Immediately after they took my father, which happened in the first weeks of the German occupation, hunger knocked at our door. My mother who worked and sewed her whole life was broken after losing father. She could not advise us on how to get food.

Pesie Mayevsky

It was late summer 1941. The front moved deep into the Soviet Union. There was still no ghetto and we were still free to leave town. The Jews of Zhetl, carpenters and tailors went to farmers in the surrounding villages and worked for next to nothing, for bread.

Our house was without a breadwinner. My mother sewed a bit but this was not enough to support us. We, the children had nothing to do. The days were long, filled with fear. We tried to find a way to run away from our house. Every morning, me, my little brother Khonyele, the youngest, my sister Hindele, and our cousins Khoniye and Tolyie would run out of town in order to collect mushrooms in the surrounding forests.

It was quiet and peaceful in the forest. As they were always peaceful, the treetops rocked against the blue sky as if nothing happened.

It's quiet in the forest. Here, a few Jewish children find comfort and protection among the trees and glades. How quickly we learn to find mushrooms and notice where they grow. We lift the moss and find yellow caps. Here and there are all sorts of mushrooms including the red capped and prestigious ceps.

We return home in the evening with baskets full of mushrooms. We clean them, string them together and hang them to dry. Evening settles on the sad window panes and we continue to dream about the free forest. This is what happened every day until the fall.

Our mother struggles to earn a living. She tries to sell our clothes but she can't. In order to do business with the farmers you need a man. They would trade anything for some food and they are hard to please.

We go digging for potatoes with a couple, with bad luck, at a farm house about 2 kilometres from the Slonim highway. The woman told us we would soon be paid for our work but meanwhile her husband tosses the potatoes on a heap and does not pay us. In the interim we are forbidden to travel so how can we go and demand our pay? They created the so–called "Jewish quarter" and you now needed a permit to leave town.

Mother once again examines our clothes and deliberates what to sell.

"Not your father's things children" she asks and lays them to the side. This was her way of ensuring our father was still alive and will return.

At the Farms in Ludzhit and Kashkali

Winter is coming. The hunger in our home is increasing. We are hearing rumours about the great slaughter in Novogrudek as they entered the ghetto. Zhetl's youth are trying to receive permits as forest workers, cutting down trees in the surrounding forests. Jewish boys arrive at farms in Ludzhit and Kashkali with permits. Girls also receive permits and work at collecting and burning the cut branches.

My mother remains at home with my eldest sister Khane. Khonyele, Hindele and I go to Ludzhit and Kashkali. A few goodhearted farmers took pity on us and gave us some food. We help the farmer's wife with housework, and since I know how to sew a bit, I take the risk and begin to sew by hand for this gentile woman and her household.

We also go to the farms and take work from the housewives. We bring it home to our mother and once it is complete we bring it back and receive peas, beans or flour. We also bring our clothes to the village and trade them for food.

[Page 321]

Armed with our permits, Hindele and I go through the frozen forest. It is still dark. Every shrub looks like a wolf or a German.

We knock on the farmer's windows and they give us their linens to sew. We prod through the deep snow. The road stretches for 9 kilometres. It's very cold and we are both shivering. We avoid Miravshchizne and walk through the forest to the Slonim highway. With our hearts pounding we walk through the field which stretches past the palace and as we cross the footbridge over the lake we arrive across from Khaim Feyvl's house.

Here we feel safe. Our house is near the stream. We quickly ran in to see our mother. Her sad and fearful face does not express good news. She takes the work from us.

"Children" she says, "it is uneasy in the ghetto, people are saying the Germans have arrived, it is not advisable to sleep here".

Mother turns around and I see she is crying. How can she send us back so many kilometres in the cold snow? And where to? But it is uneasy here and she wants to save us.

"Warm up children" says mother who is becoming thinner and smaller by the day. She fed us a bit of black noodles, and we left, out again into the deep snow.

We walk through the forests, but where to? To the farm house, to knock again and think of an excuse why we returned so quickly, because it is difficult to swallow the donated piece of bread. Hindele and I cuddle together on the hard bench covered with a bit of straw and cannot fall asleep.

Khonyele Works for 4 Kilos of Bread

Later this period would seem satisfied and happy.

Walking through the forest and fields came to an end. The winter froze our little windows. The house is empty. We are looking for a way out. They are taking Jews to forced labour. There are people who pay others to go work for them, they don't want to face danger or receive beatings.

My little brother Khonyele, the only man in the house, feels the responsibility to provide for us. He looks for the people who are willing to hire someone to work, and he goes to work using someone else's name.

They pay 4 kilos of rye flour for a day's work.

Khonyele brings his hard earned flour home and mother kneads the dough while crying. Her tears are kneaded into the bread. I know mother is crying because father is not here and she never would have wanted her only son to be the provider. My poor overworked mother. Now I understand how bitter this bread was for her.

On February 22nd, 1942 the ghetto was locked and hunger tore through our orphaned house.

Bring Potatoes

Passover is approaching. There are Jews in the ghetto baking Matzah. In our house we cannot talk about it. My uncle Yenkl brings us a bag with a bit of Matzah, so we do not feel ashamed. My mother cannot rest. She is embarrassed in front of the neighbours and won't eat anything not Kosher for Passover. We remember we are owed for the potatoes we dug. Khane receives a permit to bring the potatoes.

The ghetto is now enclosed with a wooden fence. The only entrance is the small street in the marketplace, beside the Judenrat, between Yisroel Kagan's house and Mania Dvoretzky's pharmacy.

Hindele and I go to the gentiles to get our potatoes. The couple is hesitant as they look for excuses; the potatoes are frozen, they are afraid, but finally the farmer takes small frozen little potatoes, loads them onto a wagon and takes us home. He does not give us the half we have earned.

We ride with him. He arrived in town. We go through Slonim Street. Hindele and I walk behind the wagon with our hearts pounding. In our pockets, the paper permit which should be our protection. The ghetto wall cuts through the street at Binyomin Levaranchik's house. We turn onto Hoyf Street. Krashinsky's house is now the gendarmerie. Two policemen are standing on the sidewalk. Suddenly the gentile begins to shout in his loudest voice:

"How do we enter?" I look at Hindele she is petrified. My hands are trembling. All we needed was for a German to come out of the gendarmerie and teach us a lesson for our insolence.

But a miracle happened. The police said nothing. No Germans came out of the gendarmerie, we arrived at the entrance to the ghetto in peace and then we felt secure. The gentile brought the potatoes to our house. Mother came running and we tossed the potatoes into the corner, near the small oven in order to defrost them.

[Page 322]

A pile of frozen potatoes, a treasure in our starving home! It took a lot of suffering and self sacrifice to obtain them.

Troubles

After Passover mother goes to work as a seamstress outside the ghetto. Khane goes with her. They receive a permit saying they are "useful Jews" and receive an extra portion of bread. At work they trade our clothes, but how do you bring the food back into the ghetto, when you are so helpless, without a man at home? My uncle Yenkl Dzhentshelsky helps us a lot. He comforts us saying he will not leave us. However my mother is ashamed to say how great the hunger is in our house.

After the first slaughter when the ghetto became smaller, we lived with Simkha Rabetz and other families in Pilnik's house. We were shoved into a small corner of a room. Mother struggled with all her strength to maintain her dignity. When she returned from work she would stir the noodles made from buckwheat flour and serve everyone a plate. We would sit at the table to eat.

"You have good children" called out Shifra Rabetz, who lived with us.

"Yes" replied mother with a suppressed voice, "I really do have good children". She turns her head so we don't see her cry. Then she goes outside to the steps in front of the house and allows herself to cry freely.

However this period as well was later looked upon as happy. I missed those days and called upon them in my fantasies and my dreams.

In the Zhetl Closet

On August 6th 1942, during the second slaughter, my mother, my brother Khonye and my sister Hinde were killed.

The struggle was futile, the will to be saved futile, hunger, suffering, experiencing anguish and fear. My sister Khane escaped to Dvoretz. Me and my fiancé, Hirshl Patzovsky and his brother Yenkl turned up in Novogrudek ghetto and were housed in the "Zhetl Closet".

The "Zhetl Closet" was a symbol of loneliness and hunger in the Novogrudek ghetto, but also a symbol of battle. It was crowned with the name "train station" due to the constant escaping of its inhabitants.

A few people from Zhetl brought money with them. However the majority were naked and without means to live. The portion of bread was 1/6 of a loaf, filled with straw. In addition to this, in the morning we were given a bit of black water, "coffee", cooked from burnt buckwheat, and in the evening a bit of thin soup, where with a little light we searched for a piece of potato.

The soup was brought from the general kitchen and in the closet it was divided by the light of a match. From time to time we received "white" cheese which was very sour and blue from mold. Our bosses chose to give it to us instead of throwing it out.

It was the same as a prison. The same guards and the same food. White patches with numbers were sewn on our backs. Shoemakers and tailors offer some advice because in the workshops they have contact with customers and they can steal something from work which they could later sell. The saddest is the plight of the carpenters. They swell up and die of hunger.

The "Zhetl Closet" is starving. At night we lie on top of the third bunk and dream about food. The smoke from the clay oven is suffocating, we can't bear it. Avreymke, Khaim the harness maker's son in law and his son Moishele are eating potato peels which Shmuel from Maytshet is throwing away. Hirshl and I would also like to taste this delicacy, but we are ashamed. We try to eat the burnt buckwheat from the coffee which is thrown away in the kitchen, but it is so bitter, it burns our throats. What could we do?

Soreh Lidsky and her father sleep beside our bunk. At first they cooked dumplings from white flour almost every day which they would eat from glass jars. Then they began to starve like everyone else.

We look for a solution and find an ingenious idea. There are a lot of rags in the ghetto, stuffing from pillows. We collect them, cleverly weave the holes with thread which we pulled out of the fabric. We paint the blankets, and Soreh Lidsky who sews very well, cuts them into little dresses, coats and children's blouses. Where can we find thread? We find old socks and unravel them to get thread, and secretly sew at work, in the tailor workshop.

The head seamstress in the workshop, Mrs. Zilberman, a good, kind woman from Novogrudek, helps us out. She has contact with clients on the outside and she takes pity on us seeing how we were suffering. She sells our clever patchwork items outside and we receive a small pittance.

Once, Hirshl risked his life and stole a piece of wood and sold it for a portion of bread. Wood was a rarity, there was nothing to cook on. But stealing a few pieces of wood was risky because wood is not a button, it is difficult to hide.

[Page 323]

During the day we sit in the workshop. It is lunch time. Everyone goes home, two steps away to their meagre meals. I remain in the workshop and do not go. My neighbour at the table, an older woman asks me:

"Why don't you go eat?"

"I went earlier," I replied. She looked at me in silence. The next day, when she saw I remained again, she did not ask.

I Get Sick

I got sick with pleurisy. Dr. Kagan who was in the ghetto brought me medication. He told me I must be better nourished and get more air.

I lie on the third bunk, high up. Under me the two clay ovens burn, where they cook on hotplates without chimneys. Clouds of smoke cover me, I'm actually choking.

Dr. Kagan gives us a few hundred marks. We take the money and immediately make a plan. Yenkl was still wearing a suit from home. He will sew pants from a sack and will go without a jacket. He will resew the suit and pay the debt.

Basieh Rabinovitch brings money and a bit of flour in a cup. Quite a treasure. I was refreshed. Hirshl snuck out of work and cooked me some noodles.

It is the winter of 1942. The frost freezes on the brick walls of the Zhetl Closet, but I am sweating large drops of sweat, like tears streaming from my face and hands. I am lost in thought and I realize it is good that my mother and the other children did not live to see this, because it is all futile, futile…

After I recovered, I received a stable "position", washing and cleaning the infirmary in the ghetto for a portion of bran bread.

The Last 235 Jews

It is the eve of the last slaughter in Novogrudek ghetto. We are 500 Jews. However, this is still too many for them. One fine morning, they made a list of the better tradesmen who will receive an additional portion, "meat" once a week, smelly tripe, and an extra 1/8 of bread. In the Zhetl Closet they are scrubbing and cleaning the tripe. Water is rare and one must risk their life bringing it from the pump on the other side of the ghetto.

In the Zhetl Closet they are cooking the tripe in rusty tin cans. We are delighted and think: who knows what their intentions are with this distribution. Perhaps the Germans have ulterior motives with this extra food.

One day a truck in fact arrived with additional bread. They set up two camps. On one side, the privileged who received the smelly tripe and thin slices of bread and the other side, those who did not have such luck.

From the other side of the ghetto a gang of brown, green and black bandits tore through the ghetto. They led 250 Jews across the ghetto and shot them before everyone's eyes.

The last 235 Jews. The rope around our necks is tightening. They begin to dig the tunnel from the Zhetl closet. Hirshl is sick from hunger. He is suffering from terrible stomach cramps. The doctor says he must have a diet that is nourishing. He must not eat the thorny straw bread. He is constantly vomiting. I receive a bit of flour and bake cookies on the tin sheet which he eats like a small child, small burnt cookies and boiled water.

Yenkl can no longer see as soon as night falls due to lack of vitamins. As soon as the sun sets he is blind and has to feel his way to his bunk.

God only knows where we found the strength to bear the intolerable! None of us died of hunger. Later, when we remembered these times, we longed for them.

We Escape

The tunnel is ready. The last days before our escape there was food in the ghetto. All the reserves in the kitchen were distributed. Nobody hid anything for the next day. We eat potatoes until we are full. Bread too. What more do we need? The maximum we can take with us is half a bread. We cannot take anything more with us in the tunnel where we must crawl on all four. When we get out of the tunnel we must run as fast as possible as far from the ghetto as possible.

The last day. There is excitement in the ghetto. We are leaving. While crawling inside we hear the shooting. A wet rain slaps our faces as the darkness takes us out to freedom. We run. Bullets are falling at our feet. We are together, Hirshl and I. Yenkl ran and joined a group that ran toward Zhetl, but never arrived.

[Page 324]

We are running like hunted animals. We are a group of five. Hirshl, me, Kalmen Shalkovitch, Noyekh from Fanikart and his sister Sorkeh. After an entire night of non stop roaming in a vicious circle, we remain lying in a small forest 4 kilometres from Novogrudek ghetto.

The Germans are chasing us. We hear shooting, voices. With a small pocket knife and our hands we dig a hole to hide in. It is pouring rain. Our clothes are soaking wet and sticking to our bodies. Sorkeh and Noyekh are in a hole together, Kalmen in another and Hirshl and I in our dug out hole. We were afraid to dig a big hole as it could be noticed. We are twisted and cramped.

When we begin to comprehend we had escaped from the Germans we feel hungry and there is no food. While running we both lost our bread. We tap our pockets and find wet sticky pieces of bread. Hirshl has a bit of salt and I have an onion. We eat it and we feel hungrier.

We are afraid to leave our hole during the day because the road is solid. At times we hear footsteps in the forest as well as passing wagons.

At night we crawl out and lick drops of water from the trees. Our mouths are dry and our throats are burning. The rain has let up a bit and we stretch our broken limbs. We are tired. We lie down again in our holes, even though it is crowded, it's warm.

Ten Days Without Food

One day, two days, three, four, five days! We are lying alive in a grave and rotting. We are very weak and we do not have the strength to think about taking the risk of leaving the forest.

At night, the men go into the field and return with raw potatoes. They dunk them in a bit of salt that we have and Kalmen eats twelve potatoes. Hirshl eats two, he can't eat more than that, Noyekh eats as well. Sorkeh and I absolutely cannot eat raw potatoes. I try to cut a small piece with the pocket knife, but the nauseating taste makes me vomit. I spit it out and I am envious of Kalmen as he sticks his knife into one potato after another and eats them up.

We don't have any matches to make a fire, and anyway, we are afraid to make a fire. We found, somewhere, leftover berries from the summer and acorns and we devour them with great appetite. Not far from our hiding place is a forest road where there are signs of farmer's wagons. We see holes made from wheels and in them puddles of rain water. We bend down and drink the muddy water. We don't feel the mud, we lick until the end, down on all fours.

The rain falls harder, our clothes are emitting vapour and sticking to our skin. We return to our hole. However my feet don't want to budge, they are like wood, my head feels empty and bare. I see red spots before my eyes, circles, sparks. My hands are soft as cotton. Hirshl carries me back to our hiding place. Day is breaking and we must disappear. I lie there and cry.

"Hirshl" I ask, "tell me, will we survive to tell this story in happier times?"

"Of course" he says, "of course we will survive", but he did not.

We begin to list all the foods we ate on Rosh Hashanah, Sukkot, Passover, on the Sabbath and even on a regular weekday. We list the best delicacies from home. It seems to me that a satiation is pouring through my limbs. We are drunk from talking. It is becoming warmer. I fall asleep.

The sixth day, the seventh, eighth and ninth…on the tenth day Hirshl and Noyekh left to find a house to get food. Whatever happens, will happen!

They went out and found a farmer and his wife. They were taking potatoes from the field. Their farm house was nearby. Trembling and pale they approached the couple and asked for food. They invited them into their house. They went in. Right near the door was a trough for horses and pigs. In the trough were cooked potatoes. Through the torn peels they saw a very soft dough. They threw themselves into the trough like wild animals and ate. The farmer's wife crossed herself and cried. She fed them and gave them half a bread.

With this treasure in their hands they ran back to us. Hirshl carried the bread, real black tasty bread. He sliced it like a cake and gave everyone a slice. We could not believe our eyes, nor our hands that were holding black bread.

In Bielsky's Detachment

After a few weeks of wandering we arrived at Bielsky's detachment.

[Page 325]

Apparently, who ever had experienced great hunger could not be easily coerced.

We walk through the plains of Nolibok. People are divided into groups. Each one had his supply from which he eats. We are assigned to the group of A.G. "Shushantzes". A family of uncles with their nieces and nephews. They are eating, but they do not give us any food.

Hirshl is feverish. His temperature is high. We are embarrassed to ask for food. We beg with our eyes, but no one shows compassion. The air in the forest is fresh. The pine and fir trees smell good. All of our limbs come alive. But the hunger is torturing us.

They are burning fires, everyone unpacks his package, they are slaughtering pigs, roasting, cooking and eating. From time to time I can't bear it any longer and ask, Hirshl cannot ask. They toss me a slice of bread, a few kidneys. I catch it, but have nothing to roast them on. When everyone finishes eating I swindle a tin can and roast them quickly.

This road also came to an end. We arrived at the camp in the steppe. As Hirshl overcame his illness he wanted a gun; he is after all a former soldier and not afraid. They learn however that he is a carpenter and the general staff does not allow him to leave.

He works. He chops down trees and builds many huts. Simple huts and palatial huts for the privileged. And once again the pot with a bit of thin soup, frozen potato peels without salt. Each one sits with his package and eats. Those who leave prepare food for themselves and their "households".

I go to work in the kitchen and no one sees that I steal a few potatoes which I put into my pant's pockets, which have holes. Roznhoyz, the supervisor, takes my stolen potatoes. The blood disappears from my lips.

Today, I don't recall the stealing with shame, rather with deep sorrow and pain.

The front is approaching. In the forest you can hear powerful Soviet canons. We are awaiting the victorious Red Army, and together with Hirschl, I dream about the great day of liberation. But this is when the greatest tragedy happened. Hirschl fell in battle against the Germans on July 4th 1944.

Fate dealt him the hardest blow: he died on the day of liberation.

The First Murderous Act

by Miriam Shepshelevitch (Bat – Yam)

Translated by Janie Respitz

Wednesday, April 23rd, 1941.

It was a warm beautiful morning. There were some people moving in the streets. Around seven o'clock in the morning a representative from the Judenrat came and told us the horrible news. All men between the ages of 16 and 60 must immediately present themselves at the marketplace to be "registered". Whoever does not show up will put their families in danger. They will be taken and shot in public.

This horrific news confused everyone. People gathered in the courtyards to seek advice as this was the first German trick. People tried to console one another: maybe this is really nothing more than registration in order to establish the amount of people capable of working.

Incidentally I remember that at our neighbour Khaim Tchemerinsky's the following were sitting on a bench: Zalmen Grin, the old man Hornshteyn, Khaim Meir Dvoretzky, and Leybl Dzhenchelsky. These faculty members, two of whom were refugees, were already known to the Germans, nevertheless they also went to the marketplace along with all the men from Zhetl.

Suddenly, they began to pull people out of the courtyards. Young men with childlike faces and old men with grey beards were hurried, not knowing where to. Many of them never returned.

The women, of course, felt cramped in every corner of their house, and together with their children ran to the marketplace. Already on Hoyf Street you could smell the wild dogs who were thirsty for innocent Jewish blood.

Approaching the marketplace, everything appeared black, as if there was suddenly an eclipse in the middle of the day. The entire marketplace was besieged by the military. The Germans were running around with whips, like poisoned mice, yelling, clamouring and bellowing like wild animals. They banged, pushed and kicked children, women and the elderly.

All of a sudden there was a long list.

[Page 326]

Whomever was called from the list had to stand on the other side, and from there straight into the trucks. Who ever did not move quickly enough was beaten murderously.

They read out the names of 120 men: businessmen, rabbis, doctors, bookkeepers and teachers.

When they were all seated in the trucks wives and children began to wail. I will never forget this. My father, who sat at the edge of the truck gave us a sign with his hand not to cry because we will be beaten.

Who was not crying? I think the stones on the footbridge were wet from our tears.

The Germans informed us they were being sent ostensibly to work and we should bring them food and clothing for three days. Hearing these words we breathed a bit more easily, but the murderers had this all planned out.

Returning with the small packages, people pushed toward the trucks but were immediately beaten. A minute later there was no sign of the trucks, and until today we do not know exactly where these 120 Jews died.

After that scene, all the remaining men were ordered to march through the streets singing "Hatikva". With eyes spilling blood and broken hearts our men had to drag their tired feet and obey each command: among others, dancing Hasidic dances in the middle of the street.

The Poles walked on the sidewalks and beamed with delight. Many of them even allowed themselves to spit in the faces of the tortured, which were black, like wet soil after the rain.

When the sun set, this horrific spectacle came to an end. Exhausted, tired and despondent, Zhetl's Jews returned to their homes. They could not settle down. It was hard to believe what had taken place that day.

The unlucky women felt their tragedy on the first day, and the children realized they were orphaned. They tried to talk to the farmers who would come and tell deceitful stories in order to obtain goods and make money. People would walk (since Jews were forbidden to drive) to Stushin, Grodno and Lida, but this was futile. Exhausted from the journey and lack of sleep, the women would return home with nothing.

The 120 men were the intellectuals of our town. These are the ones the Germans killed first in order to sweep away an eventual organized resistance. This was their system in all towns and cities.

The Germans killed these 120 men two days later, Friday July 25th, 1941 in Novogrudek, in the forest near the barracks.

Christians recounted how they were driven out of the prison with shovels in their hands and forced to dig a mass grave.

The First Murder

by M. Shepelevitch

Translated by Judy Montel

23rd of July 1941.

Men from 16 to 60 report to the town marketplace to register. Those who try to evade this endanger themselves and their families – thus the representatives of the Jewish Council in Zhetl announced early this morning.

This announcement boggled the minds. In the courtyards people gather and consult: What to do? Some want to persuade others that this is only registration and nothing else.

Young and old flock to the marketplace. Tension can be felt in the streets, yet when we arrived at the marketplace our eyes were dimmed. Many vehicles and Germans run about like predatory animals, creating loud noises, screaming, pushing, trampling without mercy on the aged or the young.

Suddenly there was silence. Names are read out. Those named stand on the side and from there they are put onto automobiles. They are 120 in number: shopkeepers, doctors, teachers, rabbis and accountants, from the crème-de-la-crème of Zhetl. A wail bursts out. Who didn't cry?

The cars start up and disappear. And then the shameful spectacle begins.

The Germans commanded us to line up in rows and to march while singing "HaTikva." We were also forced to dance. With eyes overflowing with tears and broken hearts, we dragged our stumbling legs and obeyed the orders. By the sides of the road our Polish neighbors were crowded, happy and satisfied. Several of them even allowed themselves to spit in our faces.

Towards evening the shameful spectacle was over. Shattered and broken we went home and found no rest.

Some time later the Poles told us that on July 25th 120 of the best of Zhetl were taken out of the jail in Novogrudok and were ordered to dig themselves a large grave.

[Page 327]

The First 120 Victims

by Pesie Mayevsky (Petach – Tikva)

Translated by Janie Respitz

That night I was tortured by terrifying dreams. I awoke with a premonition of a tragedy. Then our neighbours arrived and told us that all the Jewish men over the age of 16 must gather at the marketplace. No one was permitted to remain at home.

This was July 23rd 1941, the 28th day of Tamuz, three weeks after the Germans occupied Zhetl.

My father, feeling that he was leaving home forever, turned around three times and returned, each time, taking something else with him.

The entire town gathered at the marketplace. The gestapo read from a list prepared by the Polish municipality, of all professionals, intellectuals, students, religious men and those they suspected (as we later learned) of having an influence on life and the ability to organize things in the ghetto. They were told they were going to work.

In truth the whole procedure looked very innocent. There was a small table in the middle of the marketplace. Everyone whose name was called out had to go to the table and register. Meanwhile, the Germans photographed them.

Sadly, I saw my father among those stopped. I ran up to him at the table and my father said to me:

"My child, they are not taking everyone, Khonyele (my brother) is apparently going home".

We later heard in the ghetto that on that day the Germans were supposed to take 300 men, but they succeeded through bribes to satisfy them with 120 victims. Among them was one woman, Shifra Dunetz who they took due to denunciation by a Christian. They also took a few Jews that had been arrested and were sitting in the district jail. As well as my memory serves me I will list the people alphabetically: (according to the Hebrew Alphabet)

> Abaranek Mordkhai
> Obershteyn Leyb
> Abramovitch Khaim
> Ivenitsky Avrom
> Eynbinder Peysakh
> Alpert Volf
> Alpert Moishe
> Orlinsky Moishe
> Ornshteyn Yisroel
> Arkin Dovid
> Barishansky Avrom – Moishe
> Barishansky Aron
> Bulansky Leyzer
> Busel Hirsh
> Busel Eliyahu
> Bitensky Moishe
> Bloshteyn
> Belsky Mordkhai
> Berman Avrom – Shloime
> Berman Zelik
> Berman Meir
> Berman Khonen
> Berman Yitzkhak
> Breskin Betzalel

Ganzovitch Khaim
Gandlsman Hirsh
Gavurin Moishe Leyb
Goldshteyn Aron
Gertzovsky Yisroel
Dvoretzky Berl
Dunetz Shifra
Delotitsky Aron
Haydukovsky Gershon
Haydukovsky Zelik
Zablotsky Yisroel
Zabelinsky Eliyushe
Zasepitsky Nokhem
Zernitsky Alter
Zelikovitch Dovid
Zhukhovitsky Leyb
Turetzky Moishe
Yarmovsky Dovid
Khliebnik Yehuda
Langbart Avrom
Lusky Yitzkhak
Lusky Yehoshua
Lusky Mordkhai
Lusky Moishe
Leybovitch Yekhezkl
Leybovitch Yakov
Lidsky Khaim
Levit Moishev Levit Yosef
Levit Avrom
Levit Khaim
Levit Yakov
Mayevsky Yisroel–Asher
Mayevsky Yehuda
Mashkovsky Mordkhai
Mirsky Zalmenv
Sovitsky Ayzik
Slonimsky Avrom
Senderovsky Hillel
Senderovsky Dovid
Senderovsky Avrom
Podolsky Yosef
Podlosky Yekhezkl
Pilnik Yakov
Pergamenik Moishe
Kabak Yerukham
Kagan Yisroel
Kagan Mendl
Kagan Yitzkhak
Kovensky Leyb
Kaleditsky Mordkhai
Kaplinsky Rafael
Kaplinsky Pinkhas
Kaplan Yakov
Kapeh Yisroel
Karolishky Moishe
Karelitsky Alter
Karelitsky Avrom
Kravetsky Moishe
Rozovsky Avrom
Rozovsky Berl Moishe

Rozovsky Dovid
Rozenfeld Eliezer
Rashkin Yehuda Khaim
Raytzer Binish
Shayak Shloime
Sharlat Yitzkhak
Shushan Yehoshuav Shushan Yehuda
Shilovitsky Khaim
Shilovitsky Yakov
Shepetnitsky Dovid

[Page 328]

Those called were divided. After the Germans went through the crowd and suggested all teachers, merchants, Torah scribes and students should report voluntarily. How naïve we were then. People actually volunteered. Those who remained were ordered by the Germans to march through the streets in town singing Jewish songs. What was one of the songs sung by Zhetl's Jews? "Hatikva"!

Until today, when I hear "Hatikva" my blood freezes. I see the Jews of Zhetl marching through the marketplace singing: "we have not lost our hope" and between the Hebrew words they add in Yiddish "we will outlive you".

Oh, Jewish confidence! My brother repeated these words in chorus with all those who marched home. When my father was standing among the accused who could have thought they were going to their death, and who could have imagined what suffering awaited us, and how few would survive until the day of liberation?

The unfortunate were loaded onto trucks and driven away. The rest of the crowd was chased away with stones. I never saw my father again.

Now the great suffering has begun. When we returned to our sad empty house we began to feel our catastrophe.

The next morning the same gestapo men came and spread rumours that with gold you could ransom those sent to "work", and they told us they were being sent to Smolensk to build highways.

This resulted in chaos. Every family of those taken away began to dig up hidden jewelry, wedding rings, everything they possessed in order to save their fathers, husbands and brothers. Then we began to receive "regards" from those taken away. Some said they saw them on the road, or met them on another highway. Soon the Christians from the area began to bring so–called "letters" from them.

A delegation of women went out to the surrounding region. They said, in Karelitch and Novogrudek they let them return home. But nothing came from this. The Jews of Zhetl did not know that these 120 victims had already found their grave behind the barracks in Novogrudek.

Winter was approaching. At dawn my mother would go into the yard, look at the frozen dew, tremble and say:

"Oy vey! Your father left here naked and it is probably freezing cold now in Smolensk".

Poor mother! She could not even begin to comprehend that they took innocent people and murdered them!

…One returned: the little "Motele Idliak". The Germans ridiculed and mocked him and let him go. When I asked him once to tell me what happened he looked at me and said:

"What, your father was also among them?" That's all he said.

At the beginning of 1942, when children from Zhetl, boys and girls were hiding in the farms of Kashkali and Ludzhit, on a frosty evening when the frozen window panes were glittering in the moonlight, Yosef Khliebnik, whose brother Yudke was also among the 120, took away my last glimmer of hope. He told us that "Motele Idliak" told him that the Germans took all 120 with shovels to dig their own grave.

"And you, silly child" he said to me, "you still hope to see your father?"

I could not forgive him for a long time for taking away my last bit of hope. This did not stop me from dreaming, that someone comes to knock on our door. Tired and frozen, father tumbles into the house. On one such day there was a knock on the door at dawn, but it was not my father. It was a good friend coming to tell us we must be prepared.

"They are going to drive all the Jews into a ghetto!"

…The war ended. Remnants of Zhetl's Jews gathered. Everyone knew our most beloved were dead a long time. But somewhere in a small corner a silly hope gnawed at my suffering heart and I thought: tomorrow, or next week or next month, some of the 120 will appear. Tired and dusty he will come and ask if anyone has remained from his home.

But the road was empty and the last flame of hope had been extinguished.

[Page 329]

Zhetl at the End of 1941

by Sarah Nashmit (Kibbutz Lochem Hagetaot)

Translated by Janie Respitz

At the end of October 1941 I arrived in Lida.

Jewish homes were filled with refugees, living in constant fear, especially the new arrivals. The city was heavily guarded and the roads blocked by the gendarmes.

I arrived in Lida with a brigade of Jewish workers who were working on the highway.

I went into a Jewish house. There were seven in the family plus five refugees.

Going to Zhetl

One cannot sit in Lida. My hosts tremble from fear. They warn me, every stranger that presents himself is shot. Not presenting oneself is worse. Every few days they inspect the Jewish houses. If they find someone who is not registered they take him away with his hosts.

Where does one go?

"Go to Zhetl" they tell me, "It's calm there". But how do you get out of Lida?

All the roads that leave town are guarded by the gendarmes. Anyone caught without a permit is shot.

They point out a wagon driver to me who takes people from Lida to Zhetl for money. He has already transported about a dozen men. He had a permit and was allowed to travel. Jews are running from Lida to Zhetl…

I found the wagon driver.

"It will cost you 500 gildn".

Complaining did not help. This Jew did not want to hear it.

"Five hundred, not one groshn less". I have only my body and a short coat.

"Go to the marketplace and sell your coat," he advises me.

No choice. It is worth it in order to go to Zhetl. I quickly found a customer for my coat but they offered only 150 zlotys.

I decided to try my luck and walk to Zhetl. The wagon driver took a wealthy man from town and his family in his wagon. Approximately 8 people. He receives ten gold rubles and departs. I take a farmer's basket in my hand, tie a white kerchief on my head and walk barefoot along the highway. After walking 500 metres I see from a distance, the gendarmes stopped a wagon on the road. I get off the highway and crawl through the field, pick grass and put it in my basket…

At Fayeh's

On the third day I arrive in Zhetl, enter the Judenrat and collapse from exhaustion. There I heard they had stopped the wagon driver and his passengers from Lida. A few days later they were shot. "They arranged for you to stay at Fayeh the seamstress'" they told me, after the doctor took care of my swollen feet and drained the pus from my wounds. You will lie there for a while. Fayeh, here is your tenant.

A short middle aged woman approached me. She greeted me with a shy smile. Seeing my bandaged feet she offered me her arm.

I went in after her to a low little house, with an even lower roof. Lime falls off the whitewashed wall onto the wide wooden bed, the table and two long benches.

My hostess does not ask me. She prepares the big bed and lays me down on high folded pillows. I know this is her bed, but my protests don't do any good.

I lay there for ten days unable to stand on my feet. This quiet seamstress Fayeh cared for me like she was my own sister.

Years have passed and one forgets many meetings and personalities who we met during these sad days of wandering and fighting for our lives…but always, when I return to those years, the two mild eyes and the subtle smile of the lonely Fayeh shine from the past. I will always remember her hands and her soft footsteps, her motherly worry with which she cared for a complete stranger, a refugee, who she met for the first time in her life, the sensitive heart warming way she shared her food.

Fayeh the seamstress was not the only one in Zhetl during these bitter times to bring the homeless into their homes. It was not for nothing that thousands of refugees remained hidden in small Zhetl, among them Jews from Vilna and Congress Poland.

[Page 330]

A Quiet Island in a Stormy Sea

The fields of Zhetl stick out under a thin layer of snow, the farmer's warehouses and houses are full. In the wooden houses in the villages around Zhetl and in the small house of Zhetl's gentiles, where the homeowner lives in one half of the house and his cow in the other, they now had previously unknown housewares: the beds were covered with white shining bed sheets and blankets, and in the corner of the pillow, blushing like a drop of blood, an embroidered Yiddish monogram!…they sleep better on white shiny Jewish pillows and under a Jewish blankets.

On Sundays, gentile women and girls would go to church wrapped in the coats of Jewish daughters. When they celebrated a wedding they set the table with Jewish silver, and stuck kosher forks and knives into pork while piously saying:

"I did not steal this like the others. I gave my neighbour Yenkele a piece of bread and a dozen eggs for this…

Meanwhile in Zhetl there were three Germans who bossed around the local White Russian police. Our former neighbours, good brothers, were now holding Jewish lives in their dirty fists.

But for now, the authority in Zhetl was "good". There had not been a slaughter in Zhetl. There is an agreement with the authorities. Here a gold watch, there a diamond ring, and Jews remain alive. So called living! But in such times a moment of respite is also good.

Zhetl now has the reputation of being a quiet island in a stormy sea.

Zhetl also has a ghetto. Jews are forbidden to appear on Christian streets. They are starting to build the fence, partly from wire, partly from wood. You could still get through, you can still come and go.

Zhetl also had a Judenrat: honourable, well established men from town. The chairman was the old man Kustin, his deputy, the lawyer Alter Dvoretzky. He was the real boss. His words and opinion were respected in the ghetto.

The Judenrat in Zhetl carried a heavy burden. The town was filled with Jewish refugees. One third of the residents in the ghetto were refugees. Where do you find dwellings for them? How do we provide wood and bread?

The rooms of the Judenrat were always filled with people. They are looking for work, and not just any work but work that can provide a piece of bread for their wives and children.

Others began to do "business" with the surrounding gentiles, failed, and had to be pulled out of their hardship…

But the biggest problem was housing. How do you put a roof over the heads of so many roofless? And where do we find wood to warm frozen limbs?

The Epshteyn Family

At the Judenrat there was an active aid committee. The driving force was Dvoyre Epshteyn. Where does this thin black haired woman find so much physical strength? Her face, pale, her cheeks sunken, but her clever eyes look out with an inner fire.

Her house too was swarming with family and strangers. It was always full. As soon as one left, another came in. She and her husband, Khaim Meir Epshteyn, leave their door open. All day they run around trying to earn a living. Not for themselves, but for others. In the evening friends and strangers gather, sit around a kerosene lamp, discuss the latest news and secretly read a German or White Russian newspaper, which a former neighbour, a farmer, a good man, brought them.

The Germans boast they have captured another city. There are pitiful remnants from the Red Army. In only a few more weeks they will hang the Swastika over the Kremlin in Moscow…

The mood is heavy.

"This is what they want…it will never happen!… maybe they suffered another defeat and want to conceal it with their boasting. What do you think Dvoyre?"

Dvoyre smiles, half seriously, have mockingly,

"They say Minsk was bombed by Soviet airplanes."

"How I would love to kiss the wheels of Soviet tanks" said Khaim Meir Epshteyn sadly.

At the Rabbi's House

December 1941. The streets sink into the wet snow which becomes mud. The feet of Zhetl's refugees sink into it.

There are new Jewish mass graves in the surrounding towns. New refugees are running away from fire and the knife, wandering into the rooms of the Judenrat, filling the sad apartment with the rotted floors of the rabbi. I also go there: I want to hear what's doing…

[Page 331]

When I arrived there one evening to meet the rabbi's daughter, my childhood friend, I found a large crowd. More than usual. In the entrance women were standing with tearful eyes and sadly swaying. In the dining room, elderly Jews were wrapped in prayer shawls and were praying out loud. Among them was a mid–sized young man with a light little beard.

"Who is that?" I asked, pointing to the young man.

"That is Dr. Atlas from Kazlaishchine. His family was killed. He came here to say the mourner's prayer.

Looking at the young man who was enveloped in sorrow, no one imagined he would become a heroic Jewish partisan.

"I heard the Judenrat is choosing people to go to the Dvoretz Camp. What do you have to say about it?" I asked.

"We advise you to go there. They will in any event send all the refugees to Dvoretz. In Dvoretz you will be safe".

There was chaos among the refugees and the poor: the Judenrat wanted to get rid of them. Zhetl received an order to deliver 400 people to the camp.

"You understand who they will send? The refugees and the labourers. The wealthy will not budge from here!"

People were embittered and walked around grumbling…

That's when we heard the word for the first time: forest. It would be better for us to leave for the forest…

I no longer remember who thought up this slogan, and if it had real meaning. Here and there we heard rumours of individuals and even whole families who were in the forests. Who?…What?….It was very difficult then to find order. Everything was foggy, secretive and absurd…

Dvoyreke is distressed and worried. Each time she has to care for another.

"The matter of Dvoretz was unclear. We don't know anything about it…it is hard to learn the truth from the Germans…

"Who are they sending to Dvoretz?"

"Refugees…"

"Dvoyreke, what do you have to say about it?"

"I don't know"

Zhetl is now suffocating…they have sealed off the ghetto…Dvoretz is near the forest…

"Goodbye Fayeh, goodbye Dvoreke, goodbye Khaim Meir. Let us meet again in happier times. Thanks for everything".

From the Mouth of a Refugee who Found Herself in Zhetl

by Sarah Nashmith

Translated by Judy Montel

December 1941.

Dozens of refugees are in the building of the Jewish Council [Judenrat] in Zhetl and in the home of the local rabbi. I went there as well to hear the news.

In the entryway at the rabbi's house, I found women shaking and crying. In the dining room – a minyan [quorum required for prayer] of Jews, wrapped in prayer shawls and praying out loud. Among them a young man, of medium height with a short beard.

Who is that? I asked Dr. Atlas, from Kozlovshchyna. His family was murdered and he came to say Kaddish.

I looked at the young man who was wrapped in his grief and didn't imagine to myself that he would soon become famous as a peerless fighter and a hero of the partisans.

I heard that the Judenrat is registering people for a camp in Dvoretz. What do you think? I asked.

We advise you to register. In any case they will send all the refugees to Dvoretz. The situation in Zhetl is getting worse and worse. In Dvoretz it is safer.

An alarm spread among the refugees in Zhetl. The Judenrat wants to get rid of them.

Of course, who will they send to Dvoretz, the poor refugees. Those from Zhetl, the children of the wealthy families, won't move from their places.

The refugees walk around embittered and grumbling. And then for the first time the word is blurted out: to the forest!

Who started this word - I don't remember. There were rumors about families who had gone to the forest. Who? Where? It's hard to figure out. Everything was hazy and mysterious.

Dvora is sad. Every day she worries about someone else. Now she explains to me: The Dvoretz matter is obscure. It's

> hard to know what it smells like. You can't figure out the Germans.
>
> The atmosphere in Zhetl is stifling. They are fencing in the gate to the ghetto and Dvoretz is close to the forest.
>
> See you later, Faya, goodbye Dvora and Chaim Meir, thank you for everything. I hope we meet!

[Page 332]

The First Slaughter

by Basieh Rabinovitch – Yashir (Tel Aviv)

Translated by Janie Respitz

Worried Jews meet in the ghetto and everyone asks the same question:

What's new?

The events of the past few days have brought about more fear. A few boys, together with the lawyer Alter Dvoretzky escaped from the ghetto. The Judenrat is ordered to betray the escapees and the Christian population is called upon to help find these Jewish "criminals", but without results.

Later, notices were hung up on the streets in German and White Russian offering a large amount of money for Alter Dvoretzy's head.

Members of the escapee's immediate families were arrested. The murderous Hitlerites tried through torture and beatings to learn more, but without success. They held those arrested over night, then sent them back to the ghetto.

On April 29th 1942 a representative from the regional commissar and gendarmerie came to the Judenrat. They carried out an in-depth investigation and arrested all the members of the Judenrat.

Evening. It's getting dark. You see fewer people in the streets of the ghetto. Everyone is hurrying home since it is forbidden to be out in the evening.

Suddenly we hear shooting. Everyone ran where their eyes led them. I fell into the house of Moishe Beres. Soon we heard movement in the ghetto. The streets were filled with Germans and White Russian militia. Jews crawled into hiding places which were prepared in almost every house. The inhabitants of this house took me into their "hole".

Basieh Rabinovitch

We sit crowded and afraid. We could hear the bestial shouts of the Hitlerites and their collaborators. A little later we hear steps. They are coming closer. They are already in the house, they turn everything upside down. They take everything their hearts desire. But the main thing, they are looking for Jews. We feel their steps over our heads. A little longer and they'll find our hiding place. A few present in the hiding place begin to recite a confession of sin, traditionally said before dying. Family members say their goodbyes.

I sit as if frozen. My thoughts are with my family. Where are my parents, sisters, brothers in law? We had been together the whole time. We had decided that whatever happens, we will remain together. And suddenly, such a tragedy!

The murderers did not find us. We hear them leave the house. A half hour later all is quiet. One of us moves out about a metre and tells us all is calm, but we still hear people crying. From time to time we hear shooting.

Time is dragging. Every minute, an eternity. Finally the day breaks. I decide to go home.

The inhabitants of the house try to convince me not to go. They say I will not accomplish or change anything. When they don't succeed to convince me they tell me they categorically will not allow me to go as I will put everyone's life in danger.

Of course I had no choice but to remain.

It was day time. All around you could see frightened Jews. I ran with them.

At home I found my sister Soreh and her husband. I learned from them that they and my parents were dragged by the murderers to the old cemetery. There they were divided into two groups. One group was sent home and the other group was taken away and no one knew where.

Our sister Leah did not manage to return home. When the shooting began she was near Avrom Moishe Kravetz's house and was saved there but unfortunately not for long. She was killed in a later slaughter.

The 1000 Jews they took out of the ghetto were brought to Kurfish forest where there were prepared graves. These unfortunate people were forced to undress and were then thrown alive into the graves.

My father sat and recited the confessional prayer. My mother could not stop looking around and said to those around her:

"I am happy I don't see my children here".

Khasie Ganzovitch hugged her ten year old son and comforting him said:

"Don't be afraid Feyvele, it doesn't hurt!"

These were the last regards we received from a few Jews who succeeded in escaping the murderer's bullets.

[Page 333]

Kaddish – The Memorial Prayer

by Kahim Veynshteyn (Ramat – Gan)

Translated by Janie Respitz

Thursday April 30th 1942. I will remember this terrifying day forever!

At dawn, as I was sleeping sweetly when my father woke me up:

"Khaimke, wake up, quickly, the Germans have surrounded the Ghetto".

Maybe it's a dream, I thought and tried to go back to sleep. The panic in the house got me out of bed.

"A slaughter, a slaughter!" were the words people were saying to each other.

Khaim Veynshteyn

I quickly got dressed. My skin is trembling. We hear shooting in the street. People are running like poisoned mice from one side of the ghetto to another.

Elye Faytches from the Judenrat passes our house and says that those who yesterday received an order to work at Novoleniye should report to the Judenrat immediately. We calmed down a bit.

"If they are asking people to go to work it appears nothing will happen" comforted my father.

My father was among those that had to report for work. He said goodbye to us, took his parcel of food and left.

A short time later we heard screams. I ran out to see what happened. The German police are demanding we gather in the old cemetery.

Without giving it too much thought, I go with the others to the old cemetery. A terrifying scene unfolds before my eyes when I arrive. A mass of Jews are standing surrounded by German police. They divide us into two groups. One group to the left, the other to the right.

How useful would a twelve year old boy like me be? They send me to the left. Suddenly I hear someone shout: "Khaimke, Khaimke!"

I see my father. He is among those sent to the left.

"Why did you come here? Where is mother and Khanele. Motele and Shayndele? Why didn't you hide with them? Oy, why did you come here?" he repeated in despair.

"Papinke" I said, "it's too late. What can I do? This is my fate".

After sorting, the Germans began to push more than 1000 Jews to the graves which they had prepared in advance. They beat people with butts of guns and whips. They drove us like sheep. I held my father's hand.

Papinke, I will always remember your final road. "We betrayed You and robbed You" were his last words.

Now we are walking through the marketplace. The church bells are not ringing, the sky is blue, and the sun is shining as always, as if nothing happened. Each one of us knows this is the final road.

We walk down Novoredker Street. Here is our house. This is where I was raised.

This is the last time I'm seeing you, my dear home. You are standing empty with open doors and windows and mourn this horrible sadness.

We come to the road that leads to Kurfish. There is a small forest nearby. The bandits stop us. They stand around us with machine guns and rifles.

I look at the beautiful nature. Precisely now, in spite of everything, the day is so beautiful. The sun is shining with all its magnificence on this spring day.

The murderers take ten people to the grave. When they finished with the ten they came to get more victims. I say goodbye to my father and slide to the very end. I cannot believe that soon I will not be alive.

"It can't be!" I thought.

They are taking my father. I slide to the very end. I want to live a few more minutes.

Suddenly a taxi arrives. It is the regional commissar Taub, may his name be blotted out. He gave an order that all Jews that have a certificate saying they are "useful" should be freed with their families.

I see Nakhman the blacksmith from Ruda. I ran to him and asked if he could say I am his son. He agrees. He takes out his certificate and goes with his family and me to the murderers and shows them he is "useful". They free us.

A few Jews returned that day from death. Returning to the ghetto I found my mother, sisters and brother. They hid in the cellar and came out after the slaughter. I cannot describe this meeting. I returned from the afterlife, but father did not return.

The next day I went to recite Kaddish, the mourner's prayer…

[Page 334]

Returning from the Graves

by Yitzkhak Rubinshteyn (New York)

Translated by Janie Respitz

On the 30th of April, 1942, at three o'clock in the morning the ghetto was surrounded by White Russian police and a small group of Germans. Learning about this, everyone ran to find a hiding place, some to previously prepared places while others went wherever they could. People crawled into dark holes and pits wanting to avoid this bitter fate.

Around nine o'clock the Jewish militia announced in the streets that everyone should come out of hiding, everything will be OK, they were just checking passes. Their gathering point was the old Jewish cemetery.

I went with my family to the cemetery. There were dozens of Jews there with pale faces and pounding hearts.

Suddenly we were surrounded by armed White Russian, Lithuanian and German police. We realized we had been fooled and this was not a pass control but a slaughter.

The cries and screams of those gathered reached the heavens. The segregation began: who will live and who will die?

Finally they began to push us through the synagogue yard to waiting trucks, promising us they were taking us to work in Novolunie. However, nobody went into the trucks as they smelled of the blood they had absorbed.

Beside me, among the White Russian police was a Christian acquaintance of mine who was now wearing the uniform of a German soldier. I knew him well. He would often come into my store and I would often sell to him on credit believing he was an honest decent man. Now he was one of those leading us to the slaughter. I asked him if he would at least take my little daughter Leah, so at least she could remain alive. With the voice of a wild raging animal he responded:

"NO!"

We walked through the marketplace and Novoredker Street as sheep going to the slaughter, biting our lips with hearts of stone, not allowing a tear to fall.

"Dear God, what did we do to deserve to walk our last road on such a beautiful spring day, when everything around us is blooming? Why do our innocent children deserve to be killed in their blossoming years?

Our Christian "friendly" neighbours stood on the streets and watched our death march.

Suddenly we heard a shot. The entire crowd stood still. People are whispering to each other that Dovid Alpert's son Gedalyie ran away from the line to a field near Tcherne's mill. They chased him and shot him.

They brought us to a small forest on the Lida highway. They ordered us to sit in a row and not to budge. Beside me was Hinde Barishansky with her little one and a half year old daughter. The little girl was wearing a pretty holiday dress. Her mother gave her a piece of bread and straightened the ribbon on her head.

An S.S man with a rubber stick came to us. He counted 10 people and hit all ten on the head. All ten were taken deeper into the forest where they were shot.

They came to my row. I was among the last twenty. My mother–in–law, father in law and little daughter were with me. We were lucky. They sent us to the right side of the field where there were a hundred people, a few pulled out from every group of ten.

My wife remained with the last group of ten. Seeing from a distance they were taking people to their death I ran to the German officer and begged him to leave her. At that moment the German murderer had a moment of compassion and pulled her from those sentenced to death.

We quickly ran to the group that remained alive.

We heard bullets hailing down behind us. Soon the terrifying screams were silenced.

They brought us back to the ghetto. The houses were half empty. One thousand of our brothers and sisters met a horrible death that black morning. Those who survived were broken and depressed missing those near and dear.

[Page 335]

How Was I Saved?

by Lize Kaplinsky (Tel Aviv)

Translated by Janie Respitz

On April 30th 1942 the Germans ordered all the Jews of Zhetl to gather at the old cemetery. They said they wanted to check passes.

My husband, Shaul Kaplinsky had already been arrested. My son Rafael was shot in the operation against the 120. I was very despondent.

Lize Kaplinsky

At first I did not know what to do. Should I go to the cemetery or not? Perhaps I should hide? No, too scared. I decided to go.

I was already at the Talmud Torah. I stand among all those gathered and see, this is the devil's game. I want to go back, but it is too late. I am surrounded by militia, I am lost.

The Germans divide us left and right. I stand in the row on the left. This means: Death. I take out my hospital pass and go to the executioner Hick. I show him my pass and he answers me abruptly:

"To Novolunie, to peel potatoes".

There is a commotion and noise. They are shooting. Isar Gertzovsky's son and a few other Jews were shot on the spot. Those on the left were guarded and we were led through the marketplace to Novoredker Street.

We could barely drag our feet, but the White Russian policeman is angry:

"Walk faster, do you think you are going to Palestine?!"

We arrive in Kurfish forest, near the graves. We sit on one side of the highway, the executioners are on the other side.

We sit like stones in silence. We cannot say a word. My sister in law, Shayne Khane Zelikovitch and my cousins Itke Rabinovitch and Bayle Bom hug me crying, but without words.

The executioner Hick hits everyone on the head with his rubber whip. He hit me with the tip in my eye. I feel my eyes and my face are swollen.

The militia lines us up in rows of 30 and leads us to the graves. I was the last one in the row. At first I wanted them to shoot me as soon as possible, but then an unknown power pushed me back. Utilizing the moment I walked back about twenty metres to those still alive. Someone said to me:

"Mrs. Kaplinsky, the director of the general staff asked for you. Without thinking long, I crossed the highway and went to the director. I said to him:

"I am Mrs. Kaplinsky". He looked at a piece of paper and said:

"Yes, OK. Go Across". Later I learned this was a mistake. The director of the general staff was looking for Hirshl Kaplinsky's wife who was hiding in a cellar. But thanks to this I was saved from hell.

When the executioner Hick saw this operation was happening without resistance, he got into a taxi and left to go eat lunch. It was noon. The local authority took advantage of this situation and freed 30 Jews, including the dentist Aliyeh Kuperman, her family, Dr. Levkovitch and about ten craftsmen.

I sat with this freed group. Dr. Levkovitch came to me and wrapped my eye with a handkerchief. I sobbed.

A German heard and ran to me screaming:

"Stay calm". The freed Jews beg me:

"Stop, calm yourself!" It was hard for me to calm myself after this experience.

When I returned to the ghetto I thought: I could take revenge on Adolph Hitler, who buried our people alive.

[Page 336]

The Tragedy of My Brother's Family

by Mashe Rozvosky – Shvartzman (Petach Tikva)

Translated by Janie Respitz

The 29th of April 1942. I stand by the gate of the ghetto and look out through the slats at the gendarmerie which officiated across from us in Avrom Slonimsky's brick house. I see dozens of police doing gymnastics and are learning how to walk in line, but I don't understand why they are doing this so late at night. And why so many police? I have never seen so many. With a trembling heart, I left to go to sleep.

A sad morning woke me up. I ran through the garden to my aunt Itke Bayle to tell them what I had seen the day before. I go out to the street and hear the Jewish police:

"All Jews must go to the old cemetery for pass inspection. I return home and say:

"Come, we must hide, they want to deceive us and annihilate us".

Everyone from our house went into the stall where we had our hiding place. We sat pressed together hardly able to catch our breath. We could hear shooting and our hearts are pounding like hammers. We hear a shot! A Bang! Someone is crying, another shot! Someone screams, moans.

What is happening? Are they slaughtering Jews?

No one says a word. Minutes feel like hours. Suddenly we hear footsteps. Our hearts stop from fear. They search for us in the yard, in the house and in the stall. At that moment I felt our lives were hanging on by a hair.

But they did not search the stall for long, they left to continue to carry out their murderous task. After ten hours of gunfire all was quiet. We no longer hear crying, we no longer hear screams. But there, in the Kurfish forest, as I later learned, they cried, this is where hundreds of Jews ended their lives.

We sit with grieving hearts and wait, maybe someone will show up? Yes, someone is coming! We hear a quiet voice:

"Auntie! Come out. It's over".

This was my cousin Mikhl Gankovsky. My mother's heart immediately felt the tragedy as she asked:

"How's Shikeh?"

"I don't know" he responded sadly.

By his answer we understood my brother was no longer among the living.

I ran into my Aunt Itke Bayle's and asked: "What's with Shikeh?" They don't know.

"Come with me to his house" I asked them, but nobody wanted to come.

I ran alone. My feet are breaking under me. Night is falling. It's getting dark. Cries emerge from the ghetto houses. I arrived at my brother's house. I hear crying from each room. I go into my brother's room. I look around. Sadness is hanging on the walls. My brother was not there. My sister–in–law was not there, nor the children. I fall onto the bed and start wailing.

"My dear brother and sister! Those dear children! Why were you taken from this world so young? Why, for what sin?"

I did not stay there very long. A dreadful fear came over me. I ran home. I go into my aunt Itke Bayle's and what do I see? They are praying the evening prayers, and my father is reciting the mourner's prayer and crying after his son.

This is the first time in my life I hear my father cry.

My mother cannot be calmed. She bangs her head on the wall screaming and crying.

"My dear children, where did you go? Just yesterday I saw you, just yesterday we were together, and today you are gone".

I cannot describe my mother's sleepless nights. Her pain only grew. My imagination creates horrible scenes. I see how my brother stands with a child in his hands, my sister–in–law is also holding a child and they look at each other with pale faces and do not say a word. These were screams without words, cries without tears.

And their children? I see before my eyes my brother's children, Yosefke and Khayele with their beautiful black eyes. I cannot forget them.

Twelve years ago my brother Shike and his family's young lives ended.

These twelve years have not distanced us from them. My eyes tear and my heart aches when I think of them.

Four months later the rest of my family was killed.

[Page 337]

A Sad Summary

by Khane Mayevsky – Klar (Holon)

Translated by Janie Respitz

My father Yisroel – Asher Mayevsky was killed on July 23rd, 1941. Right after the German's occupied Zhetl, he simply lost his equilibrium, as if he had a premonition of the approaching end. He was taken with the first 120 to work, but in fact, they killed them near the Novogrudok prison.

Our family remained without a head, a body without a head. My mother was depressed and broken. She had always been affable and good natured but now she walked around quiet, silent as a shadow. Only her eyes spoke.

We, the children, saw what was happening in the ghetto, one edict after another, and no one knew what the next day would bring. We walked around locked up in ourselves trying to find a way to save our broken family.

We survived the first slaughter in the potato cellar of Tchirl Skrabun, where we were living then. Due to our initiative they built a primitive cellar: a hole in the vestibule covered on top with wood. The entrance was through a small kitchen cupboard. Thanks to us, the family of Muliye Shimanovitch from Bielitze that lived with us in the ghetto was saved.

Plans

After the first slaughter the size of the ghetto was decreased and our house was no longer within the ghetto.

Bad luck decreed that we move into the house of the Pilnik family across from Hirshl Busel.

Me, my mother, my sister Pesieh, my brother Khonyele and my little sister Hindele were given a small, enclosed corner. Besides us, living in that house were: Simkhe Robetz with his children (his wife was killed in the first slaughter), and two families from Lida. (Pilnik's family was killed in the first slaughter).

Realizing the only recourse was hiding and not "passes" we asked if we could build a cellar. No one wanted to listen to us. They said it was impossible. Later it turned out, everyone hid in the Tarbut School which was a "good" cellar.

Not seeing any other recourse we decided: I will stay with Yehoshua Levorontchik, my boyfriend and best friend. I was always in love with him and given that they were making a cellar, I will, in the event of a slaughter, bring my mother and the children and we will hide all together.

Another possibility was at Hirshl Patzovsky's. They also made a cellar and their house was closer to us.

However it happened, as usual in such circumstances, things do not go according to plan.

The tragic Thursday night (6.8.42) I awoke from a difficult night of bad dreams. I found the household awake. The following cruel news rang in my ears like thunder: "The ghetto is surrounded". No commentary is necessary. This meant: "A slaughter". There was an immediate stampede, a commotion.

Without stopping to think, I ran out the back door in order to bring my mother and the children. I soon heard shots, screams, desperate spasms, and more shooting…I didn't believe I would make it to my dearest and I returned to the house.

I did not find Yehoshua and Henekh. In the interim, they ran away. Their father Binyomin, their mother Dvoshe, their sister Frume, and the other members of the household were standing in the middle of the room confused. I tell them we should go immediately to the cellar, because soon it will be too late. The house was at the edge of the ghetto and will be the first to be fired upon. They hesitate. A while later we went into the cellar without food or water.

This was a hole covered with wood and on top, a flower bed. The entrance was a shed, closed with a small door masked with garbage. Air came in through a concrete pipe that stood at the edge of the cellar.

Days and Nights of Suffering

Besides me and the ones already mentioned, Avrom Lusky, his wife Babl, their son Itche, Babl's mother Krayne Khaye, Dovid Velvl Medvedtsky and his wife were with us in the cellar.

One day of suffering followed another. We heard from Elke Khaye's cellar next door how they took everyone out. Everyday we heard someone in the attic. Our good neighbours, the White Russians and Poles were searching for the remnants the Germans rejected. There was shooting during the day and night.

[Page 338]

We are sitting with cut wounds. I am mourning my mother and the children. They ask why I am mourning them when my fate is no better. I had such a premonition, but no idea how. I also had a premonition about my sister Pesie that she would survive.

Yishayes' parents are worried about their sons, the brothers. Everyone is despondent.

On the third day, Saturday morning we began to talk about leaving the potato cellar. I was categorically against it even though we had no water or bread.

Early Saturday morning Itche Lusky went out and brought back two bottles of water, a thin dried out bread and a knife. He told us he was outside the ghetto at Fantchik's well. The gendarmes saw him take the water and did nothing. It was hard for us to believe.

The same day, in the afternoon, he went out again. This time he did not return…

Another night passed. By Monday everyone was losing patience. Early in the morning they decided to go out. I said:

"Let's sit", although I had no expectations. However, I was sure if I went out I would be killed. We were also afraid because the house was at the edge of the ghetto. They did not listen to me. Monday, 10 o'clock in the morning we went out.

I was the last one out and felt we were doing something absurd. We went through the attic of the smaller house and instead of going down into the garden, Frume and I went up to the second attic which was outside the ghetto.

It was empty. We remained standing for a moment. Birds in the attic were singing as if nothing had happened. I took out a small mirror, examined myself and said how terrible I looked: my eyes were big, my face was black, covered in mud.

"It's a beautiful world" I said to Frume, "but not for us". At that moment she saw the gendarmes were surrounding everyone. I called Frume back to the potato cellar. She did not want to go, perhaps because she was in shock about what happened to her parents and could not figure out what was happening. I warned her again:

"Come, we must not wait, soon it will be too late". But she did not come. I went by myself, as quickly as a cat, back to the cellar. There, the old Krayne Khaye bombarded me with questions:

"Where are the children? Where did they go? Why didn't they come back?" After five days of sitting in the cellar, she was losing her mind. I calmed her down saying they would all soon return healthy and refreshed.

A short while later I heard a policeman talking to Frume. I did not hear what they were talking about but I had the impression he was interrogating her and she did not want to speak.

A moment later a man's hoarse voice called out:

"Sansevitch, there's work here!" And at the same time they blocked the opening where the air was entering from. Then they really started to work. I heard them digging. I heard shovels on the wooden boards. This was my end. At the last moment I wanted to leave and go into another hole in the same stall. But the door did not open.

Why they did not enter the cellar remains a mystery. Perhaps out of fear? There was an episode when Sholem Krashinsky shot from the cellar. Or maybe they were sure if there was someone there, they would die from starvation.

I was desperate. I sat by the tiny window which let in a bit of air and thought these were my final moments. I imagined them taking me to my death, and soon I would be shot. I thought: "I'll ask them for a little water before I die". Oh how frightening it is to realize you only have a few minutes left to live.

With these thoughts I fell asleep at three o'clock in the afternoon until 11 o'clock at night.

I awoke refreshed, with clear thoughts and a strong desire to live. I decided to go out through the opening in which the air entered. With the long knife I dug out quite a bit of earth and through the overgrown stones in the narrow concrete pipe I pushed myself through, first with one shoulder, then the other. I walked out into freedom.

In Freedom

The moon shone brightly and sacred me. I look around. Elke Khaye's house was destroyed. The garden

covering their cellar was dug up until the boards.

[Page 339]

I pick a beet from the other garden. It is tasty. I walk through the gardens, passing Mankovitch's yard.

I walk to Tzalie Patzovsky's yard because according to my calculations my closest and dearest should have been there. I call out a few times:

"Mama! Mama!", but no one answers. I walk by Rashkin's yard, past the old people's home, I run over to the other side, near Zerakh's house, and come out beside Gordon's house. I want to jump over the ghetto fence. I hear Yanek's dog bark loudly. He is beside me and grabs my dress...

I gathered my last bit of strength and jumped nimbly over the ghetto fence. I am now on the other side, on the field at Bielush's. I'm afraid they will hear me. I know them well, our former neighbours. I walk quickly on my tippy toes.

Walking along the river I ran to drink with my mouth and nose, then continued walking.

Where to?

A curve to the right, past Shaye the miner's calcium mine. I continue along the river until a small rural settlement.

Meanwhile it started to drizzle. Tired and wet, I covered myself with a small jacket, the only thing I had, and fell asleep.

I was awakened by a nearby shooting. It was a grey dawn. I found myself across from the Jewish cemetery. Two peasants were standing beside a haystack and looked at me with pity. I could not call it anything but pity. I was barefoot (one sandal got stuck in the cellar and I threw away the other) and my dress tore as I jumped the ghetto fence.

I was frightened at the sight of these Christians, but I had no choice. I asked them to hide me in the hay. They told me they were bringing it to the barn. I asked them again to hide me anywhere but they told me this was impossible. They advised me to leave quickly. I was so close to Zhetl.

"Go to Dvoretz. A lot of Jews escaped there. And don't take the main road. There is no shortage of dirty dogs".

I left. I knew the way to Dvoretz along the highway, but I was not familiar with the side roads.

It began to rain again. Once again I fell asleep and in my dream I saw my mother and the children dead. I was awakened by a joyful conversation among Christians, who were returning with trophies, Jewish goods. Luckily, they did not notice me.

I continued on through the forest near the Dvoretz highway, about 3 kilometres from Zhetl near the good Yanovitchizne. But I did not know where I was.

I sat down. A young Christian woman passed and I asked her the way to Dvoretz. She looked at me with great compassion and told me not to go there now. When it gets dark I should go first to the left, then right and I will be on the road. When she saw my swollen eyes from crying she said:

"Calm down, you will not get far in your condition. Go at night and watch out for people".

I waited for it to get dark. At dusk I continued on my way. But I made a mistake and instead of turning right, I went left.

After a half hour of walking I heard a few gunshots and saw the Zhetl church. I was a few hundred metres from the end of Dvoretz Street. My absentmindedness and short sightedness were to blame.

I quickly began to run back. I met an elderly woman. I went with her. She did not ask me anything and I did not tell her anything.

It was now really dark when I arrived 5 kilometres from the farms in the village of Muliyari. Dogs were barking loudly. I was only afraid of their masters. I had no choice and decided to sleep in the field and continue at dawn.

I took the path on the right, and lay down between two rows of cabbage. A damp chill runs through my body. It is an autumn night. The sky was clear. Thousands of stars were twinkling cold and unfamiliar. The cold does not allow me to fall asleep. It enters all my limbs.

Two Encounters

Daybreak. I get up and continue on my way. I go right, into a ditch. I continue walking. Christians are travelling in wagons, on bicycles. I see a policeman with a large briefcase and my heart stops. Luckily, no one noticed me.

Suddenly two children emerge from a farmhouse:

[Page 340]

Moishe Abramovitch's sister Libe and her little brother Itche. We were so happy to see each other and walked together.

However, the joy did not last long. About 10 kilometres from our destination, a young Christian guy appears suddenly as if from nowhere and starts to run after us. I was the closest to him and he actually grabbed my by my hair. The children managed to escape. The guy said the police placed him there to capture Jews and bring them back to town. He doesn't stop to think and starts to take me back. I cried. What else could I do?

Farmers were working in the field. They told him to let me go. What does he have against me? This does not help. He does not let me go. Suddenly, his grey murderous eyes shine: in my hair I had two brass yellow pins, made in the ghetto. He thought they were gold and began to tear them from my head. I gave them to him. He stopped.

The children return. They soon figured out what was going on. They told him we have family in Dvoretz that would give him money and things if he brought us there.

He believed them. We promised him the world just to tell us how to get to Dvoretz. Little Itche reasoned with him the most. From a bitter enemy, he became our guide. He told us he was from the village Vorevitch and under his patronage we had nothing to fear.

He took us to the edge of town. Here we met Jews from Dvoretz who after work, brought us into the ghetto. We promised the Christian guy that in the evening we would bring him lots of good stuff…

In Dvoretz

The Dvoretz ghetto was like a miniature ingathering of the diaspora. There were remnants from many Jewish communities, from Iviye, Klezk, Nolibok, Derevniyie and others.

Here, as in other ghettos, a large portion of the Jews believed they would not be touched. Dvoretz was a labour camp and they would remain alive. This was what the Germans wanted them to believe. However, there were many who were preparing to go to the forest.

Through a friend of my sister Peshke, I received a corner of a bunk in the vestibule. It was crowded with no lack of lice or fleas.

There were a few dozen people from Zhetl. A group of representatives was formed. One of them was Khaim Mikhl Roznov. They make an effort to get 25 grams of bread and soup for us from the Judenrat. We eat the bread immediately even though it is hot.

A few days later my two cousins arrived: Peshke and Khane Mayevsky. It feels more familiar. They receive a comfortable corner to live in. I still sleep in the old place but during the day we are together. They feel even worse than I do. They cannot eat and give me their bit of soup.

Shaye is Alive

One day, I learned from Soniye from Vizhank, who had just arrived in Dvoretz with her daughter Dolkeh, that Shaye is alive. He succeeded in breaking the chain surrounding the ghetto and after a few days of wandering arrived in Lipitshan forest.

His brother Henekh was shot immediately on Lipover Street. Their father who was a tanner was permitted to live. His mother and sister Frume were shot when they came out of the cellar. The murderers promised the unlucky Binyomin they would let his daughter live if he told them where he keeps his leather. Wanting to take advantage of this last chance he gave them all his leather. They did not keep their word. Binyomin was left all alone with two other tanners: Antzl Sokolovsky and Ben –Zion Peskovsky.

The news that Shaye and his father were alive gave me a new soul. I did not feel so alone. I now had something to hope for.

I did not have to wait long to see Shaye. Two weeks later on a bright morning he arrived in Dvoretz ghetto with Yisroel Zhukhivitsky to take me with them to the forest.

That day, those close to me did not recognize me. I was a completely different person. My old dress was repaired, I was washed and combed and my eyes shone with hope.

Shaye stood in the middle of a gathering of Jews telling them about the Jews in the forest and about the partisans who are organizing and ended with these words:

"Jews, why are you sitting here? Go to the forest!"

They asked him to calm down, fearing he would be arrested. They asked him why he was looking for trouble for himself and others. He does not want to be silenced.

In the company of Khaim Mikhl Roznov's family, he talks from his heart: he is not yet in a partisan detachment because he does not have a weapon. He hoped to be accepted by the detachment, but you can also live in the forest outside the detachment.

[Page 341]

There you are a free person. They listen to him with great interest. Everything he is telling them is so new.

That same night a small group of boys go out, among whom are: Yosl Gershovsky, (Khoniye the glazer's son), Yekhiel Yoselevitch, Leybl Benyaminovitch, Shepsl Lipsky, Shaye and Yisroel Zhikhovitsky.

Khane and Peshke also wanted to go, but Peshke wanted to wait for Berl Nikolayevsky, who was in Novogrudek ghetto. We part warm heartedly and wish to meet again soon.

At night, we cut the wires of the ghetto and go out. Yekhiel goes first. He knows the way. We wandered around for a few hours until we found our way. Then Shaye and Kokeh led the way.

I was impressed how our guides were so well orientated. Only rarely did we knock on a farmhouse door to ask the way. We avoided villages and took paths and detours.

At dawn we arrived at the farmhouses in Repishtche. Shaye comforted me:

"Just a little longer and we will arrive". I can barely drag myself. Feyvl Kalbshteyn approaches us. He carries me in his arms, I am half unconscious, with wounded feet.

In the Forest

Meanwhile we make a tent. Through farmers in Repishtche, Shaye contacted his father who sent us cowhide. A little later, Yosef Novogrudsky and Itche Mankovitch arrived. They had been hiding in the tannery. They bring us regards from Shaye's father. Shaye dreams about bringing him to the forest, but the tannery is heavily guarded.

Hirshl Kaplinsky, the commander of the detachment is in contact with the tanners. There was a plan to bring them to the forest, along with the leather which would be very useful for the half – barefooted Jewish partisans. However, the Germans had their own reckoning. They no longer needed these few Jews and in October, they killed them. Shaye did not achieve his goal or realize his dream.

Shaye received a gun in exchange for the cowhide. As a former Polish soldier it was not difficult for him to be accepted to the detachment. It's more difficult for girls, but he had no problems with me. The detachment needed a typist and I was the only one who knew how to use a typewriter.

This was my luck at that moment as well as later.

I worked for the 22 months I was a partisan as a typist at the headquarters of the "Barba" detachment (originally Orliansky), Lenisnske Brigade.

I found the work interesting and I did it conscientiously and accurately. I also was trusted and recognized by the leadership.

I was in the third company of the above mentioned detachment and I experienced the journey of all partisans until liberation (July 14, 1944).

Unfortunately, Shaye did not live to see liberation. He was killed sometime between July 5 – 12 1943 while carrying out an assignment. During his time serving in the detachment he carried out all his obligations exactly and precisely and participated in all the battles of the detachment.

And my unlucky mother and the children?

They were all, as we had agreed, in Hirshl Patzovsky's potato cellar. However, on the first day they had to leave, because the crying of Lidsky's child betrayed them. The result was tragic: almost all of them were killed. Only Hirshl was sent to Novogrudek ghetto. My sister Peshke was saved in an extraordinary way. After much suffering they left through a tunnel and arrived at Bielsky's detachment.

Cruel fate befell Hirshl the day before liberation. I met my sister after nearly two years of suffering. We were both broken.

The last regards from our mother and the children were given to us by Yehudis Mashkovsky. She was with them at the Jewish cemetery. She saw my dear mother near the graves, kneeling and hugging the children.

What was she feeling? What was she thinking?

Perhaps her aching heart found a bit of comfort with the hope that maybe Peshke and I were alive somewhere?

Her final thoughts were surly filled with protest and anger. And I ask: Why? For which sin was her short life ended?

Honour their memory!

[Page 342]

Two Children Fight for Their Lives

by Kalmen Mnuskin (Kfar Saba)

Translated by Janie Respitz

The noise of a truck woke me from my sleep. It was August 6th 1942. I got down from my bunk on my tippy toes in order not to wake the household who were surely exhausted before they went to sleep. Now they are sleeping and almost certainly dreaming about a better world where everyone would have the right to live.

I look around. Outside the day is dawning. Soon everyone will get up and the daily rush to slave labour will begin.

And like everyday, no eating or drinking, lined up in rows, and with beatings, returned to work. This is how it was day after day.

I look outside. There is a dead silence, like before a storm.

What happened? Do my ears not hear the song of a bird? Did they leave us in the middle of summer and fly away to a warm country? What kind of cold has suddenly fallen upon us? And what's with the dog? Why is he running confused from one end of the house to another, as if he wants to protect his masters from harm?

Yes, the sun is rising and covers its face as if it is embarrassed to look at the surrounding world. I try not to look around and suddenly, I hear a shot.

I don't panic and go wake up my parents. There is a commotion and we don't know what to do: do we wake up the small children who are sleeping so sweetly, or run to our neighbour's to inquire what's going on. Time is running out. Outside we hear the wild screams of the Hitler youth.

Kalmen Mnuskin

"Jews, get out! Jews get out!"

We are all standing together, me and my three small brothers. I, at twelve years old, am the eldest. We try to figure out how to save ourselves from the hands of the murderers.

All the children are serious, with wrinkled foreheads, as if we were trying to plan a rescue. But our minds are too weak to grasp all that was going on.

In the Potato Cellar

After a short consultation, my parents decide, of course not light heartedly, that our family will divide up. One part, our parents and my three little brothers will hide in the cellar, in the garden, so there will be a remembrance of our family in the event our parents are captured.

Hearing this, we all began to cry. No one wanted to separate. Then we heard nearby shots from a machine gun. The windows rattled. I didn't even manage to say goodbye to my parents and brothers and I was already sitting with my uncle Shmuel in his cellar.

The cellar in the garden was nothing more than a toilet hole, covered on top so no one would fall in. This is where the people were. The hole was made for 3–4 people, but when 11 people entered the situation was unbearable. Every hour felt like a year. You could not sit or stand. We sat one on top of the other. The children wanted to drink every minute and from great destitution, we had to give them urine to drink because we had no water. This is how the hours passed until night fell.

In the middle of the night my uncle Shmuel went out of the cellar and quietly went to my parent's cellar. They shared their experiences from the previous night and they decided that the following night we will all leave the ghetto. We were now fated to sit and suffer one more day in this hole.

Friday night, my uncle went out to meet my parents, as they had agreed. It did not take long for him to return disconcerted. I immediately understood that something happened to my parents, but he did not want to tell me. When I started to cry he told me he did not find anyone in their cellar. When we heard this, we all lowered our heads and cried quietly as we were forbidden to cry out loud.

I was totally stunned. I tore out of the cellar wanting to run to my parents and be with them, but they did not let me.

I remained sitting petrified. We were no longer talking about leaving the ghetto.

[Page 343]

We remained sitting like this another night, another day, without food, without air. Every minute it seemed someone was walking, that we would be discovered.

It was already the third day that I was sitting in this hole with my uncle Shmuel, his wife and two children, my aunt Shaynke and her two small children, my aunt Fridka, my grandmother Dvoyre and my uncle Shmuel's two nieces from Maytchet.

When night fell, we decided to get out of there, as it was impossible to remain in that crowdedness and there was no point to remain sitting. Sooner or later they would find us.

We Leave the Cellar

We began to crawl out. My uncle went first and then carried me out. Then one after the other. We did not waste time and divided into groups each remaining 200 metres apart from the other. The first to leave was my uncle and his household. Then my grandmother, Fraydke, me, and after us, the rest. We decided to meet at the old cemetery.

We started to walk slowly, one step after another, and after every step it seemed to me we were being chased.

Suddenly we stood still. Not far from the Talmud Torah we noticed something moving toward us. It was a dark night and we did not know what to do. My aunt Fraydke told me to run by myself and I will be saved. She had to remain with my grandmother, who experienced so much emotionally, she could no longer see.

Alone

I said goodbye to them and ran in the direction my uncle went. While running I banged into the thing that was moving and scared us. It was a German, but luckily for me, with four legs.

I ran to the cemetery where we had planned to meet. I looked around, no one was there. Not my uncle nor the others. Standing there alone I had the idea to run from the ghetto as fast as possible. I realized my fate depended on me. No one could help me now and I needed to be saved.

I began to crawl toward the slaughterhouse, not on the road, but through the gardens. I went garden by garden, fence by fence. There I was beside the slaughterhouse and suddenly, boom!...

After 20 minutes I came back to myself and noticed I had fallen into a brick hole. I cried believing this was my end.

What do I do? How do I crawl out of here? I scrambled up the wall tearing out my nails with my teeth.

After two hours of struggling I succeeded in tearing a brick from the wall and that helped me. I could crawl out. I was very tired. I dragged myself to the edge of town, not far from the new cemetery, crossed the road, ran to the rye fields and fell asleep.

When I awoke it was no longer light. I emerged from the rye, threw my shoes over my shoulder and continued to distance myself from town.

It was Sunday. The Gentiles were hurrying to church. When they saw me they were amazed. They could not understand how I dared to walk, in the middle of the day, slowly, as if nothing threatened me. They were actually right. But after what I just lived through over the past few days I was so confused, my childish mind could not foresee the danger. Suddenly, there was shooting and screaming.

Stop! Voices rang.

I awoke from my daydreaming and thought they were shouting at me. I ran quickly into the tall grass and lay down.

My heart pounded like a hammer. I could not calm down and could not understand what was going on. Later, when I looked around and did not see anyone, I crawled out of the grass.

The sun was shining brightly and I established the shooting was coming from the cemetery. I could not understand what was happening. Then a shepherd walked by and half seriously half laughing said to me:

"Jew, do you still think it's worth it? Run to the forest, you'll find everyone there. Run, run!"

I immediately understood what happened, and this non â€" Jew was not wishing me well.

Hearing the heart wrenching cries of children, women and men I discovered what was happening. Now I understood why they talked in the ghetto about graves being dug at the cemetery.

[Page 344]

I could not help myself and began to cry out loud. As I cried I began to run as far as my eyes could see. As I ran I looked back from time to time at my town Zhetl, from which I was leaving behind my parents, friends and classmates: Arele and Yisrolik, and Moishele and the school and the Tapkashes hill where we would play in the sand. Here is the priest's park and Fantchik's lake, where we would slide in the winter on horse drawn trams. Here is the Tarbut School and the horse market where we would always play football (soccer). I leave this all behind and run.

Where to? I don't know.

I ran for about 2 kilometres until the village Khadzhelan. I arrived at the Slonim Zhetl highway. I was hopeful that one of my father's Christian acquaintances from Kominke would take me in as a shepherd. Every peasant felt sorry for me, but nothing more than that. Others gave me a piece of bread and told me to run because they were afraid of the Germans.

I spent a few days going from one gentile to another. I slept outdoors in the rye fields, or the best circumstance, in a barn on some hay. But there I had to hide from the owners and the Germans as both would not let me out alive.

A Group of Two

I wandered like this for two days. On the third day, walking through Kominke from one gentile to the next begging for bread, a peasant called out to me and told me he saw a Jewish boy around my age wandering in the forest. Hearing this, I wanted to meet this child so I would not be lonely. I was sure this child ran away from the slaughter and is wandering not far from town not knowing where to go.

I returned to the forest and met the young shepherds from my street. They recognized me and told me they will bring me food in the afternoon and warned me, for God's sake, not to go far. However I decided no good can come out of this meeting with the shepherds and I must leave as soon as possible.

I quickly began to look for that child. After wandering in the forest for an hour I found him sitting near a tree and crying. I was very surprised when I realized this child was none other than my friend from Slonim Street: Yenkele Gordon.

We were very happy to see one another but our joy did not last long. Soon our faces became serious and we told each other what we had lived through the last few days.

We were now two, but also as two we had no idea what to do or where to go. I told him about my meeting with the shepherds from our street and we decided to distance ourselves, heading toward Yatzevitch.

How happy we would have been to meet a Jew, older than us who could advise us where to go. However, unfortunately, we did not meet anyone.

A week passed since I escaped from the cellar. Three days alone and three days with Yenkele. The gentiles we meet tell us of the horrible atrocities that happened in town, no one had survived and it is not advisable for us to wander like this. They told us we should return to town and perhaps the Germans will take pity on us and let two Jewish children live as a remembrance.

Understandably, we did not take advice from these Christians. We were waiting for the moment to meet a Jew, because it could not be, we thought, that the murderers succeeded to kill everyone, surely, someone managed to escape, just like we did.

A Meeting Which Disappointed Us

Walking one night on a side road, trying to find a place to sleep, we heard footsteps. We were very frightened and started to run. But then we thought: Maybe it is a Jew? We stood there and waited. What could be worse? We went into the rye, near the path and waited.

Soon we saw a figure approaching us. The figure hid under the barn, afraid of us. Lying and waiting made no sense. We went out and began to walk slowly. We were almost sure he was one of ours, and soon we heard a woman's voice:

"Jews?"

"Yes" we answered.

"Come here children, don't be afraid, I'm also Jewish".

We went to her and told her who we were. She told us she was from Bieltze, she just came from Dvoretz, and not far from

[Page 345]

We were cheered up by this woman and agreed to go to her Christian.

After two more days of dragging ourselves without food or drink, because we did not know any gentiles in the area and we were too afraid to go to a gentile we did not know, we finally arrived at the gentile, our saviour.

She asked us to wait a while outside. She would go in by herself. We agreed because we believed her, as one believes their own mother. However, after ten minutes of waiting, the door opened and the man came out of his house, a gentile with a large mustache and a dog and shouted at us:

"Jews, get out of here quickly. If not I'll call a few Germans".

Once again we were alone in a strange area. No one would even give us a piece of bread because no one knows us. We decided to head back toward Zhetl where we had Christian acquaintances. Maybe we will find one who will let us in as shepherds and give us food.

Two days later we returned. We were happy to find ourselves among familiar gentiles. We arrived during the day because we were afraid to walk at night in unfamiliar territory.

We had to hide quickly, until it got dark. Then we can go to the peasants and get a piece of bread. It had been four days since we tasted a crumb of bread.

We Bribe Our Way Out

We decided to hide in our first spot, in the forest near Kominke.

We had not yet managed to enter the forest, when a young gentile approached us, grabbed us by the shoulders and wanted to take us to the Germans. We began to cry and implore that he had nothing to gain from this. This did not help. He stood firm that Jews should be annihilated.

Suddenly, Yenkele spoke up and told him he'd give him 150 German marks. The young gentile did not think for long. When he saw the money, he grabbed it and told me to take off my shoes. I took them off right away and gave them to him. He was overjoyed with his package, kicked both of us with his foot and told us to run and that he did not want to see us again.

We were very happy we succeeded in bribing him and began to run toward the village Yatzevitch which is further from town than Kominke. We knew some gentiles there as well.

One gentile advised us to head toward Mayak. There was a quiet area called Pushtche and there we will surely find gentiles who will take us in as shepherds since the Germans do not go there often.

We headed in the direction of Mayak. After walking for two weeks without a goal, our present direction had a serious character. We now had a goal.

Despite the fact that walking during the day was dangerous we could not abandon it because we were afraid if we walked at night we would get lost and fall into German hands. We walked during the day but of course, not on the road, but through fields.

We Steal Water

Finally we arrived at the village Patsushtshine, a small village on the road to Pushtche. Being thirsty and afraid to go in somewhere and ask for a drink, we decided to steal a drink of water from a yard, even if the water would be dirty. I warned Yenkele we should abandon the water but he stuck to his guns.

He entered the yard with courage and quick steps and I followed him. He had not yet reached the tub of water which stood in the yard when a dog started to bark and there was movement in the house. The women of the house (luckily for us the men were in the field) shouted at us:

"Thieves!"

We quickly ran out of the yard and gentile kids ran after us yelling:

"Dirty Jews!"

We became completely disoriented. We were sure no one in the village would recognize us and now they were calling us: "Dirty Jews".

The gentile boys were not satisfied with shouting, they began to throw stones. It was difficult to run away because they would have chased after us and not stop until they killed us with stones. For them this was a game, but for us it was a matter of life and death.

And here our luck was favourable.

[Page 346]

We noticed a large stone lying in the field at the edge of the village, probably an old tombstone. We ran to the stone, lay down behind it and began to throw stones back at them. Our enemies were our age, but there were six of them and two of us. They were well fed and rested, we were tired and hungry. We did not lose. I had a slingshot which I found in one of the barns where I had slept. Now it came to good use. Yenkele passed me stones and I continued to sling. And just like at home, when we did not know from worries, and the only worry was the fight with our neighbours, the gentiles, who were always shouting nicknames at us and we made them pay, we continued our battle in order to give these gentiles what they deserved.

This continued until I succeeded to hit one of the six in the head with a stone. He started to bleed. These little anti –"Semites could not recount such a defeat. They ran home apparently to tell their parents to take us to the Germans which they promised as they ran away. We took advantage of the opportunity and escaped unnoticed.

At the Fire

We ran toward Pushtshe. We forgot our thirst and were happy with the outcome of our battle. Our enthusiasm drove us. Not noticing the passage of time, we arrived in a quiet forest region. Here and there stood a house in an open field. This was the so–called Pushtshe.

We decided to enter a house and pretend we were shepherds. Coming toward the house we were met by the man of the house (Matyevsky was his name), and he asked us what we wanted. We told him where we were from and what we wanted and seeing the pity on his face, something we were not used to and hadn't seen for a long time, we began to sob.

He calmed us down, invited us into his house and ordered them to give us food. We ate and drank and did not lift our heads until we were done. Then he told us there were saved Jews in the forest and he will explain to us how to find them.

We did not know how to celebrate or how to thank him. He told us to wait at the edge of the forest because every night Russian's on horseback go by that have not yielded to the army.

We obeyed him. Sitting at the edge of the forest we heard horses galloping. We cried from fear. Soon the riders approached us and asked who we were and why were we crying. We told them we escaped the slaughter, we were alone and have been wandering for three weeks through fields and villages being chased and no one would hide us. The older one comforted us and told us not to be scared. Here in the forest there are no Germans. Here the partisans rule. He told us to walk 200 metres deeper into the forest. There, we should go up to the fire and say commander Kolya sent us.

When we quietly approached the fire we did not have to say Kolya sent us, since they immediately began to hug and kiss us.

Among those kissing us were my parents and my brother Moishe. They managed to be saved, each in a different way after my younger brothers Shepsele and Berele were murdered.

We remained with this group of Zhetl Jews which amounted to 20 people in total and few guns. We all decided together not to rest by day or night and to take revenge for everything and everyone until there was total victory against the murderous nation.

August 6th 1942. Yom Hashoah in Zhetl.

[Page 347]

He Escaped From the Grave

by Shifra Medvedsky (Montreal)

Translated by Janie Respitz

Mayshke Levit was the only one to escape from the graves when they murdered 500 Zhetl Jews. For this reason I would like to recount in detail his tragic death.

When they surrounded the ghetto Mayshek tried to tear through the blockade. But when he saw people dropping from bullets that were flying over their heads, he ran back to the ghetto reaching the Talmud Torah.

There he noticed Tzirl Gershkovitch with her children, Yenkl Pinchuk's family and Noyekh the grain merchant, crawling through a cellar to a hiding place. They languished there for a week, weak and hungry. At night they would go out and get a bit of water from the Pomerayke in order to preserve their souls. They were noticed by the gentile Lazovsky who worked for the Soviets in the bathhouse. He betrayed them and the murderers discovered their cellar.

They brought them all to Sorke Haydukovsky's brick house (Yosef the barber's) where there were already many Zhetl Jews. A little later the mayor of Bielitze, Reguleh arrived with the German executioners and began their search for work certificates. Promising they would let the workers with their wives and children live, they left, leaving a strong guard composed of Latvians, Lithuanians and Germans.

In the evening the murderers arrived and began pushing the people into trucks. The cries of the children reached the sky, but this helped very little.

Mayshke was still trying to think about how to escape. Better to get a bullet in the back than to die in the grave.

During the first slaughter, Mayshke and I and our small child Kalmenke survived the fear of death. The second time, I gave Mayskhe a free hand to run and be saved. However, he did not succeed and they brought everyone to the graves.

They lined everyone up in rows of ten beside the graves and shot them. Anyone who ran away from the graves was chased and shot. Among those was Eltche Kogan, the cantor's daughter, who was severely wounded. She asked them to shoot her and they responded with beatings. She died from these beatings. They brought the Zhetl rabbi, Rabbi Yitzkhak Raytzer and his wife from Dvoretz. They tortured them and then shot them.

Mayshke could not escape from the grave. He was falling from his feet. Motte Turetzky's son, Hirshele, was holding his hand. He was already alone because his family was denounced by Shostok the shoemaker. He knew about their cellar and had their belongings. The child remained alone. He snuggled up to Mayshke and would not leave him until the last minute. When he was shot, still holding Mayshke's hand, he pulled him alive into the grave. Mayshke was covered with corpses. Blood poured on his head and he had no idea how to free himself.

After the slaughter, peasants came to the grave looking for valuables among the dead. Among the peasants was Pauluk, a lame shoemaker. When they threw aside a few corpses, Mayshke was freed and lifted his head. The peasant was frightened but at the same time recognized him and helped him throw off a few bodies until he was freed and climbed out of the grave on all fours. He remained lying in a thick shrub in the forest.

Meanwhile, they called upon the village gentiles to cover the graves and the murderers left after they got drunk on the blood of the Jews they tortured to death.

Later, the police were told people escaped from the grave. The murderers returned with hand grenades, threw them in the graves, and covered them with earth to ensure no one would return from the dead.

Mayshke lay in the forest for a long time and heard everything. He slowly returned to consciousness, stood up on his feet and began to run without a destination. Without realizing, he arrived at a farmhouse near the village Khviniyevitch. He knocked on the door. The door was opened by Prikashke, a gentile partisan for whom he worked before the war. He asked him what happened and why he was covered in blood. Mayshke told him he had escaped from the grave.

"And where do you want to go?" the peasant asked.

"I want to go to America," he replied.

[Page 348]

They realized Mayshke was confused. They fed him, washed off the blood, and took him by the hand to a forest where Peysakh Rozovsky and others already were. This is what the gentiles later told me.

Mayshke was still confused in the forest. A few days later, Artchik Alpert and his family arrived in the forest and told him I was alive. After that, Yehoshua Levoronchik told him he saw me and our child in Dvoretz. Suddenly, Mayshke let out a scream, fell to the ground and regained his awareness.

My mother, father, child and I were hiding in Yudl the ritual slaughterer's cellar. The cellar was not discovered for two days. But we had to leave because they wanted to suffocate my child worried that his crying would betray our hiding place.

We decided to go to Dvoretz. When we left, we split up. My father went on his own but we met up again in Dvoretz.

Mayshke could not remain in the forest any longer. He arrived in the Dvoretz ghetto barefoot and tattered. We could no longer remain in the ghetto and we left for the forest.

My mother could not go with us due to her sore feet and my father would not leave her alone. My father helped us leave through the wire fence of the Dvoretz ghetto and with a face filled with sorrow and tears in his eyes said goodbye to us, forever!

With great effort and fear we arrived in the forest barefoot, naked and hungry, carrying a child, and with cut up feet we left blood stains on the fields and roads.

Lying hidden in the winter mud, our feet froze. Later we found a Gypsy hut where we hid, but we couldn't lie there. We were suffering from hunger. I fainted. Our three year old child cried from hunger. We decided to go look for food.

Mayshke left. On his way he lost his shoes and had to walk barefoot. He brought some potatoes, there was no bread to be found. Meanwhile his feet froze. I was already lying with frozen feet.

It was cold in the hut. There was no one to heat it. Whoever could left to look for help. However, we remained without feet…Our voices and cries rang through the forest.

Feygl Sovitsky came and brought something for our child. She got it from Hertzke Kaminsky. After, they carried us to a hut to Shlyamke Zatzshteyn. Their eldest son Noyekh helped us. Luckily for me, Zelda Grinkovsky arrived and cooked for us. Her children died of hunger and she buried them herself.

When we asked them to save us they said some die from a gun, others from hunger. About twenty people died in this hut. Worms crawled on them alive and after they died there was no one to hide them. Mayshke also died here suffering greatly. Half his body had become paralyzed. Until the last minute he counted everyone from the orchestra in the forest and hoped to lead the orchestra one day in a liberated Zhetl.

With this thought he quietly passed away, nobody heard when.

Two weeks later our child died from hunger and filth.

I remained alone and crawled on all four, like a frog. They looked at me like a superfluous creature. But thanks to my cousin, Shifra Krayer, who sent Dr. Rokover to me, and later Dr. Miesnik, I remained alive.

I do not know how, or through what miracles I am alive and today and can impart Mayshke's experiences. It pains me that he cannot tell it himself. He lived long enough to hear that the murderers tortured my father as he worked on the ropes transporting stones in Dvoretz. His foot was broken in pieces and the murderers shot him in the Dvoretz hospital. Later they sent everyone to the village Katchke, three kilometres from Dvoretz. There you could find the mass grave of martyrs from Ivenitse, Karlitch, Lubtche, Zhetl and Dvoretz.

Mayshke's grave is in the Lipitshansk forest. Before I arrived in the forest dogs and animals of prey removed the bones. There is no remnant of their graves and we cannot even shed a tear on them.

The pain and sadness for my family will always remain in my broken heart. They were so cruelly tortured by the Nazi murderers.

[Page 349]

Zhetl Cleansed of Jews

by Tzile Zernitsky – Yoselevsky (Tel – Aviv)

Translated by Janie Respitz

After the first slaughter in Zhetl it became clear our sentence was inevitable. Different versions began to spread in the ghetto about partisans, but no one had seen them and no one believed it. People were saying that friends were organizing and Alter Dvoretzky and his group had been in the forest for a while already, but no one knew exactly. Besides all the nonsense tales like Znakher with the long beard from Novoredker Street, the table that rises and the scissors which jumps through a sieve, there was now a new fashionable belief: the partisans will show up one fine day, tear down the ghetto walls and free all the Jews.

These were merely dreams of naïve optimists.

After the news spread that Alter Dvoretsky was killed in the forest by an anti –Semitic bullet, a thick black cloud covered our sky. Every drop of hope and belief was extinguished. Only one option remained. Not to go into the grave alive, save yourself as best you could.

Human minds began to work in fresh ways. Everyone, in his own way, became an engineer, building hiding places underground. At night, people dragged sand, made man made flower beds in the gardens, under which they dug intensely. Every house had its guard, whose task it was to wake up everyone in the event of danger.

The evening of Thursday, the 5th of August 1942 did not foretell anything especially bad. As usual, the workers returned from the free world through the wooden gates, back into the ghetto. As usual, after supper, Jews would gather in houses planning new patents and constructions, worried about world politics and sharing the latest news from the front. The women, as customary, occupied themselves with household duties, sharing one small oven with 10 families, but listened to the news from the Agency.

As usual, the silver moon was out walking through the starry bright sky and as usual, the night spread its authority over the world.

That night was my tour of duty in our block in Tanah Epshteyn's house. The quiet innocent night was shameless, sneaking slyly, masking the remnants of the murderers and their bloody surprises.

At dawn, while God was still sleeping calmly, Germans and police tore into the ghetto. The entire town, in a circle of a kilometre was surrounded by a tight military chain.

"All Jews, without exception, go to the old cemetery for an inspection of work papers and passes. If you disobey you will be punished by death!!!!"

The voices of these German animals echoed in the streets of the ghetto. There was no possibility to escape. It was already daylight plus so much military traffic. Everyone tried to save himself to the best of his ability.

There were two cellars at our house. We survived the first slaughter in one of them. It was situated under the floor of a room. The entrance was in the vestibule through a covered board which was lifted under a chicken coop.

It was too late to save ourselves. The German police were already at the entrance and in the yard beating everyone with butts of guns and whips. Panic ensued.

At the Old Cemetery

They brought us to the old cemetery and set up a large, quiet, desperate mass of people. Shooting and screams reach us from the ghetto. Every minute new victims arrived and were lined up. Across from us, in the middle, stood the master of the Zhetl gendarmerie, Grifinkerl, a tall, fat, middle aged German. I am sure he had a family, a wife and children at home. He smoked his cigar and with a coldblooded kind smile, as if he was in a gallery seeing an exhibition examining an original painting: "the death throes of the town".

Police with machine guns are walking around, singing happy songs. Others go up to their acquaintances and neighbours and said: "Now they will do this to you – showing with his hand how one slaughters a chicken. Bakay, the village policeman, ran around with a little mirror, perhaps wanting to examine someone.

[Page 350]

"Make yourself pretty" he "politely" suggested.

Others were bothering young girls and dragging old men by their beards. The large mass of people stood quietly, frozen, as if this did not involve them. Neither the sound of shooting, nor the explosions in the ghetto which were accompanied by screams, laughter, cries and moans, nor the death which soared openly, shook them.

Who knows, maybe everyone was making an account of their own life.

Believers were quietly whispering the confessional prayer. Non believers were blaspheming God. Artchik Grin, the medic, was standing with his family with a bottle of alcohol sticking out of his pocket. He was totally drunk and apparently wanted to be unconscious when facing his verdict.

Two sisters, young pretty girls, pushed their way through us. They worked in the gendarmerie as cleaners. Perhaps they will find a familiar German who will save them? Are they all murderers? Is there not one good one among them?

Shoemakers, who made shoes for the Germans, tried to separate themselves from the rest. They were after all, "useful" Jews, nothing bad could happen to them. Everyone was holding his work card. Maybe they will be saved. Frightened and sleepy children were hugging their mothers. No one was crying.

More families arrived. They brought the patients from the ghetto hospital (the building of the Tarbut School), in their underwear. A woman who had just given birth dragged herself with her newborn, wrapped in swaddling clothes. Two sick men were holding each other up and a paralyzed man was crawling practically on all fours. And here among them like a phantom in white sheets, a thin pointed nose and two wild glaring eyes peeked out. This was crazy Mirke. She separated herself from the masses and stood facing the gendarme commander, waving her sheets like the wings of a bird of prey and pointing to all of us, with a non – human voice in her half mute language screamed and spat on him.

Who at that moment could understand crazy Mirke, when she opened a stream of spit on the gendarme? Who was she spitting on? Who did she mean to spit on? Us or the gendarme? Maybe she was clear and we all were crazy?

A cold shiver, like an electric shock, went through me. Two opposing thoughts flashed in my mind: perhaps she is a messenger from God, calling for revenge?!

The noise of tanks, trucks and songs shattered the air. The helpless crowd shook. Through a small door of the cemetery we saw brown uniforms, among them Royter, (the administrative commissar of the Novogrudek district). Hundreds of Germans, Ukrainians, Estonians, Lithuanians and White Russian police, coming from all sides. Royter came out in the middle and ordered the pass control and demanded everyone be disciplined and obedient. Then he called out 5 names: Elye Novoliyensky, Basie Rabinovitch, Henie Gertzovsky, Hirsh Podliosky and Tzile Zernitzky.

Everyone was sure this was the beginning of a bloody game, and the executions would take place before everyone's eyes.

A municipal policeman grabbed me from my mother's arms, hitting me with the butt of his gun, brought me to Royter, where Elye Novoliyensky and Podliosky were already standing guarded. Basie and Henie were not there. Instead of them, Fanie Dunetz and Pesie Mayevsky stepped out of line. My only desire was that my mother would not have to watch this with her own eyes. (My father was taken with the first 120).

In a line surrounded by Latvians, Royter commanded we follow him to the new cemetery.

In the Barn

Near Magelnitsky's house, where Teper Street and Bathhouse Street flow into each other, there was a quiet, bent barn. They locked us in there.

Through the rotted, moldy boards overgrown with moss we heard shooting, drunken singing by the Germans, cries from women and children and quiet moans from the wounded. Under the stall there was apparently a cellar, because from underground we heard whispering and a choking cough of a child. This gripped our hearts, none of us moved, we did not speak or cry in these last moments of our lives.

Nearby screams and cries accompanied by shooting pushed us to the cracks between the old walls. They were taking a group of 80 men captured in the cellar. Near the stall, beside a small table, stood tall S.S. men, Royter and the head of the Zhetl gendarme, Globle. They were sorting!

[Page 351]

The screams were horrific. Knowing this was their final road, Jews began to run in all directions and fell from chasing bullets. Pitilessly, Germans tore men from their wives and children, who did not want to part. The screams and cries, the pushing and shouting trembled in the air.

The quiet innocent barn which had become a boiler hole, was a silent witness to death.

Suddenly, someone from outside tore open the door and with inhumane beatings, threw in 30 more men, among whom were: Feyvl Kalbshteyn, Motl Kalbshteyn, Yoine Brestovitsky, Elye Kovensky, Zisl Kalbshteyn, Yosl Kravetz, his wife and small child.

Now we understood this was a selection for death.

When it became calmer outside, and the sentenced mass, under a hail of beatings and bullets approached the new cemetery, where the graves were already prepared, the head executioner pulled up with Traube (the commissar of the Novogrudek district). They got rid of the table with the selection points and decided to chase everyone straight to the graves so that people will be disoriented and unable to escape.

A heart wrenching scene played out during this last bloody march. Among the others I saw my mother with my little brother in her arms, and my aunt Khaya holding the hands of her two small children, Yoinele and Khanele. I saw my uncle Meir Lusky and his children, Adeh Lusky with her two year old son, bleeding with his head down. My whole family stayed together.

A bang, like thunder shook the walls. Germans tore inside. Happy with their great success they beat us until we bled, commanded us to go out in threes, undress and lie with our faces to the pavement, so they could shoot us. Fortuitously, Elye Novoliyensky recognized one of them who used to come to the Judenrat for boots. He told him something that distracted him and this saved our lives.

Twice they drove us out, and each time, thanks to another coincidence, we were saved.

How long the tension lasted in the barn, none of us can recall. Minutes transformed into hours.

At the Marketplace

In the afternoon the door opened again. S.S. men led by Royter ordered us to climb into a truck which was standing facing the cemetery.

No one doubted we were the last to cover the graves. Helpless, broken, without any hope, apathetic to everything and everyone we quietly obeyed the order. The only child with Yosl Kravetz's two year old daughter was ripped out of the arms of her parents by the murderers, then the truck turned around headed towards town.

In the light of the shining shameless sun we saw the true destruction. Through streets strewn with the dead and puddles of blood, they brought us to the marketplace which was besieged by the military. Traube stood in the middle of the boulevard (once the circle of stores), with two machine guns, opera glasses and a camera. From the cinema (Shmerke's building) until Berl Dvoretzky's pharmacy, people were laid out in fours, on their knees, facing the pavement. Beating us they led us to them and ordered us to assume the same position. We recognized those they took from the graves.

"Lifting your heads is punishable by death" shouted an officer.

Germans walked through the rows removing boots, good shoes, watches, and rings and rummaged through their pockets. When they took everything, the "public" was pleased. Our neighbours stood by excitedly with outstretched hands. When the spectacle was over there was an order:

"Stand up!"

They counted us. The last person called out 213. Two hundred and thirteen Jews were all that remained from 4000 Jews in Zhetl!

In the Cinema

The ceremony did not last long. Beating each one individually, they led us into the cinema. Royter gave a short "lecture" and promised that the next day we will all be taken to the work camp in Novogrudek, where all the "useful Jews" will not be harmed.

The door slammed, and now like a bomb, the room exploded. Parents searched for their children, husbands, searched for their wives. Children were shouting: "Mama! Screams and cries shook the walls. Here I found my little brother who returned from the graves where all of our nearest and dearest remained.

The over crowdedness and heat were terrible. People, like animals, were choking, banging their heads against the walls, losing consciousness. Others were petrified and were unable to speak.

[Page 352]

Podlishevsky had a grenade and wanted to explode the cinema. There were Jews who stopped him, believing in the promises of our life – givers.

This all happened on Thursday, August 6th, 1942, a day in hell in God's beautiful world.

All night and also the next morning the door of the cinema did not close. New victims arrived. When the hall was filled they also filled the brick houses: Peshke Langburt's and Yosef the barber's.

Friday night into Saturday was the worst. The Jews sitting in the two buildings thought those in the cinema were to remain alive so they bribed the Latvian guards to let them into the better building. This began a business with live merchandise, which every minute would fall out the window on their heads. The business took place in the back because it was impossible to open the door due to over crowdedness and besides this I think the Latvians were also afraid. These "acrobats" were only the ones who had valuables items or gold with them. The others, sadly, had to be jealous and not deny them their extraordinary good luck. However, we, the cinema Jews, understood what this all meant.

Among other news we learned that Sholem Krashinsky shot a German the moment he entered his house. He was killed running away. Shloime Busel also died heroically, killing a Latvian while trying to escape. Shepls from the House of study called out to the German as he was dying:

"You killed me, but my people will live and will take revenge!"

Saturday morning the noise of tanks and military songs shook the small windows of the dark cinema.

A New Selection

The door was suddenly opened with force and Royter accompanied by Globke and S.S. men gave a new speech:

"Nothing more will happen to anyone! There will once again be a ghetto in Zhetl, there will be workshops. In groups of 10 you will return to the ghetto, calmly, without panic!

No one trusted his words. However, there was no other option but to resign ourselves to our fate.

Holding my little brother, who at that moment was completely disoriented I attempted as always to be in the first ten. I knew that at the beginning of a selection you had a better chance to be sent to the right because toward the end everyone was sent to the left.

The desire to live brought out wild instincts in people. Tears and begging did not help. No one wanted children in their group of ten, who were not important to the murderers and had little chance to remain alive. We actually remained among the last. Included in our group of ten were: Berl Saker, Tzalie Mashkovsky, his daughter Yehudis, the idler's daughter in law Mariashke Senderovsky, me and my little brother and three old women from Bieltze.

The marketplace looked like a military front. Running back and forth in front of us, busy and sweaty were the petty bourgeois gentiles and gentiles from the surrounding villages, dragging bedding, furniture and bloodied things. Genitchke from Novogrudek Street, ran unbuttoned carrying a chair and a mirror. Apparently she came across someone stronger than her, or perhaps a better "specialist", or maybe she had bad luck and went to a "handled" house. Everything was a saleable item, you must grab what you can because when will there be another opportunity to get rid of the Jews and make a profit?!

My school friend and "good" neighbour Zasiye Veygo stood on the sidewalk arm in arm with a German. Seeing me in line she laughed loudly and heartily. I have to admit these two facts broke me more than the beatings from the Germans.

The small alley that led to the Judenrat (Kagan's house) was transformed into a narrow lane of German's who received every group of ten with beatings. When the beaten and bloodied approached the steps of the Judenrat an officer shouted:

"Men right, women left".

Right meant to the Judenrat and left, to the House of Study, to die.

There was great chaos, pushing and a stampede, screaming hysterical women. By chance, I took advantage of the storm and went right, into the Judenrat.

This all took place on Friday, August 8th, 1942. After this selection the same amount remained, but not the same people.

A truck took us to the Novogrudek camp, in the building of the old courthouse.

[Page 353]

How Did I Save My Children?

by Shaynke Mnuskin (New York)

Translated by Janie Respitz

On August 6th 1942 the Germans and their collaborators surrounded the ghetto. I hid with my children in an out house which we called an "Otkhozhe" in Zhetl. Our hiding place was under a bucket which stood on wooden boards. We sat there, as if hardened and did not say a word.

Wailing voices of women and children being brought to the slaughter were carried to us from the street.

In our hole we could not differentiate between day and night, but when the shooting stopped we understood it must be evening. From time to time we heard sounds of passing wagons and Christians walking by who had come to rob Jewish homes.

We sat there the whole night. Early the next morning we heard shooting again. They found Jews in hiding places and brought them to the graves.

This is how we spent a few torturous days and nights. The air in the hole was unbearable. My little boy who was 13 months old was half dead. Our clothes were rotting on us from the damp earth. My baby lived on a drop of sugar which I managed to bring into the hole. Thirst was torturing us and our lips were weak and cracked. With the "water" my mother in law provided from herself, I dampened their lips. We quietened our thirst but only for a few hours.

We were envious of the dead who did not have to experience this terrible suffering. Can one even imagine what it means to envy the dead?

Six days passed. We could no longer bear the suffering. My mother in law and sister in law said goodbye to us and left the hole. While in the hole my mother in law lost her eyesight and on her way out she fell, but her daughter helped her. When it became light the Germans captured them and shot them.

The second night, when the hole was flooded with human excrement, I decided it was better to be killed by a German bullet than to drown in this putrid filth. I took my little boy in my arms. It felt like I was carrying a wet rag. My other son who was two years and eight months old held on to my dress.

It is hard to describe how I felt going out of that smelly hole. I decided to go to my mother's house and stay there until they will shoot me. I thought then, if someone would ask me what my last wish would be, at that moment I would have asked for death.

My mother's house had been robbed and destroyed. A small broken oven still stood in the middle of the house from which the wind blew in. There were broken plates on the floor. It looked like a storm ripped through the four walls of my mother's house.

Where Should I Go?

I saw a Christian who had been my mother's neighbour for years.

When he saw me and my children he grabbed a shovel and waved it over my head warning me I better disappear, if not he would cut me to pieces. I asked if he would let me stay in my mother's house for a few hours, just to recover a bit. He became "softer" and advised me, since my mother's house is not far from the cemetery, I should go there because the grave is still open. He did not have the heart to kill us, but there, the peasants were ready to do away with us as they had done to the other Jews.

I obeyed him. As I walked I felt my legs collapsing under me as my heart beat weaker and weaker.

Barefoot, I walked over the glass which was strewn on the pavement. My blood dripped on the stones. I went to the graves. As I got closer I heard the rasping sounds of the dying. I avoided the graves…

Do not begrudge me my dear ones, for walking by and not stopping for a while. I was with you with my thoughts and my heart, but my feet carried me with an instinctive force forward… forward… without a destination…

[Page 354]

It was daybreak. I saw a house from a distance. Before I could get closer an angry dog suddenly attacked me.

Not far from the house I fell down and fainted near flowing water. I put my hand in the water and brought some to my children's and my weak lips.

I stood up, took my children and continued to walk. I tried again to approach a peasant. This time I received a piece of bread. He asked me to leave because the Germans can arrive at any time. I noticed, when he looked at me and my children his conscience revived.

I trudged along all morning. My head was spinning and I was lightheaded. I walked on dangerous roads. I didn't even take this into account.

Finally I entered the forest. I sat down on the ground and gave my children small pieces of the hard bread. They had not eaten anything in four days. With trembling hands they held it and quietly chewed the dry, hard bread. It did not take long before they fell asleep.

I sat, looked at the sky and talked to myself.

"God, why do I deserve to suffer for so long? Where will I go from here? Would it not be better for me to die with everyone else?"

Suddenly I heard people approaching. They were two young shepherds. As soon as they saw me they asked if I had money.

Little boys I thought to myself, and they already know how to rob a lonely Jewish woman. They took a few ruble from me and a few other things which I had with me.

Over Fields and Forests

I left there right away. I thought of going to a woman peasant who was an acquaintance, who we had been very friendly with. I would leave one of my children with her, perhaps both. I remembered she was a kind hearted woman, a church goer and had a fine character…I decided as soon as it will be dark I will try to go to her house. Maybe I'll be able to eat something before I die as I felt my soul was leaving me.

When she saw me, the peasant woman crossed herself and with tears in her eyes told me what happened in Zhetl.

She had a good heart, she gave me a shirt for the children and a coat for me and led us to her attic where we quickly fell asleep.

It did not take long before I felt someone tugging at my feet. I opened my tired eyes and that same woman standing over me with a pitchfork in her hand and shouting that I should leave the attic immediately. She heard she would pay with her life for hiding Jews.

Out of desperation I began to tear out my hair, begging her to at least allow me to spend one night. I showed her the wounds on my feet, my weak children and begged her to have pity on us.

Finally a spark of empathy was ignited in her. She advised me, since it was midnight, she would help me carry the children to a place seven miles away where two nuns lived. When I get there I should lie under the window and when the nuns wake up in the morning to serve God they will certainly notice me and maybe even help me in some way.

Without thinking long, she began to drag me by my hair and her son dragged my older son. Until today I can still picture that horrible scene of how he dragged this barely alive little boy by the neck. I carried my little boy in my arms. I walked through the overgrown field dragging my feet like sticks. Suddenly, our companions stopped. Leaving us alone they returned to where they came from.

It started to rain. We lay in the deep grass with soaking wet clothes. I heard my little boy coughing. A fear engulfed me. Someone can hear us…

Day was breaking. From a distance I saw that the nuns noticed us. They took us into their house, gave us some food and let us sleep in the barn. They bandaged my wounded feet which were bleeding. However we did not stay there long. They also heard the police were searching houses and barns. They brought us to a rye field. We lay there for three days and nights. My little boy no longer had the strength to cry. His little voice now sounded like a small bird. His face was covered with abscesses. He did not look like a human being.

Once again we continued to walk over fields and through forests until we arrived at a small river.

"God in heaven" I asked, "Give me the strength to throw myself in the water together with my children".

[Page 355]

Until today I cannot conceive how I was able to leave my little boy on the bare ground and continue. I walked for half a mile. I tried to hear if I heard any sounds.

"No, he's not crying". I was sure the child understood. I had not even walked a mile. Childish eyes were pleading with me: "Together Mama, together!"

I returned and took him in my arms.

Passing houses I noticed how Christians were turning away and others pitied us. I later heard that I looked like a crazy woman. I ran carrying both children in my arms. From time to time I would drop to the ground and lie there as if I wanted to leave the children and go off on my own. But each time I would return and take them in my arms.

At one place a Christian grabbed me and was ready to hand me over to the Germans hoping to receive a reward for delivering Jewish souls. However he changed his mind because it was too far for him to walk to town. He let us go warning me that we must quickly disappear and that he never wants to see us again. Taking his scythe in his hand he demonstrated how he could slit Jewish throats…

Running into the forest I fell to the ground. I lay there the entire night. When day broke I was once again terrified. I looked at my two emaciated children who opened their little eyes and asked for food and drink. I picked them up and we continued to wander. I went deeper and further in the forest. My bare feet trampled on twigs and sharp stones. I felt I was leaving tracks of blood…

I decided to go to a certain peasant, Varabay. I knew him to be a friend to the Jews. I thought, since he lives deep in the forest, he may not be afraid to hide us. The idea filled me with fresh courage and after a few hours we finally arrived not far from the peasant's house. I quietly whispered to my children.

"Soon, soon my darlings, we may find a corner, a place where we can hide from the death that has been chasing us".

It was evening. When he saw us he turned away as if he did not know us. I began to cry and plead with him, calling him by his name. I fell to the ground and punched my children with my fists wanting to kill them and myself. The Christian could not watch this. His wife and daughters began to beg him to allow us to stay at least one night. Finally his heart softened. He showed us to his potato cellar which was covered with straw.

The hole was far from the house, on a hill. To enter the hole you had to go down a ladder, but I fell in. He threw in my children after me. I was overcome with fear thinking at any minute he can return with a shovel and cover us up alive.

The children fell asleep quickly. I got up on my knees and listened to every rustle. I heard steps…apparently an animal… then all was quiet. My body was feverish from fear and cold. I lay down and fell asleep.

Bright rays came through slats of the cover. I realized the day was dawning…

Suddenly the hole opened and I saw my husband standing over us and crying. In his hand he was holding half a "latke" (potato pancake) which he brought for me and the children. By chance he succeeded to be saved from death and escaped to the forests. Christians told him they had seen me with both children.

He removed a pair of torn sandals from his feet and put them on my feet. He told me a small number of Jews from Zhetl miraculously managed to escape the slaughter and organized a partisan group to take revenge on the German murderers. Since they will not take me into the detachment with the children we will have to, for the meantime, hide somewhere else.

We painfully made it to a wooden stall, deep in the mud, where peasants stored their hay in the winter. There I found orphans and lonely women. They were really not happy with me and my two children. They were afraid my children would cry and divulge the hiding place.

My husband left us with this group and returned to the partisans.

[Page 356]

I Lost My Entire Family

by Yitzkhak Goldshteyn (Kfar Saba)

Translated by Janie Respitz

It is difficult for me to remember everything I experienced under the Germans. I am broken, my heart is weak and my memory doesn't serve me well. I will try to describe what I remember so that my description will serve as a tombstone for my entire murdered family.

There were three months between the first and second slaughter. We began to think about what we could do? People were not even thinking about running away. We began to build cellars. We believed this would save us from death.

I also built a cellar. Under my butcher shop I had an ice cellar. I worked hard with my two sons until our hiding place was made.

The second slaughter took place on the 25th of Av, it was Thursday at dawn. All those who survived will remember that Thursday until we are in our graves. A Christian who noticed that the little door to my cellar was open left and brought the Germans. I managed to escape to my attic, at the height of glory.

I forgot to mention that in my cellar there were a few families and it was very crowded. Therefore my two sons ran away in the middle of the night. I knew they would surely be killed.

When night fell I came down from the attic. My house was not far from the Pomeryake. It was quiet and I went down to the river. The river was very shallow. I crossed two bridges and walked along the water until I made my way to the veterinarian doctor. His wife was very decent.

At four o'clock in the morning I went into their stall where the cows and pigs were standing. I hid there in a pile of straw.

In the morning the shepherd came in to drive the cows to the field. Around eight the veterinarian's wife came in to let the chickens out. I began to talk to her. She was very frightened and wanted to run away. I told her it's me, Itche Goldshteyn. She calmed down and asked if anyone had seen me enter. I swore to her that no one saw me.

She asked me to make a place deep in the straw so no one would suspect a person was lying there. She kept me for two days bringing me food and drink three times a day.

On the third day her nephew came. I knew him. He came into the stall to get straw to lay out a bed for the pigs and saw me. He told me to leave at that minute because if they found me they would kill everyone. I began to plead with him but he went to tell his aunt that Itche Goldshteyn is here.

She came running and told me it was not good because her nephew could denounce me to the Germans. She did not trust him. She brought me bread and asked me to leave.

I left the stall that same night. The night was as dark as my heart. I walked and later sat down to rest beside a barn. It was two o'clock in the morning. Suddenly I heard footsteps. I thought it was the police. When the steps got closer I heard people speaking Yiddish. I asked:

"Who is there?"

"We are Jews" they replied.

I went to them. I saw a boy and a girl. The boy was Shmerl the wagon driver's son and the girl was Itzl Solomon's daughter, Rokhl. (Now in America).

I asked: "Where are you going, children?"

"We are going to Dvoretz," they answered. "There are still Jews in Dvoretz".

We began to walk together. Five kilometres from Dvoretz day was breaking. A peasant ran out from the wheat sheaves with a revolver in his hand and ordered us to return with him to Zhetl. However, if we had gold or other items, he would let us go. Rokhl gave him a watch and a ring. He took my boots and food from the boy and left.

The peasant's name was Matchay, I knew him well. He also caught the Zhetl rabbi who went to Dvoretz, and handed him over to the Germans. He met his end. The partisans shot him.

We arrived in Dvoretz in the morning and mixed among the workers. Our job in Dvoretz consisted of carrying stones. The Germans needed the stones and people worked very hard. We were foolish and believed those who were working would not be bothered.

[Page 357]

One night Leybl the hoi polloi (his family name was Grin) came from the forest with Berman the glazier. They came to get their wives and children. They also took me and a few others. We left late at night and at dawn we arrived at the forest.

I found my three sons in the forest. You cannot imagine my joy!

We got used to living in the forest and once again felt human. Sometimes we had food to eat, and sometimes not. In the summer we ate blackberries and mushrooms with worms, and it was good. We got used to everything.

I was together with my three sons. They wanted to join the partisans but they needed weapons. They would not accept you without a weapon.

I made my way to a group in the forest called Laptzinsky. Meanwhile my son Mikhl and I became sick with Typhus. My older son Yosef and the youngest Leyzer looked after us. We lay there for five weeks and recovered. Suddenly, my son Mikhl wanted to go look for bread. I warned him:

Mikhl, you are still weak from your illness, don't go. He did not listen to me and left. The Germans attacked him in the village Mizevetz. He did not want to be captured alive. He ran and they shot him. When I heard this I became confused and my two sons watched over me. Mikhl was the apple of my eye. Everyone from Zhetl knew him well. They thought I would lose my mind.

Mikhl Goldshteyn of blessed memory

But man is stronger than iron. After five weeks I calmed down a bit.

Then, my older son joined the partisans and within a short time my younger son and I joined as well. My older son worked in the hospital. I worked in my profession. I slaughtered animals and did everything necessary to prepare them for the kitchen.

This is how things went until the Red Army arrived. Then both my sons went into the army. I wanted to join them but they would not take me. They took away my gun and sent me home. They said they don't take older people.

I came to Zhetl. My house had already been burned. I went to live with Menakhem the butcher's children.

I began to work a bit in my profession, but I did not hear anything from my two sons.

One day I was called to "Vayenkom", and I went. A military man read from a paper that Yosl Goldshteyn fell near Bialystok for the Fatherland. You can imagine my immense loss!

I walked around in a daze and could not find a place for myself. From great heartache I began drinking. When I was drunk, I would throw myself into bed and cry so hard no one could quieten me. This lasted for a few weeks. I don't know where I found so many tears.

I became a big drinker. When I was sober I regretted it and felt ashamed. I felt I would die from drunkenness. I began to struggle with myself to overcome the drunkenness.

I succeeded. I stopped drinking and began to think about my third son. This was my last hope, my only comfort. I received a letter and a photograph from him and I was happy, but my joy did not last long. I never received another letter from him. I asked his regiment about him and they replied that Eliezer Goldshteyn disappeared and they themselves don't know where he is. Can you understand how I felt?

Eliezer Goldshteyn of blessed memory

The only one who has remained with me is my brother's grandchild, Avreyml. He was with me in the forest and after liberation he stayed with me. He is the only one who remained from my large family.

The Soviet authorities gave an order that anyone who wants can go to Poland. I immediately left for Poland and I now live in Israel.

[Page 358]

From the House of Study to the Forest

by Bashe Mnuskin (Kfar Saba)

Translated by Janie Respitz

During the second slaughter I sat in the cellar with my three children. My smallest child would often cry and I was afraid this would betray us.

Without water and very little air we sat there for three days. On the fourth day we heard footsteps. Someone moved the cabinet which blocked the entrance to the cellar and we heard shouts: "Jews, get out!!" I went out with my frightened children. Two Germans and a policeman, a Zhetl Christian, began to hit us and push us toward the cinema.

In the cinema a horrific scene unfolded before my eyes: the hall was packed with Jews who were ripping their last bit of money in order not to leave it for the murderers.

Two o'clock in the afternoon they took us out, stopped those capable of working to send them to Novogrudek, and took the rest to the House of Study. When we were inside we looked outside and saw Germans throwing Jews into trucks, separating children from their parents in order to increase the pain. They also tore away my two children from me, Berele and Shepsele and did not allow them to go with me. I remained with my third child Moishele and waited for a second transport.

The people in the House of Study walked around like shadows and together shouted: "Hear O Israel!" Every 15 minutes the trucks would return and the Germans would fill them again with people and take them to the graves. Suddenly I noticed a few Jews placed a reading stand in the corner and climbed up into the women's section. Among them was my brother in law Shleymke. I only had my Moishele with me and I was petrified after the tragedy with my two other children. However seeing how people were trying to save themselves I took my only child in my arms and began to climb up on the lectern. The first of the climbers chopped a few boards from the attic and dragged us up. We were twelve altogether. In a matter of minutes we boarded up the opening.

In the attic we were afraid we would be discovered. But downstairs the commotion was so great the murderers did not notice we went up. We saw from the attic how they were taking our brothers to their death, and I tore out my hair thinking about my two murdered children. The people in the attic comforted me saying I still had one child with me and gave me hope that my fourth child, Kalmen was hidden in another cellar.

Night fell. All was quiet. They took everyone from the House of Study. At midnight we went down from the attic. Among us were bold men like Hirshl Kaplinsky, Yosl from Kazlaytch, Pinye Grin, Shleymke Mnuskin. They went down first. I followed with my Moishele. Two women went down with us: Libe, Gershon the tailor's wife and Dvoyre Tinkovitsky. A few families remained in the attic who had been hiding there for a few days, among them, Shmerl Feyvzhinsky.

We went down one at a time. There was a dead silence outside. We walked into the Pomerayke and walked slowly with the river until the edge of town. Then we started to run. I ran holding my child with my last bit of strength.

Finally we arrived in Pushtshe. I went with two men to look for bread in Hiritch, where I had gentile acquaintances. My acquaintance filled a sack with bread and gave me things for the child.

While meeting others who had escaped from the ghetto I found my husband Mayrim and my brothers: Zisl and Mikhl. My brother Mikhl who was saved from the slaughter was killed three months later in a battle with the murderers and my brother Zisl who succeeded in saving himself was fated to die a year later on the front.

My husband and I still were hopeful about our son Kalmen. One evening, when we were sitting around the fire we heard sounds from among the bushes. We were frightened. Two from our group who had weapons went with their weapons to search the bushes. It did not take long before they returned with two tattered crying children. They were my son Kalmen and his friend Yenkele Gordon. They were the last to be saved from the Zhetl ghetto.

[Page 359]

In the Workshops of the Novogrudek Ghetto

by Pesieh Mayevsky (Petach Tikva)

Translated by Janie Respitz

In August 1942, the remaining 35 thousand Jews that lived in the Novorgudek region until 1941 were rounded up. Among them were 154 Jews from Zhetl who were brought to Novogrudek and divided into two groups: one group was brought to the so called "old ghetto" where they were all murdered in February 1943, and the second group was brought to the "workshops", near the sadly – renowned court house, where on December 6th 1941 they were rounded up with all the Jews from Novogrudek and taken to their death.

The Zhetl Jews were housed in an empty garage which was crowned with the name the "Zhetl Closet". There were approximately 100 people there including people from Bielitz and "Bezhntze". Each of them were the only surviving member of their family and they jealously looked at the "happy" people from Novogrudek who could still see their children's black eyes or an elderly person, a father, a mother.

The place was surrounded by 2 rows of barbed wire. Behind the wire was a wooden fence which was constantly guarded. On the roof of the court house, very close to the camp, stood a machine gun with a projector to ensure no one escaped.

There was no water in the ghetto. Every morning we lined up at the fence with rusty tin utensils in order to bring a bit of water from the other side of the ghetto, which had to last for 24 hours. This is where the harassment began.

A Christian guard stood behind the locked gate, a scoundrel named Subatch allowed whoever he wanted to go for water. If God forbid he did not like you, you could be sure he would hit you over the head with his stick.

In the winter we were spared from going to get water as we could manage with snow, but here we lost an essential source of existence. When we would go for water, we would often trade a shirt, a dress, a watch or anything we still had for some food, and smuggle it back in our bosom, even though it was often discovered and we would pay for it with terrifying beatings.

When we were stopped from going out for water, along with the winter days came hunger, destitution, lice and illness. It was particularly difficult for those in the "Zhetl closet". Half naked, with wooden shoes, the carpenters, shoemakers, tailors, hat makers, watch makers and a few girls would go out to work in the workshops.

Hunger was rampant. At night, the carpenters would bring some stolen wood into the ""Closet" and over choking smoke we would cook a bit of rye flour or bake some barley. A few people ate potato peels baked on a sheet of metal.

There were a few lucky ones who brought money with them. Others earned a little at work. They had enough bread to eat and even bought flour from the "Ghetto merchants". Those from Zhetl belonged to the "privileged" but most of them starved, walked around covered in lice with swollen faces.

A lonely child was attached to the "Zhetl "Closet". His name was Grishke. Except for Moishele, Khaim the saddle maker's grandson, who was there with his father, was the only child in the "closet". This 8 year old little boy was saved from a nearby town. He was always tattered, dirty and hungry and he latched on to the closet people and suffered together with them until his tragic death.

I remember one night in the "closet". It was dark. The last kindling burned out, but the dense smoke choked our throats. The bedbugs and hunger prevented us from falling asleep. Then I heard Grishke's little voice and how he turned to Soreh Lusky's whose plank bed was beside mine.

"Soreh, did Peshke eat today"? This meant he wanted me to tell him a story but he did not have the audacity to ask me if he knew I was hungry. Then he sat up and asked:

"Tell me a story, tell me Peshke".

And I told him a story about sunny fields, about my parents and familiar houses. I told him about the bad giant who chased the children from his garden causing his garden not to bloom. I told him about the "mother's tears" that ruined the palace of the evil duke who kidnapped the child from his mother. His garden withered, his palace collapsed, until he returned the child to his mother.

[Page 360]

Little Grishke decided that the German's mother's tears did not destroy any palaces, the sun shone again and the flowers bloomed again.

It's dark. No one in the "closet" is sleeping. You can hear who cannot fall asleep due to hunger and who for the hundredth or thousandth time tore at their open wounds, so immersed that it drove them crazy.

Little Grishke decided the Germans would not lead him to the slaughter and when that dark day arrived he ran away and jumped into a toilet to hide. The Germans chased him and shot him in that filth. We later removed him and buried him in a small grave in the workshop yard.

The Jews of Zhetl had a reputation of being rebels. Every day, one of them escaped through the wire. They ran to the Nakrishk forest. They had received news from there that Alter Dvoretsky and Hirshl Kaplinsky had organized a Jewish partisan unit. The majority did not succeed in their escape.

After the slaughter of May 1943 where many Zhetl Jews were killed the idea of a collective escape ripened. The main organizers of this plan were Dr. Kagan from Baranovitch and the carpenter from Zhetl, Itchke Dvoretzky. Finally, their grandiose plan to dig a tunnel was realized, dug from the "Zhetl Closet". The last Jews from Zhetl escaped through the tunnel together with the last Jews from the Novogrudek ghetto. A total of 235 people.

The tunnel was 2.5 metres deep, 90 centimetres wide, 70 centimetres high and 187 metres long. They had to work on their knees. The dug out earth was removed in special wheels onto wagons. Due to a lack of oxygen they could not burn candles or oil lamps so they installed electric lights. The lighting also served as security because twice a day there would be roll calls in the workshops where everyone had to line up in rows of five.

It would also happen, in the middle of the day a gang of "Browns" of "Blacks" would show up to inspect the camp. When this would occur, they would give a signal by flicking the electric switch which was in one of the residences, to warn those in the tunnel that the Germans were in the ghetto. The boys would immediately come out from underground, throw off their clay covered clothes which were sewn from rags, and run to the workshops.

At night, they removed the earth through the attics and used it to build double walls in the houses. When people returned from work they saw something unusual in the "Zhetl Closet": from a hole under the plank bed they passed bags of earth from hand to hand until they were brought to the attics in the other houses. Sometimes they threw earth on the floor and into their hats just to get rid of it and to ensure the guards would not notice.

The tunnel had to be supported by wooden frames in the shape of crates to prevent the thick layers of earth from collapsing. The carpenters stole the wood from the carpentry shop. They were brutally beaten when they realized wood was stolen but luckily the purpose was not discovered.

In the fall, the tunnel was flooded with water. Those who removed the water had wounds covering their bodies.

On one occasion they came up against a giant rock which blocked the way when the tunnel was already 105 meters long. A second incident was when they noticed from the ghetto a grain cutting machine on the sowed field under which the tunnel was situated. If the cutting machine would have been placed on the tunnel it would have collapsed, not being able to withstand the weight.

Two carpenters worked 13 hours under ground, without a break, to reinforce the tunnel. The cutting machine cut the grain and the tunnel withstood the test. Air entered the tunnel through tin pipes which the tinsmiths stole and placed in the ground allowing them to continue the work.

The day when 235 Jews would leave through the tunnel arrived. It was the 26ᵗʰ of September 1943. If my memory serves me, I will try to list the Zhetl Jews who escaped. Please forgive me for any names omitted. Here they are in alphabetical order:

[Page 361]

Belaus Khaim, Bielitsky Tzale, Gertzovsky Yosl, Gertzovsky Berl, Dvoretzky Yitzkhak, Dunetz Fania, Veynshteyn Shmuel Dovid, Leybovitch Yerakhmile from Bielitze, Lidsky Soreh, Mayevsky Pesieh, Novagrudsky Mikhal, Patzovsky Hirshl, Patzovsky Yenkl, Paretzky Moishe, Paretzky Shmuel, Dr. Kagan from Baranovitch, Rabinovitch Basieh, Shimshelevitch Shmuel, Shalkovitch Kalmen, Khaim Natkovitch's (the harness maker) son in law Avrom, his son Moishele, Noyekh Panikarter and Soreh Panikarter. A few Jews remained in hiding too afraid to go through the tunnel. Among them were Zalmen Gertzovsky, Leybl Berman and Khone Epshteyn. They were all killed.

We escaped through the tunnel according to a prepared list. The first and very last were young men who had weapons. We descended into the tunnel one at a time. We were ordered to not stop, even if we would be noticed by a guard.

Crawling on all fours we heard the deafening sounds of shooting. When we poked our heads out of the tunnel we found ourselves under a shower of bullets. The partisans later told us that such a dark night rarely occurred.

The Germans believed the partisans came to the ghetto so they began shooting. The surrounding police posts responded. The projector on the roof was not working because before the escape the Jewish electricians caused a defect. When the guards arrived they found the ghetto was emptied of people. This is when the real shooting began.

The Germans chased with trucks and lit up the area with rockets. Not being familiar with the region the Jews from Zhetl ran where their eyes led them, banged into Jews thinking they were Germans and the opposite. As a result of great confusion and excitement many returned to Novorudek and were killed by the Germans positions. We ran all night long without stopping. At dawn we snuggled into a small forest. We were saddened to learn we were only 4 kilometres from the ghetto.

Until today we do not know how long it took for the 235 Jews to escape through the tunnel. It is possible it did not take long, possibly a few hours.

The fate of those who escaped differed. The majority ran toward Zhetl. However, almost all were caught and shot, some by the Germans, some by the partisans.

Only a small number made it to Lipitchaner Pushtshe and a few to Nalibaker, however not all those saved lived to be freed.

The Zhetl Glaziers in Novoredok

by Zavl Mordkovsky (New York)

Translated by Janie Respitz

On a winter morning the government inspector from Novoredok, Roiter, came to Zhetl and ordered the Jewish population, within 12 hours to supply spoons, blankets, furniture clothing and other goods. Among the delivered items was 6 metres of glass and 5 diamonds to cut the glass.

Alter Dvoretsky asked me to bring boxes to pack the glass and dishes. I asked the glazier Dovid Berman to help me with this task. When everything was ready, the murderer Roiter commanded that we send glaziers to Novoredok.

We already knew what working in Novoredok meant. But because we were the youngest glaziers in Zhetl it was decided that we would go. They sent us in a special truck and brought us to "Boiteh Camp", the collection place for all stolen Jewish items. After working there for a week they sent us home.

After a short time they forced us into the ghetto. Our family lived on Novoredker Street. The ghetto was far from us. Due to the time limitation, people did not manage to bring all necessary items.

The government inspector Roiter, accompanied the Zhetl Christian Petye Bielush and other town officials from house to house and sealed each one. Everything we did not manage to take from our homes was confiscated.

We brought our few possessions in a skiff, sliding it on the snow.

[Page 362]

The same day Roiter made another order. He commanded me to take my wife and child and return to "Boite Camp" in Novoredok. Knowing that the situation in Novoredok was worse than Zhetl I asked him if my wife and child could remain in the Zhetl ghetto.

I left with the other glaziers. We worked with the Novoredok glaziers to install windows, mirrors and other glass work.

By the beginning of August we felt the slaughter was nearing. We trembled with every passing hour. One group of Jews in Novoredok were living in barracks. The second group was in the buildings belonging to the court house which were transformed into workshops. Those in the labour camp felt they would be able to evade the oncoming danger. Since they were working and producing important articles they believed the Germans would allow them to live.

On the 16th of August 1942, we left to work as usual. The tailors, shoemakers and electricians worked in the workshops, the carpenters, builders and glaziers went to the barracks. The three glaziers from Zhetl, me, Dovid Berman and Mayshke Mankovitch stayed together as always.

While working, no one said a word. We were told on that day there would be a slaughter in Zhetl. Everyone, in his heart and thoughts was with the members of his family and the rest of the Jews in Zhetl. Only our hands were working as they trembled with our hearts for the fate of our dearest and beloved.

We could barely wait for the evening when we would return to the ghetto and hear some news. But they asked us to gather and line up in rows. We were 1000 men. The Estonian soldiers looked out the window and cynically laughed. They joked about our fate.

Suddenly the supervisor appeared. He was so drunk he could barely stand on his feet. Behind him stood his officer Lovoye. Moskialyov began to call out individuals from the rows. He took aside 300 men and 10 women including the three of us. The others immediately knew they were sentenced to death.

A horrifying scream suddenly emerged from the mass facing death.

People begged Moskialyov to save them, showing how they were such good workers.

I saw Motke Kravetsky, the shoemaker shout that he wanted them to let him live: how Dovidl Kaplan cried and was completely broken, however these cries fell on deaf ears. The division of Estonian soldiers quickly surrounded us and did not let anyone tear away from our row.

The screams of the women are impossible to describe. They tore their hair and wrestled with the German murderers. Among them I saw the following from Zhetl: Leyke Sovitsky and Khane Gertzovsky. They were pushed toward the ghetto. Those sentenced to death tore away and mixed together with the other women. The tremendous chaos ensued and the Germans shot a few women on the spot.

Passing us were trucks filled with drunk Estonian, Ukrainian and Latvian soldiers with rolled up sleeves singing their grating songs. According to the direction they were coming from we understood they were the executioners that carried out the slaughter in Zhetl. We all burst out crying for our parents, families and all the Jews of Zhetl.

We were confined in a horse stall where we remained for three days without bread or water. The Estonian soldiers who guarded us brought us their dirty water which they washed with and asked us for gold. If not, they would spill it in front of our eyes.

Saturday night. It was impossible to endure due to the lack of air and a terrible thirst. Suddenly, the door of the stall opened and there stood the regional commissar Traub, Roiter, and another drunk German. They "comforted" us saying we will remain alive because we were "useful Jews".

Under strict watch they took us to the workshops. Here we found those who remained from the Zhetl ghetto: Moishe Mendl Leyzerovitch, Zalmen Gertzovsky, Motke Haydukovsky, my uncle Borukh and others who shared with me the horrible news about the death of mother, my wife and my only son.

It was here we decided that we must escape and take revenge on the murderers of our loved ones.

[Page 363]

I Escaped from the Novogrudek Camp

by Moishe Mendl Leyzerovitch (New York)

Translated by Janie Respitz

On Thursday August 6th 1942 all the Jews still alive were confined to the movie house. We were there until Saturday when they loaded us into trucks and took us to Novogrudek. On the way, in Novalyenie they sorted us once again. Some were sent to Smolensk and the rest to Novogrudek. We arrived at the camp at Novogrudek at night. We threw ourselves onto the wet grass and began to feel the great pain and sorrow.

The ground was covered with wet dew but we did not feel the cold. Under the open sky, hungry and thirsty, we huddled together and waited in silence for morning.

We looked at the buildings of the camp which were to be our new "home". The camp was surrounded by barbed wire, but behind that, life continued as if nothing was going on.

Around 10:00 in the morning a few German officers arrived and told us to line up. They showed us our quarters in dark barracks. They placed the Zhetl Jews in a large stall which was called the "Zhetl Closet".

They took us to a granary which was filled with clothing and bedding. We were supposed to take pillows and blankets and prepare our beds. Entering the granary, we were shocked by what we saw. There were blood stains on the children's clothes and men's suits. The bedding was torn and dirty, collected from Jewish houses in Novogrudek. The Jews from Novogrudek recognized their things and a terrifying cry took over. Our wounds bled even more seeing the silent witnesses of our destruction.

A day later we began to feel the beatings of the German supervisor and the strict discipline. We began working in the workshops from 7 in the morning until 8 at night. When the supervisor was not standing over us we had an opportunity to think deeply and look for a way out, how to get out of this hell.

My son and I began to think about escaping to the forest. My son connected with a group from Zhetl which already worked out a plan how to sneak out of the camp. The group was composed of 10 men. Areleh Gertzovsky, the brothers Elye and Zelik Kovensky, Yehoshua Haydukovsky, Yoine Medvedsky, Efraim Yoselevitch, Hirshl Greyzhevsky (Zhaludok), Niyanie Shelbusky (Novogrudek), Yisroel Busel and my son Areleh.

One morning my son told me the group decided what day they will escape and they decided not to take me with them. They believed because of my age I would not have the energy to keep up.

"We will face many dangers on the way" my son said to me, "and who knows if you will be able to dodge them. I give you my word" he said with tears and his eyes and assured me, "as soon as we arrive at our destination and we meet the other Zhetl Jews in the forest I will come and take you out of here".

I did not pose any more questions and did not want to prevent him from escaping death. I had already resigned from life, let him at least be saved. He is still young and could take revenge on the murderers.

Leaving the camp is even difficult to dream about. We were strictly guarded by police and it was not easy to worm out of the wires. I had the idea that perhaps it would be possible for me to go to the second camp, the ghetto, where Jews would leave every morning to go to work in town. That is where the bakery was that baked bread for our camp.

Every day a Christian would go and bring back black bread which was heavy, not well baked and mixed with bran. He would always take four or five Jews with him to help load the bread. Thanks to the Zhetl Jew Elye Novoliensky (Feytche's) who was a member of the camp committee, the group got permission to go with the Christian to the ghetto for bread, taking them out of the camp.

I said goodbye to my son who left with the group for the ghetto. The guard there was weak. From time to time the police would guard the wooden fence.

[Page 364]

With a trembling heart I waited for the Christian with the wagon of bread. I could not wait to hear how the group experienced the trip of two kilometres to the ghetto. According to their plan, they were to leave the ghetto that same night and head to the forest. Of course the suspense increased knowing they were in the ghetto and planning to leave in the evening. I waited impatiently for morning when the Christian would go for bread again with another group of Jews who would return with the news about their departure from the ghetto. I hung around the gate like a poisoned mouse, waiting for the horse and wagon.

Finally my wished for moment arrived. The gate opened and as they entered they showed me with a wink that all was fine. Now my uneasiness grew. Now I had to wait for the following day to hear news about the fate of those who escaped.

Meanwhile life in the camp became more difficult and unbearable. The regime let it be known that each day had its terrible experiences.

One day they told all the men to line up. A murderous Germans chose 100 men and forced them to march toward the marketplace on Karalitcher Street. There they told us to lift a structure and bring it to the camp. It is impossible to describe this work. Dozens fell from the beatings the German and White Russian supervisors gave all of us. When we finally brought the structure we were given 6 hours to set it up.

After hours of feverish work we saw the German murderer Roiter. He looked at the structure and did not like it. As a punishment he chose 25 men and ordered them to be publicly flogged.

They placed us in a semi circle and forced us to watch how they flogged our own brothers. Among those beaten were: Zalmen (Areh's) Gertzovsky and Tankhum Epshteyn.

I will never forget the moment when they ordered a Jew to carry out the dirty job of flogging another Jew. Sadly, he had to do this and his hands shook from fear. The bloodthirsty German was not happy, so he took the stick and flogged the victims who had already fainted himself.

The next day we were all broken and despondent.

"What is going to happen? How long will this torture last?"

The boldest looked for an opening in the wires, where at the right moment he can crawl to the other side of the camp. Some tried in the darkness of night, others, in the few moments when the guards changed. Although this step meant risking your life, some Zhetl Jews succeeded in breaking away from the camp.

It is worthwhile to stress that the desire to escape was only among the Zhetl Jews. This can be explained by the fact that there was a high percentage of young people that hoped that in the Lipitchansker Pushtche they will be able to organize a partisan detachment.

The Jews from Novoredok and vicinity did not have this desire. They thought about escaping, but where to? They did not know. Some of them, desperate and disappointed, hoped the Germans would not slaughter everyone and they could make peace with their fate. They often expressed the fear that escaping in a group can worsen the situation of those who remained.

However, the amount of people escaping increased. Every night three or four people would crawl under the wire.

Four weeks passed and I still had not heard a word from my son. One morning, a German supervisor informed us that a group of Zhetl Jews will be going to Zhetl to bring machines. I was among the ten men chosen. The same day we travelled by truck and with our hearts beating fast went to our destroyed home. I hoped to learn about my son from some Zhetl Christians. If his group was captured they would have brought them to Zhetl and a Christian would not pass up the opportunity to tell a Jew sad news.

It is difficult to describe how we felt entering our town. Every brick and stone, every small street and lonely Jewish house cried out with sorrow and pain. The cries for help and wails of our slaughtered brothers echoed in the air. Our fists were clenched and our eyes filled with bitter tears.

This was a Tuesday when the market place was filled with farmers from the entire region. We got down from the truck and the large patches on our clothing immediately attracted everyone's attention.

They surrounded us and stared as if we were exotic animals. I looked for an opportunity to hear something about my son.

[Page 365]

Suddenly, a Zhetl Chritsian whispered in my ear that he knew my son and the rest of his group were in the forest. I could not believe it but he assured me he knew this from good sources. From great excitement I became confused and did not know what was happening to me.

Now I knew it would not be long before I left, if the murderer did not get me with his slaughter knife. To take such a dangerous step was dangerous, especially at my age. Therefore I decided to form a group and make all the preparations. The chairman of the Judenrat, Ostashinsky asked us not to take this step.

"Too many Zhetl Jews have escaped. This could bring about a slaughter" he said to me.

I assured him I didn't want everyone in the camp killed because of me.

It was the first night of Sukkot. The sky was filled with stars and a cold breeze blew into the "Zhetl Closet" through the slats. I lay on my bed plank above Yenkl Dzhentchelsky's plank and could not fall asleep. It was already 2:00 a.m. My nights were filled with suffering and tears. I would cry for hours unable to stop. I had just dozed off when I felt someone pull at my feet. I heard how they woke me:

"Moishe Mendl, don't be afraid, it's me, don't make any noise, it's me, Areleh!*#148; I couldn't believe my ears, I thought I was dreaming. But I heard him talk to me. I sat up and saw Arele Haydukovsky who escaped from the camp just a few weeks ago.

"Moishe Mendl" he said to me quietly, "I have a gun with me. First hide it, then we can talk".

Meanwhile, Yenkl Dzhentchelsky woke up and when he saw the gun tossed it into the chimney. I began to ask Areleh how he entered the camp and who he came with. He told me that he and another boy from Zhetl, Borukh Alpert walked for twenty four hours from the forest until they came close to the camp. They walked 80 kilometres avoiding main roads and villages. At dawn they lay down in a potato field and observed all movement in the camp. When night fell they crawled under the wire into the camp.

"Here is a letter from your son" he said.

In the light of the moon I held the long awaited letter from my son Areleh in my trembling hands. He asked for forgiveness for not writing for so long.

"I should have come myself to get you, but they would not allow me to leave the detachment. Together with others from Zhetl, I am taking revenge on the murderers. Come at the first opportunity". These were his words.

It did not even take an hour before everyone in the camp knew of our "guests" that came to take us to the forest. Everyone looked at us with envy, that we had the opportunity to be saved.

We began immediately to prepare all that was necessary. The patrol would not be at the wire at 11 o'clock at night. Taking advantage of the moment no one would notice, Itche Sovitsky (Motche's) went to the wires behind the toilets, cut them and reattached them so the opening would not be visible. The next morning we began to plan our escape.

The guards around the camp were uniformed Christians from the surrounding villages. The young Christian boys enjoyed spending time with Jewish girls. They would often bring the girls into the patrol building.

We received two litres of whisky in the camp and gave it to the girls to bring to the guards to distract them from guarding the camp.

We gathered not far from the wires. Two hours earlier my daughter in law, her father and a few others went out. Areleh Haydukovsky shoved the gun in his bosom, Itche opened the wire and I ran out first. Until today I don't know where I found the strength to run. I ran for 200 metres before I heard shooting behind me. I felt the bullets fly over me but I did not stop running. The others from the group caught up with me and with my last bit of strength barely made it to a small forest. We rushed to the trees and fell onto the grass. After we caught our breath we began to walk toward Lipitchansker Pushtche.

[Page 366]

My Sad Childhood

by Avrom Leybovitch (Haifa)

Translated by Janie Respitz

When Hitler's Germany attacked Soviet Russia I was barely ten years old. Three weeks had not passed before the Germans arrived in Zhetl and I was orphaned. The Germans murdered my father with the first 125 Jews.

Avrom Leybovitch

I tried to help my mother. I would sneak out of the ghetto through the barbed wire, buy some food and bring it home. I was chased more than once but always managed to escape.

The first slaughter in Zhetl took place in April 1942. We disembarked a few hundred metres from the graves in Kurpish forest. The Germans led us to the graves in groups of twenty. We heard the shooting and saw how people were falling into the graves on top of which they laid wide boards. If the Jews climbed up on them, they were shot. My twin sister went to her death with the last group of twenty.

Suddenly the director of the general staff arrived to sort the people. I was among those sorted and they took us to the ghetto.

After the first slaughter the ghetto was made smaller and we lived in new housing. We were now a bit smarter and built a cellar in a bakery. Under the large oven where they would bake bread were two chicken coops. We broke the wall between the two coops and we got air through the chimney. During the second slaughter in August 1942, 60 people hid there.

After sitting for two days, almost everyone left and ran away, but no one wanted to go with children. Five children and three adults remained in the cellar. On the fifth day we left at night.

After two weeks hiding at a Christian acquaintance, we left for Dvoretz where there were still Jews. I had terrible stomach pains and my mother had to carry me in her arms. After two weeks we noticed they were digging graves in the Dvoretz cemetery. That night, 50 of us escaped to the partisans.

We arrived in Lipishanks forest. My brother Leyzer was already a partisan in the Jewish detachment led by Hirshl Kaplinsky. In the summer we lived in a tent not far from Nakrishok and in the winter we made a mud hut. During the large raid the partisans came to us. I made them pieces of kindling and they let me shine their weapons. The Germans fired upon us. We would run away and often our clothes would freeze. We were covered in lice and mangy.

At the beginning of 1943 my uncle Peysakh Feyvuzhinsky died of typhus. My brother also was infected with this disease. When the Germans would shoot at us everyone ran away but I would stay with my sick brother and another sick woman, Etke. I would pick sour bilberries in the forest and feed them.

In the summer everyone moved to summer tents. No one wanted to take us into their new place because my mother was alone with two small children. My brother had left for Bielske and Nalibok forests and there was no one to support us. I would go to the gentiles and scrounge.

The German blockade began. The front was across from us. We hid in a well disguised cellar underground. Finally we learned we were free. We stayed in the forest for two more days as we did not have the strength to walk to Zhetl.

When we arrived home we wanted immediately to return to the forest. Everything around us was ruined and broken. I saw our house from a distance, near the river still standing. Soon we were surrounded by our gentile neighbours. I grabbed a guy who was making fun of us when we were being taken to the slaughter and I beat him up. I was wild, as if I had been born in the forest.

I started going to school but I gave my teachers a lot of trouble. I would smoke in class, fight with the non – Jewish boys and drink whisky. Motl Dunetz, who was my teacher, wanted me kicked out of school , but the director said that I would become the best student. He made a big mistake.

[Page 367]

Finally they kicked me out of school. I went to the "Children's House" but I did not like it there either and I returned home. I decided to learn a trade and went to the shoemaker worker's cooperative. Avrom Alpert was there. I fought with him and left that work. I went to another place to work as a shoemaker. There I fought with Veve Zaltzshteyn and left that place as well. I went to learn hat making. I did not like that either.

Then I decided to travel deep into Russia and learn a trade there in "F.Z.O". I wrote that I was older than my true age, packed and waited for my departure. The term was postponed. At his time Jews began to leave Zhetl and go to Poland. I decided to go with them.

On May 22, 1946 I arrived in Lodz. My mother and little sister arrived one month later. My older brother who was serving in the Red Army was killed when they captured Warsaw.

I was in Poland for a short time. We went to Germany. There I studied in an "ORT" school. On April 29th 1948 I arrived in Israel.

I immediately joined the Jewish military, despite the fact that I was young. I was, however, able to hold a gun. The war with the Arabs seemed to me like a children's game compared to the war with the Germans that I had endured.

This is the end of my story about my sad childhood in Zhetl and in the forest. This was written by Avrom Leybovitch, born in Zhetl December 29, 1931, attended the Yiddish School, barely finished three grades, now a factory worker in Israel.

The Path of my Suffering

by Kalmen Shalkovitch (United States)

Translated by Janie Respitz

On June 22nd 1941 when the German – Soviet war began, I ran to Russia, but unfortunately I only ran as far as Novogrudek and had to return as the murderers were already in Minsk. This was the beginning of fearful days of edicts and great suffering. On April 30th 1942 the murderers killed my unforgettable parents, sister, brother in law and their small children. I was the only one left from our family. On August 6th 1942 the second slaughter took place in Zhetl. I was among the tradesmen sent to Novogrudek. There, there were two camps: for unskilled labour and tradesmen.

Some of us from Zhetl yearned to go to the forest and take revenge on our murderers. One evening, a large group of Jews from Zhetl tore through the barbed wire, and under heavy fire left for the forest. A short time later they destroyed the camp of the unskilled workers.

We, in the tradesmen's camp endured terrible suffering from hunger, cold and beatings. We were guarded by police day and night. We were fenced in by two wire fences and it was impossible to escape.

A while later the Germans killed half of our camp. Only 235 Jews remained.

We organized an uprising. We had a few grenades in the camp, a few pistols, and a few rifles and decided to attack the guards and leave for the forest. Unfortunately the uprising did not happen. Meanwhile a second plan was presented: the tunnel.

Thanks to the initiative of Jews from Zhetl, they began to build the tunnel from our living quarters. We worked on the tunnel day and night for 10 weeks. The work was incredibly risky. The tunnel was 200 metres long. The work was extraordinary. After our escape Hitler's generals and engineers were astonished how such exhausted hungry Jews could build such an amazing tunnel.

We all went out of the tunnel but unfortunately only a few dozen survived. The murderers immediately sent an army of police and soldiers after us. Whoever was caught, was shot on the spot. I arrived in the forest in the region of Stalptz and we were there until July 1944 when we were liberated by the Soviets.

[Page 368]

The Extermination of Zhetl's Gypsies

by Yitzkhak Epshteyn (Kfar Neter)

Translated by Janie Respitz

The Gypsy is by nature a quiet kind person. He even likes to work but persecution made them second class citizens.

The Gypsy deceives you because he has no choice, but he will never raise an ax against you, even when he is hungry. Thou shalt not murder is in his blood. But protect yourself from the gentiles, the Belarusians, Lithuanians, Germans, they and only they can lift the ax and kill you in cold blood, even when they are satiated.

This is how my father of blessed memory would talk to me in the garden, "the tanneries" during work, when I observed the life of the Gypsies who were neighbours.

Once, on a hot summer day my father sat on a bench in the garden. Our neighbour, the Gypsy Igne, came to my father and began to talk like other neighbours. However, this time, in his Gypsy words, one could feel the fear and worry, which was foreign to their psychology as they never worried about the future. Igne the Gypsy talked and sighed.

"Not good, the gentile raised his head, who knows what tomorrow will bring. They are pushing us out of our livelihoods. Only one way remains, to go elsewhere, maybe to Argentina. And if we the old folks do not achieve this, let us at least send our children, let them prepare the soil for us". This is how the Gypsy Igne spoke and my father responded:

"Not good, not good, the anti –Semitism and the persecution are poisoning our lives".

The discussion between the Jew and the Gypsy who were far apart both spiritually and economically, began long before Hitler's rise to power, however both instinctively felt a storm was approaching, and they will both be victims.

And the terrible day arrived.

The gentile raised his ax with the blessing of his teacher, Hitler, may his name be blotted out.

The Gypsies of Zhetl were confined for three days with other Gypsies from the region. The Gestapo with their Belorussian collaborators took them to the mass grave on the Kurpesh road. Each Gypsy was guarded by three policemen.

And here was the large grave. Igne was crying, Stefan raised his fists in the air, Kuntse looked into the grave and said:

"My house is big, but this house is much bigger…"

Kuntse's daughters, Luba and Mirzada fell to the ground, grabbed the feet of the Belorussian police and begging and crying pleaded with them to let them live.

…and then a bang from a shot, a second, a third, a fourth…horrifying screams shook the air. Bodies began to squirm and dance their last dance on the ground as their souls were departing. Eyes took their final glances of the faces of the Belorussian police and Gestapo. Lips moved and mumbled their last curses.

Damn you murderers, you and your children and your children's children, until the last generation! Damn the ground you walk on. And damn your God, even though we are Christians like you. But if you killed us and threw us into these death pits, and you the murderers have remained alive, you should be cursed together with your God. One hundred Gypsies from Zhetl and the surrounding region were thrown into the mass graves.

Two years later, after the war, the murderers, the same Zhetl gentiles, placed a large wooden cross on their brother's communal grave. This is the irony of fate. The murderers placed a cross on the grave of their Christian "Brothers".

On both sides of the road that leads to Kurpish there are two hills. One hill is Zhetl's Jews and on the other side of the road, the communal grave of Zhetl's Gypsies.

[Page 369]

The Underground Movement in Ghetto

by Sh. Gerling

Translated by Janie Respitz

The news about the mass murder of the Jewish population in White Russia reached the Jews of Zhetl even though the Germans tried to cut us off from the outside world. Yet, through various ways, mainly through peasants, the sad news was smuggled in.

There were a few individuals who looked a little deeper and foresaw the extermination of Jewry. They thought about organizing an armed resistance, and not go like sheep to the slaughter, but defend themselves, and if they fall, they will die as heroes.

The initiator of this idea in Zhetl was the lawyer Alter Dvoretzky. He was the initiator and soul of the underground movement in Zhetl. We must add, you had to have enough courage and talent in order to do this clandestine work under these conditions. They did not only have to guard themselves against the Germans and the local Christian population but also the majority of the Jewish population who were not in agreement with this idea.

They were against any violent act and believed you did not have to call the bear from the forest because if God forbid this failed, they would annihilate the entire ghetto. Of course, with time we saw this way of thinking was not correct.

The Germans planned to exterminate all the Jews, the good and the bad, the quiet and the revolutionaries, the so–called "useful" and the "non–useful". The intentions of this politic was evaluated by the capable, bold, intelligent Alter Dvoretzky. His goal was to awaken and organize the youth for an active resistance.

Alter Dvoretzky as a high school student

Alter Dvoretzky was a well known communal activist before the war, and an active member in the Labour Zionist movement in Zhetl and in Vilna. He was known in Zhetl for his lectures on political and societal themes and also as a devoted leader in the Labour Zionist movement. The population of Zhetl trusted him and he also served as a representative in the ghetto.

It was not an easy task to be the leader of the Jews, the liaison with the Germans and remain morally on a high level. The Germans would usually use the Jewish representative in order to carry out their vile deeds. They tried to get the Jews themselves to help carry out their extermination operations. Alter Dvoretzky utilized his community position to organize the youth and instill in them the feeling of honour, revenge and struggle against the German beast.

When we talk about the emergence of the Jewish underground movement in Zhetl we must remember the Jewish boys and girls not originally from Zhetl whose fate brought them at that time to Zhetl. Some had run away from the German occupied regions in 1939. Others came to Zhetl from the surrounding region.

Alter Dvoretzky got these refugees involved in the underground movement. A group of boys active in this service were the first to leave for the forest because they had already been driven from their homes and were not so attached to Zhetl, they did not have family responsibilities and nor material possessions which were often obstacles to going to the forest.

Among the first Alter Dvoretzky organized were: 1) Khaim Shuster from Ayshishik; 2) Yekhezkel Koren, from Lida; 3) Meylekh Saker, from Deretchin; 4) Yosef Bitensky from Kazlayshtchin; 5) Eltchik Boyarsky, form Lida; 6) Mordkhai Gantcharovsky from the village Ruda– Yovarska.

In order to leave for the forest you needed to have a weapon and this was not easy to obtain. It was very dangerous and could result in collective punishment and they did not have minimal freedom of movement.

Alter Dvoretzky conquered all these obstacles. First he organized a Jewish ghetto militia where he mobilized all those who had to teach the vanguard of the eventual resistance in the Zhetl ghetto, and if that would not happen, they would join the Zhetl partisans.

[Page 370]

He succeeded in carrying out various secret tasks, most importantly, smuggling weapons into the ghetto.

The peasants from the surrounding villages were the main source for weapons. They kept a lot of weapons when they returned from the Soviet army. But how do you reach these sources when you are isolated from the surrounding world?

To achieve this goal, Alter Dvoretzky looked for connections to Christians who could be trusted and who were willing to help get weapons either for ideological reasons or financial gain.

To achieve this goal we connected with former Soviet officers who remained in the area working for the farmers after the army retreated. They were Olenin Yurek in Beliki, Stifnaov Petye in Melniki and a Jewish first Lieutenant whose name was Bezalel who was living as a Christian in the village Yavar.

The main liaison and supplier of weapons was a Jew from Zhetl, Moishe Pazdunsky who as soon as the Germans arrived in Zhetl, went to a village and hid among Christians.

Alter Dvorestzk would personally take the weapons from the cemetery and later, with a couple of guys from the militia, take them to an uninhabited house within the ghetto.

Some of the guns and hand grenades were stored in Yoyne Medvedsky's stall.

Alter Dvoretzky worked out a plan for an armed resistance to take place the moment they would begin the slaughter of the Jewish population. The militia was divided into threes. Each group of three was its own unit and had to act independently at the time of a German operation. All the groups of three were under the command of Alter Dvoretzky. The resistance plan anticipated that Leyzer Vinarsky, Berl Yankelevitch and Sholem Pialun would set fire to Kapinksy's saw mill on Novogrudek Street. Tchernikevitch's mill on Slonim Street was to be set on fire by Peysakh Finkelshteyn's threesome. Motke Razvosky's threesome had to appropriate the machine gun which was in the work bureau (in Peshe Langbart's house). A Jewish boy, Podliasky from Warsaw worked there and was supposed to help with this task.

Aron Leyzerovitch's threesome had to take control of the home of the leader of the Sonderkommando. (Special Unit).

To carry out the above mentioned acts of sabotage and create a panic they had to paralyze the German operation and make it possible for as many young people as possible to escape to the forest.

The plan was not realized and was postponed until another opportunity because the creation of the ghetto was not accompanied by such an operation.

The underground activity in the ghetto was not paralyzed. They continued mainly to collect weapons and carry out secret money transactions.

Alter Dvoretzky with the mediation of Sholem Pialun connected with a former Soviet military man by the name of Vanye, who promised to provide weapons.

The meeting point with Vanye was at Berl Fishkes's house. Alter's most trusted people would go there and connect with Vanye. These meetings were so well organized that Vanye did not see the faces of those who came to do business.

Vanye turned out to be a shameful provocateur which resulted in a tragic failure with Sholem Pialun and other tragic events which followed.

Sholem Pialun's Failure

On April 26th 1942 Vanye sent a message to come to Berl Fishke's house because he had a plan to get more weapons. Alter Dvoretzky sent a few guys, including Avrom Alpert, the commander of the ghetto militia.

Vanye suggested they meet in the Miraytchin forest and promised to bring the weapons there.

According to what Avrom Alpert reported, this time Vanye wanted to see their faces. Avrom refused but of course reported this to Alter Dvoretsky and among other things he told Alter that he thought Vanye wanted to provoke them.

Alter Dvoretzky already had some doubts and he advised the meeting not take place. However a few of the guys, especially Sholem Pialun thought he could be trusted and that there was nothing to be afraid of. Sholem Pialun decided to volunteer to go to the designated place and bring the weapons. They informed Vanye they will meet him at the designated place.

[Page 371]

Sholem Pialun of blessed memory

In the evening, when it was dark, Sholem Pialun snuck out of the ghetto through the wires and when he arrived at the designated spot Vanye was already there. Vanye took out a revolver and allowed him to inspect the goods.

They were immediately surrounded by German gendarmes. The revolver was broken, Pialun could not shoot and Vanye handed him over to the murderers.

The joy of the Germans and this shameful traitor was great. They brought Pialun to the Zhetl gendarmerie and there began the martyrdom of this man who exhibited great courage and heroism at this tragic moment.

They tortured him severely wanting him to divulge the names of the leaders of the organization. They tore and burned his skin but he held this sacred secret locked up in him. He succeeded in sending a note through a mole which the Jewish workers brought to the ghetto. The note was written with his blood:

Friends, stay calm, I will not betray you. If you can save yourselves, continue with work and take revenge for my blood.

The news of Sholem Pialun's arrest spread throughout the ghetto. Alter Dvoretzky, who Vanye knew, as well as others from the group who were in direct contact with him, decided they must immediately leave for the forest.

On April 28th, 1942, two days after this event, and still unsure if Sholem Pialun survived his torture, Alter Dvoretzky, Yoyne Medvetsky, Leyzer Vinarsky and Peysakh Finkelshteyn left to the forest with some weapons.

Alter Dvoretzky left firmly convinced that the idea of resistance inside and outside the ghetto was planted in the youth and his work would be fruitful. By the way, he also hoped that while in the forest he could maintain contact with the youth in the ghetto, bring them to the forest to organize a Jewish partisan force in the Lipitchansk forests.

In the Forest

After two days in the forest he sent Yoyne Medvedsky and Peysakh Finkelshteyn back to the ghetto to be the links between Alter and the group that remained in the Zhetl.

The short time between Alter's arrival in the forest and his tragic death has not been totally investigated, but it was a period of feverish activity in an attempt to save Jewish youth.

To achieve this goal Alter was in contact with Christian partisan groups who were already in the forests and worked out plans to receive as many weapons as possible in order to arm the Jewish youth that would come to the forest.

There were rumours that Alter Dvoretzky was trying to convince all the Christian groups to suddenly attack the ghetto during the planned first slaughter. He hoped that such a daring step would have positive results. Shooting at the edges of town and a few fires would cause a turmoil among the Germans and the Jews could use the opportunity to escape from the ghetto. He also foresaw the possibility of breaking into the gendarmerie and other German offices, killing them and taking their weapons.

The Christian groups did not understand Alter's plan and were unwilling to accept it. They did not want to risk their lives for Jews, who they hated as much as the Germans. To that end, the Christian groups were not ideologically prepared for such an operation. They ran from the Germans because as Soviet citizens they were being murdered and tortured but they did not have any concrete goals. Their main goal was to make sure they had enough food and booze and avoid the Germans.

The leaders of the Christian groups reacted to these plans with suspicion and jealousy. Alter Dvoretzky also wanted radio – telegraphic communication with the Soviet hinterland where the central partisan command was situated at the time.

The Christian partisans decided to get rid of Alter at any price. They sent a traitorous invitation to him and Moishe Pazdunsky to negotiate in Sirataychin.

The negotiations did not result in anything and Alter and Pazdunsky returned to their base. On the way, near the village Padyaverke they came upon an ambush of Christian partisans. The Christian partisans ordered them to lay down their weapons. They of course did not obey and a battle ensued killing Alter Dvoretzky and Moishe Pazdunsky, who heroically defended themselves and Jewish honour.

[Page 372]

This is how two Zhetl Jews, pioneers in the resistance movement and the Zhetl ghetto died. They were victims of wild anti– Semitic hatred which penetrated some of the Christian partisans, who, by murdering Jews, helped the Germans in their extermination – politics.

According to all the hypotheses this occurred on May 11ᵗʰ 1942. In order to wipe away any vestiges they burned the heads of those murdered. However, the surrounding peasants later told about what happened to the Jewish partisans who were killed in the forest after the second slaughter in the Zhetl ghetto.

The graves of both these heroes are in the forest not far from the village Padyaverke.

The Underground in the Zhetl Ghetto

by S. Gerling

Translated by Judy Montel

The originator of the underground in Zhetl, it's organizer and inspiration, was the lawyer Alter Dvoretzki. It took a lot of spirit and courage to manage the activities of an underground in such conditions. Its organizers required triple caution: from the Germans, from the local Christians and from most of the Jewish population, which opposed acts of violence that were likely to endanger the well-being of the ghetto.

The development of events proved that this mode of thinking was incorrect. The Germans planned the complete destruction of the Jews, the moderates and the extremists, without discrimination. Alter Dvoretzki foresaw these intentions.

He was a well-known community activist, active in the Poelei Zion [Workers of Zion] party in Zhetl and in Vilna, a wonderful speaker and well liked by the youth. In the Zhetl ghetto he was elected to the Judenrat. It was not easy to serve in this role and to preserve a level of morality. It was known that the Germans would carry out their despicable actions using the people of the Judenrat, but Alter Dvoretzki took advantage of his status in the Judenrat to organize the youth to rebellion and struggle.

In this activity he was aided by youth from among the refugees in the Zhetl ghetto. These young men who had left their homes and lost their families and all of their possessions showed greater willingness to participate in the activities of an underground.

In organizing the Jewish Police in the Zhetl ghetto, Alter Dvoretzki enlisted his supporters into its ranks. This fact made it easier for him to smuggle munitions to the Zhetl Ghetto. With their help and the help of former Soviet officers who had found shelter in nearby villages, Alter Dvoretzki acquired arms. He would receive it in the cemetery and with the help of the Jewish police he would store it in one of the abandoned houses.

Alter Dvoretzki also arranged a plan of action in case of destruction. For this purpose, he divided the underground into thirds and gave them special jobs. One third was to set fire to Leib Kaplinski's sawmill, the second, the flour mill of Tchernikovitz. The rest were assigned to take over the house of the chief of the German police and the automatic gun in the Labor Office.

The purpose of these actions was to create alarm among the Germans and thus allow the youth to escape to the forest. This plan was not executed, because the transfer of the Jews of Zhetl to the ghetto was not accompanied by acts of destruction.

At the same time Alter Dvoretzki made contact with a former Soviet officer, Vania. In April of 1942 Vania met with the people of the underground in Zhetl and offered them arms. This offer raised fears. Avraham Alpert, the chief of police in the ghetto, recommended not holding the meeting. Alter Dvoretzki also supported his opinion. However, some of the youth, headed by Shalom Pialun, believed that no danger could be expected from meeting with Vania.

Towards evening Shalom Pialun snuck out through the wires of the fence around the Zhetl ghetto and arrived at the meeting place. Vania was already waiting for him and offered him a revolver. At that moment they were surrounded by policemen. Shalom Pialun tried to shoot but the revolver failed.

The police tortured Shalom Pialun severely, but he didn't reveal the secrets of the underground. In a note that was smuggled to the ghetto that was written in his blood he declared:

"My friends, don't fear, I will not betray you, save your lives, continue with the underground and avenge my spilt blood!"

The people of the underground in Zhetl were not certain whether Shalom Pialun would be able to withstand the torture and they decided to escape to the forest. On April 28, 1942, Alter Dvoretzki and his assistants: Yona Medvetzki, Eliezer Vinarski and Pesach Finkelstein left the ghetto and went to the forest.

In the forest, Alter Dvoretzki made contact with Christian partisans. He suggested to them to attack Zhetl, in order to save the ghetto, but the Christian partisans did not agree with his intentions. Their main goal at the time was to find food and brandy and to avoid clashes with the Germans. In addition, they had no great love of Jews.

In order to foil the daring plans of Alter Dvoretzki, the Christian partisans invited him to a meeting. On his way back from the meeting, Alter Dvoretzki and his guard, Moshe Pozdonski ran into an ambush of partisans. In the battle that

> took place they both fell at the hands of malicious and evil people as they defended the honor of Israel. Their grave was dug in the forest by Podivorka. Honor to their memory!

[Page 373]

This is How We Lived in the Zhetl Ghetto

by Pessya Mayevsky (Petach Tikva)

Translated by David Goldman

By the usual human standards of measurement the Zhetl ghetto existed for only a short time.

However, who can measure the length of even a single night in the ghetto looking through dark windows with wide open eyes shaking whenever a single leaf falls?

If it's true that in the last moment before death a person reviews his entire life, then how many lives did we go through while we were confined to the ghetto?

Originally the Zhetl ghetto comprised the following streets: Myetchansky Street, from the house of Hershel Aharon Wolfovitch to that of Gershon Hydokovsky; Slonimer Street, from the house of Chaim the strap maker to that of Binyamin Levoranchik; the Shul Court, from the house of Yisrael Kagan's wall to Lisagora near Motta Turetsky's house and one side of the main road that bordered at the Shul Court.

After the first massacre the ghetto was made smaller, and all the Jews of Zhetl were squeezed into the oldest and narrowest houses. There weren't even any trees in the ghetto, and the branch covered pear tree at the old cemetery testimony to our decline. No one prays anymore in the study halls/synagogues across from the cemetery. Instead refugees and village Jews found refuge. - A mother with six children found quarters over on the bima/platform. Her husband was killed with the first 120, and he cuddled her six hatchlings in the cold unheated synagogue.

Old decaying posts still stand next to the bathhouse. Shlyapok, the well-known *Poalei Zion* activist was looking for a piece of wood and was attempting to limp with his crippled foot. He pulled out and struck the decaying post hoping his wife could use it to cook something. Zhetl housewives displayed skillfulness with their empty kitchens. They made latkes on wax and made "herring" from hard unsalted black bread.

People threw out furniture from the houses and replaced them with beds and cots. They kept their possession packed in the event that they would be sent away to a different ghetto and needed to take along all their property. Some people buried their prize possessions in the ground. These possessions wasted away for years – with young girls' dowries and equipment disintegrating.

Other people gave their things away to Christian acquaintances hoping they would still bring some potatoes and a couple of loaves of bread into the ghetto. Just as any conceivable source of livelihood was denied to them, any source of intellectual nourishment also disappeared. The ghetto had no cultural activity organization, no schools and no libraries. Every person sought some consolation and support in his time of despair. There were some people who turned their eyes heavenward and became religious, wore tefillin, prayed three times a day and poured their hearts out before the Almighty.

Many looked for good literature. The book by Franz Werfel, *The 40 Days of Musa Dag,* the story of the heroic uprising of a group of Armenians during the Turkish massacres was passed around from person to person. Young people had the courage to collect weapons in the ghetto and created the underground movement. They did not end up massacred and fled into the forest to fight as partisans.

Spiritual seances were organized in a few Zhetl homes. In a dark room young men and women would sit together around a small table and place their shaking hands on it to get "warm" as they used to say, while asking, "little table, little table, when will we find salvation? Little table, little table, when will the war end? When will Hitler break open his head?" Then the little table started to bang and offered its answer and consolation.

There were those who believed in dreams, which they felt were either good or, G-d forbid, bad signs. At night the window shades were drawn and it became dark. When the Sabbath arrived mothers blessed the candles in potato "candlestick," or on wooden slabs. The Germans had long before removed the brass or silver chandeliers, and the pots and pans that were heirlooms disappeared along with them. Mothers made their blessings on embarrassing Sabbath candles and tearfully looked at their children.

Apparently children were never as lovely as in the ghetto. How clever and mature were they? Their mothers prepared luminaletten instead of candies for them to help the children fall asleep when they had to hide in the cellars. The little ones already knew about the horrors of ghetto life. They knew that they must not cry when the Germans searched for Jews in hiding, and that they should not run out of the ghetto.

[Page 374]

After the first massacre the children played on the roof of the Talmud Torah school, pretending there was a massacre, with one acting as a German giving order: "right, left, right left…" and childishly asking him, "Mein Herr, let me stay alive. I am still so young." But the "German" was merciless and would not listen. "He" ordered them to be killed.

At the ghetto fence Hershel Kaplinsky's little daughter was playing with a kitten. Suddenly the cat tore away from her little hands and ran away into the Aryan side. The little girl was terrified: "Kitty-cat, kitty-cat, do you have a permit?" as she shouted after the cat in child talk. The older children would wear the clothes of their older siblings to look older in the hope that the Germans would let them live as needed workers. Their mothers cut off their long hair to look younger because the Germans only let younger woman workers remain alive during the massacres.

No one went crazy in the ghetto. Some people who were very sick and crippled became well simply because of the awful experiences and trauma. Mosheke Mirsky had been blind for many years and wore dark glasses, and his niece, Zalman Mirsky's young daughter led him by the hand. At the time of the first massacre Mosheke Mirsky and his twelve-person family were in the mines. He was handsome and slim, and the dark glasses hid his open, beautiful but blind eyes. However, it was here in the inhuman horror and suffering that he got his sight back. He was now able to see the sun again and bid it farewell forever. The dark veil fell away from his eyes so he could see the mass grave before his very eyes.

Mottel Leibovitch's wife, Zlatka, had been paralyzed for many years and was bedridden. When all the Jews were herded into the ghetto she had to leave her home on the court street. She was brought into the homeo of her brother, Betzalel Patzovsky, who was lying on his deathbed. The unusual event occurred here, and she began walking, taking some first shaky steps to fall into the home of her dying brother.

[Page 375]

Remember!

by Pesie Mayevsky

Translated by Janie Respitz

I am writing these lines for you, children. When the last of the witnesses of Hitler's destruction will be gone for eternity open the pages of this Zhetl Chronicle and read about the superhuman suffering we experienced. Remember, in the deepest abyss of our suffering chasm, there were heroes who amassed weapons in the ghetto, created an underground movement and died fighting in the forests as partisans. There were also other heroes. Those who could have been saved but chose death in order to make things easier for those dearest and nearest. Many were quiet heroes, but there are no witnesses to perpetuate their memories. I will rescue from oblivion those who have remained in my memory.

Remember the 2 girls from Zhetl, the sisters Khane and Rayzl Orlinsky who the Germans wanted to let live during the first slaughter when the rest of their family was sent to die. Rayzl and Khane did not want to be separated from their parents, sister and little brother and went with them to the graves.

Remember Hadaske Leybovitch, who stood with her father Mordkhai at the graves when the Germans were allowing her to live. She took her father by the arm and faced death with him.

Remember Yetke Lusky (Orenshteyn), who during the liquidation of the ghetto was with her sister in law Feygele Orenshteyn (Goldman) and her small children. Yetke was permitted to live but she called out:

"No Feygele, I will not leave you alone, I'm going with you". And they all went to the left, to their death.

Remember Simke Sokolovsky, who could have been saved with her husband Aron Gertzovsky at the cost of leaving their child. She did not separate herself from her child and was killed.

Remember Tzale Mashkovsky, who at the second slaughter was permitted to live, but his last surviving daughter, Yudis, was sent to the House of Study to die. Tzale stood up and asked:

"Where is life and where is death?" When he learned his daughter was sentenced to die he said:

"I am going with my daughter".

I can still see today how he walked to the House of Study, tall, thin and straight. When I arrived in Bielsky's detachment, I met Yudis Mashkosky at the guard post. She did not know her father was with her in the House of Study. She was actually rescued from the graves and gave me the last news of my mother with the children. They were hugging at the graves.

Remember Areleh Barishansky, the barely 15 year old boy. When they took the first 125 Jews, his father Avrom -Moishe Barishansky was among them. Areleh went to the Germans and asked them to take him instead of his father, because his father was weak. The Germans shoved Areleh into the truck and did not free his father. One Gestapo actually suggested they free Areleh since he was young, but another decided "he was too insolent". And so Areleh was killed with his father.

Remember Dr. Vinik who the Germans, during the second slaughter sent to the cinema with his sister Malke (the wife of Hilke Senderovsky).

Dr. Vinik was sent to the right, to live, and his sister, to the left, to die. The doctor however chose death. He went to the House of Study with his sister. The only road from there was to the open graves.

Honour their memory!

[Page 376]

Kaddish – The Mourner's Prayer

by Mordkhai Epshteyn (Santiago, Chile)

Translated by Janie Respitz

You had four names,
You, small Jewish town,
Diatlava, Zdzyentzial,
Zitl, Zhetl.

From thousands of Jews
You Jewish community existed.
Like your Pomerayke River,
The people were all quiet.

For more than four hundred years,
Jews lived there.
They, the poor Jews,
Wove a culture.

Who can forget your synagogue,
Your Yeshiva?
The wealthy families
Feeding the Yeshiva boys?!

Is it possible to forget your schools,
And political parties without differences.
Your Sabbaths, holidays
Which brought joy to poor houses?!

You, a town of religious teachers, revolutionaries,
Enlighteners and many pioneers.
Your grandchildren, with Jewish feeling,
Will fight for continuity, until they reach their final goal.

You dear Zhetl!
You are no longer on the Jewish map,
Only your echo reaches us,
With the murmur of your blood.

You were martyred with other Jewish communities,
You were destroyed,
Tortured, shot and slaughtered,
Buried alive!

Witnesses tell us that your children
Fought with courage and bravery,
We confirm the 25th day of Av
Was the day of their burial.

Today, on the anniversary of their death
Swear! Townsfolk from Zhetl,
To immortalize, with deeds,
The place of your town holds!

Swear! To follow in the path
Of every pure and holy person,
Because only then will their memory
Remain for generations to come.

[Page 377]

In the forests

The "Lenin" group of partisans, 1943

First row from left to right: Yerakhmiel Likhter, Shloimele Shifmanovitch, the next three are unknown
Second row: Russian partisans
Third row from left: Aron Rozovsky, Fiags, unknown, Borukh Vismansky, Dovid Noyekh Rozenfeld,
Russian partisan, Gertzovsky

[Page 378]

Translated by Judy Montel

Many of the Jews of Zhetl escaped the holocaust on the 6th of August, 1942 to the nearby town of Dvoretz. Others went to the woods. From these refugees, the troop of Zhetl partisans came together in the Lipichen [Lipichany] Forest.

News of the troop's organization spread incredibly fast. From the nearby forests, from the labor camps in Dvoretz and Novogrudok individuals and groups began making their way to join the Zhetl partisan troop. After a short period of time the troop numbered 120 partisans, aside from hundreds of older refugees, who gathered in family groups.

The Zhetl troop was made up of three companies. The first company was commanded by Hershl Kaplinsky, the second one by Yona Medvetzki and the third by Shalom Ogolnik. At the head of the troop was a staff composed of the company commanders and the partisans: Pinchas Grin and Shalom Gerling.

The first task of the troop was to gain arms. In various ways, the Zhetl partisans fulfilled their mission. In ambushes they set for enemy forces, from foresters and with cash money, a supply of arms was collected and saved. Then the troop began to clear the nearer area of enemy forces. Many of the local farmers, who were collaborating with the Germans and their helpers in the destruction of the Jews of Zhetl, felt the force of the Jewish partisan troop taking its revenge.

Over time, the Zhetl troop integrated into the general mission: to clear the garrisons of the enemy forces from the surrounding villages and to sabotage the means of transportation. In both missions they achieved results and respect.

The troop faced a difficult test during the general attack the Germans launched on the partisan forces in December of 1942. Forty thousand troops of Germans and their arms bearers were enlisted for this mission. This attack caused bewilderment in the ranks of the partisans. In daring battles many of them fell, including the commander of the Zhetl troop, the courageous partisan Hershl Kaplinsky.

The attack had barely ended and the survivors of the troop, broken and ill, began to regroup. And then they were overtaken by the fury of the Christian partisans, who even in resistance conditions, did not hide their hostility towards Jews. As a result of this state of things, the independent Jewish troop was broken up and attached to a troop of Christian partisans. However, even in this organization situation, the fighters of

Zhetl were notable in their courage and the fire of their vengeance.

As the German armies began retreating a second German attack began on the partisans in the Lipichen forests. This attack was seven times more difficult and there were many losses of Jewish partisans, but following these the liberation arrived. At the beginning of July 1944, the partisans advanced to the liberating Soviet armies and joined their struggle against the animal Hitler. Many of the survivors of the Jewish partisans, who had been liberated by the Soviets, fell as heroes in battle at the front.

This is the history of the Zhetl troop, that fought and avenged bravely and with courage for two years and wrote a glorious page in the chronicles of the Jews of Zhetl.

Eternal Glory to the Brave Fighters of Zhetl!

[Page 379]

The Participation of People from Zhetl in the Liptchanska Partisans[a]

Translated by Janie Respitz

Jews from Zhetl who were saved from the great slaughter in August 1942 escaped to Dvoretz and the forest. Those who escaped to the forest organized the core of a Jewish partisan detachment in Liptchanska forest. The organizers or the detachment were: Pinye Grin, Sholem Gerling, Motke Gontchorovsky, Mayrim Golansky, Nosn Funt, Hirshl Kaplinsky and Velvl Rozovsky.

The news about this newly created Zhetl partisan detachment spread quickly. A group of young people came from the Nolibok forests and joined the detachment. They included: Yosl Bitensky, Sholem Ogulnik, Binyomin Yarush, Khaim Slamke and Shaul Shakhnovitch.

From the remaining labour camps in Dvoretz and Novogrudek, Jews from Zhetl, in various ways, thanks to superhuman efforts, under a hail of bullets, escaped to join the Zhetl detachment. In a short time the Zhetl detachment consisted of 120 armed partisans.

The Zhetl detachment was divided in three platoons. The leader of the first was Hirshl Kaplinsky, the head of the second was Yoyne Medvedsky, and the head of the third was Sholem Ogulnik. The general staff of the detachment consisted of the three platoon commanders and the following: Pinye Grin and Sholem Gerling. Indirectly, the Zhetl detachment fell under the command of the Christian Orliansky detachment commanded by Kolya Vakhanin.

The first task of the detachment was to find weapons. They organized ambushes and took the weapons of the forest guards. A lot of weapons were purchased for money from the peasants who had kept them after the retreat of the Red Army.

In order to move freely, the detachment decided to clear the area of undesirable elements, who collaborated with the Germans and who participated in the spilling of Jewish blood.

We will provide here a few characteristic operations of the Zhetl detachment:

The Operation in Muleri

During the extermination operation in Zhetl, many Jews escaped to the neighbouring labour camp in Dvoretz. In the dark of night they would sneak out of the cellars and head toward Dvoretz. Those escaping would pass the village Muleri where two peasants waited for them: Madjey and Anton, who, with weapons in their hands, would stop the Jews, rob them and hand them over to the Zhetl gendarmerie. This is what they did to the rabbi and his wife. They robbed them, stripped them naked and brought them to the Zhetl gendarmerie.

On September 10th 1942 a group of partisans decided to take revenge on these two Christians. Yekhiel Yoselevitch, Sholem Ogulnk, Khaim Slamke, Yehoshua Shakhnovitch, Yisroel Busel, Aron Leyzerovitch, Pinye Grin, Avrom Magid, Aron Gertzovsky, Leyzer Savitzky and Zavl Mordkovsky went to the village Muleri. After they surrounded Madjey's house they realized he was at a neighbour's distilling whisky. The partisans went to the neighbour and found a group of 18 men. They commanded: "Hands up in the air" and took Madjey out. He admitted to his crime, asked for pity and asserted that Anton betrayed the rabbi. He betrayed other Jews. He received his judgement from the partisans on the head.

After the sentence was carried out against Anton. Simultaneously they explained to the village magistrate and the inhabitants of the village the reasons for the death sentence.

Our Victory in Mirayshchine

In October a squadron of Lithuanians occupied the Mirayshchine estate (5 kilometres from Zhetl). The same day a group of our partisans received an order to block the road Luditch – Mirayshchine. A red rocket served as a sign the fight was starting. The Lithuanians put up a strong resistance but in the end they ran away. The first to tear into the estate was the small, under aged Iziye Rabinovitch who called out: "Comrades, onward, they ran away". The enemy garrison was destroyed and this fortified the partisan's region.

[Page 380]

Our Successful Battle in Zhikovchizne

At the same time the Germans began an operation to occupy the region to disrupt the partisans. They sent a larger group of military to the estate in Zhikovchine (8 kilometres from Zhetl). Our detachment and the Russian detachment decided to annihilate the German garrison in Zhikovchine.

We broke into the estate at midnight. All the German reserves fell into our hands and the German garrison was smashed. From then on the Zhikovniche estate remained under our control and the Germans did not dare return.

Our Success in Nakrishok

A few days later the Germans came with reinforcements to Nakrishok. Four of our partisans were in that village, among whom was the heroic Dr. Markus. Two partisans succeeded in escaping and warned the detachment of an attack. Dr. Markus and his comrade began a rough fight with the Germans. The Christian partisan was immediately shot dead and Dr. Markus was seriously injured. Not wanting to fall into German hands he shot himself with his revolver. A little later auxiliary arrived and with great losses chased away Hitler's servants.

The death of Dr. Markus tore from our ranks a heroic, bold partisan.

Our strength continued to grow in Liptchanska, Dubrovchin and other forests. We ruled the large region from Shtchare until the Nieman and from Zhetl until Kazlaytchine where a German foot would not walk without large military forces.

Assisting Dubrovke

There were many villages in the region which cooperated with the partisans. The Germans decided to take revenge and eradicate these villages. One bright morning they crossed the Nieman with a few trucks into the village of Dubrovke (Nakrishk district). They surrounded the village, fired upon the entire population, burned the houses, and took the cattle, pigs and all their possessions.

When we learned about this our detachment left on horse and by foot to attack the criminals. When we arrived in the village we opened fire with artillery and machine guns and forced the Germans to run away. We also succeeded in saving a few cows which we distributed among the surviving peasants.

The Battle in Matzevitch

In Matzevitch, on the right side of the Nieman (Zhaludka district), the Germans consolidated in order to make our movement difficult on the other side of the Nieman where we would go to get our food and set up ambushes. At the end of November 1942 we brought our artillery to the shores of the Nieman and shot at the German garrison.

The first platoon of the Jewish company volunteered for this attack with the two spies, Sholem Ogulnik and Shaul Shakhnovitch. The Germans opened heavy fire on them. At first our fighters turned back, but then they returned with a larger group from the first platoon on the right side of the Nieman where they found footprints of Germans who tried to run away.

We Blow Up Bridges

At the same time we began a big operation in order to destroy enemy communication lines: blowing up bridges, disconnecting telephone connections, cutting telephone poles and making it difficult for the Germans to get food.

In this operation we burned the bridge over the Malchadke, which connects the highway Slonim – Zhetl – Novogrudek. The bridge near the village Halavli – Zatshefish, Orler Bridge over the Nieman which connects Lida and Slonim and many other bridges. We destroyed 10 kilometres of telephone poles and many railway tracks. At the same time we captured the supply of prepared agricultural produce for the Germans in Yanovishtshe estate, Rahatne estate and Miendzigure estate.

The heroic Dr. Atlas from the Jewish detachment also took part in this operation along with Jews from Deretchin and Zelv. Thanks to their initiative, the Bieltz Bridge over the Nieman which connects Lida and Slonim was also destroyed.

The bridge over the Nieman was strategically very important for the Germans. After the destruction they built a ferry which they only used at night. During the day, they hid it since they were afraid of the partisans.

However, it is hard to hide such a thing from the partisans. The Zhetl detachment took on the task to destroy the ferry. After we found it, we destroyed it.

[Page 381]

The flames of the burning ferry gave the Germans the opportunity to feel the punishing hand of the Jewish partisans. They did not dare to put another bridge or ferry at that spot.

We Provide Weapons

Thanks to the initiative of Dr. Atlas and Bulak's detachment an operation began to remove weapons from Shtare which the Soviets sunk during their retreat. Our tank drivers and machine operators succeed in removing three tanks from the water. The following people from Zhetl helped in the repairs: Yisakhar Berman, Yisroel Busel, Shloime Mnuskin, Sholem Reznitsky and others. Within a short time they were repaired and prepared for battle.

The Germans were convinced they had a lot of losses in people, technical and agricultural products, so they decided to paralyze the activities of the partisan groups. To achieve this they positioned, in the heart of the forest and in the partisan village Ruda– Yovarska, a garrison of 300 Ukrainians and Lithuanians with German leadership.

This is when a large consultation took place with all the following commanders: Kolya Vakhanin, Bulak, Dr. Atlas, Boris Bulat, Hirshl Kaplinsky, Pietke from the Lida detachment and Maximovitch from the Slonim region. They decided to annihilate the garrison.

The Battle in Ruda–Yovarska

In the second half of October 1942 each detachment took up its predetermined position. At dawn, the partisan Avrom Magid, with nine other men went out on reconnaissance and returned with a report on the situation.

At eight o'clock, when it was already light the first shot from our group announced the start of the battle. It quickly turned into a 20 minute fight. After, Bronevik came from Bulak's detachment with the Russian tank driver Fishchulin and called upon the Germans and Ukrainians to capitulate. The Germans opened fire on Bronevik who while shooting retreated and gave three shots which was a sign that the Germans were not giving up and we must attack. This is when the artillery began the attack on the German headquarters.

After the artillery was prepared, and under its cover, we tore into the garrison. The rest of the partisans were lying in ambush to ensure a safe way for auxiliaries to arrive. Our partisans opened heavy fire on the confused Germans.

A few Germans surrendered, a few were killed and some ran away from this chaos without weapons. Fifty Germans were killed, many were seriously or slightly injured and 10 were taken prisoner. Trophies: 60,000 bullets, 2 maxim guns, 12 rifles, 10 machine guns, 15 pieces of short weapons, lots of grenades and food, horses, wagons, saddles and the like. From our side, two were killed and 6 wounded. We immediately took our trophies and distributed them among the detachments.

By noon help arrived for the German garrison, a few tanks and trucks with Germans. They simply established the garrison had been liquidated and quickly returned to Slonim.

Reorganizing

The battle in Ruda – Yavarska became renowned in the entire region. Shortly after, the first liaisons came from Nolibok forest, 200 kilometres from Liptchanska forest. From the groups and detachments they created one brigade named for Lenin, which was also registered through radio– dispatch at the central White Russian partisan headquarters. The Russian captain Sinitzkin was chosen as commander of the brigade. The following were united: Bulak's, Fishchulin's, Dr. Atlas', Abramov's, Lebedyenka's groups creating one detachment called "Pobyeda".

Kolya Vakhanin's (from Orliansk) and Hirshl Kaplinsky's Zhetl detachment created one detachment which they called "Barba". Within the composition of this group were two Russian companies and one Jewish company with separate commanders of platoons: the commander of the first platoon, Hirshl Kaplinsky, commander of the second platoon, Pinye Grin, commander of the third platoon, Yekhiel Yoselevitch.

The Big Raid

According to the commands from the central partisan headquarters our detachment began an intensive military action. Feeling on our own shoulders how the strength of the partisans was growing and the surrounding garrisons could not cope and were regularly sounding an alert for help, the Germans decided for once and for all to destroy the partisans. To achieve this goal they withdrew 45,000 men from the front (4 divisions) and armed them with heavy artillery and tanks. On December 10, 1942 they began their first raid in the Lipitchanska forest where they succeeded in disorganizing the partisan camps.

[Page 382]

The Big Raid of December 1942

The first group of Germans came out of Deretchin to the shores of Shtchare, attempting to penetrate the village Big Valye (Zhetl district). Bulak's and Dr. Atlas' detachments were situated on the right bank of the Shtchare in order to block the road to the forest. The other detachments were lying in ambushes on the highways which lead to the forest along the Nieman.

On the night of Thursday, December 12th, Dr. Atlas and Bulak led a heavy battle against a large German force heroically defending the river banks and raising the mood of the Jewish group. Always fighting on the first line, to set an example for all the other partisans, Dr. Atlas took a bullet to his leg. They carried him off the battlefield and on the way, he died. His last words were:

"Friends! I'm dying. Continue fighting for our unjustified spilled blood. Bury me beside my mother's grave".

The three Jewish platoons of the "Barba" detachment lay in ambushes in different directions.

The second platoon left for the road which leads from Zhetl to the village Refitche with Pinye Grin as commander.

The third platoon led by Yekhiel Yoselevitch was lying on the Nakrishk road which led to the camp.

Hirshl Kaplinsky and the first platoon were lying on the highway from Ruda – Yavarska to Kzlaytchine. Waiting for the enemy from Kazlaytchine, the first platoon was attacked by the enemy from an unexpected direction. 20 metres from our position, the Germans opened heavy fire from automatic weapons and machine guns. Some of our platoon had to retreat.

The commander Hirshl Kaplinsky with 10 men among whom were: Sholem Ogulnik, Yisl Bitensky, Avrom Magid, Zelik Kovensky, Dovid Likhter, Aron Leyzerovitch, Dovid – Noyekh Rozenfeld and Mrs. Krisiye Gerling gave an order to open a hurricane of fire on the Germans and at any price recover the machine gun which fell to the enemy. Sholem Ogulnik, Zelik Kovensky and Dovid Likhter volunteered to fight. Protected by heavy fire by the remaining 7 comrades, they removed the Katyusha from the enemy's field.

Arom Leyzerovitch was wounded in his left leg in the battle. They lay him on the Katyusha and when they were one kilometre from the shore Hirshl Kaplinsky gave an order to retreat. They waited at the meeting point for Pinye Grin to bring food for the group.

Unable to wait for Grin, Hirshl Kaplinsky sent Avrom Magid and Dovid Noyekh Rozenfeld to find out why he did not arrive. When they realized Pinye Grin was not going to come they returned to the meeting point. Hirshl Kaplinsky and Yosl Bitensky were no longer there. The others explained they went to headquarters to find out more about the situation and to receive instructions on how to proceed.

On their way they fell upon a German ambush. Bitensky died immediately. Hirshl Kaplinsky was seriously injured, but he managed to drag himself to a Christian by the name of Yablonsky. He asked him to inform the partisans of his wounds and in the meantime he hid in the barn where he would eventually die.

We later learned the peasant brought Christian partisans, but instead of helping a fellow fighter they took his automatic weapon. Before he died he managed to ask:

"Comrades, what are you doing?" They ended his life with a bullet.

The Germans later burned down the barn with his dead body inside. We later learned this, in secret, from the peasant who was afraid to talk about this event, because of what the murderers told him.

The third platoon which was on the road to Nakrishk was divided into smaller groups. Two groups of five men with Leyzer Savitzky as leader left for the Ludzhitch road. Another group went to the Fatzavshchine road. Their assignment was to control the movement of the enemy and signal with machine gun shots.

The first group of five came across German tracks. Wanting to know the exact situation Leyzer Savitzky sent Motl Bushlin to a group of Christian women wearing white kerchiefs on their heads, which he believed were returning from Fatzavishchine. He barely walked a few metres when these white, innocent kerchiefs

[Page 383]

opened a hurricane of fire. They began to throw waves of "white kerchiefs" and our guys managed to get away.

The pressure of the military divisions forced the partisans to divide into smaller groups, and leave the forest.

After the Big Raid

After the majority of Christian partisans left the forest, unable to withstand the heavy attacks from the German forces, they headed for Nolibok forest. The Jewish partisans gathered in Ludzhitch forest to decide what to do next. We decided to divide into small groups to make it easier to get out of this predicament.

One of the groups which succeeded to break away from the German predicament met the commander of the "Barba" detachment, Kolya Vakhanin, who ordered us to remain in the forest until he could make contact with Zhetl and find out the exact situation in the forest. A few days later we connected with him and he informed us that a part of the military had retreated from the forest, and the rest were slowly leaving. That is when we received the order that all the small groups should gather in the forest.

The two weeks of encircling in the swamps, without food and without footwear did not destroy our mood. We gathered once again, organized and set out on operations.

One of our comrades, Shaul Savitzky, being totally barefoot during this operation took a pair of boots from a peasant. On the command of the brigadier commander he was sentenced to death, motivated by the fact that such acts are forbidden in partisan villages. All efforts by the Jewish partisans to annul the sentence did not help. Shaul Savitzky tried to run away but as he ran he was shot by Grishka Kozak. This was the 30th of December 1942. He was buried at the Ludzhitch lighthouse. With this sentence the Jewish partisans lost a good machine gunner and a brave partisan.

This was not the only expression of anti – Semitism. At the time of the raid for example, the Christian medic Fedya from the first company did not make contact with the wounded Jewish partisan Lipeh Glikman. They also treated Jewish women badly, leaving them in God's hands.

There were grave consequences after the raid, both moral and physical. The difficult living situation resulted in various contagious diseases such as typhus, scabies and abscesses. Around 10 Jewish victims fell during this siege, besides the many victims in the family camps.

At that time a diversion group arrived from the other side of the front led by captain Kovalyov who was a very liberal man. At a general meeting of the commanders he demanded order and equal treatment of every partisan. The commanders brought to his attention that many partisans were neglected and filthy. Kovalyov agreed to take all the partisans who were still standing, approximately 50 men, a large number of whom were Jews. Time showed that all those "standing" under Kovalyov's leadership, were good fighters.

A short time later, after we prepared our winter huts, we left for a new place, in Podiyaverke, not far from Refitche.

We were better organized in this new place and at the same time showed our strength. The military front was slowly retreating, only the local police remained who realized that even with military forces they did not succeed in destroying the partisan camp. The partisans once again felt free and began to renew their activity.

We Take Revenge on a German Servant

At this time there was the slaughter of the Dvoretz camp. These were the last days of December, 1942. Many Jews managed to escape but as they were running toward the forest they were killed by local Christians who handed them over to the Germans. This happened to 10 Jews who escaped the slaughter. They were hiding in a barn which belonged to the peasant Bortko which was on a farm near the village Nahornik (Zhetl district). The peasant took them into his barn, locked the door and calmed them saying in the evening they would be able to leave for the forest. But he quickly went to the gendarmerie and informed them about the 10 Jews. Of course, the Germans came immediately and shot them all.

We decided to take revenge on this shameful murderer and his son who had helped him. A group of 7 Jewish partisan, including the Russian commander from the third company, Lieutenant Sergei Flag, climbed onto sleighs and rode toward Bortko's farm, which we surrounded.

[Page 384]

Three partisans went inside. The commander Sergei began to question the peasant, keeping his hands on the end of his gun. The peasant responded, and being irritated, he banged the gun which went off tearing the palm of the commander's hand. The partisans made him a provisional bandage, took the peasant and his son out onto the road and shot them both like dogs. All of their finer possessions were confiscated from their house.

Nine Jewish Partisans Attack Zhetl

Due to severe cold and lots of snow our fight against the Germans was weakened. We had to be satisfied with cutting down telephone poles. Later, when the frost and snow subsided the eastern first company from Nolibok which had left us, returned.

Before the first company arrived from Nolibok, our detachment, thanks to the commander Kolya Vakhanin, made contact with the oldest Ukrainian garrison in Zhetl. A group of around 20 Ukrainians from Zhetl joined us, fully armed. We accepted them, but with little trust.

The officer of the group, Shakhneh, decided this was the time to attack the Zhetl garrison which was in panic mode. The plan of this Ukrainian did not arouse trust. This is when a group of Jewish partisans received consent from the detachment commander and decided to go to Zhetl, open fire and create a panic among the Germans allowing the Ukrainians from the Zhetl garrison to escape and free their lieutenant who was arrested by the Germans.

A group of 9 Jews led by Yekhiel Yoselevitch left for Zhetl. They divided into three groups who were supposed to open machine gun fire at the same time from three sides. The group at the Jewish cemetery was supposed to give the signal.

The signal was given at the decided time by an automatic weapon and the shooting began from all directions on the gendarmerie. We noticed the electricity in Zhetl was turned off. The Germans panicked and ran to their hiding places. After 10 – 15 minutes all the groups met at a designated place in Miraytchin forest. Here we met 6 Ukrainians wearing police greatcoats. When we spoke to them we learned they were among those arrested and sent to the Zhetl jail. They took advantage of the panic and ran toward the partisans. We took them to the detachment of Ukrainians who had previously escaped.

Our Detachment takes Revenge on Koske Lubetsky

After the eastern company arrived the commanders decided to take revenge for the deaths of the brave partisans: Avrom Rashkin from Zhetl, Yoyne Arzhekhovsky from Bielitze and for the wounded Lipe Glikman from Warsaw (he had been in Zhetl ghetto). We were ordered to take Koske Lubetsky alive as a prisoner. He was the leader of the attack in the village Ayvitch, 300 metres from Zhetl. We were to take food, horses and cows away from the whole village as punishment. It was decided to carry out this plan in broad daylight.

The entire detachment left for this operation. We arrived in the village during the day. We surrounded the house of Koske Lubetsky and ordered him to come out because we wanted to take him alive. However he stretched out on the floor and opened fire from his gun. Once again we ordered him to open his door but he shouted he would not let the "dirty Jews" in. This is when our commander joined the game. He threw down his gun and said he is not a Jew and suggested they come to an agreement.

The peasant did not allow him in either. At this time we tried to set his house on fire. The peasant was terrified, opened the door and said to the commander:

"If you are not a Jew, come in! At that moment a few of our partisans entered. We tied up the peasant and took him with us, 300 metres behind the village, beside a large cross, where we stopped and our commander explained to the peasant:

"You will receive your earned punishment for killing 2 partisans here at your holy cross".

A series of automatic bullets settled the account.

[Page 385]

The First Platoon of the Jewish Detachment Organizes and Ambush against the Germans from Ruda– Yavarska

At this time there were big changes in the leadership of our detachment. From both Jewish companies a third Jewish company was created from the Orliansky detachment. One of the changes was that officers must be properly trained. At the same time many Jewish partisans were divided among Christian companies in order to weaken their influence. Our detachment was now made up of two Christian companies. The commander of the third company was Lieutenant Fantchenko from the Zhetl Ukrainians.

In order to instill fear among the surrounding German garrisons, our leaders decided to carry out a few tasks. In May 1943 the Jewish company the first platoon was sent for an ambush ½ a kilometre from Ruda–Yavarska. They added 5 Christian partisans to the Jewish platoon with the Christian commander Orlov. The ambush was placed at a spot where the Germans would pass every mooring as they went to Kurfish to buy produce.

We arrived at the designated place at 3 o'clock in the morning. Everyone was very tired from the trip. According to the orders given by the commander we set up battle positions and sent two spies in both directions.

We lay there until 6 o'clock in the morning. That is when our communications man, Itche Savitzky informed us the Germans were approaching. We all lay there. As the first German wagons approached a Christian partisan unintentionally let off a shot. The Germans immediately jumped down from their wagons and took up good positions in the ditches on the road. The premature shot caused delayed fire from our ambush. Few Germans were killed.

One of the Germans did not manage to jump in the ditch and was lying in the middle of the road protected by little hills. This German was very close to our position and began to shoot.

Wanting to liquidate the German, Pinye Grin got up on one knee in order to get him from that position but at that moment he was hit in the forehead by a bullet and died. Yekhiel Yoselevtich, protected by a tree, tried to liquidate the German. At that moment, his wife Hadasa Yoselevitch, who was taking part in the ambush, grabbed him by the collar to make sure he lay down and she was wounded in her leg. Besides her, the well known machine gunner Khaim Slamke and the commander of the ambush were also wounded.

Under the cover of the left wing we removed the wounded and brought them to the forest. Retreating to the forest we were fired upon by the arriving German auxiliary form Rada – Yavarska. On the way Khaim Slamke died. His last words were:

"Comrades, I'm dying, take revenge on the German murderers and bury me in Mayak near the grave of Dr. Markus".

The remaining wounded were brought to the central partisan hospital under the direction of Dr. Miesnik. Thanks to his devoted help, the seriously wounded Sholem Gerling survived.

The Attack on the Zhaludke Garrison

A short time later we settled 3 kilometres from the village Demyanovtze.

The "Barba" detachment and the Lida detachment "Voroshilov" were given the task, with the help of the commander of the Polish police, to attack the Zhaludke garrison. This was the second half of May, 1943.

We were transported by boat over the Nieman and stopped ½ a kilometre from the Zhalduke estate where the leaders of the gendarme lived. We laid ambushes nearby in order to cut off the arrival of eventual help. A large group with automatics went to the estate.

The first guard placed there by the Pole let us in. As we approached the house the Germans detected us so we quickly broke into the first floor. With a hurricane of bullets we killed more than half of the Germans. The rest managed to run down in the house and defended themselves with hand grenades. We decide to set the estate on fire. We brought wood and kerosene with us and burned down the house together with the Germans. We took away many trophies: live inventory from the house: horses, cows and wagons of grain.

After, the ambushes tore into Zhaludek where they annihilated all the German accomplices who had escaped from the villages and were hiding in town. We took away all their possessions and left together with the Polish police commander.

[Page 386]

We brought three German policemen alive to the forest. We later shot them. We locked up the Polish police commander and a few policemen in the camp where we checked out the new partisans before their acceptance into the detachment. However, after a short time (the White Poles broke off relations with the partisans), they used the opportunity to escape.

Diversion Work

After this operation we began collecting shells. We removed the explosives and made mines. The following mechanics excelled in this work: Yisroel Busel from Zhetl and Borukh Levin frm Zholudek. They would prepare the mines themselves and then go and blow up trains. They belonged to a group of the most heroic, bold mine layers not just from among the Jews, but the Christians as well.

Later Borukh Levin moved to commander Garelik who had his base in the Nolibok forest. Eliyahu Kovensky left with him. They were among the best known mine layers and earned the title "Heroes of the Soviet Union".

All this attention (in accordance with the commands from the centre) were given to diversion work: exploding trains, burning bridges, cutting telephone poles etc…

The Attack on the Nakrishok Garisson

The Nakrishok garrison was one of the most important strategically for the enemy and the partisans.

We tried a few times to destroy it, but without success. The attack we are talking about was done by the "Barba" detachment in April 1943.

We arrived at dawn in the vicinity of the Nakrishok garrison. We laid ambushes on the road which goes from Zhetl to Nakrishok. The ambushes were made by a Jewish platoon led by the commander Pantchenko.

The Germans managed to escape and barricaded themselves feeling very secure. Just as we were beginning to cheer the Germans opened a hurricane of fire from all types of weapons. At the same time, help arrived from the Zhetl garrison and they began a violent battle with the Jewish ambush. The ambush brought about the death of a few Germans.

During a second attack on the Nakrishok garrison we brought in an armoured car we had confiscated. The following mechanics excelled in fixing the armoured car: Yisroel Busel, Yisakhar Berman, Shloime Mnuskin and Yosef Kravietz. Due to lack of gas and ammunition we had to remove the armoured car from our battle. When we returned to camp we mined the armoured car in fear it would fall into the hands of the enemy. This resulted in a horrible event. One of the partisans, not knowing the car was mined, opened the door to remove discs for the machine gun. The armoured car exploded and the following partisans who were on guard duty were blown to pieces: Yosef Yudelevitch and Isar Likhter.

– Semitism in the "Barba" Detachment

At that time anti–Semitism was growing in the "Barba" detachment. The leadership tried as much as they could to defame the Jewish partisans. Jews were being shot more and more for the smallest things. For example the two partisans, Avrom Magid and Avrom Blakhman were accused of making a bomb and because they took a few things they were sentenced to death. At the last minute before their sentence was carried out, Avrom Magid managed to escape the bullets. The second, Avrom Blakhman, dropped dead and was buried in the swamps. This was described to us exactly by Avrom Magid in a special story.

These anti – Semitic incidents embittered us. A group of 25 partisans including: Leyzer Savitzky, Nyanye Shelubsky, Aron Gertzovsky, Alter Kagan, Shloime Goldshteyn, Leyzer Leybovitch, Itche Mankovitch, Khaye Magid and others who could not bear the anti – Semitism, attempted to express their protest against these shameful deeds. One fine morning they left the forest with their weapons, leaving behind a letter for the political director Stefan Pietrovitch where they gave their reasons for leaving. They pointed out all the anti–Semitic events and demanded the management fight such shameful stances. The group then joined the newly created detachment in Nolibok, the Ordzhenikizde Kirov Brigade.

[Page 387]

The Ambush for the Partisan Tank

At the end of July 1943 we moved to a new camp not far from Ruda – Lipitchanska and Zatchepish. This is where we began our plan to destroy the garrison in Ruda – Yavarska, which was fortified with protective walls. To achieve this we began to refurbish the Russian tank we had confiscated. We mobilized mechanical specialists and had others worry about getting gasoline and batteries. Diversion work had been strengthening. The main task was to destroy the enemy's communication with the backcountry. Each company had its mine experts who were specialists in blowing up trains.

At the same time communication with the headquarters of the partisan movement was restricted. Airplanes began to arrive from Moscow which would throw down explosives, weapons, medication and literature. Partisans arrived who had been sent to the front lines or were parachuted down. They brought greetings from the back country and a lot of explosive materials for our partisans. The small group of trained mine specialists, together with the partisans from the local detachments (who knew the area well), created new detachments which specialized in diversion work.

In August 1943 an airplane from Moscow dropped a parachutist in our camp. She was a young member of the Komsomol who brought with her a lot of explosives and told us about life in the Soviet cities during the war years. The large quantity of explosives she brought was distributed among all the detachments. They mobilized all the partisans who were able to fight and each group was assigned a specific communication line they had to destroy.

The Jewish company also played an active role in this assignment. The destruction was supposed to take place throughout White Russia at the same time, two o'clock in the morning ("Railroad War"). The Jewish company carried out their assignment perfectly.

After the "Railroad War", the work to refurbish the tank increased. This was known in all the neighbouring garrisons.

The local Germans were overcome with fear. They informed the higher authorities that a partisan attack was being prepared aided by a heavy tank. The Germans began to prepare ambushes to destroy the tank. In the first few days of September 1943 larger military divisions came to the garrisons in Ruda –Yavarska, Zhetl, Deretchin and others. We began to prepare for the ambush.

On September 2nd 1943 Bulak's well known detachment carried out a large battle with the enemy at Shlizi – Podgrebilna. They killed 40 policemen and took a lot of trophies. A few White Russian police prisoners at their interrogation, admitted that the ambush was because of the tank, but only with local forces.

On September 4th 1943 the reconnaissance team advised the Germans were approaching the forest from the direction of Ruda–Lipitchanska. A day earlier, German spies were near the village Perekop near the Nieman. This is where the Jewish partisan Hirsh Robetz was killed along with a few Christian partisans.

On the morning of September 4th 1943 the border patrol of the partisans at Perekop was attacked. Two Jewish partisans were killed: Motl and Aron Kaminyetsky. These cousins were from Stutchin. The other two posted managed to break away from this predicament, ran to the detachment and informed them the Germans were approaching from all sides.

We sent the whole detachment out for ambushes. ¼ of a kilometre from Ruda–Lipitchanska we placed mines on a bridge the Germans were supposed to cross. The ambush was set up on the edge of the forest very close to the highway.

Finally, we waited for our guests. The first to arrive was a motorcycle with three passengers. The ambush opened fire and shot them immediately. A second truck filled with Germans drove up to the bridge, however the mine did not explode. After a short battle the partisans retreated to the forest. In this battle both Jewish machine gunners were excellent: Dovid Likhter and Yosl Gershovsky. They fittingly inserted a few discs in the truck and killed a few dozen Germans.

The second company lay in ambush at another place. Later we all gathered at the headquarters of the brigade and together with other groups arrived at the shore of Shtchare where we found a portion of Bulok's detachment and together under the protection of the tank we crossed the Shtchare.

[Page 388]

After crossing the Shtchare we removed the motor from the tank and mined it. Then we all ceded our places in order to arrive at the old camp of Bulok's detachment where we were going to rest for a day or two.

However, they did not let us rest. Already the next day we received an order to leave. During the day, for the second time we crossed the Shtchare near Tchorni – Bur (Zelv district) and headed toward Slonim where Zaytzev's detachment was situated.

We rested during the day and at night we marched 40 –50 kilometres. We moved through the regions of Slonim, Maytchet, Baranovitch, Polanka and later in the direction of Novogrudek. We had to cross a highway and some railway tracks but we did this safely.

When we arrived in the village Botchkevitch we sent out reconnaissance in the old region to learn what was going on. The first spies informed us the Germans had burned the village Moskoli and destroyed a few peasant farms which they suspected were protecting partisans. The main thing our spies told us was that there no longer were any Germans there. The brigade decided to return to the old region. After 11 days of marching through villages and forests we cut through the train line Yatzuki – Lida.

On the 15th of October 1943 we arrived again in Lipitchanska forest. We settled into the camp not far from Ruda– Lipitchanska, not far from the partisan airfield. Once again we began to organize, renewing the administration and erecting tents.

Revenge on Police Families

At that time, according to an order from Moscow, there was permission to take revenge on police families. Jewish partisans had been waiting for this moment for a long time as they had a large account to settle with them. We must realize that earlier such acts of revenge were forbidden and partisans were shot for taking these matters into their own hands.

In order for the police families not to know what was going on we decided to carry out all these acts of revenge in one night.

We were divided into groups of eight. Each group with its commander had to kill police families, burn their houses and confiscate their possessions. All the groups carried out their tasks perfectly.

However with one group there was a tragedy where the Jewish partisan Yehoshua Haydukovsky of blessed memory was killed by his own bullet. The commander of this exercise was Yitzkhak Kravetz from Zhetl.

When the partisans arrived in the village Khatki, 3 kilometres from Ruda – Yavarska, and went to the police family, they were all so nervous about taking revenge on the bloody murderers, they forgot about certain military precautions. After they lined up the Christians to be shot there was a lot of screaming. When the commander Kravetz shot, the lights went out in the house and in the darkness the Jewish partisan was shot.

These shameful German accomplices behaved differently. They fell to the feet of the Jewish partisans begging and kissing their feet to let them live. They lost the heroism they displayed in the Jewish ghettos during the slaughter of helpless unarmed Jews. The Jewish partisans felt no pity for them. They remembered very well the time when their dearest cried and the police laughed cynically and sent the unfortunate to the graves.

We Fight the White Poles

Meanwhile we began to prepare for winter. We sent out groups of partisans to prepare huts and on the 11th of November 1943 we moved to our winter camp, 3 kilometres from the village Golubi where we organized provisions, baking ovens, a bath etc…

At that time, White Polish bandits were gaining strength on the other side of the Nieman. They would lie in wait for the partisans as they returned from diversion work and ambush them. In many respects they were as dangerous as the German garrisons, because we never knew where they were and who they were. During the day they were regular peasants, and at night they would carry out acts of revenge on Christians who provided protection for partisans and Jews. Many partisans and Jews were murdered by these White Poles.

During one such attack the partisan from the "Barba" detachment, Dovid Hirsh Mekel, the leader of the third company, was killed. This occurred during a farm operation in the village Zatshefitch near the Nieman. While everyone was resting the guard on duty noticed they were surrounding the village. He immediately gave a signal with one shot and everyone except Dovid Mekel, with weapons in hand tore through.

[Page 389]

The White Poles greatly restricted the movement of our partisans. The commanders of the "Barba" detachment with captain Davidov decided to destroy the Polish village where the headquarters of the White Poles was situated.

In the second half of November 1943 the entire detachment together with Davidov's group, armed with highly calibrated machine guns which were left on the left side of the Nieman, arrived in the Polish village Voltchki. Awe were met by fire of the White Poles who had been hiding. In accordance to an order we received from our commander we lay prepared for battle and a larger group went in the direction the bullets were coming from. We opened heavy fire during which time 10 White Poles were killed. We also did not spare the village.

The Jewish Company is Liquidated

At the beginning of 1944 a new detachment was created under the name of "Krasna – Gvardaysky", as a part of the Lenin Brigade. All detachments had to send some partisans to the new detachment. The anti –Semitic commanders of "Barba" once again used the opportunity to get rid of Jewish partisans and gladly liquidated the third Jewish company. In their selection they did not even spare the old partisans who had participated in many praiseworthy actions in the detachment. Among those sent out were the former platoon commanders Yekhiel Yoselevitch, Sholem Gerling, Yoyne Medvedsky, Motl Gontdherovsky, Aron Leyzerovitch and others.

Comrade Shulman from the Vilna ghetto (a communist before the war) protested energetically against the way things were handled and showed how this was blatant anti –Semitism. They arrested him, but he was later released. The protests did not help and all the Jews were sent to the "Krasna – Gvardaysky" detachment.

It turned out to be a good thing for the Jewish partisans. The commander of "Krasna – Gvardaysky", Lieutenant Kolashayni did not discriminate according to race. He evaluated each partisan according to his fighting ability and accomplishments. This encouraged the Jewish partisans to fight, and many who were expelled and not allowed to fight in "Barba", excelled and even received government recognition. For example: at the ambush set up not far from the German garrison in Mielkovitch.

The Ambush against the Mielkovitch Garrison

We received information that the police from the Mielkovitch garrison were setting up an ambush. Our partisans also set up an ambush ½ a kilometre from the German garrison.

Being close to their garrison the Germans were feeling secure. The partisan ambush was very close and opened a hurricane of fire where 15 Germans were killed. Then the detachment commander ordered us to chase the Germans who were running away. The first one to attack was the young partisan Khaim Shapransky from Zholudek. Shooting the escaping Germans he encouraged the other partisans by example. They totally destroyed this German group capturing many trophies, and taking 6 policemen alive. The other Jewish partisans played an active role in the ambush and the commander expressed his gratitude.

A New Enemy: The Vlasovtzes

The German military began changing their fighting methods with the partisans. The experience taught them they cannot destroy partisan camps with more forces. So they decided to create, from the Russian masses, folk– traitors, the famous Vlasov – Army. The Germans began to occupy the villages with these Vlasovtes and created garrisons near the partisan zones. This was a big blow to the partisan movement since it made diversion work more difficult as well as farm operations.

The "Barba" detachment carried out an attack on the Vlasov garrison in Zatcheptich but the Vlassovtzes already managed to fortify and the partisans had to retreat with small losses.

The large victories of the Red Army forced the Vlasovtzes to think about their future. A few of them began to make contact with the partisans, providing us with information. In the garrison on Ruda–Yavarska there were a few policemen who connected with the commander of the Lenin detachment and helped us destroy the garrison.

At the end of April 1944 the entire Lenin detachment left on assignment. The guard of the enemy was one of the police connected to us and he let us in. The Lenin detachment began immediately to fight. They threw grenades into one bunker and set fire to another. Two bunkers with 72 men surrendered.

[Page 390]

The headquarter's Russian official who was supposed to occupy the German headquarters began the operation a bit late. During this time a German went out on the street to warn the other Germans who managed to run into the bunkers to open fire on us with machine guns. The commanders decided to take the bunkers at any price. Our partisans crawled to the opening of the bunker and threw in grenades. This was a life threatening job.

During this operation those who excelled were Yerakhmiel Likhter, the machine gunner from Zhetl, a young partisan from Deretchin and the brave young Shloimele Shifmanovitch form Zholudek. He crawled right up to the bunker, but was seriously injured and later died in hospital. In this assignment three Jews were killed and 5 injured. The attack was of great significance. It weakened the spirit of the German collaborators and things became calmer on the road to the forest.

The Last Ambush

In June, 1944 the enemy began its last big ambush against us. A few Vlasovtses searched for partisans where no human foot had walked. Our situation was hopeless.

The amount of wounded increased, we lacked ammunition and we hardly had any food. We began to eat dead horses as we could not undertake any farm operations.

We began to look for a way to break away from this tight ring and make our way to the Dubrovchin forests, but no success. Every attempt to break away resulted in many casualties. Our headquarters now commanded two detachments: "Krasna – Gvardaysky" and "Barba " to break through the blocked roads back to the forest in order to evade attention of the enemy from the Dubrovchin forests. A few attempts ended without results.

Finally we received an order to break away at all cost. At night we approached the highway. Receiving a sign from a reconnaissance we all began to run forward. We were immediately fired upon by all types of weapons, but thanks to the plan of the spies (one was a Jew Nosn Funt), to shoot in the opposite direction, we diverted the enemy's attention which allowed the detachments to reach the other side of the highway.

At four o'clock in the morning we crossed the Podyavark small river and approached the old, former camp near Karshuk. 25 partisans died that day including the girls from Zhetl: Henie Gertzovsky, Miriam Levenbuk and Maliye Kravetz.

Finally Liberated!

At this time Marshal Rakosovsky began a lightning speed attack on the White Russian front. This saved our situation after a long, difficult six week ambush. Individuals from the Vlasovstes began to retreat and we returned to our old camps.

We cannot describe the joy we felt at our meeting with the first swallows of the Red Army. Under a hail of bullets we kissed them. We were finally liberated!

800 Jews From Zhetl Escaped to the Forest

"Dvoretzky's seed in the Zhetl ghetto did not fall on empty soil. Right after the second slaughter (August 6th 1942) over 800 Jews succeeded in leaving under the cover of night to the Lipitchanska forest.

It is clear, without the activity of Alter Dvoretzky and the Zhetl partisan organization so many Jews from Zhetl would not have been saved. The resistance organization prepared the Jews of Zhetl psychologically to join the partisans".

Excerpt from "Jewish Participation in the Partisan Movement in Soviet Russia" by Moishe Kaganovitch, p. 83.

Original footnote:

a.   This work was written by: Dr. Avrom Alpert, Lipe Glikman, Avrom Magid and Yekhiel Yoselivitch and was corrected by a group of partisans in Israel.

[Page 391]

Revenge for the Blood of our People!

by Eliyahu Kovensky, Petach – Tikva

Translated by Janie Respitz

April 30ᵗʰ 1942 people were being sent to the left and right at the Zhetl cemetery. Everyone sensed the scent of death. We just did not know from which side it came: right or left.

Eliyahu Kovensky

The Germans took 1,800 men one kilometre from town. Here, the unfortunate Jews found prepared, large graves which the inhabitants of the village Kurfish dug during the night.

The Jews of Zhetl were shot in groups or twenty but there was no space for the last 60 men in the graves, so the Germans brought them back to Zhetl.

When they returned they told about the terrifying execution and how before dying Jews tore their hair out of their heads and Germans knocked out their teeth.

The air around the graves trembled with wailing and spasms. They told how one of the rabbis was standing and praying, reciting psalms and asking for his congregation. But seeing how Jews were being shot and thrown like slaughtered calves into the graves, with great rage he raised his hands to the sky and blasphemed the Almighty. With his last bit of strength he shouted:

"This is Justice? This is our God of mercy and compassion? How did our congregation sin?"
Then he tore the hair from his head and beard and tore the shirt off his skin. The machine gun interrupted his bloodied screams. With clenched fists toward heaven his life ended and he fell into the grave.

About my uncle, Eliezer Kovensky, a happy clever man, among the most respected in town and my other uncle, Shmuel Kovensky, we were told, before they died, they drank a bottle of whisky which they took with them, said the confessional prayer lay down together and were shot together.

This terrifying execution lasted two hours. Those who remained returned to their houses without husbands, wives or children.

Barely a few months passed and the ghetto was surrounded again and once again the Jews had to go to the old cemetery.

My family and 50 other Jews hid in a bunker. However this time the Germans found us and led us to the marketplace.

I Lost my Wife and Child

At the marketplace we found 500 men, barefoot with their faces to the ground. They commanded us as well to remove our shoes and lie face down.

We lay like this for half an hour. Then they commanded us to stand up and walk to the graves.

The men parted from their wives and children with heart wrenching sobs. Some actually went mad. On the way to the graves we saw bloodied bodies lying in the gutters. The S.S. commander was standing on the edge of the road which led to the slaughter. I was among the few Jews they removed from the group. When they saw me they said:

"A saddle maker! Come here!"
My wife and child hung on to me tightly and did not let me go. Suddenly a shot filled the air. They shot my wife…she fell like a sheaf at my feet…My son cried and begged:
"Don't shoot me, I'm only eight and a half years old!"
A bullet ripped through his clothing as well. The hangmen threw me and 30 other men into a stall. Everyone else was shot at the graves. Peasants told us the soil moved for three days and blood did not cease to flow.

There were no Jews left alive in town. The hangmen sent me and 212 other Jews to Novogrudek where there were 4,000 Jews divided into work groups.

After one week I realized the camp was in despair. They were not feeding us and beatings were not spared. In the middle of the night 14 of us crawled through the barbed wire and escaped to the Zhetl forests.

We Arm Ourselves

When we escaped we only had one automatic pistol. During the day we lay in the forest and at night we left to look for bread and something with the bread.

We knew the area well and we knew which peasants had hidden Soviet weapons.

[Page 392]

In the middle of the night we would wake a peasant from his sleep and force him to give us his weapons. Whoever refused had to take a shovel and dig his own grave…

It is important to note that we received food easily but we had to fight for the weapons until children would beg their fathers with tears:

"Give them your gun, if not, they will shoot you!"
This is how we all were armed. After 14 days in the forest we sent 5 men to make contact with the partisans.

At night we visited one of my peasant acquaintances and asked if partisans would come to the village. He showed me the way to the partisans.

We Join a Partisan Group

We followed the dirt roads deep into the forest. After trudging around for a few hours we found an armed Jewish patrol. When he saw us he aimed his gun at me.

"Stop, Jew!" I cried out. "After I had seen so many slaughtered Jews, you are the first ready to shoot me with a bullet. I ask you, tell me, how can we reach your commander?"
I told him who I was and that's when he gave me the password for the commander.

Deep in the forest, sitting around a fire, there were a few hundred armed people, Jewish partisans, soldiers from the Red Army, and among them a commander, a Russian lieutenant. I introduced myself, told him where I was from and informed him I had 14 men with me, all armed.

"I permit them to come here" was his response.
Two from our group returned to bring the remaining 9 friends.

Together with Dr. Atlas

Next to us a group of Jews from Deretchin were operating under the leadership of Dr. Atlas. They did not want to join us. They were well organized and carried out their battles independently.

One day Dr. Atlas came to us with another 5 men and suggested we blow up a bridge on the Nieman. Our commander agreed and sent me and another Zhetl Jew, Yitzkhak Medvedsky to help Dr. Atlas.

We pulled out shells from the river and dried them. Then we got hemp from the peasants and 6 bottles of turpentine and in the middle of the night left for the Bielitz Bridge.

As we approached the bridge we threw the German patrol into the water so he could get to know the roaches in the Nieman, and as we said the blessing for fire we set fire to the bridge.

Dr. Atlas was very pleased with our work. It did not take long for him to approach my commander to allow me to command one of his groups. My commander agreed and I took on my new post.

Coincidently, there were many Jews in the group from Kazlaytchine who were burning with the desire to seek revenge for their brother's blood.

We decided to run an operation. We gathered all the commanders in the forest and decided we had enough strength to attack the town.

At dawn, before the sun rose, we attacked Kazlaytchine and fought for 4 solid hours. The Germans put up a strong resistance. But we tore into the town, set fires on all sides and shot 30 German policemen.

The S.S chief that ran the slaughter in Zhetl was tied up and brought alive to the forest. We hung him from a tall tree, just like Haman. This is how the Jews from Kazlaytchine took revenge for their old rabbi who the murderers tied to a wagon, dragged around and buried alive.

The attack was led by the Russian lieutenant Bulat, who was missing a hand.

Meanwhile we received new greetings from the partisans. A large force was put together to build mud huts, and take care of getting cows, horses and a lot of weapons. A short time later we attacked Deretchin, surrounded it from all sides, set the houses on fire, shot and took many Germans prisoner.

The Death of Dr. Atlas

At the end of 1942 the Germans sent a giant force against us which surrounded the forest. We withstood bloody battles for three days. Many of us fell heroically, among them Dr. Atlas, the famous Jewish fighter and hero who did not know fear or danger.

[Page 393]

He died in my arms. His last words before he died were:

"Hang in there brothers, take revenge for the spilled blood of our misfortunate people!"

We buried him on a hill in the forest. Giving him the last honours of a partisan we fenced his grave with shell cases.

Let the surviving partisans know and remember that here rest the bones of their commander, and perhaps one day he will have a Jewish burial?

Shoot, If I Deserve it

Realizing we could not oppose the German forces we took down our encirclement and left for the Slonim forests. Potatoes and peas were all we had to eat during the days of the siege. People were starving. The Russian commander sent people to bring food from the surrounding villages however they gave the Jews smaller portions. I sent people from my group to find food. On the way the Germans were shooting so they returned empty handed. Due to anger and bitterness I took my group back to the previous forest.

The next morning the angry head commander asked:

"Who gave you permission to leave the brigade?"

"My people are starving, therefore we can no longer be with you".

Noticing two partisan girls without weapons he asked again:
"Where are your guns?"
The girls explained when they ran from the siege they threw down their weapons. With lightning speed the commander took his automatic off his shoulder and shot the girls. Then he aimed at me.
"Shoot," I said,: "if I deserve it". Putting down his automatic he said:

"You're right, you don't deserve it. Remember this time I forgive you.

We returned to the brigade.

A short time later a group of parachutists came from Moscow led by Captain Kovolov. This was a group of officers and soldiers that took over the running of the partisan movement. They demanded our commander give 4 people who were very skilled and knew the region's highways and railroads well.

My commander chose me as a guide. I joined the commando group where I carried out various operations. The Red Army crossed the White Russian border and within a few weeks we stopped the German trains from Minsk to Baranovitch. Under our leadership a partisan army of 70 thousand was assembled in the Nolibok forests.

This army ruled the entire region. They received weapons and explosives by airplane and sent the wounded to hospitals in Moscow.

I am Wounded

One beautiful bright day in 1943 a German division supported by tanks and aviation, seized the forest. We fought them for 15 days.

Being familiar with the area I excelled in many battles. As recognition I received a first rank partisan medal, the "Red Star" medal and the "Fatherland War" medal, second rank.

In 1944 they honoured me with the medal "The Order of Lenin".

On January 19th 1944 in the battle behind Stolptzi, I was assigned to a tank group whose task was to blow up armoured German bunkers made of iron and cement. After a four hour battle we partially succeeded to finish off the bunkers. The Germans consolidated and responded with heavy fire. Then we received an order:

"Enter the bunkers immediately with grenades!"
I succeeded in throwing in two grenades through a little window of the bunker where there were 18 Germans. They were all blown up.

Retreating quickly from the bunker, a bundle of bullets from another bunker cut off all the fingers from my right hand. In these fiery moments I jumped on my horse, I was a rider, and swam across the Nieman with a boot full of blood.

I arrived at a partisan aid station on the other side of the Nieman. There they bandaged my hand and sent me to another medic station.

The doctors explained they had to amputate my fingers but they did not have any narcotics. I practically broke my teeth from such pain. Then my friend came to me, the partisan Borukh Levin, shoved his fist in my mouth and said:

"Bite my hand!" Then he turned to the doctor and said: "Cut!"
[Page 394]

When things lightened up I was already at the airfield in the forest and flew by plane to Moscow.

I lay in various hospitals for 8 months. My hand was operated on a few times. As a hero of the Soviet Union I was well looked after with great devotion.

In Zhetl and in Volkovisk

When I recovered I returned to our old towns which had been liberated. However I did not find anyone, only graves. I returned with the few surviving partisans to Zhetl. We erected a monument in memory of our brothers and sisters who were annihilated and whose wails and screams, until today, still fill the air over their graves.

From Zhetl I went to the city where my best years flowed, where I got married and had the honour of becoming a father of dear children, in Volkovisk.

There I didn't even find graves. The honest and dear Jews of Volkovisk were burned, transformed into ashes in the ovens of Treblinka and Auschwitz. I wanted to fall to the ground and cry without stopping!

An acquaintance peasant, Boris Sharyako, met me and invited me to come in and sit down. Then he asked if I wanted to eat. I replied:

"I'm full. In the name of our old friendship, give me a bit of ash".
I covered my head with the ashes, went out on the street and sat on a stone. I sat "Shiva" (Jewish mourning period) for my wife and children and all the other dear, beloved Volkovisk Jews who will never return. The Christians looked at me with compassion.
"So" I said to them, "Now it's good for you. The Jews are no longer here, now you are happy!"
They responded that they were innocent and they did not get involved.

There, where the sickle and hammer rules, it is still possible for a Jew to hold a small position, his life is not abandoned. However, after all the problems I said goodbye to everyone, took my backpack on my shoulders and went on my way. I passed through destroyed cities and towns, all without any Jews!

My feet took me toward the east, to the Alps, on my way to the Land of Israel.

[Page 395]

We Fight!

by Azriel Shilovitsky, New York

(became Irving Shiloff upon immigration to US)

Translated by David Goldman

Around the 8th of August, 1942, 20 men appeared in the forest, the first refugees from the Zhetl slaughter. There was no food and every rustle made us nervous. It seemed, if we were found, our lives would end.

However, destitution teaches. We began slowly to go out at night and bring food from the nearby villages and began to adapt to our new life. The small advantage of the forest Jews, was they immediately understood they had to organize and collect weapons in order to provide food and in order not to remain unprotected.

The Organization of the Jewish Military Detachment

On August 20th 1942 the first group was organized in the forest near Ludzhitch. Hirshl Kaplinksy was chosen as commander. After dividing into groups of ten the commanders were: Yisroel Shilovitsky, Pinye Green and Sholem Ogulnik. We began immediately to organize these "tens" with military training and provided weapons.

Meanwhile, Jews from Zhetl who had escaped the camps in Novogrudek began to arrive. The groups grew. We received a lot of support from the Russian First Detachment in Lipitchansker Pushtche, under the leadership of Nikolai Vakhanin.

The influx of Jews in the forest rose with the arrival of Zhetl Jews from Dvoretz.

The Jewish detachment now had 200 Jewish boys and girls. We put up tents and camps. We already had almost enough weapons. Our group had 5 machine guns and rifles for everyone.

There were already about 600 partisans in the forest, besides 400 men who lived in small family groups not far from the detachment and each in his own way supported his family.

The groups created an autonomous region on the backs of the Germans and this was beneath their dignity. It went so far that we did not allow grain, potatoes or meat to reach Germans anywhere in the region of Zhetl and Kazlaychsin.

German patience exploded when partisans began to drag out weapons and artillery which the Russians abandoned when they retreated. Not far away was the White Russian village Valiye. The Christians in that village removed the weapons or showed the partisans where they were.

This is where the partisans in general and the Jews in particular made a living in weapons, especially, bullets. The Germans saw this and waited for the opportunity to take revenge.

The Rudeh Battle

In the heart of Pushche was the so–called partisan capital city – the village of Rudoyovarske. There were many partisans all around the village including our Jewish detachment. The village was swarming with partisans.

The Germans knew very well what Rudeh meant to us and they actually prepared to capture our "capital city" and give a death blow to the partisan movement. They thought about installing a strong garrison in Rudeh which would control the roads and restrain our development.

We would receive news that the Germans and their servants, the Ukrainians and Belarusians, were preparing an offensive against our headquarters. This happened at the end of 1942. As usual, we were sitting in the forest near Palatka, each doing his own work. Some were cleaning weapons, some were sleeping as they were exhausted after completing a job such as: cutting telegraph poles, bringing weapons and food for themselves and the dozen horses. Others prepared food, sang, sewed and mended clothing and shoes. Suddenly, we heard from Rudoyovarkse violent shooting from machine guns. As always, at the time of an alarm we received the following order:

"In five minutes be prepared to fight!"

We immediately sent out an intelligence group to find out what happened. I was in this intelligence group.

With great effort, one behind the other, we headed in the direction of the shooting. No one spoke a word. We only heard the orders of our commander. We arrived at a small house, approximately 200 metres from the village. A peasant peeked out of the window. We called him out and asked what was happening and who was shooting. We learned that Germans and Ukrainians arrived at Rudeh and people were saying they wanted to install a post.

[Page 396]

This is where we met the intelligence group of the Russian detachment led by Nikolai Vakhanin.

When we learned the news we returned to tell the leadership of our camp. The situation in our detachment became strained. Everyone understood that a battle would ensue the next day in order to chase out the Ukrainians.

The order for our detachment was: strengthen your posts and prepare dry food for the trip.

Meanwhile all the commanders of the detachments in Pushche were consulted: Hirshl Kaplinsky, Nikolai Vakhanin, the famous Bulak, for whom the whole world trembled, and it was decided that tomorrow, everyone jointly would chase out the enemy from the village. They also worked out an exact assault plan.

After releasing a communique about the joint assault, the moods were happy. We hoped we would win the battle.

The next day, very early in the morning, we marched to the battle field. Women and the elderly stayed behind in the camp. They remained dignified, they did not cry and wished well and said we would meet again after our victory. We went to the battle one after the other, and spent the night in a house, 250 metres from Rudeh, in order to begin the battle at dawn.

At exactly 6 o'clock the first sounds of the cannons echoed. This was the sign our assault must begin. Soon after shooting began from all types of weapons: cannons, automatic machine guns, which lasted 5 minutes. The assault stunned the enemy and they barely responded. Immediately we received this command:

Attack! We streamed into the village from all sides. Together with the stream of people, our only tank stormed in which belonged to Bulak. This was the culminating point. When the Ukrainians saw our tank they ran away. There was an extraordinary panic.

Dozens of dead and wounded Ukrainians lay on the streets who we had shot with great excitement. Out of the 160 men that were in Rudeh, 50 were killed, 12 were taken prisoner and the rest managed to escape.

The village celebrated with joy. We took some weapons and supplies which the Germans managed to bring in and left in the village. Upon our return to the detachment we were greeted with songs appropriate for the victors.

The Big Raid

After the great victory the Germans planned a raid which was to smash all the partisans.

The raid fell on us unexpectedly. Besides which at that time we did not have experience in open battle. Therefore the success was sad. The main problem was our spirits fell.

Our commander Hirshl Kaplinsky fell in this battle. It seemed our end had come. The Germans captured our camps and burned food and items.

The raid had a particularly bad effect on the so–called family groups who lost around 70 men, besides those who died from frozen feet and typhus.

After the Big Raid

The raid lasted for three weeks. Then the enemy withdrew from Pushche.

A few weeks passed. The partisans regrouped and began to reorganize but there had been great losses in weapons and artillery which we felt.

The Germans left us alone until the fall of 1943. Until then many changes took place in our partisan lives. Firstly, our Jewish detachment merged with the Russian detachment led by Nikolai Vakhanin. We began diversion work which greatly harmed the enemy. We blew up trains, bridges, made ambushes, attacked German garrisons, activated a tank which the partisans captured and due to this the Germans organized the raid on August 15 th 1943. This raid was not very big. Its goal was to destroy the tank.

We burned the tank ourselves in Pushche. We then returned and settled into a camp where we would remain until liberation.

From September 1 st 1943 until July 1944 we were busy with Russian traitors who ceded from Russia in fear of the Russian army. The Russian traitors' goal was to annihilate, although at the last minute, the partisans. They organized a big raid which lasted an entire month. This was the worst raid we experienced.

[Page 397]

Years in the Forest

by Khane Mayevsky – Klar (Cholon)

Translated by Janie Respitz

The end of October 1942. Lipitchanska forest. A frosty night. I lay on a pile of straw covered with a fur pelt. In the six weeks I had been in the detachment we changed our location three times. We built half winter huts. The work goes quickly. I am used to living in the forest. In the evening we gather around the fire and tell stories of our horrific experiences. Sometimes we sing quietly and sadly.

Female Typist at Headquarters

I go to work at the headquarters of the detachment. The commander Hirshl Kaplinsky tells me to type attestations which we give to the peasants as receipts for the food we take.

Vertilo, the leader of the Christian partisan detachment, calls me to work at his headquarters. I type notices for the October celebrations which will take place on the 7–8 of November. In the evening I go home. The same every day.

Unexpectedly the winter arrives, cruel with severe cold and snow. Some in our detachment are building earthen huts in the winter camp, large, comfortable completely underground so as to not feel the cold.

On November 12th 1942 Vertilo came to take me to work for a few days at his headquarters. They already have nice winter huts. So I will not feel alone, he introduces me to the Jews in his detachment.

I type a long command about uniting the two detachments, with exact lists according to companies, platoons. At night I am informed a large military force of 35,000 Germans and Ukrainians are concentrated in the forest.

The Big Raid

December 12th 1942. The guys left for ambushes. A battle takes place very close by. Artillery shots mixed with machine guns echo through the air. We sit in a wagon and ride: Vertilo, Dorosh, Dr. Miesnik, Feya the medic, the nurse from Leningrad and me. The canons are loud and seem to be quite near. The horse begins to gallop wildly and we turn over.

We run where our eyes take us. I ran after Dr. Miesnik. We reached the group of Minke and Yakov Senderovsky. All the roads to the detachment are occupied by Germans. We stay with them and hide in their caves.

Minke had a few potatoes and shared them. We also eat raw peas. We hear the shooting nearby. The surrounding farm houses are burning. This lasted for more than two weeks. The raid is not yet over but the shootings are less frequent. A group of our friends arrive including Yishayahu Levorontchik.

The rest of our detachment groups together in Nakrish forest. We go there. There sad news awaits us: many have been killed, our commander Hirshl Kaplinsky, Yudl Krugman, Sonia and Fruma Shilovitsky, Soreh Shulevitch, Dr. Garber and many more.

Many partisans have frozen feet and are despondent. There is talk that many women will be excluded from the detachment.

Podyavorke

January 1943. We moved to Podyavorke, an island surrounded on all sides by swamps. I find myself in a platoon with Yoyne Medvetzky. Our hut is two stories, the only one of its kind in the detachment. It is extremely cold. We hardly have any clothes to change into. We have to share our bunks, my hands are covered in scabies, my feet with abscesses.

The hut is mixed, men and women together. One by one, when everyone is asleep, we rub our scabies with pitch ointment and dry them in the tin oven.

The straw on our beds is full of lice. Typhus is spreading. There is little food. At that time there was an attempt to get food by the partisan from the Lida detachment, Mayrim Dvoretzky, who was killed. Mayshke Mankovitch's hands were wounded badly and Soreh Alpert was tortured to death.

February 23, 1942, the day of the Red Army, 23 Ukrainians ran to us from the Zhetl garrison. They were still wearing Ukrainian uniforms. There was great joy. They were highly skilled in diversion work.

[Page 398]

Yisroel Busel works with them and displays great heroism, destroying many trains until he is killed carrying out a diversion operation.

The beginning of March 1943. We moved to our summer camp near the village Krufitzi. The huts are nice, airy and on the ground surface.

Our detachment grew. We took back the girls which had been sent away after the raid.

March 8th 1943. They are preparing a second raid. People said whoever does not have a gun should remain in the camp. Many girls were kicked out of the detachment. A tragedy! We leave in the darkness of night.

After the village Gezgali we cross the train tracks on our backsides so as not to leave footprints.

We arrived at Kushelyevo near Novogrudek. A boy goes into the ghetto. I gave him a letter for my sister Peshke. After a few weeks of wandering we return to the forest.

May 1st 1943. There is a celebration and many of our comrades receive honorary distinctions. At this time the Nakrishk battle took place. There was a strong fortified German garrison. Moshke Senderovsky was killed.

In the middle of June the following were killed: Isar Likhter, Yosef Yudelevitch, and a Christian from Zatshepitch. Dovid Alpert was severely wounded.

July 1st 1943 a group goes to the "Third Reich". A few of them return 10 days later. The following were killed: Yishayahu Levorontchik, Khonen Gonshor, Mendele, and Meir Rozhansky. No one even knows under what circumstances.

July 15th 1943. Our detachment is divided. A portion joined the "Lenin Detachment". The commander of our third company is Panchenko. His assistant and commander of the first platoon is Sardak, a tall, barefoot guy with a long stick in his hand. He walks around with Pushkin's works and quotes him at every opportunity.

On the Eve of the Raid / End of August 1943

The so–called Railroad War is raging throughout White Russia. Our comrades are actively participating in this fight. Dozens of trains are blown up with the Germans, weapons and ammunition. We were extremely satisfied. On that day Hirsh Robetz and Hillel Levenbuk were killed.

September 4th 1943. We prepare for the raid. Our men prepare a successful ambush. A lot of Germans are killed. There is a decision to bury the typewriter as I cannot carry it. I took Yosef Mankovitch as a witness. In the event something happens to me, he will know the spot…

We continue to wander. We arrived at the Shchtara. We cross it by foot. The water is up to our chests. Someone almost drowned. On the other side of the river we divide into groups. We lit small fires and dried our things. During the day we rest. At night we walk 40 kilometres. It is pitch black. In the morning we arrive at the high mountains near Slonim.

September 18th 1943. After two weeks of wandering we return "home". I dig up the typewriter, dry it, and return to work.

September 1943. The victory in Stalingrad affects us like a charm.

November 7–8 1943 the October celebrations begin. Many express their gratitude. The commander of our company Fantchenko was so drunk he almost shot me.

Some troops under the leadership of Captain Davidov, a Jew, set up beside us in the forest. I go into their headquarters. Their goal is: to fight the White Poles on the other side of the Nieman and in the Third Reich.

In December 1943 we moved to our winter camp. The headquarters of the brigade is near us. I go there often to see my uncle Yakov Dzhenchelsky. Before every raid he gives me boots.

We now have nice comfortable huts. In the other company there is an oven to bake bread, and in the first, a bath. Only the men wash there. The women wash in the hut. We hang a curtain in the corner, send everyone out and wash in a washtub with hot water. In the summer we wash outside.

In January 1944 a group of comrades went over to the newly founded Red Guards Detachment.

In the middle of January parachutists begin to arrive regularly from the other side of the front. They come night after night at the same time. They bring weapons and explosives for the brigade. The guys go out and lay ambushes for the train. The parachutists lodge near us.

[Page 399]

In the evenings we arrange entertainment with them.

The two boys Aron Haydukovsky and Shloime Itzkovitch lay mines on the Lida – Grodno train tracks. On their way back they are killed by the White Poles.

February 13th 1944. There is a celebration for the anniversary of the Red Army. I was happy to be included among those recognized for excellence: "Partisan Medal 2nd Class", for dedication and precise work.

Recently I have been working a lot. First of all, reports told about the victories of the Red Army are written in hundreds of copies. Every battle is registered. There is also information distributed to the detachment and with the Christian villagers. We also prepare two weekly wall newspapers with exact lists of partisans who were killed.

May 1st 1944 there is a celebration. After the official celebration everyone continued to celebrate in his own way. Some danced the Kosatzka while others danced a tango or a waltz.

End of May. There is talk about a new raid. At night we often have battle drills. Food is scarce. One stormy June night all the men left on an ambush. The women guarded the camp. We were all together in the large hut of the third platoon. We change every few hours. It is thundering and lightning. It's pouring buckets. I felt the world was ending. In the morning all was calm. Our comrades returned safely.

Blockade

The 15th of June 1944. We learn the forest is blockaded. Once again I bury the typewriter. We bury food and a few other things in a big hole. Everyone is nervous. German airplanes circle low over our heads. We prepare for battle. We send a Christian, Vasya, on reconnaissance. He does not return. A second goes. He too does not return. Whose turn would be next?

We were lucky to avoid the German raid. We received an order not to leave the forest. Given that the front is approaching we will have to help the Red Army. The forest is so blockaded it is impossible to leave.

The allies of the Germans are after us in the biggest swamps. We wander at night and their rockets light up the entire forest. On one such night the Soviet airplanes bomb the German garrison in the forest. A radio technician sits near our tent, receives information and transmits.

Once again we have courage and hope. In the morning we continue. It is more than three weeks. The emergency food is finished. A horse was standing in the marsh. We killed him and made lunch.

The Fate of the Women

The third platoon leaves on an assignment. Maliye Kravietz, Mirke Levenbuk and Lyuba Inderstheyn decide to join them. It is not a good time to separate from the platoon. I help Lyuba get ready. They leave quickly. This was their road to their death. They walked into a German ambush. The men managed to escape. The women fell into the hands of the murderers.

We take our last desperate steps. We decided to go to the Durbrovchin forest on the road to Kazlaytchine. However we have to pass the Slonim highway which is filled with German bunkers. We cross safely. We practically ran across the highway. For the first time in my life I feel pain in my heart. It stabs me and I cry against my will.

Our sister Hindke Mirsky gives me valerian drops and tells me to put cold water against my heart. Later we washed some laundry in lye from ashes. We dragged water from a kilometre away. Again I don't feel good. I started to cry. I don't tell anyone. Who would be interested? And who could help me? That same night we were shot at with artillery. We decided to return, taking the same road we came on.

We are led by Elye Glazkov. He ordered the women to go last. Each woman received a pail with a bit of food. Quiet, without saying a word the train moves on. Here we are, the last ones, we crossed the highway and entered the forest. Suddenly artillery fire opens on us. It's very dark. We run. I trip over a fallen tree, I fall and lose my pail. I look for it but I can't find it. I get up and all I see around me are shadows. I don't recognize anyone. I ran after the disappearing shadows. The shooting stops. We were lucky: the very tall trees in the forest protected us. There were no human losses.

And then the tragedy happened. As usual, in difficult times, they realized there were too many women. From company headquarters, without any reason, they abandon Henie Gertzovsky, Malke Smulevitch and a few Christian women.

[Page 400]

From the second company they want to abandon Lyuba Yoselevitch and a Christian woman because they lost their pails. Lyuba tells me to bring her a pail from another group.

The commander from the Panchenko company knows I lost my pail. There were two more pails in our group and there was enough to cook our lean breakfast. But how do you pass such an opportunity and not teach a Jewish girl a lesson? They sent me to Commissar Kavyazin. He sends me back and says: "Go Khanke to the company. Tell them I sent you".

I return to the company. Panchenko decides to punish me by not giving me food. No is no. When everyone sits down to eat I walk 200 metres away, I turn my back and sink into sad thoughts…

Later, when I looked at the place where everyone was sitting I noticed no one was there. They left and left me alone. Is this possible? Did Panchenko go against the commissar's decision? Will no one look for me? Where are my Jewish friends? I lay in the bushes and felt the hair on my temples was turning grey.

Suddenly I remembered that Abrashe Garber and Kokeh Zhukhovitsky went somewhere as liaison officers and will most certainly return. I calm myself saying I can go five days without food…

Three hours later Kokeh and Abrashe actually return. My joy is immense. They know where everyone is and we go to the detachment. I cry from joy and resentment.

The abandoned women are not with the detachment. The Christian women calmly returned to their villages. But our misfortunate Henie Gertzovsky and Malke Shmulevitch were caught by the German murderers at the Shchtare, brought to Zhetl and tortured to death.

From the Forest to the Front

The front was getting closer. The forest was filled with retreating Germans. We are milling flour with a hand mill in the first company. In the second company, Motke Zakraysky is baking bread for the detachment. And here, the last days before liberation, he was killed.

Vanya and I dig up the typewriter and once again I can earn my bread.

Retreating Germans march out of order. We take revenge on them for innocent spilled blood. They are thrown into the Shchtare.

Practically the entire detachment went to Zhetl. The Red Army is already there. A military division marches through the forest. Our leaders hand them over to the partisans. Everyone, except the highest leaders go to the front. All night I type battle characteristics for our friends. In the morning they return from Zhetl and inform us they are going to the front. There is no shortage of silent tears.

They are standing in formation. Everyone, the entire brigade. I wanted to scream, cry. After so much suffering, we have to separate again? One more look, one more smile, and they left.

Final Requests

I will repeat their final requests: Mayrim Galiansky asked me to take care of Mashe. Yoyne Brestovitsky asked me to send regards to Khane –Layke (the women remained in Zhetl).

We return to our former home, Zhetl.

Three days later, July 18th 1944 the first of our partisans fell victim on the front. Among them are Dovid Likhter and Zaydl Finklshteyn. They were killed crossing the Svislatch River near the village Khomutovzky, in the Grodno region.

Zhetl Jews are wandering around. I feel I can't live without them. I cannot remain here where everything which is so dear and close to me is no longer.

I go with the current!

July 7–11 1944, all Zhetl partisans and family camps were liberated by the Red Army.

[Page 401]

Between Life and Death

by Tzile Zernitzky – Yoselevsky (Tel Aviv)

Translated by Janie Respitz

The surrounding villages had already been blocked for a few days. The peasants told us there is a great concentration of German forces, Ukrainians and police. All the roads are cut off. The situation worsens from minute to minute.

Winter is in full force. It snows during the day and the nights are freezing cold. There were still no tents in the detachment. The armed comrades were more or less prepared for winter, some with boots and shoes, others with pelts and other warm things, but the majority were naked. The summer clothes we were wearing when we ran from the slaughter tore during the few months we were in the forest.

Our third company, one of the three companies in the Jewish detachment led by Hirshl Kaplinsky, stood between the first and second companies near the villages Ruda – Yavarsky and Refitch. There was no lack of food. The famous "Host Group" provided meat and bread. The kitchen, supervised by the head cook Dvoyre Tinkovitzky, worked non stop. The large pots are cooked three times a day. Everyone had his job. Some fought and others hosted.

Suddenly something tore through the silence. There was a command: "To the battle!"

All the detachments in the forest left to fight the enemy. In our company 12–15 remained, girls, the sick and the unarmed. The work in the kitchen intensified. We prepared lunch in good spirits as we were sure our comrades would return from battle victorious as had happened a few times before.

Although every finger was wrapped individually with rags, our hands froze and the knife out of habit cut the potatoes on its own. We tap our feet and sing a song. The bonfire is crackling and the soup with pieces of meat is bubbling. From time to time we glance in the direction from which our victors should return.

And suddenly, the sky lights up as if it is lightning, the air trembles, there is a shot. Very close by. We look around and hear a voice from a nearby tent. We are terrified. Another shot, even closer. "A series of machine gun fire aimed at us and stop! Stop!" They are shouting. They are shooting from all directions. We hear screams and heart wrenching sighs.

It is too late to do any reckoning. Our brains have stopped thinking. We begin to run disorientated, not knowing where to go. The forest is unfamiliar to me and I do not know the area, except for the bonfire and the half frozen potatoes. This is all I did in the 2 Â½ months.

I see girls from other companies. Here is the road that leads to Karshuk's farmhouse. They are also shooting from that side. Germans everywhere.

"Save me", "Mother"! "Stop! Stop!" I hear people scream. We ran along the road seeing dead bodies. Soreh Shmulevitch is already dead. A minute later the sisters Sonia and Frume Shilovitsky are also killed. Running beside me are Khane Gertzovsky, Muliye, her brother, Mirke Levenbuk, Khayke Savitzky (Magid) and Yudis Mashkovsky.

Realizing we could not cross the highway that would take us to our winter camp in the Nakrishk forest, we turned right, among the young birches near Karshuk, right near the main road which leads to Zhetl.

Everything is becoming more difficult, our feet no longer serve us, as if someone was pulling them back. We are sinking into the deep mud and snow. We tried to penetrate deeper into the marshes, and all five of us intertwined, like young birch trees, and each one hearing the other's heartbeat. The shooting does not stop. We hear screaming and the barking of bloodhounds.

It gets dark. The dark December night is lit up by rockets, projectiles and fires in the surrounding farmhouses. The dense shooting is mixed with cries and shouts from peasant women and children who the Germans are shooting near their homes for helping and collaborating with the partisans. We hear the creaking of wagons, the squealing of pigs, the bellowing of cows which were confiscated by the Germans.

"Kids! Rub your feet!" Mirke whispered constantly. During the day when the sun warmed up the ice in the marsh melted, but at night, in the cold our feet froze with the water. However we did not feel it. The one common thought and feeling that dominated: not to be taken alive by the murderers.

[Page 402]

We sat like this for three days and four nights, tortured by hunger, cold and danger. By the fourth night things calmed down. We decided to crawl out of the marsh and go to our old camp with the hope of finding surviving partisans. Holding each other, we heard whispering sounds from a distance. The assuredness that these were ours and not Germans gave us courage, and with our last bit of strength, we dragged ourselves to the camp.

We saw a white horse near the burnt kettles, which in the darkness looked like a ghost, moving and licking the ground. Beside him there were moving black shadows scraping the kettles. Who are they? People or ghosts? They were neither ghosts nor Germans. They were hungry, frightened Jews from the family groups near Mayak who came looking for food in the local kitchens.

Here, we actually found, in a non destroyed tent, a few armed partisans: Zelik Kroyer, Sholem Ogulnik, Veveh Kravetz and Shaul Savitsky of blessed memory. Our joy was interrupted by the sad news they shared with us: the German army withdrew two divisions from the front in order to eradicate the partisans. The surrounding villages were still blocked, all the farmhouses burned, the family groups were murdered, and the partisan groups chased away. There was no way out and no hope.

At that moment I did not think about the future. These people have to eat. We light a few fire sticks, it warms up and we feel it in our limbs. We fall asleep. But day breaks and we must leave this place. I wrap my feet again in the wet rags and then shoes, but I can't get my shoes on. My feet are swollen, my shoes are wet. There is no time to make a fuss, I see they are leaving. The situation is such that everyone worries about himself. Whoever can stand remains, without sentimentality or feelings.

Small groups form, no one tells the other where they are going. Everyone wants to be close to those who are armed.

I leave my shoes, wrap my feet in rags and try to follow them, not noticing that they are chasing me away, even threatening me with the butt of a gun.

We had not even crossed the first ice hole when dense shooting echoed in the forest.

The Germans attacked our camp. Those who had not managed to escape were killed.

We wandered for a few days and nights, often under a hail of bullets, until we arrived at the Nakrishk forest, where our winter camp was supposed to be ready. At that spot we found many partisans, Jews and Christians, exhausted from battle. Some had weapons other did not, beaten, with frozen feet, wounded, covered in lice, hungry and depressed. At that moment of disorganization and lack of discipline anti – Semitism flared up with edicts, persecutions and victims. And on top of all this a typhus epidemic breaks out.

Approximately one kilometre from the camp was a family group with 50 –60 Zhetl Jews. These were unarmed families, elderly people and small children. In calmer times they scrounge for food in the surrounding villages. Some reclaimed their hidden items from the peasants, others had acquaintances or children in the fighting groups who supported them. Now in the heat of the raid, they shared the same fate of all the partisans, to a certain extent, more terrifying and fearful.

Frozen and hungry I crawled to one of their tents from which the "owners" ran away. It was hard to notice it from outside as it was so well masked.

"There are people inside sick with typhus. Where are you going?" someone asked.

This did not interest me or scare me. Life and death stood in balance. What was important to me was to warm up my feet, which I could no longer feel. Perhaps I could also get a piece of bread?

I enter the tent through the little door and I'm standing in water. Darkness, dampness and the moaning of the sick is what welcomes me in the tent.

I'm overcome with fear. I feel like I've fallen into a live grave. Touching the wooden bunks I feel the difference between feet and clothing. I haven't seen anyone but they noticed me from the light when I opened the little door. Suddenly, someone grabs me and calls out my name. We both begin crying hysterically. We recognized each other: my little brother, the only one I had left from my whole family. He was saved in the last battle and was now battling typhus. His hands quickly fall hard, his cries transform into heavy sighs and incomprehensible speech. He's burning with fever and loses consciousness.

[Page 403]

The tragedy hardens me and gives me energy and courage. With the help of a thin ray of light I recognize a few other people on the bunk including Khane and Muliye.

Everyone is breathing heavily and rambling from the fever. Between the bunks and both walls, on a low plank of wood, someone is sitting like an iron statue, not moving. From the gasping and moaning one feels the angel of death is lying in wait for his prey.

This was the beginning of desperate, fearful days. No one opens the little door to bring good news, or medical aid. It's cold, dark and damp.

Khane, who got better, and I wet the lips of the weak and feverish with the filthy water that reached as high as the bunks. Every morning we removed the only covers, the pelts off everyone and tried to remove the countless lice. We would have had much better results if we had a fire but such a luxury was not possible. Two lonely helpless girls like us, without any tools could not possibly cut down trees for wood. We had to freeze in this dark cave.

Meanwhile the typhus epidemic controlled the entire forest. The amount of graves in our group, near the little Mayak, grew by the day. Little children without their parents wandered around swollen from hunger, frozen and in pain. Those with typhus were fighting death.

Sometimes, Jewish partisans returning from a task would toss bread or meat into the family camp. But this rarely happened. And you had to be able to actually catch anything.

Early in the morning, in a helpless state, typhus stopped me in my tracks with fever and unconsciousness and frozen feet. My fight to exist ended. I began a bitter terrifying battle between life and death.

The amount of "inhabitants" in the dark cave was dwindling. Some went to the detachment while others went to the family group. My brother who had a weapon with him was taken half sick back to his division.

There were three dying people in the tent waiting every day for inevitable death.

From time to time the little door would open and someone, without pity, would toss in a piece of bread, or a loaf, but no one could enjoy it, it was too late. The bread lay in the dirty water nourishing the worms and cockroaches.

Opening the cave, I would still recognize the "statue" in the corner, but this time, no longer breathing or sighing. This was Borukh Lipsky, a 16 year old boy. He died sitting quietly, with eyes half open, as if he still wanted to see our suffering. The boards of the bunk in the two corners held up his dead body in a sitting position not allowing it to fall into the filthy water.

Yosef Busel (Avreymche the blacksmith's son) lay beside me on the bunk. He came to the forest after the slaughter in Dvoretz. During the raid both of his feet froze. Finding this chaotic tent, he moved in. Worms ate his open wounds. He rotted away and this is where he breathed his last breath.

The horrible smell in the hole carried far on the surface of the earth. It was dangerous for people who came close to the place. I heard later from stories from friends that people would pass by daily to to see for themselves if there were still moans coming from the hole or if they should close the door for good and place a pile of sand in its place. This happened in the family group in "Lapchinske" where an entire tent died of typhus and the dead, in their bunks, found their mass grave.

Apparently miracles do happen. Such a miracle happened to me thanks to Mineh Senderovsky. If there are people who sacrifice their lives for another, Mineh Senderovsky is one.

Walking by one day she heard a cry from the "House of Death". Paying no attention to the danger which faced her and her family, she came the next day with Hilye Zhukhovitsky and took me on a sled to their tent in another forest.

Thanks to her motherly devotion she succeeded, despite fate, to rescue me with force, from death.

My strength returned very slowly. In May 1943 I returned to the detachment.

[Page 404]

Taking Revenge on a Maytchet Murderer

by Yekhiel Yoselevitch (New York)

Translated by Janie Respitz

We were a group from Zhetl that set out on the road. However, when we examined the situation we realized if we went to Nolibok forest we would lose contact with Zhetl and would not be able to bring the kids over. So we decided instead to create a group that would go to the neighbouring Bork and Rahat forests.

The forest was not big but there was no other recourse because we could not go to Lipitchansk forest due to the event with Alter Dvoretzky. The Bork forest is near Dvoretz and from Dvoretz we can make contact with Zhetl. There was a large Jewish work camp in Dvoretz where people lived in better conditions than in the Zhetl ghetto.

Around July 15th 1942 I went with Shepsl Nakhmanovitch, Dovid Kantarovitch, Shloime Shifmanovitch, Shaul Shakhnovitch, Binyomin Yurush, Khaim Slamke, Frenkl and Sholem Ogulnik with 6 rifles to the Bork forest.

When we arrived in Bork forest we met 3 boys from Maytchet, including Moishe Daykhes, who ran away from the slaughter in Maytchet and thanks to a few guys with guns they succeeded in escaping the encirclement and getting to the nearby forest.

They also told us the surrounding Christians, led by the secretary of the township and his son, capture escaping Jews, rob them and hand them over to the gendarmerie.

After a brief consultation we decide to take revenge on the secretary and his family and at the same time convince the surrounding Christians there is a punishing hand for the murderers who spill Jewish blood.

On July 25th 1942 at 9 o'clock in the evening our group armed with 6 rifles, sticks and a litre of benzene set out for the secretary's house. By one o'clock in the morning the secretary's farmhouse was surrounded. Each window was guarded by two men and a gun waiting for my commands.

We sent comrade Daykhes to the window to ask for bread. We thought the secretary and his son would run out as they had always done to capture the unarmed Jews and turn them into the gendarmerie.

However, the proprietor this time felt the danger and his wife threw some bread out the window. Then Daykhes said he is not a dog and they should let him into their house. At this point the secretary and his son began shooting out the window from automatic guns. We were not afraid and responded with fire while Moishe Daykhes took the benzene and set the house on fire. From a distance, we did not stop shooting until the house was engulfed in flames.

Meanwhile the Maytchet garrison opened heavy fire on us. We retreated. The next day we learned from our contacts the secretary and his family died in the flames. The only one rescued was the five year old boy who the mother probably threw from the window when she was shot.

After this act of revenge I sent the following four comrades to Zhetl: Shepsl Nakhmanovitch, Dovid Kantarovitch, Shloime Shifmanovitch and Frenkl, to bring more friends and weapons which were in Yoyne Medvedsky's cellar. These listed men, except for Shloime Shimanovitch who remained with wounded feet one kilometre from Zhetl, were killed on August 6th, 1942 at four o'clock in the ghetto.

An hour later the Zhetl ghetto was surrounded by German military.

The three comrades led by Shepsl wanted to break through the barrier with stones and clubs (when they did not receive the weapons) not far from Mogilnitsky's gate. Dovid Kantarovitch was killed by a murderer's bullet. The brave 19 year old Shloime Busel also broke through the barrier with a pistol in hand. As he shot he tore through one but at the second he was shot. Shepsl was wounded in the stomach. He managed to stand up on his feet and shout with his last bit of strength:

"Murderers, you will pay dearly for this spilled blood!"

The murderers wrapped wires on a stick and beat his wounds until he died from pain. His last words were: "Death to the murderers"!

[Page 405]

We Take Revenge on a Murderer from Maldutch

by Zavl Mordkovsky (New York)

Translated by Janie Respitz

I escaped from the camp in Novogrudek with Dovid Berman, Yenkl Mankovitch and his three sons: Moishe, Itche and Yosef. After three days of wandering through fields, not knowing where we were going, we arrived in Lipitchansky forest.

The first Jewish partisan we found was Sholem Ogulnik. He informed us that in order to be accepted into a partisan detachment we must have weapons.

We remained where we were and tried to acquire guns in order to join the detachment.

One day, walking through the forest we met a group of partisans from the detachment. They suggest we go with them to Faretch, a village where they produce whisky, to burn the rye depot, so they will give us guns.

Zavl Mordkovsky

When we arrived in the village they sent me with one other guy to scout the place. I learned that a large group of German soldiers arrived that day and fortified the village. I tell this to the commander and we decide to return to the depot where we received three guns. We were happy to leave and go join the Jewish partisan group.

On a winter night in 1942 we received an order from our commander, Hirshl Kaplinsky, to go to the Novoyelniye highway to destroy the telephone communications, cut down the posts and cut the telegraph wires. Nosn Funt was chosen as the leader. He was the nephew of Alter Dvoretzky. The others in the group were Zelik Grayer, Motke Haydukovsky, Yisroel Burda, Areleh Leyzerovitch, Leyzer Savitzky and me.

It was a very dark night. Our assignment had to be carried out near the village Maldutch. When we completed our diversion work we decide to enter the village and settle accounts with the village murderers, first and foremost the village magistrate, Matusevitch.

We had many accusations against him. He sent a Christian to Maytchik the baker to buy his scale. After the Christian paid him for his scale he came back with a German, demanded his money back and took the scale for free.

Saturday evening, when my uncle Borukh and I sat at Meir the tailor's in the small prayer house, Matusevitch came with a German and demanded glass for 16 windows from my uncle. Understandably, with the help of the German, he got what he wanted from my poor uncle.

Matusevitch also betrayed an entire Jewish family to the Germans. This happened right after the first slaughter. The carpenter Yirmiyahu Kravetzky built a house for Matusevitch and considered him a friend.

Hiding from slaughter in a cellar, he ran out with his family at night to Maldutch with the hope Matusevitch would hide them. When they arrive Matusevitch let them into his barn and promised to bring food. Instead of food he brought the German police who shot them all on the spot.

We walked into the village and asked where Matusevitch lived. We knocked on the door and after a few minutes nobody answered. Leyzer Savitsky noticed through the window someone was moving in the house. We barged into the house.

When I opened the door the light in the house shone on us. We saw the big Matusevitch standing beside us. We took him inside and asked him if he remembered sins he perpetrated against Zhetl Jews.

He did not deny he did all those things, but he claimed he was innocent. He said the Germans forced him to behave this way.

Nosn ordered him to come with us to headquarters. He began to argue. We tried to take him by force but we couldn't. He then began to scream like a wild man. We assessed the situation and realized we were only a few kilometres from Zhetl and his screams could be heard from far away. I loaded my gun, held it to his temple and shot. Matusevitch dropped dead.

This is how we took revenge on an enemy of Israel who helped the German murderers kill our brothers and sisters.

[Page 406]

The Battle in Dubrovke

by Sholem Gerling (Ramat Gan)

Translated by Janie Respitz

It was September 1942. Two peasants informed our headquarters that 40 German trucks crossed the Nieman and surrounded the village Dubrovke.

The Germans, with their machine guns, drove the peasants into a few large barns, loaded all the possessions of the village onto trucks and crossed to the other side of the Nieman.

What was now going on, they did not know. They barely managed to escape. We understood this was a punishment for the village that helped the partisan movement.

The partisans went to help.

All of our weapons consisted of three cannons, one high caliber machine gun, around 10–12 machine guns and rifles. There were about 250 people.

The day was hot, the road was sandy. The place was far, about 30 kilometres away. We rode there, two on one horse. Only the reconnaissance team of 35 were privileged to each ride on their own horse. The trip took five hours. When we arrive we saw the entire village was burning.

The reconnaissance team returned with information that the Germans were still in the village. However they had no details about their numbers or location as they did not meet any civilians in the area.

Without thinking too long we continued on closer to the enemy. In the lead were 40 men, all Jews led by the company commander Hirshl Kaplinsky. The situation was such that the group I was with was distanced from the remaining group.

Our group stopped at a sparse small forest on a hill. Upon receiving a certain signal we were to spread out and take our positions. However, before we could managed to carry out the order bullets came pouring down on us. We were so close to the enemy we heard the reloading of weapons, however it was impossible to go back.

In truth, we were not very afraid of the bullets because due to our proximity they fell beyond us. However, we were worried that at any moment they could surround us and that would be worse than meeting a bullet.

Lying near me were Sholem Ogulnik and Shaul Savitzky. A little further away were Yoyne Medvedtsky and Khaim Slamky. Our commander Hirshl Kaplinsky was far from us on the left. I quickly oriented myself and quietly gave the order: "Fire!!"

Luckily our artillery understood to open fire at that moment. The Germans were sure they were fighting against a large unit and began to retreat.

The shooting lasted 15 –20 minutes. Later it became quiet. I crawled to the top of the hill to observe the area. I did not see anyone. We waited a bit then began to move forward. We arrived at the Nieman.

We gathered at the river bank with everyone we had lost during the sudden enemy fire. Hirshl Kaplinsky kissed us when he saw us. The same with Binyomin Yurish. They were sure we were killed.

Meanwhile we noticed a ferry on the other side of the river, probably used by the enemy to run away. Four of our comrades got into a half broken boat, rowed to the ferry and set it on fire.

We return.

We walked through the village. All of Dubrovke was burned. Among the embers and ashes from the burned stables we saw human bodies, peasant boots and burned feet.

We arrived too late…

The entire village, all the peasants and their families were killed in the flames.

We met our detachment behind the forest. The partisans were astonished that in such an open fight and overpowering enemy forces we all returned safely without casualties.

They shook our hands, kissed us and praised our boldness and cold bloodedness.

For a long time after the commanders used us as an example for the detachment.

"Learn cold bloodedness and endurance from the Jewish detachment "Orliansky!"

"Remember Dubrovke!"

[Page 407]

Four Victims

by Lialeh Kalbshteyn – Yakhas (Johannesburg)

Translated by Janie Respitz

After the second slaughter, when Zhetl had been cleansed of Jews, I left for the Ludzhit Forest. At night I would go to Christian acquaintances in the villages and ask for food.

One time I went with my mother Rokhl. It was late at night. The moon was shining, the stars sparkling and the snow squeaked under our feet. From a distance we saw the glimmer from Christian houses. We approached a small house and knocked on the door. The Christian opened the door for us. As always our first question was:

"What's new in town?"

The Christian tells us it is calm in town. There is no military. However the non Jews in town are saying a raid is being organized on the forests and bunkers have been built on the roads. We feel we are surrounded by two wolves that want to devour us.

The Christian gave us some grain and milk for those gravely ill in the forest. Another Christian gave us potatoes and flour. By the way he told us the same thing as the first Christian.

We take the bit of food and return "home".

The question bothering us is: "Will we eat this?"

With sacks on our shoulders and quiet steps we approach our forest. The moon and stars have disappeared, dawn is breaking and our hearts are pounding from fear. Who knows what the day will bring?

On the highway we met a man wearing a black coat. We did not see his face. He was wearing a hood and his feet were bound with rags. It appeared he was going from town to the forest. This man made a bad impression on me and I told my mother he must be a spy.

We quickly crossed the highway. I stopped and looked in the direction of the stranger. He also stopped to see where we were going.

We continued. When we were in the forest I looked around. The covered man was not there, he disappeared.

Everyone was sitting around the tents waiting impatiently. I shared the sad news with them as well as our encounter on the highway. I threw off my boots and the wet rags from my feet and made a fire to warm up and cook something for the sick. I cooked the milk and went to feed the sick, Yente Riveh Gal and her uncle Kalman Savitsky, who were sitting on the hill. As I approached the hill German buttons and greatcoats flashed before my eyes. I shouted:

"Germans!" and ran.

Shooting began. Running out of strength I fell and remained lying under a bush. The sick were shot on the spot.

While lying under the shrub I saw how Mertche Gal, Yente Riveh's mother, came out of a hiding place talking to herself:

"If Yente Riveh is gone, I don't want to live any more." She barely walked a few steps and they shot her. My only desire was: not to fall into the murderer's hands alive. I dragged myself until I was able to stand up and run.

I ran to a marsh with fallen trees and sat down to rest.

From time to time I heard shooting. Suddenly I heard someone crawling through the trees. I was sure it was a German murderer, but to my great joy it was my little brother Moishele.

We crawled together under a birch tree and spent the night. From there we went to Ludzhit forest where we knew the following fallen victims during the attack: Mikhal Rozovsky (Tuviya Idl's son), Yente Rive Gal, Mertche Gal and Kalman Savitsky.

That same night, after we buried the victims we returned to Lilpitchansky forest and continued our difficult struggle to exist.

[Page 408]

In the Family Camps

by Shmule Mnuskin (Kfar Saba)

Translated by Janie Respitz

The few Jews saved from the second slaughter who escaped to the Lipitchansky forest organized a partisan group under the leadership of Hirshl Kaplinsky in the first days of August 1942. At first they did not have weapons, but the desire to take revenge on the murderers of our people and the need to defend themselves from a German assault forced us to think about where we could acquire weapons.

It was decided everyone had to figure out how to obtain a weapon and newcomers to the partisans must have a gun. As a result, many women, children and the elderly remained outside the detachment.

Those who were not organized and unarmed were called "Semayns". They were mostly concentrated behind the partisan camps in order to benefit from their protection as well as their food.

Concentrating in one place risked being discovered by the enemy which could have, easily and quickly surrounded all of us. The unarmed and elderly had to spread out in small groups throughout the forest. Another looming danger were the Christian partisans who in masses romped through the forests often attacking and robbing them. There were incidents when defenceless women and children were attacked by the Christians who often raped young girls.

This situation did not last long. In time there was order and discipline among the organized partisans and such acts were severely punished.

As a result the food problem grew worse. During the day they lay hidden in the bunks, listening with perked up ears for approaching danger. At night, when a dead silence took over the forest, some would crawl out of hiding and leave for a piece of bread, a few potatoes or a glass of milk.

Shmuel Mnuskin

We Go Begging in the Villages

Many Jews had Christian acquaintances in the villages who would toss the hungry, ragged beggar a piece of bread or some black flour to cook. At first begging did not come easy to well off men and women, but with time we were forced to make peace with the concept.

And this is how they went, in the darkness of night through the forest roads and paths with a sack on their backs. Looking for ways to stay alive, women, children and the elderly, walked barefoot, shivering from cold with chattering teeth. The shadow of a tree and a tweet from a night bird frightened them. They avoided dirt roads and waded through plowed fields and swamps. The earth was soft and the bare feet would bang into a stone, often sharp, and suddenly it would feel warm between their toes…with careful steps, quietly, holding their breath, they would approach a peasant's house. A light tap on the window and a sleepy voice asked from the dark house:

"Who's there?" (In Russian)

A small window opens and a sleepy face looks out.

"What do you want and why did you wake me up in the middle of the night?" asks the angry peasant. He does not wait for an answer. He knows what the poor hungry person wants. He disappears immediately and a few minutes later returns with a piece of bread or a few potatoes in his hands. Some peasants did this out of pity, others, out of fear.

Sometimes we would come across a peasant we knew well. He would open his door for Jews. The peasant would light a kerosene lamp or a dry piece of kindling and a pleasant warmth would embrace the cold bodies. The peasant would roll some tobacco in a piece of newspaper and smoking the cigarette would warm and soothe the soul. The warmth of the house, the long wooden table with benches, and the smells of the evening supper awakened a longing for home. The heart gnaws and almost explodes with jealousy.

At times, the peasant would tell some happy news from the front providing a ray of hope.

[Page 409]

Then, when there is a piece of cheese, a bottle of milk and a piece of bread in your sack, your feet feel lighter, the road seems shorter, and the weight on your shoulder, easier. You even allow yourself to sit under a tree and catch your breath.

The sky slowly becomes lighter, the stars are dimming. The forest is echoing with the songs of birds and the branches are swaying with the early morning breeze. A rabbit runs by pricking up its ears detecting a person. Frightened, it jumps away, leaving on the sand, small, dainty tracks. You want to shout:

"Little rabbit, don't run away! We are persecuted by the same fate, hunters are lying in wait for us…

The sun rises in all its magnificence. A fragrant scent of resin fills the forest. The tired body inhales it and sleepiness takes over. The eyes stick…you fall asleep for a while, but suddenly, you are overcome with fear, you glance at your bag of food and remember someone is waiting for you with a trembling heart.

The First Raid

The first raid began in December 1942. Forty five thousand well armed Germans were removed from the front to fight the partisans. The battle lasted three days. When the partisans began to feel the lack of bullets the resistance was broken. The Jewish commander Hirshl Kaplinsky was wounded and later beastly murdered. The partisans spread out throughout all corners of the forest and the result was sad. Hundreds were wounded or killed. The store houses of ammunition and food were depleted. One by one the partisans, hungry and tattered, dragged themselves through the forests and marshes.

Those who suffered the most were the "Semayns", those who were unorganized and unarmed who lived near the detachments. The murderers agitated the unarmed women and children, shooting them on the spot. During the attack the panic among this group was so great, as they ran from danger they ran into the hands of the Germans. The German newspapers wrote that hundreds of partisans were shot and the forest was strewn with corpses. Of course their losses were not stated.

This operation lasted a few weeks. Those who survived in the forest were starving. The filthy cold tents were rampant with typhus. Not having the necessary medication and suffering from hunger, people dropped like flies. The forest was filled with graves of those who avoided bullets, but not typhus. When everyone in one tent died, it was transformed into a communal grave.

It was a strong, angry winter. The epidemic stopped with the advent of spring. A freshness and happiness dominated the people in the forest. Detachments once again began to organize and rebuild the destroyed camps. Those unarmed were forbidden to live near the partisan camps. Now they had to hide in more dangerous places, like at the edge of the forest, near the roads. Every step the Germans made resulted in casualties.

At the beginning of the summer the Germans began to place police garrisons in all surrounding villages. This forced the unarmed, unaffiliated, to learn from mistakes after the first raid, and build well camouflaged hiding places.

The Last Raid

Our situation improved in the first months of 1944. We were more acclimatized and were more familiar with all the pros and cons of the forest. The food situation was also easier. Everyone now had their source for food. Spring was approaching. The berry bushes were blooming and the birds were singing. Who knows, perhaps they were songs of freedom for us, the chased and tormented.

Then we were informed the camps of German bloodthirsty murderers were besieging the forest. The peasants told us the Germans were threatening to rid the forest of the last partisan.

We began to prepare ourselves for difficult dangerous days. We began to build caves but food was still an issue. Nothing remained from the winter and going to a peasant was impossible. Dvoyre Gorodaysky and I tried to leave the forest a few times but the Germans opened fire on us from all sides and each time we had to turn back empty handed.

One quiet morning the reconnaissance informed us the raid was beginning.

My hiding place was almost completed, I just needed a door to close it up. With my last bit of strength I dragged over a few trees and placed them at the opening. My wife and I and our three children lay in the hole with pounding hearts and held our breath.

[Page 410]

My sister in law Shayndl Mnuskin and her children, Khane the gentile, Rive Novoprutsky and Motl Dunetz were hiding in a cave not far from us. We lay there all day.

The sun set. It became quieter. My brother Shleymke and I stood under a tree and watched the bullets which flew over us like fireworks. According to where they were flying and landing, the Germans were not far from us.

It grew dark. We called the women and the children to come out of the cave. My wife lit a fire to cook a few potatoes and warm some water to freshen up our weakened hearts. I went to the people from Zhetl whose cave was half a kilometre from ours. When I arrived at their tent, no one was there. There was a frightening silence, as if everyone had sunk. I went to the cave and called out quietly:

"Moishe! Moishe! Come out, it's me Mulke!"

Suddenly I noticed, from behind a shrub, the blond disheveled hair of Moishe Abramovitch. After him, his brother Itche crawled out and one other. They stared at me with fear in their eyes and waited for me to say something comforting, or bring good news. I told them the Germans are half a kilometre from my cave and I'm afraid the children who range in age from 2 –6 will cry and disclose our hiding place. I stayed with them for a half hour and returned to my family.

Upon my return I met a few people from Zhetl standing around a fire. They asked me what I was planning to do. They wanted to move to another place because there were too many footprints from living people. I told them it would be difficult for me to leave with small children.

"You are all adults. Do what you feel is best".

We hid our few potatoes in a hole and the few pieces of bread behind a thick shrub and returned to our cave as day was breaking. The children were sleeping sweetly on the grass. They did not feel the mosquitos sucking their blood.

We went into the cave and masked the entrance with branches and grass. I lay down with the children and tried to sleep. I lay with my eyes open while thousands of thoughts ran through my mind.

My wife Yokheh asked me if it was day yet. I tried to lift the little door to our cave. Bright rays of light blinded me. Yes, it is day, probably around 10 o'clock. It is very quiet. We heard the loud noise of a motor. Trucks and tanks are driving through the forest. We hear frightful voices.

In the evening I crawl to my brother's cave. They are still sitting confined and apparently don't know the sun is already set. I called him out. He asks me:

"What's new?"

How should I know? I was lying all day in a cave.

I surmised the Germans had besieged the forest and were driving around on the forest roads. When it was really dark we called the women and children to come out. Our nightlife started again. They prepared something to eat as well as food for the whole day.

People arrive from other tents. We discuss politics and what's happening on the front and try to prophesize. The Germans are only 500 metres from us. We can actually hear them talking. They continue to shoot and the bullets fly over our heads. But we are in the forest and are protected by the dense trees.

At dawn we return to our caves. It is impossible to breathe. The children are sweaty and itchy. The mosquitos and lice are eating their skin. The air is damp and heavy. Our new enemy are the conditions in the cave.

At dawn I crawl out and try to listen to the noises. It is quiet. I only hear the birds singing. I tell my wife and children to come out for some fresh air. Who knows how much longer we will be tormented?

I consulted with my brother Shleymke. My opinion is that we must change our location. We are too close to the road and the Germans will most certainly come here.

We Search for a Better Place

It is calm and quiet in the forest. We decided to look for a better place. Tzviya Lantzevitsky, Khane the gentile, Moishe Abramovitch and Motl Dunetz went with us. On the way we picked some berries and were happy to find the first mushrooms. I noticed a newspaper beside a bush. I picked it up and my eyes quickly scanned the German lines. It was dated just a few days before. We were quite sure Germans had been at that spot. I took the paper with me. It could be used to roll a cigarette.

We soon crawl closer toward the edge of the forest. Suddenly we hear shooting from artillery. We notice the bullets are headed toward the Lida detachment.

[Page 411]

We did not understand the reason for the shooting as we knew the Lida detachment had left long ago.

We decided to return to our tents. Suddenly we heard singing from a distance. Was it a drunk group of partisans? Who knew?

We were not far from our tents. I sat down for a minute. Then I saw my friends running. I stood up and saw three standing with guns. Instinctively I began to run. I ran to the left, they shot. I ran to the right, they shot. My brother Shleymke and the others ran to the right. I understood we were surrounded.

I caught up to my brother and the group. As we ran we decided, not far from where we were there was a Jewish cave and we must run there. We are anxious about the women and children. We left them at the surface, they should at least know how to cover up the opening.

We ran to the cave, we looked for the door. We whispered quietly for them to open the door and let us in.

However, no one answered, and the shooting was getting closer and closer. Finally we managed to open the door. We crawled into the cave.

We saw 18 people sitting pressed together and afraid. We told them what brought us. They were not happy we were there. Maybe the cave will be discovered. Maybe the Germans followed our footsteps.

By evening things were a bit calmer. We lifted the door and crawled out. We hurry to our wives and children. At first we crawled on all four but slowly we stood up. It was calm and quiet. My brother Shleymke walked behind me.

We were approaching our tents. There was smoke winding behind the trees. My heart was jumping from fear for the fate of our loved ones.

We crawled on our knees. Perhaps the Germans were still there waiting for human skeletons to crawl out of the caves. I crawled to the cave and called out:

"Yokheh!

I heard a reply. I could not believe it. Yokheh crawled out of the hole. We fell into each other's arms and cried from joy. She told me that right after we left they decided to return to the cave because they were afraid to remain alone. The Germans had come to the tents and were close to the cave. Luckily they did not notice our tracks. Before they left, they set the tents on fire.

On that day many Jews from the family groups in the corners of the forest were killed.

Heroic Dates in the Battles of Zhetl's Partisans

August 20, 1942 – the first Jewish detachment was organized.

December 12 1942 – the first big raid against the partisans.

June 7 1944 – the second large raid against the partisans.

July 7 1944 – the partisans from Zhetl were liberated.

[Page 412]

The Partisan Hospital

by Sholem Gerling (Ramat – Gan)

Translated by Janie Respitz

One of the issues among the partisans was caring for the sick and wounded. In "normal" times we found a solution, we arranged for the sick to be placed with local peasants. At first the amount of sickness was small and the roads to the farm houses were relatively calm and safe.

It was a different situation during the hostile raids, especially when they lasted a long time. For example, in 1942, when from the 12th of December the Lipitchansky forest was surrounded by tens of German divisions, and as a result of heavy bitter battles many partisans were wounded. At the same time there were many sick with typhus and 90% of our comrades were leprous! By this time there was no talk about arranging for the wounded and sick to be placed with peasants. Everyone agreed they would not be safe and the few partisan doctors would not be able to visit them. It was also impossible to burden the surrounding population with so many severely wounded and sick. One solution was: to open our own partisan hospital. And this is what we actually did.

We Found a Place

Finding a place for a hospital on the backs of the enemy was easier said than done. After a long difficult search the choice was a secluded corner of the forest between the villages Ruda Lipitchanska and Zatchefish. The place was shown to us by a local peasant, in an area of approximately 6 square kilometres of marshes that no one had ever stepped into. The above mentioned peasant stumbled across it in the winter of 1940 when he went hunting. At the time it was extremely cold and the soil was frozen. If not for his own footprints in the snow the peasant would not have known how to return.

At the general meeting it was decided that each partisan detachment should supply four people who would help organize the hospital and serve as medics and security in the event of an attack.

This newly created division took to their work energetically. The first thing they did was create a camouflaged approach.

At the very end of the marsh was a small hill. As a result of storms and trees which were dynamited they laid two planks for a footbridge which one could barely cross. They placed the fallen trees in a way that it looked like that is how they fell. When the planks were not being used they were taken away. The branches of the trees were camouflaged with moss and tobacco so even dogs would not smell traces of human steps.

At the same time they prepared pieces of cotton, field beds, dirty and bloody bandages which would be scattered at the hill in the event of an alarm to fool the enemy that the hospital was there. This proved to be very smart. Thanks to this the hospital was actually saved a few times.

A special armed detachment was placed at the hill to protect the hospital, and whenever possible, fool the enemy.

At Work

Later, when all the preparations were ready we began to "build" the hospital.

Four tents were erected. There was no room for more in this limited space. One tent was designated for severely wounded, the second for lightly wounded. The third for the bakery and the medics and the fourth was where the doctors lived. There are a lot of good things to write about partisan doctors, especially the Jewish ones. I would like to mention a few of them that worked in the hospital.

Dr. Rakover, an internal medicine specialist from Novoredke ghetto gladly accepted the suggestion of the partisans to go to the forest. He was devoted and worked intensively. Until the hospital was founded he did not avoid any battles. He was always there to offer first aid.

Dr. Khaim Miesnik, a surgeon left the Lida ghetto, with his wife and a small child on a cold snowy day, and came to the forest. Thanks to his great professionalism, hundreds of severely wounded partisans were saved from death.

[Page 413]

Dr. Avrom Alpert left with his wife and small child on a terrifying journey in search of a resistance group which together with them would fight against the enemy. Later he would become the brigade doctor of "Fabieda".

We must also mention the doctors: Rozentzveyg, Golombovsky and Pupko. It is difficult to describe their working conditions, because even now it appears as a dream to those who experienced it.

The newly wounded were brought to the same tent as those who had already been operated on. The screams of the new arrival mixed with the moans of the others.

Carrying the sick over the narrow footbridge in rain, and freezing cold temperatures, and then to a crowded, damp tent with the most primitive means to administer first aid and often an immediate operation was no easy task.

Until August 1943 there was no anesthetic. The most difficult operations were done without narcotics. For a long time we did not even have cotton or gauze.

The Hospital is not Discovered

The German murderers knew about the existence of the partisan hospital in the forest. They devoted a lot of effort to discover and liquidate the hospital, but without success. There were times when they almost discovered our tracks. We believed they knew exactly where we were and would wander through the swamps with rubber boots and face nets against the mosquitos, searching, but returning with nothing…

On a few occasions we were able to hear their voices and curses from the hospital. Those were frightening moments.

The only comfort was the bullet that each of us had.

The Germans tried other ways to discover the hospital. However we only learned about it later after the following incident:

In the spring of 1943 a gorgeous Russian girl appeared in the village Demianovtse. She said she escaped from an echelon of deported Russian girls and we should direct her to a partisan group. Incidents like this happened often and we believed her.

That same day a partisan group from Varshilov's detachment returned from their assignment through that village. The commander of the detachment showed interest in the girl, questioned her, talked to her and took her with them.

In the forest, the commanders, as usual, began a rivalry to gain the sympathy of the beautiful girl. To everyone's surprise, she kept her distance while conscientiously and seriously carrying out the work she was given.

After three weeks with the detachment she asked them to give her work in her profession. She was a nurse. The partisan hospital needed nurses, so they fulfilled her request.

She immediately gained everyone's trust with her devotion to her work at the hospital. The patients would gladly talk to her, opening their hearts…

One night, a patient happened to hear her talking to another patient. The conversation sounded suspicious to him, particularly the issues she was asking the patient about. In the morning he told everything to the commander. They began to observe the girl. The suspicion was confirmed and she was immediately brought to an interrogation.

During the first few days she denied everything, but in the end she admitted her guilt and told the truth. This is what we learned:

The Germans set up a special school in Minsk for spying and diversion work. The school recruited young, beautiful Russian girls and taught them to spy on the partisans. They provided the girls with good food and drinks and for their parents as well so they could not resist the temptation. She was one of forty girls at the school. Each was trained for a specific task. Her assignment was to find the partisan hospital in Lipitchansk forest.

We received a lot of important information from this "nurse" on the last night of her life.

Early the next morning a partisan bullet settled accounts…this was the last attempt the Germans made to find our hospital.

[Page 414]

Partisan Heroes

by Sholem Gerling (Ramat – Gan)

Translated by Janie Respitz

Yisroel Busel

Yisroel Busel, a locksmith, was born and raised in Zhetl. His father was a blacksmith. He was one of the many unknown and forgotten Jewish partisans, who fought bravely and fell heroically in battle.

Let these lines about him, written by a friend, serve as a memorial light.

Lipitchansk forest. Partisan detachment "Barba". Commander: Kolya Vakhanin. The year, 1943. Yisroel Busel and I were in a Jewish company. Later the company was dissolved and scattered among various divisions. Yisroel Busel was sent to a company where he was one Jews among 65 Russians and White Russians. His company was taught special instructions, led by Captain Kovaliov and first Lieutenant Alexander Gorelik, they had special assignments: blow up railroads, block viaducts and send echelons flying through the air. This was difficult and dangerous work.

Besides mining railroads these guys would refurbish mines from old shells. An important source for raw material were the 25 kilogram bombs which they stole from the airfield between Shtutchin and Lida. The bombs were without explosive capsules, they were very large and difficult to transport and not easy to mine. Therefore they had to be refurbished and this cost a few lives.

Yisroel Busel was one of the most talented "mine producers". He quickly mastered the technique and devoted heart and soul to it. His comrades respected his work and he was loved by all.

At first everything went according to plan. After preparing the sufficient amount of mines they began the actual work: mining the railroads. The command was: not to allow enemy echelons to reach the front! The rail lines: Lida – Baranovitch, Baranovitch – Minsk, Volkovsky – Bialystock were seeded with explosives, and tens of enemy echelons began flying through the air…

The Germans were becoming more cautious. Every kilometre there was a guard who every minute would shoot a light rocket and light up the area. Every metre of the railroad was checked every morning by German military engineers who were specialists in mine searching. Among the various means the Germans used against mines, they thought of one which was practically impossible to solve. They would place very thin pieces of wood along the entire rail line which could not be seen in the dark. The partisans, laying the mines, would unknowingly step on these pieces of wood and in the morning it would be easy to find the spots where the mines were hidden and remove them without danger.

Tens of mines were lost because of this, with no results. It became harder to blow up the railroads which became more important by the day as they led directly to the front, Kursk – Ariel – Belograd, where the main assaults took place.

Our comrades were distraught, including Yisroel Busel. He would disappear for hours, tinkering with something but no one knew what. One day he called me aside and said:

"I want to trust you with a big secret. A finally invented a mine which explodes right after you place it, set off by the lightest movement. It is impossible to remove it from its spot without it exploding". I suggested he tell the commander about his invention.

Commander Gorelik was very excited and showed great interest. In his presence and the presence of other commanders and partisans Yisroel Busel, pale from excitement, demonstrated his mine and explained its construction. It was different from other mines because the explosion was not caused by pulling out a wire from the capsule, or strong pressure. His mine contained two capsules attached by a thin black thread which would explode from a gentle movement of the thread.

The results of the test surprised everyone. They lifted the inventor up in the air three times and in his honour shouted hurrah and kissed him…He later received a special gift from Moscow for his invention, a new pistol and an automatic rifle.

Soon there were results from Busel's important invention. Already on the second day of using his mine, two Ukrainians and two Germans were blown up on the spot.

[Page 415]

The same was repeated a second and third time resulting in chaos among the Germans. We received information from all sides that the Germans feared this secret mine. The Germans were afraid to approach these mines. Once again the enemy echelons began to fly through the air.

Yisroel Busel was not destined to enjoy the results of his invention for very long. In the summer of 1943 (around June), while carrying out an assignment on the railroad tracks from Lida to Baronovitch, not far from Novolieniye, he was killed by one of his own mines.

Six men went to the railroad. Busel and his friend Vasili Bashko buried the mine. The others were standing guard. It was a dark night and it was raining heavily. At a certain moment everyone shuddered from Busel's cry and right after a big explosion. They all ran away.

At the spot where they had decided to meet after completing the task, only 4 arrived. Yisroel and Vasili were missing.

After a few hours the four decided to return to the place of the explosion and look for their missing comrades.

Feeling their way in the darkness they found, near the exploded tracks, the limbs torn from Busel's and Vasili's bodies. Searching further, they stumbled across two massacred bodies of German patrols. It was clear: The attack by the German patrols was so unexpected, in order not to fall into enemy hands alive only one solution remained: blow themselves up with them…

He was 29 years old. Let his memory serve as a blessing.

Izye Rabinovitch

Izye Rabinovitch was born in Zhetl in 1928. He escaped from the ghetto and arrived in the forest in 1942. At first he was in the family camps.

Little Izye Rabinovitch did not like the family camp. He would come to our "post" every day and ask:

"Take me into the partisans".

Of course we sent him back. One day he snuck in to see the commander:

"Take me into the partisans! I will go with you everywhere. I can't sleep at night. I dream about terrible things…fear drives me out of the tent… take me in!"

"You are still a child, go "home"," answered the commander. He cried, fell to his feet and did not budge. They took him and sent him to feed the horses.

We were preparing a defence for an attack by the Brown Bandits, who were trying to penetrate the forest. We set up an ambush near the village Luditchi. Little Izye, now our coachman, brought us food every day with two female cooks. On the fifth night we were informed that 7 kilometres from our "ambush" at the Mirayshchine estate, a company of Latvians had consolidated. In order to liquidate this enemy we had to increase our strength. It was decided three ambush groups would gather secretly and work out a plan of attack. Our commander explained the assignment and ordered us to go to the meeting point. Little Rabinovitch was there, listened and said:

"I will go with you!" The commander, as usual in such a serious moment shouted at him angrily:

"You go back and bring back the women and the dishes!" Izye stood at attention and stammered: "The women can go on their own…coming here they held the reins very well…"

He said this in such a childlike, naïve way, everyone burst out laughing. The commander also smiled and softened.

"You don't have a gun, they will be shooting there. You could be killed. You better go home!!"

The little guy shook his head, tears welled up.

"How come you can all go where they are shooting and I can't? The commander should lend me his revolver…he also has a pistol…"

Even Yisroel Busel stood up for him:

"Let him come along. He'll help carry my reserve bullets for my machine gun". Finally the commander agreed.

With great joy little Izye grabbed the bag of reserve discs and headed out with quick steps.

During the attack on the Latvians which began exactly at 12 o'clock at night, Izye displayed rare boldness and fearlessness.

"Quick, lie down, bullets are flying!" shouted Yisroel Busel more than once. He didn't make a big deal of it and asked:

"Give me your machine gun for a while, I'll shoot once through the window, just once!"

After a 4-5 hour battle the Latvians ran away.

[Page 416]

We did not enter the estate right away as we were not sure if their silence was just a trick to fool us. We were also afraid of hidden mines.

Meanwhile, little Rabinovitch disappeared. We were waiting for it to become light (there was no longer any shooting), and then we saw, how he rode out from the estate on a horse and complained to everyone:

"What are you waiting for? The stable is full of horses!"

After that incident little Izye was assigned to a battle group in my division and alongside everyone else fulfilled many difficult and important tasks. His work was still to carry reserve discs for machine guns. He learned how to handle a machine gun and understood its construction. He also had his own gun which he protected with his life. It was always shining, was always in order, even in 1942 during the fiercest raids when there was not even enough time to wash your face.

It did not take long before he received something he didn't even dare dream about: his own machine gun.

I was successful in obtaining another machine gun and knowing that Izye could handle it, and no one would care for it like him, I decided to give it to him. Are there words to describe his joy?

A short time later we left for the Kurfish forests to build a new camp. One day, Izye came running and told me that Boris (with the wart), a well known partisan, asked him to lend him his machine gun because they were going on an assignment on the other side of the Nieman.

"You can lend it to him, but take a gun in return so you don't remain unarmed".

"No," said the little Jewish partisan. "I will not let the machine gun out of my hands, I prefer to go with them on this assignment"…and he left.

There were six men. Five Russians, and he was the sixth. They crossed the Nieman and arrived at the designated place. Three went into the house and three remained standing on the street on guard. Izye was among the last. He stood with his machine gun at the crossroad. He stood there with no idea what danger was looming.

"Good" neighbours immediately informed the German guard at the nearby headquarters. In less than an hour they were surrounded. Disguised in peasant's clothing the murderers snuck behind Izye's back and shot him. The others did not hear the shot and did not know what happened. They too were soon surrounded and they could not defend themselves. They were burned together with the house. One of the guards managed to get away.

Despite all our efforts, we did not find the corpse of the young Jewish partisan Izye Rabinovitch. We were not destined to give him the last honours he deserved. May his soul be bound among the living!

Areleh and Shloymeleh

On a cold February night two black boxes were brought by boat to the village Golubi on the Nieman. We unloaded them very carefully and put them on the shore. According to information received by our detachment we understood the boxes were the coffins of two young Jewish partisans, Shloyme Itzkovitch, who was born in Baranovitch in 1928 and Arel Haydukovsky, born in Zhetl in 1927, who were carrying out an assignment on the other side of the Nieman and were killed.

Arel Haydukovsky arrived in the forest along with all the other Jews who escaped from Zhetl, on August 8th 1942. Disregarding his young age, from the very first day he was ready to participate boldly in all dangerous operations. He was loved right away by all the partisans in our detachment and gained respect, like an equal adult comrade.

When Jewish partisans, with the permission from the commanders entered the surrounding ghetto to rescue Jews and bring them to the forest, the young, small Arel was among the first to report for this mission. Together with two other Jewish partisans we went to save the Jews from Novogrudek.

It was far, approximately 50 kilometres, and we had to go through various dirt roads and detours. The biggest danger loomed around the ghetto. It was surrounded by an open field watched carefully by the armed enemy!

Arel and his friends entered the ghetto with those returning from work. Disregarding all the dangers connected to leaving the ghetto, many Jews turned to him.

[Page 417]

Unfortunately, the first time they were only able to save 8 – 10 people.

The best specialists and professionals were in Novogrudek ghetto, having been selected from other surrounding ghettos which had been liquidated. They all lived in a few houses and wore a number. They were counted a few times every night. Besides this, their clothing was so apparent, every peasant would recognize them immediately making it very risky.

During the day when the ghetto was least guarded the barbed wire was cut in a specific spot, and at dusk, before they lit the large projectors, those chosen to leave crawled out one at a time. The first to leave were the three partisans and they prepared for any incident.

This is how many Jews were saved.

A few weeks later, Areleh Haydukovsky and four others left for the second time. Once again, with the help of this young man Jews were saved from the murderer's claws. Among others, at that time Dr. Rakover joined the partisans and later did a lot for the partisan hospital.

The young Arel Haydukvosky did not display any less heroism in other operations which as a minor he participated in on his own free will. He voluntarily presented himself and asked them to let him go along. He took part in and excelled in the liquidation of the German garrison in Zhaludek, 25 kilometres on the other side of the Nieman (April 1943); and participated with the others in the famous "Train track attack".

This is when his friendship began with Shloyme Itzikovitch, the second young heroic partisan in our detachment.

There is a lot to tell about Shloyme Itzikovitch. It is simply astonishing how this small Jewish boy was so bold and fearless. I remember, among others, this incident:

It was around April 1943. Our detachment took up a defence position near the Nieman, protecting ourselves from the White Poles on the other river bank. Having been in one place for a long time we decided to send out reconnaissance to the enemy. Shloyme Itzkovitch took this mission upon himself. He presented himself to the company commander with the request for permission to sail across the river. They wanted to send an adult with him because he could not row.

When they arrived on the other side, his comrade sat in the boat and Shloymele left for the village. He went into the first peasant farmhouse and asked from the doorstep if there were any Poles in the village. Here was an unfamiliar boy, in broad daylight, with a gun bigger than him. Understandably this was cause for concern in the farmhouse. The woman there asked him with compassion:

"What's your name, little boy?"

He replied curtly and audaciously:

"Me? Partisan!"

That's when the woman cried out in fear:

"Run away, run away! They are in the village, the Poles…"

But Shloymele Itzikovitch asked calmly: "How many are there and how often do they come to the river bank?"

The peasant's warning for him to leave quickly did not help. He told him to go to the river and he will tell him everything.

The little partisan wanted everything on the spot and to be informed immediately. Then he demanded: prepare food for a few partisans and two pairs of underwear! He stood at the door:

"Nobody can leave the house, if you do, I'll shoot!"

At first glance the whole thing appeared comical, but when the little guy grabbed his gun, opened the lock, loaded a bullet in the barrel and put his finger on the trigger, everyone present in the house became very serious.

They sailed back late at night. No one slept. Everyone, including the company commander, lay in the barn anxiously waiting. As soon as they heard movement, everyone got up.

"Who's there?" Then they heard a child's voice answer:

"it's us!…"

The joy in the barn was indescribable. We took him in and the commander hugged him with true fatherly love.

"So, tell us!"

In the darkness, no one noticed the package under his arm. He told us what happened calmly and leisurely, not leaving out a detail about what he did and what he managed to learn. The more he spoke, the more it sounded like a made up story.

It was quite amazing! To cross the river where no other partisan dared to go and returned safely!

[Page 418]

Some people doubted his story, until Shloymele spread his arms and with a mysterious smile said:

"People, come and eat!" (He said this in Russian).

And to everyone's surprise he opened the package that was lying beside him, untied a peasant kerchief and took out a jar of honey, a large pack of butter and a few pieces of hard cheese. He kept the two pairs of underwear for himself and his friend Haydukovsky.

The enthusiasm was great. They grabbed him, kissed him and threw him up in the air. After the feast they made him a full fledged partisan and gave him an honourable place to sleep. However he refused and said:

"It's my turn at the guard post".

"No!" everyone shouted spontaneously, "go to sleep, we'll go instead of you".

A command came: Blow up the railroad tracks in all of White Russia. Explosives were sent by airplane for this purpose from Moscow. Everyone received 3 pieces of explosive material and we had to use it to blow up around three miles of three separate train lines.

Arel Haydukovsky and Shloymele Itzkovitch decided to carry out this mission together. The successful completion of this assignment brought them even closer and strengthened their friendship. From then on they were always seen together. They also went together to their last assignment!

January 1944. The train tracks from Rozhon to Baronovitch, which goes to Minsk, and was located in our region and had to be blown up at any cost!

The difficulty was not only in mining the tracks, but in swimming across the Nieman to the place where there were not only Germans rampant, but White Poles as well. Due to a lack of explosives, not everyone could be trusted with such a mission. When discussing who should take on this special task, from almost 300 partisans, two children's voices called out:

"We will do it!" This was Arel Haydukovsky and Shloymele Itzkovitch.

They left that same night. We never saw them alive again.

Opening the boxes, a horrific picture unfolded before our eyes: Arel Haydukovsky's skin was covered with bruises and shot in a few places. Clearly, he fought back against the enemy. Shloymele Itzkovitch was lying still, as if sleeping, with a smile on his face. It felt like he would soon wake up from his sleep.

They were buried together in a common grave in the forest at a crossroad. The entire detachment was present including the leadership. The commissar delivered a sad eulogy, enumerating the heroic deeds of these two young partisans who fell in the name of freedom and for humanity while honouring their people. Their coffins were lowered into the grave and a command was given:

"Salute!"

Three shots rang out in the quiet forest from diverse weapons.

A provisional tombstone made from wood was placed on their grave with the following inscription (in Russian) "Honour these heroes for eternity".

Shloymele Shifmanovitch

Shloymele Shifmanovitch came to Zhetl from the nearby town of Zholudok after the liquidation of that ghetto in 1942. He managed to escape as he did not look Jewish.

Having no place to live, young Shloyme went to the House of Study. He lived there barefoot and hungry. After a while, three other boys he did not know "moved in". They had escaped from the work camp in Novogrudek: Binyomin Yursih, Khaim Slamkeh, Yosl Bitensky and Shepsl. (They would all be killed as partisans except for Yurish).Through them the partisan headquarters in Zhetl had secret contact with Peysakh Finklshteyn.

Shepsl, a tall healthy young man, with a serious proud expression on his face, would often, with tear filled eyes, tell his comrades about his wife and child who were killed. Shloymele, who heard this story more than once, could not understand one thing: where did Shepsl and the other three disappear for the whole night? Not able to fall asleep in the empty House of Study he lay there and waited for them.

"Tell me" he asked Shepsele quietly when he returned, "you always talk about your wife and child, but then you go out all night to have a good time?"

Shepsl smiled at him and thought: "Can I tell him the truth?"

One day, Shepsl and Yosel left on a mission from headquarters to the village Kashkali, to a certain peasant Pranyuk, to get some weapons.

[Page 419]

Berl Monkovitch went with them. The trip there and back was around 45 kilometres. They left the ghetto at 9 o'clock at night and returned at dawn with the entire treasure: 3 hand grenades, a few bullets and an "Otrez", (a gun cut off at both ends making it easier to mask). The weapons could not be placed at the regular spot so Shepsl brought the "Otrez" to the House of Study and hid it in a lectern.

Later, when Shepsl got up Shloymele went to him and embarrassed said:

"Now I know you don't go out to have a good time".

"What do you know now that you did not know before?" asked Shepsl with a smile.

"I saw what you hid in the lectern". Shepsl became serious.

"Someone as young as you should not know about these things! Don't you dare tell anyone! Bad things will happen to you! Do you hear?"

Shloymele swore on all things holy he wouldn't tell anyone. Then he asked:

"Take me with you, wherever you go. By all means test me. I am very familiar with the roads. I will do everything you ask of me. Will you take me along?"

"We'll see" answered Shepsl, a little gentler.

He looked at the little Jewish boy who looked like a gentile and thought to himself: with his curly hair, bare feet and tattered clothes he looks like a true shepherd…he can even go on missions further away and during the day.

We must discuss this.

Shepsl spoke to me about this the next day.

"Good," I said. "Send him to me".

And this is how Shloymele became our trusted man.

Quiet, serious, compliant and very secretive he was very useful in our underground work. He did not talk a lot or make a lot of noise. He did not interfere. He carried out everything we asked him to do with precision.

One day he was sent on a mission to the forest. When he returned to the ghetto the next day he said to me:

"I will not remain here. I'm going to the forest. I don't want to be here any longer!"

What will such a young boy do in the forest" I thought to myself, but then said aloud:

"Go, and may you be guided by a lucky star!"

And he left.

We heard he was a shepherd who brought horses to pasture that belonged to the artillery. We did not know if this was true.

One night, when I was already in the forest, the partisans carried out a large operation. They had to destroy a large alcohol factory which was located in Mayontek Zhukovchizne.

It was late at night. The companies began to arrive at the meeting point. The artillery were also approaching. I was deep in conversation with my friend, a partisan, and suddenly someone fell on top of me and started kissing me.

"Shloymele Shifmanovitch! How did you get here? And how did you recognize me in the dark?"

"From your voice" he said, and told me he was in the partisan artillery.

The resistance of the enemy was weak, and after one hour of fighting we entered the estate. Our trophies were meaningful: live inventory, wagons of tobacco, bottles of alcohol, butter and cheese. What we were not able to take, we destroyed.

Shloymele Shifmanovitch, like an old artillery man, rode among the first. From that day on I met him often.

In July 1943 a new detachment was formed whose task was to block the newly established German garrison in the village Ruda – Yavarska. Shloymeleh was assigned to that detachment as reconnaissance. Soon this little "spy" was popular among all the partisans. He would never return from a mission without exact information. With his joy, and his childlike heartfelt smile he was loved by all. It would never have occurred to anyone that he was a spy.

In February 1944 we went with the detachment to assault the German garrison in the above mentioned village. In the first attack they captured two bunkers taking 76 prisoners. The remaining two bunkers were desperately defended.

Yerakhmiel LIkhter (machine gunner number 1) and Shloymele Shifmanovitch (number 2) crawled up to the little bunker window the Germans were shooting out of. Yerakhmiel Likhter was killed on the spot.

Shloymele was badly wounded in the stomach. They barely were able to remove him alive from the hail of bullets.

They took him directly to the partisan hospital where after two days of suffering, he died.

[Page 420]

Short Biographies of Zhetl's Partisan Heroes
Who Fell Fighting Hitler's Bandits

Translated by Janie Respitz

Berl Ivenitsky of blessed memory

Berl Ivenitsky was born in Zhetl in 1921. He graduated high school and was a bookkeeper by profession. He was loved in the detachment and was a happy fellow. In the evening he would sing by the bonfires and bring pleasure to his friends with his beautiful voice.

In September 1942 he arrived in the forest from Novogrudek ghetto. He belonged to Kaplinsky's group, and later the third Jewish company in the "Barba" detachment.

He participated in almost all battles. Then he was sent to the headquarters of the brigade and its economic group. Due to anti – Semitic tendencies he was sent to one of the detachments of the Varashilovsky Brigade where he remained until liberation.

After liberation he was mobilized in battle against Nazi bandits and in 1944 he died heroically fortifying the Narev River. He was buried in that region.

After experiencing so many battles, he did not survive to see the total downfall of German fascism.

Avrom Hirsh Indershteyn of blessed memory

Avrom Indershteyn was born in Zhetl in 1892. He arrived from the Zhetl ghetto in August 1942. He worked in Kaplinsky's group as the detachment's tailor. He was a quiet, modest man. He clothed all the partisans. He was killed during the big raid of 1942 and was buried in the forest, not far from the hamlet Karshuk.

Yosef Alpert of blessed memory

Yosef Alpert was born in Zhetl. As a boy of 14-15 he arrived in the forest right after the first slaughter and settled into the family camp. A few months later, when his two brothers arrived from Novogurdek ghetto (Avrom and Berish) and joined Kaplinsky in his division, they took him from the family camp and he became a shepherd in the "Barba" detachment of the Lenin Brigade.

At the beginning of 1943 when the Lenin Brigade created the Lenin detachment, little Yosef and his brother Avrom and his sister in law were sent to the new detachment. There he was used for small operations as well as local guard duty.

One evening, when the young Yosef was at his post, he fell asleep and the anti –Semitic commander, Volentin, not taking his young age into consideration, shot him for this "crime". He was buried in the Lipitchansk forest.

Yitzkhak Alter of blessed memory

Yitzkhak Alpert was born in Zhetl in 1920. His was a harness maker. He arrived in the forest from the Novogrudek camp in October 1942 and joined Kaplinsky's Jewish group. He participated in almost all the battles. Besides this he worked as a saddle maker for the detachment and would make saddles, combat knives, pocket weapons etc…

He was a quiet, calm, modest and obedient partisan. He had a warm relationship with the family groups, to whom he would give everything he had. In July 1943 he escaped with 25 men to Nolibok forest due to the frightful anti –Semitism which dominated the Orliansky detachment.

In Nolibok he joined the Ordzhenkidzhe detachment where he proved to be one of the best partisans. After liberation he worked for a while in Baranovitch and then joined the Red Army and was killed in battle against the Germans. It is not known exactly where he fell and where he was buried.

Sholem Bom of blessed memory

Sholem Bom worked as a teacher in the Yiddish school in Zhetl. As a graduate from a Polish teacher's seminary he came to Zhetl in 1935 – 1936 from a town in the Vilna region.

[Page 421]

He was very talented especially as a music and art teacher. He organized magnificent choirs with the school children as well as adults, who would often perform for the benefit of the Yiddish school. I can see him standing before me, black haired, energetic young man who possessed an incredible amount of energy and was very ambitious. He put much of his talent into the choir as well as amateur circles at the school.

This is how his life flowed until the outbreak of the German – Soviet war. When the war broke out in 1941 he found himself in the ranks of the Red Army. During a retreat to the east his division was probably surrounded by the Germans and they were unable to unite with the Red Army.

It is not known how he arrived in the Lipitchansk forest, either he escaped from German captivity or broke away from the siege. In general, this period of his life and his further heroic activity is draped in mystery.

There were a few opinions. Some said he betrayed the Jewish people for a "whisky". I will make an effort to evaluate his personality objectively, paying attention the material which has remained about him. I will make an effort to briefly impart his heroic struggle in the partisan movement and his tragic death.

He arrived in the Lipitchansk forest at the beginning of 1942, when the amount of partisans could still be counted on your fingers. He came from around Lida where he had previously operated as a legendary commander under the Polish name "Khadzietsky". As a Pole it was easy for him to move through the Polish regions where he was loved by the Poles who provided him with information and weapons.

When he arrived in Lipitchansk he was already a commander of a detachment which was called "Lider". Later, the Varashilovsky detachment emerged from the "Lider" detachment in the Lenin Brigade, which was known for its anti –Semitism and killing Jews.

We were told he would walk around in a long leather coat with a belt, armed with an automatic gun. His attitude toward Kaplinsky's Jewish group was cold. This resulted in hatred and disdain toward him but in his situation he could not behave differently. The Christian partisans did not know the brave commander Khadzietsky was a Jew. This was his luck. Thanks to this he was able to play this leading role. However the secret could not be kept for long. At the time there were many Zhetl Jews around who knew him. This passed from Jewish mouths to Christian ears.

Khadzietsky also began to feel uncomfortable. It must be said that pretending to be a Pole was useful. He was loved and received an exceptional amount of weapons. His group was the richest in war materials thanks to his personal influence and respect by the Poles.

Hearing what was happening to Jews in the surrounding towns and seeing the problems Jewish partisans were facing in the forest, he began to revise his attitude regarding the Jews.

He also remembered his gorgeous wife and child who were in the Zhetl ghetto. He sent messengers a few times to his wife wanting to bring her to the forest. However his wife betrayed him with a White Russian policeman who was serving the Germans. Disregarding this fact he sent a few trusted messengers to get her. She never left the ghetto.

This all affected him. Analyzing the Jewish situation in the ghetto and the forest, remembering his ties to the Jewish masses, he decided he devoted his efforts to the fight against the German occupant, however his energy and talents were given to the Jewish partisan groups helping them obtain a dignified position.

He then decided to secretly go over to Kaplinsky's group but he did not want to go with empty hands. He wanted to bring all the ammunition he had hidden.

The Christian partisans from his group learned about this as well as the subsequent leader, Commander Petiye Makorov, for who Khadzietsky was like a thorn in his side. Makorov and a group of anti- Semites decided to get rid of their Jewish commander. Commander Khadzietsky had a devoted adjutant, Leonke, who never parted from him and stood beside him until the last day like iron and steel.

Petiye Makorov and his comrades decided to kill Khavdzievsky and his adjutant. In order not to have any witnesses they invited him on a walk in the nearby village, and riding there on horses they shot Khadzievsky and Leonke in the back with an automatic gun and buried them in the marshes.

The shameful murderers later defended their actions saying Khadzietsky wanted to betray them and wanted to go over to the Jews and give them all the weapons.

[Page 422]

The truth was, it was a power struggle.

The crime was kept secret and even after liberation Petiye Makorov was not held responsible.

This is how one of the creators of the partisan group in Lipitchansk forest was killed. This man could have achieved so much more in the fight against the German fascists. His character must be eternalized as a partisan commander who brought the Jews a lot of honour.

Sholem Busel of blessed memory

Sholem Busel was born in Zhetl. He was a locksmith by profession. While in the ghetto he was the first one ready to join the partisans in order tot take revenge on the German murderers.

He was very helpful to the Zhetl underground organization. He stored the collected weapons in his cellar and was always busy polishing and repairing the weapons. He had his own pistol which was more precious to him than anything else thinking he could take revenge with it.

During the second slaughter, together with Shepsl, Frenkl and Kantorovitch, with the revolver in his hand, he broke through the first and second barriers and died heroically at the third. The Germans paid dearly for his life.

Yosef Bushlin of blessed memory

Yosef Bushlin, the son of a Zhetl blacksmith was born in 1923. He was of middle height with a solid build, a blacksmith by profession. He came to the forest from the Novogrudek ghetto with his father and brother. They joined Hirshl Kaplinsky's Jewish group. His father and brother settled into the family group, and later in the third company of the Orliansky detachment. He participated in many operations and diversion assignments.

Together with a group of 25 he left for the east in 1943, later in "Ordzhenikidze". He displayed great bravery in battles with the White Poles and received government distinction for ambushes against the German and Ukrainian police not far from "Hute Shklame" (in the Lida region), and a second distinction for the battle with the White Poles in Dokudova (Lida region).

Ruven Berkovsky of blessed memory

Ruven Berkovsly arrived in August 1942 from the Zhetl ghetto. He was 35 years old. He worked as a cutter of shoe leather, first in the Jewish company and later in the general detachment. He also took part in battles with a weapon in hand. He helped to make sure the Jewish partisans did not go barefoot.

He was killed before liberation during the last raid in 1944. When the entire ghetto was blocked a group of partisans decided to tear through the blockade. A group of 25 which did not succeed get away were besieged by the enemy and a few were captured alive by the Germans, including Ruven Berkovsky. They brought him to Zhetl and shot him one day before the arrival of the Red Army.

Mayrim Dvoretzky

Mayrim Dvoretzky was born in Zhetl in 1914. He came to the forest from the Zhetl ghetto in August 1942 and was killed in February 1943 on his way to carry out an economic assignment for the detachment as the first sergeant of the division.

He was killed under the following circumstances: He was in the village Romanovitch (Zhetl region) with Yoyne Brestovitsky, Moishe Mankovitch and Soreh Alpert who belonged to the family groups. They were sitting in a peasant's house and talking to three partisans from the bandit –like neighbouring detachment (Lida detachment). Suddenly, the Lida partisans took their revolvers out of their pockets, aimed them at their heads and demanded they hand over their weapons and go outside to the street. Once outside on the street they opened fire where Mayrim Dvoretzky was first seriously wounded and then killed.

Moishe Mankovitch was wounded in his hand and managed to escape under a hail of bullets. Mrs. Alpert was dragged, raped, shot and thrown into a hole filled with potatoes. The murderers were Kolke the bandit and Vanke the bandit.

The Russian commanders and Captain Sinitchkin knew very well who the murderers were, but they did not take any measures against them. There is one witness of this incident still alive today: the partisan Moishe Mankovitch who remained an invalid his whole life.

Dvoretzky participated in many battles as first sergeant. He was very diligent, disciplined and provided the partisans with all necessities. They brought him from the village Romanovitch and buried him near the Ludzhitch lighthouse, with a military salute.

[Page 423]

Alter Dvoretzky of blessed memory

Alter Dvoretzky was born in 1906 in Zhetl. He was the son of well off parents. At a young age he graduated from high school in Grodno and in 1922 went to Germany to study in a polytechnic institute. During years of great inflation he had to stop studying due to financial reasons. He quit his studies and returned to Poland.

He entered a Polish high school, completed his matriculation and tried to get accepted to medicine, but because he was a Jew, he was not accepted. He spent one year auditing courses at Warsaw University. However this did not satisfy him so he went to Vilna to study law.

This is where he began to show interest in communal work. He joined the Zionist – Socialist association at the student union. Soon he was in the top ranks of the Zionist association, giving lectures and getting involved in broader political work. He was loved by his friends.

During his vacation he would come to Zhetl and carry out diversified work for the Labour Zionists, organizing various cultural events, communal trials, where he would appear as the accuser or the defense. He possessed rare talents, was very smart, intelligent and was loved even by his opponents. He was interested in everyone and everything. He was interested in sports, and believed in the expression that only a healthy body could have a healthy spirit. He organized a sports team, a football (soccer) team and participated himself. He was considered one of the best athletes among the youth in Zhetl.

"I will now break an old conception of small town Jews, that believe that sports are not appropriated for grown ups, especially a student who will soon be a lawyer" he would say.

His university studies proved to be very difficult due to great anti- Semitic tendencies which dominated the professors at Vilna University. They tried through all possible means to make things as difficult as possible for Jewish students in order to reduce the amount of Jewish lawyers. However, he persevered and a after a few years receive the title Master's of Law. But this is when his real suffering began. He could not earn a living and had to undergo a difficult path to get clients and practice law.

At this time he married and had a little son. His parents were impoverished and he had to try to get by. He did not lose his courage or energy. He continued to work, becoming a court intern and at the same time, was active in the party where he devoted a lot of time, energy and love. After many long difficult years he finally, on the eve of the fall of the Polish state, received the title of lawyer.

The year 1939 brought upheaval. The Soviets arrive. He must now, as a political activist with Zionist tones, only involve himself in his professional work. He quickly became one of the most beloved and talented lawyers in the Baranovitch region.

However, this did not last long, only until the arrival of the German hordes. When they had to, in these dark bitter times choose a representative from the Zhetl Jewish community, he was chosen as the chairman of the so called "Judenrat" (Jewish Council). He displayed exceptional organizational talents and did the job keeping the Jewish youth in mind. The clever, farsighted Alter Dvoretzky foresaw, this was the devil's game and not the way to save Jewish lives and Jewish honour.

He had the idea to organize the Jewish youth in the ghetto to fight. His idea was to collect weapons and prepare the Jewish youth to go the forest as an armed force to take revenge on the German executioners and to save those who could not fight.

His idea was grandiose. He was not only thinking about the youth from Zhetl, but all the Jewish youth from surrounding towns. To achieve this goal he secretly organized a partisan headquarters in the Zhetl ghetto. He led this work in incredibly difficult conditions having to deal with opposition from many Jews who were afraid to call the bear from the forest. He understood, in any case, what he needed to do. Therefore, disregarding everyone, carried out his holy work, risking his life at every minute. While in the ghetto and having contact with the Germans, he was always armed with an automatic pistol, so he could, at the appropriate moment, take revenge on a fascist murderer. For details about his secret work, the partisan headquarters and his heroic death, you can read about it in the section about the History of Zhetl in the article about the underground movement.

Aron Haydukivsky of blessed memory

Aron Haydukovsky was born in 1928 in Zhetl. He came to the forest from the Zhetl ghetto in August, 1942.

[Page 424]

He had a brother in the same detachment and his father, sister and another brother in the family group. He was short, had an athletic build and black hair, somewhat myopic. He was very cheerful.

He was killed in January 1944 in a village across from "Golub" on the right side of the Nieman, walking with his friend Shloymele Itzkovitch with a mine to blow up the train tracks.

He was one of the brave partisans, participated in all battles and ambushes. He had a kind heart for the family groups always felt the responsibility to support them, even though it was dangerous to remove himself from the detachment. He was buried together with his friend Itzkovitch near the lighthouse, in the partisan cemetery, near the farmhouse of the peasant Matzukevitch.

Yehoshua Haydukovsky of blessed memory

Yehoshua Haydukovsky was born in Zhetl in 1906. He came to the forest in August 1942. He lost a wife and two children in the ghetto. He was a leather cutter by profession. He was killed carrying out an act of revenge on a police family in the village Trikhotky near Ruda – Yavarsky under the following circumstances:

When the partisans started shooting, someone from the police family ran through the door where Haydukovsky was standing. His friend who opened fire on the escapee accidentally hit Haydukovsky who died on the spot. They brought him to the detachment and buried him in the partisan cemetery near the lighthouse not far from Matzukevitch's farm.

Ruven Khlebnik of blessed memory

Ruven Khlebnik was born in Zhetl in 1915. He was a Yeshiva student. He arrived in the forest from the Zhetl ghetto on August 1942. He belonged to Kaplinsky's group and participated in a few battles until the second raid in 1943.

During the spring raid he was left in Baylsky's family group because he did not have a good gun. Later, when a group of 25 Jewish partisans escaped from "Barba" in the Nolibok forest, they took him with them and he joined the Ordzhenikidzhe detachment, Kiravk, which was active in the Lida region.

After liberation he left for the front. He was wounded twice and met his heroic death fighting the German executioners. His place of burial is unknown.

Leyzer Leybovitch of blessed memory

Leyzer Leybovitch was from Zhetl (Tcherne the miller's grandchild). He arrived in the forest from the Zhetl ghetto after the second slaughter and joined Kaplinsky's Jewish group. Although he was just a boy of 16-17 he was among the talented fighters, participating in a few battles and ambushes. Together with the 25 who escaped from "Barba" he joined the Ordzhenikidzhe detachment and was later killed on the front near Warsaw.

Mendl Mankovitch of blessed memory

Mendl Mankovitch was born in 1922 in Zhetl. He arrived from Zhetl ghetto in August 1942 and died from typhus in March 1943. The great typhus epidemic broke out during the large raid in December 1942. Due to the difficult sanitary conditions people had to live in, there were many victims.

He participated in all the battles and ambushes until he got sick. He was very brave and courageous and excelled in cold blooded attacks. He took upon himself all the difficult spying operations even when they were extremely dangerous. He was not afraid and completed all of his tasks. As a partisan and comrade he was disciplined and devoted. He was buried on the hill near the partisan hospital.

Yoyne Medvedsky of blessed memory

Yoyne Medvedsky was born in 1918 in Zhetl. He belonged to the secret partisan movement in the Zhetl ghetto. He helped to collect weapons in the ghetto and stored them in his cellar. He was sent a few times as a messenger from the ghetto to the forest to Alter Dvoretzky. In the end he was captured in the slaughter in Zhetl at which time he was sent with another 200 workers to the camp in Novogrudek.

He escaped from Novogudek and in August 1942 came to the forest and joined the Jewish group. For a long time he was commander of the division. Later, when Kaplinsky's group united with the Christian partisans, he remained division commander.

He participated in all the battles and ambushes in the forest. He excelled in battle, collected weapons for the detachment and in the first half of 1943 was sent with many others to the Lenin Detachment. There, he was among the outstanding partisans. Four blown up echelons can be attributed to him.

[Page 425]

At the end of 1943 he moved to the newly created Red Guard Detachment, where he remained until liberation. In this detachment he partook in two great battles against the Germans, and two train explosions and a difficult battle against the White Polish bandits at the Nieman, near the village Stukali (Zhalud Region). The battle lasted two hours. In the interim they destroyed the boat he used to cross the Nieman and he fell into the river. Barely alive, he managed to save himself and return to his detachment.

After liberation, he went with the entire unit to the front. He fought at Volkovisk, Lomzha, Zambrov, and Ostralenka. It was there he was wounded. Once he recovered he was wounded again, sent to hospital and provisionally released. He settled in the town of Bialo – Podloska with his wife (Sholem Pialun's sister) who had also been a partisan the entire time.

He died under the following circumstances:

Travelling by train, he was attacked at the station near Mezritch by Polish reactionaries and shot. At the same time a Jewish girl was also shot and a Jewish boy was severely wounded. This was in 1945. He was buried in the Jewish cemetery in Mezritch.

After experiencing so many battles, this is how one of the bravest partisans died.

Yitzkhak Sovitsky of blessed memory

Ytzkhak Sovitsky was born in 1914 in Zhetl. He arrived in the forest from the Zhetl ghetto in August 1942. He was short with blond hair and full of life. He was a house painter by profession and was killed under the following circumstances:

During the attack on the garrison in Aruda – Yavarska at the end of March 1944 he was accused of retreating too quickly from the battle and as a result of a command from the commanders of the Lenin detachment, he was shot.

The commanders, with the anti-Semitic commander Volentin were not successful in the battle. According to their plan they were supposed to liquidate the entire garrison, however due to poor organization they only succeeded in destroying one bunker and 80 men were taken prisoner.

There were many losses among the partisans. Six partisans were killed who were sent to destroy the German bunker with grenades. Included among the dead were: Shloyme Shifmanovitch, Yerakhmiel Likhter and Bekenshteyn from Deretchin.

Volentin, wanting to wipe away the failure and find a scapegoat to blame, took advantage of the moment and killed Itche Sovitsky, accusing him of retreating too quickly. He was buried in the forest not far from the village Ruda – Lipitchanska.

As a partisan in the "Barba" detachment, in November 1942 with a group of friends: Nosn Funt, Shaknovitch Yehoshua and others, he went to the Lida ghetto and brought 10 men, including Dr. Miesnik and his family who was our head surgeon and performed many complicated operations in extraordinarily difficult and primitive conditions. The famous partisan Borukh Levin also arrived with them.

Shaul Sovitzky of blessed memory

Shaul Sovitsky was born in 1917 in Zhetl. He arrived in Novogrudek labour camp in September 1942. He fell victim to anti – Semitism during the first raid.

During the large, terrifying winter raid, the partisan split. In the freezing cold and snow they were without shoes and socks. On his way to an economic operation, Sovitsky took a pair of boots from a peasant who was a German collaborator. He put them on right away and left his old pair for the peasant to repair. The commanders used this opportunity to kill another Jewish partisan while raising the level of discipline among the partisans. In accordance with a command by commander Sinitchkin, he was sentenced to death.

The verdict was supposed to be carried out by the commander of the detachment Kolya Vakhanin and the official at the time Vorotilo and his assistant Grishko Kozak. However the condemned managed to escape before the sentence was carried out under the following circumstances:

He asked if his death sentence could be replaced by dangerous diversion work, but they refused. They searched him and found a gun hidden under his belt. They suspected he was planning to attack them. Sovitsky once again asked commander Kolya to change his punishment, and when he once again received a negative response he requested a final wish before he died: a smoke. They permitted it and taking advantage of the moment, he escaped.

[Page 426]

They began to hunt him down. Participating in the hunt were Grishko Kozak and Misha Kretov. He was wounded in the chase, and from the blood stains in the snow, they found him in the family group in Ludzhitch forest at Berl Yokhe's from Zhetl.

Grishko Kozak demanded he come out of the tent. If not he would throw a grenade and kill all the others who were in there. Not wanting innocent people to be killed because of him he came out and took off the boots. His last request was they give the boots to his wife. He said goodbye to all the Jews, lay down in the snow with his face down and the bandit Grishko Kozak carried out his sentence. Sadly, he struggled for a long time with death. The murderer took the boots for himself.

In the detachment he carried out his duties as a good machine gunner, took part in many battles, ambushes and diversion assignments, was a disciplined comrade and was killed due to the anti –Semitism of the enemy. He was buried near the lighthouse in Ludzhitch.

Hirshl Patzovsky of blessed memory

Hirshl Patzovsky was born on October 30th, 1915 in Zhetl. He died fighting in Nolibok forest on July 9th 1944 and was buried the same day in a communal grave in Bielsky's detachment.

He was one of the working boys who after a day of hard work spent the late hours reading books to deepen their knowledge.

Hirshl Patzovsky of blessed memory

At a young age he lost his mother and looked for comfort in communal work. He was a member of Hashomer Hatzair. Later, he connected his fate with the socialist movement and became active in the professional activity in Zhetl.

In 1937 he was arrested as a member of the board of the Building Union and was sent to jail in Novogrudek.

After his release he was mobilized to the Polish army.

During the Polish – German war in 1939, he fought near the Prussian border and later was one of the defenders of Warsaw. On the 28th of September, 1939, when Warsaw capitulated, he was taken prisoner by the Germans.

Later, when the Soviet army liberated western White Russia and the Ukraine, he returned home. On August 6th, 1942, when Zhetl became rid of Jews, he was sent, together with 150 Jews to the Novogrudek ghetto workshops.

He suffered from hunger and beatings. He became sick, swollen and began spitting up blood. This is when the grandiose plan was made to build a tunnel. He was one of the 235 to escape from the tunnel.

After much wandering he arrived in Bielsky's detachment. He suffered both morally and physically, due to the great contrast in living standards of people. They knew in the detachment he was a carpenter, and not a bad one. He harnessed all his energy and built tents, actually palaces, a theatre, workshops, the headquarters, the sausage department, the bakery and tent after tent.

From time to time he left on operations. His comrades could not praise his boldness high enough. Often when he was standing ready with his gun prepared to leave, headquarters would stop him from going as something needed to be built. When the German defeat was approaching he was sent with others to guard the nearby airfield and roads. His group fought the Germans. During an outing they met the Red Army.

On July 9th 1944 he was sent with his group to guard the headquarters. At dawn a German division attacked the camp. A Russian major led a group of partisans shouting hurrah against the enemy. A battle ensued. Shamefully, many armed men from the Bielsky detachment ran away, together with the women and the elderly. Those who remained fought an uneven battle. Among those who fell were Hisrshl Patzovsky. He had a terrible death. His stomach was completely torn open and one eye was shot out.

It is hard to know what he was thinking during the final minutes of his life. Perhaps he had grievances against his fate, which delivered the harshest punishment, being killed on the day of liberation. Or maybe during his horrible dying pains he found the strength to understand that he witnessed with his own eyes the power of the Red Army liberating the regions.

Who knows? This is a secret he took with him to his grave.

Peysakh and Zaydl Finkelshteyn of blessed memory

Peysakh Finkeslshteyn was a carpenter in Zhetl and belonged to Alter Dvoretzky's secret partisan movement.

[Page 427]

He was also with Alter Dvoretzky in the forest. He spent three weeks in the forest and then was ordered by Alter Dvoretzky to return to the Zhetl ghetto with Yoyne Medvedsky, to take out the rest of the people. However, he remained in the ghetto unable to carry out his assignment and was killed in the second slaughter, August 8th, 1942.

His brother Zaydl spent more than two years in the Orliansky detachment. After liberation he joined the Red army and fell in battle against the Germans.

Alter Kogan of blessed memory

Alter Kogan, the son of the Zhetl cantor was born in Zhetl in 1923. After he lost his family he escaped to the forest with the first partisans of Kaplinsky's group (August 1942). He was always in the first ranks, in battles, ambushes and planting mines on train tracks. He was very bold, brave in battle and cold blooded in the most difficult moments. He belonged to the first Jewish company of the Oriliansky detachment.

Unable to withstand the horrible anti –Semitism, he left with a group of 25 men to Nolibok forest. First he joined Bielsky's detachment and after the newly created "Ordzhenikisde" detachment. He took part in many battles and diversion work.

Hirshl Kaplinsky of blessed memory

Hirshl Kaplinsky was born in Zhetl in 1910. His parents made and effort to give their only child a good education. Due to the worsening of their economic situation, Hirshl left his studies at the Tarbut High School in Lida and returned to Zhetl.

In 1927 he founded the Hashomer Hatzair in Zhetl and was the leader until 1932 when he was called up for military service.

He displayed many educational and organizational talents and his influence was felt throughout the movement. He held an important place in Zionist work in town in general and particularly in the Tarbut School, where he was secretary from the founding of the school until it was liquidated by the Soviets.

With a strong character and filled with wisdom he always found a way to influence the youth.

During the last action in the ghetto he escaped from the gathering point at the old cemetery together with 50 other young people, who organized themselves at the last minute, under the slaughter knife of the bandits. He arrived with them to the forest and it was obvious Hirshl Kaplinsky would lead the Jewish partisan groups that were organizing in Lipitchansk forest.

The qualities he excelled with in Hashomer Hatzair and in his communal activity in town served him well in his fight with the Nazi murderers. His military experience helped him to organize diversion operations for the partisan groups. Within a short time attacks were carried out with great success.

During the large raid against the partisans in Lipitchansk forest he headed the partisan division at the Shtchare and pushed back the enemy's attack. That same evening, he went out with a friend on a spy mission looking for a way to make contact with headquarters. As they walked, they stumbled across a German ambush. After a short struggle his friend was killed and Hirshl was wounded. With his last bit of strength he crawled to a partisan group. As he approached them he was met by the traitorous Russian partisans who shot him and he died on the spot.

Hirshl Kaplinsky did not manage to realize his aspiration of going to the Land of Israel. He died a hero, fighting for Jewish honour and for Jewish existence.

Hirshl Robetz of blessed memory

Hirshl Robetz was born in Zhetl in 1919. He arrived in the forest in August 1942. On the 3rd of September 1943 during an uneven attack by Germans on their post, he was killed and brought for burial not far from our partisan camp, 4 kilometres from the village Ruda – Lipitchanska (Zhetl region). He partook in many battles and ambushes.

The Sisters Frumeh and Sonia Shilovitsky of blessed memory

The two sisters, Frumeh and Sonia Shilovitsky hid in a cellar and later came to the forest with their brothers Ezriel and Yisroel. At first they were with Kaplinsky and later in the Orliansky detachment. Frumeh Shilovitsky worked as a cook.

They were both killed during the large raid in December 1942 under the following circumstances:

During the raid, running toward Karshuk's farmhouse, they fell upon a German ambush and were both killed. Right after the raid their bodies were found and buried in the forest, not far from Karshuk's (near the Lipitchansk forests). Their father and mother died in the forest from hunger and hardship.

[Page 428]

"Kokes and Shakhmaniyes"

by Tzila Zernitzky – Yoselevsky (Tel – Aviv)

Translated by Janie Respitz

Oy, oy, oy, "Kokes and Shakhmaniyes"
Oy, oy, oy, have pity on them.
They walk around like chickens without a rooster
And they have nothing to do.

The first anti partisan division goes on assignment
The third rides on horses.
The third builds tents,
And the first sleeps with his mistress.

Characteristic of the forest, the lines above were written by an unknown poet…

Today, when the noise of weapons has been silenced, when trenches are even with the ground, graves are grown over and life calls, we read these lines with a smile and contempt.

However, at the time, this song had deep meaning where anger was expressed as well as the embitterment of the "forest society". At the time, this song was sung by all the partisans, some triumphantly with laughter while for others, it was their last song…

When describing the chapter on partisans and their heroism it is worthwhile to remember a little about the mutual attitudes of the forest people.

The words "Kokes and Shakhmaniyes" date from approximately the end of 1942. Within the armed elements as well as the family groups there was "class" distinction.

It is tragic, but unfortunately true. What is even more painful is the fact, that after the shared dark past, when people lost everyone and everything they had, and lineage, honour and dignity were buried in one mass grave, they continued in the forest to distinguish between better and worse off people.

From the beginning this had more a physical character. The younger elements found it easier to find solutions and cope under these new conditions.

In the family groups this was understandable. The groups consisted of various people: young and old, those alone or with families,the rich, and those who were fed themselves by scrounging in the surrounding villages. Lifestyles divided the "forest society" into regions, where the rich and poor lived separately. For example: the poor lived in Nakrishok and Luditch forests and near the lighthouse. They were tattered, barefoot, and hungry. Even a relative, an armed partisan, would avoid going there because what pleasures awaited him there after a difficult task, except for cold, hunger, complaints and emaciated distressed girls. However, the Germans would often go there and put and end to their pain and suffering.

On the other hand, in the heart of the forest, closer to the detachments, in Grafsk and Demianovetz forests, lived the rich, the better ones, the higher sphere of society. The people that lived here were the ones who managed to escape with money or their hidden belongings, or even did some business. One of their tents was called Handwork and Culture. They had a much better existence in the forest.

These two classes were distinguishable outwardly and inwardly. During the freezing cold winter and in the summer when the forest smelled nice and beckoned life, you could see people walking on the forest paths and immediately notice which class they belonged to.

In fact, on these paths you could meet a boy swollen from hunger with his feet wrapped in rags, an older person bent over, a despondent broken shadow of a man, formerly a successful businessman, but now lonely, neglected and disappointed. You would also see pale, withering young girls.

They would come face to face with healthy, fresh people filled with life and hope, well fed children and well dressed clean, glowing, charming young girls.

Members of the better class would look cynically at the pitiful poor. How great was the resentment and bitterness of the poor man, when not long ago, he was among the better off. But the city and its past were far away.

Here, all the inhabitants of the forest met on the narrow plodded through paths where a variety of emotions, joy and tears were absorbed. A drop of blood would fall there from a wounded or dead partisan whose comrades carried back from battle to the camp.

[Page 429]

There you would also hear the ringing of triumphant songs when partisans would return after a victory against the enemy.

It was in this camp, within the fighting groups, that the above mentioned song was born: "Kokes and Shakhmaniyes".

There, in antithesis to the family groups, the concept of money did not exist. Rich and poor did not exist. Here, everyone paid a dear price, selling their lives to the enemy. If in the family camps they fought to survive, here there was a bitter bloody fight with death.

Despite this, here as well, on the surface, there were two classes: one, the better and privileged, the second, the lower and ignored: the so called Kokes and Shakhmaniyes. Here, as in the family groups, common sense and talent played a role. The first candidates were the remnants, those who remained from the underground in the ghetto (some came with weapons). The rest began to concentrate around them. Those who had a chance to join the detachment were the ones with weapons, those who had served as soldiers and had military experience, and those who were recommended, or better said, had connections.

The situation was more difficult for young boys and even worse for young girls who hadn't yet, or were unable to adapt to these new surroundings.

If such a boy succeeded in entering the detachment through a friend or broke through a barrier, his following journey was marked by great moral and physical suffering.

Due to a shortage of weapons, such a boy would have to remain doing unskilled work, chopping wood for the kitchen, fetching water, harnessing and unharnessing the horses, building tents and often endure the whims of the higher authorities. Standing guard duty was a great achievement.

They did not take these boys to ambushes where you could take the weapons from a fallen German, as these weapons were distributed among the "Experienced".

Of course, they were not very hopeful about worming out of this situation. Very often you would see one of these water carriers or wood choppers wearing two different boots or torn shoes and a greasy jacket that an "Experienced" guy would give him when he received a new one, as these items would disintegrate from age and filth and such a "poor item" would be mocked and humiliated. All of this impacted him morally and the boy would become resigned, apathetic and discredited by others and himself and would continue to drop lower and lower.

It is worthwhile to point out, the majority of these boys who only recently left their mother's supervision and whose understanding of life came from books and stories, were disappointed with the cruel reality they had to experience in this difficult crisis. Many of them were jealous of the "Experienced". Not of their boots or their warm fur pelts or even success with the weaker sex, but their guns, the only key for revenge.

The best fact was, that after the reorganization of the detachments, with the influx of weapons and good commanders, the majority of "Kokes and Shakhmanyies" comprised a large amount of the heroic fighters. Like many of the "Experienced", many of them ended up taking credit for blowing up bridges and killing Hitlerites.

One question remains: who bears the blame and responsibility?

The anarchy created at the beginning?

The "Koke and Shakhmaniye" himself?

Or the disdain of their commanders?

Honour Eternally:

The Zhetl partisans and the Red Army who fought, took revenge and died in battle with Hitler's murderers.

[Page 430]

Before Liberation

by Lizeh Kaplinsky (Tel Aviv)

Translated by Janie Respitz

Once again there were rumours about raids and again there were difficult days. There was nowhere to hide. The forest was once again crowded. Every day we searched for a new hiding place.

The mood was stressful. After long searches our "architects" Zhamke Fin and Aron Leyb Kovensky went to build a new cave. They found a nice dense forest of nut trees near the river.

A few days later we moved to this "summer residence". It was difficult going from one forest to another. However we organized ourselves well at the new place. Everyone had his own bunk. This was the greatest comfort in the forest.

It was already very warm. The forest was blooming but something gnawed at us, things were not calm. It continued like this for a few weeks until the large raid began. It flared up in all corners of the forest.

One day we saw Jews running through the forest with packs on their backs shouting:

"The Germans are already in Demianovtze". This was a nearby village. We were all confused. What were we to do? We immediately began to hide and bury our potatoes.

It was noisy. Everyone was running not knowing where to go. We understood the raid was serious and it hung over our heads like black cloud.

However, thanks to our brave partisans, we were able to finish building our caves under heavy fire. The women buried themselves underground. Each one of us had a few black crackers.

The situation in the forest was becoming worse by the minute. Jews were flying from one end of the forest to another. Jews came to us frightened, with red sweaty faces, disheveled, with packs on their backs asking:

"Where should we go? Where can we hide?" It was not long before the cave was ready. We received news that the forest was under siege. We heard them shooting up the forest. People were panicking.

We were 22 people underground, without air. It was so suffocating, we sat with our mouths open. We breathed like stuffed geese. No one dared to speak. It seemed we would be captured at any moment. The air became more dense and hotter. We undressed down to our underwear. Our bodies were wet. When someone touched another person he was disgusted.

We suffered in this underground hole for an entire month. There was no possibility to see daylight. This happened to be the nicest time of year. Red berries were blooming as if there was no shooting. It felt like the earth was splitting and the sky was falling.

The enemy surrounded us from all sides. We were desperate. The hunger was great and we were only able to breathe fresh air at night.

As soon as it became light, they sent us back into the cave. No one wanted to return to this live grave and the horrible stench. It was dark, low and we had to crawl on all fours.

As soon as we went down into the cave we were overcome by the heat. Mosquitos drank our blood.

We were prematurely dried up, our eyes were dark and our faces jaundiced. The cave sucked out all the colours from us. We slept all day due to hunger and weakness.

We received horrible news. We envied the dead. We lay underground covered with lice and filth. As we lay there we suddenly heard Russian. We all froze. There was a dead silence in the cave. There was no pulse.

These were the collaborators. They were walking on top of our cave. Each one of us awaited death. We thought they would throw grenades into the cave. They disturbed our cover and shot a bit of food under the bushes.

For a long time we were afraid to come out of the cave. We feared they were waiting for us under every bush. After this experience we felt dejected. Are we animals being ambushed?

[Page 431]

We did not believe we would be freed from this darkness, from life in the forest and that a day would come when we would stand under the sky and look at the sun.

One day, as we were sitting in the cave we heard movement not too far away. We made an effort to listen.

"What could this be?" Everyone said their own prayer and thought about death. Suddenly a few people stuck their heads out. They had a good premonition. They began to dig: they saw the partisan Senka Payte. He shared the good news with us:

"The Red Army is here! The first partisan detachment marched in and freed us from the German, bloody criminals!"

Two of our friends went closer to the partisans, not believing their luck. The partisans shouted:

"You are freed!" The two boys ran breathless to the cave and announced:

"The Red Army is here, come out!"

We all froze. We wanted to break down the wall, the door seemed too narrow.

Finally we left our dark graves and were freed. We could not believe the day arrived that we could move freely and visit our loved ones who were tortured.

From the forest to our home was the second tragedy. We gathered our forest remnants and began to walk to our destroyed town.

We walked all night, about 22 kilometres. The road was difficult. At six o'clock in the morning we arrived at our old home after two years of living underground in the forest.

The town was unrecognizable. More than half was burned. Everything was covered with wild grass. The rest of the houses were in ruins. Windows were torn out. The houses without doors appeared orphaned. The Christians looked at us in astonishment as if we had returned from the afterlife.

We made our first visit to those tortured in the Krufish forest. We went to the large graves. Heart –rending screams tore from our hearts:

"Father! Mother! Darling children! Beloved brother!…"

Unfortunately our screams were futile.

There were human bones strewn on the graves. Beside them a dried out skull. I looked at it. It gave witness to our great Jewish tragedy.

While we were in the forest banished from everything, we never even thought that we, small, weak people would resist the powerful bloody Hitler, may his name be blotted out, and we as free people would arrive in our own Land of Israel.

The Last Months in the Forest

by Soreh Ovseyevitch (Holon)

Translated by Janie Respitz

We had already been in the forest for 22 months. It seemed like an eternity, it felt like we never had a home and that we were born in the forest. The rustle of the trees was our lullaby, our beds, the hard planks of wood and our home, a hut made of wood. Beside the hut was a shallow pit, this was the well from which we drew water to cook and wash.

The days in the forest drag on. We do not see the end. The night, our saviour, does not want to come. The night is our day. That is when we rested our broken bones and stressed nerves. At night we were able to move a bit and were sure there would not be an attack.

According to the latest news, the Red Army was attacking on all fronts. The Germans were retreating and the front was getting closer to us. Now the will to survive was stronger, to live to see the German defeat.

Meanwhile our lives were in danger. The Russian People's Army that collaborated with the Germans under general Kaminsky, was in Zhetl.

We prepared every day for a raid. We built caves. We carried heavy bags of sand far into the forest in order not to leave tracks of freshly dug earth. We built our hiding place but we begin to doubt:

[Page 432]

Is it not visible and is it covered? Perhaps we should begin to build another one somewhere else?

We did not have to wait long. The raid began on June 7th, 1944. In our cave were Khane Gertzovsky, Lusik, Khane Volotinsky, Feyvl Kalbshteyn and Gruniye from Novogrudek. When we entered the cave no one believed we would ever come out. It was damp and the walls were covered with thick mold.

The door to the cave was closed all day because the Russian collaborators walked around the forest all day. Every rustle of the trees sounded like footsteps.

We waited impatiently for nightfall. At night, we would quickly cook, wash and prepare for the following day. We had very little water. It was very hot and the "wells" dried up.

One day, when we returned to the cave I was carrying a small pot of food. We stopped, not far from the cave, to gather a few branches and leaves to cover up our footprints. When I put my pot down a bit of the food spilled out. After walking a bit further I thought that the next day when the Germans walked by these traces could lead them to the cave.

I told this to Khane Gertzovsky quietly. We decided to go back. With our hands we raked the ground and wiped away the signs of the spilled soup. I was still unsure if there were traces. Sitting in the cave I thought fearfully that if we were found everyone would be killed because of me. I was very happy when night fell again.

There was another cave not far from ours where Dvoyreke Gorodaysky was. Once, during the day when it was quiet and we were sure no one was near she came to our cave. She wanted to smoke a cigarette and did not have a light. The door to our cave was open and we were all dozing. As soon as Dvoyreke was inside we heard shouting from horse riders. Dvoyreke quickly closed the opening to our cave.

The riders rode over our heads. We heard them talking. We all held our breath. Nothing scared us more than being captured alive. Now, as the day of liberation was nearing, we heard sounds from the front, precisely now, our lives were in danger!

The day does not end. Every minute feels like an eternity. It was as if the earth stopped spinning on its axis and night would never come. Finally it was night. We breathed a little easier. Another day of fear and torture had passed.

July 7th, 1944. Like every other day we crawled back into our lair at dawn. It did not take long before we heard shouting. We trembled:

"Nu, this is surely our end. The murderers are above our heads and we will be captured. To our great astonishment we heard the voice of Hirshl Kaplinsky who told us all to crawl out. Hirshl told us divisions of the Red Army were already in the forest.

No one could believe this. We thought he had simply gone mad, or that it was a dream. Had our hour of liberation actually arrived?

We decided we must leave the forest as quickly as possible because Germans who had been hiding from the attacking Russians could suddenly appear.

Our group consisted of: me, Khane Gertzovsky, Notteh Sokolovsky, Shifra Shabokovsky, Feyvl Kalbshteyn, Lizeh and her daughter Mireh Rozovsky. We walked slowly and did not say a word. Everyone was deep in their own thoughts. Rows of soldiers passed us but we did not see them. We were still afraid the soldiers would attack and shoot us on the spot. We could hardly believe we were walking freely on the road toward Zhetl. The Christians stood in front of their houses looking at us, overgrown and tattered.

Where exactly were we going? Home?

Now everyone realized our home no longer exists. All our dear and beloved had been killed before we left for the forest.

We were two kilometres from town. We could see the top of the church. Instinctively we slowed down our pace. Someone suggested we rest a bit. Everyone agreed as we all wanted to delay the moment we actually entered town and stood before the bitter truth.

We sat for a long time. No one dared say: "Let's go".

How good would it have been if I could have heard my mother's kind words, if I could have found a lap upon which to lay my head and have a good cry.

We picked ourselves up and continued our walk. We looked toward the graves, the only thing that remained.

[Page 433]

My Last Day in the Forest

by Hindke Mirsky (Montreal)

Translated by Janie Respitz

This took place on July 16th 1944. The last commander of the "Barba" detachment, Ilya Glazkov, gathered all the partisans and marched with them to Zhetl. He left a few sick partisans in the forest together with: Dr. Rakover and his wife Manye, Alter Orlinsky ("The Mother"), Moteh Zakraysky, Mayshek Mirsky, Yenkl and his wife, Vanye and me. After feeding the sick I went to pick berries, meeting many Red Army soldiers on the way.

The day was sunny and calm. After lunch Dr. Rakover went out for a walk. Mayshke MIrsky, Manye Rakover and Moteh Zakraysky remained in Misha Krestov's tent. I remained with Yenkl's wife sitting with the patients in another tent. Alter and Vanye were in the bakery.

Suddenly we heard loud shooting from machine guns. When I looked out the door I saw Dr. Rakover running without a hat shouting:

"Save yourselves. The Germans are in the camp!"

We all ran, leaving one patient behind who could not be moved. The shooting was vigorous, bullets flew over us. While running, Yenkl was wounded in his foot but he continued running until we arrived at the swamp at "Golubi Rashtshe", from which we barely pulled ourselves out.

In the evening we arrived in the village of Golubi trembling over the fate of those who remained in the forest. Later we learned those who remained did not leave the tent. Upon hearing the shooting only Moteh Zakraysky ran out and was shot on the spot.

Mayshke Mirsky and Manye Rakover pushed the guns through the door and began to shoot. The Germans, thinking they were partisans, threw a hand grenade on the tent which luckily did not explode and they quickly retreated. In the village of Golubi we asked for help to bring the patients and the others that remained in the forest. We needed a lot of intervention to get some people from Davidov's or Severnem's military groups. Some of them promised to help in the morning. Having no other recourse we went into a peasant's house, bandaged Yenkl's foot and decided to wait until morning.

I will never forget that night. We cried for our dear ones, quite sure the Germans had murdered them.

To our great surprise the door suddenly opened and Sonia (translator's note: previously referred to as Manye) and Mayshke Mirsky came in. They shared with us the sad news about Moteh's death.

In the morning we all returned to the camp where we buried Moteh, took the patients and left the forest.

This is how our year long partisan life in the forest ended.

On the way to Zhetl, not far from the village Demyanovetze we once again met Germans, but now they were being led by the Red Army soldiers. They gave us the "privilege" to take them to Zhetl. We, 6 Jews led 8 Germans to Zhetl. How pathetic they all looked. Watching us, they tried to figure out what we would do with them. When we told them we were Jews they began to cry and beg for "mercy".

Many Red Army soldiers approached us. They asked where we were taking the Germans. When they heard our answer, that we were taking them to Zhetl, they laughed.

"Why should you drag them with you, give them to us "at our expense".

We happily handed them over ignoring their pitiful faces which begged for protection from Jews…

With broken hearts, crying eyes and deep sorrow we entered the ruined and massacred Zhetl.

[Page 434]

Zhetl Partisans in the Soviet Army

by Khaim Sovitsky

Translated by Janie Respitz

On July 1st, 1944 the blockade in the Lipitchansk forest ended. Tired and hungry we returned to our camp.

We received information that the Red Army was close. We received a command to stop the retreat of the German army by blowing up train tracks between Razhanke and Skribova on the road from Slonim to Bialystok.

We waited for nightfall and went on our way. At the Nieman we received an order to cross to the other side and wait there for further orders. When we received a report from the reconnaissance group that all was good, we began our work. We mined the line at various points and quickly left. On our way back we rewarded ourselves with some food and returned to the camp.

On July 7th we learned the Russians captured Novolenyie, the district city Zhetl and the entire region. We could not believe our ears, the last hour before our liberation had struck.

The artillery from the front was moving toward the Shtchare. We received an order: to take various roads to Zhetl. When we were 10 kilometres away from the Red Army, riders from the main brigade caught up with us and ordered us to return to camp. We turned around to return through the village of Nakrishok. Only a few days earlier there had been a strong German garrison there. We attacked them more than once, but each time we had to retreat, leaving behind victims. However we always left them with greater losses both in men and ammunition. The most important thing was they were always afraid of us.

July 8th. First thing in the morning they informed us the Red army had advanced further and none of us could leave the camp. They gathered us in an empty field near the Shtchare where almost all the detachments of our brigade were gathered. They told us we must spend the night there and wait for further orders.

July 9th. High ranking Soviet officers arrived and greeted us as dear devoted soldiers in the fight against the German enemy. After listening to a few patriotic speeches they accompanied us with songs to the other side of the river.

As we did not find any food in that region, I and 12 other men were sent back to the camp to bring bread from the camp bakery. As we approached the camp we heard loud shooting from machine guns. We could not understand the reason behind the shooting as the army had advanced forward. We went to the peasants who lived near the forest, but their houses were empty. Everyone was hiding from the frightful shooting. Finally we found a few Christians who told us the forest was full of Germans who were running from the attacking Red Army. Their divisions were defeated and in small groups they were going through the forest. The peasants advised us not to return to camp as they were surely more powerful than us. We listened to them and returned to our detachment.

July 10th. We were awoken at dawn. We prepared to march. We did not know where. Peasant women came to say goodbye to their sons and husbands. They told us that overnight a group of Germans shot Moteh Zakaraysky (Avrom the tinsmith's son) in the camp bakery. They found a group of partisans baking bread. The entire group ran away but Moteh was not fated to be saved in the last minutes before liberation.

We marched toward Volkovisk. We had not eaten in 48 hours. Hungry and tired we stopped to rest three kilometres from town in the Zamkov forest. There we were informed Volkovisk had been captured by the Red Army.

At eleven o'clock in the morning an army major came from the second White Russian front, led by Marshal Rakosovsky. He greeted us warmly as devoted fighters. He informed us, for our service, we would receive appropriate recognition and meanwhile we will be allocated to the "best" division of the 339th regiment.

[Page 435]

They divided us into groups. Our group consisted of one hundred men including the following 20 from Zhetl:

Avrom Alpert	Yisroel Burda
Yoyne Brestovsky	Zelik Haydukovsky
Hillel Zhukhovitsky	Yosef Novogrudsky
Yisroel Zhulhovitsky	Zaydl Finklshteyn
Yekhiel Yoselevitch	Velvl Kravetz
Efraim Yoselevitch	Zelik Kovensky
Feyvl Lontzevitsky	Yosef Kalbshteyn
Dovid Likhter	Doivd Noyekh Rozenfeld
Yitzkhak Mankovitch	
Yosef Mankovitch	

The following men from Zhetl served in other detachments:

Berl Ivenitsky	Yekhiel Yoselevitch
Hirshl Indershteyn	Ruven Khlebnik
Yisakhar Berman	Aron Leyzerovitch
Nokhem Berman	Shepsl Lipsky
Khaim Bekenshteyn	Hillel Levenbuk
Mayrim Galinsky	Yoyne Medvedsky
Leyzer Goldshteyn	Berl Nikolayevsky
Shmuel Gertzovsky	Meir Sovitsky
Yosl Gershovsky	Khaim Epshteyn
Sholem Gerling	Zisl Kalbshteyn
Borukh Volfevitch	Shmuel Shabakovsky
Moishe Aron Zernitsky	
Khaim Yatvitsky	

The next morning they took us to another place where we had to meet our new leaders. We spent the whole day lying in the field and when night fell we spread out on the grass and slept. They woke us in the middle of the night and told us to go to headquarters to register.

There was a small house in the corner of the field. When we entered we saw a table lit by a small candle, an older Red Army man who wrote down everyone's name. He also wanted to know where we came from and the names of our close relatives. I did not know how to answer this question: who should I give in the event I am killed in battle. I could not provide an answer. I asked myself that question and for a long time was lost in my thoughts.

"Why are you silent?" he asked, "Why don't you answer me?"

"I don't have anyone to give you" I finally managed to say.

"Give me anyone you want".

I gave him the following address: All surviving Jews from Zhetl.

July 13th. It was still very dark when they woke us up. The officers from each division arrived. They gave us some food, the first time in a few days we had a chance to fill our stomachs. It did not take long before we were marching. According to all the signs on the roads we felt the enemy was not far away. Within a short time we received the order:

Attack! Forward!

The shooting was heavy. We shouted: Hurrah! And ran after the enemy. However, when we came to the bank of the Svislatch River we had to stop. The enemy had dug deep trenches on the other side and was shooting at us. We received an order to drive the enemy out of the trenches at all cost. Again we advanced shouting:

"Hurrah! Death to Hitlerism!"

We stormed their bunkers and tens of soldiers dropped dead. Some of my closest friends fell in this battle: Zaydl Finkelshteyn, Dovid Likhter and Yoyne Brestovitsky. The number of soldiers in our division was greatly reduced.

We moved forward on the left side of the train tracks which ran from Volkovisk to Bialystok. The whole road was seeded with dead Germans. We came across a smaller enemy group and succeeded in staving them off. We moved forward capturing village after village, town after town.

August 19th. We continued to march onward. We received an order from our colonel Raznov to cut through the forest road that leads to the train tracks. One battalion from the Red Army was already fighting there and needed help as the resistance of the enemy was great.

We snuck closer to the edge of the forest but the enemy chased us away. This was the only road upon which they could retreat therefore they were defending it so relentlessly.

When night fell they provided some food but while eating we were attacked by German airplanes and had to be satisfied with our first bites. When it was really dark they regrouped us and told us to continue our attack.

[Page 436]

The commander of our division talked to us with a pistol in his outstretched hand. He explained we had to cross a small river, fortify it on the other side and not omit any enemy trucks. He ordered us to spread out through the field and cross the river one at a time. Then he warned us that whoever lags behind will be shot by his own comrades. I knew what he meant. I was very familiar with such cases.

The distance was not great, around 500 metres. We walked about 300 metres and everything was calm. Luckily it was a dark night and the Germans did not notice us.

After walking a little further they suddenly opened fire on us and we were drawn into a battle with the enemy. We received an order to retreat 100 metres and bury ourselves at the edge of the forest. The group which collected the fallen arrived. We collected them like fallen corn stalks under the peasant's reaping hook, shot and riddled with bullet holes. Among the pile of corpses I recognize two of my Zhetl partisan friends: Yosef Novogrudsky and Zisl Kalbshteyn. Yosef's body was torn to pieces, hard to identify. He was blown up by a mine.

The shooting did not stop. They sent us to defend the hill. We captured it without casualties. The German artillery shot at us without interruption. We had to retreat. We buried ourselves in the field and lay there for half a day. The enemy discovered our position and hailed mines from mortars upon us. One mine landed not far from the hole I was lying in. A sliver twisted my gun and I was covered with pieces of earth.

I remained lying there until darkness fell. Then I got up and went to the commander to inform him. He gave me a machine gun and we marched on. After marching all night we arrived at a tar factory 25 kilometres from Bialystok.

August 21st. The enemy was in the village not far from the tar factory. After reciprocal shooting they retreated. Our commander sent a reconnaissance group out to find the remaining Germans. Just as the spies entered the village, shooting began and two of them were immediately killed. One of the two was Zelik Haydukovsky from Zhetl.

The enemy was chased out of the village, but dug into the nearby forest. Before we attacked them a group was sent to determine their strength. One man in this group was Efraim Yoselevitch. A battle ensued where Efraim was wounded and could not move. Lying in terrible pain he was hit by a grenade and died. The attack by the enemy was repelled and we moved on.

August 23rd. During the day we moved closer to the village Yanove, 5 kilometres from Bialystok. We stormed the village and partially pushed out the enemy. The enemy defended the other part of the village relentlessly. I received an order to chase out the enemy with the help of my machine gun. I took a strategic position and after a long fight the enemy retreated.

August 24th. They brought us breakfast very early because soon we had to attack the enemy again. A fog covered the fields. It was cool and damp. I led with my machine gun with Zelik Kovensky behind me. The enemy began to fire bullets at us. We shot back. A bullet hit Zelik and he fell dead beside me.

After a short time we were ordered to storm the enemy. We approached and were one hundred metres away. I had not yet managed to stand up my gun when I felt I was wounded in my hand and foot. I fell to the ground and called for help.

A few soldiers ran to me including Borukh Vismansky from Bielitziye. They quickly pulled off my boot and bandaged my foot with a rag.

It was impossible to drag me off the battlefield as the enemy was shooting over our heads. I remained lying on the field the whole day. In the evening they carried me to the village where I spent the night. The next morning they took me to the field hospital where I lay for six weeks. After they sent me deep into the hinterland, to the Urals, to the city Upa.

I remained there for two and a half months and then they sent me back to Zhetl as a discharged soldier.

[Page 437]

A Zhetler in the Red Army Recounts

by Shloyme Sharlat (Haifa)

Translated by Janie Respitz

June 22nd, 1941. A shrill voice disturbed our rest. The blankets were lifted and the soldiers went out to hear the news.

Molotov spoke at noon. A strong speech. Military and civilian songs instilled courage and called for action. Molotov spoke slowly, clearly and with conviction.

"The enemy has attacked, we must defend. Our cause is justified. Victory will be ours".

Just yesterday there was peace. Today, war. Human blood had already been spilled and widows and orphans are being born. Just yesterday I received a letter from Zhetl and responded quickly. I grab the letter and read the greetings from all my friends in the Iron Guard. The news from Zhetl was filled with joy and hope. This was all suddenly disturbed as they are so close to the border! Who knows what they will do?

Our division received an order to leave for the front. By the first of July we were already in echelon. We approached the front. The closer we were to the front the more refugees we saw.

We went through Bransk. We were greeted by German airplanes, which instilled great fear on the roads filled with military and civilians. Among them, a large amount of Jews, women and children.

Everyone was running. I look for a familiar face. It seems to me I will find someone from Zhetl that will tell me what's happening there. I understand that even if I find someone from Zhetl they also won't know anything because every day, every hour, the radio brings fresh, sad news.

The Germans advance. They capture city after city. Lida and Baronovitch are already captured. The Germans are nearing Minsk. The hope that I will be at the defence of our province disappears.

Our regiment is defeated. Meeting points are created with formations from other regiments. The Germans are going to Smolensk. The days are difficult. The population is running to the east. We walk with our backs to the east and wait for a miracle.

German airplanes drop leaflets saying the war is only against Jews and commissars. However, people that escaped from a prisoner camp 388 kilometres from Moscow said the Germans were not picky and death was sure for everyone.

On the 3rd of October we fall into the third siege. A German troop landed and we were surrounded. Everyone walked on foot, even the commissars and generals. Heavy weapons were destroyed and some were left in secure hands with the hope that if we could not break through the siege we will have something to fight with in the partisan groups.

We walked at night, and during the day we were forbidden to stick out our heads. German airplanes were pursuing individuals.

Meanwhile the Germans were experiencing a Russian winter. With frozen noses, hands and feet they were not even able to run away. The peasants beat them with sticks and took away everything they had not yet sent to their wives and lovers.

The roads were burdened with Germans. Thousands of Germans died. It was a difficult winter. Stormy winds buried the roads under the snow. On the sides of the road we would often see Germans with their heads in the snow and their leather boots sticking up.

The front stopped at the Agra River. Battles of strategic significance resumed. More attacks, pushing the enemy further and freeing millions from the German cannibals.

The occupant put up a strong resistance. He did not want to leave behind the Russian and White Russian warehouses of bread, meat and honey. He did not yet complete his extermination operation against the Jews. He had not yet satiated his thirst for blood. We are now very close to Minsk, Baranovitch and Zhetl.

The summer of 1944 was approaching. The roads have dried after the wet spring. The rye was growing.

[Page 438]

The fields were green. The army was ready to take revenge. Plans were prepared. Our brothers behind the enemy front were working hard to spread fear among Hitler's heroes who were afraid of every shrub and of their own shadows. The army put hope in its patriots on the other side of the border.

The hour was nearing. Minsk is already behind us with 56 thousand German prisoners. The front pushes forward, Baranovitch, Stolptz and Novogrudek. We are only a few kilometres from Zhetl. We can already see the great destruction caused by the Germans. We see the destroyed Houses of Study and torn Torah scrolls. Our hearts our broken. We cannot ask anything to anyone. There is no one to offer consolation!

I met Jewish partisans from Novoredok. They told me a bit about Zhetl and its fighters, but my head did not grasp what my ears were hearing.

I could not rest. With great impatience I waited for the moment when Zhetl would be liberated.

I get closer, Kisheleve, Novoleniyie, Halavli, where we would always meet Aron Leybke the wagon driver, Mayshke the Turkey and Yoshke Ishieles'. The forest near the saw mill where the youth of Zhetl would gather in the summer.

The saw mill stood like a large tombstone, stripped of wood. The Germans took it all. They would have taken the ground if it were possible.

The truck turned right, to the Nieman where difficult battles are still taking place. I turn left, with my pack on my back and my weapon on my side.

I am already in Zhetl. I start to walk, where do I go? Who shall I look for and who will I find?

I walk on both side of the street. Jewish houses, but peeking out of the windows are unfamiliar, non - Jewish faces. I walk and cannot believe what I see. Zhetl without Jews?

It is unbelievable. Is it really true what the newspapers and people said? Vinarsky's house, where Feygele Kaplinsky lived, empty. Zaydke's house, destroyed. Khaytche's, destroyed. Ruins on top of ruins!

The war had already hardened me, but fell apart completely. Where are the Jews of Zhetl? The Jewish town with its culture, with its friction between religious and secular, Zionists and Yiddishists, the youth from the "Bund" and "Hashomer Hatzir"? Where is everybody I loved and didn't love? Are they all really in the Zhetl cemetery? I will go to them, spend the night and after, with my pack on my back, I will go to my war comrades and take revenge for all the innocent who were killed. But then a miracle happened. People recognized me and called to me.

"Do you see who came? Shloyme Sharlat! Shloyme Sharlat!"

This took me out of my despair. I kissed the people who I did not previously know, people I had never spoken to before. One thing united us: we were Jews from Zhetl.

They began to ask me many questions: had I seen this one's brother or this one's sister, or had I met anyone from Zhetl? So many people from Zhetl escaped, was I the only one who survived? Others pointed out with heavy sighs:

"See, this is all that has remained from my entire family!"

I walked to the marketplace. On the way, at Leybke Kaplinsky's house I found a few Zhetlers who asked if I recognized them. From my old friends from the Iron Guard that played an important role in Zhetl, I found almost no one.

What value do the houses in Zhetl have if they are empty, without Jews? What good is the synagogue if there is no one to pray?

The ground is soaked with Jewish blood burning under our feet. We cannot remain in Zhetl which looks like a graveyard. We must leave and settle in the land of our forefathers.

[Page 439]

In a German Prison Camp

by Berl Goldberg (Montreal)

Translated by Janie Respitz

The eve of Passover, March 1939. Standing in my store I received a telegram to report immediately for military duty.

There was a feeling of mourning as on Tisha B'Av in our home. My family cried as if they knew they would never see me again.

I left that same day for Baronovitch. From there I was sent to the Polish German border where they taught us to shoot and how to slaughter one another.

Friday the 1st of September we received the sad news: War!

We were sent immediately to the front where German machine guns were awaiting us. We fought them in Sherftz and Plotzk. We then received an order to march toward Otvotzk.

German cannons and airplanes shot at us from all sides. The entire road was sown with the dead. Finally we arrived in Otvotzk. After we rested a bit we marched toward Warsaw.

There were already German paratroopers in Warsaw. After a short time we rid the city of diversionary agents.

Resting from our battle in our lodgings we heard shooting. The Germans began bombarding Warsaw. Within a few hours Warsaw was transformed into a large cemetery. We fought in the suburbs, but realizing our situation was hopeless we broke through the front and marched to Modlin.

In Modlin we received the sad news, Warsaw fell. However we continued to fight until the 27th of September. On that day I was wounded and sent to a prison camp: Stalag A.

Our situation was not an enviable one. During the day they tortured us with hard labour, at night, beatings. Dozens of prisoners could not withstand it and died. One day a miracle occurred. A Wehrmacht officer entered our room and saw how a Nazi officer beat a Jewish prisoner to death. The Wehrmacht officer slapped the Nazi across the face and phoned a higher authority to replace the Nazi. They actually sent another officer who treated us humanely.

A while later they received an order to send us home, to regions occupied by the Russians. However, instead of sending us home, they sent us to an airfield not far from the border. The living conditions were terrible. Thousands of prisoners died from typhus.

I was also sick with typhus. I lay in bed for 10 weeks. Mulye Sovitsky from Zhetl sat by my bedside day and night until he too got sick. Miraculously, we both survived.

From there they sent us to Konskavalye where we worked hard paving highways.

After the Nazi occupation they sent us to Bendzin. We worked there for a year under difficult conditions. Hunger dominated the camp. Mulye Sovitsky bribed a few German soldiers and would go to the city to buy food. One time they betrayed him and they found the food I had. With great trouble I crawled out of this mess. I claimed the food was from the kitchen and not from town.

From there they sent us to Vielitchok and Plazhov. In Plashov we exhumed those tortured to death and burned them.

When the Russian front drew nearer they packed us like herring into wagons and sent us to Gras –Rozn and Brilnitz in Czechoslovakia.

There we worked in an ammunitions factory. The Czech workers put us in contact with the Czech underground movement who provided us with weapons. When the Nazis learned of this they fled and this is how we took over control of the camp until liberation.

The Russian regime sent us home. Travelling with Sovitsky home to Zhetl we stopped in Lublin. Mulye found his wife. I found Manye Rabinovitch and she told me no one from my family survived and all the Jews left Zhetl.

That is when I decided to leave Poland a search for a new home.

[Page 440]

Partisan Heroes From Zhetl
Who Died in the Forest and on the Front as Soldiers in the Red Army

(**Translator's note:** the list is according to the Hebrew Alphabet)

Translated by Janie Respitz

א

Ozhekhovsky Yoyne
Ivenitsky Berl
Indershteyn Shloyme
Indershteyn Lyuba
Alpert Berl
Alpert Borukh
Alpert Hirshl

Alpert Yitzkhak
Alpert Soreh
Arkin Yakov

ב

Boyarsky Eliyahu
Bom Sholem
Barishansky Brokha
Busel Yisroel
Busel Frume
Busle Soreh
Busel Shloyme
Buslin Yosef
Bitensky Yosef
Blakhman Avrom
Blakhman Shmuel
Beknshteyn Khaim
Bermnan Yisackhar
Berman Leyb
Berman Nokhem
Benyaminovitch Yosef
Benyaminovitch Yitzkhak
Benyaminovitch Leyb
Benyaminovitch Soreh
Berkovsky Ruven
Brestovitsky Yoyne
Breskin Avrom Aron

ג

Gal Miriam
Gal Yente Rivka
Goldshteyn Eliezer
Goldshteyn Yosef
Goldshteyn Yerakhmiel
Goldshteyn Mikhal
Galinsky Miriam
Goldberg Feygl
Garber Dr.
Gertzovsky Heniye
Grin Pinkhas

ד

Dvoretzky Alter
Dvoretzky Miriam
Dzhenchelsky Naftali

ה

Haydukovsky Aron
Haydukovsky Zelik
Haydukovsky Yehoshua

ו

Volfovitch Yakov
Volfovitch Dvoyre
Vinarsky Eliezer

ז

Zatzshteyn (Two children)
Zakraysky Mordkhai

ט

Tchemerinsky Khaim

י

Yoselevitch Efraim
Yudelevitch Yosef

ל

Likhter Isar
Likhter Dovid
Likhter Yerakhmiel
Leybovitch Eliezer
Levit Kalman
Levti Moishe
Levarontchik Yehoshua
Levarontchik Mendl
Levenbuk Hillel
Levenbuk Miriam

מ

Mankovitch Mendl
Medvedsky Yoyne
Mekl Dovid

נ

Novogrudsky Yosef

ס

Sovitsky Khonen
Sovitsky Yitzkhak
Sovitsky Meirv
Sovitsky Shaul
Solomyansky Mashe
Saker Meylekh
Slamke Khaim
Senderovsky Khaye Rokhl
Senderovsky Moishe

ע

Eliashev Meir

פ

Pazdunsky Moishe
Pialon Sholem
Feyvuzhinsky Peysakh
Finklshteyn Zaydl
Finklshteyn Peysakh
Peretz Avrom

ק

Kagan Alter
Kagan Libe
Kovensky Zelik
Kalbshteyn Zisl
Kaminsky (Hertzke's wife)
Kaplinsky Nutta
Kaplinsky Yente
Koren Yekhezkl
Kuperman Yudl
Kravetz Yitzkhak
Kravetz Malka
Krugman Yudl

ר

Rabinovitch Izye
Robetz Hirsh
Rozvosky Mikhl
Rozvosky Laye Mikhle
Rozvosky Khane Rashkev
Rashkin Avrom

ש

Shuster Khaim
Shilovitsky Khaim
Shilovitsky Sonye
Shilovitsky Frume
Shifmanovitch Leyb
Shmulevitch Soreh
Shmulevitch Malke
Shraybman Noyekh

Honour Their Memory!

[Page 441]

People From Zhetl Throughout the World

Zhetl Book Committee in Canada

Seated: Moishe Mirsky, Mineh Shiluvsky
Standing: Hinde Mirsky, Yisreol Goldberg, Sholem Lisagursky

The Board of the Zhetl Interest Free Loan Society in Israel

Seated from right to left: Fraydl Berman, Dvoyre Shkolnik, Borukh Kaplinsky, Yekhiel Kuznietsky, Yehuda Ostrovsky, Abba Levenbuk
Standing: Mayrim Lusky, Alteh Kuznietsky, Yosef Berman, Yitzkhak Yalon, Shabtai Mayevsky, Arye Cohen

[Page 442]

Zhetlers in the World

Translated by Judy Montel

Dzyatlava may still exist, but Jewish Zhetl is gone. The Pomereika may still overflow its banks before the Passover holiday, but no Jewish possessions are damaged by the stormy waters.

It may be that in the summer, children still flock with hammocks in their hands to the grove of the Christian cemetery to breathe fresh air, but they do not chat together in Yiddish.

The firemen may still practice in the streets of Zhetl, rolling barrels of water, climbing roofs that aren't burning, but Chayim Meir the fireman doesn't rally them with his bugle.

Jewish Zhetl found its rest in two cemeteries after 450 years of creation and struggle. However, in the larger world, many offshoots survived from the town. We will mention them briefly.

For many years before its destruction many of the children of Zhetl sensed the end that was drawing near. Hundreds took up a wanderer's staff, set off on the seven seas and reached all five parts of the world. Where can they not be found today? They make up the settlements of Zhetl in the larger world.

The largest settlement of Zhetl descendants can be found in the United States. According to the reckoning of Ephraim Pesoff, some 600 families from Zhetl made their new home there. The pioneers of this settlement arrived in the United States already in the 1870s and 1880s. In 1890 they organized and founded a synagogue called: Chevre Mishkan Israel People of Zhetl. In 1904 they created the

Organization for Extending Aid to Zhetl and its Institutions. In the 30s they founded the Organization of Women of Zhetl.

The organizations were successful in strengthening the ties among the Zhetlers in the United States and in sending aid to Zhetl institutions until 1939.

In Israel, some 250 families from Zhetl integrated into the fabric of life. When did the first people from Zhetl arrive in Israel? We don't know. We assume that in all the generations and all of the times. Five gravestones on the Mt of Olives testify to people from Zhetl who lived in the Land of Israel in the second half of the 19th century and perhaps even in the first half.

With the first Aliya (wave of immigration) to the Land of Israel, R' Elimelech Izraelit arrived, one of the founders of Kastinia. In 1884 Shaina Michla Moshkovski arrived in Israel from Zhetl, and she died in 1936 in Ekron. In 1886, R' Gershon Shlomo Kaplinsky arrived from Zhetl. His grandson is R' Shmuel Zakif, head of Magdiel. In 1887, R' Yehoshua Eizenshtat-Barzilai arrived from Zhetl, one of the founders of Bnei Moshe and an activist who did much in the country. In 1895 R' Moshe Eizik Ostrovsky arrived. His daughter and her husband founded a business for building materials known as L. Glikman.

Many people from Zhetl arrived with the second Aliya and the third Aliya up to the survivors of the Sho'ah who arrived between 1945 and 1950.

In 1943 the Organization of Olim from Zhetl in Israel was founded and in 1951 a Charity Fund. Over time 1500 trees were donated to the forest in memory of the martyrs of Zhetl.

A third settlement of people from Zhetl, some 70 families, is in Argentina. The first immigrants arrived in Argentina from Zhetl after the first World War. Today, there is a busy Organization of People from Zhetl in Argentina which has done much for the members of our town who survived the Sho'ah.

In Canada, some 40 families from Zhetl found a home. Dozens of families built their homes in England, France, Australia and South Africa. In total, around the world over a thousand families from Zhetl found homes, who number at the very least 4000 people.

Such a number of Jews never lived in Zhetl. The Jewish population of Zhetl ranged between 3000 to 3500 souls. It turns out that in fact, the settlements have a greater population than Zhetl, their place of origin.

Let us cultivate the emotional connection between the children of our town in every place they are found, strengthen it and bind it so that the embers of Zhetl around the world stays alight.

[Page 443]

Jews From Zhetl in the United States

by Efraim Pasaf (New York)

Translated by Janie Respitz

It is not known when the first Jews from Zhetl walked on American soil as no registration from those days remain. I believe it was at the end of the 70s or early 80s of the last century.

Many small town Jews, suffering from poverty were forced to wander into the new big world, some from Zhetl among them. By 1890 there were so many Zhetl Jews in America they felt the need to establish a Zhetl Society and a synagogue which was called "Chevra Mishkan Yisroel Anshei Zhetl".

Efraim Pasaf

For the early arrivals that were religious and found everything so foreign and non –Jewish, the synagogue was a treasure. They prayed together, distributed honours and studied Mishna. They attempted to create a familiar Zhetl atmosphere in a small corner of the new world.

Even the non – religious, the Enlightened, looked at the synagogue as a safe haven where they could meet with their townsfolk, receive regards from home and ease the longing for their loved ones they left behind in their old home.

In fact, membership in the synagogue grew. On Saturdays and holidays the synagogue was packed. Apparently loneliness brought these two groups together despite their differences.

For the religious this was a synagogue in the true sense of the word, a place to pray and learn. For the non-religious, it served as a club where they gathered to enjoy themselves in familiar surroundings.

In 1902 -1903 a younger group arrived from Zhetl, driven away from the old home due to hardship. Some of them were absorbed in the revolutionary spirit, belonged to revolutionary parties and ran away from the old home because they were being persecuted by the Russian police. For them, joining the synagogue was out of the question.

A large portion of these young people came from families of shop owners and businessmen. They did not have a trade. Even those who did have a trade could not put it to use, for example, scribes.

Wanting to chase away their loneliness, they would gather in the homes of older Zhetler, who already climbed the economic ladder, and poured out their hearts. They would debate political and social issues of the day and sometimes play cards.

What was characteristic in those years was the devotion and connection they all felt to one another, not taking into account their parentage, or social standing back home. As soon as they learned someone arrived from Zhetl, the townsfolk were ready to help, first and foremost with lodging, and the next day, take him the factory, and teach him a trade so he could support himself. Until this happened they were prepared to share their last morsel.

Slowly, every immigrant found work, the majority in the women's clothing industry, which was then almost entirely run by Jews. The gathering of Zhetl Jews was happening more often and now, was better organized.

In 1904 they had the idea to establish the Zhetl Society with the long name: "Independent Zhetl Young Men's Benevolent Association", which still exits today.

At first the organization had more of a social and communal character, but slowly it was more focused on financial support for needy members. The members were constantly concerned about the difficulties of daily life and worried about the future.

We must remember this happened in the time of the Sweat Shops, when people slaved twelve to fifteen hours a day. The shops were dark holes, barely letting in a ray of sun, the walls dripped and many workers contracted illnesses under these conditions, particular tuberculosis. Salaries were pitiful, barely enough to live off. No one was ever sure of his job, and in times of unemployment people would starve. There was no one to turn to for help, as friends and relatives were on the other side of the ocean.

[Page 444]

The Book Committee in the U.S.A

First row from right to left: Volf Kravetz, Efraim Pasaf, Moishe Mendl Leyzerovitch, Dovod Sovitsky
Second row standing: Mikhl Kivelevitch, Yisroel Shilovitsky, Aron Leyzerovitch, Ezriel Shilovitsky, Zavl Mordkovsky

Therefore, the Society was the most important institution to help a brother in need, to support him in the event of illness and provide for his wife and children in the event of a tragedy.

Right after the First World War in 1918 the local Jews from Zhetl set up a Relief Fund to support the needy in Zhetl. They collected money and sent a delegate to Zhetl to distribute the funds. Between the two World Wars the Relief sent money to support various institutions like the Talmud Torah, the Tarbut School, the Yiddish School, the Interest Free Loan Society and the Fire Department. Every year they sent Matzah for Passover for the poor and so on. In the 1930s the Zhetl Women's Organization was established to help in this work. This work continued during the Second World War.

I do not know how many Zhetl Jews are living in America. I believe around 600 families because in the mid 1930s the Society had 400 members, the Zhetl synagogue had 100 and approximately 100 Zhetl families did not belong to any of our organizations.

Unfortunately, the Zhetl family in America is becoming smaller and smaller. The older generation is slowly disappearing. The tragedy is even greater because they have not left heirs to take their places, as the younger generation, those born in America have assimilated, not merely with language but also spiritually and belong to other organizations. They don't know and don't want to know about Zhetl and it people. The doors of America are locked for new immigrants and slowly, 70 years of the history of Zhetl Jews in America is being obliterated.

[Page 445]

Jews From Zhetl in Argentina

by Moishe Man (Buenos Aires)

Translated by Janie Respitz

By the time the First World War broke out there were 4-5 Zhetl families in Argentina.

A larger immigration began after the First World War. A few families arrived in 1922, many more in 1923 and it continued like this until the outbreak of the Second World War.

The first immigrants arrived without trades or prepetition and endured difficult times as labourers and slaughterers. However they soon began to take on various trades. Tailors left unskilled jobs. People without trades began to work in carpentry and worked their way up. Others became peddlers, starting off by selling on installments and ended up doing well.

Today there are close to 70 families from Zhetl in Argentina.

The Zhetl Townsmen's Society was established in the 1920s. It attracted people who were needy and lonely. When you get together with people you know loneliness is not as bad.

I do not know how long the society existed. It was dissolved shortly after and no archive has remained.

In 1937 the society was re-established. At first we were very active and even created an Interest Free Loan Society. Every member received an interest free loan of 100 pesos. That was a substantial amount at the time for the lonely, sick and needy.

We also sent financial aid to the rabbi's address in Zhetl for the: Yiddish School, the Tarbut School, the Talmud Torah and other institutions. The secretary of our society was Feyvl Bielitzky.

During the war our work gradually decreased until it totally stopped.

In 1945, at my initiative, a general meeting was called. We elected a new board. I was elected secretary and kept in touch with the Zhetl Society in Israel and with their instructions on how to help survivors who were in Austria and Italy.

At first we sent cash to Italy. At the time it was the only way we could help, but without success. We never received any receipts. It appeared that whoever in the camp took the envelope with the money, kept it for himself. When we learned of this we stopped sending money and began to send packages to Austria and Italy. Unfortunately, the same thing occurred.

The Zhetl Committee in Argentina 1950

Seated from right to left: Hirshl Sovitsky, Shloyme Lusky, Avrom Levit, Khaim Velvl Sovitsky, Moishe Man
Standing: Moishe Lusky, Hirshl Shilovitsky, Ozer Kaplan, Izik Epshteyn, Pinkhas Medvedsky, Berl Kravetz, Eliezer Lusky

[Page 446]

After these failures we decided to send aid to Israel and allow them to distribute it according to their discretion.

We began to send large sums of money but when it was forbidden to send money out of Argentina we started to send packages of food according to instructions from the committee in Israel.

We decided to do this in order not to create a recommendation system which unfortunately exists in many institutions and societies.

We found kind people who would find friends and offer heaven and earth. But when it came time to send something they would turn to the Society and ask them to do it. These were people who could have done it on their own.

In order to stop this, we decided, only as per instructions from Israel, to send packages and continue to do it this way.

We sent everything in a respectable manner. We sent things out of moral obligation and not, God forbid, as alms.

Here as well, locally, we help our townspeople morally and financially, although thank God, no one needs financial help.

At this time we learned of the date of the mass extermination of Zhetl's Jews, the 25th of Av. We mark the anniversary and remember our nearest and dearest who were so brutally murdered.

We also have a tradition of holding a banquet every year for everyone from Zhetl. In the first years we would enforce a contribution, but over the last few years we stopped as there is always left over money after the banquet.

For the past five years we have been organizing a quorum for prayer. On the High Holidays everyone comes and remembers the old synagogue back home while at the same time, strengthening our community. The banquet and the prayer quorum have created a homelike atmosphere for the Jews from Zhetl. We must stress that many townsmen societies cannot boast like this.

The Jews from Zhetl are not especially involved in other organizations, but when called upon by the Zhetl Society, they respond immediately, both for happy and, God forbid, sad occasions. We serve as an example for others.

Almost all Zhetl Jews in Argentina live in Bueno Aires, where we have planted deep roots with our children and grandchildren.

The Society of Zhetl Jews in Argentina, 1954

Seated right to left: Moishe Man, Hirshl Sovitsky, Shmuel Shilovitsky, Yekhiel Sovitsky, Moishe Lusky
Standing: Yosef Sovitsky, Ozer Kaplan, Eliezer Lusky, Hirshl Shilovitsky, Yehoshua Lusky, Izik Epshteyn

[Page 447]

Jews From Zhetl in Israel

by Borukh Kaplinsky (Tel Aviv)

Translated by Janie Respitz

When did Jews from Zhetl arrive in the Land of Israel?

I believe in all generations, at all times and in all manners. Unfortunately there are very meagre written sources. We were successful in finding traces of Jews from Zhetl in the Land of Israel from the 19th century.

In the book "The Zoning Registrar" by Asher Leyb Brisk there is a list of tombstones on the Mount of Olives. Among the thousands of tombstones we found 5 belonging to Jews from Zhetl.

Here is a chronological list:

Reb Yitzkhak Ben Asher from Zhetl, died on the eve of Rosh Hashanah, 1860.
Reb Yisroel Zuber Bar Mordkhai from Zhetl, died in 1879.
Itkeh Bat Yisroel Katz from Zhetl, widow of Reb Mordkhai Lufler, died in 1886.
Libe Gitl Bat Duber from Zhetl (widow of Reb Berl from Zhetl), died in 1892.

Thanks to Rabbi Yakov Glubshteyn form the Burial Society we received a list of Jews from Zhetl buried in Jerusalem:

Reb Yisreol Bar Shmaya, died on the 12th of Elul, 1907.
Rabbi Eliezer Bar Moishe Papeh, died on the 23rd of Iyar, 1909.
Reb Yitzkhak Zelik Bar Eliezer Dvoretzky, died on the 13th of Tishrei, 1910.

Reb Asher Yunigster and Reb Alter Shub sent the following list of Jews from Zhetl who received aid from the Society of Vilna Jews: Reb Yerakhmiel Nager, Rabbi Gershon Shloyme Bar Yehuda HaKohen, and Reb Khaim Nager who was shot by Arabs and his place of burial is unknown, and Reb Yekhiel Nager.

The above mentioned Jews from Zhetl lived in Jerusalem but unfortunately we do not know what they did in Zhetl, when they immigrated, how they earned a living and if they left behind children here.

Zhetl Jews Who Arrived in The Land of Israel with the First Aliya (Immigration)

Many Jews from Zhetl came to the Land of Israel with the First Aliya. We only know about a few. One Jew form Zhetl who arrived here in the 1880s was Reb Elimeylekh Izraelit. He was one of the founders of Castina (Be'er Tuvyia). He devoted himself to agriculture. He died in Rehovot in the 1930s. His grandchildren live in Haifa.

Shayna Mikhle Moshkovsky arrived from Zhetl in 1884. She married and lived in Ekron. Her husband was a farmer and she helped out. She died in 1936. Her two sons Shmuel and Noakh Shedshevsky live in Ekron.

In 1887 the well known Lover of Zion activist, Reb Yehoshua Eyznshtat – Barzilay came from Zhetl to the Land of Israel. He was born in Kletzk but married a woman from Zhetl. His father in law was the Zhetl businessman Reb Leyzer Fraydkes. He died in 1918 in Genf on his way to Germany to help work for a German Balfour Declaration.

His daughter Shifra was born in Zhetl in 1880. She married Reb Yisroel Tzurba in the Land of Israel and died in the 1930s.

Reb Yehoshua Eyznshtat – Barzilay, who has a street named for him in Tel Aviv (Barzilay Street near Kikar Hamoshavot),visited Zhetl in 1898 and gave passionate speeches which resulted in the organizational revival of the Lovers of Zion movement. (See "Hameilitz" vol. 232, 1898).

In the 1880s Reb Yekhiel Nakhman Bar Zvi Alpert escaped from exile to the Land of Israel. He was a carpenter from Zhetl, the grandfather of Avrom Levit of Argentina. Reb Yekhiel died in 1920 in Jerusalem. His daughter Masha Peres lives in Ekron.

In 1895 Reb Moishe Izik Bar Yosef Yoyne Ostrovsky came from Zhetl to the Land of Israel and settled with his family in Jerusalem. His daughter Miriam married Yehuda Leyb Glikman and in 1918 they opened a business in Jaffa which developed quickly and is known today as "Building Materials L. Glikman".

Reb Moishe Izik died in Jerusalem on the 20th of Iyar 1901.

Reb Gershon Shloyme Bar Yehuda Hakohen Kaplinsky came to the Land of Israel with his wife in 1886. He died in Jerusalem in 1902. His daughters: Rokhl and Mikhle, the mother of Shmuel Zhukhovitsky (General Magdiel), supported him. His grandchildren are: Diyun Hinde (Haifa), Rokhl Tzirl (Tel Aviv) and Shmuel Zhulhovitsky, (Tel Aviv).

[Page 448]

His great grandchildren: Yaffa Grushevsky (Kiryat Amal), and Gdalya Zakif (Tel Aviv). Reb Gershon lived in Old Jerusalem on Chabad Street, in the building belonging to Yeshayahu Salant. The House of Study he learned in was there as well.

Jews Form Zhetl Who Arrived with the Second Aliya

In 1906 Reb Avrom Yakov Mirsky the scribe arrived with his son Zalman Mirsky. Reb Zalman wrote about the reasons they came in his article in this book.

The Mirsky family arrived on the same boat as our former foreign minister Moshe Sharett. At first the Mirsky family settled in Jaffa, but then they moved to Jerusalem. They could not adapt to the Jerusalem climate and after half a year returned to Jaffa. Reb Avrom Yakov Mirsky opened a store but still continued his work as a scribe. Among other things, he wrote the tfilin (phylacteries) for Rabbi Kook.

Before the First World War, around 1909 three Jews arrived in the Land of Israel from Zhetl: Reb Yidl Lusky, the prayer leader from the old House of study Reb Berl Zhizhayker, and Reb Yisroel Dvoshkes.

Reb Yidl Lusky lived in Jaffa for nine months, his wife Zlate lived in Kfar Saba and died during the First World War.

In 1913 Miriam Kovesnky arrived. She was the daughter of Reb Meir Kovensky and the wife of Khaim Ariab, of blessed memory who was a member of Knesset.

That same year Sonia Feyge Dzhenchelsky also arrived. She is the daughter of Naftali Dzhenchelsky and lives in Moshav Tel – Adashim.

Zhetl Jews that Arrived with the Third Aliya

The First World War, followed by the Polish – Bolshevik war put a stop to immigration to the Land of Israel. However by 1920 three pioneers left Zhetl: Avrom Shepetnisky and the brothers Moishe and Nekhemia Aminoach (Rovovsky).

They all came to the Land of Israel through Vilna, Kovno, Konigsberg, Berlin, Munich and Trieste. At first they were unemployed but eventually found work with farmers in Rishon Letzion.

After two years in Rishon they moved to Kfar Uriah where they worked for four years. After leaving Kfar Uriah, Avrom Shepetnitsky went to Kfar Khasisidim and Moishe and Nekhemia moved to the outskirts of Tel Aviv.

That same year, 1921 the first female pioneer from the Grodno region arrived, Hadassah Vernikovsky, today, Zaks. At her farewell banquet organized by Zhetl Zionists, her father, Reb Menakhem Vernikovsky said the following:

"Today is the happiest day of life. Now I can die in peace".

Avrom Ivenitsky said:

"Hadassah, I'm envious of two things. One, you are realizing your ideal and two, that your parents are going with you, hand in hand".

Mayrim Epshteyn said:

"I want to be the coachman that drives the first female pioneer from the Grodno region to the Land of Israel".

Dr. Shapiro said:

"It is crazy to allow a 19 year old girl to travel to the Land of Israel".

Reb Menakhem Vernikovsky smiled and with a smile answered the question posed to him:

"We understand a man risking his life to immigrate, but a woman? Is that possible?

"I have no sons" replied Reb Menakhem, "so my daughter is going".

Hadassah Vernikovsky missed her train in Egypt and as a result arrived in Jaffa after the tragic events of 1921. At first she lived with the Ostoshinsky family in Rishon Letzion. However, Ostoshinsky wrote to Reb Menakhem Vernilovsky in Zhetl telling him his daughter was a communist. Hadassah then moved to Tel Aviv where she worked with a donkey transporting sand to straighten the Rothschild roads.

After the Yefuar events when the workers left "Hadassah Hospital", Hadassah Vernikovsky was hired at the hospital. At first she worked as a cleaner but later as a manager.

Reb Menakhem Vernikovsky was proud of his daughter, and when Jews in the House of Study would ask him what his daughter was doing, he would reply: "She's working in place of Arabs".

Yekhiel Kuznyetsky arrived in 1922. The first Jews from Zhetl he met in Tel Aviv were the Aminoach brothers and Avrom Shepetnitsky. They took Kuznyetsky into their room which they rented from a Yeminite Jew. Besides all these people their donkey also slept in their room. During the day the donkey would help transport gravel from the sea.

At first Yekhiel Kuznyetsky worked in the carpentry shop of the Zeliviansky brothers and later for the mayor of Ramat Gan, A. Krinitsky. Later he opened his own carpentry workshop on the road Tel Aviv – Jaffa.

[Page 449]

In 1922 Solomon Lubtchansky's family arrived. At first he worked as a teacher in the "Shulamit" conservatory. In 1924 he opened a musical instrument store.

Yehuda Ostrovsky arrived in 1923. He lived in Gdera for his first year at Moishe Kaplinsky's and worked in the groves. Later he found work as a teacher. In 1924 he came to Tel Aviv and worked for the firm "L. Glikman".

That same year the following arrived: Shmuel Dunetz of blessed memory, and Nokhem Cohen, may he live long. They both left Zhetl in 1920 travelling through Vilna, Kovno and Vienna and arrived in the Land of Israel in 1923.

Shmuel Dunetz began working in construction but later went to work in the "Argoz" factory where he was killed in a tragic accident.

Nokhem Cohen first went to Kibbutz Givat Hashlosha, then worked for two years in construction and then moved to Moshav Herut where he lived and worked for more than 20 years.

Shloyme Zalman Dunetz arrived in 1924. Even here he continued to fight for Zionism. Thanks to the help from a few Zhetl families, he moved into an old age home in Jerusalem and died there in 1933.

In 1925 Reb Menakhem Vernikovsky arrived. Together with Rabbi Aronson he taught Talmud in the old peoples' home where he donated his vast library. He died in Tel Aviv in 1930.

Miriam Droyshevitch arrived that same year and works today in Moshav Herut.

Arye Cohen arrived in 1926. At first he worked in construction, later on a kibbutz, then worked as a carpenter for a short time in Tel Aviv, delivered gas and today is an agent for "Delek".

The following arrived that same year: Abba Levenbuk, Henye Pekelny, Tzvi Lusky who is now a sergeant in the port of Tel Aviv, Arye Leybovitch, an employee in the municipality of Tel Aviv.

The following arrived in 1933: Shmuel Rabinovitch. His profession was porger, one who removes veins from meat to make it kosher. He lives in Herzliya. Ruven Mirsky is a farmer in Ramat Hasharon.

Rokhl Rabinovitch arrived in 1934. She lives in Tel Aviv and is a seamstress.

The following arrived in 1935:

Rivka Rabinovitch, today Zaks, from the founders of the large textile factory " Mashi – Zaks", Yitzkhak Rabinovitch who lives in Haifa in Kiryat Eliezer, and works at the "Nur" factory. Sorhe Epshteyn – Shoer, lives in Natanya and works at "Yachin – Hakal".

The following arrived in 1936: Arye Zelikovitch, a bookkeeper at "Yachin – Hakal" and lives in Natanya. Ahuva Yoselevitch – Pomerantz, a seamstress by profession and lives in Rishon Letzion, and Moshe Rabinovitch, an officer in the IDF.

Right after the Second World War, in 1945, Basia Rbinovitch arrived. She lives in Tel Aviv and works as a bookkeeper at Bank Leumi.

The following arrived in 1946: Shabsai Lipsky, a carpenter in Even Yehuda, Khane Mayevsky who lives in Holon, Yosef Kravetz who lives in Tel Aviv, founder of "Taxi Atid", Eliezer Sovitsky who lives in Givatayim,

**Shmuel Dunetz at the tomb of Dr.
Theodore Herzl in Vienna**

[Page 450]

and is an upholsterer, Berta Sovitsky, lives in Givatayim and is a nurse, Khane Epshteyn, lives in Hadera and is a teacher, Dovid Zakroysky, lives in B'nai B'rak and works in the port of Tel Aviv, Khaye Alpert, lives on Kibbutz Yifat and works as a bookkeeper.

The following arrived in 1947: Khaim Vaynshteyn, a carpenter in Ramat Gan, Dvoyre Gorodaysky – Shkolnik, lives in Kfar Saba, Eliezer Senderovsky, is a member of Kibbutz Kinneret, Pesieh Mayevsky – Nadel, a bookkeeper, lives in Petach - Tikva, Aron Gertzovsky a carpenter in Givatayim, Magid Khaya and Avrom, an upholsterer in Givatayim.

The following arrived in 1948: Borukh Kaplinsky, lives in Tel Aviv, an employee at the community centre, his mother Layeh Kaplinsky, Yitzkhak Mankovitch who lives in B'nai B'rak and is a glazier, Miriam Shepelevitch – Rozvosky, lives in Bat – Yam, Khane Alpert, lives in Kfar Saba, Lusky Yehuda, works at the cooperative shop in Natanya and Yehuda Gafanovitch, lives in Ramat – Gan, and works for the Ministry of Labour.

The following arrived in 1949: Dr. Avrom Alpert, lives in Ramat – Gan, and works as a doctor in Kupat Holim, Avrom Alpert, lives in Hadera, works in cement production, Bushlin, Yokeved and Mordkhai, live in Zichron – Yakov, he works as a blacksmith, Shaul Rozovsky, a bookkeeper in "Solel Boneh", lives in Kfar –Saba, Efraim Shepshelevitch, works at the post office, lives in Bat – Yam, Levit Yosef, a construction worker, Rozovsky Zelda and Shloyme a worker, live in Kfar – Saba, Miriam Rozovsky, lives in Kfar – Saba.

Yisroel Kapel arrived in 1950 and works as a bookkeeper in "Kupat Holim" in Raanana.

No one from Zhetl has arrived in Israel since 1950.

The Organization of the Association of Zhetl Jews in Israel

Moishe Rabinovitch was one of the first to organize the Association of Zhetl Jews in Israel. The first meeting took place in 1943 in a room at the National Bank, the following were elected onto the committee: Yehuda Ostrovsky, Yekhiel Kuznyetsky, Abba Levenbuk amd Moishe Rabinovitch.

At that meeting it was decided to collect items and money for refugees from Zhetl.

In 1944 the association received its first letter from Zhetl written by Sasha Zabelinsky, about 13 Jews from Zhetl that had survived. The association immediately sent things. Packages were also sent to Jews from Zhetl who spent the war years in Russia.

The third general meeting of the Zhetl Association took place during the interim days of Sukkot, 1945. Rabbi Zalman Saratzkin participated as well as the first person to arrive from Zhetl after the war, Basia Rabinovitch.

Three Areas of Activity of the Zhetl Association in Israel:

1) Interest Free Loan Society; 2) the Zhetl Memorial Book; 3) the Forest in Memory of Zhetl's Martyrs.

The Interest Free Loan Society of the Zhetl Association was created in 1951. Today its capital has reached 8,000 pounds. They distribute loans of up to 200 pounds.

The Zhetl Memorial Book is the second accomplishment of the association of Jews from Zhetl. Just as in the Interest Free Loan Society, Zhetl Jews in the United States, Argentina and Canada provided help to publish this Memorial Book.

The Forest in Memory of Zhetl's Martyrs was the third accomplishment of the association. So far, there have been 1,500 trees planted in memory Zhetl's martyrs.

Occupations of Jews from Zhetl in the Land of Israel

There are 240 families registered in the Association of Zhetl Jews in Israel. We are interested in their occupations but unfortunately we do not have all the information. We have succeeded in collecting the information on 215 families.

Employees	56 families	26%
Craftsmen	48 families	22%

Merchants and small businesses	35 families	16%
Labourers	23 families	10%
Workshops	17 families	8%
Farmers	12 families	5.5%
Kibbutz	11 families	5%
Professionals	7 families	3%
Householders	4 families	2%
Drivers	2 families	1%
	215 families	

We learn from these statistics that more than a third of Zhetl families were employees and labourers, almost two thirds were independent working in various areas: handicrafts, small industry, agriculture and professionals.

[Page 451]

The Zhetl Interest Free Loan Society in Israel

by Shabtai Mayevsky (B'nai B'rak)

Translated by Janie Respitz

It was 1943 when we began to receive terrible news about the slaughter abroad. A group of Zhetl Jews, among them: Yehuda Ostrovsky, Yosef and Fraydl Berman, Yitzkhak Yalon, Arye Cohen, Soreh Lev – Leybovitch, Efraim Klin and Moishe Rabinovitch met at Yekhiel Kuznyetsky's and decided to create a committee to help survivors from Zhetl. Right after a meeting was called of all Zhetl Jews in Israel and everyone was asked for a monthly contribution of membership fees. We also turned to our townspeople in America and Argentina for help.

Jews from Zhetl in Israel and other countries responded warmly.

In 1944 we received the first letter from Zhetl informing us of a few Jews from Zhetl who were saved. We immediately sent clothing and food.

In 1946 a few Jews from Zhetl succeeded in breaking through the blockade and arrived illegally in the Land of Israel. The Zhetl committee helped them with long term loans.

However, not everyone succeeded in breaking through the British blockade and were sent by the British to Cyprus. We sent them clothing and food.

Refugees from Zhetl began to stream in from 1948-1950. They came from Cypress, Germany, Italy and Poland. Almost all of them turned to the committee which helped everyone with loans.

In 1951 a few members of the committee felt our work was over. The Jews from Zhetl who came were now settled and there was no reason to continue with this work. Opposing this were the members: Y. Yalon, Y. Berman and H. Khabibi who felt the work should continue and an Interest Free Loan Society should be created.

H. Khabibi was at that time visiting America and our townspeople there suggested the creation of the Interest Free Loan Society in Israel and offered financial help. It was then decided to create the fund.

In August 1951, during the meeting to observe the anniversary of the deaths, a temporary committee was chosen: Y. Kuznyetsky – chairman, P. Berman – vice chairman, Yalon – treasurer, and Sh. Mayevsky – secretary. Members: H. Khabibi, Y. Ostrovsky, D. Shkolnika and A. Levenbuk. They also worked out a statute for the Interest Free Loan Society. Here are a few points from the statute:

A. The name of the fund is: The Interest Free Loan Society of Zhetl in Israel in Memory of Zhetl's Martyrs.
B. The purpose of the fund is to provide loans to Jews from Zhetl interest free.
C. A member of the Society can be anyone who requests and pays 6 pounds membership.
D. The amount loaned is limited to a maximum of 200 pounds over a period of 12 months.
E. There will be a general meeting once a year in order to confirm the balance and choose a new committee.
F. The base capital of the fund comes from the monies owed by Zhetl Jews in Israel and from membership dues paid by Zhetl Jews in Israel and around the world.
G. Loans are distributed against promissory notes with two guarantors.

During the interim days of Passover 1952, the first general meeting of the Interest Free Loan Society took place where a committee and revision commission were chosen.

In 1953, 1954 and 1955 the annual meeting of the fund took place on the same day as the memorial evening, on the 25th of Av.

During its five years of existence the Interest Free Loan Society gave out 250 loans at the sum of 35,000 pounds.

The capital of the fund now stands at 7,500 pounds. This money comes from membership fees and donations from Zhetl Jews in America, Argentina and Israel and the paid back loans from previous years. The amount is not enough to meet all the requests of our townspeople who sometimes have to wait a long time to receive a loan.

It is worthwhile mentioning that our townspeople are punctual with paying their promissory notes, except for a few individual cases, when we had to apply a bit of pressure to get the money.

At the last general meeting it was decided to turn to Jews from Zhetl all over the world to become involved in the Interest Free Loan Society.

[Page 452]

The Zhetl Forest

by Yehuda Ostrovsky (Tel-Aviv)

Translated by Judy Montel

The first activity of the Organization of Olim from Zhetl in Israel was sending food and clothing to the survivors of the Sho'ah in Zhetl. When the survivors of the Sho'ah moved to Israel in the years 1945-1950, we began the second activity, which was to offer them aid and help to ease their integration in the country.

Simultaneously with these two activities, we began the third activity: creating a memorial for our town and to perpetuate the people of Zhetl who had been wiped out.

To this end we set up the Zhetl Charity Fund, whose goal was to give loans to those of our town who needed it. Later on, we announced the publication of the Zhetl Book, that would reflect the life of the town and perpetuate its social, cultural and economic character for future generations.

However, we did not stop with these activities. We felt we were obligated to create an endeavor that would join the incredible work that was being done in Israel in bringing the wilderness to life, that would also perpetuate the memory of our town. In order to achieve this idea, we decided to plant the Zhetl Forest.

On the 23 of Adar, 5710 [March 12, 1950], we obtained agreement to this proposal from the Keren Kayemet LeYisrael and we began to collect donations for the trees.

The members of our town in Israel and all over the world donated hundreds of trees and thus we were able to create a memorial for our town. However, to this day we have not collected enough donations that would allow us to begin to plant the forest and we have a long way ahead of us before we reach our goal.

With the foundation of the two important endeavors: The Zhetl Charity Fund and the Zhetl Book, we are commanded to devote all of our strength to realize the third endeavor: "Zhetl Forest."

Every family event can be marked by planting trees in the Zhetl Forest and thus it will become a tradition for our children. They too will continue this important endeavor and our town will not be forgotten by the coming generations.

Also, we must mark the anniversary of the destruction of Zhetl by planting trees in the names of the members of our families who died.

The trees in the Zhetl Forest will grow and perpetuate the memories of our fellow townspeople, who dreamed of the Land of Israel but never reached it.

We will increase the donations of trees and the Zhetl Forest will be planted in the entry to Jerusalem.

Keren Kayemeth Certificate on the planting of 15 trees in the Zhetl Forest

[Page 453]

At a Memorial Gathering in Tel Aviv

by Shimon Berniker (Even – Yehuda)

Translated by Janie Respitz

It is hard to get together with people from Zhetl in Israel. Everyone is busy with his daily life, building and establishing his personal life while at the same time building and establishing the country for the future of the Jewish people.

In addition, the few people from Zhetl are spread out throughout the country in cities and villages, Moshavim and Kibbutzim. Old timers and new arrivals, all trying to be honest citizens of the State of Israel.

Only on the memorial day for our holy, innocent, murdered Zhetl Jews, which takes place every year in the month of Av (August) at Bet Hachalutzot in Tel Aviv, almost all the Zhetler in Israel get together. All those who remained from their torn and unfortunate families

> Keren Kayemet LeYisrael
> The Local Committee in Tel-Aviv
> Tel-Aviv
> 23 Adar, 5710
> 12.3.50
> To: The Organization of Olim from Zhetl in Israel
> To H' Yehuda Ostrovski
> 29 Gedud HaIvry Street
> Here

> Sir,

> We confirm receipt of your letter from 19 Adar and welcome your decision to plant the "Zhetl Forest" in memory of the victims of your town.

> We will willingly record all of the trees that will be planted by your organization and its members to the account of "Zhetl Forest" and will provide certificates for them.

> We wish to emphasize that it is customary to complete the collection of donations for special plantations within two years, however, considering the goal of this plantation, to memorialize a Jewish community, we have agreed that you will fulfill the quota of 10,000 in a period of five years.

> We wish you success with your endeavors.

> Respectfully,

> The Local Committee of the Keren Kayemet LeYisrael in Tel-Aviv

Participants at the memorial gathering in Tel Aviv, 1955

At these gatherings we feel the specific familiarity with the others from Zhetl: the joy of seeing one another after a long time; the common sadness of our losses. All have sadly lost those near to them and come together to honour their memory.

And meanwhile, until everyone arrives and until the cantor begins chanting the memorial prayer, everyone stands outside and greets old friends with whom they experienced so much. Slowly, everyone arrives. We meet acquaintances who we thought were lost, remembering past days and years, the quiet days of our past as well as the bitter years of the cruel Hitler bandits.

Slowly all the survivors from our town gather and we are ready to begin the memorial ceremony for our holy martyrs.

Black candles are lit. The lights in the hall are turned off. Everyone covers their head and the cantor chants in a heart rending crying voice the El Maleh Rachamim (The prayer for the souls of the departed).

The hall is dark. There is a dead silence. A shiver goes through the crowd. You can hear people crying softly and sighing deeply.

Our thoughts take us far away and it seems all those who were tortured, burned and buried alive have gathered together. The hall becomes filled with their souls and they appear before our closed eyes as if they are alive.

Here they are, the women and children, brothers and sisters, relatives and friends, in life and death, not separated.

And the voice of the cantor wails: "May they rest in heaven".

All of our friends soar before our eyes, our almost forgotten neighbours who had the good fortune to die normally before the wild animal Hitler, may his name be blotted out, arrived. Every one of them is now in this hall, standing before our eyes and filling our hearts with grief. Everyone is afraid to move because if we move, they will disappear.

We are only a few families that have remained and are witnesses of the great tragedy. We must memorialize these martyrs at least once a year and eternally see them alive through spiritual eyes.

The cantor concludes with a few chapters from the Book of Psalms.

The light in the hall is switched on. We open our eyes. The holy souls have disappeared. The words of the Kaddish (memorial prayer) recited in the hall ring in our ears.

Life continues, but the pain in our hearts remains. Many are standing with red teary eyes. The dream disappears and daily life returns.

[Page 454]

From Zhetl to Petach – Tikva

by Pesiye Mayovsky (Petach – Tikva)

Translated by Janie Respitz

Summer 1945. There is peace in blood-stained Europe. Wagons are crossing the Polish plains carrying remnants of murdered Polish Jewry. The Jews of Zhetl lie slaughtered in two mass graves on either side of Zhetl.

In Novolenyie, at the train station, there are long lines of military transport trains. The graves shout: Remain! The transport trains shout: Come, go out into the world, join your people!

Everyone took with him the last cry of their parents, the last moans of sisters and brothers. They absorbed the blood shed in the forests, in the swamps, and set out to cities and villages, countries and borders, individuals from large families, setting off on their wandering.

> When the autumn night extinguishes
> One star after another,
> When quiet shadows of dawn
> Crawl out of earth,
> I lay still with blinded eyes
> And look far away.
> I hear the night barely whispering;
> You are alone…alone….
> Alone… my voice whispered
> Alone…my heart trembled
> Alone… my heart wrapped in my sorrow
> In the depths of the night's darkness.

A misfortunate mother searched for her child, her husband, a lonely girl searched for her sister, her friend, wanting to find comfort. Strangers became family, hugging each other. No one asked another: Where are you from? A closeness from a shared tragedy.

> Oh, don't cry my sister, don't cry so bitterly
> Your sadness rips out my heart, poisons my blood,
> Lift your head, your dark beautiful eyes
> And look at me with belief and courage.
>
> Lay your head on my lap, I'll kiss you,
> I will kiss away your anguish and suffering,
> I will whisper words to you, gentle and loving
> And awaken in you a quiet joy.

The wagon wheels are noisy. The ground runs away under them. Here is Lodz, drawing in the survivors of Polish Jewry. Notices from Mordkhai – Khaim Rumkovsky still hang on the ghetto houses, to the Jews of Lodz whose ashes have been spread over the fields of Auschwitz. In Lodz we search for family.

"The Folk"! is the Jewish promise.

Kibbutz "Dror" at 18 Poludnyove Street. "Shalom!" Enjoy yourselves tired survivors, the Kibbutz welcomes you. So many Jewish children, so many youths! The bloodied heart strengthens, beams with delight. Courage is increasing.

> I chase away the cutting sharp pain
> Far away from my heart,
> The phantom disappears
> Let my fear disappear!
> In the black abyss of suffering
> I will search for sunshine,
> We will pick flowers in the fields
> And braid a wreath…

And trains continue to take illegal wanderers to the borders. It is crowded in the train cars, dark. You can see in many eyes the fear of "those death trains". Now they are taking us to a new life.

The Polish Czech border. They take us as Greek repatriates. While travelling we repeat the Greek names, we try to learn "Greek", which means passages from the bible and the Prophets.

"Strange people" say the Polish border guards shrugging as they search for hidden diamonds, dollars and pieces of gold, throwing around our meager knapsacks which are exuding laughter about our poverty.

Hearts are pounding! These survivors do not have any gold, but someone hid a partisan "certificate", a medal for heroism.

We cross the Polish Czech border safely, red roofed houses, spread out, growing like mushrooms in the Czech fields. The wheels are noisy…hearts are pounding…

Prague, the city of the legendary Maharal that formed the Golem!

[Page 455]

Here is the Prague synagogue and the old cemetery.

Carlsbad. In an abandoned Jewish villa where the Germans murdered the homeowner, we lay down our tired heads to rest. Once again our packs on our backs, more inspections, fear.

The Czech –German border. We wander in the dark without stopping, long unending kilometres, holding hands. Someone holds onto an old man, who can hardly take a step in the darkness. A young man offers his hand to a pale girl who is exhausted.

Quietly, I hold my breath, we look for each other in the darkness and whisper:

"Are you here? Is everyone here"?

The night is gone and our tired feet walk upon the ritually unclean German soil. Trains, trains, a stampede, a rush over the fields.

Here is Landsberg, the city where Hitler, may his name be blotted out, wrote "Mein Kampf". Grey housing blocks, military barracks and beer cellars have been transformed into housing for uprooted, displaced persons. (D.P)

The children, survivors, hug each other. Young boys and girls who have never experienced happiness in their lives. Men and women who lost everything, with young faces wrinkled from worry and strands of silver hair webbed through their temples. There are very few old people who were miraculously saved. Everyone has large black eyes from the terrifying years they have just experienced.

Young Kibbutzim are growing, they cheer us up and call for a new life. Young people sit at the long tables with radiant faces, and bright eyes. It seems they are growing wings, as a powerful song emerges from the breast;

> Do you hear the noise, drumming in the air?
> Do you hear that powerful song? -
> We sing about your land, the new life,
> The proud, courageous cheerful Jew!

Bringing in the Sabbath on the Kibbutz. Sabbath candles are burning in their candle sticks, eyes of Jewish boys and girls light up, twinkle, there is great hope. It is still worthwhile to live, for something and someone…

But where is the crying coming from? Who is moaning like that, who is writhing in agony? Souls flutter around…somewhere violins are crying, strings are quivering…where is the music coming from? An orchestra of concentration camp inmates, wearing striped clothing is performing a concert in the Landsberg camp:

> Play the fiddle and cry out
> The songs of the concentration camp,
> Corpses dance, soaring about,
> In a death ballet…
>
> The saxophone dies out
> In the space of sounds; -
> The heart yearns to be free
> Through the barbed wire.
>
> An orchestra of Jews plays -
> Corpses come to sing;
> May the wails from the graves
> Ring throughout the world.

But the world is deaf and mute. They do not hear the screams of the remnants of the Jewish people, who must continue to sit confined in camps and tread on the unclean German soil.

There is peace in land of murder of the Germans, the snow is melting. Everything comes alive, as if nothing ever happened; the fields are sown with bread which children will eat.

> It's spring in Germany
> The Birds are singing,
> The sky is smiling,
> Its blue is so clean,
> The trees are adorned with
> All types of blossoms –
> And blend with the whiteness
> Of human bones…

The cursed German soil burns under our feet. It is cramped here for the Children of Israel, where everything is soaked in Jewish blood. They need to leave here as soon as possible.

We continue to wander at night. Once again a stampede, a rush, during hot days and dark nights. We ride in overfilled trucks over the snowy Alps near the Swiss border toward France.

Here is French soil. The city of Marseilles. The sea is a marvelous blue framed by a mountain chain. Again we sit for months in preparation camps waiting for our turn to leave. The back packs become smaller, they are measured and weighed as not to encumber the sea trip.

[Page 456]

Broken little boats, like canoes, wait for the immigrants. In the dark of night we sneak to the boats, facing the stormy sea…we surrender to the foamy waves trembling in their laps, without fear, without a quiver, but with immense faith in the truth to which we are striving.

On stormy nights and cloudy days, the caravan of ships take us home…home…

> The sea is stormy and angry,
> Spilling snow white foam.
> Oh sea, be calm and quiet
> Let me spin my dreams.
>
> Clouds are spreading over and
> Are being carried by the wind,
> Where are you, my only sister,
> Where is your boat now rocking?
>
> If you are free and proud
> In your own sunny land,
> Wait for me in the quiet morning
> Prepare to squeeze my hand.

The journey to the Land of Israel is far and filled with pitfalls. We are chased by pirate ships. The Imperial naval fleet of His Majesty, the King of England persecutes the child survivors, the immigrants to the Land of Israel. The snouts of the battle ships cut into the stomach of the groaning immigrant ship. It falls to the side, the English throw tear gas. Everyone cries. Our eyes close but our hearts open. Spontaneously a song tears from our throats, a song filled with hope.

From a distance we can see the houses winking from Haifa. Jews are lying on the roofs and watching. Tired feet walk along the longshore but the soldiers from the British Imperial army tear away the immigrants from the Land of Israel and drag them to expulsion ships that will take them to Cypress. From a distance we see the contours of the island and the walls of the old fortress.

> The sun had not set
> From the blue sky,
> It has not covered its face from the shame
> Of those past days.
>
> They chase us wildly away
> From the yearning shores
> Walls of barbed wire,
> Blocking our way.
>
> Oh, your black wires
> With the sharp bent nails –
> While still in the ghetto
> You poked out my eyes with these wires.

Blindly we take each other's hands and descend on to the island of exile. But where is the fear? There is no sign of despair. Everything is like a sad fantasy children's story.

Searches, refugee camp. A forest of canvas tents. We break out in song: "How lovely are your tents, O Jacob" – Can our love of freedom be shackled? Can our impulse to live be confined by wire? We continue to dream about freedom in these canvas tents.

At night, when the light of projector burns and pierces our hearts like needles, the pain of being persecuted and chased awakens and the old unanswered question hangs in the air:

Why? And how much longer?

> Why has spring once again been delayed
> It has forgotten to come to my garden,
> The garden bed is withering and deserted.
> Without sprouting grass or blooming flowers.

My heart has been plowed, with sadness,
I plant in it happy songs like flowers
And stand like a guard by the empty flower bed
And wait for the golden spring to arrive.

Purified in the fires of hell from inhumane suffering, with hearts longing for joy and happiness, the refugees face new suffering. The sharp twisted nails of the barbed wire pierce our hearts and remind us: you are once again a prisoner, confined like a criminal on a far off island.

It is winter on Cypress. Rainstorms are raging, fiery lightning tears through the sky. The tents are falling down. But we are far away in thought, not present. Far off behind the mountains lies the Land of Israel we long for. We are carried off to the plowed fields where bread grows, sowed by Jewish hands. It seems the wire disappears and we dream we are free, free…

The fields are inundated with flowers
The golden sun shines on the slim cypresses

[Page 457]

A heavenly song hums in my ear;
Be happy for a moment, forget, forget!

I throw myself on the grass, and sink into the meadow,
I hug myself like a child sitting on a lap,
I close my eyes and choke from pleasure
Oh, today I feel good, my joy is great!

But the guard opened the gate,
A harsh grating sound, like a spider on the wire.
The jingling of keys, the scraping of a bolt –
The joy flows away like the foam of the sea…

One ship arrives after another. There are many refugees. The Jewish settlement calls to us. The British proclaim a blockade. The rebellious refugees go on a hunger strike. It continues day after day.

Revolt! Revolt! Enough sitting behind fences. Let us have our long awaited freedom. The British tents are burning. The British shoot, one falls dead, many are wounded.

A Hellish red flame
Burns the bent poles of the wire fences,
Smokey souls are flung to the sky-
The sun is wrapped in fire and flames.

The last hours. Is this really the last journey? The ship slides over the smooth backs of the waves.

Adieu Cypress! One by one the tents disappear, the last guard tower. We can see the contours of the shores of Israel.

But there is still a long way to go for our yearning for freedom. The gates of Atlit open and devour us again. Large sad barracks, made of wood with bed bugs. Once again barbed wire and English, Arab and Jewish police.

Like a spider crawling in a dusty spider web,
Rocked by the shadow of the guard, back and forth
And every heavy step he takes, so blunt,
Tears a wound through my heart, bloody and pinched…

Long difficult months of anguish and suffering. It is a thousand times worse to be confined in your land. The road from Atlit goes to Kiryat Shmuel. Jewish guards. Although they are Jews, they are still guards, guarding behind barbed wire.

The day arrived for true redemption. The last gates are opened. The road to our country is open. For the last time, we put our knapsacks on our backs.

We are standing at the threshold of our new life. Somewhere deep in our hearts is our longing for our dear ones which fidgets with the pain of our lost joy. With sorrow filled, but bright eyes, these child survivors walk into a new life. Their lips are whispering a prayer for the Land of Israel:

> Flood my soul with light and sun,
> Let your juices run through my veins,
> May your springs which extinguish the desert red glow
> Refresh my weak heart…

Petach – Tikva. Groves are soaked in greens and gold, wide green fields. Orange trees grow in my little garden. The aroma is intoxicating. My little girl, a Sabra, born in Israel sits on my lap and I tell her:

"There once was a small Jewish town, my little daughter, a town called Zhetl, with narrow streets, low houses, with kind Jews and happy little children. It was, and is no longer!

Over 100 families from Zhetl survived the war and made their home in Israel.

[Page 458]

Remember!

By Mordecai Dunetz, Flint – United States

Translated by Janie Respitz

> Canons are no longer resounding in the fields,
> The sword is resting after the bloody battle.
> Graves are overgrown with hills and forests,
> Spring has covered the world with its beauty.
>
> Children are no longer screaming in Auschwitz,
> The ovens in Majdanek now stand cold.
> Fathers in Treblinka and mothers in Dachau
> Are no longer shouting "Help!"
>
> The earth is irradiated with bright white sun luster,
> The sky sinks into a blue – grey abyss.
> The wind plays a nature dance at night,
> The stillness of the forest is wrapped in death.
>
> Shrubs whisper on hills and in valleys,
> Rivers wash the ancient shores.
> The currents in the seas, in the chasms,
> Will make the stains of dark days disappear.
>
> The streets are noisy with human sounds,
> Life continues down a stormy path.

But we cannot forget our sisters and brothers,
Who were slaughtered in the forest on the trail.

The nights carry terrifying screams,
The air is cut by howls and wails.
Heads are greying and hearts are splitting,
From sorrowful pain which will never heal.

They awaken people with patched skulls,
And clench fists of tattooed arms.
They call out: Remember the millions,
That were shot, tortured and burned!

On roads soaked with sacrificial blood,
On trails in forests, dead silent in the night,
Through borders and outposts, territories and zones,
No powers frightened us.

Mothers could not rest in the places,
Where "Mama" is cried everywhere.
Where Lamentations cried: now deafened from the laughter,
Of drunken murderers of past "glory".

Trenches and fences could not stop us,
Every minute was dear.
Our brothers call out to us from their rows,
To build a memorial to the blood spilled.

A memorial for our dearest, beloved,
Who were exterminated by murderers for eternity.
A memorial for Zhetl – our ravaged home,
Whose respectability was supplanted by the destruction.

Eternally we will, with honour and quiver
(the years may flow like currents),
Until the end of all generations we will remain the guards,
Of your beloved and cherished names.

[Page 459]

Zhetl in April 1957

Greeting from Mireh Volpovsky – Gontchorovsky

Translated by Janie Respitz

Dear Motl!

You asked me to write a few details about our last visit to Zhetl. I am doing it gladly. Please send it over to the Memorial Book.

On April 4th 1957, before we left Grodno on our way to Poland we stopped in Zhetl in order to say our goodbyes to those alive and dead in our destroyed home town.

The sadness and emptiness in Zhetl instill a horrific sense of fear and mourning. It immediately opens the unhealed wounds and your broken heart breaks even more.

At the end of Novoredker Street you can see the old bent houses that stand hunched like war invalids. It seems to me familiar faces of Zhetl Jews are looking out the windows. Unfortunately it is just a mirage. You meet nothing more than unfriendly gentile stares.

Here stands Ben – Tzion Poskovsky's house, across is Tzalye Vinorsky's, near the highway and an empty lot where Munakhme Lusky's house once stood.

I pass some houses where I stop for a while trying to remember who lived there. All along Novoredker Street I do not see one familiar face. Close to the marketplace I meet Borukh Leybovitch (Pertchikh's son in law). He has a wife and two children. Shaul Yoselevitch lives in his old house.

On the small street of the head of the Yeshiva Hertzke lives with his daughter Henieh Kaminsky who married Gdalye Krulevetsky.

On that same street a new house was built by Yoel Novogrudsky (Avrom Moishe the shoemaker's son) and Moishe Alpershteyn (Petrikier) and their families.

Rivele Levit (from Nakrishkok) lives in Leyzer Elye's house with her husband and two children.

A little further down Novoredker Street is Mariashke's house where Shmulik Niselevitch (formerly Pinkhas Lusky's son in law) lives with his wife Feygl Kaplinsky, their three daughters and the old man Yisroel – Yenkl Kaplinsky.

Elye Shmulevitch – Kanapka lives in Yasha Leybke's house with his wife and three daughters.

Shmuel the shoemaker lives on Dvortzer Street.

Aron – Leyb Kovensky lives in Yenkl Kaplan's house. Zhamke's half a house was bought by a Christian and he and his daughter moved to Minsk. Bayle Barishansky lives in her own house with her husband and two children.

When I passed the spot where our house stood I saw the entire destruction. Even the Pomerayke has dried up. I remain standing and the cobblestones become wet from my tears. There is no sign left at the place that used to be our home, where my parents lived for so many years with their family. At the spot where our large brick house once stood and Yisroel Lusky's house, there is now a large beautiful orchard. In the middle stands my sister Zelda's house like a castle that shines in the spring sunshine. My heart is torn from pain and longing.

Leah Gitl Tzalye the blacksmith's daughter lives on Slonimer Street in Izik Hirshl's house with her family. Hodl, Itche the butcher's daughter lives in the same house with her family.

Moishe Aron Zernitsky lives with his wife and three daughters in Khaim Levit's house.

Yoel Dovid's (Dunetz) house has not aged. They dug a well in the yard with flowers growing all around.

Dovid Epshteyn lives in Sholem the blacksmith's house.

Yisroel Kaplinsky (the bird) lives in Yudl Levit's house at the very top of the street.

Hillel Zhukhovitsky built a house on Lipaver Street.

These are the people who remained from Zhetl Jewry and are suffering today in Zhetl.

The mass graves of the second slaughter are at the large cemetery and are under the supervision of Hertzke who has taken the position of official gravedigger chosen by the Soviet authorities.

There is a terrifying scene in the Kurfish forest at the graves from the first slaughter. There are still today scoundrels and beasts who come at night and dig through the graves looking for gold teeth or a ring on a dried out finger. When we were there the graves were covered. The thought that our martyrs have no rest destroyed me.

The Jews of Zhetl turned to the local authorities to take interest in the graves. Bayle Barishansky made a particular effort.

[Page 460]

My friend Borukh!

Today in Zhetl there are 20 Jewish families originally from Zhetl and 9 families that came from other towns. Financially, the Jews in Zhetl live well but they have no spiritual satisfaction. There is no communal Jewish cultural life.

What are the professions of the Jewish families in Zhetl?

4 families are government employees.
3 families live off shoemaking.
3 families from carpentry.
3 families from smithy.
2 families from tailoring.
1 – Driver.

All the Houses of Study and small prayer houses were destroyed. Only the new House of Study has remained. Of course no one prays there. The building was taken over by the Zhetl Fire department.

The building of the Tarbut School was destroyed. The old Yiddish School is now a cinema. Rashkin's house is now the Russian School. The post office is in Rabinovitch's hotel and Berl Dvoretzky's house is a bank. The hospital is in the palace, the saw mill works but the steam mill was burned.

The majority of Jewish homes were burned. The houses that remained are inhabited by Christians or Jews or have been transformed into government institutions. Rarely has a destroyed house been rebuilt by a Christian.

Market days take place now only on Sunday. The marketplace is now at Glovotsky Place across Levashke's former mill. There is no city administration in Zhetl.

On the anniversary of the murders all the Jews of Zhetl gather at the graves for a memorial.

The Jews of Zhetl know about the memorial book Zhetl Jews around the world are preparing. They also received the prospect sent to them by the book committee in Israel.

We were all astounded by the prospect and I came to Zhetl from Grodno especially to see it with my own eyes. We were all curious to hear some news from Israel.

I have a favour to ask. When the book will be published please send me a few copies. I will mail you as much as it costs.

Recently, a few Zhetl families came to Poland. I will list them here:

Henyie Zaltzshteyn and her husband Meir Alpershteyn and a child.
Veveh Zaltzshteyn and his wife Rivka Medvedsky and two children.
Leyb Zalzshteyn with his wife and child.
Mayrim Zaltzshteyn.
Masheh Zaltzshteyn with her husband and child.
Hertzke Kaminsky.
Henyie Kaminsky and her husband.
Shloyme Kaminsky.
Gdalyeh Krulevitzky and two children.

How Many Jews From Zhetl Live In the World?

600 Zhetl families live in the United States
250 Zhetl families live in Israel
70 Zhetl families live in Argentina
40 Zhetl families live in Canada

Dozens of families are spread out throughout Australia, South Africa, South and Central America, England, Soviet Russia, France, Poland and other countries.

[Page 461]

Bricks have Fallen – We will Rebuild with Hewn Stone

by Baruch Kaplinsky (Tel-Aviv)

Translated by Judy Montel

At the crossroads, between Novogrudok and Slonim, in the heart of White Russia [Belorussia], there was Zhetl.

Zhetl was surrounded by forests and it sat in the heart of a plain. We were born in its houses. In its streets we spent our childhoods. There we were educated and grew up. Some in the "cheder" of Yossele Mendes, some in the Talmud Torah with Yudel the Shochet and some in the study hall of Noach Ellis. In later years, we learned in the Folks-Schule guided by Yiddishists and in the Tarbut school run by Zionists.

In this town we took our first steps in public life, some in the Keren Kayemet committee, some in the school committee, some in TO"Z and some in the Cooperative Credit Bank.

In this town we were also stifled by a lack of perspective, and this was the worthwhile side for those who studied with Yossele Mendes and at the Folk-Schule, to those active in the Shomer HaTza'ir [Young Guard], Freiheit and Beita"r.

And from this town we also moved to the Land of Israel. Some in the thirties with certificates of the Land of Israel Office and some in the forties with a number from Auschwitz carved into their arms, some from the partisans in the Lipichan forests and some from the distant Siberian exile. Some via Romania and Italy and some via Cypress.

And thus, we gathered in Israel, embers snatched from Zhetl, the praiseworthy, to tell you, and the following generations, the history and hardships of a town of Israel.

When you were traveling to Zhetl, from a distance of several kilometers from the town, the cross of the Catholic church could be seen. However, this cross did not rule Zhetl and the town did not dwell under its wings. It also didn't determine its character and tendencies.

The character of the town was determined by the Schulhof, (the courtyard of the synagogues) with three study halls, the Talmud Torah and the Chassidarnia (Hasidic prayer house), the character of the town was determined by the three schools and they were purely national [Jewish].

This truth you quickly learned when you got off the bus that arrived from Novoyielnya (the train station before Zhetl). You would be immediately surrounded by the quick people of Zhetl who would take your pulse: Who are you? Are you of the Tarbut people or the Folks-Schule people?

If you were of the Tarbut people, they would put you into Berl Rabinowitz's inn. There they would house you in a nice room and before you had a chance to rest, the heads of the Tarbut in Zhetl would arrive to engage you in conversation.

The first to arrive: The elderly, learned and honorable R' Herz Leib Kaplinsky, a grandfather who had much to discuss with sons and grandsons.

Here he stands in front of my eyes, his face overflowing with splendor. He walks erect, doesn't lean on his stick, despite his age. This grandfather takes off his hat, sits bareheaded, rubs his bald head and begins a philosophical discussion about elevated matters.

After him, my father, R' Sha'ul Kaplinsky, loyal Zionist and lover of the language of the past, a man of stature who faithfully does much community work.

With him, R' Feivel Epstein would arrive, the youngest of the group and loyal to the movement. He was an educated man and generous to every Zionist activity and institution.

Who doesn't remember Chaim Levit? The chair of the commercial association, a young man full of energy and initiative, calling meetings, reaching authorities and pleading the case of his people.

And here is Avraham Langbort, the Keren Kayemet representative in Zhetl, a Torah student, educated and Zionist, sunk head and shoulders into matters of funds and Aliya to the Land of Israel and living the life of Zionism with all of its victories and failures.

And here stands the image of Yo'el Cheplovodsky, the youth representative, a man of the "Hitachdut", an entrepreneur and eager for every Zionist enterprise.

And how could I not mention Betzalel Moshkovski, David Sendrovski, Moshe Reuven Mordkovski and dozens of martyrs of the evil kingdom, who devoted their time, money and hearts to Zionist, to Aliya and to Hebrew culture.

Before they could begin a conversation, here on the doorstep stands Yisrael Ozer Brishensky. Thin and faded was the man, but his heart shone with love, his mind with cleverness and all his being spoke of energy and initiative that positively overflowed. It was he who built the power station and he who absorbed the curses of the women over every problem in the electrical system. It was he who built the Talmud Torah and who aided in building the Tarbut school. It was he who took care of the bath-house and mikveh, the women who gave birth and the widows, the elderly and, in case of a catastrophe, when one needed to be driven to Vilna for treatment. It was he who delayed the Torah Reading in the study hall, in order to add to the salaries of the Rabbi, the Shochet [ritual slaughterer] and the doctor. It was he who went house to house to gather funds for this one, who's horse collapsed. He, who was called in daily life "Yisrael Leizerkeh", was a symbol of community work for its own sake.

However, it happened sometimes that one of the great activists of the Folks-Schule arrived in town. Then an entirely different scene unfolded.

To the inn Avraham Moshe Brishenski, Shaikeh Ovsivitz, Chayim Ganozovitz, Gedalyahu Shevdesky would arrive as well as dozens of other townspeople.

They were our rivals. For decades they fought us, wrestled with us. This struggle created a lot of bitterness, but it was conducted in accordance with beliefs and opinions and innocently. They were the dreamers and fighters who believed in the diaspora and not in Zion. They preferred Yiddish and turned their backs to Hebrew. They championed socialism as a solution to the national question and denied the value of Jews gathering in the Land of Israel. From here came their battles against Aliya, the national funds, against Zionism and the pioneers.

Yet even if our methods differed, we were united in one goal: to move our lives forward. And even though their path was proven false and ours was proven true, there is no denying that they were pioneers in several endeavors.

[Page 462]

They were the first to form a theater and a secular school in Zhetl. They were also well-known for their solidarity and care for one another.

However, at times both sides were sorely disappointed. The guest, who came to the inn, was neither an activist for Tarbut nor for the Folks-Schule, but a simple agent for linen stockings from Lodz.

Yet even this disappointment did not cool off the spirits of the rivals. The battle of the schools was the main battle in Zhetl, which divided the town in two and whose arrows hit all areas of life. When the Folks-Schule built a beautiful building near Tcherna's flour mill, immediately the Tarbut activists rolled up their sleeves and built a no less beautiful building near the old-age home. A successful bazaar was held by the Keren Kayemet LeYisra'el in the Tarbut school, immediately the people of the Follk-Schule organized and held a splendid production of Mirele Efros.

These were the faces of the daily battle in Zhetl. Behind it stood two contradictory viewpoints about the life of the people of Israel: Zionism on the one hand supporters of the diaspora on the other.

All these battles were scattered by the wind. The nailed boot of the enemy trampled, destroyed and wiped them out. It had no mercy on the elderly, on women, or on youth. And of all the battles only graves were left in reality and precious memories in our hearts.

These memories flutter, beseech and give us no rest. They cry out for expression, for memorialization. Can we deny them, hide them, condemn them to be forgotten?

* * *

Here they rise from behind the fog. Images of the youth march first. They have just finished the Friday night meal, and they are already filling the streets of the town with noise and tumult. Thus, they make their way, arm in arm, to the castle that is called "Palatz". On the way they eat sunflower seeds, drink soda in the basement of Alter Gertzovski and lift their voices in song.

Sometimes this youth is seized by the dance craze, and then all of Zhetl dances. Sometimes this youth is seized by political fervor, and then all of Zhetl danced the "hora" and went to house meetings. Sometimes this youth is seized by the football craze, and then all of Zhetl kicked a soccer ball in the horse-market square. Sometimes this youth was seized by the "Hachshara" craze, and then they attended programs to prepare for the life of a pioneer, chopping wood and drawing water in Klosova and in Shachariya. Sometimes this youth was seized by the craze of Aliyah, and then dozens and hundreds of them made Aliya to the land of Israel. This youth was noteworthy also in the forests and as partisans, there they amazed with the fierceness of their spirit and the courage of their hearts. They were famed in command and campaigns, taking revenge and their hands still ready for more. These children did not let down their parents with their love of Israel and their dedication.

And the mutual aid in Zhetl? Can we forget that? It was indeed somewhat primitive in form, but how wonderful were its intentions? It was not based on taxes, requirements, the government or authority. These were missing from the life of a Jewish town in White Russia, but as a candle to their feet they were guided by: generosity, volunteering, care for others.

Do you remember the hospital, the Visiting the Sick, the Aid to the Sick, the Support for the Needy, the Charity for Brides, the Old-Age home and the Orphan Aid societies? Each organization and its goals, each group and its mission.

And how can we not put to paper the mothers and the fathers, who collected and saved one penny and another in their red kerchiefs for those who give birth, for the brides, for the orphans and the widows, for those burnt out and for those cursed by fate.

This on the one hand. The traditional institutions that the Jewish diaspora created in Eastern Europe. And on the other hand, the modern institutions for mutual aid like: the TO"Z, for keeping one's health, the Cooperative Credit Bank, and the Commercial Associations and the Artisans Guild.

Who can count all the ways our ancestors and parents endeavored in order to encourage mutual aid in all of its forms and goals?

* * *

One sheaf of memories. Shabbat in Zhetl.

It began with Shabbat evening. The sun is making its way down the sky. The shops are closed and locked up. Columns of dust rise up from the paved road (bruck – in Yiddish), one can already see men, women and children all scrubbed and ironed, wearing holiday clothing and hurrying to receive the Shabbat Queen.

From the Kleizl (small prayer-house) on the banks of the Zhetlka, the hoarse voice of R' Hershl the Blacksmith can be heard, grappling with his god and asking for mercy for the people of Zhetl who barely earn their livelihood. Yudl the Shochet [ritual slaughterer] is leading prayers in the Chassidarnia (Chassidic synagogue). In the *plosh* (the synagogue corridor), children gather and show off their Shabbat clothes. They call one another names that can be heard in the air: "Trembos" (Tarbut) and "Klakshuleh" (a name for the Folks-Schule), an echo of the parents' struggle in the mouths of babes.

It has become dark and the Shabbat Queen has spread her wings over Jewish Zhetl. Every home receives the Angels of Peace, the Angels of Service.

And here the song of the angels is over and your ear hears the clatter of plates, forks and spoons. Zhetl is eating its Shabbat meal.

Those who are quick and always early can be found in the streets of the town. They eat sunflower seeds, sip soda, gather on the balconies (*briklech* in Yiddish) and discuss the events of the town so: *wos darfstu mer, ch'vell dir dertzeylen a bessereh maiseh* (why do you need more, let me tell you a better story). And from the conversations the rolling laughter of the youth can be heard, as they make their way to the castle or in the direction of the sawmill.

The following day: The holy Shabbat. The entire town gathers in the synagogue. They have just reached the reading of the Torah and from some distant corner the figure of Yisrael Ozer pops up. He slaps the *stender* [where the prayer leader usually sets their prayer book] and announces a delay in the reading. Sometimes he delays the Torah-reading and demands a raise in the price of yeast by 2-3 pennies a "loyt" (a unit of weight) so that the local rabbi can have an honorable living and not a meager one. On another Shabbat he rallies public opinion against the butchers, who don't want to pay "karavke" fees at the agreed upon amount. At times he inflames the congregation in the matter of the doctor who receives the poor according to a note, and demands additional payment from his customers. Another time he arouses mercy for an unfortunate family, who must be taken to Vilna for medical treatment and can't afford it.

To begin with, the congregation listens intently, but has only grasped the matter and is all unsettled when, from a distant corner a hand is raised and the cry rings out: *Yungatsh* (ruffian), desecration of god's name, get out! The respectable people and the moderate ones try to calm the passionate spirits and meanwhile, Yisrael Ozer continues with his persuasive talents towards a solution. Will he not achieve it?

[Page 463]

The congregation has been standing in the silent prayer of "Musaf" for a while, but Yisrael Ozer is still arguing with his rivals in the *plosh*. The battle has not ended for the rabbi, for the ritual slaughterer, for the doctor or for those whom fate has stricken with illnesses.

After the midday Shabbat meal, the committee meetings begin, in Tarbut, and in the school, the committees sit. In the Talmud Torah the *gabbaim* [deacons] meet. The committee that sets the salary of the doctor sits separately and the debates and arguments continue until the third meal.

* * *

Do you remember the fundraising bazaars for the Keren Kayemet, Tarbut and for the Yiddish school? Zhetl prepared for them for months. Hundreds of women sewed and embroidered in the evenings. Dozens of girls ran about, getting donations, carrying baskets full of all good things.

In the home of R' Avrabam Langbort the committee is meeting and considering how to raise the status of the event. Telegrams and letters come and go urgently to centers in Warsaw and Vilna saying, more or less: "For heaven's sake, send us the important speaker, So and So".

And when the day arrives, set for the opening of the bazaar, the hall is full and crowded. It overflows with abundance and a selection of excellent things, the fruit of donations from hundreds of donors and collectors. The bustle is great and there is no end to the joy.

And here, decorated and ironed Zhetl flocks to the large hall. Who can't you see there? From the crème-de-la-crème of Zhetl, the respectable people and the simple folk. Even the rivals haven't overcome their curiosity and they come to witness the reality and to dance joyfully.

But the main members of this event are, of course, the children. They crowd through the doors and the windows. They are inside and outside. You can chase them away, but they come back. The pennies are jingling in their pockets, pennies they drew from every possible source, in order to win the raffle or a small pocket knife that they've been yearning after for ages.

On the stage, the important speaker stands, the representative of the center in Warsaw. His speech is impressive and exciting and thrills the crowd. He describes the situation generally and particularly, uses foreign words and makes a great impression. Next to him the organizers are sitting and enjoying this. The fruit of their handiwork is glorious. They beam with joy and are delighted by the hall full of people, the celebratory event and especially, the hoped-for income.

And here, the official part has ended. The buying and selling are at their height. The payment register is crowded, there is a lot of activity in the cafeteria and the teens are excited: when will the dancing finally begin?

This great celebration continues all the days of *chol hamo'ed Pesach* [interim days of the Passover holiday] and *chol hamo'ed Succot*. Every evening Zhetl celebrated and was joyful and with them the respectable activists most of whose worries were about the new and old deficits their institutions were facing, institutions they were honored to run, and for them the bazaar was a lifeline.

This is a modest paragraph, taken from the daily life of the vibrant Zhetl of 20 or 30 years past, and offered to our sons and daughters who are growing up in the free and independent state of Israel.

And even though the minister of the nation has compensated us for our losses, and new youth has arisen and new charity organizations, new battles and problem, that are of greater importance, more dynamic and of greater breadth, even so, the heart aches, longing for what is past, and is unable to be comforted.

And it seems to me, that with this aching heart we will pass on to the netherworld and no one will understand the nature of the wound, which didn't heal.

Life is hard with the memory of graves and in the shadow of the destruction. And therefore, it is natural that the days of horror are gradually forgotten, and in their stead new life is formed.

In this new life, you, our sons and daughters, who did not know Zhetl and its life, have a central role. For you – the future and happiness. But also, in moments of happiness and success, listen, let us sit together for just a moment, let us together recall a chapter from the struggle of the diaspora and observe the commandment: And you shall teach [your children]!

With all that is dear that surrounds us in the independent state of Israel, let us leave a hidden corner – sacred to the diaspora, and nourish it with the pages of this volume.

With our joint efforts, we will be diligent in building new lives without horrors and without terrors. For here, we see that the words of the verse are taking shape: Bricks have fallen – we will rebuild with hewn stone.

REMEMBER!

Remember 450 years of creativity of our ancestors in the town of Zhetl!

Remember generations that educated your parents to Torah and to deeds!

Remember the tragic death of our loved ones in Zhetl!

Remember and don't forget!

[Page 464]

List of former Dzyatlava residents living in Israel

Transliterated by Judy Petersen

Surname	Given name	Place	Page
ABERNOK	Yakov	Kibbutz Netiv L"H Doar Na Harei Yehuda	464
ABERNOK	Sarah	Kibbutz Netiv L"H Doar Na Harei Yehuda	464
OZCHOVSKY	Dov	Akko	464
OZCHOVSKY	Shlomo	Akko	464
OSTROVSKY	Ita	Tel Aviv	464
ORLINSKY	Zelik	Tel Aviv	464
AZBORNITZKY	Natan	Rehovot	464
ELIAV	Avraham	Tel Aviv	464
ELIOVITZ	Chaim	Ramat Gan	464
ELIOVITZ	Tuvia	Tel Aviv	464
ALPERT	Avraham	Hadera	464
ALPERT	Avraham	Ramat Gan	464
ALPERT	Chaya	Kibbutz Yifat	464
ALPERT	Shmuel	Kfar Saba	464
ANDERSTEIN	Yakov	Kibbutz Eilon, Nahariya	464
ANDERSTEIN	Tzvi	Ramat Gan	464
ANDERSTEIN	Shlomo	Haifa	464
ESTERKIN	Raya	Tel Aviv, near Yad Eliahu	464
EPSTEIN	Zelik	Lod	464

EPSTEIN	Chaim	Pardes Katz	464
EPSTEIN	Channah	Kfar Saba	464
EPSTEIN	Yehoshua	Petach Tikva, Kfar Ganim	464
EPSTEIN	Yitzchak	Kfar Neter	464
ETZKOVITZ	Chaim	Petach Tikva, Kfar Ma'as	464
ETZKOVITZ	Shmuel	Petach Tikva, Hayovel	464
ARIAV	Miriam	Tel Aviv	464
BUSEL	Peretz	Beersheva	464
BUK	Chasida	Ramat Gan	464
BUSCHLIN	Mordechai	Zichron Yakov	464
BUSCHLIN	Moshe Zelik	Zichron Yakov	464
BEGIN	Sarah	Jerusalem	464
BITANSKY	Zev	Kfar Saba	464
BICHLER	Meir	Tel Aviv	464
BITAN	Moshe	Tel Aviv	464
BEN ARI	Yakov	Tel Aviv	464
BENDER	Devorah	Hertzlia	464
BENYAMINI	Yisrael	Kibbutz Ramat HaKovesh	464
BROIDA	Nachum	Tel Aviv	464
BROIDA	Shamai	Kibbutz Ein Harod	464
BRURMAN	Yaffa	Raanana	464
BERMAN	David	Netanya	464
BERMAN	Yosef	Tel Aviv	464
BERMAN	Avraham	Tel Aviv	464
BERNIKER	Shimon	Even Yehuda	464

BARKAN	Chaya	Tel Aviv	464
BERKOVITZ	Yakov	Rishon Letzion	464
GIBORI	Yitzchak	Tel Aviv	464
GOTLIEB	Leah	Kibbutz Alonim	464
GOLDSTEIN	Yitzchak	Kfar Saba	464
GORODTZER	Malka	Tel Aviv	464
GENOZOVITZ	Yehudit	Yaffo	464
GEFENOVITZ	Yehuda	Tel Aviv	464
GRIN	Aryeh	Kfar Saba	464
GRITZER	Luba	Holon	464
GERLING	Shalom	Ramat Gan	464
GERENDA	Sarah	Petach Tikva	464
GERTZOVSKY	Aharon	Givataim	464
GERTZOVSKY	Aryeh	Kiryat Motzkin	464
GERTZOVSKY	Gitel	KfarSaba opposite Egged Beit Rizenbach	464
GERTZOVSKY	Shmuel	Kfar Tavor	464
GERSHOVSKY	Yosef	TelAviv, Hadar Yosef	464
DWORETZKY	Yosef	Tel Aviv, Yad Eliahu	464
DWORETZKY	Tzipora	Kibbutz Kfar Menachem	464
DWORETZKY	Shlomo	Haifa	464
DAVIDOVSKY	Miriam	Givataim	464
DZENCELSKY	Yakov	Kfar Saba	464
DIYUN	Hinda	Haifa, Hadar Hacarmel	464
WOLFOVITZ	Pesya	Tel Aviv	464
WOLFOVSKY	Tzvi	Raanana	464

WOLKOVITZKY	Lipa	Petach Tikva	464
VILENSKY	Gita	Tel Aviv	464
VILKOMIRSKY	Shmuel	Nachalat Yehuda	464
VEINBLAT	Lula	Tel Aviv	464
VEINERSKY	Betzalel	Kfar Saba	464
VEINSTEIN	Chaim	Ramat Gan	464
VEINSTEIN	Rabbi Yitzchak	Jerusalem	464
VASILEVSKY	Tzipora	Hertzlia	464
VERNIKOVSKY	Rakhel	Tel Aviv	464
ZABLOTZKY	Shlomo	Tel Aviv	464
ZABLOTZKY	Shmuel	Tel Aviv	464
ZADROYEVITZ	Miriam	Moshav Cherut next to Tel Mond	465
ZAHAVI	Channah	Hadera	465
ZOCHOVITZKY	Yisrael	Jerusalem	465
ZONENBERG	Yehudit	Tel Aviv	465
ZELIKOVITZ	Aryeh	Netanya	465
ZAKS	Hadassah	Tel Aviv	465
ZAKS	Rivka	Tel Aviv	465
ZEKROISKY	David	Bnei Brak	465
HAVIVI	Helena	Tel Aviv	465
HAZAN	Menachem	Tel Aviv	465
HERMONI	Golda	Tel Aviv	465
TOPELBAND	Freidel	Givataim	465
YOSELEVSKY	Tzila	Tel Aviv	465
YOSELEVITZ	Reuven	Jerusalem	465
YELIN	Mila	Tel Aviv	465
YITZCHAKI	Tzvi	Hadera	465
YASHIR	Batya	Tel Aviv	465
COHEN	Aryeh	Tel Aviv	465
COHEN	Nachum	Moshav Cherut	465

		doar Tel Mond	
LUBETKIN	Betzalel	Tel Aviv	465
LEVI	Malka	Kibbutz Yakum	465
LEVIT	Zelik	Bat Yam	465
LEVIT	Yosef	Tel Aviv	465
LEVIT	Sarah	Netanya	465
LEVIN	Leah	Tel Aviv	465
LONBUK	Abba	Tel Aviv	465
LONBUK	Shlomo	Bnei Brak	465
LONBUK	Reuven	Shavei Tzion next to Nahariya	465
LUSKY	Aryeh	Netanya	465
LUSKY	Chaim	Netanya	465
LUSKY	Yehuda	Tel Aviv	465
LUSKY	Channah	Tel Aviv	465
LUSKY	Yehuda	Netanya	465
LUSKY	Miriam	Tel Aviv	465
LUSKY	Tzvi	Bnei Brak	465
LUSCHCHIK	Yitzchak		465
LUSCHCHIK	Miriam	Tel Aviv	465
LEIZEROVITZ	Aryeh	Tel Aviv, Kfar Salome	465
LEIZEROVITZ	Asher	Kfar HaRoeh doar Hadera	465
LEIZEROVITZ	Avraham	Kfar HaRoeh doar Hadera	465
LEIZEROVITZ	Chaim	Akko	465
LEIZEROVITZ	Yechezkel	Kfar HaRoeh doar Hadera	465
LIBOVITZ	Avraham	Haifa	465

LIBOVITZ	Aryeh	Tel Aviv	465
LIBOVITZ	Chaim	Bnei Brak	465
LIBOVITZ	Khasya	Petach Tikva	465
LIBOVITZ	Yitzchak	Rosh HaAyim	465
LIBOVITZ	Roza	Haifa	465
LIBOVITZ	Sarah	Petach Tikva	465
LIBOV	Esther	Tel Aviv	465
LICHTIGMAN	Lyuba	Tel Aviv, Givat Aliya	465
LIPSKY	Shabtai	Even Yehuda	465
LACHMAN	Yaffa	Petach Tikva	465
LAMKIN	Bavel	Tel Aviv	465
LANGBURT	Yehoshua	Tel Aviv	465
LANDAU	Etel	Haifa	465
LANVAL	Tova	Tel Aviv	465
MAGID	Avraham	Givataim	465
MOTZNIK	Shlomo	Tel Aviv	465
MIVSKY	Channah	Petach Tikva	465
MIVSKY	Shabtai	Bnei Brak	465
MIVSKY	Chanan	Ramat Yitzchak	465
MIRSKY	Zalman	Tel Aviv	465
MIRSKY	Reuven	Ramat HaSharon	465
MAN	Binyamin	Kfar Saba	465
MALCHIELI	Chasida	Ramataim	465
MANUSHKIN	Miriam	Kfar Saba	465
MANUSHKIN	Shmuel	Kfar Saba	465
MANUSHKIN	Kalman	Kfar Saba	465
MANKOVITZ	Yakov	Ramat Yitzchak	465

MANKOVITZ	Yitzchak	Ramat Yitzchak	465
MANKOVITZ	Moshe	Haifa	465
MERLIN	Chaya	Tel Aviv	465
NADEL	Pesya	Petach Tikva	465
NIGNIVITZKY	David	Hertzlia	465
NIGNIVITZKY	Yitzchak	Ramat Gan	465
NIGNIVITZKY	Sarah	Tel Aviv	465
NIKOLIVSKY	Dov	Rishon Letzion	465
NIRENBERG	Grona	Tel Aviv	465
NAMIOT	Eliezer	Kiryat Chaim	465
SAVITZKY	Eliezer	Givataim	465
SAVITZKY	Hertzel	Tel Aviv	465
SOROTZKIN	Rabbi Zalman	Jerusalem	466
SOROTZKIN	Rabbi Elchanan	Jerusalem	466
SOROTZKIN	Yisrael	Petach Tikva	466
SOROTZKIN	Bentzion	Jerusalem	466
SLUTZKY	Miriam	Tel Aviv	466
SENDEROVSKY	Eliezer	Kvutzat Kineret	466
SENDEROVSKY	David	Yaffo	466
SKAROVON	Eliahu	Ramle	466
AMINOACH	Zalman	Tel Aviv	466
AMINOACH	Moshe	Petach Tikva	466
AMINOACH	Nechemia	Petach Tikva	466
POMERANTZ	Ahuva	Rishon Letzion	466
FEIGIN	Reuven	Tel Adashim	466
PIKELNI	Yosef Eliahu	Kfar HaRoeh doar Hadera	466

FELDHORN	Yaffa	Tel Aviv	466
FELDLAUFER	Channah Glika	Kfar Saba	466
FRUMKIN	Yosef	Karkur	466
FRANK	Ahuva	Tel Aviv, Kiryat Shalom	466
TZEIG	Chasida	Rehovot	466
CHIMERANSKY	Avraham	Azar	466
TZIMERMAN	Tzipora	Givataim	466
TCHERNY	Yirmiyahu	Kfar Saba	466
KUZNITZKY	Betzalel	Tel Aviv	466
KUZNITZKY	Tuvia	Ramat Gan	466
KUZNITZKY	Yechiel	Tel Aviv	466
KUZNITZKY	Shlomo	Tel Aviv	466
KOVENSKY	Eliahu	Petach Tikva	466
KOVENSKY	Aharon		466
KOCH	Leah	Holon	466
KOLINSKY	Elka	Petach Tikva	466
KOPELEVITZ	Iga	Tel Aviv	466
KALBSTEIN	Feivel	Ramat Gan	466
KLAR	Channah	Holon	466
KLEIN	Tova	Tel Aviv	466
KLEIN	Efraim	Tel Aviv	466
KAPLINSKY	Baruch	Tel Aviv	466
KAPLINSKY	Zelik	Tel Aviv	466
KAPLINSKY	Chaim	Ramat Gan	466
KAPLINSKY	Leah	Ramat Gan	466
KAPLINSKY	Menachem	Tel Aviv	466
KATZLINSKY	Tzipora	Tel Aviv	466
KARBECHOK	Moshe	Tel Aviv	466
KRAVITZ	Yosef	Tel Aviv	466

KRAVITZ	Shlomo	Ramat Gan	466
KARBETZKY	Mordechai	Tel Aviv	466
KRUGMAN	Yitzchak	Akko	466
KARPEL	Yisrael	Raanana	466
KRUSHINSKY	Shalom	Lod	466
KARTZMAN	Max	Petach Tikva	466
RABINOVITZ	Yitzchak	Haifa	466
RABINOVITZ	Moshe	Tel Aviv	466
RABINOVITZ	Rakhel	Tel Aviv	466
RABINOVITZ	Shmuel	Hertzlia	466
RABINOVITZ	Sarah	Tel Aviv	466
RADZINSKY	Luba	Petach Tikva	466
ROSENBLUM	Henya	Raanana	466
ROSENFELD	David Noach	Kibbutz Sarid	466
ROSENTAL	Khinka	Netanya	466
ROMANOVSKY	Tzviya	Rishon Letzion	466
ROMANOVSKY	Shoshana	Tel Aviv	466
ROZEVSKY	Aharon	Holon	466
ROZEVSKY	Wolf	Raanana	466
ROZEVSKY	Tzvi	Petach Tikva	466
ROZEVSKY	Shaul	Kfar Saba	466
ROZEVSKY	Shlomo	Kfar Saba	466
REZNITZKY	Shalom	Tel Aviv	466
REZNIK	Zelik	Herut	466
REICHENBACH	Miriam	Lod	466
RAF	Shlomo	Raanana	466
RATZENDOR	Bilha	Ramat Gan	466
SHEVKOVSKY	Shmuel		466
SCHWARTZMAN	Moshe	Petach Tikva	466

SCHOCHET	Nachum	Holon	466
SHOER	Sarah	Netanya	466
SCHACHRAIT	Zelda	Kibbutz Shefaim	466
SHTEINHAUZ	Miriam	Bitan, Doar Kfar Vitkin	466
SHTRUCH	Mordechai	Tel Aviv	466
SHLOVSKY	Moshe	Ramat Gan	466
SHEFTANITZKY	Yitzchak Avraham	Kfar Chasidim	466
SHAPIRA	Raya	Tel Aviv	466
SHEPSHELOVITZ	Efraim	Bat Yam	466
SHKOLNIK	Devorah	Kfar Saba	466
SHARLET	Shlomo	Haifa	466
SCHERTZER	Tzila	Tel Aviv	466

[Page 467]

List of former Dzyatlava residents living in the US

Transcribed by Genia Hollander

Surname	Given name	Place	Page
ABRAMS	Irving	New York, NY	467
ABRAMS	Morris	Brooklyn, NY	467
ALBERT	Nathan	Bronx, NY	467
ALBERT c/o BRAVIN	Rose	Bronx, NY	467
ALPERT	Aron	Chicago, IL	467
ALPERT	David	Lakewood, NJ	467
ALPERT	Eizer	Chicago, IL	467
ALPERT	Harry	Bronx, NY	467
ALPERT	Joseph	Bronx, NY	467
ALPERT	Mike	Bronx, NY	467
ALPERT	Meyer	Brooklyn, NY	467
ALPERT	Morris	Bronx, NY	467

ALPERT	Rebecca	Bronx, NY	467
ALPERSTEIN	Albert	Bronx, NY	467
ALPERSTEIN	Meyer	New York City	467
ALPERSTEIN	Solomon	Bronx, NY	467
AREN	Sam	Bronx, NY	467
ARLINSKI	Alter	San Francisco, CA	467
ARNER	Sam	Bronx, NY	467
BAYAR	Harry	New York, NY	467
BERKOWITZ	Abraham	Bronx, NY	467
BERMAN	Joseph	Brooklyn, NY	467
BERMAN	Meyer	Brooklyn, NY	467
BERMAN	Morris	ForestHills, NY	467
BERMAN	Rubin	Brooklyn, NY	467
BERNICKER	Rabbi Myrem	New York City	467
BERNIKOFF	Morris	NY City. NY	467
BLUM	Harry	Bronx, NY	467
BOJARSKI	Irene	Bronx, NY	467
BRESKIN c/o KROPKOFF	Nachman	Brooklyn, NY	467
BREVDA	Moses	Brooklyn, NY	467
BRODSKY	Fanny	Brooklyn, NY	467
BUSEL	Rabbi Joshua	Brooklyn, NY	467
BUTENSKI	Isidore	Poughkeepsie, NY	467
BUCIEL	Dorris	Bronx, NY	467
DAROFF	Marc	Philadelphia, PA	467
DEMBOFF	Celia	Brooklyn, NY	467
DITKOWSKI	Isidore	Brooklyn, NY	467
DONEFSKY	Abram	Brooklyn, NY	467
DUNETZ	Max	Flint, MI	467

DWORETZKY	Hyman	Brooklyn, NY	467
DWORK	Betty	Brooklyn, NY	467
DWORK	Harry	Brooklyn, NY	467
DWORK	Isidore	Bronx, NY	467
DWORK	Jacob	Bronx, NY	467
DWORK	Solomon	Bronx, NY	467
EPSTEIN	Benjamin	Brooklyn, NY	467
EPSTEIN	Joseph	Brooklyn, NY	467
EPSTEIN	Max	Farmedale, NJ	467
ETZKOWITZ	Louis	Bronx, NY	467
FAIGENBAUM	Rose	Bronx, NY	467
FARBER	Max	Brooklyn, NY	467
FEINE	Julius	Bronx, NY	467
FEINE	Soul	Bronx, NY	467
FISHKOWITZ c/o MARGULIS	Izidore	Philadelphia, PA	467
FRIDMAN	Louis	Rockaway, NY	467
GAIR	Abraham	Bronx, NY	467
GAVRIN	Mr.	Bronx, NY	467
GERSHOWITZ	Harold	Bronx, NY	467
GERSHOWITZ	Isidore	Bronx, NY	467
GERSHOWITZ	Sam	Brooklyn, NY	467
GERSHOWITZ	Sam	New York, NY	467
GERTZOW	Mayer	Bronx, NY	467
GERCOWSKI	Aron	San Francisco, CA	467
GOLDBERG	Ann	Bay Side, NY	467
GOLDFEDER	Max	Bronx, NY	467
GOLDBERG	Nathan	Brooklyn, NY	467
GOLDMAN	Abraham	New York, NY	467
GOLDSTEIN	Sam	New York, NY	467
GOODSON	Jacob	New York, NY	467

GROSSMAN	Morris	Bronx, NY	467
HAIDUKOWSKI	Hirsh	Brooklyn, NY	467
HIDEN	Max	Bronx, NY	467
HOLINSKY	B	Bronx, NY	467
HOROWITZ	Fannie	New York, NY	467
JOSELL	Irving	Brooklyn, NY	468
KAPLINSKY	Isaac	Brooklyn, NY	468
KANTOROWITZ	Abraham	New York, NY	468
KAPLAN	Charles	Bronx, NY	468
KAPLAN	Meyer	Neptune. NY	468
KAPLAN	Sam	Bronx, NY	468
KATZER	Abe	Bronx, NY	468
KAUFMAN	Abraham	Detroit, MI	468
KIVEL	Max	Bayside. L.I..	468
KOLEDICKI	Abraham	Detroit, MI	468
KOLEDICKI	Israel	Detroit, MI	468
KRAWIETZ	Wolf	Jackson Hi, NY	468
LANCEWICKY	Philip	Bronx, NY	468
LARO	Aron	Brooklyn, NY	468
LAZAR	Rubin	Memphis, TN	468
LAZOWSKI	I.	Brooklyn, NY	468
LEIZEROWITZ	M.	Brooklyn, NY	468
LEVENBACH	Louis	Long Island, NY	468
LEVENBACH	Sam	New York, NY	468
LEVITT	Eisel	Brooklyn, NY	468
LEVITT	Philip	New York, NY	468
LEVITT	Sam	Boston, MA	468
LIDSKY	Albert	Brooklyn, NY	468
MALACHOWSKY	Max	Brooklyn, NY	468
MARCO	Sol	Bronx, NY	468

MATLOW	Joseph	Cleveland, OH	468
MEADOW	David	Brooklyn, NY	468
MINUSKIN	Noach	Los Angeles, CA	468
MINUSKIN	Sam	Bronx, NY	468
MISHKIN	B	Brooklyn, NY	468
MISHKIN	Julius	Bronx, NY	468
MISHKIN	Victor	Bronx, NY	468
MOSS	Rabbi J.	Providence, RI	468
NAMIOT	Morris	Brooklyn, NY	468
NORMAN	Shelub	San Francisco, CA	468
NICHOLS	Gabriel	LosAngeles, CA	468
NOVACK	Max	Brooklyn, NY	468
NOVACK	Philip	Brooklyn, NY	468
OVSON	Morris	Detroit, MI	468
PASSOFF	E	Brooklyn, NY	468
PASSOFF	M	Brooklyn, NY	468
PALAY	Sam	Mt Vernon. NY	468
PEARL	A	Brooklyn, NY	468
PERRY	Jacob	Brooklyn, NY	468
POLLACK	J.	Bronx, NY	468
RABINS	J.	Brooklyn, NY	468
RABINOWITZ	Morris	Hartfort, CT	468
RABITZ	Moshe	Detroit, MI	468
RAZNOV	Morris	San Francisco, CA	468
RECANT	R.	New York, NY	468
REINER	S.	Brooklyn, NY	468
RESNICK	S.	Brooklyn, NY	468
RUBINSTEIN	Itzchak	Brooklyn, NY	468
SAKIER	B.	NY	468

SAVITZKY	B.	NY	468
SAWITZKY	Chaim	Newark, NJ	468
SAVITZKY	Dave	Bronx, NY	468
SAVITZKY	Isidore	Bronx, NY	468
SAVITZKY	Fay	Bronx, NY	468
SAVITZKY	S.	Brooklyn, NY	468
SANDER	Cila	Philadelphia, PA	468
SELTZER	M.	Brooklyn, NY	468
SETLER	M.	Baltimore, MD	468
SENDER	Jacob	Brooklyn, NY	468
SHALCOVITZ	Kalman	N.Bergen, NJ	468
SHELL	Sam	Bronx, NY	468
SHILOVITZKI	Israel	Brooklyn, NY	468
SHMIDT	Ida	Brooklyn, NY	468
SHULKIN	L.	Bronx, NY	468
SHILOFF	Irving	Brooklyn, NY	468
SIEGEL	H.	Brooklyn, NY	468
SILVERKLANG	R.	Brooklyn, NY	468
SKYDEL	Sam	New York, NY	468
SMALL	Harold	Chicago, IL	468
SOKOL	L.	Vineland, NJ	468
SOROTZKIN	B.	Cleveland, OH	468
SOROTZKIN	L.	Cleveland, OH	468
STOLAK	Sonia	Brooklyn, NY	468
STOLOFF	B.	Bronx, NY	468
TINKOWITTTZKY	D.	Brooklyn, NY	469
TURECKI	B. Mrs.	New York NY	469
TURGEL	L.	Bronx, NY	469
WOLK	Osher	Bronx, NY	469
WOLK	P.	Bronx, NY	469

ZABITZ	Philip	East Orange, NY	469
ZABITZ	S.	Brooklyn, NY	469
ZAVIN	R.	Bronx, NY	469
ZEIDMAN	Bella	Chicago, IL	469

[Page 469]

List of former Dzyatlava residents living in South America

Transcribed by Genia Hollander

Surname	Given name	Place	Page
ABRAMOVICH	Aron	Buenos Aires	469
AIZENSEHLAS	Amalia	Buenos Aires	469
BELA	Zelik	Buenos Aires	469
BERMAN	Jonon	Buenos Aires	469
BERMAN	Naun	Buenos Aires	469
BIELICKKY	Pablo	Buenos Aires	469
BRAVERMAN		Buenos Aires	469
BRESKIN	Bernardo	Buenos Aires	469
BUCHHALTER	E.	Buenos Aires	469
DERCHINSKY	Szyfra	Buenos Aires	469
DOBRY	Leon	Buenos Aires	469
DOBRIN	Elias	Buenos Aires	469
DOBRIN	Raul	Buenos Aires	469
DWORECKI	Dobe	Buenos Aires	469
DUBKOWSKY	J.E.	Buenos Aires	469
DUNIEC	Isaac	Buenos Aires	469
EPSTEIN	Aizik	Buenos Aires	469
EPSTEIN	Isaac	Buenos Aires	469
EPSTEIN	Max	Chile	469
EPSTEIN	Ita	Buenos Aires	469
FRIDENBERG	Carlos	Buenos Aires	469
FURMANSKY	Jose	Buenos Aires	469
GERCOWSKY	Abraham	Buenos Aires	469

GERCOWSKY	Max	San Martin	469
GERCOWSKY	A.M.	San Martin	469
GERCOWSKY		San Martin	469
GOLDSTEIN	Dr.	San Martin	469
GOLDSTEIN	Jacobo	Buenos Aires	469
GORDON	Elias	Buenos Aires	469
GUSOVSKY	Roberto	Buenos Aires	469
GUSOVSKY	Salomon	Buenos Aires	469
HAIDUKOWSKY	Israel	Buenos Aires	469
ILEVICKY	David	Buenos Aires	469
IWENIETZKY	Samuel	Buenos Aires	469
JOSELEWICZ	Meilaj	Buenos Aires	469
KAPLAN	Abraham	Buenos Aires	469
KAPLAN	Janke	Buenos Aires	469
KAPLINSKY	Aron	Buenos Aires	469
KAPLINSKY	Jacob	Buenos Aires	469
KOTIK	Simon	Buenos Aires	469
KRAWIETZKY	Braine	Buenos Aires	469
KRAWCHUK	Abe	Buenos Aires	469
KRIGUAL	Zjarie	Buenos Aires	469
KUZNIETZKY	Faiwl	Buenos Aires	469
LEIBOWIC	Izrael	Buenos Aires	469
LEIZEROVIICH	Jacobo	Buenos Aires	469
LERMAN	Saul	Buenos Aires	469
LEVIT	Abraham	Buenos Aires	469
LEVIT	Richke	Buenos Aires	469
LUBCHANSKY	Salomon	Buenos Aires	469
LULINSKY	Roberto	Zarate	469
LUSKI	Bernardo	Buenos Aires	470
LUSKI	Beile	Buenos Aires	470
LUSKI	Jorge	Buenos Aires	470
LUSKI	Max	Buenos Aires	470
LUSKI	Moises	Buenos Aires	470
LUSKI	Lazaro	Buenos Aires	470

MAN	Moises	Buenos Aires	470
MEDVETZKY	Ana	Buenos Aires	470
MEDVETZKY	Pedro	Buenos Aires	470
MEDVETZKY	Sara	Buenos Aires	470
MEDVETZKY	Simon	Buenos Aires	470
MISZKIN	Szolem	Buenos Aires	470
MOSZKOWSKI	Robert	Buenos Aires	470
NOVODVORETZ	Abraham	Buenos Aires	470
NOWODWORSKY	Izrael	Buenos Aires	470
NOWODWORSKY	Simon	Buenos Aires	470
ORZEJOVSKY	Vijne	Buenos Aires	470
ORZEJOVSKY	Gedale	Buenos Aires	470
PESCOWSKY	Isaac	Buenos Aires	470
RAJMAN	Rajmiel	Buenos Aires	470
SAVITSKY	Abraham	Ramos Mejia	470
SAVITSKY	Benjamin	Ramos Mejia	470
SAVITSKY	Carlos	Mercedes	470
SAVITSKY	Hirsch	Buenos Aires	470
SAVITSKY	Jamie Wolf	Buenos Aires	470
SAVITSKY	Jose	Buenos Aires	470
SAVITSKY	Julio	Buenos Aires	470
SAVITSKY	Leon	Buenos Aires	470
SAVITSKY	Moises	Buenos Aires	470
SCHAPIRO	David	Buenos Aires	470
SCHAPIRO	Oscar	Buenos Aires	470
SCHARVAT	Jacobo	Buenos Aires	470
SCHARVAT	Leon	Buenos Aires	470
SILOVISKY	Gregorio	Buenos Aires	470
SILOVISKY	Mario	Buenos Aires	470
SILOVISKY	Samuel	Buenos Aires	470
TURGUEL	Hirsch	Ramos Mejia	470
WELKANSKY	Max	Buenos Aires	470
WOLFOWSKY	Israel	Buenos Aires	470

WENZOWETSKY	Henaj	Buenos Aires	470
ZDZIENTZENLSKY	Max	Buenos Aires	470
ZAMOSHCHYK	Israel	Buenos Aires	470

[Page 470]

Former Dzyatlava resident living in Canada

Transcribed by Genia Hollander

Surname	Given name	Place	Page
FREIDEREICH	Bascha	Winnipeg. Mann.	470
MEDWETZSKY	Abram	Montreal. Canada	470
MIRSKY	Moshe	Montreal. Canada	470
MONTSCHAK	Riwka	Winnipeg. Mann.	470
PINSKI	Herzel	Winnipeg. Mann.	470
PINSKI	Ruwen	Winnipeg. Mann.	470
PRAZOFF	H.	Octremont. Can.	470
SERLIN	Leah	Winnipeg. Mann.	470
SILVERMAN	S.A.	Ontario. Canada	470

Former Dzyatlava resident living in England

Surname	Given name	Place	Page
CALPSTEIN	M	Cardiff. England	470

Former Dzyatlava resident living in France

Surname	Given name	Place	Page

WALDMAN	M	Paris. France	470

[Page 471]

Families From Zhetl

Translated by Janie Respitz

Over six hundred families lived in Zhetl. We will perpetuate the memory of many of them in these photographs. Take a good look at them and remember Zhetl! Remember the martyrs, do not forget the survivors!

The Rabinovitch family with their sons, daughters, sons in law,
daughters in law and grandchildren

First row: Mirele and Sorele Epshteyn, Rabinovitch: Izyele, Khanele, Rokhele and Nyanye
Second row: Efraim Rabinovitch, Yitzkhak Epshteyn, Rozeh Daykhovsky, Hirshl and Rivka Rabinovitch
Third row: Feygl Epshteyn, Frume Simeh and Berte Rabinovitch, Khaim Ganuzovitch
Last row: Soreh Rabinovitch, Mayrim Epshteyn, Rabinovitch: Feygl, Leyb, Lazar, Mikhl, Khashke
In the background: Three cousins

First row: Nosn, Arl and Khayele Lirsky, Rokhele Kaplan, Leyb Ivenitsky, Yisreol
Kovensky, Avreyml Kaplan, Arl Kovensky, Poliya Kaplinsky, Ruven Katz, Henyele Shalkovitch
Second row: Herzl Ivenitsky, Tuviya and Shmuel Kovensky, Soreh Ivenitsky, Meir, Khane and
Khaye Yudis Kovensky, Sahyne and Avrom Busel, Khienke Bielitsky, Rokhl Shalkovitch
Third row: Nakhman and Libke Lidsky, Yakov and Leah Kaplan, Shaul Kaplinsky, Khaim
Aryev Shalvovitch. Fourth row: Miriam Ivenitsky, Eli Busel, Leybl Kovensky, Zviya Kovensky,
Rokhl Ivenitsky, Leah Busel, Khienke Ivenitsky, Sonieh Shalkovitch
Fifth row: Rivka Ivenitsky, Tzaliye and Motke Bielitzky, Kalman Busel

[Page 472]

Savitsky family
Seated: Yehoshua, Esther, Khaim
Standing: Yakov Shimen, Feygl, Babl, Herzl

Kaplinsky family, Hirshl and Khatye

Ganuzovitch family
Seated: Khaye Leah, Yisreol
Standing: Rokhl, Moishe, Khaim, Feygl

Khatke and Leah Kaplan, Libe Khane Benyaminovitch

Shalkovitch family
Seated: Itke Bayle, Yitzkhak, Henyie, Rokhl, Hillel
Standing: Esther, Shmuel, Frume, Moishe, Mikhliye

Shefshelevitch family: Avrom and Frayde

[Page 473]

Epshteyn family
Khaim Meir, Basieh, Dvoyre

Kaplinsky family
First row: Rokhl, Libke and Leah Shvedsky, Hertz Leyb Kaplinsky, Soreh, Esther and Berl Ivenitsky
Second row: Gdalye Shvedsky, Itche Yosl Eynshteyn, Avrom Invenitsky

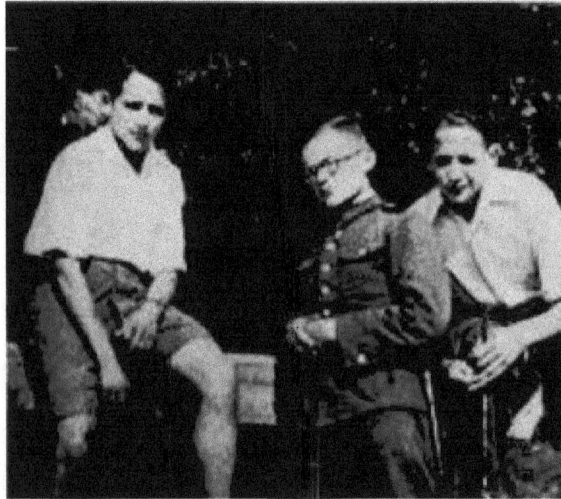

Kovensky family
Yisreol, Leybl, Aron

Kravietz family
Seated: Minye Kravietz, Kantorovitch, Avrom Moishe Kravietz
Standing: Fraydl, Hirshl, Shimen and Manke Kaplinsky, Veveh,
Yosl and Shloyme Kravietz, Yehoshua, Soniye, Asher and Yisroel Shushan

Rozovsky family
Lizeh and Berl Moishe

Zelikovitch family
From right: Yakov, Dovid, Leyb and Shayneh Khane

[Page 474]

Levit family
Seated: Shifra Fridnberg, Rokhele Stolovitsky, Avrom Levit. Tzipora Berman
Standing: Yentl Stolovitsky, Bashke Fridnberg, Fraydl Berman, Rivka Stolovitsky

Langbart family: Tzi Hirsh and Avrom

Rozovsky family
From the right: Noyekh, Shloyme Zalmen, Yehoshua Bar Meir

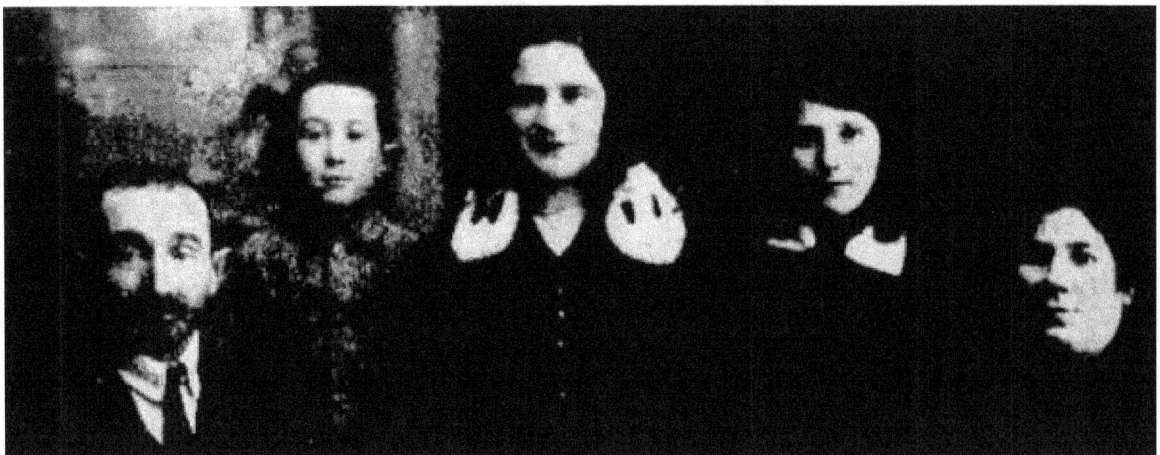

Slutzky family
From the right: Khaye Rokhl, Zeldeh, Frumeh, Zelik, Leyzer Eli

Rozovsky family
Yitzkhak and Minyeh Brokha

Yisroel and Mariasheh Senderovsky

Eliyovitch family
Seated: Avrom Leyb, Rayzl, Giteh Minyeh
Standing: Tuvyia, Feygl, Khaim Velvl, Eshekeh, Aron, Kayleh, Yisroel

Levenbuk – Sheluvsky family
From the right: Yosef and Mikhleh Levenbuk, Nekhameh and Khaim Sheluvsky

[Page 475]

Grin family
First row: Binyomin Aron, Shmulik, Zalmen, Ginyeh, Masheh
Second row: Rivka, Henyeh, Lizeh

Yitzkhak Shalkovitch with his grandchildren

Berman family
Yisakahr, Avrom, Nokhem, Lyubeh, Milyeh

Leybovitch – Elyovitch family
First row: Eliyahi Leybovitch, Yisroel and Rokhl Elyovitch, Brokha Leybovitch
Second row: Polkeh Leybovitch, Khaim and Lyubeh Elyovitch, Yakov and Siamkeh Leybovitch

Rozovsky family
Seated: Yosef, Yakhne
Standing: Kayleh, Dovid, Berl Moishe, Itkeh, Shloyme, Aron Leyb

Gertzovsky – Bielsky family
Seated: Etkeh & Moishele Bielsky,
Unknown, Isar & Mulvieh Gertzovsky,
Avryml Bielsky

Gal family
Yente, Rivka, Nakhman,
Mershetch, Soreh

Zatzepitzky – Savitzky family
First row: Mineh Zatzepitzky, Avreyml Savitzky,
Asneh Zatzepitsky, Hindeh Savitzky, Bezalel Zatzepitzky
Second row: Khaye, Yakov Shimen, Avrom, Feygl and Dena Sovitz

[Page 476]

Zablotzky family
From the right: Yisroel, Shifra, Shloyme, Mulyieh, Pesheh Levit, Golde Zablotsky

Dvoretzky family
Seated: Henyieh, Rayeh and child
Standing: Yakov Meylekh and Alter

First row: Shaynele and Alte Shepshelevitch, Velvele and Moishele Solman, Mikhl and Soreh Libele Shepshelevitch
Second row: Hirshl and Yakhne Indershteyn, Shloyme and Khane Guzovsky, Baylke and Yishayahu Solman

Henyieh Gertzovsky – Shokhat

Epshteyn family
First row: Frumeh Rayzl, Moishe, Henyieh Minye, Yisroel Ber
Second row: Meylekh, Khaim Meir, Yehoshua

Dvoretzky family
From the right: Pesyieh, Mordkhai, Fraydl, Khane Leah, Feygl

[Page 477]

Khaim and Menukha Leyserovitch

Dzhenchelsky family
From right: Naftali, Yakov, Miriam, Soreh, Khonen

Senderovsky family
First row: Hindeh, Shloyme Yuakhadler, Khashke
Second row: Motke, Leah, Esther, Aron

Rabbi Yakov Nisn Gorodaysky

Senderovsky family
First row: Henke, Rishe, Bashe, Minke
Second row: Elke, Kalmen, Avreymke, Asher, Yenkl, Rivka, Shepsl

Gertzovsky - Shmulevitch family
Seated: Alter Gertzovsky, Khaye, Mulyieh and Ben – Zion Shmulevitch
Standing: Lyube, Khaye and Hirshl Gertzovsky, Soreh Shmulevitch, Fanyie Levin,
Yisroel Shmulevitch, Arl Gertzovsky, Malke Shmulevitch

[Page 478]

Shmule and Feyge Mereh Levit

Cohen family
Seated: Nokhem, Yisroel, Marishke, Frayde
Standing: unknown, Golde Cohen

Dunetz family
Seated: Basheh, Soreh Rokhl, Antzele, Yoel Dovid
Standing: Rozele (Minyate's daughter), Shifra, Shmuel, Brokheh, Fanyia, Motl

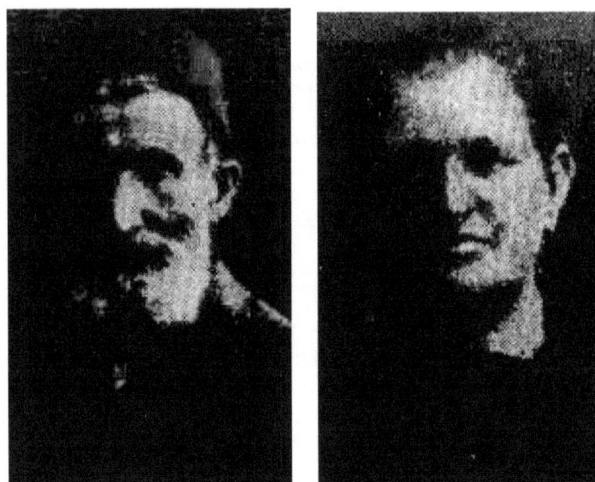

Gitl and Eliezer Berman

First row: Mirl Zernitzky, Khanele Levit, Leyb and Bayle Lusky,
Yoel and Khaye Levit
Second row: Zernitzky, Alter, Tzile, Moishe Aron, Khaim Levit

The Lusky family with their daughters,
sons in law and grandchildren

[Page 479]

Grash family
Seated: Moishe Kravetzky, Velvl the doctor's wife, Khane Lusky, Khaye Kravetsky
Standing: Nignevitzky, Malke Grash, Malke Nignevitsky

Khane, Bayle, Leah, Khane, Meir Kontesbrat

Dovid Hirshl Medvedtzky and wife

First row: Leah and Rishe Zhukhovitsky, Zlateh Goldshteyn, Brokheh Vilkansky, Shloyme Kahim,
Yosef, Mulyieh and Ladkeh Goldshteyn
Second row: Zelde Zhukhovitsky, Bashe, Rivka, Avrom and Henyie Senderovsky, Yitzkhak and Khaye
Leah Goldshteyn
Third row: Kalmen Senderovsky, unknown, Libke and Motke Turetzky, Alte Vilkansky, Yisroel and Rishe
Senderovsky

Kravetzky family
Seated: Moishe Kravetzky, Velvl the doctor's wife, Khane Lusky, Khaye Kravetzky
Standing: Gutke Karvetzky, unknown

Nokhem Elye, Yisakhar and Elek Berman

Name Index

Solman, 641
Solomansky, 148
Solomiyansky, 11, 337
Solomon, 33
Solomyansky, 575
Soloveichik, 305
Soloveitchik, 306, 308
Sorke's, 345, 346
Sorotskin, 79, 170
Sorotzkin, 73, 127, 152, 185, 294
Sorotzkin, 616, 624
Sovitsky, 115, 200, 222, 224, 236, 345, 349, 388, 437, 465,
     482, 485, 556, 557, 567, 568, 573, 575, 581, 583, 584, 587,
     588
Sovitzky, 200, 237, 556
Sroyleyzer, 325, 326
Stesl, 108
Stifnaov, 491
Stolak, 624
Stoloff, 624
Stolovitsky, 635
Stravinsky, 120, 122, 151, 283, 329, 332
Strindberg, 246
Stukolsky, 278

T

Taneh, 241
Tankhum, 53, 113, 484
Tchatchina, 27
Tchemerinsky, 433, 575
Tcheplavodsky, 225
Tcheplovidsky, 289
Tcheplovodsky, 117, 118, 199, 205, 206, 207, 209, 227, 228,
     229, 246, 252, 255, 257, 284, 287
Tcherne, 245, 293, 332, 344, 355, 356, 362, 378, 448, 555
Tchernikevitch, 491
Tchernikhov, 138
Tcherny, 617
Tchertches, 290
Tentzer, 118, 119, 130, 134, 141, 220, 231, 254, 260, 329,
     330, 347, 348, 353, 395, 398
Tevli, 306
Tikachinski, 82
Tikachinsky, 198
Tiktinsky, 157
Tilevitch, 27
Tinkovitsky, 229, 478
Tinkovitsky, 27
Tinkovitzky, 527
Tinkowitttzky, 624
Tinlovirsky, 263
Topelband, 613
Tosfaa, 68
Traub, 306, 482
Treger, 27
Trepov, 108
Trivush, 306
Trotsky, 27
Tseitlin, 35

Tsinovitch, 53, 69
Tules, 119, 181, 401
Turecki, 624
Turetsky, 115, 116, 168, 199, 289, 496
Turetsky, 27
Turetzky, 200, 243, 244, 436, 464, 649
Turgel, 624
Turguel, 627
Turkov, 283
Tzalye, 603
Tzederboym, 237
Tzeig, 617
Tzimerman, 617
Tzinovitch, 64, 145, 187, 308
Tzinovitz, 86, 302
Tzinuvitz, 310

U

Urseyevitch, 287

V

Vafner, 119
Vainstein, 376
Vakhanin, 502, 504, 505, 506, 507, 520, 521, 522, 543, 557
Valdman, 391
Vanyshteyn, 222
Vapner, 249
Vasilevsky, 613
Vaynshtein, 153
Vaynshteyn, 222, 224, 251, 588
Veinblat, 613
Veinersky, 613
Veinreikh, 280
Veinstein, 613
Velikansky, 25
Verenikovsky, 348
Vernick, 25
Vernik, 219
Vernikovski, 78, 98, 152, 185, 316
Vernikovsky, 96, 97, 103, 111, 115, 118, 132, 133, 134, 141,
     144, 145, 153, 158, 167, 187, 188, 189, 191, 192, 193, 198,
     204, 208, 237, 238, 243, 245, 250, 251, 282, 315, 319, 329,
     348, 353, 586, 587
Vernikovsky, 613
Veygo, 470
Veynshteyn, 97, 105, 146, 445, 446, 480
Veysbrum, 310
Veysenberg, 147
Vilensky, 253, 290, 377
Vilensky, 613
Vilkansky, 649
Vilkomirsky, 613
Vilkovsky, 399
Vilner, 150, 251, 272, 273, 278, 279, 385
Viltchuk, 48
Vinakur, 230
Vinarsky, 114, 116, 120, 219, 263, 388, 491, 492, 572, 575
Vinarsky, 25

www.ingramcontent.com/pod-product-compliance
Lightning Source LLC
Chambersburg PA
CBHW062020090426
42811CB00005B/911